'Here is that marriage of good writing to good scholarship that one seldom comes upon. Peter Brune's prose crackles and sparkles and he has done the hard work on the ground. You can smell the jungle. If Papua was a bastard of a place, this is a pearl of a book.'—Les Carlyon, author of *Gallipoli*

'Brune is that rare combination of a great researcher, powerful historian and good writer, and *A Bastard of a Place* brings all those qualities together on the canvas of Australia's greatest war story.'—Peter FitzSimons, *Sydney Morning Herald*

'Any Australian high school that lacks a copy of this book in its library has ceased to teach Australian history.'—Peter Ryan, *Weekend Australian*

'They are the custodians of the Australian Digger legend, typified by mateship, compassion and selflessness forged at Gallipoli . . . Triumphant is the Australian soldier to whom this book is dedicated.'
—Christopher Bantick, *Canberra Times*

'With the skill of a great storyteller, Brune blends these high-level strategic command issues with riveting accounts of combat and its aftermath, often letting soldiers speak for themselves . . . Brune's book is a timely reminder that, despite the warmest alliances, nations sometimes have to stand up and save themselves.'—Geoffrey Barker, *Weekend Australian Financial Review*

'. . . *A Bastard of a Place* undeniably ranks as the best book ever written about Aussie battles in Papua . . . Very highly recommended, and certainly one of the best books of the year.'—Stone & Stone Second World War Books website

'Few are more qualified to write of the Papuan campaign than Brune.'
—Chris Brice, *The Advertiser*

Peter Brune is one of Australia's leading military historians. He is the author of the bestselling and highly acclaimed *A Bastard of a Place: The Australians in Papua*, as well as *Those Ragged Bloody Heroes: From the Kokoda Trail to Gona Beach 1942*, *The Spell Broken: Exploding the myth of Japanese invincibility*, and *We Band of Brothers: A biography of Ralph Honner, soldier and statesman*, and is co-author with Neil McDonald of *200 Shots: Damien Parer and George Silk and the Australians at War in New Guinea*. He lives in Adelaide.

PETER BRUNE

DESCENT INTO HELL

The Fall of Singapore—Pudu and Changi—
the Thai–Burma Railway

ALLEN&UNWIN
SYDNEY · MELBOURNE · AUCKLAND · LONDON

First published in Australia in 2014

Maps by Ian Faulkner

Allen & Unwin
Sydney, Melbourne, Auckland, London

83 Alexander Street
Crows Nest NSW 2065
Australia
Phone: (61 2) 8425 0100
Fax: (61 2) 9906 2218
Email: info@allenandunwin.com
Web: www.allenandunwin.com

Cataloguing-in-Publication details are available from the National Library of Australia
www.trove.nla.gov.au

ISBN 978 1 74114 534 2

Typeset in 11/15 pt Minion by Midland Typesetters, Australia
Printed and bound in Australia by Griffin Press

10 9 8 7 6 5 4 3 2 1

The paper in this book is FSC® certified.
FSC® promotes environmentally responsible, socially beneficial and economically viable management of the world's forests.

CONTENTS

———⇥►◄⇤———

PART III   PUDU AND CHANGI PRISONS ... purgatory

PART IV   THE THAI–BURMA RAILWAY ... the gods
            don't give a damn

PART V   SINGAPORE ... the orphan

FOREWORD

———⊷⊶———

I first encountered Peter Brune in early 2007 when he rang to request an interview with me. He wanted to discuss my experiences as a Medical Officer in the 8th Australian Division, AIF, during the Malayan Campaign, 1941–42 and, later, as a prisoner of war of the Japanese during World War II. During that initial phone call, Brune informed me that he had already written six books concerning the Papuan Campaign (July 1942 until January 1943), and that he was now writing a book on the 8th Division in the Far East. I was immediately interested and we agreed to meet soon after. Throughout our first interview, I was impressed by Brune's dedication and determination to search for the truth. A few days later, I received a letter from him containing more than 40 questions to clarify his understanding of the medical terms and medications I had referred to during our interview. Brune is the kind of author who wants to make sure that even the smallest of details are correct.

This first interview marked the beginning of my friendship with Brune: a man who is committed to obsessive fact checking and unafraid to ask awkward (but important) questions. His questions have kept coming ever since. We have had countless telephone conversations to clarify details in each chapter of *Descent into Hell* and it has been my privilege to follow the extensive research and cross-checking that has taken place to ensure the accuracy of this book. I am now delighted to have been asked to write this foreword.

When considering the members of the 8th Division, we must remember that, first and foremost, they were true fighting soldiers who upheld the highest tradition of the Anzacs both in action against the Japanese and in captivity. These soldiers possessed courage and bravery, as well as the ability to improvise in even the most challenging of circumstances. Mateship was an outstanding quality of the Australians. I never saw a sick Australian who did not have a mate or somebody else to look after him.

Since World War II there has been an abundance of books published on the experiences of these men. Some accounts, especially autobiographies, have relied on memory as a primary source of information, while others have been based on diaries and personal or official documents. It is my view that the books based on diaries and other documents are more likely to be authentic than those whose authors have relied on memory alone. During captivity, many men kept diaries in the optimistic hope that their words might one day be used in evidence in War Crimes Trials. After the war, original or expanded diaries were published by these men for two main reasons: first, for the information of family members and, secondly, for their historical value. Some diaries were published just as they were written while others were used as 'aides memoir'—to facilitate expansion in the diary format or to permit conversion to a narrative format. Mostly they were strictly personal, describing their hunger, a broken denture, missing home and family, or other private feelings.

Among the earliest books to be published was *Behind Bamboo* (Angus & Robertson, Sydney, 1946) written by Rohan Rivett, a military journalist. (For a short period Rivett and I were in the same camp in Tavoy in Burma.) In 1951 Roy Whitecross wrote *Slaves of the Son of Heaven*, a personal account of his experience as a typist in 8th Division Headquarters during the Malayan Campaign and in Anderson Force in Burma during the construction of the Burma–Thailand Railway. I was the Medical Officer of Anderson Force and appointed Whitecross as a part-time medical orderly in my Regimental Aid Post to protect him from the working parties when his health was deteriorating rapidly. His book is a truly authentic account of only one man's experience of the Railway. I knew him very well and can verify his story.

Now we have *Descent into Hell*, a forensically written book by an academic historian, Dr Peter Brune. He writes objectively as an interested critical observer, without personal or family involvement in the war. Written over a period of nine years, *Descent into Hell* is based on more than 50 recorded interviews, diaries and official documents (some of which are held in the Australian War Memorial and National Archives), papers made available by participants or members of their families, and numerous books.

In this compelling book, Brune tells the history of the 8th Division in the Malayan Campaign. His introduction describes the futile planning, construction and weak defence of the 'impregnable fortress of Singapore'. It also features a commentary on the formation of the 8th Division, including a summary of the senior division and brigade officers eligible to command the Division. Brune records their animosities, especially the disgraceful conflict between some Regular Army Duntroon graduates and the Citizen Force Officers.

After a description of some of the men in selected battalions who fought in the Malayan Campaign, Brune then reviews the fate of men in selected Forces who were prisoners of war in Malaya, Singapore, Burma and Thailand. He focuses on the Malayan Campaign, Changi and the construction of the Burma–Thailand Railway; he does not attempt to provide a comprehensive history of all elements of the 8th Division (for example those who were in Borneo, Rabaul, Ambon and Timor).

Descent into Hell gives us an insight into the stark difference between the experience of prisoners in Burma and Thailand based on the contrasting geography in each country. In my experience of the Railway in Burma, there were initially neither villages nor shops, only occasional clusters of a few dwellings linked by ox-cart tracks through the dense bamboo and teak jungles. As the Railway progressed the tracks were enlarged to allow the Japanese trucks to carry supplies and material for the Railway construction. During the wet season the tracks became little more than ruts in thick mud.

By contrast, in Thailand from the Burma border to Bangkok, the Railway ran alongside a road and navigable river (in effect a 'four-lane highway' with nothing comparable in Burma). Together, the road and river enabled vehicles and barges to deliver supplies to the several sizable towns, villages and shops, and the growing construction camps (both in number and size). These construction camps received a regular supply of rations and supplementary supplies of food and medicines. Such supplies were made possible by the operation of a highly organised black market of food and life-giving drugs.

The 44 Australian Medical Officers and their medical orderlies who served on the Railway come in for special recognition by Brune. He acknowledges and praises their dedication and, in particular, their remarkable efforts in improvisation: without essential medical supplies or equipment, they treated men who suffered from a variety of diseases. Brune also stresses the importance of the need for close cooperation between the POW Commanding Officers and their Medical Officers. The Medical Officers who receive special mention in this book are: Lieutenant-Colonel Albert 'Bertie' Coates, Major Bruce Hunt, Captain Roy Mills and Captain Dave Hinder. (I saw Albert Coates in a jungle camp in Burma battling the effects of severe dengue fever. Such was the dedication of this doctor that he insisted on being carried on a stretcher to visit his sick patients. He was outstanding among remarkable colleagues.)

Brune gives credit to some officers and condemns the disgraceful behaviour of others. He also gives credit to the courage with which the men (who were forced to undertake slave labour while being starved and denied adequate accommodation, rest and clothing) faced up to the shocking treatment they received from the Japanese and Korean guards. I was particularly impressed by Brune's account of the different kinds of cruelty inflicted by the Japanese—and by some camp commanders and other officers—on our men.

The author concludes this book by summarising the results of his research and revealing important facts that have previously remained unpublished or unverified. Having also studied other campaigns fought by the AIF in World War II, he assures readers that the fighting soldiers of the 8th Division hold a record second to none in the 2nd AIF despite statements to the contrary.

This remarkable book, with its extraordinary commitment to accuracy and detail, is the only one of its kind relating to the 8th Division; it will fill missing gaps in the knowledge and understanding of most readers. This book is a chronicle of man's unpredictability and man's inhumanity to man (both Australian and Japanese) overwhelmingly overshadowed by genuine life-saving mateship. I thoroughly recommend *Descent into Hell* as essential reading for all Australians.

Dr Rowley Richards, RAAMC Maj (ret.) MBE OAM KStJ ED MID MBBS HonMD Caus MD, FRACGP FACOM FASMF ACSM FAIM, RMD of the 2/15th Field Regiment, Anderson Force (Thai–Burma Railway) and Sakata Force (Japan)

Sydney, August 2013

LIST OF MAPS

PROLOGUE

Driver Joe Nimbs, 4th Reserve Motor Transport Company, 8th Division Australian Imperial Force (AIF):

It's dawn in Singapore City, Friday the 13th of February 1942. There is another stinking hot day coming up. The sky has a red glow, partly from the rising sun, but mainly from reflections of fires raging around the city and the docks at Keppel Harbour. As daylight starts to appear the air raid sirens keep wailing as Jap planes carry out their bombing missions unopposed. Between them and their artillery they are blowing the guts out of Singapore. We haven't seen any of our aircraft for many days. The lack of air and land support are our main problems. The Japs have our forces, the civilian population and countless numbers of refugees, jammed into the south-eastern corner of the island.

Our ambulances are in the grounds of St Andrew's, the beautiful one hundred-year-old Church of England Cathedral, a landmark of the city. The Cathedral's been converted into an emergency military hospital, and we've got the job of driving the wounded from the CCSs [Casualty Clearing Stations] to the church. Large red crosses have been painted on sheets and put on the roof to let the Japs know that

1

this is a hospital and in the corner of the grounds the cooks are set up, giving anyone from any unit a feed.

These beautiful Cathedral grounds, with their colourful tropical shrubs and well kept lawns are changing in appearance. The lawns are disappearing as graves are dug to lay to rest battle casualties that were too badly wounded to survive—the crosses are quickly growing in number.

A Bren gun carrier pulls up in a cloud of steam at the entrance to the cathedral. It . . . has a big dent on the driver's side and a bashed-in headlight, and the radiator is dripping water. It has brought in two badly wounded troops, one with a leg so badly torn it looks like he will lose it, and his mate is suffering from chest and facial wounds. The driver is a tall, thin, sunburnt Australian, his face red and peeling. He's no more than twenty and the bandage on his arm is red from blood that has seeped through. He's absolutely buggered and should be in hospital himself. Catching our stares he says, 'The bloody Japs dropped a shell amongst us about two hours ago and killed three and badly wounded my two mates who I've brought in. And they gave me and some others in the area a few cuts.' He shrugs his shoulders as he fills the radiator and then gets back into the Bren gun carrier and heads back to the front line.

The ever decreasing perimeter our forces are holding is becoming a shambles. It's swelling to bursting point by the stream of refugees. Many have arrived some time ago by rail, or by car or truck or even bike. Others are on foot carrying baskets on their shoulders, piled to capacity with everything they can carry. And their children are carrying bundles nearly as big as themselves.

Mothers show their terrible strain, babies in their arms or on their backs, just able to shuffle along as their toddlers hang onto their clothing. Others are caring for elderly and wounded relations, while all panic at the sounds of the bomb blasts and the rumble of the heavy artillery in action, the screaming of the air raid sirens, and the wailing of the wounded. The dead pile up as the living look for somewhere safe. And where would that be?

A stream of cars loaded with families, mainly European, is trying to get to the wharves. They find they have to abandon their cars a long way off, adding to the enormous tangle of vehicles that have been dumped in the area. Near the wharves, some have been let run into the sea, others left on the road by their owners before leaving the country where they stand with those of later arrivals hoping to get away on anything that floats. The pile of vehicles ranges from trucks to the most luxurious sedans some of which have been chauffeur driven. The British with their ladies and families, whom most of the population used to have to bow and scrape to, get no right of way. These days it's everyone for themselves. We have heard all sorts of rewards are being offered by the Europeans to anyone who has anything that looks like it could get them away from Singapore Island.

The rosary beads are getting a hammering while many believers in other denominations are bending the knee as the black smoke blowing across the island blocks out the sun and gives the area an eerie look that seems to spell doomsday. I feel for the troops who are holding the lines while suffering enormous casualties, their main support being their big hearts. Friday the 13th is drawing to a close, and it'll be one we remember for the rest of our lives.

It is Saturday morning, the 14th of February. At St Andrew's Cathedral an elderly English lady is playing 'Nearer My God To Thee' and similar hymns on the mighty Cathedral organ. The sound of the organ is all consuming, playing to a packed congregation—not of orderly rows of occupied pews, but full of doctors, and orderlies, over-tired with make-shift gear working like hell attending to the many wounded. Some of the stacked pews do come in handy, as they are used to rest a number of the incoming and post-operative patients. But it is an up hill battle—the gardens are quickly giving way to more fresh earth and crosses.

Another beautifully spoken prosperous looking English lady is standing near the Cathedral entrance with a couple of Pekinese dogs in her arms, the only worry she seems to have is the noise of the air raid sirens and bomb blasts which are cowering the dogs. She is the wife of a Malayan rubber plantation manager. They have evacuated their two daughters back to England a fair time ago, but she wouldn't go, and her husband doesn't know she's still in Singapore because he's been fighting with the Malay Volunteers. He gave her instructions to drive to Singapore, dump the car and then get on anything carrying passengers to England or, failing that, to get to India. It would have been easy to get a passage then. But she had decided to stay on with a friend to help the wounded and the never-ending stream of refugee children who get separated from their families in the panic that goes on when shells are bursting close by. The poor things, mostly uneducated, don't seem to understand what is going on. They just run—it doesn't matter where just as long as they run. Some finish up getting hurt falling into shell holes or bomb craters, while others get knocked over and trampled on.

As we pick up more wounded, we hear that Japanese snipers have now infiltrated the perimeter. Are they fifth columnists who have been living and spying in Singapore and have now taken up arms? Rifle fire can be heard from the tops of some city buildings.

Some of the wounded in the Cathedral are asking what is going on. What can we tell them? Most seem to pin their faith on us receiving air support or being evacuated. What courage these men have. The staunchest of the 'hopers' are beginning to wonder what our fate will be as the smell of blocked and busted sewers, decomposing bodies in building rubble and the many fires raging in refuse that could not be disposed of, are causing fear of an outbreak of some serious disease.

Today, Sunday the 15th of February 1942, the dawn breaks with the sun rising in a ball of fire as it did yesterday, is today, and will tomorrow. The distance to the front lines to load wounded is only a few miles.

As night approaches the flares and gun fire seem more spasmodic than they have been. The latest battle casualties are very low in morale. Some think we will all be annihilated, others have no idea what will happen. All agree with what one bloke said, 'They've got us buggered.' For days now we've had little sleep, snatching a few hours whenever we can. My mate Nelson Potter and I have been using a truck that has been put out of action on a road alongside St Andrews. Later in the evening I wake up, turn over, and am about to go back to sleep again when I sense something is different. I sit up and rub my eyes. Not a sound. I wake Nelson up.

We stand up and peer down the road. To confuse things there are a lot of Chinese on the move, heading eastward. We jump down from the truck and run across the Cathedral grounds. Some of our unit and other troops are sitting with heads bowed in their hands. Others are walking about stunned by the news that Singapore has surrendered.

What can you say in a situation where you stare into space without recognising anything? You have a shocked, choked feeling, your heart is beating like hell pushing blood up into your head until your brain seems as if it will burst. Everything is in a whirl and you just can't think straight. Hell, let's get the head down somewhere.

We wake up on Monday the 16th of February to see men pouring beer and spirits down the drain from the Adelphi Hotel across the road. A lot of the troops still seem too dazed to realise what has happened. Those of us affected this way snap to reality later in the morning when we either see or hear that the Japanese flag has been unfurled at Fort Canning—'the blazing arsehole'.

What will they think at home? Will they know the truth about the non-existence of air and naval support, the shortage of essential arms, the fifth columnists in Singapore? Some of us are asking questions, while others are trying to find answers.[1]

Driver Joe Nimbs wasn't the only one trying to make sense out of the fall of Singapore. Historians in Britain and Australia—and Singapore itself—have been asking how and why this disaster occurred for over 70 years.

PART I
PRELUDE TO WAR

. . . the stresses and strains

———⊷⊷⊶———

Absorbed in building the temple of peace
They neglect to take into account
The stesses and strains the edifice may have to bear . . .

Liddell Hart, *Thoughts on War*, 1925

1

THE SUN NEVER SETS . . .

After landing at Singora and Patani in southern Thailand and Kota Bharu in Malaya, the Japanese, in just ten weeks, were able to dominate the seas, command the skies and crush all land resistance, culminating in the surrender of Singapore on 15 February 1942.

The fall of that city remains the largest military capitulation in the long, proud history of British Arms, and remains a controversial and painful episode in both British and Australian history. The immediate cost was easy to count: over 50 000 British and empire troops surrendered and a significant amount of their equipment was transferred to Japanese hands. But there were also long-term consequences. The prestige of European colonial rule was severely eroded and the cause of Asian nationalism thereby significantly enhanced. In blunt terms, the long-dominant white master had not only been beaten, but totally humiliated by those he considered his cultural and racial inferiors.

Such massive defeats and consequent humiliations, and the loss of prestigious commercial colonies, are rarely received with measured objectivity and much less with compassion. Scapegoats had to be found, particularly by politicians who endeavoured to absolve themselves of their responsibilities by shifting the focus upon generals; while a number of senior officers in turn attempted to cover up their actions often by adopting a rather flexible attitude to the truth. In the case of the Australians, some of these officers wrote their lines in the compulsory and prolonged detention of Changi, while one, who had escaped back home to Australia, faced the wrath of elements of his army with whom he had been warring for years.

And then capitulation had its price. The consequence of defeat could not have been imagined by the vanquished. Pudu and Changi prisons and the Thai–Burma Railway would constitute a different fight, a protracted fight to survive, to come home and to start again.

Much has been written about life in Changi and its subsequent work parties on Singapore Island. But Changi's overriding significance lies far beyond its university and entertainment programs—and pinching all manner of items from the docks at Keppel Harbour. The real issues have more to do with the black market and the nature of leadership in that jail. The experience of Australians in Pudu Prison in Kuala Lumpur will shed much light on these matters.

For Australians, the Thai–Burma Railway has become a fourfold legend: there are the stories of 'Weary' Dunlop; the mateship and survival techniques of individuals; the brutality of the Japanese and Korean guards; and Hellfire Pass. All are legitimate legends, but the Thai–Burma Railway also teaches us so much more about the very essence of leadership.

To a very large extent, the chances of survival for a prisoner of war on the Thai–Burma Railway came down to a deadly game of chance. The POWs often endured the monstrous and widespread brutality of the Japanese and Korean guards, and the effects of prolonged slave labour while on a grossly inadequate diet exacerbated the chance of disease. In such circumstances, two people could greatly enhance their chances of survival: their unit's commanding officer and doctor.

A brave and efficient commanding officer worked hand-in-hand with his doctor. That CO's administrative acumen, his courage and sheer guile in managing the limited force or battalion funds—often, incredibly, a substantial portion of it brought from Changi—could mean the difference between life and death for his men. And then there was the black market, both along the River Kwai and in local villages. The barge traffic on the River Kwai brought some supplies of nutritious food, but, above all, supplies of critically important drugs, such as emetine hydrochloride, the miracle saviour for the biggest killer on the Railway: bacillary and amoebic dysentery. There were never anywhere near enough food supplements and fewer drugs, but such resourceful commanders and dedicated doctors could often tip the balance in favour of survival.

The experiences of three battalions from different forces on the Railway will demonstrate that some officers who shine in battle are lost in the POW experience, while others who make no particular impression in action, come to legendary status amongst their own in the crucible of incarceration. Field Service Regulations and the Geneva Convention were essentially redundant documents on the Railway of Death. There was no handbook for leadership. Sadly, our story will also examine the dire consequences for POWs when they found themselves under the command of docile, indifferent or neglectful senior officers who were quite simply useless in that unique environment.

Each of the five parts to this story explains another, and helps us to understand the continuum that led to the tragedy of the fall of Singapore, the POW experience in Pudu and Changi, the Thai–Burma Railway, and the postwar political and military aftermath of that crushing defeat. But our story must start at the end of the First World War, where the folly of Versailles, the interwar years of misplaced idealism, disjointed defence policy and neglect conspired to place one of the greatest empires the world has seen on its knees.

When, on 11 November 1918, an armistice was signed to end the most destructive and costly war in history to that time, the Allies stood in triumph on, and in some cases across, the borders of the once powerful Germany. But that victory masked a number of long-term physical, economic and psychological wounds that the victors had incurred in their 52-month ordeal. France had borne 25 per cent of the Allied killed in its total of over 5.5 million casualties, Britain had suffered around 885 000 dead and about 1.6 million wounded, while Australia had sacrificed around 60 000 killed and approximately 150 000 wounded.[1] The cream of a generation had been put to the sword for victory. And despite this heady triumph it was realised, particularly by the French, that within a generation Germany would again be able to muster an army twice the size of the French Army and that it remained the largest homogeneous nation in Europe.

The economic cost of the war was on a scale never contemplated by any of the participants. Billions of pounds of Britain's wealth had been strewn across the killing fields of France and Belgium. The victorious but exhausted and mourning masses of the Allied powers demanded that Germany must pay and never rise again. Three mechanisms were employed to this end: the Treaty of Versailles; a form of international government where the perceived power of the many might in future control, by sanctions and collective military might, the aggression of the few; and international disarmament initiatives amongst the world's great powers.

On 21 November 1918, the Royal Navy set sail along with two squadrons of American and French ships into the North Sea, for the purpose of intercepting the German High Seas Fleet. From their bases at Kiel and Wilhelmshaven 91 German warships put to sea for the last time. Escorted between two columns of Allied ships, the German fleet was interned at the British naval base at Scapa Flow, while the Allies at Versailles determined their fate.

Fearful of the future deployment of their ships, the German officers hatched an audacious plan, the scale of which had not been witnessed before, nor seen since. On 21 July 1919, while the British Fleet were on exercises, the Germans scuttled 52 of their ships at Scapa Flow.

The Treaty of Versailles allowed France to shelter behind the natural barrier of the Rhine. It provided for the virtual dismantling of the German armed forces by the reduction of its army to a mere 100 000 men; it forbade the already dismembered German Navy, much of which was lying on the seabed at Scapa Flow, to possess no more than six battleships, six light cruisers, twelve destroyers and twelve torpedo boats, and no Dreadnought class capital (battle) ships or submarines; and it further prohibited either the army or navy possession of any air forces.[2] In addition, a massive series of reparation payments was proposed. Perhaps Field Marshal Foch best summed up the ruthless nature of the treaty when he said: 'This is not peace. It is an Armistice for twenty years.'[3]

The League of Nations was created as a part of the Treaty of Versailles on 28 June 1919. Its covenant contained a number of lofty, ambitious articles.

It laid down a process for the peaceful resolution of international disputes by the means of an international court; it allowed for the isolation, both politically and economically, of a transgressor by the world community; and critically, it allowed for military intervention by a selection of nominated members against an aggressor, with the costs of such involvement to be shared amongst all members. But arguably its most ambitious aim was disarmament. Article 8 stated that the maintenance of peace would require general armaments only to satisfy national safety and as a contribution to collective peacekeeping. Further, the members of the League undertook to exchange full and frank information as to the scale of their armaments, their defence programs and the state of their industries which were adaptable to the pursuit of war.

Despite these undertakings the immediate postwar years were marked by a resumption of the race for naval dominance. While the British Parliament, which had looked to a reduction of capital ships after the German scuttling at Scapa Flow, now scrapped more than a hundred ships, including the groundbreaking HMS *Dreadnought*, the United States embarked upon a massive capital ship-building program. By 1921, six battle cruisers and twelve of the largest and most powerful battleships ever conceived were either on the drawing board or under construction, which reflected that nation's position as the new industrial giant of the world. Once completed, the American fleet would outnumber, outgun and outrun any of the remaining world's principal naval powers.

In the Far East, Japan watched this American naval expansion with apprehension. It saw the United States as a serious impediment to its growth in the Asia-Pacific region. Japan now went down the same costly capital ship-building path that the United States had taken. And this initiative consumed approximately two-fifths of the Japanese budget.

Britain, still recovering from the First World War's drain upon its wealth, could neither financially afford to participate in this race, nor strategically afford to lose it. The British now embarked upon a capital ship-building program that demanded larger, faster and more heavily armed capital ships that could compete in a global war.

After the First World War, Britain was faced with a further problem. British governments had long maintained a strong relationship with Japan, which had been strengthened by the Anglo–Japanese Alliance of 1902. That union had delivered British neutrality for Japan during the Russo–Japanese War; it had committed either signatory to go to the assistance of the other in defence of their interests in the Far East or India if attacked by any other power; and as a consequence, in 1917, it had seen Japan provide much-needed convoy protection for British ships in both the Mediterranean and the Indian Ocean. As a result of the alliance, and the desire to increase their European fleet, the British were also able to reduce their China Squadron fleet based at Hong Kong. In return for this assistance, Japan had occupied the German concession of Tsingtao on the Shantung Peninsula in China, and had occupied the German Pacific possessions of the Marshall, Caroline and Mariana Islands, which were retained as mandated territories after Versailles. A continuance of the Anglo–Japanese Alliance would place Britain in an invidious position, since potential antipathy between the US and Japan over the balance of power in China and conflicting interests in the western Pacific could harm its relationship with the United States. The problem was how to end the alliance without antagonising the Japanese.

It is ironic that the United States was the first major power to offer a solution to the then current runaway naval arms race, and also the answer to Britain's alliance with Japan. In 1921, the United States Secretary of State, Charles Evans Hughes, called a conference to be convened in Washington during November of that year, for the prime purpose of a capping of the construction of capital ships.

On 6 February 1922, the United States, Great Britain and its empire, Japan, France and Italy agreed to the following tonnage of capital ships: the United States 525 000 tons; Great Britain and her empire 525 000 tons; Japan 315 000 tons; France 175 000 tons; and Italy 175 000 tons. The provision of aircraft carriers was broadly on the same ratio and all replacements of capital ships were restricted to prescribed tonnages. Under Article 14 of the Washington Naval Agreement, the three major powers in the Pacific region—the United States, Britain and Japan—agreed to confine their spheres of influence to specific areas and not build any new bases or facilities outside them.

For Britain, this meant 'Hong Kong and any limited possessions east of the meridian 110° E, except those adjacent to Canada, Australia and New

Zealand'.[4] This undertaking maintained British assets in the Far East and the integrity of her sea routes to them, but meant that Britain could not build naval bases east of Singapore.

The United States was restricted to 'the insular possessions in the Pacific, except those adjacent to the coasts of the USA, Alaska (not including the Aleutian Islands), the Panama Canal zone and Hawaii (Pearl Harbor)'.[5] The United States could henceforth not build bases west of Hawaii. The Japanese retained 'the insular territories and possessions of Japan in the Pacific Ocean, to wit the Kurele, Bonin, Ryukyu Islands, Formosa and the Pescadores'.[6] But Japan's great gains were the mandated Mariana, Caroline and Marshall Islands—granted by the League of Nations—which were not mentioned in this treaty. By retaining those islands, Japan had potential bases across the American lines of communication to Guam and the Philippines, and there-fore critical control over the north-west Pacific region. It was agreed by the signatories that the Washington Naval Treaty was to remain in force until December 1936.

This treaty was followed quite quickly by two further agreements. The first was the Four-Power Treaty, signed by the USA, Britain, France and Japan, which provided for the 'status quo in the Pacific',[7] and the determina-tion to solve each of the signatories' disputes, instigated from within or by an outside power, by peaceful means. The second was the Nine-Power Treaty where 'the nine signatory powers agreed to respect the sovereignty, the rights and interests and the integrity of China'.[8]

Within four years of the end of the 'war to end all wars', the victori-ous Western Allies could look to a recently defeated and militarily defunct Germany, which, by the conditions of the Treaty of Versailles, could not rebuild or maintain armed forces capable of any significant military action on the Continent or on the high seas; they could look to reparation payments as compensation for their crippling war costs; they had created the League of Nations as an instrument of collective international security; and in the Pacific, they saw the Washington Naval Treaty as a timely handbrake upon the costly and runaway naval arms race, and a recognition of each signatory's interests and spheres of influence.

As a consequence of the Treaty, the Royal Navy was bound to scrap 22 capital ships and four partly constructed battle cruisers, while the United

States pledged the scrapping of four existing capital ships and a further seventeen under construction. From an Australian perspective the treaty was particularly ruthless. The fledgling Royal Australian Navy was considered a part of the British Navy and under the ratio of Britain and its empire to the US and to Japan of 5:5:3 in capital ships, Australia was duly forced to scuttle her battle cruiser HMAS *Australia* off Sydney Heads in April 1924. That battle cruiser was Australia's only capital ship.

Amongst all the idealism and optimism of the Washington Naval Treaty, in the end it was Britain who stood as the colossal loser. During the later part of the nineteenth century the Royal Navy had been capable of defeating any two of the world's next great sea powers. 'The sun never sets on the British Empire' were not idle words—Britain had a far-flung empire across the globe, and the industrial, political and military might to protect its interests. But after the First World War and then the Washington Naval Treaty, the Royal Navy's influence had to now encompass the Pacific as well as the Atlantic and Mediterranean. Britain's considerable Far Eastern commercial interests lay fairly and squarely in that now exposed eastern hemisphere. Its commercial sea power and trade routes still existed, but the naval might required to protect them was in decline.

In Europe, further feelings of security were established by the signing of the Locarno Treaties, negotiated in Locarno, Switzerland between 5 and 16 October 1925, and signed on 1 December of that year in London. Its purpose was to maintain the integrity of the postwar territorial settlements and an eventual diplomatic return of the German Weimar Republic to western European affairs and membership of the League of Nations.

Procedures and time had now been created to mend the physical and economic wounds of the First World War but the psychological impact of that conflict lingered. It remained to be seen whether each of the victors would have the resolve to make the League of Nations work by enforcing its charter, and further, whether they would have the determination to provide for their own defence capabilities upon which the idealism of the League of Nations depended. But in the end the victors got off to a feeble start.

President Woodrow Wilson had been the guiding hand in the agenda for the Versailles Treaty. He had delivered his famous 'Fourteen Points' address to the US Congress on 8 January 1918, in which he proclaimed amongst his framework, the abolition of secret treaties, free trade, disarmament, freedom of the seas, the establishment of Poland with access to the sea, and critically, the formation of the League of Nations. However, Britain questioned his assertion of freedom of the seas, France desired colossal reparation payments from Germany, and his own Congress was wary of the League's potential to interfere in the jurisdiction of Congress to act in time of war. In the end, a number of the Fourteen Points were not accepted by the European powers and the United States Congress did not vote to join the League. Therefore, arguably the world's greatest power had failed to join that organisation at its inception, a grave handicap to both its potency and therefore its credibility.

The United States now withdrew into a period of isolationism. This policy had two broad precepts. The first was that the US would henceforth avoid all foreign alliances, and therefore potential wars, that did not relate directly to its own territorial security. The second was that the US believed that it could operate as an independent, self-reliant economic power, lying behind a wall of protectionist tariffs. Three consecutive Republican presidents— Harding, Coolidge and Hoover—stuck rigidly to this doctrine. Perhaps President Calvin Coolidge best summed up the plan: 'the chief business of the American people is business.' After a period of economic turmoil, the United States entered into a period of unparalleled wealth. The business of business was booming. The United States had, for all intents and purposes, turned its back on the rest of the world.

2

THE FAR EAST AND
NEAR NORTH

In 1921, believing that a major war was unlikely for a period of at least ten years, the British Government decided that maintaining a fleet in both the western and eastern hemispheres was too costly, and in the end, unnecessary. Further, there was no naval base in the Far East capable of servicing a modern fleet, that is, a fleet still dominated by the massive Dreadnought class (and now further advanced) battleships of the time. Hong Kong was not an option, since it lacked the docking and repair facilities needed, and was also seen as being indefensible because of its isolation and close proximity to Formosa, a Japanese base. It was therefore decided that a central fleet would be held in European waters, from which the Far East could be reinforced in time of war, and that a new base would be built in that region to accommodate it.

In selecting the location of a new Far Eastern naval base five factors were of paramount importance. The first was the need to be able to protect the enormous commercial maritime traffic which ran from Britain, through the Mediterranean, the Suez Canal, and then on to Ceylon, before diverging on two paths: one going south-east to Fremantle, Adelaide, Melbourne, Sydney and on to New Zealand; and the other through the Strait of Malacca, to Singapore, the Dutch East Indies, Borneo, Indo-China, Hong Kong and

Shanghai. The second factor was the potential to deploy a capital ship-dominated navy quickly in the sea lanes described. In other words, the British fleet should be in reasonable proximity to the potential area of operations. The third factor was a consequence of the second: the fleet would have to be close enough to an existing network of refuelling points and oil production. The fourth was the need for a skilled pool of labour for the repair facilities provided. But it was the fifth factor that was most critical. Given that the first four factors were satisfied, 'there would be an undesirable lapse of time between the moment that an emergency necessitated the despatch of a part of the fleet to the Far East and its arrival there'.[1]

This final factor became known as the 'Period before Relief', and it described the period during which any British or empire army or air force stationed at the new base had to be able to withstand an attack until well after the relieving naval force could engage its adversary. When the Committee of Imperial Defence applied these five prerequisites to possible base venues, two locations became worthy of close examination: Sydney and Singapore.

Sydney possessed three advantages. The first was a more than satisfactory supply of skilled labour; the second was that it seemed at the time to be almost invulnerable to a Japanese attack—in 1921 the full potential of carrier-borne aircraft operations had not been fully appreciated nor developed; and third, that it possessed a suitable climate. But Sydney was judged to be too far from the sea lanes it would need to protect, and also too distant from the necessary oil fuel stocks needed to sustain its fleet.

At the time the very criticisms of Sydney's case were perceived as Singapore's chief advantages. A naval base at Singapore would sit neatly near the fork on the Indian Ocean, where on the one hand, the commercial sea lanes veered away through the South China Sea to Indo-China and Shanghai, or south-eastwards to Australia and New Zealand. Singapore also lay close to its supplies of fuel oil. However, Singapore did not possess Sydney's skilled labour pool, and it was nowhere near as secure as that Australian location. It also possessed a far more enervating climate.

In the end, the committee decided on Singapore, as it was considered that a land-based assault upon that island via the jungle terrain in Malaya was unlikely. Further, it perceived that the rich deposits of Malayan rubber and tin, the Dutch East Indies oil supplies and the security of the sea lanes

themselves were far too distant from a proposed Sydney naval base. But
there were dissenting voices.[2] Writing in the London *Daily Telegraph* in
July 1923, Colonel Repington, a respected British military commentator,
said:

> It is of little importance where ships are distributed in peace. The
> only test is war. It is the tradition of Japan to seize the initiative, and
> begin when the flag falls or a little before. We must expect the loss of
> Singapore and Hong Kong before our Grand Fleet sails out there. We
> must also expect the appearance of Japanese submarines in the Sea
> of Malacca. It is useless to send a battalion to Singapore when Japan
> has shown herself capable of capturing a first class fortress like Port
> Arthur, defended by 45,000 men.[3]

Few took note of Repington's critique in those first heady years after
Versailles.

With the successful negotiations for the Washington Naval Treaty
completed late in 1921, plans began for the new base at Singapore. A fundamental question was its location on that island. Two venues were considered.
The first was the already established commercial site at Keppel Harbour on
the south-eastern point of the island, while the second was to the northern
side at the Johore Strait. The latter location was chosen, and reflected the
current thought that any Japanese assault on Singapore was liable to come
from the sea. The decision was finalised in February 1923.

No sooner had this decision been taken than a Labour Government under
Ramsay MacDonald replaced the Baldwin Conservative Government in
January 1924. And with that change of government in the United Kingdom
came a radical foreign policy shift: there was an immediate suspension of
funding for the Singapore naval base. G. Hermon Gill, *Royal Australian Navy
1939–1942*:

> ... the decision not to proceed with the Singapore Base was on the
> grounds that to do so would be inconsistent with its policy of inter-
> national cooperation through a strengthened and enlarged League
> of Nations, the settlement of disputes by conciliation and judicial

arbitration, and the creation of conditions which would make a comprehensive agreement on limitation of armaments possible.[4]

This policy reflected two thought processes. The first was a lofty, idealistic aspiration towards a world community where war was to be virtually outlawed by negotiation, collective security and disarmament. But surely the widespread optimism of the period was underpinned by the still lingering psychological wounds incurred during the First World War: the cost in young lives and a crippling economic burden that must be avoided at almost any cost.

Reflecting this idealism and hope, severe cuts were taken to British defence spending. In 1921–22 the Royal Navy had received funds for expenditure of £95 000 000 which was reduced to £52 000 000 in 1923–24; in 1921–22 the British Army had received £80 000 000 which was cut to £50 000 000 in 1923–24; and for the same period, the Royal Air Force funding had been slashed from £13 000 000 to £9 000 000.[5] Therefore, the total defence budget reduction amounted to £77 000 000 or 41 per cent in two short years. This critical funding blunder was compounded by a political mechanism to maintain limited defence spending for the forseeable future. A 'ten year rule' had been introduced in August 1919 which had, as its cornerstone, the assertion that Britain would not be involved in a major war for a ten-year period. In the event the forecast was proven accurate, but the damage done to Britain's long-term ability to protect its empire, and critically, to maintain its industrial infrastructure in the event of a future war, was severely impaired. In the end, 'the ten year rule' was nothing more than a concerted political ploy for successive governments to abstain from adequate military funding.

However, the MacDonald Labour Government had a short period in office when, in November 1924, Stanley Baldwin led the Conservatives to a resounding victory. The new government immediately announced a continuance of funding for the Singapore Base. A subcommittee of the Committee of Imperial Defence reaffirmed the site of the Johore Strait as the location of the base and then proceeded to examine the best means of defending it. The decision came down to an ongoing and spirited argument as to whether the emphasis should be on fixed guns or aircraft cover. Kirby, in *The War Against Japan*:

The Royal Air Force was the worst offender in this respect, for, having seen their wartime strength waste away after 1918, they tended, under the leadership of Sir Hugh, later Lord, Trenchard, to make claims they could not substantiate, claims which brought them into head-on clashes with the other two services.[6]

The Royal Air Force argument was based on the belief that heavy coastal guns were obsolete and that torpedo bombers, guided by reconnaissance planes and protected by fighters, were capable of a much greater range and were both a greater deterrent and a more potent offensive weapon. Further they argued, unlike the option of fixed guns, aircraft could be deployed elsewhere in times of peace and moved to Singapore as the need arose.

The army and navy took the view that torpedo planes were yet to prove their ability to sink capital ships, that there was no established reinforcement route to Singapore, and critically, that the Royal Air Force did not possess the logistical capability to deploy the necessary ground crews at short notice.

At the time of these deliberations, Singapore had five 9.2-inch guns to protect Keppel Harbour, which were predominantly located to the south on two islands. In the end, the subcommittee placed an each way bet. In July 1926, it recommended the installation of a number of close and medium guns and three 15-inch heavy guns, and that the issue of torpedo planes should be examined in the future. These decisions caused ongoing animosity between the British Army and the Royal Air Force and were to prove an impediment to the long-term defence of Singapore.

The two years prior to the Great Depression were marked by further indecision and delay. When in 1927 the War Office sent a committee under Lieutenant-General Gillman to Singapore to determine the size of a garrison for that island, the location of its fixed defences, and the number of batteries, the committee immediately came into conflict with the government of the Straits Settlements. The civil administration demanded an assurance that the cost of developing the base would be in no measure dependent upon a contribution from them. Delay now ensued.

On receipt of the Gillman Report in March 1928, the War Office reaffirmed its belief that Singapore would not be attacked via the Malay Peninsula, and that resources should therefore be concentrated upon the defence of a seaborne assault. Four months later the Committee of Imperial Defence recommended that the 'Ten Year Rule', which had been implemented in 1919, should be extended with an annual assessment. But worse was to follow. A second Labour Government came into power in 1929, again under the premiership of Ramsay MacDonald. That Prime Minister's idealism and pacifist tendencies had not deserted him since his brief period in office in 1924.

The Kellogg–Briand Pact of 1928, named after its architects, American Secretary of State Frank B. Kellogg and French Foreign Minister Aristide Briand, was an international treaty which asserted that the renunciation of war should be an instrument of national policy. Fifteen nations, including Germany, Japan and Italy, were the original signatories, with numerous other nations joining months after. But with the idealism of the Kellogg–Briand Pact as a perceived guide to the prevention of war for the foreseeable future, the MacDonald Government 'decided that further efforts should be made to obtain international agreement to "general" disarmament, despite the failure of the League of Nations to do so hitherto'.[7] As a result, that government offered to decrease the number of Royal Navy cruisers agreed to in the Washington Naval Treaty of 1922, and also suspended construction of the Singapore Base while waiting for the outcome of the Naval Disarmament Conference, which was to be held in London in 1930. More delay.

The London Naval Treaty, signed in April 1930, provided for the British Empire, the United States, Japan, France and Italy not to replace capital ships during the period 1931–36, under the agreed ratio prescribed in the Washington Naval Treaty signed eight years previously. It further set the cruiser ratio between Britain and her empire, the United States and Japan at 10: 10: 6—and, in addition, allowed for equal numbers of submarines and destroyers. The signatories to the treaty agreed to meet again in 1935.

From the end of the First World War to the onset of the Great Depression, Britain was the second strongest economic power on earth, still deriving enormous wealth from its far-flung empire. In terms of its financial position, therefore, it could still maintain a navy capable of both a domination of European waters and the protection of a considerable source of its revenue: its Far Eastern possessions. But the Washington Naval Conference amounted to a signing off on Britain's ability to protect its assets. To this end it was decided to build a naval base at Singapore capable of servicing a portion of the fleet released from European waters in time of need. The reality was that the ratio in capital ships between Britain and Japan dictated that 60 per cent of that home fleet would have to be sent to the Far East to merely match an enemy fleet in time of war. Such a promise would amount to an empty gesture should Britain become immersed in a war in two hemispheres.

However, the most disturbing aspect of British foreign policy during the decade after the war was the idealistic and misplaced notion that the League of Nations, disarmament and gestures of goodwill through treaties would bring about world peace. Such treaties were merely pieces of paper, and sincere speeches at the League of Nations and disarmament conferences simply became empty rhetoric, unless there was to be a keen vigilance and an unshakable fortitude to back them up with action. Subsequent events would prove there was not.

When Australia's Prime Minister William Morris (Billy) Hughes attended the negotiations for the structure of the Treaty of Versailles and the subsequent birth of the League of Nations, he had one ambition: the physical and social integrity of his nation. To this end, and using Australia's great sacrifice during the war and its military prowess during that conflict as his bargaining strength, Hughes set about gaining control of the former German New Guinea and the maintenance of the White Australia Policy.

Hughes wanted the outright ownership of the German New Guinea possessions, but in the end, the League granted German New Guinea to Australia as a mandated territory.

Despite Japanese efforts to gain international recognition for the principle of racial equality, and the fact that the majority of delegates favoured the motion, Hughes, with the help of President Wilson, was able to see the Japanese proposal defeated. For the first time Australia had, through Hughes's ability to operate both within the British Empire delegation and independently of it, a voice on the international stage.

Although Hughes was an advocate of the League of Nations, he saw Japan's growing power in the Pacific with apprehension. At the Imperial Conference of 1921 he argued that:

... the Pacific problem is for all and practical purposes the problem of Japan. Here is a nation of nearly 70 millions of people, crowded together in narrow islands; its population is increasing rapidly, and is already pressing on the margin of subsistence. She wants both room for her increasing millions of population, and markets for her manufactured goods. And she wants these very badly indeed. America and Australia say to her millions 'Ye cannot enter in.' Japan, then, is faced with the great problem which has bred wars since time began ...

But where are the overflowing millions of Japanese to find room? Not in Australia; not in America. Well, where, then? ...

These 70,000,000 Japanese cannot possibly live, except as a manufacturing nation. Their position is analogous to that of Great Britain. To a manufacturing nation, overseas markets are essential to its very existence. Japan sees across a narrow strip of water 400,000,000 Chinese gradually awakening to an appreciation of Western methods, and she sees in China the natural market for her goods. She feels that her geographical circumstances give her a special right to the exploitation of the Chinese markets. But other countries want the market too, and so comes the demand for the 'Open Door' ...

This is the problem of the Pacific ... for which we must find an answer ... Talk about disarmament is idle unless the causes of naval armaments are removed.[8]

If the Washington Naval Conference had brought reassurance to the British, it also engendered a feeling of great security in Australia. On 26 July 1922, Hughes proclaimed that 'this treaty establishes an equilibrium in the Pacific. As far as any action of man can do so, it ensures peace for the next ten years for Australia.'[9] And as had happened to British funding, the Hughes Government took a similar financial axe to its armed services. In short, this would amount to a reduction of the navy and army, and a postponement of the expansion of the infant air force.

The Royal Australian Navy was ordered to submit alternatives for a £500 000 cut in spending for the financial year 1922–23. The government opted for the Naval Board's second of four alternatives: the scrapping of the RAN submarines. The RAN establishment in commissioned ships was now three light cruisers (unchanged), three destroyers (reduced by one), one sloop (reduced by one) and various ancillaries.

The blade also fell heavily upon the Australian Army. Seventy-two regular army officers out of a modest total of 300 were retired; the staff of the permanent army was cut to 1600; the strength of the Australian Militia— five infantry divisions and two cavalry—numbered only 31 000, which was a mere 25 per cent of their war strength; and funding for training of that undersized organisation amounted to a paltry six days in camp and four days at local drill halls per soldier per year.[10]

On 9 February 1923, the Bruce–Page Coalition Government came into power with Stanley Bruce as prime minister. Bruce saw three challenges for his government: the need for a rapid growth in Australian economic development, improved federal–state relations and national security.

During the period 1923–29 the government adopted the theory that increased capital works programs would facilitate a modern and efficient transport network and therefore lower production costs, which would make exports more competitively priced. By developing the nation's resources, enlarging its industries, providing the necessary labour force through a migration policy, and aggressively seeking larger markets through lower costs, the economy, protected by tariffs, would expand. The migration policy and the funding for these programs were essentially imperial by nature, and mainly financed by English loans. In the economic sense the 1920s were fundamentally the years of borrow, build, protect and prosper. But the reality of a growing public debt and its attendant interest payments was ignored in the euphoria.

Bruce believed that an improvement in the federal system through healthier working relationships between the seven Australian governments, and the creation of mechanisms for improved guidelines for public borrowing, would enhance Australia's appeal to British investors.

In agreement with the former Hughes Government and similar prevailing views in Britain, the Bruce–Page Government saw Australia's defence strategy in its traditional imperial form, with an emphasis on naval rather than on military defence. Before leaving for the Imperial Conference of 1923, Bruce addressed the parliament:

Then we have to face the question of defence. Do we propose to insure our own safety, and not look to the Empire for help? Or are we going to provide our own defence within the Empire, believing that the best way to defend our own country is by entering into close relations with the Motherland and the other Dominions.[11]

The resulting resolutions of the Imperial Conference of 1923 became the essential foundation of Australian defence policy for the period between the world wars. They identified the need or desire to protect both the empire's dominions and territories, and their trade routes. Significantly, the conference resolved that it was the right of any or all of these countries to determine the extent of foreign policy or military action that should be undertaken by them. Further, each country was to be essentially responsible for its own local defence, and was to assist in 'the provision of Naval Bases and facilities for repair and fuel, so as to ensure the mobility of the fleets'.[12] They were also required to maintain the naval integrity of the Washington Treaty and the development of air forces, as far as possible, using 'a common system of organisation and training . . . patterns of arms, equipment and stores . . .'.[13]

There were two other points of interest concerning these resolutions. The first was Australia, New Zealand and India's strong desire to build the Singapore Base, and the second was the desire to maintain the impetus for not merely the existing limitation of armaments, but for further reductions.

When in January 1924 the newly elected MacDonald Labour Government took office in Britain and immediately proceeded to cancel plans for the building of the Singapore Base, the reactions of the empire's dominions clearly reflected their geographic locations, and therefore their vested interests. The South African Government agreed with the MacDonald Government, while the Canadians stated that 'it was not in any position to offer any advice'.[14] The protests came from Australia, New Zealand and Newfoundland. Lord Jellicoe, the Governor-General of New Zealand, made the pertinent point that without the Singapore Base, the closest base from which a relieving fleet could operate would be Malta, some 6000 miles away. He also informed the British Government that the New Zealand Parliament had pledged £100 000 towards the building of the Singapore Base, 'and would not stop at that'.[15]

The Bruce–Page Government protested strongly concerning the suspension of the Singapore Base. Prime Minister Bruce told the British Government that:

> We think ... that if the proposal ... is abandoned by your Government, incalculable harm will be done to the Empire's prestige, the confidence of smaller nations will be shattered, the ambitions of lesser powers will be increased, and deep distrust will be caused throughout the whole Empire. Not by these actions having such results as these can we hope to bring about further reductions in armaments ... Therefore, on behalf of our Commonwealth, which has on every possible occasion proved its loyalty to the Empire, we urge you even at this late hour to reconsider your decision.[16]

The British determination to forgo the building of the Singapore Base, and therefore place the defence of the empire in some jeopardy, forced the Australian Government to look to another part of the 1923 Imperial Defence resolutions: the need of each member of the British Empire to provide for its own defence.

The Australian 1924–25 budget initiated a five-year defence plan costed at £36 250 000. By 1929 the Australian Navy had added two cruisers, two submarines and a seaplane tender, giving it a total of some 28 ships and serving personnel in excess of 5000. During the five-year program, the RAN received £20 000 000 or roughly 55 per cent of the allotted defence funding.

Given that one of the resolutions of the 1923 Imperial Conference had been to develop each dominion's air force, the Bruce–Page Government's response during its five-year plan was pedestrian to say the least. Towards the conclusion of its five-year program, the government invited Sir John Salmond, who had been commander in the Field of the RAF during 1918–19, to assess the fledgling RAAF in terms of its training, equipment and administration. Paul Hasluck, in *The Government and The People, 1939–1941*:

> While kind enough to say that the existing force had been built on firm foundations and developed on sound lines, and giving credit to

those responsible, he also said bluntly that, due to the obsolete type of service machines in use, the entire absence of any reserve equipment, and the low standard of training in the operational units, he considered the R.A.A.F. would be totally unfit to undertake war operations in cooperation with the navy or army even after the permissible period of training for the latter had elapsed.[17]

In response to the shortfalls identified, Salmond recommended a virtual doubling of the government's funding to around £2 000 000 a year for nine years. But before the Bruce–Page Government could instigate a portion of Salmond's recommendations, a change of government occurred.

Nor were the small increases in defence force funding during the period 1924–28 to the benefit of the army. Lieutenant-General Sir Harry Chauvel was the Inspector-General of the Australian Military Forces from 1922 to 1930. His reports during the period 1923–28 are a damning indictment upon the plight of permanent and militia soldiers alike, and portray a lamentable neglect of even basic resources.

A professional soldier in the Australian Army during the 1920s pursued his career because of a number of reasons: his love of soldiering; a high sense of patriotic duty; and, critically, with the perception that the First World War had most certainly not been the war to end all wars, that another war would quite possibly come to Europe and most likely to the Far East also. There was little else to entice him to remain, as the rapid promotion gained in the 1914–18 War had degenerated into stagnant promotional opportunities for a ten-year period, and a reduction in rank and pay. Warrant officers were now denied access to the Officer Corps, 'entry to which was reserved to pre-war regular officers and graduates of Duntroon, and became, at the best, quartermasters, wearing without the corresponding pay and without hope of promotion the rank that they had won in the war'.[18] The only real mechanism for the Staff Corps to engage in further professional study came in the form of service with the British Army in Britain or India for junior officers, and exchange duty or specialised study in British schools, or perhaps at places such as Quetta in India. In 1927, roughly one in every six of the permanent army had spent time overseas studying for at least a portion of the year.[19]

Nor was the ailing army well equipped. Gavin Long, in *To Benghazi*:

Gains in equipment were microscopic: in 1926 the army obtained its first motor vehicles—five 30-cwt lorries, one for each military district except the Sixth (Tasmania), and eight tractors for the artillery; in 1927 four light tanks arrived. Nor could the army comfort itself with the reflection that, when the need arose, it could commandeer enough horses . . .[20]

There was also often a certain social stigma attached to military service. To the idealist of the 1920s, and there were no shortage of them, the soldier and his political supporters were 'brass hats', 'war mongers' or 'militarists'. They merely perpetuated the capitalist struggles between peoples, and whose inevitable victims were the working class, who were denied social progress in terms of working conditions and pay, and who inevitably provided the cannon fodder for war. It was a common Australian perception of the times that the great issues facing the young federation were immigration, increased land settlement, the discovery and utilisation of the nation's resources, a transport infrastructure, and, importantly, in conjunction with those economic issues, came the social question of industrial relations. Issues of foreign policy and defence were the realm of the League of Nations, of international disarmament and arbitration. These were the intellectual initiatives, the intelligent mechanisms of a pursuit of peace—a new social order and a brave new world.

If there had been dissenting voices in Britain over the location of a naval base in the Far East and the nature of its defences, Australian military strategists were also debating the issues.

In a remarkable and far-sighted lecture entitled, *The Strategical Inter-Relationship of the Navy, the Army and the Air Force: An Australian View*, delivered to the Royal United Service Institute in Melbourne on 1 September 1926 and published in the *Army Quarterly* in April 1927, Lieutenant-Colonel H. D. Wynter, Staff Corps, Australian Military Forces, outlined his perspective concerning imperial naval defence and the Singapore Strategy.

He began with the relationship between the navy and army:

... in the British Empire—mainly a maritime empire—the Navy is
the first consideration. First, because of the territorial security which
it affords to the heart of the Empire; secondly, because freedom of the
seas is essential to the food supply of the United Kingdom; and thirdly,
because in a maritime empire it is only by means of a superior navy
that the mobility of the decisive instruments of war—land forces—
can be assured.[21]

Wynter then went on to mention the need for a potent defence of naval
bases by land forces 'on which the fleet depends' and that a maritime
empire would depend upon 'the proper development' of both the navy and
army and the mutual recognition of both.

He then discussed, with great foresight and an equal measure of common
sense, the relationship of the air force to the other services:

... there does not yet appear to have been established any generally accepted doctrine on this subject; on the contrary, there appears
to be much difference of opinion, not to say confusion of thought,
upon the whole matter. There are those who maintain that not in
any circumstances can an air force have a completely independent
strategical role, and, on the other side, there are those who maintain
that air-power is the only power which counts and that the other
Services, if not actually redundant, are at any rate strategically
subordinate.[22]

The above portion of his speech alluded to the then passionate debate
between the services of the time concerning the role(s) of air forces. There
were those strategists who maintained that an enemy's ability to conduct a
war hinged upon his industrial capacity. By massed air force attacks upon
industry and a destruction of an enemy's civilian morale, some strategists—
mainly air force—believed that nations could be brought to defeat. Wynter
maintained that: '... attacks of this kind can only be of secondary and
subsidiary importance, since the really decisive act in war is the battle itself,
and no amount of destruction in an enemy's rear territory will be of much
use if the main battle is lost.'[23]

In concluding this portion of his address, Wynter identified the need for the three services to develop a common understanding of the requirement for training of officers of all services in the 'broader aspects of war upon common lines and the building up, if possible, of a common doctrine of war to which they will all subscribe'.[24] Profound words indeed, and words subsequently ignored by many in Britain and Australia with regards to future events concerning the Singapore Base.

Wynter then turned his attention to the empire's naval defence. Predicting that the Singapore Base would eventually be built, he identified two critical points. The first was the obvious change in the balance of naval power. He correctly stated that the British Navy could no longer reign supreme across the globe, and that, from an Australian perspective, its Pacific strength was therefore 'merely a potential force' and would not become 'an actual force' until it had been moved to the Pacific. And then came, as Colonel Repington had foreseen in Britain nearly three years earlier, Wynter's realistic statement:

> ... the question arises whether under all circumstances reasonably likely to arise it can be confidently relied upon by Australia that the British Navy will be able to operate in the Pacific in sufficient strength to ensure the security of Australia. It is a reasonable assumption that, if war were to break out with a Pacific Power, it would be at some time when Great Britain was involved in war in Europe.
>
> Even though the British Navy is preponderantly superior to any one existing European Navy, is it likely that the British Government would sanction the despatch of sufficient naval strength to the Far East to ensure superiority there until the local problem had been dealt with? The security of Great Britain—the heart of the Empire—is the primary consideration of Imperial defence. Even if other interests suffer, that supreme interest must be kept inviolate ...
>
> Moreover, even assuming that a British Government were willing to accept whatever risks were entailed in the dividing of its naval forces, what would be the attitude of British public opinion at a time when there existed a real or a fancied threat to its food supply? The public pays the piper ...[25]

Given these circumstances, Wynter still maintained that the Australian Navy should remain as a part of general empire defence—that is, working in conjunction with the Royal Navy—since it could not hope to operate in a Pacific confrontation as an independent operational force. As a consequence, Wynter argued that the local defence of Australia would come down to its army and air force, and that both should be funded accordingly and operate under a unified command. He then stated or identified the additional issues of 'the production of war material and internal communications'[26] which he chose not to elaborate upon, but which would obviously be critical to his stated aims for army and air force development.

Thus, as had been the case in Britain, Australia too had its dissenting voices concerning the Singapore Base, the Royal Navy's ability to react to a genuine world war, the paucity of funding for the army and air force, and critically, the need for a united or interrelated doctrine for all service arms. These assessments were level-headed and responsible but, in the end, were lost in a sea of idealism, pacifism, interservice rivalry and, above all else, a desperate longing for an avoidance of a repetition of the slaughter and financial cost of another World War.

When in 1929 industrial disputes in Australian reached their highest point since the end of the First World War, Prime Minister Bruce called a double dissolution of parliament. The resulting election saw a Labor Government take office with James Scullin as the new prime minister. In terms of defence policy, the new Labor Government differed markedly from its predecessor. Within months of this election result, however, the Great Depression began to affect the world economy. And with that catastrophe, global forces were unleashed that would change the world's political and social landscape— forces that would also drastically change the complexity and urgency of defence considerations.

To the cash-strapped British, their commercial possessions across the other side of the world yielded much-needed financial gain, but were not to the forefront of their defence planning, and were therefore aptly referred to as the 'Far East'. To a young, only recently federated and increasingly anxious white Australia, Britain's 'Far East' was now increasingly seen as Australia's 'Near North'.

3

SINGING FROM DIFFERENT
HYMN SHEETS

The Malay Peninsula is approximately six-tenths of the area of Victoria, and is about 640 kilometres (400 miles) from its northernmost point to its southern extremity. It varies in width from roughly 95 to 320 kilometres (60 to 200 miles). Thailand, then known as Siam, lies across its northern border; the South China Sea is to the east; Singapore lies at its farthest southern point; and to its west and south-west, across the narrow Strait of Malacca lies the then Dutch East Indies island of Sumatra.

A mountain range 'generally 4000 feet high and rising to 7186 feet'[1] (about 1220 to 2190 metres), forms the spine of the Malay Peninsula and prewar the coastal plains to the east and west of this feature contained most of the population and commercial interests—particularly on the western plain. As a consequence of Malaya having a close proximity to the equator, and also a very high tropical rainfall, the vegetation in the mountains was essentially untouched virgin jungle. On the plains virgin and secondary jungle, cleared for cultivation, abandoned, and then allowed to regenerate, gave way in part to regional towns, villages (kampongs) and their associated cultivated areas of rice fields, coconut, pineapple and rubber plantations. Tin mining, mainly on the western plain, was also an extremely profitable commercial pursuit in prewar Malaya. Most of the rivers on the peninsula ran from the mountainous spine east or westwards to the coast, where poor drainage often resulted in jungle swamps.

Singapore Island is not unlike the ball of a ball-and-socket joint—it sits neatly across the Straits of Johore, varying from about 550 to 1830 metres (600 to 2000 yards) from the curved, concave southernmost tip of the Malay Peninsula. Roughly a quarter of the size of the Australian Capital Territory, it is a mere 22 kilometres (14 miles) from south to north and approximately 40 kilometres (25 miles) from east to west.[2] However, by the outbreak of the Pacific War in December 1941, the roughly 520 square kilometre (200 square mile) island had grown out of all proportion to its modest geographical dimensions. Colonel Masanobu Tsuji, Imperial Japanese Army, provides us with a succinct assessment of the island's prewar significance:

> Singapore was Britain's pivotal point in the domination of Asia. It was the eastern gate for the defence of India and the northern gate for the defence of Australia. It was the axis of the steamship route from Europe to the Orient, north to Hong Kong and through to the south and east. Through these two arteries alone, during a period of many years, Britain controlled the Pacific Ocean with Singapore as the very heart of the area.[3]

To service and administer Malaya, the British had constructed a most impressive (for the times) commercial infrastructure which flowed from Singapore, along the Malay Peninsula and through to Thailand. A single one-metre gauge railway line ran from the extensive docks of Keppel Harbour in Singapore Town, past the village of Bukit Timah, through Bukit Panjang and then to Woodlands, before crossing the roughly 1000-metre (1100-yard) long causeway built in 1923 into Johore. Johore Bahru lay on the other side, the railway then passing through Rengam, Kluang, Labis and Segamat to the town of Gemas. Here the railway took two paths. The first, serving the western part of the peninsula, ran past, and had branch lines to, the ports of Malacca, Port Dickson, Port Swettenham, Kuala Selangor, Teluk Anson, Port Weld and Perai (near Butterworth, which serviced Penang Island). The line then passed through Sungei Patani and Alor Star before reaching the Siam (Thailand) border at Padang Besar. From that town, the railway continued on to link with the second branch line from Gemas, which had wound its way inland across the states of Pahang and Kelantan past the town of Kota Bharu (with a branch line to it), and then on to link with the other line near Singora. From there, the line made its way to Bangkok.

The road system in Malaya—for its time, and particularly in Asia— was widespread and of high quality, especially on Singapore Island and Johore, its nearest Malay state. The main roads were bituminised and about one-and-a-third lanes wide, necessitating trucks having to partly leave the roads when passing.[4] These roads were marked with mile pegs (every 1.6 kilometres). Like the railway on the western plain, that region's road system was well served by many feeder roads to ports and inland towns, and numerous dirt roads had been built for access to the lucrative rubber estates and tin mines. On the eastern plain the road network was less impressive, with basically three main roads: the first ran from Johore Bahru to Kota Tinggi, Jemaluang, Mersing and then to Endau; the second linked the west and east in Johore via a Trunk Road at Ayer Hitam through Kluang and Kahang, before linking with the first at Jemaluang; and the last linked the west to east from Kuala Kubu to Raub, through Fraser's Gap in the mountains to Jerantut, and then to Maran, before reaching the eastern coastal town of Kuantan.

In 1940, the Civil Government in Malaya consisted of three independent states. The first was the Crown Colony known as the Straits Settlements, which comprised Singapore, Malacca and Penang with Province Wellesley. Singapore was the administrative centre for the Straits Settlements. The second was the Federated Malay States of Selangor, Negeri Sembilan, Pahang and Perak. This state was administered in general terms by a federal government from Kuala Lumpur in Selangor, although each state also had its own rulers who were assisted by British residents. The third state was the Unfederated Malay States of Johore, Perlis, Kedah, Kelantan and Terengganu, which were governed by their own sultan, who was also assisted by a British Advisor. Presiding over this fragmented and awkward system was the Singapore-based Governor of the Straits Settlements, who also doubled as the High Commissioner of the Federated and Unfederated States.

Major-General Kirby has observed that this civil administration was 'complicated, cumbersome and markedly unsuited to war conditions'.[5] However, the salient point is that the whole system was perpetuated by the

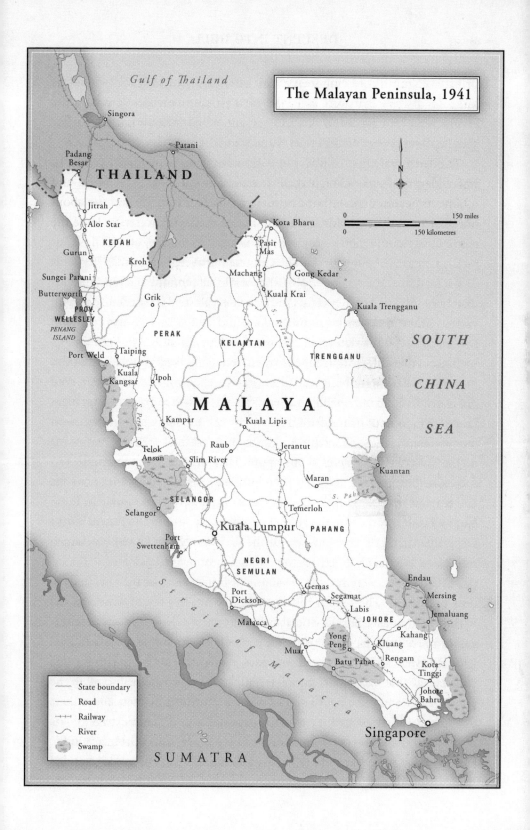

The Malayan Peninsula, 1941

Gulf of Thailand

Singora

Patani

Padang
Besar

THAILAND

Jitrah

Kota Bharu

Alor Star

Pasir
Mas

KEDAH

Machang

Gong Kedar

Gurun

Kroh

Sungei Patani

Kuala Krai

Butterworth

Grik

Kuala Trengganu

PROV.
WELLESLEY

PENANG
ISLAND

PERAK

KELANTAN

SOUTH

Port Weld

Taiping

TRENGGANU

CHINA

Kuala
Kangsar

Ipoh

SEA

MALAYA

Kampar

Kuala Lipis

Raub

Jerantut

Telok
Anson

Slim River

Maran

Kuantan

S. Pahang

SELANGOR

Temerloh

Selangor

PAHANG

Kuala Lumpur

Port
Swettenham

NEGRI
SEMULAN

Endau

Mersing

Gemas

Segamat

Jemaluang

Labis

JOHORE

Port
Dickson

Kahang

Yong
Peng

Kluang

Malacca

Muar

Rengam

Kota
Tinggi

Batu Pahat

Johore
Bahru

Strait of Malacca

Singapore

SUMATRA

0   150 miles
0   150 kilometres

State boundary
Road
Railway
River
Swamp

British as a means of being seen to not interfere—unless absolutely necessary—in matters that were not vital to their commercial interests, while
maintaining a divided and unwieldy system of administration in Malaya.
This kept wages at a minimum level and therefore costs down, and critically,
it inhibited a real sense of Malayan nationalism on any significant scale. In
essential terms, it was very 'colonial' and good for business.

The composition of the population of the Malay Peninsula and Singapore
Island prior to the Pacific War was also fragmented and diverse. In 1940, the
approximate population of Malaya was nearly 5.5 million, of which Singapore comprised about 550 000. The Chinese numbered around 2 379 000 or
43 per cent; the Malays about 2 278 000 or 41 per cent; the Indians approximately 744 000 or 13.5 per cent; the Eurasians about 48 000 or 0.87 per cent;
various other nationalities numbered around 58 400 or 1.06 per cent; and
the European population totalled some 18 000 or about 0.33 per cent.[6]

Most of the Malays, indigenous to their peninsula, lived in small kampongs
in homes which were built on stilts with thatched roofs, where they eked
out a relatively comfortable and easy-paced existence by growing vegetables, rice, coconut palms, fruit trees and by fishing. The Chinese, in general
terms, were the most adaptable and industrious race of the non-Europeans
on the Malay Peninsula and in Singapore. They worked in the tin mines, ran
successful businesses, plied their keen business sense to all manner of shops
and worked as coolies on the docks. The Indians were predominately Tamil
labourers who worked on the rubber estates as tappers, in the Public Works
Department and on the railways. Of the various other nationalities, which
numbered around 58 400, there were a small number of Japanese.

In 1940, there were roughly 14 400 British in Malaya or 0.26 per cent of
the population.[7] The British in the public sector were essentially members
of the Malayan Civil Service and also 'forest officers, civil engineers, doctors,
surveyors, educators, police officers, harbour masters and the like'.[8] Such
vocations were secure in tenure, well paid, essentially routine in nature, and,
with a wage that had a most impressive purchasing power, the British in the
public sector enjoyed an affluent lifestyle. Although the planters and miners
in the private sector had, to some degree, felt the economic pain of the
Depression years, they too now enjoyed a very prosperous existence. On the
rubber estates or near the mines, they—not unlike the public sector—tended

to live in well-furbished bungalows with ample servants, access to clubs and other recreational facilities. They often sent their children back home for their education, and if all went according to plan, many of them could look forward to the odd holiday in Britain and eventual retirement there.

In 1819, when Sir Thomas Stanford Raffles had gained a treaty for the acquisition of Singapore for the East India Company, he had dreamed of a new, powerful free trade port that might rival Batavia (Jakarta) and become a secure base for British trade in the region. By the onset of the Second World War, his dream had been realised far beyond his expectations. Malaya had become a seemingly bottomless well of strategic raw materials—over half of the world's tin and 38 per cent of its rubber—with Singapore as its administrative and logistical hub.

***

After the Wall Street crash on 'Black Tuesday' in November 1929, the western world fell into a period of low profits, deflation, high unemployment and poverty. The Great Depression provided the economic, social, and as a consequence, the political and military environment in which fascism and communism flourished. In Japan that economic calamity provided impetus for already established expansionist ambitions.

For the western powers, the ideal of world peace through arbitration, disarmament and the collective security provided by the League of Nations would soon become an illusion. And following that optimism and corresponding defence funding cuts of the 1920s came the anxiety and further spending cuts of the Depression, and as a consequence, an even more desperate measure to prolong the peace: appeasement. In 1933 Nazi Germany withdrew from the League of Nations and the Geneva Disarmament Conference, while also having initiated a rapid rebirth of its military forces. At the same time Japan was engaged in its expansion in Manchuria and also gave notice of its intention to withdraw from the League of Nations. It then promptly occupied the province of Jehol and moved into northern China. The next year, Germany renounced the Treaty of Versailles and told the world she was to rearm, while the Japanese condemned the Washington Naval Treaty, which meant that by December 1936 when the London Naval Treaty was due to expire, there would be no restriction upon another explosive naval arms race. In June

1935, in anticipation of the naval arms conference of the following year, Germany and Britain signed a treaty allowing the German Navy to 'build up to 35% of the surface tonnage'[9] of the Royal Navy, while in 1936 Hitler occupied the Rhineland and the Japanese militarists gained political control over their government. Italy in turn then snubbed the League of Nations over its condemnation of her invasion of Abyssinia, and then proceeded to align itself with Nazi Germany, and finally in November 1936, Japan and Germany signed the Anti-Comintern Pact, which in essence was an attempt by both countries to isolate Russian communism. By the signing of this pact Japan was further portraying her aggression towards China. All of this constituted a three-year roller-coaster ride towards disaster.

If the ten-year rule—Britain's decision to base one fleet in European waters and none in the Far East—and the Washington Naval Treaty had severely diminished its ability to protect the Empire, then the Anglo–German Treaty of 1935 compounded an already difficult situation. When the British Government boasted that this treaty limited the Germany Navy to 35 per cent of the Royal Navy's surface tonnage, which was a victory for the ongoing aim of armaments limitation and therefore the preservation of peace, it was a view expressed through purely European eyes. The undeniable truth was that in the event of war in both the western and eastern hemispheres, Britain would henceforth be forced to retain the majority, if not all, of her naval strength in European waters. A striking illustration of Singapore's now precarious security was to be the subsequent lengthening of its 'period before relief': from six weeks during the 1920s to ten weeks in 1937, to nearly thirteen weeks in June 1939, and finally, at the outbreak of war in September 1939, to almost 26 weeks or nearly a half a year.

Against this frightening and rapid deterioration in the economic, political and military scene in Europe and Asia, the development of the Singapore Base had continued to proceed at a disjointed and pedestrian pace. By 1931, eight idle years had passed since Britain had decided to retain her fleet in Europe and build a new naval base in the Far East. Japan's expansion in China caused the British Chiefs of Staff to strongly advocate the abandonment of the 'ten-year rule' which had, they rightly maintained, inhibited Britain's ability to defend its Far Eastern interests. Although in March 1932 the Committee of Imperial Defence accepted their recommendation, the

Government, immersed in the economic crisis, duly informed them that this should not be misconstrued as a pledge for greater funding.

But the initial problem was not just funding but the well-worn debate between the British services as to the emphasis of that spending. Kirby, in *The War Against Japan*:

> In December 1931 a sub-committee of the Committee of Imperial Defence, presided over by Mr. Stanley Baldwin, had been set up to examine the question of coast defences and the security of defended ports throughout the Empire, with special reference to the employment of air forces in that particular role ...
>
> The Service Ministries reiterated the views they had expressed in 1925–26.[10]

The recommendations by the Baldwin Committee in May 1932, and subsequently approved by the British Government, need further attention. First, as in 1925–26, the fixed gun was chosen as the main prevention against an attack from the sea; second, the plane was acknowledged as an important addition to those guns, and further, as a potent means of offensive action; and last, the RAF was to 'take part in all aspects of the defence of the Singapore Base, including fighter defence and offensive action against ships'.[11] The first recommendation clearly portrays the expectation at the time that any attack on Singapore would be a direct seaborne one, that is, that a landward assault via the Malay Peninsula was still not contemplated. Hence the ongoing reliance upon fixed guns. The second is self-evident. But the third point sadly depicts the ongoing lack of cooperation and joint planning, and petty interservice rivalry.

It was now decided, with some sense of urgency, to build the naval base and the first stage of Singapore's fixed defences, which were to be completed by 1936–37. The construction of the graving dock at the naval base was put to tender and the necessary infrastructure for a skilled labour force— accommodation, workshops and ammunition storage—was undertaken. In planning to protect Singapore Island from an amphibious landing, the fixed defences were concentrated in two areas. The first was near the east coast at Changi (Changi Fire Command) and would consist of three 15-inch, three 9.2-inch and eight 6-inch guns; while the second was Faber Fire Command, situated in the south and west with two 15-inch, three 9.2-inch and ten 6-inch guns. These sites provided for excellent observation posts from Changi Hill and Mount Faber respectively. Their share of big guns, smaller weapons for close defence and modern communications adequately covered the entrances to the naval base via the Johore Strait and Singapore's commercial port at Keppel Harbour.[12] This work was completed in 1939.

While the Admiralty was thus engaged, the Air Ministry set about constructing airfields on Singapore Island at Tengah, about thirteen kilometres northwest of Singapore City; at Sembawang, about two kilometres south of the navy base; and at Seletar, about five kilometres east of Sembawang.

As the political and military turmoil of the mid-1930s was unravelling, a new General Officer Commanding Singapore was appointed. Major-General William Dobbie, a man known for his 'straightforwardness and simplicity of character, based on his strong religious beliefs',[13] assumed command in August 1936. Born in Madras (Chennai) on 12 July 1879, Dobbie had been educated in England and qualified for a military career at the Royal Military Academy Woolwich, and the Royal School of Military Engineering at Chatham. He had seen service during the Boer War and the First World War.

It is at this point that a key character—and a controversial one—enters our story. Shortly after Dobbie's appointment, Colonel Arthur Percival was appointed as General Staff Officer, Grade 1 (GSO1) to HQ Malaya Command. Percival had had a distinguished career. Born at Aspenden, Hertfordshire on Boxing Day 1887, Percival attended Bengeo School before proceeding to Rugby School (1901–06), where he was a member of the cadet and rifle corps.[14] He began his working life for Naylor, Benzon and Company, in the City of London, which was 'one of the 40 or so London firms of iron ore dealers trading to support the still massive British iron and steel industry'.[15] Lionel Wigmore, in *The Japanese Thrust*:

... Percival had been commissioned at the age of 26 upon the outbreak of the 1914–1918 War, in which he rose to command a battalion,

then to temporary command of the 54th Brigade, and won three dec-
orations [MC, DSO and Bar]. His service between the wars included
four years (1925–29) with the West African Frontier Force . . .

He had the unusual distinction of having graduated not only at the
Army Staff College at Camberley but at the Naval Staff College, and
having attended a course at the Imperial Defence College. This had
made him a member of a relatively small group from which senior
commanders and chiefs of the general staff were customarily drawn.[16]

Wigmore described Percival as 'unassuming, considerate, and conciliatory',[17] while a more recent English historian, Peter Elphick, describes him
as 'something of an athlete, yet his appearance belied the fact. He was tall
and of slight build. He had a soft voice, and his most obvious facial characteristic was a pair of protruding upper teeth . . .'[18] General Key, who served
under Percival during the Malayan Campaign, acknowledged that he 'did
not have a dynamic style of command',[19] but stated that Percival was 'as
straight as a die with a very good brain'.[20]

Upon his arrival in Singapore, Dobbie was faced with a multitude of
problems. The first was the growing realisation that the defence of Singapore
and its naval base now depended on defence in depth, that is, the possibility
that the Malay Peninsula might be used by the Japanese to attack Singapore
'through the back door'. Dobbie and Percival ordered an extensive reconnaissance of the peninsula and planned an exercise to assess the possibility
of the Japanese conducting an amphibious landing during the north-east
monsoon (October–March) of 1936–37. This proved that not only was the
landing quite feasible, but that the poor visibility during this period would
impede British air reconnaissance. Consequently, Percival requested before
his departure for England that he be permitted to submit an appreciation
from the Japanese view of an invasion of Malaya. Dobbie consented.[21] Kirby,
in *The War Against Japan*:

This appreciation drew attention to the fact that before launching
an attack the Japanese would be likely to establish advanced air bases

in Siam, and pointed out the possibility of their making landings
on the mainland. Among the landing places mentioned as possi-
bilities were Singora and Patani in Siam and Kota Bharu [sic] in
Malaya ... in such circumstances the security of the Naval Base was
dependent on the defence of northern Malaya and Johore ...[22]

Here we have a GOC in Singapore in July 1938, three years and five
months before the Japanese invasion of Malaya, warning that the likely
Japanese approach to the capture of the base and island would come from
landings in Siam and in Johore; that the assault was highly probable during
the north-east monsoon, whereby the enemy would have the potential for at
least a partial screen in his approach; and that the jungle in Johore was not
impenetrable. Further, Percival noted that in their war in China, the Japanese
were using significant numbers of sophisticated landing craft; had built
landing ships to transport them; had integrated the use of tanks in these
operations; and were constructing 18-knot merchant ships which could
be used for such operations in addition to their obvious use.[23] As GSO1
to Dobbie, this was Percival's appreciation, and subsequent events were to
prove that it was professionally undertaken, detailed and, above all, accurate.
Moreover, the appreciation was undertaken on the ground and the assertion
that the timing of an invasion might be during the north-east monsoon had
been put to a practical test.
    When Percival left his appointment to head home to England, he
was instructed by Dobbie to present the appreciation to the War Office.
However, the appreciation was nothing new, in the sense that during the
1930s the Directing Staff and students at the Imperial Defence College had
repeatedly turned their minds during war games to the likely methodology
of a Japanese attack in the Far East.[24] The students were further ordered
to predict this scenario against the neutrality of the United States. Their
conclusions, in the light of future events, are illuminating. Kirby, in *The
War Against Japan*:

Year after year the students, as the result of examining Japanese
military history, came to the conclusion that she would attack without
a previous declaration of war during the north-east monsoon and

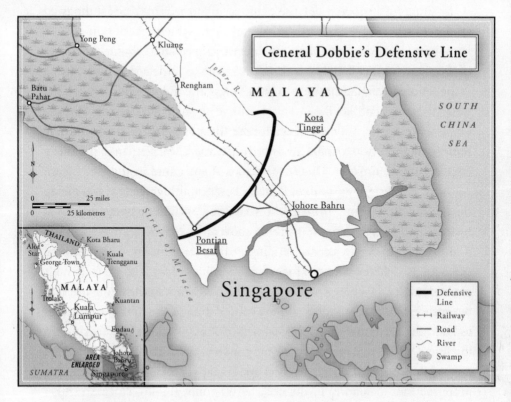

would effect a landing or landings well to the north of Singapore in southern Siam or northern Malaya with the object of gaining control of existing airfields . . . and then advance southwards . . . along the main road and railway.[25]

Also, as Kirby has pointed out, the students' appreciations were always available to the service ministries. As to the notion that the Japanese might attack before a formal declaration of war, this had a precedent: they had done so on 8 February 1904, when the Imperial Japanese Navy had attacked the Russian Fleet at Port Arthur.

On the basis of the appreciation, Dobbie advocated two initiatives: the first was planned to complement the existing beach defences and those for Singapore City by the construction of a defensive line of pillboxes in Johore; and the second was a significant build-up of the garrison in Singapore to enhance the potential to deploy additional troops in Malaya.

In siting his proposed defensive line of pillboxes, Dobbie saw the need to place them far enough north to put Japanese artillery out of range of the naval base and the reservoir and pipeline which produced about 40 per cent of Singapore's water supply. He therefore envisaged a defensive line starting at the Johore River and running to Kota Tinggi and thence south-west to the western coast at Pontian Besar. This defensive line had been astutely devised. On its eastern extremity it had the Johore River as a natural barrier; to the north-east there was coastal swamp, which made an outflanking eastern coastal landing unlikely. Due in part to a slight curve in the line before reaching the western position of Pontian Besar on the west coast, and due to the fact that the distance from that town to the southern tip of the peninsula further limited an enemy outflanking movement (to the rear of the line), it also made an enemy coastal landing in the west unlikely. The proposed defences also had the potential for ample assembly points, with cover, to stage counterattacks. Dobbie planned to use army engineers in the construction of the defensive works and sought the cooperation of the rubber companies to build the roads at cost price. He sought £250 000 for the construction of the line. Dobbie was later granted the conservative sum of £60 000 for the task of the construction of defences on Singapore Island, Penang and his proposed line in Johore. In the end, he was only able to allocate £23 000 to the Johore Line, and as a result, it was destined to run no further than a short distance west of Kota Tinggi. Another rational initiative to defend the vital ground of southern Johore in the defence of Singapore had been lost through negligence, apathy and a resulting lack of funding.

The second of Dobbie's recommendations was for an increase in the size of the army. At the time, there were two British battalions and artillery and engineer units in Singapore, and one Indian battalion and two reserve units in Malaya: the Straits Settlements Volunteer Force (SSVF) and the Federated Malay States Volunteer Force (FMSVF). The fact that both units were under-manned, poorly trained and poorly funded was a fair reflection of the civil government's commitment in both policy and spending. Each of these units was funded by a budgetary system that operated on a fixed revenue for some years at a time, which made no allowance for the rapidly changing defence climate, and further, the civilians were not taxed and were concerned that increases in defence spending would instigate taxation.[26]

Many of the British civilians in Singapore and Malaya had not experienced the First World War and, sheltered away from Europe and its political climate, had enjoyed and still wanted to enjoy their commercial and lifestyle pursuits. According to Percival's biographer, it appeared to Percival that the colonial administration, 'instead of adjudicating between the competing priorities of defence and commerce, saw its role exclusively as that of protecting the latter against the former'.[27] It was crystal clear to both Dobbie and Percival that the main priority of the civil administration was the preservation of the economic and commercial life of Singapore and Malaya. Business was, as always, to come first and the likelihood of war in Singapore and Malaya in 1937 seemed remote. After all, through the ignorant eyes of the local population, there was a seemingly impressive naval base taking shape right under many of their noses, and they were reassured by the potential British naval presence which had ruled the waves for hundreds of years. As a result of Dobbie's plan, however, the War Office did retain the Indian Army battalion that was due for relief while the training and establishment of the volunteer battalions was in progress.

The threat from within was another issue Dobbie faced during his tenure in Singapore. Concerned at the Japanese presence in Malaya, he requested the posting of a defence security officer from MI5. At this time the Japanese owned one of the principal iron ore mines in Malaya and transported their ore to Japan in Japanese ships; they owned numerous rubber plantations, particularly abundant in Johore, some of which were run by 'retired Japanese officers';[28] there was a considerable Japanese ownership of photographic and barber shops, a number of fishing boats which operated out of Singapore and plied their business up and down the peninsula; there was the odd brothel; and, as Sergeant Jack De Loas of the 2/19th Battalion AIF was later to discover, an undercover Japanese major played a fair game of tennis before hostilities began.[29] The Japanese were thus well placed to gather comprehensive military intelligence throughout Malaya.

The British officer posted to Singapore as the defence security officer was Colonel Francis Hayley Bell. Briefed in London before his work began in Singapore in October 1936, Hayley Bell was directly responsible to Colonel Vernon Kell, who was Head of MI5 in London, and not General Dobbie.[30]

Hayley Bell was 58 years of age, attractive and 'a splendid man, courageous but impetuous . . .'.[31]

Not long after his arrival in Singapore, Hayley Bell called on the Governor, Sir Shenton Thomas, to present his credentials. He was in for a shock. According to Hayley Bell's daughter, her father came home from the meeting with the Governor to proclaim that when the subject of Japan came up, Thomas had said that only a fool would think Japan would want Singapore.[32] And worse was to follow.

Just preceding Hayley Bell's arrival in Singapore, Major Kenneth Morgan had been appointed as the first head of the Japanese Section of the Singapore Special Branch. Morgan did not impress Percival. Clifford Kinvig, Percival's biographer:

> Morgan was an odd man, sickly, secretive and paranoid, who stead-fastly refused to share his intelligence with the Services . . . In Percival's view Morgan had 'an eccentric mentality, ill-balanced judgement, muddled thought, lack of general common knowledge and uncalled for reticence . . .', and was 'not fitted for the appointment he holds'.[33]

Malaya Command, the RAF and the Royal Navy had their own intelligence operation: the Joint Intelligence Bureau. From early 1937 Major Herbert Vinden was the Malaya Command representative in that bureau.

It would seem that Vinden's endeavours formed the intelligence basis for the excellent appreciation written by Percival for Dobbie. Vinden was the officer who had tested the potential of an enemy landing during the north-east monsoon. He not only landed 'on several beaches from a dinghy and came close inshore all the way along the coast,'[34] but discovered that 'several thousand Chinese [illegal immigrants] landed on the east coast every year'[35] during this period. Vinden had therefore not only personally tested the potential of a Japanese landing during the monsoon, but had discovered that the Chinese had been employing this procedure for years. He also travelled to Singora in Siam and noted the excellent harbour and facilities which were 'suitable for the establishment of an invasion base.'[36]

In his subsequent appreciation of enemy intentions, Vinden accurately forecast the Japanese landing points and subsequent advance down the

Malay Peninsula. He further predicted that the operation would not occur until Britain was immersed in a European war, and that Japan would attack without a declaration of war.[37]

Morgan's contribution seems more clouded—apart from some useful work in the deportation of some enemy agents and the instigation of contacts elsewhere in the Far East.

Hayley Bell's work in the period 1936–39 was so thorough and so relevant—and controversial—that it cost him his job. He criticised the continuity and standard of successive military leaders and their subordinates in Singapore, asserting that their tenure was too short, causing ever-changing plans and disjointed responses to those plans. Furthermore, he reported that they did not travel widely enough during their tenure to learn about the countries they had to defend.

But Hayley Bell's most damning indictment of the security structure in Singapore came when he, in cooperation with Vinden and other interested officers, conducted an exercise to test the security of vital installations in Singapore. They were able to 'blow up' the naval base graving dock; 'destroy' the aviation fuel stocks on the island; 'sink' the moored fleet of RAF flying boats near RAF HQ; 'wipe out' the telephone exchange; and 'demolish' the lighting and power supplies to Singapore. Hayley Bell later commented that the navy took stock after the exercise, but that the 'challenged civil utilities slumber on'.[38] To add further insult to a growing range of injuries, Hayley Bell further asserted that the Thais were in close accord with the Japanese, which deeply offended Sir Josiah Crosby, the British Minister in Bangkok. The civil utilities may have 'slumbered on', but the Governor, General Bond (who had succeeded General Dobbie) and Crosby were incensed. Using their not inconsiderable collective influence, they succeeded in having Hayley Bell sent back to England in May 1939. Here was one of the most competent prewar officers engaged in the sad saga of Singapore's defence, who was removed for displaying energy, acumen and common sense. The grandfather of the British actress Hayley Mills, Colonel Hayley Bell died in 1944, having seen many of his predictions materialise.

During their tenure in office, Dobbie and Percival also had further difficulty with the RAF. In light of the fact that there was no British naval presence, the air force was confronted by a number of challenges. Its first task was to detect enemy seaborne convoys sailing from the Gulf of Siam and/ or the South China Sea, and then, having found them, to be in a position to offer multiple attacks on their shipping before they could land their invasion troops. The only airfields in Malaya were along the western coast and were used to service the commercial route from Calcutta to Singapore. The Air Ministry therefore decided to build two new strips: one at Gong Kedah, about 45 kilometres from Kota Bharu, which was in turn roughly sixteen kilometres from the Siam border; and the second at Kuantan, about halfway between Johore Bahru and the Siam–Malayan border. A third strip, which was privately owned, was purchased at Kota Bharu. But in an appalling and high-handed decision, the air force did not consult the army—which was responsible for the protection of the RAF personnel and their planes and strips—as to the selection of these airfields, which had been sited 'in areas unsuitable for defence and highly vulnerable to enemy landings, since they were close to the coast'.[39]

Percival debated this issue repeatedly with his RAF colleagues, Tedder and Peck, but got absolutely nowhere. The obvious problem was that given the scattered nature of the proposed RAF airfields in Malaya, the RAF would have had to deliver such a resounding blow to a Japanese invasion that it would be rendered virtually impotent before its arrival. And that was never going to be the case, given the number and quality of its planes. In turn, therefore, the army was now given a task which was beyond its meagre capability.

Meanwhile, the situation in Europe was deteriorating rapidly. On 15 September 1938, Hitler demanded the Sudetenland from Czechoslovakia, the integrity of which had been guaranteed by France. When Britain mobilised her fleet and war seemed likely, the Prime Minister of Great Britain, Neville Chamberlain, flew to Munich to mediate a settlement. The ultimate catch-cry of appeasement, 'Peace in our time', was just another feeble attempt at peace. It engendered temporary relief in many quarters—except the Czechs—but had merely delayed the inevitable. In March 1939, German troops swept into Czechoslovakia and during the next month Albania was invaded by Italy. Growing in confidence, and sure that France and Britain would remain indecisive, Hitler then demanded Danzig and denounced the Anglo–German Naval Agreement signed only four years earlier.

Whilst these events were rapidly unfolding, the Chiefs of Staff framed another appreciation in February 1939. Essentially, nothing much had changed since their assessment two years earlier. It was still recognised that a fleet would have to be despatched to the Far East to respond to a Japanese threat to India, Australia and New Zealand, and that such a fleet's size and date of deployment would depend upon the available resources and the state of war in Europe. Of course it would. The point is that defence professionals, observers and commentators had been predicting this exact scenario for over twelve years and had been ignored. And with these rapidly changing events, it was further realised Japan had overtaken Italy as a major threat to British interests. Not long after Germany and Italy proclaimed a pact.

In July 1939, the Committee of Imperial Defence decided to act. Realising that they were in no position to release a fleet, or a substantial portion of one to the Far East, they increased the period before relief to 90 days and ordered that 'the implications of stocking Malaya with food reserves for the civil population and garrison for a period of six months should be investigated'.[40] In August 1939, they further recognised the need to reinforce their army in Malaya and Singapore by posting the 12th Indian Infantry Brigade Group under Brigadier Paris (consisting of the 2nd Argyll and Sutherland Highlanders, the 5/2nd Punjab, the 4/19th Hyderabads, the 122nd Field Regiment and the 15th Field Company) and two bomber squadrons from India. In addition, in September 1939, two further bomber squadrons arrived from the United Kingdom.

When the Second World War began in Europe in September 1939 the naval base and Singapore's coastal defences were operational but some engineering work was still to be done on the 15-inch heavy gun emplacements; there were three British, one Indian, one Malay and two volunteer battalions; three anti-aircraft artillery regiments; two heavy coast defence artillery regiments; and four engineer companies on Singapore Island. Penang's defences included one Indian battalion, one volunteer battalion, a heavy coast defence battery and one engineer company. Kirby, in *The War Against Japan*:

The defence of northern Malaya was entrusted to the Federated Malay States Volunteers, and the defence of Johore to its State Forces. The

12th Infantry Brigade and 22nd Mountain Regiment were retained
as a mobile reserve for the defence of Johore. There were six air force
squadrons of fifty-eight first-line aircraft.[41]

The time from the outbreak of war in Europe, until the beginning of the
Pacific War, was a critical 27-month period in the preparation of Malaya
and Singapore for war—critical because the very scenario that had been
predicted by a significant number of the serving military, strategists and
observers alike, had now come to pass. The foreseen inability of a British
western hemisphere fleet to come to the aid of British interests in the Far
East had now occurred; the necessity of addressing the issue of defending
Singapore by holding the Malay Peninsula with Johore as the vital ground
was acknowledged in most circles; the methodology and even the timing
(the north-east monsoon) of Japan's probable invasion of Siam and Malaya
had been foreshadowed. Moreover, an accurate appreciation of the Japanese
landing points and subsequent movements had been made, and made in
a number of circles. Therefore, it was realised that the coordination of all
parties involved in the future fight—the three services and the civil administration—would be instrumental in mounting a successful defence.

The truth is that the use made of this 27-month period was an abject
failure. There was poor, uncoordinated and therefore dysfunctional decision
making in London and in Singapore. In essential terms, by the end of 1939,
the administrative and military power base in the defence of Singapore and
Malaya consisted of five key figures: the Governor, Sir Shenton Thomas; the
Secretary of Defence, Charles Vlieland; the GOC, Major-General Bond; the
Air Officer Commanding, Far East, Air Vice-Marshal Babington; and later,
when the British withdrew their China Squadron from Hong Kong and
deployed it at Singapore, Admiral Percy Noble, representing the Royal Navy.

Thomas had been appointed to the position of Governor and Commander-
in-Chief in 1934, after having spent all of his prior colonial service in Africa.
He was not an authority on matters military and had not served in the First
World War; in fact, his colonial service had virtually shielded him from war
and its effects entirely. His biographer described him as 'by character and
upbringing . . . a sincere churchman, always honest and direct, not devious
in any way'.[42] Mr V A Bowden, who had served in the British Army from

1915 to 1919 and had worked in Japan and China for 25 years, including six years as Australian Government Commissioner in China (1935–41), was the Australian Government Representative in Singapore between 1941 and the capitulation of Singapore. He described Thomas as 'more ready at producing reasons for not doing things than for doing them, and in the Malayan Civil Service there seemed to be too much of the old bureaucratic doctrine that action means to risk blunders, and inaction means safety'.[43] Kirby was even harsher:

> ... Thomas proved to be a man who was inclined to be influenced by the opinions of those with whom he was in daily contact, in this case his senior Malayan civil servants and in particular the Colonial Secretary ...
>
> Events were to show that the Governor was a weak chairman of the War Committee, incapable of enforcing measures which would prepare Malaya for war.[44]

Thomas was the Governor and Commander-in-Chief of the Straits Settlements, High Commissioner of the Federated Malay States, and, through his indirect power, also a critical influence over the Unfederated Malay States. He was therefore in charge of a cumbersome, inefficient government organisation that was ideally suited to placing export dollars or pounds into Britain's coffers, but not structured or inclined in any way towards a contribution to a major war effort.

It will be remembered that in August 1938 the Chiefs of Staff had recommended the stockpiling of six months' food supplies for Malaya should war break out in the Far East. Charles Vlieland was given the job of assessing this problem. Educated at Oxford, he had joined the Malayan Civil Service in 1914 at the age of 24. Like Thomas, Vlieland did not possess a military background. According to Shenton's biographer, Vlieland 'was not renowned for his tact, and certainly made no attempt to curb his intolerance of inefficiency or ignorance wherever in his view either existed'.[45] In some circles this rather superior manner earnt him the nickname of 'Starchie Archie'. As a basis for undertaking his study, he requested the plans for the defence of Singapore and Malaya. After studying those plans, Vlieland formed the view that in the event of war, the Japanese would land in Siam and that the Malay Peninsula must therefore constitute the vital ground. He also advocated that the existing Defence Committee be abolished and that a new committee be established with the Governor in the chair; that a Secretary of Defence be appointed who would be responsible for the coordination of the civil administration in time of war; and that the remaining members of the committee be the commanders of the three services. In the event of war, the Defence Committee was to become the War Committee. Thomas embraced the proposal and appointed Vlieland to the position of Secretary of Defence.

Vlieland claimed that he had developed 'a considerable knowledge of the varied terrain of Malaya by hunting game in its forests, shooting over its open countryside and round its coasts'.[46] Further, he claimed his own unique intelligence network consisting of 'planters, miners, prospectors, foresters and game rangers', who he said, 'could send word of strange things which were happening in odd places'.[47] He would later assert that the best forecast he received concerning the eventual disasters in Hong Kong and Malaya was from a Chinese servant who 'had worked for British masters in both territories for thirty years'.[48] Military intelligence made easy—go hunting and listen to your servants.

It is interesting to note that Dobbie was still in Singapore at the time of Vlieland's appointment but did not object. Dobbie probably saw the potential of the committee, but failed to perceive the incompetence and vested interests of its civil component. Vlieland was in a unique position of power. He had, as Secretary of Defence, direct access to Thomas and great influence over the conduct of the civil service in respect of defence issues. In an extraordinary procedure, Vlieland also proposed that the Defence Committee 'should be a purely consultative body with no secretary, no agenda and no minutes and that its members should be free to take action or not as they pleased within their own spheres of responsibility'.[49]

Under the old system, the GOC had been chairman of the Defence Committee. With Thomas now as chairman, Vlieland was able to do two things: use his influence and ready access to the Governor; and side with the RAF representative on the committee, whose views he shared. This isolated an increasingly stubborn GOC, Bond, and tended to inhibit progress. In blunt terms, Vlieland was clearly manipulating the Governor, cultivating the RAF representative's friendship, and thereby seeking to weaken Bond's influence.

The RAF representative on the Defence Committee was the Air Officer Commanding, Far East, Air Vice-Marshal John Tremayne Babington. During the First World War Babington had been a member of the Royal Naval Air Service. In early January 1920 he had been removed from the navy list and given a permanent commission in the Royal Air Force. From 1929 to 1934 Babington had been the British Air Representative to the League of Nations; from 1934 to 1936 the Commander, RAF Station Halton and Commandant, No 1 School of Technical Training; and from 1936 to 1938 Commandant at the RAF 24 Training Group. He was posted to Singapore in 1938.

Babington was a passionate advocate of the theories of Lord Trenchard who was often referred to as the 'Father of the RAF'. Given the current inability of the Royal Navy to defend Singapore and Malaya, he had a rather inflated opinion of the RAF's ability to accomplish that task, and consequently, a poor perspective of how the three service arms might best coordinate their endeavours for the common good. In Babington's eyes, the army's role was nothing more than to guarantee the security of the RAF and its bases. In order to detect, and subsequently attack, an enemy seaborne operation both at sea and then at its landing points, the RAF required dispersed bases stretching as far as the Siam border. The greater the range of aircraft, he argued, the earlier and more decisive the defence would be.

From August 1939, Dobbie's successor as GOC Malaya was Major-General Lionel Vivian Bond. Born in 1884, Bond had begun his military career in the Royal Engineers in 1903. He had seen action in India in 1908, had fought in Mesopotamia during the First World War and he had seen further service as Chief Engineer, Aldershot Command, Commanding Officer Chatham Area, Commandant Royal School of Military Engineering and Inspector of Royal Engineers, War Office. According to the Official British Historian, Bond was 'a man of sterling worth and character', but 'was lacking in personality' and 'kept himself aloof and was inclined to exercise control from his office chair'.[50]

Bond's views concerning the defence of Malaya and Singapore differed markedly from those of Babington and Vlieland, and therefore, by extension,

Thomas. Aware that consultation had not occurred concerning the RAF's widely dispersed airfields on the Malay Peninsula, that they were poorly sited, and further, that he did not possess the resources to adequately protect them, Bond steadfastly refused to comply with the plan. In his view the vital ground for the defence of the Singapore Base was Johore. Given this assessment, it is surprising that Bond did not see the need for the defensive line of pillboxes which Dobbie had designed in southern Johore, and had in fact begun to build. Here is a clear example of Hayley Bell's contention that the short tenures of GOCs in Singapore had inhibited astute, continuous defence planning and implementation.

When in September 1939 the Defence Committee automatically became the War Committee, it was thus composed of Thomas, Vlieland, Babington and Bond. Later, when Headquarters China Squadron was transferred to Singapore, the Royal Navy representative became Admiral Sir Percy Noble.

The reader could be forgiven for thinking that upon the outbreak of war in Europe, this committee, entrusted with such critical challenges and a decided lack of resources to confront them, might have pulled together for the common good. There was not a bit of it. A number of these issues were new, but others were ongoing, and together they constituted a tragic catalogue of recalcitrant, self-serving and narrow-minded decision making and behaviour that brought little credit to the committee's members.

Manpower allocation was the first. At the outbreak of the European war, the Governor was instructed to increase the supply of rubber and tin from Malaya to help fund, and therefore offset, Britain's deficiencies in raw materials, military hardware and food. Naturally, this meant that the civil administration was now under great pressure. The initial confrontation between the members of the committee came in September 1939 when Major-General Bond advocated conscription to expand and train the Volunteer Forces, which comprised an important portion of his meagre garrison. Thomas at first agreed but withdrew his approval when Vlieland protested. The Governor, finding himself in the middle of an argument between Vlieland and Bond, lacked the resolve to make a decision, and therefore referred the issue to the Colonial Office in February 1940.

It is at this time that ample evidence of the ongoing conflict between the members of the War Committee is clear. Thomas sent his views on the defence of Singapore with his despatch concerning the conscription of manpower. Babington in turn sent his appreciation to the Air Ministry at around the same time. Bond, not to be outdone, later sent a memorandum of his own. The Governor's stance was little more than an endorsement of the views held by Vlieland and Babington: that in the absence of a British naval presence, Malaya must be held by the RAF, supported by 'any submarines and other naval vessels on the station'.[51] Thomas therefore called for a large increase in the RAF garrison—if need be, at the expense of the army. Major-General Woodburn Kirby, in his *The Chain of Disaster*, provides a near perfect summary of the Governor's stance:

> There is no doubt that in the absence of a fleet the strengthening of the RAF was essential for the security of Malaya. The view that the RAF alone could secure Malaya and that the role of the army was purely that of guarding the airfields from which the RAF would operate was, however, fallacious.[52]

The thrust of Babington's despatch recognised the present inability of the Royal Navy to protect Singapore. It therefore saw its defence in terms of the RAF being able to operate from bases near the Siam border and northern Malaya in order to attack an enemy fleet before it could land; that in order to accomplish this, the RAF would need substantial reinforcement; and, finally, that the army should be made to provide a secondary role of merely protecting the RAF's bases. Babington further asserted that if the Japanese gained a foothold on the Malay Peninsula, Singapore was doomed.

Bond's later memorandum was a far more precise, realistic and uncompromising document. It contained three basic points. The first was that as the Japanese now had control over southern China and Hainan Island, they were in a position to construct airfields in Siam and Indo-China as a means of covering an assault upon Malaya and Singapore. He conceded that all of Malaya should therefore be held. His second point considered the resources required by the army to accomplish this: 'a minimum of three divisions, two tank battalions, two machine-gun battalions and a pool of 20 per cent reinforcements'.[53] Further, Bond argued, if it was decided to invade southern Siam in order to resist a Japanese invasion, he would require a further two divisions. Bond's third point was, in effect, an attempt to force the RAF to take full responsibility for its stance on Malaya and Singapore's defence: if the Governor and Babington's views for the defence of the whole Malay Peninsula by the primary means of air power were to be adopted, then the RAF should accept total responsibility for the detection and annihilation of the Japanese invasion fleet at sea, or at worst, the prevention of it being able to facilitate the construction of bases within range of the British airfields in Malaya.

If this course of action were to be adopted, Bond maintained that the army's role would then be the protection of Penang, the airfields in northern Malaya, and possible enemy landing points on its east coast. He estimated that the resources required by the army to support this plan would constitute around seventeen battalions and a company of tanks. The thrust of Bond's memorandum, therefore, was that London must decide which of the two defence plans was to be implemented and resource it appropriately.

The Overseas Defence Committee gathered to assess these conflicting and contentious memorandums on 16 May 1940. Only two days earlier, the Dutch had surrendered to the Germans, and, with the German breakthrough to the English Channel only an additional two days away, they thus convened under the most extraordinary pressure. Clearly, with Britain virtually on her knees, the Chiefs of Staff were going to be most reluctant to send either air or army reinforcements to the Far East—where peace, however threatened, still prevailed. The Overseas Defence Committee sent an insipid response. It now advocated a conscription of local manpower in Malaya, while at the same time requesting that any such measure should not prejudice the output of tin and rubber production.

These horrendous events, and corresponding decisions, caused further friction between the army, air force and the civil administration in Singapore. To compound these problems, Thomas now undertook extended leave in England, delegating the role of Acting Governor to the Colonial Secretary, Stanley Jones.

As a consequence of the weak reaction from the Overseas Defence Committee, Stanley Jones was now faced with increased tension on the War Committee. Bond continued to state that he could do no more than defend his vital ground—southern Johore and Singapore Island—and deploy a battalion at both the crucial airfields at Alor Star and at Penang. Babington, on the other hand, knew that any RAF-dominated defence of Malaya and Singapore depended upon the security of the air reinforcement route from India, and therefore, airfields such as Kuantan and Kota Bharu as well as Alor Star. Jones, caught in the middle, and understanding the plight of both Bond and Babington, referred the argument to the Chiefs of Staff in London.

When, on 4 June 1940, the last ships crossed the English Channel from Dunkirk with their human cargo, the fate of France was sealed. Although some 338 226 British and Allied troops were returned to England most of their equipment was left behind.[54] On 10 June, Italy declared war, and twelve days later France signed an armistice with Germany. Britain's darkest hour had arrived.

The ramifications of the fall of France upon Britain's ability to defend her Far Eastern interests were grave indeed. It had been anticipated that in the event of war in Europe, the French Fleet could defeat or at least contain the Italian Fleet, thereby enabling the promised portion of the Royal Navy to sail to Singapore. The Royal Navy was now faced with war against the Italians in the Mediterranean, and a desperate war against German U-boats in the Atlantic, to allow much-needed equipment and food supplies to reach the island fortress. In June 1940, the period before relief of 180 days— established at the outbreak of war in Europe—must have seemed a distant dream. The period before relief was now 'indefinite'.

When the Chiefs of Staff convened in late June 1940, their assessment of Britain's Far Eastern strategy was made against the fall of France, Britain's resulting isolation, and, therefore, Japan's increased potential to expand her presence in Indo-China. They recommended the withdrawal of their garrisons in China and advised against any attempt to reinforce Hong Kong. Clifford Kinvig has left us with a succinct description of their changing assessment: 'The Chiefs of Staff were at last signing the death certificate of Britain's Far Eastern strategy. It had been a sickly infant when the naval base decision was first adopted in 1922, terminally stricken since 1935; now it was declared stone-cold dead.'[55]

Turning to the defence of Malaya, the Chiefs rightly concluded that in the absence of a Far Eastern fleet, the whole of Malaya would have to be defended and that that task now lay mainly with the RAF. In addition to providing aircraft to confront a Japanese land attack upon northern Malaya via Indo-China or Siam, and an amphibious landing on the Malay Peninsula, they were also obliged to protect their airfields in British Borneo and the empire's trade routes in the Indian Ocean. To meet these responsibilities, the Chiefs of Staff estimated that no less than 22 squadrons comprising 336 first-line aircraft would be required. At the time of their assessment, the RAF's actual strength in that theatre was a paltry eight squadrons consisting of 88 first-line aircraft—which were predominately obsolete.

Kirby, in *The War Against Japan*:

> They recommended that, as soon as possible, and certainly not later than the end of 1940, two squadrons of fighters and two of reconnaissance aircraft should be despatched to the Far East, and that the squadrons in Malaya should be re-equipped with modern aircraft and brought up to establishment. The increased air forces, up to the total of 336 aircraft required in the area, should be provided if possible by the end of 1941 . . .[56]

This Chiefs of Staff appreciation was made in late June 1940. When the Singapore strategy was reliant upon the Royal Navy during the period 1922–39, much use of the term 'period before relief' was used by the powers that be in determining the time needed for the arrival of a European-based fleet. The pertinent point is that in June 1940 the Chiefs of Staff were now also imposing an RAF 'period before relief' of six months for the arrival of two further squadrons—to therefore bring the air force establishment of squadrons to ten—and a further 'period before relief' of another twelve months, before the desired total squadron strength would be reached at 22. They further estimated that once this air force component had been reached, an army garrison of six brigades would be required to protect it. Another division was therefore needed, and, with none available from Britain or the Middle East or India, the Chiefs of Staff recommended that Australia supply one.

Two critical points should be made regarding this RAF 'period before relief'. The first is that at the time of the Chiefs of Staff recommendations, the Battle of Britain was about to begin. For the next five months, the grossly outnumbered RAF was faced with the massive task of denying the Germans control of the skies over Britain as a prelude to a possible German invasion. So much was indeed about to be owed by so many to so few. And Churchill and his War Cabinet were hardly going to make the soon to be famous 'few', 'fewer', by transferring valuable aircraft and pilots to Singapore and Malaya.

The second point concerns the lamentable lack of cohesion of thought and policy between Churchill and his advisors. To all but Churchill, the days of Singapore being defended by the Royal Navy had passed. Singapore was not a fortress, it had long been recognised that it was vulnerable to a landward assault via the Malay Peninsula, and, after the surrender of two colonial powers (Holland and France) in mid-1940, it was further recognised that the Royal Navy's 'period before relief' was now indefinite. As late as August 1940, and at complete variance with his advisors, Churchill, the 'former naval person' and now the Prime Minister of Great Britain, cabled the prime ministers of Australia and New Zealand:

> The combined Staffs are preparing a paper on the Pacific situation, but I venture to send you in advance a brief foreword . . .
>
> I do not think myself that Japan will declare war unless Germany can make a successful invasion of Britain. Once Japan sees Germany has either failed or dares not try I look for easier times in the Pacific . . .
>
> We are about to reinforce with more first-class units the Eastern Mediterranean Fleet. This fleet could of course at any time be sent through the Canal into the Indian Ocean, or to relieve Singapore. We do not want to do this, even if Japan declares war, until it is found to be vital to your safety. Such a transference would entail the complete loss of the Middle East, and all prospect of beating Italy in the Mediterranean would be gone.[57]

Later in the cable, Churchill made a most significant point. Speaking of Britain's growing military strength, he made mention of the air arm: 'Our fighter and bomber strength is nearly double what it was when I cabled you, and we have a very large reserve of machines in hand. I do not think the German Air Force has the numbers or quality to overpower our air defences.'[58]

Given this statement, the despatch of even two squadrons of Hurricanes or Spitfires, and perhaps one bomber squadron, to Malaya or Singapore might surely have accomplished two vital defensive measures. The first would have been a significant improvement in the RAF's ability to wage war, and the second would surely have been a priceless opportunity for both present and soon-to-arrive Far Eastern pilots to begin training with these planes, pending potential reinforcement with further aircraft. But it would have been beyond Churchill's comprehension to implement such an achievable and not too costly plan, when his misguided—and entirely faulty—plan for the defence of Singapore remained focused upon the Royal Navy.

In another extraordinary display of his ignorance towards the problems of defending Singapore, and further, his ignorance of the Japanese, Churchill, in a signal to General Ismay on 10 September 1940 stated that:

The prime defence of Singapore is the Fleet. The protective effect of the Fleet is exercised to a large extent whether it is on the spot or not ...

The fact that the Japanese had made landings in Malaya and had even begun the siege of the fortress would not deprive a superior relieving fleet of its power. On the contrary, the plight of the besiegers, cut off from home while installing themselves in the swamps and jungle, would be all the more forlorn.

The defence of Singapore must therefore be based upon a strong *local* garrison and the general potentialities of sea-power. The idea of trying to defend the Malay peninsula ... cannot be entertained.[59]

And concerning the Japanese, Churchill wrote some further prophetic words:

The presence of the United States Fleet in the Pacific must always be a main preoccupation to Japan. They are not at all likely to gamble. They are usually most cautious, and now have real need to be, since they are involved in China so deeply.[60]

There are a number of significant points in regard to Churchill's cable. In relation to his pledge that his government would, if necessary, cut its losses and send its Mediterranean fleet to the aid of Singapore, he qualified his statement by stating that 'we do not want to do this, even if Japan declares war, until it is found to be vital to your safety'. Given his assessment of the Japanese ability to capture Singapore, the term 'until it is found to be vital to your safety' is nothing more than a justification for inaction. Churchill's statement that 'the idea of trying to defend the Malay peninsula . . . cannot be entertained' also flies directly in the face of his Chiefs of Staff assessment, his service heads stationed at Singapore, numerous appreciations conducted by people such as Percival, Bell, Viden, and, for that matter, even numerous war games conducted by the Staff College. To all but Churchill, Malaya had to be defended for Singapore to survive; to all but Churchill, the Royal Navy was a redundant mechanism for Singapore's defence; to all but Churchill, 'the plight of the besiegers, cut off from home while installing themselves in the swamps and jungle' was a fanciful notion; and to an ignorant Churchill, forecast after forecast had warned that in the event of the Japanese gaining a foothold on the Malay Peninsula, two months was about the maximum time that Singapore could hold out.

Percival's biographer, Clifford Kinvig, in a masterly piece of understatement, has said that: 'The Prime Minister and the Chiefs of Staff seemed to be singing from different hymn sheets.'[61] The Prime Minister and the Chiefs of Staff were, in reality, not only 'singing from different hymn sheets', but were singing in garbled rounds.

During the period 1922–40, a number of British governments had held divergent views regarding the defence of Singapore. Much has been made—except by Churchill—of the inability of the Royal Navy to defend Singapore. As the emphasis of that defence shifted to the RAF, the same old problem of 'the period before relief' reared its ugly head.

It will be remembered that it was at this point that the Australian Government was asked to supply an infantry division. Our story now returns to Australia, and the raising and leadership of the AIF division designated for service in Singapore and Malaya.

4

RAISING NEW DIVISIONS

⟶◆⟵

On 15 September 1939, just twelve days after his declaration of war against
Nazi Germany, Australia's Prime Minister Robert Menzies announced the
formation of a second Australian Imperial Force (AIF). As the Australian
Militia at that time had four divisions and elements of a fifth, the new formation was to be called the 6th Division AIF. This volunteer force, with its auxil-
iary units, would together number 20 000 men for service either in Australia
or overseas.

There were seven candidates for command of the new division. In order
of seniority they were: Major-General Henry Gordon Bennett, 52 years of
age; Major-General Sir Thomas Blamey, 55; Major-General John Lavarack,
53; the Adjutant-General, Sir Carl Jess, 55; Major-General Phillips, 57;
Major-General Drake-Brockman, 55; and, Major-General Iven Mackay, 57.
Of the seven, there were probably three main candidates: Bennett, Blamey
and Lavarack.[1]

Bennett's credentials as a fighting commander were unsurpassed in
the original AIF. Born in Balwyn, Melbourne on 5 April 1887, he joined the
Australia Military Forces as a sixteen-year-old; at 21 he was commissioned
in the Australian Infantry Regiment and gained a captaincy in less than three
years; and at 25, not long after the introduction of compulsory training, he

had reached the rank of major with the 64th (City of Melbourne) Infantry. He was 'of middle height (five feet eight and a half inches), wiry and active, with the abundant energy which, as well as a quick temper, so often goes with red hair . . . ideally suited, both by physique and temperament, for soldiering'.[2]

His service in the first AIF began in 1914 as second-in-command of the 6th Battalion of the 2nd Brigade. Lionel Wigmore, in *The Japanese Thrust*:

Bennett established a reputation for personal courage and forceful leadership under fire from the first day at Gallipoli . . . in the famous though ill-fated advance on Pine Ridge, when his men realised that plans had miscarried, he characteristically rejected the suggestion that he should retire, and led an advance to a position where a party of enemy troops came into sight, in front of Turkish guns. Bennett stood to direct his men's fire, opened a map, and was shot in the wrist and shoulder. Although, when he went to the rear to have his wounds dressed, he was sent to a hospital ship, he was absent without leave from the ship next day, and back in the front-line. Ten days later Bennett led the 6th Battalion in a final attempt by Anglo–French forces to capture the peak of Achi Baba . . .

When the brigade was relieved from the line, Bennett alone remained of the original officers with the battalion, and succeeded to its command. In 1916, at the age of 29, he was appointed to command the 3rd Brigade; and thus became probably the youngest brigadier-general in any British army at the time . . .

Bennett's reputation continued to rise during his service with the A.I.F. in France, and on several occasions before the war ended he temporarily commanded the 1st Division.[3]

After the First World War, Bennett became chairman of the New South Wales Repatriation Board and subsequently commanded the 9th Infantry Brigade from 1921 to 1926. From that appointment he commanded the 2nd Division as a major-general for five years before–as was the custom—being stood down and placed on the unattached list. Bennett's successful postwar public service saw him as president of the New South Wales Chamber of Manufacturers in 1931, and president of its federal counterpart in 1933.

The second senior candidate was Sir Thomas Blamey, and, like Bennett, he had had a most distinguished military career. Born at Lake Albert near Wagga Wagga in New South Wales on 24 January 1884, Blamey had won a commission in the Commonwealth Cadet Forces in 1906; he had joined the Australian Military Forces in 1910 and had subsequently furthered his professional training at Quetta in what was then British India; he had been attached to the British Army in England; and at the outbreak of the First World War he was working in the War Office in London.

A colleague described him thus: 'Short of stature, rugged in appearance, it took some little time to discover that behind that broad forehead there was well seated an unusual brain, and that the square jaw denoted not obstinacy and lack of tact, but quiet resolution and a calm and definite power of expression.'[4]

After a number of staff appointments during the war, Blamey's abilities and performance came strongly to the fore as General Monash's chief of staff. The fact that this period saw such stunning Australian successes, and that General Monash rose to such prominence both in and outside his own force, is also in part a reflection of Blamey's ability and performance as his chief staff officer.

The last of the three prime candidates was Major-General John Lavarack. Born on 19 December 1885 at Kangaroo Point, Brisbane and educated at Brisbane Grammar School, Lavarack later gained high grades for a commission in the Permanent Military Forces. Of an imposing physical appearance—five foot eleven-and-a-half inches, (181 centimetres) in height, well built, and blue-eyed and dark in complexion—his first appointment was as a lieutenant, Royal Australian Artillery.

In early 1913, Lavarack attended the Staff College at Camberley, England until the outbreak of the First World War. After a posting at the War Office, he was assigned as brigade major to the 22nd British Divisional Artillery in 1915. He then saw service in France and Salonica, and became a staff officer in the Royal Artillery at XVI Corps Headquarters.

In July 1916, Lavarack was posted to the AIF 2nd Division for operations at Pozieres. He subsequently commanded two field batteries and was the brigade major of the 5th Divisional Artillery during the fighting on the Somme and the offensive on the Hindenburg Line. He was later promoted to lieutenant-colonel and GSO1 4th Division, in which he fought during 1918 at Dernancourt, Villers-Bretonneux, Hamel and Amiens.

After the First World War, Lavarack's career continued to advance. In 1919 he was posted to Duntroon as director of military art; in 1924 he became a staff officer on the HQ of the 2nd Militia Division in Sydney; in March 1925 he was posted as director of military training at Army HQ in Melbourne; and in 1927 he went to London and became the first Australian officer to complete the course at the Imperial Defence College. In 1929 Lavarack became the director of military operations and intelligence at Army HQ; in January 1933 the commandant of Duntroon; and, in June of that year, achieved the highest serving defence post of Chief of the General Staff. At the time of deliberations over command of the newly formed 6th Division AIF, he was on a tour of Britain.

The reader could be forgiven for thinking that all three of these officers had impeccable records and were deserving of the position of GOC 6th Division. But other factors had come into play. The circumstances of the selection of Major-General Blamey as the GOC of the first raised 6th Division and then the subsequent choice of Major-General Gordon Bennett as GOC 8th Division AIF—and the ensuing behaviour of a number of other senior officers—are clouded in considerable controversy.

Both during the First World War and between the wars, Bennett was a strong advocate for the command aspirations of the citizen soldiers of the Militia. Based on his experience, he had come to believe that certain senior permanent officers, in contrast to the British, lacked the ability to lead their men, that they lacked the 'common touch', and should therefore be confined to staff operations. Bennett would later write that:

> The great lesson learnt during the War was that the staff was the servant of the fighting units. There were unfortunately signs that there is a drift to the pre-war idea that the units are the servants of the Staffs.
>
> This can only be overcome by firmly establishing the principle that *all* commands shall be in the hands of Citizen Force Officers and

that even a Citizen Force Commander be appointed over the whole Australian Army.[5]

But it was in 1937 that Bennett's criticisms of the Staff Corps reached their peak. In November and December of that year, he wrote three articles for the Sydney *Sunday Sun* and *Guardian*. The first was published on 28 November under the headline, 'No More Monashes: General Hits Staff Corps' and contained two subheadings, 'Citizen Army Excluded From High Command' and 'Major-General Bennett Charges Jealousy in plans for Militia Leaders'. The article began by pointing out that recent events in China—the Japanese were, at that time, closing in on Nanking—'must make every Australian ask what is the true position of Australia's Army'.[6] Bennett then pointed out that in the event of an invasion Britain 'could not lift a finger to save us. Our air force and our army will be our first line of defence'.[7] After pointing out that the Australian Army was 'inefficient and insufficient', he once again made his assessment of the Staff Corps brutally clear:

What of our military leaders? Nothing effective is being done to train senior Citizen Force Officers for high command. It would appear, on the other hand, that senior Citizen Officers are not wanted. They are not given the full rank they are entitled to when commanding brigades and divisions.

Only two of the four divisions are commanded by Citizen Officers, and it is well known that attempts have been made to hand the command of all divisions to permanent officers.

Experience has proved that citizen officers can handle our Citizen Army more efficiently than permanent officers.

Our permanent officers are trained as staff officers and not as commanders.

The last great war showed our permanent officers to be efficient staff officers, and our citizen leaders to possess the capacity to lead.

Of late there seems to be an inclination to create a situation so that citizen officers will be excluded from the high command.

Fortunately that policy did not exist in the AIF. If it had we would not have produced General Monash—a world famous leader.

It is well known that he was regarded very jealously by certain Staff Corps officers after the war.

And the present trend makes it appear that they have decided that there will be no more 'Monashes' nor any senior commanders from the Citizen Forces.[8]

The second of Bennett's articles, published on 5 December, was also controversial, but not towards the Staff Corps—it concentrated more upon criticism of the size and equipment of the army and air force and the need for a munitions manufacturing infrastructure 'before and not after war breaks out'.[9]

From the Military Board's perspective enough was now enough. On 12 December 1937, the *Sunday Sun* ran the headline, 'Military Gags General Bennett' with the subheading, 'Prohibits Any More Articles in "The Sunday Sun"'. The paper also stated that:

The best English newspapers regularly engage Service men, of the reserve or retired lists, as their experts on Service matters . . .

A man of that character approaches the Australian democracy when Major-General Bennett expounds his views through 'The Sunday Sun'—and the first and only impulse of the Australian Military Board is to make him shut his mouth![10]

After the first article, the Military Board, consisting of the permanent officers Major-Generals Lavarack, Jess and Phillips, and its civilian component, suggested that Bennett be 'retired under Defence Act 26 in the interests of the Service'.[11] The second article they claimed, 'constitutes an additional reason why, in the interests of the Service, he should not be retained'.[12]

In the end, Bennett was 'retained'. There are a number of interesting perspectives regarding Bennett's stance. He would later comment that:

I sought to arouse public interest in Australia's citizen forces, so that there would develop a wave of enthusiasm in recruiting or even a call for a more efficient system than the present voluntary enlistment. I foresaw the likelihood of attack by Japan developing within the

measurable future and was convinced that Australia could not meet it
with her existing system of military organisation or with her industrial
organisation still unprepared for war in spite of the pledges given by
politicians. I felt I voiced the feelings of citizen force officers concerning certain policies which they felt to be operating against them.

In consequence, the Military Board, which has never forgiven
me for my promotion at the instigation of W.M. Hughes some years
before, and which could not abide any criticism from a civilian, even
though that civilian had a good fighting record, now turned on me the
full force of its fury.[13]

In the end, the selection of the GOC 6th Division AIF came down as
much as anything to political influence rather than merit alone. Despite his
impeccable professional training for the position, Lavarack did not have the
support of the Prime Minister Robert Menzies, nor the Treasurer Richard
Casey, nor the influential Defence Secretary, Frederick Shedden. Although
the Military Board had nominated Lavarack for the position,[14] Menzies's
mind had already been made up. It should also be recognised that Lavarack
did not have any real political support—far from it, as he had antagonised
his political masters as Chief of the General Staff.

On 28 September 1939, the War Cabinet appointed Blamey as the GOC
of the 6th Division, and Lavarack as the GOC Southern Command.

However, from Bennett's perspective, worse was to follow. On 28 February
1940, the War Cabinet decided to raise a second division for overseas service:
the 7th Division AIF. Blamey's command was now to be expanded to that of
a corps, and consequently two divisional commanders were to be appointed
under his command. In the process of planning for the raising of the
7th Division, Sir Brudenell White became the new Chief of the General Staff.
When the Army Minister recommended that one regular and one citizen
soldier should be appointed, Mackay and Lavarack were appointed to the
6th and 7th Divisions respectively. Bennett had not been short listed.

On 2 May 1940, the Military Board was asked to recommend two further
divisional appointments, which were to the 1st and 2nd Divisions, Eastern
Command (New South Wales)—these were Militia appointments. The board
considered seven candidates of which Bennett was most senior, and second

youngest. It consulted Major-General Vernon Sturdee—a Staff Corps officer and GOC Eastern Command—concerning these appointments. Sturdee claimed that Bennett was 'from a purely local military standpoint' most suitable to command a division and 'train it for war'. Further, he stated that his relationship with Bennett had been 'most cordial', and that his 'personal enthusiasm, energy and ability'[15] were beyond question. The board duly recommended Bennett to command the 2nd Division. The recommenda-tion was signed by General White and Major-General Miles.[16]

Having made their decision, one or both of these signatories decided that additional scrutiny was called for. Miles rang Sturdee on 9 May 1940 with four questions. Sturdee's replies are illuminating. Miles's first query was, 'Is General Bennett fit in all respects to take command of a Division?' In his *The Fall of General Gordon Bennett*, A. B. Lodge quotes the first sentence of Sturdee's reply: 'Yes, this officer is probably the most efficient senior Militia Officer in the Commonwealth.'[17] But Sturdee's following two sentences—not cited by Lodge—are surely worthy of mention: 'He continu-ally tries to keep himself up to date by study, notwithstanding that he has not been actively employed since 1931. When a Div. Comdr. he was most active and is the only Div. Comdr. in 2 M.D. [New South Wales] who has taken effective measures to train his senior Comdrs.'[18] These last two sentences fly in the face of criticism Bennett would later receive concerning his training, modern technical knowledge and training of his senior commanders. It was customary for Australian citizen commanders during the interwar period to be placed on the unattached list after a period of service. Sturdee refers to Bennett 'trying to keep himself up to date by study' and also identifies Bennett as the only officer in NSW to have 'taken effective measures to train his senior commanders'—high praise indeed.

The second query was 'How is he regarded in the Militia Forces?' Lodge quotes Sturdee's full reply: 'He is looked up to as an excellent leader and organiser and one who maintains the dignity of a senior officer. He is a good mixer and popular amongst those who know him personally, largely because everyone realises he does his utmost to get efficiency. He is regarded as fair in judgment and decision.'[19]

Miles's third question was 'How is he regarded in the civil community?' Lodge does not cite Sturdee's answer: 'He is regarded as a man of undoubted integrity, clean living and of temperate habits.'[20] Sturdee then mentions Bennett's civil background which we have identified earlier in this chapter— except for two additional points:

> His selection as a City Council Commissioner during the period 1928 to 1930 to clean up the affairs of the Sydney City Council indicates the high esteem in which the then State Government held him. His work on this Commission is reported to have been outstandingly brilliant.
>
> He is President of the N.S.W Golf Club which is indicative of his general popularity. He is generally regarded as a good energetic citizen with plenty of fighting spirit and organising ability. Like all energetic public spirited men, he has some critics, especially amongst the less efficient.[21]

Again, high praise indeed. The fourth and last question was 'Do you consider his Press and other criticisms in the past should now be taken into consideration?' Other than the first word, 'No'—a significant omission— Lodge quotes most of Sturdee's first paragraph:

> whilst his methods may not have been orthodox, I am convinced that his motives were sincere. His outlook both in civil life as well as in the Army is to obtain maximum efficiency. His strongly worded criticism of the Staff Corps was, I gather, mainly directed against certain senior officers whom the Government subsequently proposed to retire . . .[22]

But Sturdee, after the word 'retire' states that: '(this action was partially interrupted by the war, but the majority of them have now been removed to less responsible positions or retired).'[23]

Sturdee's comment is surely—in part at least—a vindication of Bennett's motive for writing his public criticism of certain elements of the Staff Corps. Sturdee is admitting to a significant amount of deadwood in the system, and points out that some of these soldiers have been moved or 'bowler hatted'.

Following this sentence, Sturdee—quoted by Lodge—goes on to say:

His other personal criticism of Army matters was an effort to obtain greater efficiency in the defence of Australia. The fact that he pressed for a senior appointment in the Army for himself was probably due to his opinion that he was capable of making improvements in the Army's efficiency. It seems improbable that he was seeking such an appointment merely for financial reasons . . .[24]

The remainder of Sturdee's sentence—after the word 'reasons', and not cited by Lodge—continues: '. . . as I understand his emoluments from director-ships and his private practice would exceed any salary that he would be likely to receive in an Army appointment.'[25] The balance of Sturdee's last sentence provides further substance to its beginning.

Sturdee's frank and detailed assessment of Bennett's command quali-ties was admirable. Here we have a Staff Corps senior officer who appears capable of rising above the Staff Corps versus Militia command issue. But three further points should be raised. The first is the fact that in their recom-mendation of Bennett and Fewtrell for the command appointments of the 2nd and 1st Divisions respectively, Generals White and Miles quoted Sturdee as saying that Bennett was suited 'from a purely local military standpoint'. In other words, to a militia or local command position. The fact that Bennett had shown—and successfully, according to Sturdee's personal experience—his ability to work with and for Staff Corps officers in NSW surely should not have precluded him doing so in an AIF command overseas.

The second point is that White and Miles withdrew their recommenda-tion for Bennett on 6 June 1940, and proposed that Cannan be appointed to command the 2nd Division. After first officially recommending Bennett on 2 May, and then placing him under further intense scrutiny by contacting Sturdee with four further questions after that recommendation, White and Miles were obviously going far, far out of their way to look for any means of not appointing Bennett. Third, neither could fairly claim that Bennett's nine-year absence from an active command disqualified him, since they recommended Cannan as an alternative appointment, who had had a fifteen-year absence from an active command.[26]

On 22 May 1940, the War Cabinet approved the formation of the 8th Division AIF, the third Second AIF Division to be raised. Major-General

Vernon Sturdee was given command. Clearly, Major-General Gordon Bennett had some powerful enemies. The first was White. As Chief of the General Staff, he was determined to use his not inconsiderable power to ensure that regular soldiers were to be given command postings whenever possible. When Bennett went to see White regarding a posting, White told him that he had 'certain qualities and certain disqualities' and made it quite clear to him that he could not anticipate a command during his time as CGS. Clearly, Bennett had committed two sins: the first was the fact that he was not a permanent officer; and the second, and it would seem the more grave, was that he dared to question White's policy of wanting to appoint only permanent officers to high command positions. The second enemy was almost certainly Blamey, who as corps commander of the Second AIF and a passionate enemy of Bennett's, would have had no small say in such matters; the third were various government ministers who would have most certainly resented Bennett's newspaper criticisms of defence policy and spending in the media; and the last was the Staff Corps as a group.

On 1 July 1940, Bennett was given command of the Eastern Command Training Depot. During that same month, the newly formed Volunteer Defence Corps—made up of ex-soldiers and run by Army Headquarters and the RSL—was also placed under his command. In effect, Gordon Bennett was now in charge of a training depot and a unit of 'Dad's Army'.

On 13 August 1940, the command career of Major-General Gordon Bennett was resurrected by a national tragedy. An aircraft crashed near the Canberra airport, killing a distinguished passenger list: the Chief of the General Staff, Sir Brudenell White; the Minister for the Army, Mr G. A. Street; the Minister for External Affairs, Sir Henry Gullett; and the Minister for Air and Civil Aviation, Mr J. V. Fairbairn. Also killed were White's Staff Officer, Lieutenant-Colonel Thornthwaite, Mr Fairbairn's Private Secretary, Mr Elford, and the RAAF crew of four.

For the second time within a year the post of Chief of the General Staff (CGS) required a new appointment. Blamey lost little time in cabling Menzies offering his services back home in any capacity Menzies deemed fit. Northcott, who was at that time Deputy Chief of the General Staff, might have considered himself a chance for the position, and so might

Lavarack, who had filled the post before the war. In the end Sturdee was given the job on 30 August 1940.

Not to be outdone, Bennett also put his case before the Prime Minister in a letter dated 2 September. In part, his letter stated that:

> When this war commenced, I was the senior officer in the Australian Army, but was superseded by Blamey, Lavarack, Mackay and Sturdee.
>
> My age (53) and my service in the last war and in the Citizen Forces since then, surely justify my appointment. The only reason for my supersession is the attempt on the part of the Permanent Staff to have all higher appointments in the AIF reserved for themselves. This is not in the interest of the AIF nor the Citizen Force Officers.
>
> I would appreciate your support when your Cabinet considers the matter this week and would like my appointment, if made, to date my seniority in the AIF so that my position on the list will be restored.[27]

A. B. Lodge in *The Fall of General Gordon Bennett*:

> Such a letter of demand, permeated with evidence that Bennett still harboured a deep resentment of regular officers, served only to highlight those aspects of his character which indicated unsuitability for a command in the AIF. Had he been prepared to come to terms with a new situation in which prewar position in the army carried little weight and stressed instead his desire to work with officers regardless of their service backgrounds he may have had more success.[28]

Sturdee, now acting as the new CGS, suggested that Gordon Bennett be given command of the 2nd Division (a militia appointment) and that Northcott fill the vacant 8th Division command. The War Cabinet delayed its decision pending Blamey's counsel—the substance of which can well be imagined. In the end, Bennett was appointed to command of the 8th Division on 30 September 1940.

It is at this juncture that a new character enters our story. Wilfred Kent Hughes was born in East Melbourne on 12 June 1895. He had served with distinction during the Great War at Gallipoli, Palestine and in Syria: as staff captain of the 3rd Light Horse Brigade he had won an MC in 1917; and he had served as the Assistant Adjutant and Quartermaster-General (AA&QMG) of the Australian Mounted Division during 1917–18. Kent Hughes was mentioned in despatches four times. During the period 1927–49, he would serve his state of Victoria as a MLA (for Kew); after the Second World War he was destined to become the Minister for Transport and Electrical Undertakings and Deputy Premier of Victoria from 1948 to 1949; he was further destined to serve his nation as a Member of the House of Representatives from 1949 until his death in 1970. During his period in federal politics, Kent Hughes was the Minister for the Interior and of Works and Housing from 1951 to 1955. Perhaps one of his greatest achievements was as chairman of the Olympic Games in Melbourne, for which he would be awarded a KBE—he was indeed a distinguished Australian. Wilfred Kent Hughes will influence our wartime story in Singapore where he was subsequently a prisoner of war and will prove a major character in events after the war.

Major Wilfred Kent Hughes had been appointed to the Headquarters of the 8th Division by Sturdee. The day before Bennett arrived to assume command of the division, Kent Hughes was a witness to an extraordinary display of antipathy towards the new 8th Division commander: Major-General Gordon Bennett.

In a letter written on 24 January 1952, as the Minister for the Interior in the Menzies Government, Kent Hughes told the Minister for Defence P. A. M. McBride that:

> I was the first Staff Officer to go into camp in Rosebery Racecourse when the 8th Aust. Div. was first formed. I was both ashamed and disgusted when two Duntroon [Staff Corps] Officers stated publicly in the Mess the day before General Gordon Bennett arrived to take over his Command, that they disapproved of his appointment and were not prepared to cooperate with him.[29]

The two officers were Colonel Henry Rourke, GSO1 8th Division, and Colonel Ray Broadbent.[30]

Lodge has claimed that Bennett's forthright letter to Menzies requesting command of the 8th Division 'served only to highlight those aspects of his character which indicated unsuitability for a command in the AIF'. Further, he has stated that Bennett should have 'stressed instead his desire to work with officers regardless of their service backgrounds'. Sturdee's recommendations to White and Miles, and his answers to Miles's four questions in his letter of 9 May 1940—that is, the full answers—surely adequately answer Lodge's allegation.

But given Kent Hughes's observation in the Mess at 8th Division HQ on the day before Bennett's arrival to assume command, such an accusation might have also applied to Rourke and Broadbent. Here we have two so-called 'professional soldiers' who have two very clear alternatives: the first is to give absolute loyalty to their appointed superior officer, or secondly, to request an immediate transfer. At no time did Bennett proclaim that he would not work—or 'co-operate'—with anyone, which is more than can be said of Rourke and Broadbent. Further, in an interview with the Official Historian in June 1952 in Melbourne, Rourke claimed that 'we tried to see that Bennett was not appointed'.[31]

Lodge also points out that it was 'rumoured' that a senior officer of the Staff Corps had 'threatened that the 8th Division would never function as a complete formation under Bennett's command'.[32] He then states that Bennett believed this officer to be the Adjutant-General, Major-General V. P. H. Stantke.[33] Bitter conflict between Bennett and Stantke will unfold after the former's arrival in Malaya, and during the postwar controversy of his escape from Singapore.

A part of the predicament Bennett found himself in was of his own making. His attack on the Staff Corps was ill-considered and, put simply, flawed. Lavarack, Rowell, Berryman, Vasey, Clowes and Robertson were distinguished examples of regular officers who performed well as senior commanders.[34] Bennett's assessment of regular soldiers as fighting commanders was thus inaccurate. Second, he should have been astute enough to realise that by criticising the Staff Corps, he was in fact alienating a significant portion of the very power base of the army, who had a direct say in the selection of field commanders. Third, his criticisms of government defence policy and funding did not endear him to a number of his political masters. Bennett could have, and indeed should have, suggested that all appointments to senior commands be decided *on merit*, and softened his criticisms of government policy—in short he was not diplomatic. There aren't many 'feathers' in a small army, and it is therefore best to ruffle as few as possible.

When General Gordon Bennett assumed command of the 8th Division, he inherited a staff which had been selected by Sturdee. The Division's Chief of Staff (GSO1) was Colonel H. G. (Henry) Rourke, who had served as a major in the artillery during the First World War, and had 'passed through the Staff College at Quetta, India. Later he instructed at the Royal Military College Duntroon and at the command staff school established in Sydney in 1938'.[35] The senior administrative officer (AA&QMG) was Colonel J. R. (Ray) Broadbent, who had also graduated from Duntroon and had served at Gallipoli. Broadbent had resigned from the army in 1926 and become a grazier. It will be remembered that Rourke and Broadbent were the two Staff Corps officers whom Kent Hughes has identified previously as having stated that they 'disapproved of his [Bennett's] appointment and were not prepared to cooperate with him'.[36]

The 8th Division's artillery commander was a Militia officer, Brigadier C. A. (Boots) Callaghan—nicknamed 'Boots' because he owned a number of shoe shops—who 'in the 1914–1918 war had won his way to command of a field artillery brigade. This was followed by continuous service in the militia, including command of the 8th Infantry Brigade from 1934 to 1938'.[37]

The senior signals officer was Lieutenant-Colonel J. H. (Jim) Thyer and the senior engineer was Lieutenant-Colonel E. G. H. Scriven. Both were permanent soldiers. Lieutenant-Colonels Byrne and Stahle, the commander of the Army Service Corps and the senior ordnance officer respectively, were both Militia officers, while Colonel A. P. (Alf) Derham, the 8th Division's Assistant Director of Medical Services (ADMS), was also a Militia officer.[38]

On 4 July 1940, the headquarters of the new 8th Division was established at Victoria Barracks in Sydney, and on 1 August it was transferred to the Rosebery Racecourse. The three brigades of the 8th Division were originally the 22nd, 23rd and 24th. As the 23rd Brigade did not serve in Malaya or Singapore, it is beyond the scope of our story, and therefore will not be examined. In September 1940, it was decided to raise the 2nd AIF's fourth division—the 9th. Rather than use corps troops and reinforcements from Australia, General Blamey recommended that Bennett's 24th Brigade be transferred from the 8th to the 9th Division. The 27th Brigade was soon raised as its replacement for service with the 8th Division. Bennett's 22nd and 27th Brigades are therefore at the heart of our infantry journey. The 22nd Brigade consisted of the 2/18th, 2/19th and 2/20th Battalions. It was commanded by Brigadier Harold Taylor. Lionel Wigmore:

> He had gained a commission in the militia in 1913 and, during the war of 1914–1918, served with distinction in France as an infantry officer. After returning to Australia he resumed militia service and, in 1939, when he was given the 5th Militia Brigade, had successively commanded the Sydney University Regiment, the 18th Battalion, the New South Wales Scottish Regiment, and the 56th Battalion. In civil life the quality of his mind was evident in his having become a Doctor of Science in 1925. He had become Deputy Government Analyst of New South Wales in 1934.[39]

Taylor chose commanding officers with First World War experience, 'young militia officers as seconds-in-command, and a sprinkling of veterans among his N.C.O's and men'.[40] This provided each unit with a sound core of experienced soldiers who, it was thought, would have a decisive influence in both early training and in initial action. He also gave permission for each CO to enlist recruits from their own areas. Thus, the 2/18th Battalion, commanded by Lieutenant-Colonel Arthur Varley, had a strong Armidale contingent, while Lieutenant-Colonel Jeater's 2/20th Battalion had a large number of recruits from Newcastle and Sydney. Lieutenant Jim Howard, 2/19th Battalion:

> There was a Militia Brigade in a ninety-day camp in Wallgrove. And they were the 56th Battalion which was Riverina; the 54th Battalion which was Central West; and the 20/19th Battalion were Newcastle

and the northern side of Sydney. Now ... the country blokes, the
56th Battalion—there were quite a lot of officers and NCOs—enlisted
in the 2nd AIF, and went straight into the 2/19th Battalion. About
July or August 1940, we got a trainload, some hundreds of blokes, like
400, or 450 out of Wagga Showgrounds, which was a reception depot
for the Riverina. These blokes ... some had full uniforms, some had
giggle suits on, and some were in civvy clothes. The greatest ragtail
mob you'd ever want to see! We equipped them though, and that's
how the battalion was formed. They were top blokes, top blokes, and
most of them could shoot. They'd been popping rabbits with a twenty
two rifle from about the age of eight. A bloody rifle—it fitted, second
nature.[41]

From 15 July 1940 the officers and NCOs of the 22nd Brigade went into
training at Wallgrove Camp, about 40 kilometres from Sydney, and just
south of the main road to the Blue Mountains. The Brigade moved to Ingle-
burn from 20 August. In broad terms, the leadership of the Battalions of
the 8th Division and their training in Australia followed a familiar pattern.
The 'bull-ring' method of basic training was adopted, whereby instructors
repeated lessons as section-sized groups of recruits rotated through their
roughly hour-long lectures and/or demonstrations.[42] A number of these
22nd Brigade soldiers had already had some Militia experience.

During the course of the Division's training, General Bennett's influence
was substantial. The very qualities that Sturdee had identified in his letter to
White and Miles in May of that year were shown in abundance during the
last months of 1940 and during early 1941: an aggressive attitude to training,
efficiency and physical fitness, and as Sturdee had noted, to the training of
his officers.

During this period both Bennett and Rourke made frequent trips
through New South Wales, Queensland, Victoria, Tasmania and South
Australia inspecting the 8th Division's far-flung units. In addition to
the administration and training of the Division, General Bennett was in
charge of all corps troops in New South Wales. On 13 November 1940, the
HQ of the 27th Brigade opened at the showgrounds in Sydney. The Brigade
was to consist of the Queensland 2/26th Battalion (Lieutenant-Colonel

Boyes), which went into camp at Grovely in Queensland; the 2/29th Battalion (Lieutenant-Colonel Robertson), which went into camp at Bonegilla in Victoria; and the 2/30th (Lieutenant-Colonel Galleghan), which went into camp at Tamworth in New South Wales. By the end of 1940, therefore, Bennett had his 22nd Brigade in camp at Bathurst in NSW; his 23rd Brigade in camp at Bonegilla in Victoria; and his 27th Brigade spread through NSW, Victoria and Queensland.

During January 1941, Bennett conducted TEWTs (Tactical Exercises Without Troops) at his HQ and held a conference of commanders. In addition, he gave exercises for Divisional HQ in daily movement for up to five days at a time. These exercises were also used to test the signals from division to brigade and to units.[43] By the time the 8th Division left Australia, it was at least as well trained as the 6th and 7th Divisions.[44]

After the decision was made in October 1940 to send an Australian brigade group to Malaya to operate directly under the British Malaya Command, Brigadier Taylor's 22nd Brigade was chosen for the task. But that plan 'had given way to a decision to send also a part of the divisional headquarters, on the ground that the staff of a brigade was insufficient to handle an Australian force in an overseas country'.[45] In his book, *The Fall of General Gordon Bennett*, Lodge claims that the decision to send a portion of the 8th Division's HQ to Malaya 'probably stems from Bennett's distrust of regular officers'.[46] According to the Official Historian, the units which sailed on the *Queen Mary* were: the 22nd Brigade (the 2/18th, 2/19th and 2/20th Battalions); the 2/10th Field Regiment; a battery of the 2/4th Anti-tank Regiment; the 2/10th Field Company; the 8th Division Signals; the 10th Advanced General Hospital; the 2/4th Casualty Clearing Station; the 2/9th Field Ambulance; the 2/2nd Motor Ambulance Convoy; the 2/5th Field Hygiene Section; the 2nd Bacteriological Laboratory; the 17th Dental Unit; the 4th Supply Personnel Section; a Reserve Motor Transport Company; a field bakery; the 2/4th Field Workshop; the 2/2nd Ordnance Store; the 8th Division Cash Office; the 8th Division Provost Company; the 8th Division Postal Unit and other headquarters details—in all around 5750 personnel.[47]

Major Kappe, GSO2, left Australia on 31 January while General Bennett flew out four days later. The 22nd Brigade and its attached units— codenamed 'Elbow Force'—departed Sydney on board the *Queen Mary* on

2 February 1941. With the *Queen Mary* sailed the *Aquitania* and the Dutch ship *Nieuw Amsterdam*, which were carrying troops to the Middle East. The convoy was escorted by HMAS *Hobart*. Two days out from Fremantle, the *Mauretania* joined the convoy.

The Unit Diarist of the 2/18th Battalion has left us with a stirring account of the eventual splitting of the convoy on 16 February 1941, with one part heading for the Middle East, and the other to Singapore:

Day dawned hot and steaming and Ships ploughed their way through the placid sea at 14 knots ... At 1430 hrs a ship, which we later knew to be H.M.S. Durban, appeared dimly outlined on the N.W. Horizon. As we came closer she crossed our bows and swung into line abreast to starbd [sic] of H.M.A.S. *Canberra*. This was the dispersal point for the Convoy and on two blasts of the "Queen Mary's" siren the "Q.M." swung to the port making a complete circle behind the other ships of the Convoy. After they were in formation again the "Queen Mary" increased her speed from 14 to 30 knots in 10 minutes and soon overtook first, the "Mauritania" [sic] and then the "Aquitania". As we passed the "Mauritania" about 300 yds on our port side we noticed that the soldiers had gained every vantage point, with the Nurses amidships at the highest and best point of all, as though at a given signal, wild bursts of good Aussie cheers and cooees rent the air, and was fittingly replied to in a similar manner by the entire personnel of this marvellous ship., the "Q.M.". We soon left the "Mauritania" and overtook the "Aquitania" where again this most inspiring and never-to-be-forgotten performance was repeated. To most of those who were capable of fine and deep feelings will remember this day forever and all must have been almost overcome with emotion and after these last farewells, the convoy consisting of "Aquitania", "Mauritania" and "New Amsterdam", headed by H.M.A.S. Canberra, circled to the west and set course along the path of the sinking sun. The "Q.M." and H.M.S. Durban on the other hand, moved in N.E. direction ... [48]

Perhaps Lieutenant Jim Howard's sentiments were those of many on board: '... very emotional. I suppose one of the things that goes through your mind is, "I wonder how many of us will see this out?"[49] None of them could have guessed that in a symbolic sense, they were amongst the last of the empire's men. If the sun was setting on the *Queen Mary*'s horizon, irresistible forces were at work against a continuance of European colonial rule in Asia—the sun was indeed setting. And the cost to Britain and two of her dominions would be horrendous.

The *Queen Mary* arrived at the naval dock at Singapore on 18 February 1941. Among the multitude of coolies and British troops on the wharves was a gathering of British dignitaries to greet them: the GOC Malaya Lieutenant-General Bond, and the Governor Sir Shenton Thomas and his wife. According to Don Wall, 2/20th Battalion, the troops 'showered them with coins'.[50] Perhaps Reg Newton was a little more explicit when he decribed a number of 'practical jokers' who engaged in 'the heating of pennies and throwing them down onto the wharves among the coolies and British troops'.[51] To another onlooker aboard the *Queen Mary* the multitude of uniforms worn by the welcoming party 'might well have come from the wardrobe of a theatrical company'.[52]

The 22nd Brigade was packed into railway carriages and taken to the state of Negri Sembilan: Brigade HQ and the 2/18th and 2/20th Battalions to Port Dickson on the west coast of Malaya and about 320 kilometres from Singapore; and the 2/19th to Seremban, roughly 32 kilometres inland from Port Dickson and about 330 kilometres from Singapore. The HQ of the 8th Division and its signals were established at Kuala Lumpur, the capital of the Federated Malay States, while the artillery, general hospital and supply units were based at Malacca. The motor ambulance convoy was stationed at Kajang, about halfway between Seremban and Kuala Lumpur.

The Australians were stepping into a world totally new to them. There was no following in the footsteps of the ghosts of the First AIF here: through the training grounds of Egypt and the Bible Lands; or the fields of Flanders or leave in the 'old country'; and there were no train convoys with original AIF autographs cut into the timber of the rail trucks. On the basis of their limited education in geographical and cultural terms, this was an alien world.

Probably the troops' first impression of Singapore was the heat and humidity, the resulting heavy perspiration and the on and off again rain. And there were sights and sounds and smells unique to this new world:

the predominant vivid green of the palms and striking colours of tropical gardens, the multitude of aromas of the crammed open-air food stalls—some curious and others, such as the drying fish and their accompanying flies, utterly repugnant. Then there were the streets. Through a seething mass of hawkers, food stall owners and coolies moved a seemingly dysfunctional mass of bikes, rickshaws and horn-blowing cars—all making their hurried way against a background of crammed and densely occupied buildings with washing hanging from bamboo poles high above the busy scene below.

On leave in Singapore, the Australian soldier could venture to the Great World, the New World or the Happy World, which were the Singaporian equivalents of Luna Park. Here the usual sideshows and stalls were prevalent as well as picture shows. But there was another attraction. Soldiers could buy their alcohol and visit the taxi-dancers in dance halls. For around 25 cents each, tickets could be bought and honoured by either attractive local or Eurasian women who danced with the soldier for a set period of time. To those seeking 'horizontal refreshment', there was the lure of Lavender Street—the extensive red light area of Singapore.

At the time, as the other ranks of the 22nd Brigade 8th Division began training and adjusting to a totally new military, physical and cultural environment, few—if any—could have contemplated the undercurrent of hostility, and at times intrigue, that was to be played out within 8th Division HQ.

When Major-General Henry Gordon Bennett arrived in Malaya, he knew that he had been overlooked three times for command positions he felt he was both qualified for, and entitled to; he knew he had both bitter and powerful enemies; and critically, that his arch enemy Blamey was in command of a corps in the Middle East. And if all this were not enough, he was to be forced to work with two Staff Corps officers on his staff—Rourke and Broadbent—and one of his brigade commanders, who were not appointed by him, and it will be shown, would prove to be recalcitrant subordinates.

5

MALAYA COMMAND

When General Bennett and Brigadier Taylor's 22nd Brigade Group arrived in Singapore in February 1941, a number of critical changes to Malaya Command had been made in the context of events in Europe and a rapidly escalating potential for war in the Far East.

By October 1940, the Chiefs of Staff had become acutely aware of the antagonism and resulting lack of cooperation in Singapore between General Bond and Air Vice-Marshal Babington. They now recommended to Churchill that a Commander-in-Chief Far East be appointed with the responsibility for the land and air defence of Singapore, Malaya, Burma, Borneo and Hong Kong. The Commander-in-Chief's command did not include the Royal Navy. On 17 October 1940, the Chiefs of Staff nominated Air Chief Marshal Sir Robert Brooke-Popham.

Lionel Wigmore in *The Japanese Thrust*:

From 1898 to 1912 Brooke-Popham had been an infantry officer. Then as a captain he had joined the Air Battalion, Royal Engineers— the beginning of a British Military air force, later to become the Royal Flying Corps and later still the Royal Air Force. He gained distinction as an air officer in the war of 1914–18 and when it ended was one of its senior leaders. In the following nineteen years he held a series of high appointments, including command of the R.A.F. Staff College and the Imperial Defence College (school of future senior commanders of all three Services) . . .

Three years before the war he had retired from the post of Inspector-General of the Air Force to become Governor and Commander-in-Chief of Kenya.[1]

There would seem to be two major criticisms of this appointment. The first was the nature of Brooke-Popham's responsibilities. He had no control over the navy in the Far East; that whilst Bond and Babington were subordinate to him, both retained control over their respective finances and administrations; both were still to report directly to their service chiefs in London; he had absolutely no control over the civil administration in Singapore; and, although he had access to intelligence from the Far Eastern Intelligence Bureau, he had no operational control over it. Further, Brooke-Popham had a miserly sized staff of seven. The second point concerns the suitability of Brooke-Popham for the position. At 62 years of age, and given the nature of his preceding appointments—and recent retirement—he was hardly an energetic or inspiring appointment. As Wigmore has pointed out, 'General Gort, who had commanded the British Expeditionary Force in France, was aged 54; General Wavell, then C-in-C Middle East, was 57; and General Auchinleck, soon to become C-in-C India, was 56.'[2]

If Brooke-Popham's powers were limited, and his staff small, he deserves great credit for one of his very early initiatives: the removal of the troublesome Defence Committee Chairman, Mr Vlieland ('Starchie Archie'). Brooke-Popham would later state that: 'I have seldom met anyone who is, with two or three exceptions, so universally distrusted', and that Vlieland had developed "procrastination as a fine art".'[3]

After being briefed in London, Brooke-Popham acted swiftly after his arrival in Singapore. Obviously the Governor, Sir Shenton Thomas, had also been briefed in London and then by Brooke-Popham in Singapore, and knew what was coming. Vlieland has left us with his account of the fateful meeting of 13 December 1940:

When I entered the council chamber and took my old seat at his right hand, Sir Shenton did not greet, or even look at me. He opened the proceedings by inviting B.P. [Brooke-Popham] to speak. The C-in-C Land and Air then made a savage attack on me. It was, in effect, more of an attack on Sir Shenton's previous regime than on myself. No one else said a word. Bond and Layton nodded their approval and my friend the A.O.C. [Babington] could not rally to my support in defiance of his Air Chief Marshal. Sir Shenton remained silent with bowed head.[4]

It would seem highly likely that 'Starchie Archie's' fate was sealed by two unforgivable misdemeanours. The first was his obvious efforts to isolate Bond on the Defence Committee by siding with Babington, and thereby acting as a divisive influence upon a coordinated defence plan. But his second transgression—Bond and Babington must bear most of the blame for their poor professional and personal relationship—was by far the more serious. We have noted that as early as August 1939, the Chiefs of Staff had recommended the stockpiling of six months of rice supplies. On 2 July 1940, the Colonial Office had asked for information on the stocks of rice; on 14 July, 'they told Jones that all possible steps should be taken to increase food stocks to the utmost extent practicable';[5] and that the War Office 'considered that the storage and milling capacity for rice should be dispersed throughout the country'.[6] Jones was also told to consult Bond concerning these arrangements.

Jones's reply was extraordinary: on 2 October he stated that no action had been taken, nor planned, to implement the request because 'the policy of retaining rice stocks in the north appeared to be consistent with the views expressed in the appreciation by Chiefs of Staff, which pointed to the fact that the whole of Malaya should be held rather than only Singapore Island'.[7] According to Kirby, Jones's reply was based on Vlieland's advice. After further pressure from London, although Jones finally acted, it was discovered that Vlieland had 'failed to inform the Food Controller in Malaya that stocks had to be built up to 180 days; a decision taken a year earlier'.[8] To label Vlieland's participation during the fateful months before the war in the Far East as mischievous is to understate his negative influence.

After witnessing the acrimonious relationship between Babington and Bond, Brooke-Popham's next initiative was their removal. Babington's replacement was Air Vice-Marshal C. W. H. Pulford. Pulford had seen service during the First World War with HMS *Ark Royal* at Gallipoli during 1915; as commander of 1 Squadron 1917–18; and 201 Squadron during 1918. Prior to his appointment in Singapore, he had been AOC 20 Group during 1940–41. Bond's replacement was Lieutenant-General Arthur Percival. It will be remembered that Percival had been General Dobbie's GSO1 in 1937, and had submitted an astute appreciation on a possible Japanese invasion of Malaya. Lionel Wigmore in *The Japanese Thrust*:

> He [Percival] had gone to France with the British Expeditionary Force soon after the outbreak of war in Europe; but in April 1940 had returned to London to become one of the three Assistant Chiefs of the Imperial General Staff. After the fall of France he asked to be transferred to a field formation and was given command of the 44th Division, recently evacuated from France and needing extensive reorganization.[9]

It is highly likely that the Chief of the Imperial General Staff (CIGS), General Dill, chose Percival for four reasons. First, he was a protégé of Dill's and had his complete professional and personal trust; second, Percival had graduated from the Army Staff College at Camberley, the Naval Staff College, and had attended a course at the Imperial Defence College. Given the poor relationship between the services in Malaya, Percival would have been seen as being able to relate to, and establish cordial relationships with, each of the services. Third, having served under Dobbie in Singapore/ Malaya, Percival would have been only too well aware of the pedestrian and muddlesome workings of the civil service and the Governor, Sir Shenton Thomas, as well as having had prior opportunity to experience the unique conditions of service in the Far East. Last, he must have been aware of the current policies of the Chiefs of Staff to the Far East.

If Brooke-Popham's decisive action in removing Vlieland, Babington and Bond deserves high praise, then his subsequent appraisal of the ability of the RAF to defend Malaya and Singapore from a Japanese invasion, and his resultant decision making, were at best flawed, and at worst, incompetent.

In considering the RAF's chances of successfully defending Malaya and Singapore from a Japanese invasion, four areas deserve close scrutiny: the disposition of airfields; the quality of the protagonists' planes; the relative training and experience of their pilots; and the RAF's infrastructure—leadership, intelligence, communications and airfield defence.

The ongoing arguments between the army and air force regarding the location of airfields in Malaya have been described. There were three airfields in Kelantan on the north-eastern coast of Malaya: Kota Bharu, Gong Kedah and Machang. Kota Bharu lay a mere three kilometres from the coast, and only sixteen kilometres from the Siamese border. Gong Kedah, about 48 kilometres south-east of Kota Bharu, lay only about 9.5 kilometres from the coast, and Machang was at that time not operational. Clearly, the RAF chose these locations to provide maximum range for reconnaissance and offensive strikes over the Gulf of Siam and Indo-China. But if the Japanese, undetected or at least partially screened by the north-east monsoon, managed to bomb or shell these airfields, and land on the coast at or near these sites, the airfields would more than likely fall, and fall quickly. Further, the only ground supply link to Kota Bharu was by a single line railway—also highly vulnerable.

The main airfield on the west coast of Malaya was at Alor Star in Kedah, which was a mere 48 kilometres from the Siamese border. Further south lay the airfields of Sungei Patani and Butterworth, while two airfields in Perak were to be found at Taipang and Ipoh.

Airfields at Kuala Lumpur in the west and Kuantan in the east served central Malaya while further south in Johore was to be found an airfield at Kluang and a landing ground at Kahang. Three RAF bases were located on Singapore Island: at Seletar, Sembawang and Tengah. There was also a civil airfield at Kallang. It is now pertinent to examine the RAF's ability to carry out its allotted task.

The front-line fighter on which the British placed their faith was the American designed and constructed Brewster Buffalo. Rejected for service in Britain—considered not good enough for service against the Luftwaffe over Britain, or in the Middle East, but a match for anything Japanese—some

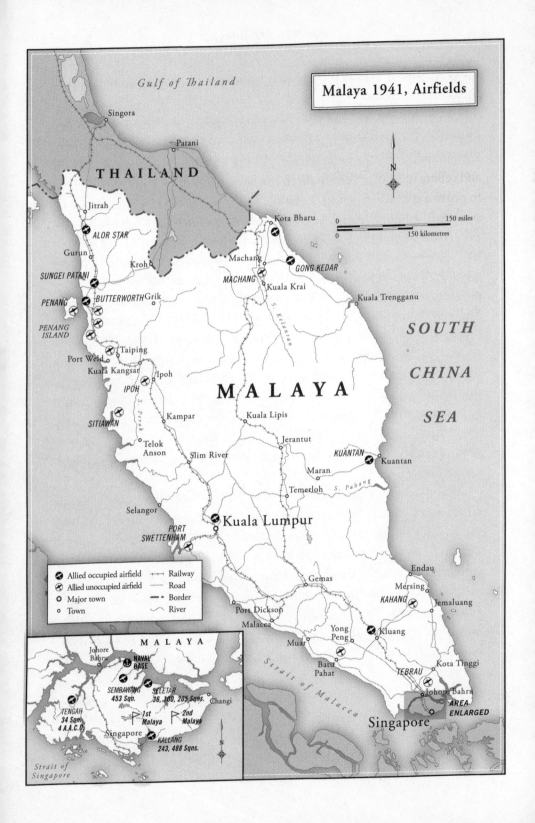

Malaya 1941, Airfields

Gulf of Thailand

Singora

Patani

THAILAND

Jitrah

ALOR STAR

Gurun

Kroh

Kota Bharu

Machang

MACHANG

GONG KEDAR

Kuala Krai

SUNGEI PATANI

BUTTERWORTH Grik

PENANG

PENANG ISLAND

Kuala Trengganu

Taiping

Port Weld

Kuala Kangsar

Ipoh

IPOH

Kampar

Kuala Lipis

MALAYA

SITIAWAN

Telok Anson

Slim River

Jerantut

KUANTAN

Kuantan

Maran

Temerloh

S. Pahang

Selangor

Kuala Lumpur

PORT SWETTENHAM

SOUTH

CHINA

SEA

0 ——— 150 miles
0 ——— 150 kilometres

N

Endau

Gemas

Mersing

KAHANG

Jemaluang

Port Dickson

Malacca

Yong Peng

Kluang

Muar

S. Perak

S. Kelantan

Batu Pahat

Kota Tinggi

TEBRAU

Johore Bahru

AREA ENLARGED

Strait of Malacca

Singapore

Allied occupied airfield	Railway
Allied unoccupied airfield	Road
Major town	Border
Town	River

MALAYA

Johore Bahru

NAVAL BASE

SEMBAWANG 453 Sqn.

SELETAR 36, 100, 205 Sqns.

1st Malaya

2nd Malaya

Changi

TENGAH 34 Sqn. 4 A.A.C.U.

Singapore

KALLANG 243, 488 Sqns.

N

Strait of Singapore

167 were sent to Malaya from February 1941 to form four squadrons. This aircraft had numerous faults—the adaptation of the original model used by the RAF had been 'developed beyond the limits of the airframe'[10]—and with a more powerful engine and increased weight caused by such additions as armour, radio and more armament, its top speed, manoeuvrability, climb and ceiling were all adversely affected. Known as 'the flying beer barrel' it was to prove a disaster in action. As late as November 1941, 21 Squadron RAAF stationed at Sungei Patani reported that 'the undercarriage of the Buffalo gave frequent trouble by sticking in the locked position; even the manual release device was not efficient'.[11] Further, difficulty was experienced with the Buffalo's .5-inch guns: 'two of which were synchronised to fire through the propellers, were affected by corrosion and rusting in the electrical system which meant that the squadron "never had efficient armament".'[12]

The Japanese were to deploy a number of fighters in their air arm during the Malayan campaign. One of the most prominent was the Army's Nakajima ki 27, code-named 'Nate' by the British, which was the most numerous of the Japanese fighters during the campaign. Its great advantage over the Brewster Buffalo was its superb manoeuvrability. But it was another fighter which captured the imagination of the Japanese people and the great respect of the British during the early part of the Pacific War: the Japanese Navy's Mitsubishi A6M Zero-Sen, which became universally known as the 'Zero'. Christopher Shores and Brian Cull, in *Bloody Shambles*: 'It combined almost unbelievable agility with a tremendous range, a fair top speed, a rocket-like climb and the heaviest armament yet carried by a Japanese fighter. Undoubtedly the A6M was the supreme fighter in the Far East at the start of the war, and its achievements were to be substantial.'[13]

Another formidable Japanese fighter was the Mitsubishi A5M or 'Oscar'. Often confused with the Zero, the Oscar also performed admirably during the fighting. In their detailed summation of the fighters used in the Malayan Campaign, Shores and Cull, in *Bloody Shambles*, point out that the attributes of Japanese superiority in fighter performance were not speed nor ceiling but in 'the lightness of their aircraft, which thereby enjoyed greater manoeuvrability, higher climb rates and faster acceleration'.[14]

Four squadrons of Brewster Buffalo fighters were destined for use during daylight operations against these Japanese fighters, while one squadron of

Bristol Blenheim I medium bombers was modified and used as a night fighter squadron. The Blenheim I was 'old and in poor condition'[15] and suffered from poor armament and a modest bomb load.

Turning to a comparison between the Japanese and British bombers, the British relied upon two squadrons of Blenheim I and IV light bombers and two reconnaissance squadrons of Hudson bombers. The Blenheims were not a formidable opponent to the Japanese aircraft, and further, while the Hudson operated with a reasonable armament of five machine guns and an acceptable bomb load, all four bomber squadrons were required to operate on both reconnaissance and bomber operations during day and night. This decision affected both the quality and duration of training for either. There were also two torpedo bomber squadrons consisting of Vickers Vildebeeste biplanes—ruled obsolete by the RAF in 1940 and due for replacement.

But the most telling Japanese advantage over the RAF, RAAF and the RNZAF came down to arguably the most critical component of air warfare: the training and operational experience of the pilots. Douglas Gillison, in *Australia in the War of 1939–1945: Royal Australian Air Force 1939–1942*:

... at this time [7 December 1941] about 6,000 Japanese pilots had graduated from training units, 3,500 of whom were assigned to the navy and the remainder to the army. About 50 per cent of the army pilots had been in combat either in China or in the border fighting against the Soviet air force, while 10 per cent of the land-based navy pilots had been engaged in the China operations. About 600 of the best navy pilots were assigned to aircraft carrier units. Japanese pilots were receiving about 300 hours in training units before going to tactical units. The average first-line Japanese pilot in 1941 had about 600 hours and the average pilot in the carrier groups had more than 800 hours.[16]

In contrast, the training of the RAF, RAAF and RNZAF pilots varied enormously. By late 1941, the Australian content of the total squadron strength in Singapore and Malaya was around 25 per cent. As late as September, 21 Squadron RAAF was still converting to Brewster Buffaloes, and 'experienced' pilots were still being transferred to other units for training purposes. Douglas Gillison:

In the same month a temporary advanced flying training unit was formed at Kluang in central-southern Malaya in an endeavour to meet the training needs of Australian and New Zealand pilots who were arriving direct from flying training schools. More than four months of training was required before such airmen could be expected to be ready for operational flying. To help in the establishment of this unit five of No. 21 Squadron's most experienced pilots and six of its Wirraways were transferred to it. The squadron was handicapped also by a decision of Air Headquarters, made simultaneously, that it should change its role from general reconnaissance and become a fighter and army cooperation squadron. Not all the pilots were readily adaptable to the change—they had not been selected as fighter pilots in the first place and inevitably some were unsuitable.[17]

By December 1941, three-quarters of all personnel serving in the RAF Far East Command had been posted direct from a training school and were new to the unique conditions found in Malaya. Further, from January to September 1941, there were some 67 flying accidents across Far East Command which resulted in 48 deaths.[18] This must surely be, in part at least, a reflection of the training of the pilots.

If the equipment of the air forces in the Far East was substandard in terms of both quality and quantity, then the shameful truth is that the authorities gave their aircrews little assistance in other critical areas. Their intelligence gathering—and failure to use what they did get—was a classic case in point.

Brooke-Popham's chief intelligence service was the Far Eastern Combined Bureau. In basic terms, both the bureau and its intelligence recipients in Singapore were amateurish, unprofessional and probably incompetent. Administered by the Royal Navy, and with a naval officer in command, army and air force intelligence ran a distant second and third to naval intelligence. Japanese fighters had been involved in combat missions over China and Manchuria for some time, and, when the soon to be famous Zero began to appear over the same skies from around July 1940, the proficiency of Japanese aircraft and their pilots were obvious to any interested parties. Further, in May 1941—seven months before the Pacific War began—a Japanese fighter was shot down by anti-aircraft fire near Chengtu in China, a major US Army

Air Force base. Data on its armament and range were passed onto Air Headquarters in Singapore, and, after the British Air Attaché stationed in Chung-
king sent his estimates as to the Japanese fighters' performance, this too was
passed onto Air HQ Far East. Shores and Cull, in *Bloody Shambles*: '. . . but
at Air HQ, Far East, lack of intelligence staff resulted in this data failing to
be extracted from a mass of general intelligence information.'[19] No excuse.

Given that the pilots in the Far East were often very inexperienced, and
that they were to be further handicapped by an inadequacy of both numbers
and quality of aircraft, to deny them the opportunity to become familiar
with the performance of Japanese army and navy aircraft, their operational
tactics and the abilities of their pilots was unforgivable, given that much of
this information was readily available.

Brooke-Popham made two visits to Australia to confer with the Australian Government and service representatives. The first was in February
1941, when he informed the Australians that Churchill had told him that
he would not let Singapore fall, and that he was to hold the 'fortress' for six
months until capital ships could arrive. This was an empty gesture given
that the Chiefs of Staff had extended the period before relief to 'indefinite'
after the fall of France—over six months earlier. Further, Brooke-Popham
told the Australians that the Japanese were not 'air-minded' and particularly
so against 'determined opposition'.[20] He also said that the Malayan air force
would put up 'a good show'. Determination is an admirable quality—but
competitive aircraft and trained pilots and adequate intelligence are the
necessary prerequisites for 'a good show'.

But it was at the second conference with the Australian Advisory War
Council on 16 October 1941—under the new Prime Minister John Curtin—
where Brooke-Popham's comments became culpable. He stated that the
Buffalo fighters were superior to their Japanese counterparts, and that the
Buffalo was well suited to Malayan conditions. But he 'admitted a shortage
of long-range and torpedo bombers'.[21] Brooke-Popham also stated that
the Japanese were more likely to move against the Soviet Union while
that nation was immersed in fighting the Germans. This would delay any
Japanese move southwards by at least three months. Prime Minister Curtin
was not convinced. Pointing to the still deficient numbers of aircraft needed
to defend Singapore and Malaya, Curtin urged a stronger stand against

Whitehall. Brooke-Popham took 'umbrage' at this statement and said that he had 'made all representations short of resigning' and that the British Chiefs of Staff were 'not neglecting the Far East and that probably they have made a fair allocation from the resources available'.[22]

In an extraordinary footnote to Brooke-Popham's statements at this conference, Douglas Gillison, in his *Australia in the War of 1939–1945: Royal Australian Air Force 1939–1942*, has stated that:

> Apart from complaints about this aircraft's inefficiency from pilots in his own command, of which he must have been aware, Brooke-Popham in his official despatch admitted that the Buffalo's performance at heights of 10,000 feet and over was relatively poor, a fact which he had already demonstrated (in September) by a test in Burma. This showed its inferiority to the American Tomahawk which members of the AVG [American Volunteer Group] doubted would be a match for Japanese fighters. Yet at this time there was Intelligence information to show that the Japanese Zero was powerfully armed (two 7.7-mm guns and two 22-mm cannon), had a maximum speed of 345 m.p.h. and a range, with maximum fuel load, of 1,500 miles—an impressive performance by any standards then known and one which, clearly, was far beyond that of the Buffalo. Brooke-Popham should not have lacked this information which in fact was issued with a noteworthy review of the origin, organisation and development of the Japanese Navy and Army Air Services as a RAAF Intelligence memorandum, just ten days before Brooke-Popham's comments to the Advisory War Council.[23]

This is astonishing evidence. Brooke-Popham must have been aware of this data. It would seem that David Day, in his *The Great Betrayal*, provides the only plausible answer to Brooke-Popham's statements.

> ...Brooke-Popham acknowledged that the Labor Government was more critical of Britain and more conscious of its predicament in the Pacific. He warned London of the importance of making Australia 'feel that we, in England, look upon them as definitely part of one

Empire and we must do everything we can to keep them in the Empire and not run any risk of their slipping out of it'.[24]

And how would that be accomplished? By 'spin' and generalities, and if need be, by untruths.

But there were failures that were more localised in nature. The animosity between General Bond and Air Vice-Marshal Babington has been identified. Poisoned senior command relationships permeate to subordinate commanders and the other ranks, and further inhibit common policy, common objectives and cooperation. Therefore, despite the lack of funding from London, muddled and uncoordinated efforts in Singapore caused further grave difficulties. Although by 1941 around 22 airfields had been built, the RAF was faced with a number of inherent local weaknesses, in addition to its flawed airfield locations, inferior aircraft and inexperienced pilots.

Although all airfields were allotted eight light and eight heavy anti-aircraft guns by the end of 1941, only 17 per cent of these guns had been deployed.[25] Thus, the poor siting of the airfields was compounded by equally poor protection of them against enemy air attack. In mid-1941, Flight-Lieutenant Burlinson RAAF was appointed group defence officer. During an examination of the airfields on Singapore he noted that they were:

. . . defended on the old principles of the 'thin red line'; as a friend said, 'very thin and not much of a line.' One clause in the orders for the defence of each of these stations appeared in identical words in each set of orders. This clause referred to the Mobile Relief Column which was to rush to the aid of the station garrison in the event of pressing need. This force was referred to in . . . general terms and inconclusive detail . . . Major Peel Thompson of the Manchesters . . . General Staff Officer II, Headquarters, Singapore Fortress . . . gave me all the help it was in his power to give . . . When I outlined my question [about the relief column] he smiled and said, 'My friend, you have been reading the papers, you have entirely the wrong idea of the defence of Singapore.' [Thompson then showed Burlinson a map of the disposition of troops on Singapore Island] . . . Somewhere inland from Singapore was a cluster of four pins. Pointing to these the GSO II said, 'Here my friend, you have the whole of the reserve of which you spoke—of four platoon strength. It is NOT mobile and has seventeen different roles to perform.'[26]

Burlinson's tour of the Malayan airfield defences was hardly anymore encouraging. Douglas Gillison, in *Australia in the War of 1939–1945: Royal Australian Air Force 1939–1942*:

> On arrival at the northern most airfield, Kota Bharu, he was taken to meet Brigadier Key, who was charged with its defence. Key had three battalions of infantry dispersed along 45 miles of frontier and 40 miles of coastline. The R.A.F. station was less than a mile and a half from the coast. As the artillery available consisted of one servicable field gun, it was obvious that so far as army defences were concerned, enemy destroyers might lie off shore and shell either Kota Bharu or Gong Kedah (where a new airfield had been constructed 30 miles to the south) without risk. Asked by Burlinson whether he could guarantee that these two airfields could be maintained in service in the face of an enemy attack with one full division, the brigadier replied that he could give no such guarantee and that, anyway, the enemy naval escort could render both airfields untenable without any troops landing.[27]

The RAAF Official Historian then proceeds to record a disturbing British trait, which, when viewed through Australian eyes, comes down to little more than professional snobbery. When Burlinson sent in his report to Pulford, it was passed on to General Percival. The general's reply was subsequently shown to Burlinson by Pulford: 'the General was satisfied with the dispositions and that in any case he was not accustomed to receiving critical reports signed only by a second lieutenant.'[28] Burlinson was 'merely' a second lieutenant; he was not a 'professional'; but he was an experienced business man 'of some standing at home',[29] who probably was, therefore, more than capable of identifying structural weaknesses in organisations. Further, Pulford would surely not have passed the report on to Percival had he thought it lacked substance.

Another officer of equally unimpressive rank—but, it seems, with keen powers of observation—was Flight-Lieutenant Bulcock, who observed that the RAF station at Seletar facing the Johore Strait 'was staggering for those seeing it for the first time—palatial messes, barracks, tennis courts, football fields, swimming pool, golf course, picture show and yacht club—all situated within the seven-mile steel boundary fence enclosing the aerodrome . . .'[30] When posted to the RAF station at Kuantan, he observed that 'nearly all the buildings had been completed and stood out like a fire on the ocean, for that excellent camouflage the rubber trees had been ruthlessly shorn away'.[31] After repeated requests for additional equipment, and a visit by a group captain, Bulcock was told to 'put all his troubles in writing'.[32]

If the RAF airfields in Singapore and Malaya were poorly protected by the army, and often poorly camouflaged, as well as lacking quality anti-aircraft gun cover, then the RAF's ability to provide early warning of enemy aircraft and then operate with a sound communication system was also severely flawed. Although there were two radar units on Singapore, only two more would be in use by the end of 1941 in eastern Malaya, with another five under construction. The communication channels in the RAF Command comprised the telephone network, teleprinter, wireless telegraphy and radio-telephone networks. As the telephone network passed through the civil exchanges and there was a paucity of emergency lines, the whole tele-phone network was extremely vulnerable. Also, the RAF internal telephone system lacked a repair and maintenance field signals system, which impacted upon both station and unit communications, while there was a shortage of teleprinters and, they too, depended on exposed land cables.

As the Pacific War drew ever closer, the air war was to become a most unequal contest. The Japanese were superior in numbers and aircraft and had highly trained and experienced pilots. They also had the initiative and had concentrated their resources and their force. Above all, they possessed a high sense of plan and purpose. The RAF on the other hand was a poorly trained and equipped formation with an inflated sense of its own ability to engage its enemy. It had a poor intelligence system, was vulnerable to concentrated strikes in terms of early warning and airfield protection, and was to be further inadequately protected by an army it had failed to consult and to work with. While the British services argued almost endlessly over the strategic and tactical roles of the RAF in shaping defence plans in the Far East, the Japanese Army and Navy each had their own air arm, and each controlled its own training, tactical use and deployment of that resource—which would prove decisive.

——◦◦◦——

General Percival took over as GOC Malaya Command on 16 May 1941. Any fair assessment of his performance before the outbreak of war—a seven-month period—should be based on two criteria: first, the resources (both human and material) at his disposal; and second, the impact he made upon his command.

By December 1941, the total strength of the army—including the administrative and line of communication units—was around 88 800. Of these soldiers, about 37 000 were Indian, 19 600 British, 15 200 Australian and approximately 16 800 were locally enlisted Asians. This force consisted of three divisions (each composed of two brigades): the 9th and 11th Indian, and the 8th Australian, and a modest allocation of supporting artillery. There were also 'two reserve brigade groups, two fortress brigades for Singapore Island and a battalion as garrison for Penang'.[33] In addition to a number of airfield defence and local volunteer defence units, Singapore Island possessed its fixed coastal defence guns and anti-aircraft batteries. In all, the army defence of Malaya and Singapore numbered around three and a half divisions—a shortfall of about seventeen infantry battalions and two tank regiments which Generals Bond and Percival had estimated were the minimum army requirement until the air forces had reached their promised strength. But the really damning deficit in the structure of the army defence of Singapore was the absence of armoured units. Percival had requested two tank regiments as early as 1937, whilst serving as General Dobbie's GSO1, and had repeated his request when GOC Malaya in 1941. They would not be forthcoming.

The 'locally enlisted Asian' forces aside, by far the biggest army formation in the defence of Malaya and Singapore was III Corps—primarily the Indian Army's 9th and 11th Divisions. III Corps was over twice the size of the British and Australian formations put together. Its commander was Lieutenant-General Sir Lewis Heath. Known as 'Piggy', Heath had had a distinguished career. Born in Poona India on 23 November 1885, he had, whilst serving with the 59th Scinde Rifles, been wounded in an attack on the

Dujailah Redoubt, Mesopotamia on 8 March 1916, which had left him with a withered arm. Promoted to Major-General in 1939, Heath had commanded the newly raised 5th Indian Division to a decisive victory against the Italians at Keren during the Eritrean Campaign. He was an attractive man, two years older than Percival, senior to him until Percival's promotion to GOC Malaya, and had been knighted with the distinction of having conducted the first British offensive of the war. He had recently re-married to a 'New Zealand nurse many years his junior whom he had "smuggled into Malaya" as he put it, as his fiancee'.[34] By the time the fighting commenced, Heath's wife was expecting a child and was subsequently allowed to remain in Malaya.

III Corps was not, at the outbreak of hostilities, in any fit state to fight a war against an adversary of the standard of the Japanese. The Indian Army had originally been formed as a limited professional formation designed for the defence of the North-West Frontier. Prior to the First World War, it was an organisation made up of officers and other ranks who often had 'family ties binding them to their regiments'.[35] Thus, despite differences in religion or caste, the army had a strong *esprit de corps* and a proud tradition. In 1921, it was planned that each Indian regiment should be capable of a doubling of its size. There were two conditions to this proposed expansion: the first being that it should be limited to a 'doubling' of units, and the second that there should be ample warning of such an expansion and a sufficient time span for the training of both officers and other ranks before such units were committed to action. Neither of these sensible prerequisites for expansion came to pass.

In September 1939, the Indian Army was a little over 200 000 strong. By 1941, it numbered some 900 000 officers and other ranks and would increase to 1 800 000 by the end of 1942—in other words, within a period of a little over two years it would increase its prewar strength by nine times.

The fall of France was the catalyst for this rapid growth. The Indian Government offered the establishment of five new divisions immediately and a further five after the departure of the first five formed. During 1940–41 therefore, the 6th, 8th and 10th Divisions had set sail for the Middle East, and the 9th and 11th Divisions were sent to Malaya. Lieutenant-General Heath's III Corps HQ was established in Malaya during May 1941; the 11th Division (Major-General Murray-Lyon), consisting of the 6th, 15th and later the 28th Brigades, became operational in late 1940; and the 9th Division (Major-General Arthur Barstow), consisting of the 8th and 22nd Brigades, was established in Malaya during early 1941.

An Indian Army battalion was, understandably, modelled on the British Army establishment of four rifle companies each of three platoons, with a headquarters company composed of its various specialist platoons. At the brigade level, two of the three battalions were Indian and the third was usually a British battalion. In the case of the 12th Brigade the British unit was the 2nd Argyll and Sutherland Highlanders. As expansion occurred, this time-tested practice became harder to employ. By December 1941, of the six Indian brigades in Malaya only three—the 6th, 12th and 15th—contained a British battalion. Lionel Wigmore in *The Japanese Thrust*: 'It seems strange, therefore, that three British regular battalions—2/Loyals, 2/Gordons and 1/Manchester (a machine gun battalion)—were all relegated to the Singapore Fortress, a direct attack on the island being the least likely probable course of action.'[36]

Presumably, there were two benefits in having a British battalion in each Indian brigade: the obvious advantage of it being well trained and well led, and therefore being a decisive influence on the fighting quality of that formation; and second, its potential as a tool of training for its two fellow battalions. Wigmore's point is therefore relevant, since the three British battalions stationed on Singapore Island could have fulfilled both needs for those three Indian brigades.

Any resemblance between the 4th and 5th Divisions of the Indian Army which fought with distinction in the Middle East during the period 1940–41, coupled with the sterling service of the Indian Army's contribution to the British 14th Army's fighting in Burma later in the war, and elements of the same army in Malaya during late 1941 and early 1942, was near impossible to discern.

The Official British Historian offers the term 'milking' as the reason for the demise of the Indian Army during the Malayan Campaign. The term refers to the mechanism used by the British to expand the Indian Army. 'Milking' involved the transfer of regular and experienced officers and other ranks to newly established units. It was widespread and occurred even after some had arrived in Malaya. In order to understand the severity of this 'milking' process, it is well worth examining some of the unique qualities of the Indian Army structure.

The other ranks of the prewar Indian Army were drawn from less than five per cent of the population; had strong ties to the Punjab Province; were often recruited from the same families and villages as existing soldiers; were recruited at a young age, with the result that the army and unit became their home; and were concentrated in companies by their particular race, religion, caste, dietary peculiarities and other cultural similarities.[37] An Indian infantry battalion's junior leadership relied upon two types of officers, named jemadars and subedars. Each held a Viceroy's Commission. Alan Warren, in *Singapore 1942*:

> VCOs were Indians promoted from the ranks, usually after at least ten years' service. These men were junior to all officers with King's or Indian commissions, but wore the same rank insignia as lieutenants and captains. Jemadars commanded platoons, and a subedar was the senior VCO in a company. The senior VCO in a battalion was the subedar-major. VCOs were the principal link between the army's mostly British officers and the sepoys [other ranks] ...
>
> One shortcoming of the VCO system was that, without the western education that British and Indian officers took for granted, even the most talented VCO was to some extent isolated from his superiors by culture, language and some aspects of training.[38]

The Indian Army's senior battalion officers—around twelve to sixteen—held a King's Commission. They were British apart from a small number of Indians who had graduated from Sandhurst (from 1919) and from Dehra Dun from 1932.

The 'milking' process involved a removal and reposting of a number of these junior and senior officers to other units of a rapidly expanding Indian Army. In fact the term 'milking' rather understates the severity of the process. 'Gutting' would seem a far more apt term. It is at the company and platoon level where basic training and leadership impacts most. To 'gut' at a battalion level such junior, and to an extent, senior level commanders is to retard the training process both in terms of quality and time—and there was not much time available. So severe was this process that by the outbreak of war many Indian battalions had failed to reach a satisfactory level of unit training, let alone brigade and divisional training. A further problem was the basic quality and diversity of the newly arriving recruits. Kirby in *The War Against Japan*:

> What mechanisation meant to the Indian Army will be apparent when it is realized that the first thing many a recruit had to do was to discard his mother tongue or provincial dialect and learn Urdu—the language in which all instruction was imparted. Then, after basic training, he had to become proficient in a number of new and complicated weapons. To teach all this to a man who on joining was often completely illiterate, and then expect him in addition to learn to drive and maintain a heavy mechanical vehicle was asking a lot.[39]

Similar problems faced the Indian Army's ability to enhance both the quantity and quality of its signals, artillery, technical corps and schools of instruction. There was only one answer to the problem: time. The raw product, as stated using the examples of the Middle East and later Burma, was more than satisfactory. But given the time between their arrival in Malaya—and the prior and ongoing 'gutting' of their formations—to their deployment in action, the task was beyond them. And III Corps under Heath was to be the vanguard of the defence of Malaya.

During the interwar period, the majority of British Army units serving in the Far East garrison had been stationed in India and Singapore. In comparison with garrison service elsewhere in the Empire, it was not a bad life—especially for officers. In terms of social standing, British officers serving in Singapore and Malaya could look to a similar existence to English businessmen, planters and civil service personnel. This lifestyle included an impressive purchasing power for their wage; membership of exclusive clubs and hotels; impressive sporting facilities; and, for a minimum outlay, a seemingly endless supply of servants. In blunt terms, it was a leisurely paced, privileged and sheltered life. And periodic leave back to Britain tended to diminish the isolation of prolonged tropical service.

While the other ranks were denied access to such exclusive clubs and bars, they too enjoyed a lifestyle better than at home or, for that matter, than elsewhere in the British Empire. Alan Warren, in *Singapore 1942*:

> Life was unhurried but the army had evolved a routine to fill in the day that commenced early in the morning. There were end-less parades for any number of reasons ... Men still wore a pith helmet (sun helmet or sola topi) that had been part of a soldier's equipment in the tropics since Victorian times. The hottest hours of the day were spent indoors in large, airy barracks with only limited privacy. ...
>
> Yet, in small ways, junior servicemen enjoyed a social status higher than they might have enjoyed in Britain. Native staff were employed for menial tasks ... Off duty men could visit cinemas, bars, amuse-ment parks, dance halls and the red light districts.[40]

British units in Malaya and Singapore also suffered from a 'milking' of experienced officers and NCOs to Britain and the Middle East. Further, these officers were often not replaced, and to compound the problem there was not an adequate supply of trained reinforcements 'accustomed to the climatic conditions in Malaya'.[41]

And Percival had further challenges. The first was the size and quality of his Malaya Command HQ. Although the size of the army in Malaya and Singapore had increased since 1939, the Command HQ had not. Further, the standard of its work was inevitably poor, since promotions and the transfer of officers to the Middle East and Britain had impacted upon the level of experience found in it. Instead of such personnel being replaced by officers who had recent service in these theatres, Malaya Command was forced to fill its vacancies by promotion from within its own ranks. Kirby has also cited the differing rates of pay between the Indian, British and Australian forma-tions as an impediment towards the transfer of suitable officers from one formation to another.[42] Kirby has claimed that:

> ... there was no training directorate with a senior and experienced officer in charge; instead, training was in the hands of a comparatively

junior officer of the staff duties department, which was already heavily overloaded . . .

Moreover, the newly raised Indian formations reached Malaya only partially trained, and neither these formations nor the British battalions from China nor the Australian formations had had any experience or training in warfare in close country almost entirely covered by trees and jungle.[43]

Further, while schools and training centres had been established in the Middle East, no such training infrastructure existed in Malaya—a further barrier to systematic, effective training. Training was therefore left to individual brigade and unit commanders, the standard of which was going to vary.

Kirby draws a similar conclusion about the intelligence branch at Malaya Command HQ. 'This was in the hands of one second-grade and one third-grade staff officer who, because of their rank, had no direct access to Percival.'[44] It should be recognised that Percival had two easy choices with regards to these officers: either replace them, or promote them so that they at least had access to him!

It is blatantly obvious that in terms of strategy, Malaya HQ Staff, the available equipment and the quantity and quality of personnel allotted, the task of holding Singapore and Malaya was always going to be extremely difficult. When General Percival's biographer, Clifford Kinvig, claims that Percival was a scapegoat for these multitude of sins committed both in London and Singapore, he is essentially right. Percival's difficulties were diverse. However, it is also true that the pages of history bear ample testimony to commanders having to operate with such disadvantages. One of the great tests of command, therefore, is surely how any given commander confronts his challenges—how he either delays his eventual defeat, or perhaps, how he may triumph against adversity.

Percival's first problem was how best to conform to the existing RAF-dominated plan for the defence of Malaya and Singapore. His second was how best to train and then utilise his army in the field if, and when, the army became the prime weapon for the defence of Malaya and Singapore. And this eventuality must surely have been clear to him given the naval period before relief and the extreme shortfall of aircraft numbers in Malaya and Singapore at the time.

The Japanese had occupied southern Indo-China in September 1940. This brought their bombers within range of both Malaya and Singapore Island. Any Japanese advance staged down the Malay Peninsula would necessitate the capture of airfields in southern Siam (Thailand) and northern Malaya. The British were well aware that such Siamese fields existed at Singora and Patani and at Kota Bharu and Gong Kedah in northern Malaya. But it was the acquisition of Singora and Patani that posed the greatest threat. If these were captured, the Japanese would be in a position to advance along two roads—the Patani–Kroh road and the Singora–Alor Star–Kuala Kangsar road—which would have two critical consequences. The first would jeopardise the defence of Kedah and Perlis, which were the main rice production areas of Malaya; and the second, and more serious consequence, was the fact that any defending force in the area ran the risk of envelopment.

To counter this potential Japanese thrust, first General Bond and later Brooke-Popham advocated a crossing of the Siamese border to capture Singora and Patani. They also stated that additional troops would be needed to mount the operation. When Percival replaced Bond, the operation was examined again. Percival changed the plan to enable it to be undertaken without additional troops. The 11th Indian Division would now have one of two tasks: either a movement into Siam to capture Singora (code-named Matador), or the defence of the Alor Star airfield. Given that the existing resources did not enable an operation against Patani as well as Singora, Percival now advocated the occupation of a position on the Kroh Road called the Ledge. Located around 40 kilometres inside the Siamese border, the Ledge was a portion of the road which had been cut through a steep ridge. The force designated to occupy the Ledge was to be codenamed Krohcol.

In the end, Matador and Krohcol suffered from severe political and military handicaps. Both operations involved a violation of Siamese territory. At the time, British policy in the Far East was to avoid war with Japan. Should Matador and Krohcol be undertaken before a Japanese landing at Singora, the British would be seen as violating Siamese neutrality, and just as importantly, such an act of aggression might affect the attitude of the Americans. The Japanese must be seen to be making the first move.

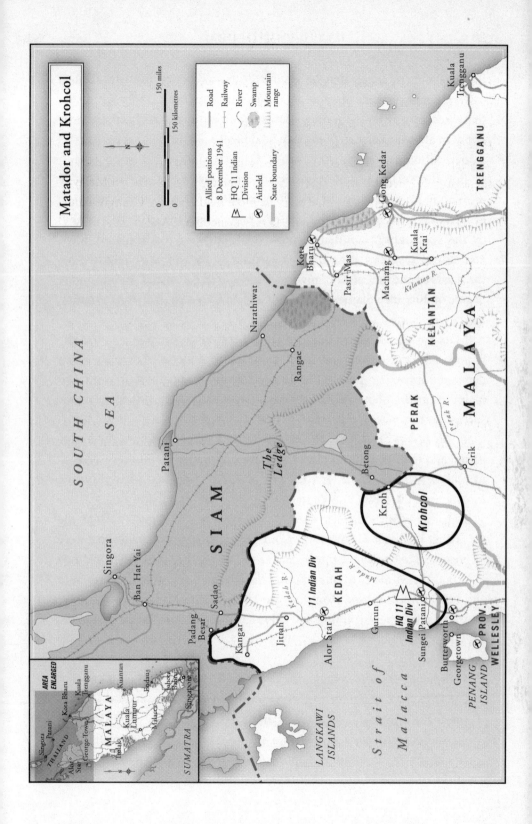

Matador and Krohcol

150 miles

150 kilometres

0

0

N

Allied positions
8 December 1941

HQ 11 Indian
Division

Airfield

State boundary

Road

Railway

River

Swamp

Mountain
range

SOUTH CHINA

SEA

Kuala
Trengganu

TRENGGANU

Gong Kedar

Kota
Bharu

Pasir Mas

Machang

Kuala
Krai

Kelantan R.

KELANTAN

Narathiwat

Rangae

M A L A Y A

Perak R.

PERAK

The
Ledge

Betong

Grik

Patani

Kroh

Krohcol

S I A M

Singora

Ban Hat Yai

Sadao

Kedah R.

Mudu R.

KEDAH

11 Indian Div

Gurun

HQ 11
Indian Div

Sungei Patani

PROV.
WELLESLEY

Padang
Besar

Kangar

Jitrah

Alor Star

Butterworth

Georgetown

PENANG
ISLAND

Strait of
Malacca

LANGKAWI
ISLANDS

SUMATRA

AREA
ENLARGED

THAILAND

Singora
Patani

Kota Bharu

Kuala
Trengganu

Endau

M A L A Y A

Kuala
Lumpur

Malacca

George Town

Singapore

Alor
Star

Kota Bharu

Brooke-Popham stated that he needed 36 hours' notice from the British Government before the operations could be implemented. He also estimated that once permission to mount Matador and Krohcol had been given by London, at least a further 24 hours would be needed for the troops to arrive at these locations.

But the real flaws in these operations were military. Any British movement into Siam would involve detailed staff work to facilitate speed of movement for not only the infantry, but also for the material required by the engineers to combat Siamese demolition of roads and railways, and also to repair existing bridges. Further stores would be required for the needs of the defence of Singora. Time would be crucial. To add to the degree of difficulty, Siamese border guards, followed soon after by infantry, might well contest the advance.

Matador was an ill-conceived plan—ill-conceived because it defied the bounds of common sense as much as military prudence. Any plan which demands unrealistic political and time restraints, superb staff work and highly trained troops will fail dismally when those very prerequisites for success are so obviously lacking.

In his book, *The Chain Of Disaster* (1971), Kirby examines these very issues, and then goes on to offer a possible alternative plan for the defence of Malaya and Singapore. A vital part of Kirby's analysis is based on the evidence provided by a new character who now enters our story.

Brigadier Ivan Simson arrived at Singapore on 5 August 1941 as the new Chief Engineer Malaya Command. His qualifications for his post were impressive. He had spent three years at the War Office (1937–39) and one (1940) at the Ministry of Supply 'after the Master General of the Ordnance and his Branches moved from the War Office to the Ministry of Supply'.[45] Simson's subsequent training and knowledge for his posting to Singapore are well worth quoting.

In both places I served under the Director of Mechanisation as Assistant Director of Engineering with continuous and close liaison with the Staff Duties and Military Training branches at the War Office on the engineering requirements of the Army. This also involved frequent visits to establishments of the Royal Engineers and Signals

Board (as it was then called). The R.E.S.B. had specialist research and development staff for the complete modernisation of all R.E. equipment and the techniques and training necessary for using such new equipment in the field. This covered railway, road, and personnel bridges of all types, floating and rigid (including the Bailey Bridge); water supply; petrol storage; demolitions and new demolition explosives; camouflage; obstacles against enemy tank and infantry landings from the sea and their advance on land; 'disappearing pill boxes' to protect airfields etc. against paratroops and plane landings; searchlights and sound locators (and radar which was being developed there); barbed wire of various sorts; booby traps . . . etc.; and how best to deal with similar enemy items when we were attacking. In fact the engineering equipment of the army was being brought up-to-date after intensive troop trials.[46]

To complement his theoretical knowledge, Simson had subsequently spent 'about five months in 1941'[47] as Deputy Chief Engineer (Operations) at the Headquarters of Scottish Command, working on the installation of 'many such items [identified above] on airfields and seaward attack against tank and infantry landings—and advance on land if they got established ashore'.[48]

It is of little surprise that Simson was told he had been selected as the new Chief Engineer Malaya Command because of his 'up-to-date knowledge and experience in the development and installation of modern defences'.[49] His orders were simple: he was to bring the defences of Malaya and Singapore up to date 'specifically against possible beachlandings and against tank and air attack'.[50]

Simson claims that he was warned of two problems that were to confront him: that friction had existed between the Chief Engineer's Office and Malaya Command HQ; and that an officer in the Works Service of the Engineer's Department had recently been convicted of malpractice. To compound this situation, he was not issued with written orders to place before Percival on arrival, but instead was assured that the Chief of the Imperial General Staff would forward a letter to Percival explaining Simson's role and his suitability for the task. No such document was ever forthcoming.

Simson received a correct but indifferent welcome from General Percival and his BGS Brigadier Torrance. 'I at once became conscious of an indefinable restraint on their part—as if they never trusted the Chief Engineer or his staff.'[51] And he could only ponder the reasons for their extraordinary behaviour. Perhaps, he thought, it was 'partly because of strained relations prior to my arrival—and partly because they—already adverse to any defences—suspected that I was bluffing about my instructions from the War Office to modernise and extend defence works'.[52]

We have noted the close relationship between Percival and the Chief of the Imperial General Staff, General Dill. Percival could so easily have cabled Dill and sought a clarification of Simson's role(s). He appears to have not done so.

After a lengthy reconnaissance of the defences in Singapore and Malaya, Simson sought an interview with Percival in mid-October 1941. He claimed that the meeting ran through 'the entire morning' and that Torrance was 'present most of the time'.[53] Before offering his plans, Simson made three key observations. The first concerned the labour required to build the fortifications. He stated that all fortifications approved by Percival could be built by civil labour or by contract, and that all works could be readily supervised by Royal Engineer officers and NCOs, who were trained in such work. Simson added the obvious point that such work should begin immediately, since the tasks would become far harder after the outbreak of hostilities. His second point concerned the required materials for the defences. Simson:

> There were large quantities of defence stores in Singapore and up country which had been shipped out in 1938–39. They included steel loopholes for pillboxes, sandbags, pickets, old and the latest types of barbed wire, including much high tensile steel anti-tank Dannert wire ... The War Office had shipped such materials to Gibraltar, Malta, Aden, Singapore, etc., knowing that after war had started, there was invariably a strain on shipping and shipping routes to such oversea garrisons.[54]

In essential terms, therefore, General Percival had the materials at hand. Simson's third point was profound—he gave five historical examples of 'constructing permanent and field defences whilst time, labour, supervision and material were available and long before the defences were needed'.[55] The five examples were Torres Vedras (1810), Sebastopol (1854–55), Port Arthur (1904), field defences used by both sides during the First World War, and the Givenchy Redoubt (1915–18). But it was the Port Arthur example that should have hit home to Percival. Simson pointed out that the Japanese attacked Port Arthur with no warning and no declaration of war; that Japan had its air bases in Indo-China within range of Malaya and Singapore; that the below strength RAF and no naval presence would not prevent enemy landings 'up country'; and that the Russians at Port Arthur had held out for nine months. These points made, Simson then made his recommendations:

1   Anti-tank and machine gun positions in depth across roads and railways at as many natural defiles down the Malaya peninsula as possible; to prevent deep tank penetration as had occurred in France in 1940. I had noted many such natural defiles on my tours and I now indicated them on the map. Also I recommended detailed demolition plans to be prepared in advance and mine chambers built for all major bridges. Since they had already used tanks in China, it was expected that the Japanese would use them in Malaya, should they attack.

2   Any of the above positions selected to have some flank protection. Some flanks could be canalized for ambushes; others blocked by anti-personnel mines. Additional protection would be barbed wire, trip wires, booby-traps and such-like, all aimed at forcing casualties, delay and longer detour on the enemy and warning by the explosions. I specified some points where our flanks could be thrown forward to ambush the main enemy advance along the road or railway from three sides. In other positions the flanks could be refused.

3   A complete ring of permanent and field defences round Johore Bharu to keep the naval base out of shell range. A detailed reconnaissance had found several M.G. pillboxes in jungle about a mile or two apart near Kota Tinggi. This was the line now suggested for full development with flanks on the sea and Johore Straits.

The history of these pillboxes was unknown to the G.O.C., B.G.S., or myself. Years later from the Official History (p. 16), I learned that they were built in 1939 by General Dobbie when G.O.C. His successor (General Bond) must have stopped this work as the Official History records that only £23,000 out of £60,000 allotted by the War Office was actually spent.

4 For the north shore of Singapore Island covering the waters and opposite shores of the Johore Straits, I proposed field and permanent defences in depth consisting of mutually supporting wire trenches, switch lines, pillboxes and various underwater obstacles, mines, petrol fire traps, anchored but floating barbed wire, and methods of illuminating the water at night. Rivers and mouths of rivers up country could be provided with similar defences also. The idea was that the water surface and shore line should always be the main killing ground.

5 To organise Chinese and Malays into guerrilla bands to operate behind enemy spearheads. To use various aboriginal tribes as guides and to give warning of enemy movement through the jungle.[56]

There is but one flaw in Simson's argument. He mentioned to Percival that the labour requirements for his proposed fortifications could be acquired by 'civil labour directly, or under contract'. As Percival's biographer has claimed, Percival had tried to grapple with 'the stranglehold which the Treasury maintained, via the War Office, on every aspect of expenditure in Malaya Command'.[57] And the main problem was the poor rates of pay that the Colonial Office was prepared to pay—rates of pay that prohibited significant local labour recruitment.

Of all the service appreciations during the interwar period, there was but one measured and practical effort: that by General Dobbie. It was Dobbie who, in 1938, had made an accurate assessment of the Japanese options for the assault on Singapore via the Malay Peninsula; it was Dobbie who had tested his appreciation by exercises during the north-east monsoon

(October–March); and, critically, it was Dobbie who had identified southern Johore as the vital ground.

On the basis of this appreciation, Dobbie had rightly concluded that a line of fortifications across southern Johore would give his limited and largely untrained garrison a set-piece defence of that vital ground; that such a location for these fortifications would offer protection for much of Singapore's vital water supply; place Japanese artillery out of range of Singapore Island; and further, and most importantly, his line would severely restrict the Japanese from outflanking him from the sea by landings behind his line. Such a strategy would still enable him to defend northern air bases to some degree, by the posting of garrison forces at those localities. And this was a plan that would be relatively easy to enhance if future aircraft and more troops became available. General Percival had been Dobbie's GSO1 and, as such, had planned and written this appreciation. To Percival's credit the Japanese were destined to almost exactly conform to his appreciation.

Such a policy still allowed for a naval base servicing a fleet *if* it came, and still allowed for an RAF-dominated defence of Malaya and Singapore *if* it became reasonably resourced. Dobbie's plan was the only arrangement that covered the failure of both and the reality of events as they existed *at the time*. Professional appreciations are easy to make—having a plan that is based on one's existing resources and the quality of manpower is a much harder but more realistic exercise.

The pages of history bear ample testimony to the fact that after the senior commander, the most important soldier in a fortress is the chief engineer. And Percival had a newly posted, highly trained and motivated chief engineer on his staff: Ivan Simson. In his *The Chain of Disaster*, Kirby says that:

Percival refused point blank to consider these [Simson's] proposals. He cannot be held entirely to blame for his refusal at a time when both Brooke-Popham and the Governor held the view that the danger of war with Japan was remote or even had passed. He was clearly committed to a defence plan approved by the War Office; he had great difficulty in getting financial approval for any expenditure, the wholesale construction of defences would have needed War Office policy and financial approval, and labour was in short supply. He knew that the civil administration would offer every objection to the construction of defences, both because they would be bound to encroach on private property, and on the grounds that his proposals were a sign that the army did not intend to fight for northern Malaya, the old cry that had bedevilled the deliberations of the War Committee throughout 1940.[58]

It has been established earlier in this chapter that Brooke-Popham had no control over the administration or finance of the army or RAF in Singapore. Besides, as Simson has pointed out, much of the material for his lines of fortifications had already been delivered to Singapore by the War Office in 1938–39. Further, the War Office could hardly have complained about building a line of fortifications in southern Johore and at key defiles along the north–south communications axis, enhancing airfield defences and deploying garrison troops at airfields, since they had in fact posted Simson to Singapore with express orders to improve fortifications. Kirby's point concerning the civil administration's possible complaints is thin to say the least—Percival was not responsible to the civil administration for either his policy or its implementation.

But the one real problem remained a labour supply for the construction of the fortifications. There could only have been one plausible—if undesirable —solution: to employ the limited available labour and machinery, along with the over 80 000 troops themselves. What was needed was a dynamic, determined, inventive approach. Percival seems to have possessed none of these traits. His failure to rapidly employ Simson on a coordinated, large-scaled and urgent building of fortification construction flew in the face of his former GOC's (Dobbie) appreciation and their own joint plan.

———— ✵ ————

The term 'jungle training' is misleading prior to, during, and for that matter, for at least a year after the Malayan/Singapore Campaign. The term 'doctrine' is essentially the repository of military knowledge.[59] The truth is that there was no great jungle doctrine or repository of knowledge concerning jungle warfare in December 1941. Given that General Percival had only one second-grade and one third-grade staff officer in charge of his training at Malaya

HQ, his task was always going to be difficult—and not helped of course, by the fact that their junior credentials gave them no direct access to their GOC. But there were two answers to Percival's dilemma, and they existed in his own command: one British and one Australian. We will examine the Australian source in the next chapter.

There was only one real way of acquiring a jungle doctrine: train rigorously in it, apply the principles of war to its unique environment, and thereby begin the task of obtaining a repository of knowledge. Lieutenant-Colonel Ian Stewart had been promoted to command of the 2nd Argyll and Sutherland Highlanders in February 1940. Of slim physique and known as 'Busty' to his predominately Scottish troops, Stewart was a born leader. While other British battalions were performing standard drills and often confining themselves to the confined and repetitious garrison work of service on Singapore Island, Stewart was confronting the potential for war in a new environment.

The inactive troops on Singapore Island christened the Argylls 'the jungle beasts' and derided their commander as having had 'a touch of the sun', and when Malaya Command proclaimed that the Kranji River on Singapore Island could not be crossed by infantry, Stewart and the Argylls promptly 'staged a battalion exercise, and got the whole lot across the horrid muddy affair'.[60] If all this was poor enough, it was the attitude of a number of senior officers in Singapore that displayed the ignorance, lethargy and sheer ineptitude to the question of training for war in Malaya. When Stewart had the gall to challenge the notion that Singapore might not hold out until relieved by the Royal Navy, a brigadier told him 'to shut up and sit down, adding for good measure that everyone regarded his ideas as dangerous fanaticism'.[61] But the most damning indictment of Percival's attitude to training comes from the Chief Engineer, Ivan Simson. After having had a fruitful interview with Stewart concerning his thoughts on tactics, Simson then met with Percival and his BGS Brigadier Torrance: 'I mentioned this meeting to General Percival and Brigadier Torrance in late November, only to be told by Torrance, without any remark from the General, that Stewart's ideas on jungle training were those of a crank.'[62]

It is well worth summarising what the 'crank' had discovered. Stewart quickly ascertained that the jungle was not impassable and that six months provided adequate training time in it; that it was ideal for the attacker, since it offered 'a universal covered approach';[63] that most of the standard doctrine of defence applicable elsewhere—'good fields of fire, secure flanks, and above all, secure communications'—did not apply in the jungle if the commander's control was broken. And his words concerning this issue were prophetic:

> The jungle enormously increases the difficulties of control at all levels, for it prevents even visual means beyond the section. In Malaya, too, there was no wireless within battalions, while maps and compasses were lamentably short. Control, therefore, depended entirely on keeping open the single artery of the road. It became absolutely the dominant tactical feature, the only one to attack or defend. The battle was always for control, and therefore always for 'the road'.[64]

Given his appraisal, Stewart also identified the exact Japanese tactics that were to be used in Malaya:

> Control can be cut either by encircling attack on to the road, or by ripping it up by frontal attack straight down the road . . . itself. Such a narrow frontage allows of great concentration of artillery and other resources, and has the effect of scattering the enemy into the jungle on either side, where all means of control are lost.[65]

After this description of the Japanese tactics—which came to pass—Stewart then examined the best means of countering them. He saw the answer in 'Tiger patrols', which were three to five soldiers trained to venture out into the jungle and 'lie in wait on the enemy's road, there to attack his control and morale'.[66] It would later be found that while Stewart's 'Tiger patrols' were entirely feasible, such tactics were applicable to much larger sized forces, from platoons to battalions. And that notion implied ambush on varying scales. Ivan Simson: 'The Australians sprang a most effective ambush along these lines at Gemas . . . but it was apparently the only one during the campaign. This could well have been repeated in many defiles both north and south of Gemas.'[67]

However, in basic terms, Lieutenant-Colonel Ian Stewart and his Argylls were applying common sense to the question of jungle fighting—they engaged in cross-country movement through the jungle and living in it 'for days at a time'[68]; wide encircling movements were practised; control of varying sized forces was rehearsed; and even the ration establishment and the value of hot sweet tea 'five times a day'[69] was recognised and later applied with great success during the campaign.

According to Simson, Stewart had, during their meeting, also foreseen the potential for static lines of defence:

> There were only two places in all Malaya where static defences would have had no real flanks to go around without the enemy coming under fire from other defences:
>
> (a) General Dobbie's concept of the line in front of Johore Bahru and Kota Tinggi, and
>
> (b) The north shore of Singapore Island.
>
> In both cases the flanks rested on the sea, but neither defensive position was ever developed, though both were repeatedly suggested.[70]

In blunt terms, General Percival had a magnificent jungle training tool and the latest British Army engineering skills for a set-piece defence right under his very nose. He quite simply failed to identify them, much less employ them.

We have identified the extreme degree of difficulty that confronted General Percival during his seven-month period of command in Singapore and Malaya prior to the outbreak of hostilities. The varied quantity and quality of his resources—in terms of his soldiers and their equipment—have also been examined. It has also been noted that his staff was small and, in key areas such as training, of poor quality. But we have also highlighted the units in his command that did possess the necessary standards of unit training that would have allowed them to then train in the jungle and prepare themselves for demanding operations such as Matador and Krohcol.

However, the really damning indictment of Percival's command was his absolute failure to marshal his best troops for either defence or attack from prepared, static defensive positions at defiles along the Malay Peninsula and the critical defence line in Johore. Further, as identified, his Indian Army battalions were best suited to a static role along the Johore Line or on Singapore Island—and perhaps, at some defiles along the Malay Peninsula. The comprehensive jungle training of his best units—the 22nd and 27th Australian Brigades, the British battalions on Singapore Island, and the Leicesters and Surreys—would have given him both a strong offensive weapon and a dogged defensive one. But they were not allowed to deploy their newly acquired skills. Lieutenant-Colonel Ian Stewart was, after all, a 'crank', and Brigadier Ivan Simson was simply a redundant voice in the wilderness.

The truth is that none of the constructive criticisms mentioned in this work constitutes brilliant military thought; none is revolutionary in design or in suggested execution; all were staring Percival in the face; and all were, in a large measure, either a part of, or a consequence of, thinking that had been initiated by Dobbie and Percival himself years before. And, critically, they were suggested to him at the time. The truth is that to a large, and damning, degree the excessive complacency, the lack of thought and purpose so rampant amongst the civil administration had spread to the armed services in Malaya Command and amongst many of its formations. And, according to Lieutenant-Colonel Galleghan, 2/30th Battalion, there was 'an unrealistic atmosphere . . . before Pearl Harbour [sic]'. As late as August 1941, he was requested by the British at Changi to stop playing reveille because 'it would wake British officers' wives . . .'.[71]

6

INTERNAL DISSENSION

On 28 February 1941, the Deputy Chief of the Australian General Staff (DCGS), Major-General John Northcott, arrived at Bennett's HQ with the disconcerting news that the 8th Division was to remain scattered: Brigadier Taylor's 22nd Brigade Group was stationed in Malaya; the 23rd Brigade's three battalions were to be deployed at Darwin, Ambon and Timor; and the 27th Brigade's probable destination was Alice Springs. Northcott then told Bennett that he (Bennett) must 'either arrange with Malaya Command to take over an area command in Malaya, or return to Australia to take command of the larger part of the division'.[1]

Bennett's response was both immediate and understandable. In his diary he noted that: 'I must expect to stay here unless Japanese situation cleared up. I asked that a complete Div HQ be formed here or alternatively my DHQ be sent from Aust & that I be authorised to form a complete Base HQ. He said he would recommend it to Mil Bd [Military Board].'[2] At this meeting Bennett also asked Northcott for a casualty clearing station, more equipment, interpreters of Japanese, certain staff officers including Colonel Derham, his senior medical officer, a VD hospital and various reinforcements.[3] Three days later, in an effort to bolster his chances of securing his requests to Northcott, Bennett cabled Melbourne requesting further units including a second infantry brigade and a pioneer battalion. The next day, 4 March 1941, he sent yet another letter to Sturdee requesting again that his 8th Division be kept intact; he sent a letter to Brigadier Callaghan, his artillery commander, urging his support for these issues in Australia, and yet another to the secretary to the Minister for the Army, H. V. Howe, who had been one of his First World War staff officers. On 11 March, Bennett received news from General Sturdee that his force in Malaya would not be increased, but his staff there was enhanced later that month by the arrival of Major Wilfred Kent Hughes, his Deputy Adjutant and Quartermaster-General.

It was to take some three months before General Bennett was allotted an area command: in mid-April 1941, the then GOC Malaya Command, General Bond, told him that until his force consisted of at least two brigades, it would come under the command of General Murray-Lyon's 11th Indian Division; and, in early May, he was told that this role would probably be undertaken in the far north of Malaya—perhaps even as a part of a movement into Siam to counter possible Japanese landings there (Operation Matador). Bennett, suspecting that both he and his HQ would be left out of such an operation, then registered a strong protest with Bond, who decided to recommend to his successor, General Percival, that Bennett be given an Indian brigade and responsibility for the defence of Johore. When Percival arrived on 16 May Bennett's worst fears were realised. At the end of that month, Percival told him that his 22nd Brigade would be kept in reserve, and as such, liable to be deployed in any area but most likely at Kedah in the north. However, on 19 June, Bennett received the news that his 27th Brigade—at the time still training in Bathurst—was to be sent to him. It arrived in Malaya in mid-August. And that decision had only been made after the British Government had requested that the remaining two brigades of the 8th Division be sent to Malaya. That British request had been refused by the Australian War Cabinet and the arrival of the 27th Brigade was therefore a compromise. At the end of August 1941, Bennett assumed command of the defence of Johore with the 22nd and 27th Brigades under command.

The most pressing challenge facing General Bennett and Brigadier Taylor on their arrival in Malaya was the immediate training of the 22nd Brigade and, later, the 27th. Although the 22nd Brigade's 2/18th, 2/19th and 2/20th

Battalions had completed their unit training in open country in Australia and had also undertaken a number of brigade exercises there, the terrain and vegetation found in Malaya presented new challenges. As Lieutenant-Colonel Ian Stewart and his Argyll and Sutherland Highlanders had discovered, the best method of acquiring these skills was to confront the new environment, assess its unique characteristics and then undertake rigorous training to operate within them.

Both Bennett and Taylor—to the credit of both—quickly realised that Malaya's environment offered restricted fields of fire; that defence in depth of roads and rubber plantation dirt tracks was all-important; that all-round protection of a perimeter was vital; and that in the closed environment of jungle and rubber the section and platoon commander's ability to exercise command would be essential to success. The subsequent training of Taylor's 22nd Brigade and, later, the 27th Brigade was based on these considerations. Lieutenant Jim Howard, 2/19th Battalion carriers, recalled:

> When you get down to it, your section corporal is the last person in authority that sees the enemy. He controls ten men who directly have a responsibility for disposing of the enemy, rendering him neutral, shooting, killing or wounding him. And good section commanders are vital. If he [the platoon commander] has briefed his section commanders adequately, they can possibly carry on.[4]

The unit diaries of the 22nd Brigade provide ample testimony to the disciplined and varied syllabus that was applied to the Australians' effort to overcome these challenges. Apart from standard weapons training, fire and movement, and extensive practice in reconnaissance and fighting patrols, the emphasis was upon control of a section, platoon and company in rubber plantations, villages and at defiles with carrier support; navigation by compass reading; river crossings and section and platoon movement by night and day and over extensive distances; village fighting in both attack and defence; and exercises over a number of days to acclimatise to the environment.[5] And as Lieutenant-Colonel Stewart and his Argylls had also discovered, the Australians' enthusiasm for the task met with a studied indifference from both the British military and the civilian population.

Lionel Wigmore, in *The Japanese Thrust*, has quoted one 22nd Brigade officer:

... its early preparations for jungle training received little encour-
agement from Malaya Command, 'and they assured us that if we
were not drowned in the seasonal rains, we would be decimated by
malaria'. Training manuals were 'pompous, heavy, often platitudinous
and other wise equivocal', and accordingly, 'everyone had completely
different tactical conceptions or else none at all'.[6]

And the Australians' attitude to labour in the tropics was also un-
orthodox:

On one occasion a ship arrived at Port Swettenham with 800 tons
of frozen meat and many motor vehicles for the AIF. The Australian
officers in charge, keen to get the unloading done swiftly, worked the
native wharf labourers hard for six hours until they were wilting,
whereupon Australian troops who had been sent for took over, despite
the fact that it was not considered desirable politically or medically to
employ white men as labourers in Malaya. These moved cargo at three
times the rate achieved by the poorly-nourished coolies, and emptied
the ship in record time.[7]

By December 1941, the Australian 22nd and 27th Brigades had had
the opportunity to acclimatise to service in the tropics and had, to a large
measure, examined the problems of training to fight in a Malayan war.

Very early after his arrival in Malaya, Major-General Gordon Bennett
had realised that movement and communication were going to constitute
major challenges to any force operating on the Malay Peninsula. His diary
for the period confirms this.

Lionel Wigmore:

The 22nd Brigade took part in March in a 'Far Eastern Defence
Exercise', staged by Malaya Command, and aimed at testing all stages
of transition from peace to war by the civil authorities and Services.

On the theoretical assumption that an enemy had landed at Mersing, where the 12th Indian Brigade was stationed, the Australian brigade was to move from the Seremban–Port Dickson area via Kluang to help repel the invaders. This necessitated a movement by road and rail over a distance of about 150 miles.[8]

Major-General Bennett and Brigadier Taylor had never got on. Bennett's biographer has left us none the wiser as to the cause of this antipathy, other than to assert that 'Bennett would never have selected Taylor as one of his brigadiers'.[9] The trouble began almost immediately. On Sunday 9 March 1941, Bennett noted in his diary:

Decided to sleep at H.Q. tonight. Rang Taylor re details of exercise. He wants 3 hours to move his men. Told him it was too long. At 10 pm told Taylor to stand by train & M.T. [motor transport] ready to move at moments [sic] notice. Night disturbed with constant stream of messages—slept at office. Everything ready for move tomorrow.[10]

Bennett wrote one diary entry for Monday 10 and Tuesday 11 March:

Exercise going as per plan. Messages rather slow in coming through from Malaya Cmd. At 9.30, men still waiting for order to move. At about 11 order to move arrived. MT moved 1st party at 1230 & last . . . at 3.30. Train parties left 12.45, 1315, 1345 . . .

Trains arrd [sic arrived] well on time 1730, 1750, 1830 M.T. started arriving 2000 hrs with bulk at 0700 & 20 Bn group 0400. The last group were, in my opinion, started too late. Had words with Taylor. He resents receiving orders & does his best to thwart me. He states that he was well equipped mentally for his post, that I knew nothing & that the last war was useless experience. The humour is that he has been a Bde Cmd for less than 2 years.

He was to move 1 bn etc [sic] by M.T. at 0700 . . . He wants to start them at 0500 . . .[11]

Bennett's diary then claims that Taylor was placing his transport person-nel under unnecessary strain by moving them too early. He then alludes to the reason for the complete shambles that followed:

He upset the show by a wrong map reading and Situation report. This prevented his move. He wanted to walk out of the exercise with his Bde to 'do a bit of housekeeping' I ordered his move at 1100. I went to Kulung [sic] & found his unit not yet started at 1200 hrs. Told him all about it.[12]

Taylor maintained that 8th Division HQ had not sent the code for deciphering the map references. He further stated that:

Div Comdr arrived in a towering rage, wanted to know why column was not on move . . . ordered me to move the column whether it was ready or not. I tried to point out that it was far better for the advanced guard to move complete with its commander and not for me to send it off into the blue. He would not listen and ordered me again to move it. I refused on the ground that such an action on my part would only cause chaos. I was then told that either I or he would go back to Aust over this and it would not be him . . .

I was perfectly polite all the time and did not even raise my voice. I wonder what he will be like in action.[13]

Lodge in *The Fall of General Gordon Bennett* has stated that 'Taylor seemed largely unperturbed by the affair, which reflected his unflappable character'.[14] One wonders whether the term 'unflappable' might be used to describe a brigadier who tells his divisional commander that he is 'well equipped mentally for his post, that I [Bennett] knew nothing & that the last war was useless experience'. True, this is Bennett's recollection of the confron-tation. But worse was to follow. It seems that both soldiers saw the need for some form of reconciliation. After the altercation both men approached Lieutenant-Colonel Thyer to mediate. The two then exchanged civil letters, and on 14 March, Taylor drove down to see Bennett at Kuala Lumpur. Lodge cites Taylor as referring to their meeting after dinner as a 'ding dong go'.[15]

In his diary, Bennett stated that:

Recd letter from Taylor. He is to dine here tonight.

    Taylor still endeavouring to control show—far from respectful—
inclined to bluff. After long discussion he agreed to 'play'... Decided
to restrict his activities to cmd 22 Inf Bde only. Kent Hughes joined in
the discussion helpfully.[16]

Lodge neglects to mention Bennett's last sentence above: 'Kent Hughes
joined in the discussion helpfully.' In a letter to Gavin Long on 18 June 1953,
Kent Hughes—not cited by Lodge—gives us an insight into the 'unflappable'
Brigadier Taylor and his behaviour at the post-dinner meeting on 14 March
1941:

This Far Eastern defence exercise was the cause of the clash between
the G.O.C. and the Brigadier . . . I was present at the subsequent interview between the G.O.C. and the Brigadier in what I remember as one
of the nastiest evenings I have ever spent. The Brigadier flatly refused
to obey the G.O.Cs. orders on the grounds that he was in charge of
the Brigade group and the A.I.F. Headquarters had no business to be
in Malaya in his opinion. The difference was not patched up. Colonel
Rourke, a friend of Brigadier Taylor's and an enemy of the G.O.C.,
splashed some paint over the scarred surface . . . The quarrel did not
'emphasise a fundamental difference in the character and outlook of
the two men' [Lionel Wigmore's interpretation in a draft of the Official
History]. The G.O.C. was too kind-hearted. If any Brigadier had
refused to obey my orders he would have been home by the next boat,
S.N.L.R. [Services No Longer Required]. Brigadier Taylor remained a
disturbing element in the A.I.F. Malaya both before, during and after
active operations.[17]

Taylor and Bennett have recorded their interpretation(s) of that meeting.
It would seem extraordinary that Lodge has not cited a third person's
account—from one who was present.

Brigadier Taylor certainly disobeyed direct orders from his superior during the exercise. To not adhere to an established timetable for movement of such a significant sized force during an exercise constituted poor command; to then speak to one's superior officer in the manner in which he did would seem gross insubordination; to then seek to heal the wounds as both men did, and to then behave in the manner in which Kent Hughes describes that meeting, would seem to be far, far from 'unflappable' behaviour from Brigadier Taylor. Lodge's failure to even mention, let alone take account of Kent Hughes's evidence, seriously distorts his treatment of the conflict between Taylor and his superior officer.

On 20 March 1941, 'Bennett was informed by Army Headquarters that his whole divisional headquarters was to join him, and also a field park company, stores depot, reserve motor transport company and convalescent depot.'[18] On 6 April, the senior officers of the 8th Division Headquarters Staff arrived from Australia. Colonels Rourke and Broadbent were among them.

Much has been made of Bennett's supposed negative relationship with both the Staff Corps officers on his 8th Division Staff and his rapport with the English officers both on Malaya Command and in British combat formations. However, it would appear far more than a coincidence that the real friction between some members of the 8th Division HQ Staff and Bennett occurred with the arrival of Rourke and Broadbent. According to Bennett's diary—and not cited by Lodge—the general was well satisfied with his staff prior to the arrival of Rourke and Broadbent. On Friday 7 March 1941, Bennett stated that: 'Staffs learning much, gaining practical experience. Still behind what I call War Tempo.'[19] In other words, although it is hardly surprising that Bennett would see his staff as being 'behind war tempo', he was quite content with their progress. On Saturday 5 April 1941, Bennett wrote that: 'Everything cleaned up at office. In retrospection, have had a satisfactory time since arrival—good team work . . . Everyone kept me in the picture. This is the result of constant pressure on my part. I hope this continues in future.'[20] Nor, it seems, was Bennett prejudiced against his new Staff Corps arrivals enjoying a brief sojourn in Singapore. On 4 April 1941, Bennett's diary records that: 'Broadbent rang from Singapore & asked if his party might stay on another 24 hours—excuse—to complete matters given them by Northcott. I agreed—except for Head. Of course, it seemed unnecessary for Rourke & Derham to stay too. Still, it is natural to want to look around.'[21]

The 'trouble' at 8th Division HQ began with the arrival of Rourke, Broadbent and, to a lesser degree, Colonel Derham (the senior medical officer). While enjoying their extra day's stay in Singapore, Rourke and Broadbent were visited by Taylor, who stayed overnight. When they arrived at 8th Division HQ, Bennett discussed the Taylor situation. On Tuesday 8 April, Bennett wrote that:

> Discussed my problem with Rourke & Broadbent. Both agree that I have been over tolerant & see no alternative to suspending Taylor. Have decided to do so on grounds that he is temperamentally unfitted for cmd. I have given Rourke permission to see Taylor to let him know what is coming. If Taylor adopts a repentant attitude, then I may reconsider my attitude. Rourke leaves today & will return this evening.[22]

Bennett's term, 'permission to see Taylor', would seem to indicate that the initiative for this meeting was Rourke's. Colonel Rourke had lunch with Brigadier Taylor at Seremban. Taylor then decided to visit Bennett at Kuala Lumpur that evening. Rourke's 'initiative' for his meeting with Taylor may well have been driven by their time in Singapore before Rourke and Broadbent arrived at 8th Division HQ. Bennett's diary:

> Taylor has just rung to ask if I would see him. He will be here 5.30 or 6.—at residence . . .
> Saw Taylor—Broadbent present. Taylor very humble & assured full support etc. Regretted his recent action. Stood firm & said I must be quite satisfied this time & could take no more risks. He gave every assurance. Told him I would hold over my letter to Melb till after Easter and then see him to confirm his attitude. I still doubt if he can alter a temperament that it has taken many years to develop. Rourke later came home & gave his opinion that Taylor wd [sic] be straight in future.[23]

After the meeting, Taylor wrote that:

> The Gen. appears to believe all rumours and looks for ulterior
> motives in everything I do and say. [I] gave way to the extent of
> saying that I had been foolish and would like to remain in comd
> of Bde. He finally said he would hold letter up for [a] week. Col.
> Broadbent was present at interview. I have two very good friends in
> Rourke and Broadbent.[24]

Two points should be made regarding the Bennett–Taylor incident
during and shortly after the 'Far Eastern Defence Exercise'. The first is that
both soldiers sought a resolution to the conflict for the sake of their careers.
Had Bennett sent Taylor home, the latter would have been in a position
to severely undermine Bennett's already precarious position within the
Australian Army—Bennett already had enough enemies in Australia. But
at 50 years of age, had Taylor been sent home, he would almost certainly
have missed another AIF brigade command. Neither man would have gained
a lot had Bennett's letter been sent. In the end a cease-fire was called. On
Tuesday 15 April 1941, the two had tea together. Bennett later wrote in his
diary that: 'Told Taylor had decided to allow the trouble to die. He asked
that I forget everything & start a fresh. I agreed.'[25] It was an uneasy truce
that would survive until the last days before the capitulation on Singapore
Island. Secondly, however, it also appears that Rourke and Broadbent used
the incident to destabilise both Bennett and his 8th Division HQ.

Lodge has selectively quoted Sturdee's assessment of Bennett prior to
Bennett's command of the 8th Division; he has not cited Kent Hughes's
direct and repeated evidence as to Rourke and Broadbent's disloyalty upon
hearing of Bennett's posting to the division; he has not cited Kent Hughes's
first-hand evidence as to Taylor's behaviour after the Far Eastern Defence
Exercise; he has neglected to quote Bennett's contentment with his staff
before the arrival of Rourke and Broadbent; and, in the absence of the just
mentioned evidence, he then uses a number of Bennett's diary entries to
attempt to portray a general who is solely responsible for any disharmony
in 8th Division HQ. Furthermore, Lodge implies that Bennett was obsessed
by the notion that Rourke and Broadbent were being disloyal to him, or

conducting a 'whispering campaign'. In the context of the above, the reader is left to judge Bennett's diary entries:

Saturday 12 April 1941:
Find Rourke, Derham & Broadbent inclined to discuss among themselves the Taylor incident. Apparently based on investigations by Derham during recent trip. Not sure that Derham's investigation & opinion will be sound—inclined to be swayed. So far he has not discussed the episode in detail. Broadbent came to me today & suggested that unless complete confidence betw [*sic* 'between'] T & me is restored then the healing of the breach is not desirable. He considered the cause a clash of personalities. I resent this slightly. Surely in an army such a clash must show the junior to be wrong. A junior must be subservient to a senior & shd [*sic* 'should'] not clash with him. I don't like the whisperings that are going on behind my back. It is un military.

Thursday 29 May 1941:
Secret & confidential letter from Percival was addressed to me personally but was opened by Rourke who must have seen the address which was written in large lettering & enclosed in 2 envelopes. Was annoyed that he shd [*sic* 'should'] open it.

Friday 30 May:
Strange how Rourke and I always seem at cross purposes. I find that he is all the time watching my words to see if I am agst [*sic* 'against'] his kind & he comes straight back with an unhesitating contradiction. He still has the Staff Corps complex agst [*sic* 'against'] mere civilian soldiers—inferior beings, ignorant etc etc. It is really a sign of inferiority complex [on Rourke's part]. I feel sure he will get over it—especially when fighting starts, if, indeed, he is here then. I feel that he is all the time working with his friends in high places for another appointment. He is against Kappe & Beale the only others on Div HQ. who are permanent officers . . .

They have their failings—like the rest of us myself & Rourke included.

Saturday 31 May 1941:

My mind has been running on Rourke, who impresses me as an arch intriguer, spending more time worrying about his position & prestige than on his work. He resents me dealing with any member of G Staff. Yet he omits to keep me in touch with things himself. He has told at least one of his staff that I am unapproachable & must not be worried with any matters . . . He seems to have his mind engrossed with defending the regular soldiers against the mere civilians. That is a subject that never intervenes with me. I fear that he realises his own incapacity in certain directions & allows this obsession to obtrude itself.[26]

However, a change was coming. On Friday 4 July, Bennett noted in his diary:

Rourke & Broadbent out for dinner. That left Kappe Gordon & self. How different the atmosphere! R is evidently ill either physically or mentally or both. He is unnecessarily harsh with his own G. officers. He snaps at Walker re the Mess. He whispers to Broadbent & Derham & succeeded in making them disgruntled though Broadbent is too loyal & sensible to be party to intrigue. If Derham was not so ill, he too wd [sic 'would'] refuse to be drawn in. I fear that Rourke is a very unhappy man.[27]

And three days later, when Rourke was temporarily in hospital, Bennett noted that: 'Spirit at HQ . . . cheery once again. All on their toes & keen. What a difference one man makes!'[28] On Wednesday 16 July, Bennett wrote:

During dinner recd wire—appointing Rourke to AIF [as Commander Royal Artillery 7th Division] with para 'propose THYER as G1.' Alls [sic] well that ends well. Told Kappe he was to be cmd Sigs. Sent for Thyer & we all celebrated. It seems to me most likely that this has been engineered [Bennett had 'for some time' after this sentence but had crossed it out].[29]

The next day Bennett stated that:

Rourke doesn't seem too happy at the idea of going to M East. He told me that he wd [sic 'would'] just as soon have gone to Aust: that he was beyond the age when he wanted to be in the fighting zone. He also told Kappe that his health was far from good.[30]

Colonel Henry Rourke left for the Middle East on 21 July 1941. From the time of his arrival in Malaya he had acted upon his pledge made at the 8th Division HQ in Sydney the day before Bennett arrived to take command. Rourke was subsequently appointed as BGS (Brigadier General Staff) to General Rowell at Ist Corps during 1942 and saw out the war as a liaison officer to the Joint Planning Committee at the War Office London from 1942 to 1945. For a considerable portion of the war he attained his ambition—that he was 'beyond the age when he wanted to be in the fighting zone'.

Rourke's departure, however, did not assure harmony. Broadbent, Derham and Bennett clashed during late August over the AIF's transfer to the area of responsibility for the defence of Johore and Malacca. The subject was the incidence of malaria. On 22 August 1941, Bennett wrote that:

Broadbent discussed changeover and made an appeal about some alteration & said 'I am afraid there will be a great deal of Malaria & I want you to realise the position so that if there should be an investigation from Australia as to the cause of so many cases the blame will be attached to you' [sic].
I hit the roof & made mention of people 'covering themselves as they were afraid to take responsibilities.' He said that A.D.M.S. and Malaya Command were against it. I asked who on Mal. Comd. And he answered 'Hill'. Now Hill is Fortress Q—who has tried to block our taking over the area at all. My comments on A.D.M.S. [Derham] were terse. I saw I'd have to make a change if he could not become more military and less namby pamby. Then Broadbent asked if Taylor had been one to protest. I said No, and that Taylor did

not seem to mind sending his men out on 5 day treks into unprotected areas.[31]

By 'coincidence' Broadbent told Bennett the next day that Brigadier
Taylor had requested a meeting to discuss the malaria question. Bennett—
understandably—wrote:

Broadbent said Taylor had rung & wanted to see me personally on
the malaria question—arranged Monday. I suspect the thing is due
to Broadbent's wrangling. If so, there is a lack of loyalty that cannot
go on.[32]

The subject of malaria in the 8th Division in Malaya has been covered
by the Australian Official Medical Historian, Allan Walker:

During the first phase of the Malayan experience the incidence of
malaria was low in the A.I.F. Control was good in the settled areas, and
the influence of the Institute of Medical Research at Kuala Lumpur was
most valuable. When jungle training began the incidence of malaria
increased, particularly where troop movements were not correlated
to anti-malarial measures. When the Australian troops took up battle
stations, malaria became common.[33]

Broadbent's outburst to Bennett lacked substance and was delivered in
an insubordinate fashion. The War Diary of the 8th Division Administrative
HQ for the period August–October 1941 clearly shows that either Broadbent was a very poor judge of the issue of malaria, or that, perhaps, he had
other motives. The entry for 2 September cites the wastage report for malaria
as 'good'—and for mumps 'on the decrease' and VD 'fair'; on 15 October
the diary stated that there had been only 35 cases of malaria in six weeks,
that VD was down to a very low level, and that hospital admissions were
as low as they had been since the arrival of the 8th Division in Malaya. On
30 October, the diary stated that the malaria position was 'quite satisfactory'
as the total cases of the disease since the 8th Division's arrival in Malaya—
some eight-and-a-half months—was 297 compared with 76 new cases in

Johore in two months.[34] These figures must reflect favourably on Derham's work in the clinical sense, but very poorly on his and Broadbent's behaviour—and motives—in their treatment of Bennett regarding the subject of malaria.

In early September 1941, Bennett was confronted by enquiries from Australia. Bennett's diary 6 September:

> Recd cables Aust—complaining about food for tps replied accordingly
>   Ano [*sic* another] cable—suggesting concessions for travel on leave etc
>   Ano cable Military Bd concerned lack amenities etc very annoyed—cabling reply—looks as if Stantke is trying to pillory me.[35]

Bennett had long suspected that the Adjutant-General at Army HQ in Melbourne, Major-General Victor Stantke, had been doing all in his power to frustrate his command of the 8th Division. Lodge has noted that Bennett's assessment 'was probably correct'.[36] Further, we have noted that during the interwar period, not just Bennett, but even Blamey had also suspected that Militia officers were being sidelined for key promotions in the army. The truth is that, rightly or wrongly, the Staff Corps exercised considerable control over the Australian Army through its power on the Military Board. Major-General Stantke's hindrance to Bennett's command of his division continued through 1941: when in March he communicated directly with the Minister for the Army, Percy Spender, he was told to refrain from doing so by the board; his request for a VD hospital was denied; his request that he be allowed to grant promotions within his division was also denied, which resulted in some of his requests being allowed and others turned down. In short, Bennett was being thwarted by fellow officers both in Australia and in 8th Division HQ.

It is questionable as to what real damage Rourke, Broadbent and, to a lesser degree, Derham had imposed upon the working efficiency and morale of 8th Division HQ. Lodge states that '. . . there could be found on the staff of Headquarters 8th Division several key officers who shared Taylor's opinions of Bennett, some of whom, like Taylor, were also militia officers'.[37] During the period January–December 1941, 'several' were, in fact, Rourke, Broadbent and Derham. There may have been others who privately held varying views, but there seems no evidence of conflict or disloyalty—or a failure to work together. Further, there were certainly other officers who were quite content working under Bennett: for example, Kent Hughes, Stahl and Maxwell. The truth is, as David Horner has pointed out in his examination of the Staff Corps vs Militia argument, that there were widespread instances of various Militia officers not getting along, just as there were examples of Staff Officers doing likewise. The plain and simple truth is that Rourke, Broadbent and Derham were negative influences on Bennett's staff; that Taylor and Bennett had never got on, and their poor relationship in Malaya was primarily the result of Taylor's insubordination.

In a further attempt to discredit Bennett, Lodge states twice within a page-and-a-half in his book that: 'Bennett apparently was oblivious of the irony in arguing that he was not against regular officers while having only three on his staff.'[38] And 'It must be remembered, however, that 8th Division Headquarters nevertheless had the fewest staff college graduates of any of the AIF divisions, including the 9th which was still then in the process of being formed.'[39] Yet, a mere 30 pages before these comments, Lodge acknowledges that the original GOC General Sturdee—a Staff Corps officer—chose the staff of the 8th Division.[40] Furthermore, when Rourke left his post, Bennett proceeded to appoint another Staff Corps officer to replace him. The Official Historian has also made it very clear that Sturdee chose the 8th Division Staff.[41]

The Second World War had not begun well for Major-General Gordon Bennett. Possessed and driven by enormous ambition, he had seen himself overlooked to command the 6th, then 7th and, initially, the 8th Divisions. And if this perceived injustice was not galling enough, he had been forced to witness the promotion of his arch enemy Blamey to raise and then command the 2nd AIF and its 6th Division, to be followed by a further promotion to the command of a corps. A frustrated but determined Bennett was lagging behind.

By the outbreak of hostilities in early December 1941, during his roughly eleven-month period as GOC 8th Division in Malaya, Bennett had experienced further testing times. Denied the concentration of his three brigades in Malaya, he had experienced the wrath and resentment of Staff Corps officers both within his midst in Malaya and in positions of power on the Military Board. He even had to gain permission of the board to be able to communicate directly with the Minister of the Army.

It is an inescapable conclusion that the sheer hatred and devious behaviour of the likes of Rourke, Broadbent, Derham and Taylor in Malaya, and Stantke at home, were, in simple terms, a fundamental breach of loyalty to both Bennett, and the army and nation they all purported to serve. There was a war on—and another on the horizon.

Gordon Bennett has received criticism for his attitude towards, and dealings with, the British in Malaya and Singapore during his tenure of command before the Pacific War began. Such criticism deserves close scrutiny.

At the outbreak of the Second World War, and when, as GOC 6th Division AIF, General Blamey realised that his force was to go overseas, he 'knew that occasions would arise when an Australian force commander would have different views from those of the British theatre commander under whom he was serving'.[42]

The experience of serving under the British in the First World War had convinced Blamey 'of the necessity of a very firm statement'.[43] That he took the matter seriously is demonstrated by the fact that he consulted Generals White and Squires, and Sir Owen Dixon, a Justice of the High Court. Meanwhile, Charles Bean, the Official Historian for the First World War, had written to Prime Minister Menzies 'about the problems of cooperating with the British'.[44] General Blamey's charter became the basis for a similar document for all independent Australian commanders serving overseas. David Horner: 'It was a declaration that Australia was an independent nation, whose forces remained under its command even when operating under a British commander.'[45] Blamey's charter was formally recognised by the British Government on 26 March 1940 and the Minister for the Army issued it to him on 19 April.

Blamey's desire for a charter was shrewd and was put to the test on a number of occasions. His Chief Staff Officer 1, Colonel Syd Rowell, would later write:

... the national commander is given a charter by his government which is agreed to by the senior partner. While this charter usually places the national commander's force at the disposal of the superior commander, it also imposes on the former certain very specific obligations. It gives him the right and indeed the duty of direct communication with his government ... Most importantly, the charter provides that the main force may be broken up into smaller formations only with the express concurrence of the national commander.[46]

Therefore, it is important to realise that Major-General Gordon Bennett's charter was nothing new, and that problems with its implementation were not peculiar to himself or the challenges he faced in Malaya and Singapore. Bennett's charter stated that:

(a)   The Force will retain its identity as an Australian force;

(b)   No part of the Force is to be employed apart from the whole without your consent;

(c)   Should the G.O.C. Malaya in certain circumstances of emergency insist on an extensive operational dispersal of your Force you will, after registering such protest as you deem essential, comply with the order of the G.O.C. Malaya and immediately report the full circumstances to Army Headquarters, Melbourne.[47]

Given the range of Bennett's First World War service, both the need for, and the content of such a charter, would have been appreciated by him no less than people such as Blamey and Bean. We now examine Bennett's implementation of his charter.

The first problem concerned Malaya Command's desire to involve the AIF in breaking a plantation workers' strike for improved pay. Bennett's diary, 14 May 1941: 'Attended King's House at request Governor who had asked that AIF supply tps to quell strike. I refused & explained Australia's policy. He asked me to attend daily conference at 9 am.'[48] The next day, during a clash with troops, four workers were killed. Bennett recorded that he 'Recd letter Malay Comd saying that AIF was legally bound to prevent civil strife

& cd [could] not refuse duty and asking for my views . . .'.[49] Malaya Command also pointed out that the Governor would examine his 'views'. But Bennett was not about to be intimidated: 'Have wired Aust. and also replied.' One week later Malaya Command received notification from Australia that the AIF was not to be used for strike breaking. According to Lionel Wigmore, 'Bennett learned subsequently that India had also objected.'[50] It is of interest to note that the British Government had ratified Blamey's charter in March 1940. It would therefore seem that, in the interests of both harmony and efficiency, the British might have seen fit to enlighten all subsequent commanders of the Australian charter.

The second problem Bennett faced was the discipline of the AIF in Malaya. On 4 April 1941, the AIF opened its detention barracks. Bennett: 'Port Swettenham detention barracks commenced. Was told by staff to expect 100 prisoners. I divided this by 2 as my estimate. Actually there are only 7. It is said that the name "sweetin 'em" has frightened away a lot of crime.'[51] The truth is that the AIF's behaviour from the 22nd Brigade Group's arrival in January 1941 until the outbreak of hostilities on 8 December 'caused little trouble for the [Australian] military police'.[52] It would only be during the final stages of the campaign—especially after the troops had withdrawn across the causeway onto Singapore Island—that the trouble and controversy began.

Glenn Wahlert, in *The Other Enemy? Australian Soldiers and the Military Police*, has argued that:

If the AIF had any problems with the military police in Malaya, it was with the British Red Caps rather than with the Australian Provosts. The Australians viewed the British MPs as inflexible, intolerant, and unnecessarily harsh. As one Australian saw it, they were 'pure bastards: they gave their own no quarter.' As had occurred in the Middle East with the 6th Division, in at least one incident in Malaya the actions of the Red Caps so incensed the Australians that a near riot occurred: 'One of our fellows [from the 4th Anti Tank Regiment] had been beaten up by the Red Caps in Singapore, not far from the Union Jack Club . . . He was probably drunk and a bit cheeky to the Brits, but he didn't deserve the hiding he got . . . When we got the news we all grabbed our rifles and headed out to shoot the bastards [the Red Caps]. Just as well they had been warned off.[53]

Wahlert has pointed out that the incidence of arrests, offences and courts martial within the 8th Division in the period February 1940 until January 1942 was far less than for the AIF in the Middle East—even allowing for 'differing activity rates and methods of recording offences . . .'[54] Both Bennett's diary and the diary of the 8th Division Administrative HQ reveal two critical points concerning discipline in the AIF in Malaya: the heavy-handed attitude of the Red Caps and the behaviour of a number of British troops.

Bennett's diary, 9 August 1941: 'Heard of several cases where British MP are trying to irritate our men & apparently deliberately.'[55] The 8th Division Diary for the same day was more illuminating: 'Received information that British Military Police (Red Caps) deliberately irritated our men, result—a fracas in Kuala Lumpur. Similar irritation tactics in Singapore.'[56] It did not take Bennett long to react to the incident. The Division Diary stated later on the same day: 'Arrangements were made with the G.O.C. 3rd Indian Corps and the G.O.C. Malaya Command, that Military Police [British] should not in future touch members of the A.I.F.'[57] The 'fracas' apparently involved soldiers of the 8th Division Signals, under the command of Lieutenant-Colonel Kappe. Bennett's diary the next day (10 August): 'Kappe called—apologetic re fracus in KL in which his men went out in a mob to deal with red caps. He fined them £3 & 14 days CB.'[58] However, it seems that the problem continued to a degree through late August and October 1941. The 8th Division Diary on 22 August:

G.O.C. called on Major-General Keith Simmons formally re hand over to the A.I.F. He showed the G.O.C. a letter from the Union Jack Club, complaining of misconduct of Australian soldiers 15th, 16th and 17th August. Investigation showed that the report was grossly exaggerated, and proved a prejudice against Australians by the secretary of the Club.[59]

It would seem that the Union Jack Club was an ongoing concern, and by mid-October, soldiers of the Argyll and Sutherland Highlanders—most of whom were tough troops indeed—became embroiled in conflict with members of the AIF, and significantly, a second party. The 8th Division Diary:

> The relationship between British and Australian troops is giving concern. A number of men of the Argyll and Sutherland Highlanders severely handled four of our men at the Union Jack Club. This threatens to be followed by several organised displays. The R.A.A.F reports similar experience with the Argylls.[60]

On 17 November 1941, General Percival complained to Bennett about the behaviour of the AIF at the Union Jack Club. Bennett told him that 'we were blamed for all the trouble & that Secry [secretary] was biased against A.I.F'.[61]

Bennett had every right to demand sole authority over the behaviour and discipline of the AIF troops under his command. Given his First World War experience of the 1st AIF—a volunteer, citizen army—and his observations of British soldiers during that war, he understood the differences between the two. On 22 October 1941, Bennett attended a conference concerning the shortage of enlistments and difficulties in training of the Malayan Volunteers. He drew a broad comparison between the Volunteers and the AIF: 'The British regular cannot realise that Volunteers must be catered for on a different syllabus from regulars. Percival realises this but others not.'[62] He also pointed out that AIF volunteers were not raised in the same mould as the British regular. Glenn Wahlert has surely left us with a thoughtful explanation of Bennett's reasoning: 'To the Australians, the British MPs were simply too heavy-handed and officious, and their formality and bearing often brought out the worst in the Australians.'[63] And added to this 'cultural' problem came the age-old conflict between different forces, such as the Argylls and the AIF, either at or near the Union Jack Club.

While apportioning blame for such clashes is futile, the value in each army defusing the situation by imposing its own discipline measures is not judgemental but simply pragmatic. Percival's biographer has criticised Bennett for 'refusing even to have their [the AIF's] off-duty behaviour regulated by the British Military police'.[64] The reader can imagine the reaction of a number of Britain's allies—such as the Americans—if the British had sought the right to 'regulate' the behaviour of their troops on leave. It would seem that Malaya Command, and a number of British postwar historians, have confused the difference between the terms 'colony' and 'dominion'.

Another matter concerned the use of motor transport for recreational purposes. When General Percival attempted to apply British regulations to the Australians' use of motor transport—strictly limited regulations where the cost was to be borne by the troops—Bennett explained to him that it was Australian Government policy that morale and health, and therefore vehicles for leave, were to be provided at government cost. Bennett's diary, 11 November 1941: 'Wrote fully to Min For Army on use of M.T. for recreational purposes & the controversy with the War Office.'[65] Once again, Bennett was acting within the bounds of his charter, in the best interests of his troops, and communicating his decisions to the Australian Government.

Malaya Command's attempts to interfere in the internal administration of an independent force even extended to the Australian ration scale. When Percival wanted the Australian meat ration reduced to a comparable level with that of the British, Bennett once again informed him that it was an 8th Division AIF and Australian Government matter.

Another sore point with the British seemed to be Bennett's relationship with the press. Lionel Wigmore in *The Japanese Thrust*:

The arrival and activities of Australian troops in Malaya, with their unusual characteristics, naturally had made a newsy subject, useful for emphasising Imperial solidarity and the accumulating strength of British defences in the area. Thus the force was given extreme publicity, and Australian news was increasingly featured in the Malayan newspapers with the aid of a service established by the Australian Department of Information. At one stage, however, steps were taken by the Services authorities to soft-peddle news about the A.I.F. on the ground that the prominence given to the Australians tended to create ill-feeling on the part of other troops who had gained less recognition.[66]

Wigmore acknowledged that while a 'soft-pedalling' of such publicity pleased the British, it aggrieved both Bennett and 'newspaper correspondents who gathered in increasing numbers in Malaya as the Far Eastern crisis approached its climax'.[67]

The point is that, according to Wigmore, there was a need for an expert press to foster a 'favourable influence upon the American public', increase awareness of events in the Far Eastern area, but most importantly, to instil in the civil population of Malaya and Singapore a sense of realism and vigilance. In short, the Services Press Bureau was frequently in conflict with the press because it lacked officers who had experience in dealing with it.

Gordon Bennett most certainly had a number of problems to deal with as a commander of an AIF division under overall British command. But there is little evidence that such matters were not conducted with a measure of goodwill and certainly, from an Australian perspective, with correctness. Brett Lodge:

> Although he appreciated the consideration he had received from Bond on his arrival and the strengths of Barstow, the commander of the 9th Indian Division, Bennett disliked most other senior British officers and their conversation. In many ways he seemed to regard the British as much as adversaries as allies.[68]

Bennett's actual diary entries concerning the above tend to offer far more illumination: On 8 April 1941, on hearing of Bond's replacement by Percival, Bennett 'Wrote him a letter of regret. He has been considerate to me.' On 3 April 1941 he 'Called on ... Barstow—9 Ind Div & discussed tactical plan. Seems good sort.' And on 17 July 1941: 'Gen Barstow (9 Ind Div) dined with me. Very tall & very lean, blue eyed, thin—very charming. Doesn't stand on ceremony.'[69] Such entries would seem to indicate both a respect and liking for these officers. In a letter to Kent Hughes on 25 August 1947, Bennett stated that both Shenton Thomas and Percival 'were unusually kind to me'.[70] But there exists far more substantiated evidence as to Bennett's relationship with the British.

Major Charles Moses began his service in Malaya with the 2/20th Battalion. He was subsequently posted to 8th Division HQ as a liaison officer in August 1941. The fact that Moses was born in England and had graduated from Sandhurst might suggest that he was an astute choice as a LO, whether

Bennett personally selected him or not. Moses communicated by letter with Lodge for his research for *The Fall of General Gordon Bennett*. Given that he was a liaison officer and therefore had frequent contact with British officers, it might have been opportune for Lodge to have asked Moses his thoughts on Bennett's relationship(s) with the British. Sir Charles Moses:

> . . . the criticism that he didn't get on with the British, that he didn't get on with various other people—I can say this: that his relationship with General Barstow was a friendly one. Now Barstow was highly regarded in the British Army . . . I know that he and General Bennett got on extremely well. Colonel Coates who was the G1 of that division spoke very highly of our general in Sumatra after he got away . . . Now the AQ of that division was Colonel Trott—by the way an Australian— he later became the brigadier commanding the 9th Indian Brigade when Brigadier Lay was removed from his command . . . now those men couldn't have spoken more highly of General Bennett . . . And this suggestion that is through this book [*The Fall of General Gordon Bennett*] that he didn't get on with the British; well, I'm sure there were times when he felt that he would have disliked some of them or not agreed with some of the things that were done. I wonder what the author of that would like to say about Montgomery—a very difficult man in his relationships with the Americans . . . and some of his own people. Our general got on extremely well with the British who were working with him and the only exception being Brigadier Duncan of the 45th Indian Brigade.[71]

Major-General Gordon Bennett was, in some ways, a difficult sub-ordinate: he was strong-willed and certainly forthright, and at times lacked tact. But throughout history there has been a significant number of army commanders who have often not been docile, even-tempered men, but highly ambitious and forthright. Lieutenant-General John Lavarack, Major-General Jack Stevens and Brigadiers 'Tubby' Allen and Arnold Potts are Australian examples—but all were considered capable commanders. Major-General George Vasey's diary entries and letters concerning many of his peers during the Second World War—both regular and citizen soldiers alike—also bear ample testimony as to the ambition, competition and personal opinions of high ranking officers. Moses's point concerning Montgomery would seem entirely fair—and General Patton might readily be added to such a list. Further, it will be shown that Lieutenant-General Heath also had disagreements with General Percival. The plain truth is that antipathy between commanders and subordinates in wartime is hardly rare. Surely the issue is whether or not General Gordon Bennett was in any way guilty of injustice towards either his 8th Division HQ or Malaya Command. On the balance of all the evidence it would seem that he adopted an even-handed approach to both his own HQ and the British.

7

THE ENEMY

After China's eventual defeat in the Opium Wars, Britain, followed by other European powers, forced the Chinese to sanction a string of treaty ports along the Chinese coast, which enabled European trade into the interior to prosper. Shanghai and Hong Kong became lucrative symbols of British growth in the region. The Japanese saw the so-called 'Unequal Treaties' and the resulting 'open door' policy towards trade with the Europeans as a humiliation to the Chinese, and determined that Japan would not go the same way.

When Commodore Perry and his American squadron of four steamships arrived in Japan in 1853, Perry was under instruction from President Fillmore to 'obtain from the government of that country some relaxation of the inhospitable and anti-social system which it has pursued for about two centuries'.[1] His diplomacy was in fact an ultimatum: the Tokugawa shogunate had to conform to the demand that Japan allow trade and diplomatic rights to foreign nations or suffer a display of force that it was clearly unable to counter. Upon his return to Japan seven months later, this time with seven ships, Perry received a signed treaty. The Japanese door was now open to the 'western barbarians'.

The subsequent Japanese transformation from a disjointed feudal collection of autonomous domains ruled by the shogun overlords and administered by the samurai into a modern industrial and military power was extraordinary in both its methodology and time frame.

In 1868 the shogunate was overthrown and a central government was formed under the authority of the Emperor Meiji. Japan's leaders during the Meiji period set out to redefine the very nature of their country's politics, its economy and the nation's armed forces, chiefly for the purpose of giving it the strength to resist the West. Their methodology was simple: they utilised Japanese tradition to protect them against the potential poison of westernisation.

Rather than construct a duplicate of the democracies of the West, they adopted the Shinto principle of the divinity of the Emperor. Japan and its people had been created by 'other gods' and were both of divine origin, and therefore racially superior to other countries and their peoples. Further, and most important of all, the first Emperor Jinmu was an earthly descendant of the Sun Goddess Amaterasu. It followed that the present Emperor and his descendants were also the worldly and spiritual descendants of Amaterasu. The Japanese, therefore, lived on sacred soil; they were led not by a mere monarch but by a living God; and, critically, they saw their path in life as a dedicated exercise in complete and utter servility to that order. From around 1905, this Shinto belief became much more than a premise for a constitution, but more a means of social unity. And through this social unity shone the family, the community and the nation.

> By vesting the emperor with absolute sovereignty, making the imperial line the ultimate repository of spiritual and secular authority, and not allowing for the existence of any external moral or religious authority capable of sanctioning alternative thoughts or actions, the ruling elite claiming to act in the name of the emperor achieved a monopoly of the symbols of power and effectively made opposition into treachery.[2]

Japan's economic growth during the Meiji period began with enormous strides in transport and communications. By 1871 an expansion of postal services had begun; six years later Osaka, Kyoto and Tokyo had railways connecting them to their closest deep-water ports; a national telegraph system had been installed; and foreign competition in shipping was restricted by the emergence of Japanese coastal and overseas services. A number of shipping firms amalgamated into the formidable shipping company of Nippon Yusen Kaisha, whose business grew rapidly; by 1880 the Bank of Japan had been created to regulate a national currency and the banking system in general, and a further bank had been established to control foreign exchange.

The agricultural sector began to achieve higher production through the advent of agricultural schools and experimental farms, which in turn led to better strains of crops, the employment of fertilisers and greater efficiency. In basic terms, after 1900, the growth and increased profits of the Meiji period and the fact that a central government could now more efficiently collect revenue allowed Japan to develop a major change in economic development: the growth of heavy industry.

By the onset of the Great Depression, Japan created about 60 per cent of its requirements in pig-iron; it produced around 70 per cent of its steel needs; it had a growing shipbuilding industry; at the turn of the century its engineering capacity had begun to produce steam trains and electrical equipment; and by 1930 it had over 13000 miles of railway.[3]

Japan's rapid industrial development was also fostered by a willingness to learn and adopt procedures and technology from overseas missions and paid experts brought in from abroad. But the nation lacked raw materials, a key ingredient of a modern industrial power. As Japan's economy grew so its appetite for the resources of industry increased. This predicament was a major influence upon her foreign policy and the growth of her armed forces.

The slogan that inspired the resurgence of the Japanese armed forces before and during the Meiji period was *sonno joi* ('restore the Emperor and expel the barbarian').[4] The Japanese armed forces, therefore, were not merely an instrument of national integrity, or the later means of the acquisition of an empire. They were primarily committed to the protection of the chosen land of the Gods and Amaterasu's descendant: the Emperor. They were to be a shield against the corruption and impurity of the outside world. Here was a fundamental racial and cultural chauvinism of a rare intensity.

As Japan's successful modernisation gained momentum, and its armed forces became more professional and potent, its gaze turned ever more towards mainland Asia and its two potential adversaries: China and Russia.

On 8 February 1904, in a sign of things to come, the Japanese attacked the Russian fleet at Port Arthur three hours before their declaration of war. Employing a torpedo boat attack, Admiral Togo badly damaged the two biggest Russian Far East Fleet battleships and a cruiser. After dealing with the Russian Far East Fleet, the Japanese plan was that one army would land in Korea and advance on Manchuria by an advance across the Yalu River, while a second was to land on the Liaotung Peninsula and move on Port Arthur. A third army was to later land between them.

The Battles of Liaoyang (September 1904), Port Arthur (2 January 1905) and Mukden (March 1905) were the final yet costly Japanese victories, and the final Russian Army humiliations. Undoubtedly, a major outcome of the Russo–Japanese War was the psychological impact within Japan and Asia. Japan now saw itself as a legitimate imperial power, whose international status and sense of pride had been earnt in battle against a traditional, powerful European foe; whose considerable military, economic and political growth had transcended a struggle for its own safety, and had now become a means of expanding its economic power; which saw a future outcome of this status and strength in the potential emigration of its people to new territories; and, critically, its victories reinforced its ethnic view of its Emperor, nation and people as being superior to others. Such arrogance not only applied to the white man, but applied in equal measure to other Asians. Through Japanese eyes, the future proclamation of 'Asia for the Asians' was really a racial decree of 'Asia for the Asians with the Japanese as masters'.

The onset of the Great Depression in 1929 created the economic and social and, therefore, the political environment in which the Imperial Japanese Army broke up Japan's liberal power base and then took control of the nation. In political terms both the extreme right and left questioned the old order: capitalism. The Great Depression caused many to doubt the fundamental basis of free enterprise: had international trade collaboration, which had degenerated into nations and empires falling back on collective trade barriers, not become redundant? Further, could democratic processes solve the problem? That questioning was not unique to Japan, and as the crisis worsened, the fear of communism gripped much of the world. Japan needed a guaranteed supply of raw materials and a resulting secure market for its products. The remedy appeared close at hand and entirely feasible: Japan once again looked to China.

In November 1930, Prime Minister Hamaguchi was assassinated and numerous secret societies were created by Imperial Army officers. When another prime minister went Hamaguchi's way in 1932, Japan's 'convulsive period' was in full swing.

An opportunity for expansion now presented itself. When the local warlord began to hinder Japanese interests in southern Manchuria, after having formally recognised the new Chinese Nationalist Government in Nanking, Japanese officers in the Kwantung Army in Manchuria decided to act. Kirby in *The War Against Japan*:

> On the 18th of September 1931 the extremists, taking advantage of the fact that Japanese troops were stationed in southern Manchuria as guards for the Southern Manchurian Railway . . . staged an incident in such a way that national feeling in Japan would support their policy. A carefully arranged explosion—ostensibly the work of the Chinese—destroyed a part of the railway track with the consequence that Japanese and Chinese troops came into conflict.[5]

The incident gave the Japanese an excuse to occupy Mukden and later the whole of Manchuria. Japan now had possession of an area of land 'larger than France and Germany combined'.[6] China did what it had done before: it appealed to the West, this time through the League of Nations. The Americans joined the protest. On 30 September 1931, the League ordered Japan to withdraw its forces. It was met not only with a refusal to do so, but also with the creation by the Japanese of the puppet state of Manchukuo. The League's Commission of Enquiry condemned the Japanese aggression. The situation then deteriorated further.

China's appeal to the League of Nations formed the first of two reactions to the Japanese state of Manchukuo. The second was a boycott of Japanese goods, which, in the context of the already deepening Great Depression, bit hard on Japan. Japanese living in China were threatened, assaulted and in January 1932 violence broke out. After a riot in Shanghai on the 18th, the Japanese demanded reparations and the assurance that all anti-Japanese groups be disbanded. The Chinese simply ignored the ultimatum. The international city of Shanghai now became the focus of events that further isolated the Japanese in the eyes of the world community.

After the Japanese had mobilised their considerable local population and their Marines, had bombed a Chinese armoured train and station, and deployed forces within foreign sectors of the city, the situation deteriorated further. Following an artillery engagement in early February, the Japanese decided to send a division and a brigade, which were subsequently reinforced by a further two divisions, to the north of Shanghai. It was only after the Japanese had driven the Chinese about ten miles inland that the Shanghai European community was able to mediate a halt to the fighting.

The formation of the Japanese puppet state of Manchukuo and the Shanghai incident resulted in the League of Nations censuring the Japanese as an aggressor. But the Japanese were no longer terribly interested in world opinion and gave notice, in February 1931, of their intention to withdraw from the League. Their decision became effective in 1935. Japan then proceeded to move southwards from Manchukuo, occupied the province of Jehol, and then crossed the Great Wall into northern China.

In May 1933, a truce was signed between Chiang Kai-shek's Chinese Nationalists and the Japanese. The Great Wall became the basic line of demarcation with a buffer zone further south. Japan had, within a few short years, become the principal foreign player in China.

At this time, there existed numerous ultra-nationalist groups within Japanese society—and within the Imperial Army—which were determined that Japan should go further along the path of expansion. One such group, the Young Officers, staged an attempted coup on 26 February 1936. Meirion & Susie Harries, *Soldiers of the Sun*:

At a stroke, the rebels removed several of the leading proponents of constitutional monarchy in Japan, and provided a display of military brute force vicious enough to guarantee the cooperation of others who might otherwise have challenged the army ... the army

needed partnership with other technocrats, so it was never to assume
an absolute dictatorship, but direct and overt opposition ceased after
February 1936.[7]

The uneasy truce between the Chinese and the Japanese in China
came to an abrupt end in July 1936. From Chiang Kai-shek's perspective a
final showdown with the Japanese was inevitable. Groups within his own
Nationalist movement had been pushing him to forestall his war with the
communists. They argued that the Japanese threat in northern China and
the continued Japanese use of the rich resources in Manchuria were far
greater political and military issues than the communists or any remaining
war lords. It was time, they argued, for all Chinese to combine and defeat
the common and hated enemy. To this end, Chiang now had some 30 divisions which had been trained by German advisors, and he could also call on
various other Nationalist formations elsewhere in the country.

On the night of 7 July 1936 elements of a Japanese unit near the Marco
Polo Bridge at Peking was fired upon. Fighting ensued between the Japanese
and Chinese and although local mediators were in the process of securing a
cease-fire, both the Japanese and Chinese Governments were drawn into the
fight. Chiang Kai-shek exhorted his people to war and occupied the buffer
zone in north China, which forced the Japanese hand. Within two months of
the Marco Polo Bridge incident, the Japanese had deployed 200 000 troops in
northern China and had made impressive gains in the Peking–Tientsin area;
between August and October 1936, the Japanese became embroiled in heavy
fighting around Shanghai; and in an attempt to break the deadlock, a further
three divisions of the Tenth Army were landed south of that city and one on
the Yangtse on 13 November. The three-month fight for Shanghai cost the
Japanese around 9000 killed in action and approximately 30 000 wounded.

After having pursued the retreating Chinese Nationalists from Shanghai
some 300 kilometres upriver, the Japanese found themselves at the gates of
Nanking, Chiang Kai-shek's capital. After the infantry had entered the city
on 13 December 1937, and their support units had arrived the following
day, the Imperial Japanese Army instigated a campaign of premeditated,
cold-blooded and systematic murder, rape, looting, and terror that became
infamous in both its intensity and scale: the Rape of Nanking.

At and around the Chinese capital, the Japanese sought to destroy the Chinese ability to wage war by the systematic looting and burning of factories, plant, commercial venues, housing and the confiscation of food and fuel. But it was the elimination of members of the Chinese Army who had gone to ground in the city that interested the Japanese commanders most. During the campaign preceding the fall of Nanking, the Japanese had sustained some 72 000 casualties of which around 18 000 had been killed in action. As would be the case so often through the coming years of the Pacific War, when the Imperial Army took heavy casualties, brutal reprisals against both captured combatants and innocent civilians followed.

Under officer supervision, the Chinese were rounded up and taken to execution points around the city. The machine gun, rifle and bayonet were worked overtime as these concentration points, and numerous watercourses became additional slaughter sites. As the scale of the murder intensified, so the selection of victims became less disciplined and indiscriminate. Any male, not just suspected former combatants, was put to the sword or bayonet or was simply shot. And as Christmas passed and the New Year came, alcohol became a chief factor in the behaviour of the Japanese. The rape of the Chinese women in Nanking was rampant and it is difficult to imagine the scale of their suffering. Roaming bands of drunken and largely unsupervised troops engaged not only in pack rape, but subsequent murder. After the streets had been cleared of potential victims, homes, hospital and university quarters were ransacked. The process went on for weeks.

The Rape of Nanking shocked the western world. European and American missionaries, businessmen and diplomats had witnessed and recorded much of its carnage first hand. The fact is, however, that this incident was not isolated, as it had been both preceded by and would be later followed by further widespread atrocities during the Chinese and Pacific Wars.

The Japanese soldiers who were to fight against the British, Indians and Australians in Malaya and Singapore—and who became their masters in Pudu and Changi Prisons and on the Thai–Burma Railway—had a moral and martial code that at the time defied western comprehension.

The conscript who presented himself for Imperial Army service was used to subservience to superiors. He was born into a family where early submissiveness towards his father and elder brothers was instilled and demanded of him, and where this concept of dutiful service was then transferred to the Emperor through the institution of *chu*. Upon joining the army the conscript became 'one already dead'.[8] The recruit had thus renounced any right or privilege or ambitions for his own life. Ei Yamaguchi, Japanese Imperial Army:

> We were taught that dying was lighter than a bird's feather. That it was easy to die. That's how we were trained. So we weren't scared of dying. Even when a comrade died all we thought was, 'What a pity for him.' We just thought he was unlucky. We used to say, 'I'll be joining you soon', because that's how we saw it.[9]

A soldier's death was thus seen as an inspirational and pure act which was likened to the precise moment of perfection of the fall of the cherry blossom. Sublime death, if it came, brought honour to his emperor, nation and family. Correspondingly, surrender to an enemy brought disgrace and humiliation not only upon the Japanese soldier, but upon his emperor, nation and family. It followed, therefore, that through Japanese eyes, enemy prisoners of war had shamed themselves and deserved contempt and ill-treatment.

Corporal punishment was an accepted form of discipline throughout the Imperial Army and took many forms. Standing at attention in front of a superior for a misdemeanour might involve a few forceful slaps across the face, a particularly angry officer or NCO might resort to punching or a 'king hit',[10] and, on occasions in China, soldiers might be lined up for collective failure and be ordered to slap their opposite number's face.

The Japanese officer saw himself as a latter-day samurai, and his reverence for his sword held an almost spiritual hold over him. Masao Maeda, Japanese Imperial Army: 'In those days we naturally accepted the tradition that Japanese samurai in olden times fought with the sword. I believe that by carrying swords ourselves we became samurai.'[11] And the sword was often used to 'blood' or test a new officer who had just arrived from officer training school. In a remarkable oral history interview with Haruko and Theodore

Cook, Second Lieutenant Tominaga Shozo of the Imperial Japanese Army described the 'blooding' of Japanese officers and other ranks.

Shozo reported for duty with the 232nd Regiment of the 39th Division on service in the Yangtze Valley in July 1941. When he was introduced to his men he was struck by their 'evil eyes'.[12] After a guided tour of a recent battle-field, Shozo was informed that the next day he and the other new officer arrivals would be given a trial of courage, a test to see if they 'were qualified to be platoon leaders'.[13]

The next day twenty emaciated Chinese prisoners were brought to an area where a large pit had been dug. Present were the regimental (brigade) commander, the battalion commanders and the company commanders—obviously an important occasion and an equally important test. The officer presiding over the demonstration was a Second Lieutenant Tanaka, who proceeded to unsheath his sword, pour water over both sides of the blade, and then with a shout of 'Yo!' removed a prisoner's head with a clean cut. Shozo's reaction is illuminating: 'The scene was so appalling that I felt I couldn't breathe.'[14] Here, surely, was the reaction of a man who did not at that point have 'evil eyes'. Shozo's reaction when his turn came is also illu-minating: '. . . the only thought I had was "Don't do anything unseemly!" I didn't want to disgrace myself.'[15] He need not have worried. Shozo passed his test by decapitating his victim with one swift slice. He then claimed that something inside him changed—he no longer felt uneasy in his men's eyes, but now 'felt I was looking down on them'.[16]

Shozo's experience portrays the obedience of all ranks to their superiors; it depicts the extreme Japanese determination to not lose face, to be loyal and submissive; and it also portrays the spiritual strength of the sword and its empowerment to the individual Japanese officer or NCO. And no less a ritual was used on occasions for the private soldier through the public practice—in front of their peers and superiors—of running at and then bayoneting blindfolded prisoners of war tied to poles. The empowerment was the same and only the tool of execution differed. According to Shozo, any new, 'unblooded' arrivals who experienced difficulty with their first execution, who might have 'stopped on their way' were kicked and 'made to do it'.[17] Perhaps the difference between the use of a sword and bayonet was a depiction of privileged power and status. But the end result was the same.

Given the Japanese soldier's concepts of racial superiority, of death, his attitude to surrender and prisoners of war, and the method of his 'blooding', he was consequently indoctrinated to believe that any means justified victory. He was taught that his war was total war. Shiro Azuma, Japanese Imperial Army:

> War was about winning or losing. We didn't think about humanity at all. We believed we could do anything to win. When we won the war against China, because we'd won all our previous battles, we were very arrogant . . .
>
> Kick a chink, kick a dog, kick a stone. It was all the same! We were arrogant. Killing a Chinese person was just like killing a dog.[18]

This racist Japanese view was to have dire consequences for the entire Asian Chinese population and will touch our story dramatically in Singapore.

Another Japanese Imperial Army imperative through much of its campaigning in Asia was the edict that its troops should live as much as possible off the land. This practice brought indescribable suffering upon the civilian population in China and throughout South-East Asia. And such a philosophy had an implication for women. Shiro Azuma: 'When we went searching for food, we found women hiding. We thought, "Ah, they look tasty!" So we raped them. And every single time a woman was raped, the soldiers would kill her.'[19]

Such behaviour was embedded in the Japanese male's psyche. He came from a society where the female was subservient to her husband and sons. The mother and sister's every waking hour was focused upon being a faithful family servant and a moderate, diplomatic communicator at all times. Given the status of the Japanese woman, those from 'racially inferior' countries were at great risk when uncontrolled troops descended upon them to confiscate, loot, pillage and burn. Rape and murder all too often became the final acts of disgrace, and, when alcohol and the psychology of the pack or group of soldiers came into play, as at Nanking, the result was horrific. And in another appalling display of their contempt for women, around 250 000 Korean and numerous numbers of Chinese and Formosan females—and some European—would be press-ganged as 'comfort women' into cruel prostitution across the lands of Japan's conquests.

The Imperial Japanese Army's officers were drawn from three sources. The first, comprising senior commanders and 'in peace, most of the junior ones',[20] was drawn from the military academy where, in most cases, soldiers had undergone extensive training over a seven and a half year period before graduating with the rank of second lieutenant.[21] The reserve officers formed the second source. They had usually served in the conscript ranks; were invariably amongst the best educated of the conscripts; were then trained at officer reserve schools; and, after gaining their commissions, were normally put into the reserve at home ready for active service when required. Second Lieutenant Tominaga Shozo was an example of this category. The last group of officers were those NCOs who were promoted through the ranks on merit after distinguished service.

The other ranks in the Japanese Army were tough troops indeed. They were prepared to follow orders without question, and, therefore, death was a much more acceptable end than was the case with other nationalities. This attitude manifested itself in a number of ways: a soldier, when ordered, dutifully presented himself as a target before his foe in order to draw fire and thus expose enemy positions; snipers willingly penetrated an enemy perimeter during darkness to climb trees or coconut palms and later snipe at the enemy, fully understanding that death was almost inevitable; and others would lie 'doggo' amongst their dead in already forfeited positions, waiting to rise and strike at their foes as they passed by.

The Japanese plan to secure a large South-East Asian empire was based upon an audacious and speedy naval dominance of the Western Pacific. In order to accomplish this task, the navy planned to deliver a crippling blow against the American Pacific Fleet at Pearl Harbor and bomb Malaya and the Philippines. The Imperial Japanese Army's task was to then invade Malaya and Singapore, the Philippines, Borneo, Sumatra and the Dutch East Indies. The outer limit of this huge empire was to stretch from the Indian–Burmese border, around the Dutch East Indies, north-east to the Marshall Islands, Wake Island and then north-west to the Kurile Islands.

By the speedy acquisition of such an enormous empire, the Japanese believed that the cost of winning it back for the Allies would be so prolonged, and therefore so costly in human life and material, that a prolonged fight would be totally unpalatable. They believed that in the long term the Allies would not have the stomach for such a fight and would negotiate. It was also anticipated—not without some confidence in November 1941—that Germany would triumph against the Soviet Union, finally defeat or at least further isolate Britain in Europe, and thereby confine the Japanese fight in the Pacific to isolationist America and an exhausted and unaided China.

The naval plan to destroy the American Pacific Fleet at Pearl Harbor and shield the landings in South-East Asia was devised by Admiral Isoroku Yamamoto. After having studied at Harvard and having been posted as a naval attaché to the United States, he was under no illusion as to the long-term war potential of that nation. According to Admiral Toyoda, Yamamoto had stated that the Imperial Navy could: 'carry through for one year, some way; but after that I don't know'.[22]

At no time did the Japanese have any intention of invading Hawaii. But Yamamoto's study, training initiatives and profound belief in the potential of naval aviation as a means of inflicting long-term damage on an enemy fleet inspired his planning. And the striking British carrier success against the Italian Navy at Taranto barely a year before added substance to that planning. Vice-Admiral Nagumo, Commander-in-Chief 1st Air Fleet, was to command the carrier attack upon Pearl Harbor. Vice-Admiral Kondo, commander of Second Air Fleet, was to command the Southern Area Fleet which was responsible for operations against the Philippines and Malaya. The carrier attacks upon Pearl Harbor and the invasion of the Philippines and Malaya were timed for 8 December 1941 (or for operations east of the international date line 7 December).

Japan's Southern Army HQ (General Terauchi) was established at Saigon in late 1941. Each of Southern Army's four objectives was allotted to an army group: Fourteenth Army was to be responsible for the capture of the Philippines; Fifteenth Army was to take Thailand and Burma; Sixteenth Army was to overrun the Dutch East Indies; and Twenty-fifth Army was to capture Malaya.

On 15 November 1941, Lieutenant-General Tomoyuki Yamashita was appointed to command the Twenty-fifth Army. Yamashita had had a most impressive career. Born in 1885 in a remote village on the island of Shikoku, he had entered cadet school in Hiroshima at fifteen; had attended the Central Military Academy in Tokyo; at 32 years of age, he had graduated from the War College; he had been a military attaché in Switzerland and Vienna; in 1936 he had been Chief of Military Affairs at Imperial HQ; and had seen service in Korea and China as a divisional commander. He was a tall, thickset soldier with a shaven head, thick neck and swaggering stance. Colonel Masanobu Tsuji described him variously as 'of dignified appearance', and a man 'who had a keen insight into human nature [which] created a level of morale which spurred men forward on scores of battlefields and in many campaigns'.[23]

To those Allied soldiers and strategists who had studied the potential for war in the Far East, the German invasion of Holland and Belgium on 10 May 1940, followed by the fall of France on 22 June, must have confirmed that all of their predictions were coming to pass. With two of the major colonial powers defeated and occupied by Germany, and Britain on its knees, a roller-coaster ride to war in South-East Asia had begun. In September 1940, Japan had been granted bases in Indo-China; later that month Germany, Japan and Italy had signed the Tripartite Pact.

In late June 1941, the Germans had invaded Russia, and within a mere 32 days of that momentous event, the Japanese had felt confident enough to land troops in southern Indo-China. Two days later the Americans froze their assets in the United States.

At an Imperial Conference on 6 September 1941, the Japanese decided that diplomatic efforts must continue to stop the Americans supplying aid to China; that the British and Americans must agree to no further build-up of their forces in the Far East; that they should allow Japan a free hand in Indo-China; and, most importantly, allow them the acquisition of raw materials. If the western powers did not comply with these demands, the Japanese were prepared to go to war by the end of October. After negotiations between Admiral Nomura and the American Secretary of State, Cordell Hull, reached a deadlock on 2 October, Prime Minister Konoye—who had advocated peace—resigned and was replaced by General Tojo, who now held

the posts of Prime Minister, Minister for War and Minister of Home Affairs.
The Japanese militarists now held almost total power. At an Imperial
Conference on 5 November 1941, the Japanese determined that unless
their conditions were met by 25 November, they would go to war.

While these events were unfolding in Japan, further muddled thought
occurred in Singapore. In September, Duff Cooper, who had been the
Minister for Information in the UK, arrived in Singapore as a Minister of
State to 'investigate the situation in the Far East, and to inquire into the feasi-
bility of setting up an authority to deal on the spot with political questions
which were then being referred to the British Cabinet for decision'.[24] Cooper
chaired a meeting on 29 September. Those present were: Air Chief Marshal
Brooke-Popham; Vice-Admiral Layton; Sir Shenton Thomas; Sir Earle Page
(the Australian Minister of Commerce, who was on his way to London); the
British Minister to Thailand, Josiah Crosby; and the British Ambassador to
China, Sir Archibald Kerr. The conclusions reached at this conference could
not have been more misguided: Japan's attention was upon Russia; it would
be most wary of war against the United States, the British Commonwealth
and the Netherlands East Indies; and, incredibly, the conference decided that
the Japanese would not attempt an invasion of Malaya during the north-east
monsoon. Surely such thoughts made absolutely no allowance for the fact
that the vital factor governing Japanese strategy was composed of two words:
raw materials.

The die had been cast, and cast over years of poor planning, low-priority
funding and resourcing, and constant changes of leadership in Singapore
across the three services. Most of all, interservice conflict had retarded
common purpose and policy for the best use of those scant resources to
defend Malaya and Singapore.

In December 1941, the Japanese were about to attack at three landing
points already forecast; as predicted years ago and by no shortage of observers, they were also about to attack 'before the flag falls';[25] they would surely
land at around this time, during the north-east monsoon; they would have
the initiative; they were attacking—through the predicted backdoor of
Malaya—a naval base without a navy; they were to fight against a British
Empire air force grievously depleted in both number and quality of planes
and pilots; and they were to be met by a largely under strength, ill-trained,

dispersed, and therefore ill-prepared Empire army. And surely, when another Dunkirk, another Greece and another Crete had come to pass, there would be the now familiar talk of 'glorious withdrawals' and 'brave stands'.

War was imminent. To those soldiers and strategists who had for years been predicting this scenario, it must have felt as if they were part of a selected, exclusive playhouse audience, where the actors were playing out a humiliating but all-too-familiar tragedy and the characters striding that stage were in fact themselves. And all that could now be done was to watch, to sit there transfixed, paralysed in both thought and action.

PART II
THE CAMPAIGN

. . . in the cleverest way

＝⟩●○⟨＝

Our opponents are even more feeble than the Chinese Army . . .
Victory is certain, and the only problem is how
to win in the cleverest way.

Colonel Tsuji, Chief of Operations and Planning Staff,
25th Japanese Army

8

AN UNPLEASANT
SURPRISE

The British and Dutch had reasoned that the most likely Japanese approach to an invasion of Malaya was through the South China Sea. Accordingly, the Dutch Naval Air Service assumed responsibility for reconnaissance patrols in a roughly rectangular area from Singapore, northward to Kuantan, eastward to Natuna Island, to Kuching in Sarawak and back to Singapore. Three Catalina flying boats based at Seletar airfield on Singapore Island undertook this task. The RAF was responsible for an area from Kota Bharu, north-east to Cape Cambodia, south-east to Natuna Island, due west to Kuantan and then back to Kota Bharu. They employed their three available Catalina flying boats—also based at Seletar—to provide an overlap between the Dutch and British reconnaissance areas, while the RAAF was made responsible for the remainder of the British section.

The Australians were to fly their patrols using two squadrons of Hudsons. Number 1 Squadron was based at Kota Bharu, where it had served since August 1941, while No. 8 was deployed at Sembawang. The joint Dutch and British air reconnaissance plan relied upon the principle that an enemy invasion fleet might be detected whilst still 'beyond night steaming range of the coast',[1] which would allow for bombing and torpedo missions against it that might either cause it significant damage at sea and

force it to turn away, or severely maul it at its landing points. Douglas
Gillison:

> To provide for coordinated action, three degrees of readiness were laid
> down by General Headquarters: the third degree of readiness was the
> then existing war state of the command; the second—to be assumed
> if the international situation deteriorated so far that it was justified—
> required all units to be ready to operate at short notice; the first would
> call for readiness for immediate operations with all units prepared for
> enemy air attack without warning.[2]

No. 8 Squadron RAAF was to move from Sembawang to Kuantan to
complete the concentration for the RAAF reconnaissance duties once the
second state of readiness had been reached. On 1 December 1941, that
degree of alert was given, but it took—because of a lack of air transport—
until 4 December before eight Hudsons flew in and the squadron advance
party arrived by road. Four aircraft had remained behind at Sembawang,
while much equipment and the ground staff were still travelling north
by sea.

In early August 1941, Winston Churchill had sailed to Newfoundland on
board the *Prince of Wales* to meet with President Roosevelt. The Atlantic
Charter was the end result of their meeting. But during their deliberations
the subject of the Far East was also raised. It was decided that both the US
and Britain would take a tougher stance against Japan. Upon his return to
Washington Roosevelt was to hand the Japanese Ambassador the following warning: 'Any further encroachment by Japan in the South-West Pacific
would produce a situation in which the United States Government would be
compelled to take counter-measures, even though these might lead to war
between the United States and Japan.'[3]

Churchill returned to London on 19 August. Six days later he sent a
minute to the First Sea Lord advocating the formation of an Eastern Fleet.
He envisaged 'a deterrent squadron in the Indian Ocean' which would consist
of the 'smallest number of the best ships'.[4] Churchill believed that such a fleet

'might show itself in the triangle Aden–Singapore–Simonstown' (a naval base near Cape Town) and that such a fleet would 'exert a paralysing effect upon Japanese naval action'.[5] The proposed squadron was to consist primarily of a modern, fast battleship (he suggested the *Duke of York*), an aircraft carrier and an old but fast battle cruiser.

The Admiralty were at odds with Churchill's assessment. G. Hermon Gill, in *Australia in the War of 1939–1945: Royal Australian Navy, 1939–1942*:

> [The Admiralty] proposed to send to the Indian Ocean between mid-September 1941 and the end of January 1942 the battleships *Nelson* and *Rodney* and the four 'R' class ships *Revenge*, *Royal Sovereign*, *Ramillies* and *Resolution* (the 'R's' being ships of about 2,500 miles endurance at 20 knots in smooth water), and the battle cruiser *Renown*. The aircraft carrier *Hermes* was already there, and it was proposed to send there *Ark Royal* in April 1942, and *Indomitable* in an emergency.[6]

It was believed that this force should perform four roles: it could be used in the Indian Ocean as troop convoy escorts; it would discourage the Japanese from deploying raiders in the Indian Ocean; these ships would be relatively free from enemy aircraft and submarine attack; and, eventually, they would become a part of the long-term plan for an Eastern Fleet of seven battleships, one aircraft carrier, ten cruisers and around 24 destroyers. The Admiralty argued that the Prime Minister's proposal of the 'smallest number of the best ships'—including only one battleship—would not be in any position to effectively counter an enemy fleet sailing south which they estimated might contain at least four battleships.

Churchill yet again dismissed the notion that the Japanese would invade Malaya, and preferred instead to attempt to counter potential Japanese raids in the Indian Ocean against British trade routes. In the end, Churchill's political expediency—bolstered by the British War Cabinet, Singapore, the Australian Government and the British Foreign Office—far outweighed professional advice. In late October the Admiralty agreed to the aircraft carrier *Indomitable*, the battleship *Prince of Wales*, and the battle cruiser *Repulse* being sent to Singapore. After 2 December 1941, the Eastern Fleet was to consist of the above-named three ships and the destroyers HMS *Revenge*, *Electra*, *Express*, *Jupiter*, *Encounter* and HMAS *Vampire*. It was to be codenamed Force Z after its arrival in Singapore. But on 3 November 1941, the *Indomitable* ran aground while sailing into Jamaica and had to be docked for repairs. Nor was HMS *Revenge* destined to serve from Singapore, but, after convoy work to the United Kingdom, would eventually sail to Bombay and finally arrive at Trincomalee (Ceylon) on 13 December 1941.

On 24 October at Greenock in Scotland, Admiral Sir Tom Phillips raised his flag aboard HMS *Prince of Wales* as Commander-in-Chief Eastern Fleet—a posting that was to make him the senior naval commander in the Far East. Phillips had had a most distinguished and rapid rise in the Royal Navy. Only five foot two inches in height and known as 'Tom Thumb' to subordinates, he was recognised as having a sharp wit and a rigid belief in both himself and the power of capital ships. His confident and forceful nature caused Churchill to refer to him as 'the Cocksparrow', while Admiral Somerville christened him 'the Pocket Napoleon'. Phillips was 53 years of age when appointed to command the Eastern Fleet. G. Hermon Gill:

> He was an officer of considerable destroyer experience afloat (he was commodore (D) [Deputy Director] and later Rear-Admiral (D) Home Fleet Flotillas from April 1938 to May 1939) and he had been in closest possible touch with the naval side of the war at sea. But he had no actual experience of that war, especially as it was being fought under the conditions imposed by naval aviation. Only three days elapsed between his relief at the Admiralty after a period of years there as Director of Plans and Vice Chief of the Naval Staff, and his hoisting of his flag in *Prince of Wales*.[7]

In fairness to Phillips, no admiral at that time had had extensive experience of being attacked by land-based or fleet-based aircraft whilst at sea. Most theorists (and certainly Phillips) believed that the bombing of capital ships from high altitudes was extremely difficult, and that, while torpedo assaults on capital ships were possible (such as had occurred at Taranto), such an attack had been made against ships anchored in port. The potential of the *Indomitable*'s 60 aircraft—including a number of

Hurricanes—critically important for the dual roles of a self-contained air screen for his fleet and as a potent strike force, had been lost in Jamaica.

Admiral Phillips sailed to Colombo on the *Prince of Wales* before leaving by air for Singapore. The arrival of the *Prince of Wales*, *Repulse* and four destroyers at Keppel Harbour at Singapore on 2 December 1941 caused an unrestrained euphoria amongst the local population. Against an inspiring background of the massive guns of the Island, poised to devastate any approaching enemy fleet, and with brass band anthems and a sea of glamorous white uniforms lined up on the decks, Singapore seemed secure. After all, here was the long-awaited fleet, complete with the latest British capital ship which was less than a year old. To the uneducated, the size and composition of that fleet was lost in a proud tradition of past glory, and in a racist perception of an enemy whose ships and seamanship must surely be inferior to the greatness of the Royal Navy. While the press in Singapore had a field day, the ships were met at the naval base by Singapore's who's who: Sir Brooke-Popham, General Percival, Air Vice-Marshal Pulford, Duff and Lady Diana Cooper, Sir Shenton and Lady Thomas, and a whole host of other civilian and military dignitaries. Phillips entertained them on board the *Prince of Wales*, during which time Percival renewed acquaintances with his host and the captains of the *Prince of Wales* (Captain Leach) and the *Repulse* (Captain Tennant). Percival and Phillips had known each other during their time at the War Office, and Percival knew Leach and Tennant during their service at the Greenwich Staff College.

If the arrival of the two capital ships had caused a local sensation, then the Admiralty was more circumspect: it contacted Phillips on 1 December suggesting that his ships leave Singapore, believing that the Japanese might find the presence of those vessels far more of a concern if they were at sea, and their location therefore harder to determine. *Repulse* sailed on 5 December bound for Darwin and screened by the destroyers *Vampire* and *Tenedos*, while *Prince of Wales* remained temporarily in dry dock. Number 453 Squadron RAF was assigned to Phillip's Eastern Fleet to provide fighter cover along the eastern Malay coast. By 8 December 1941, the squadron was to have one flight at Kota Bharu and another at Kuantan.[8]

At 5.30 am on 4 December 1941, nineteen Japanese transports with around 24 600 troops on board, and escorted by Rear-Admiral Kurita's 7th Cruiser Squadron, sailed from Samah Harbour, Hainan Island. Skirting the Indo-Chinese coast to avoid detection, they initially sailed southwards, and then north-west, heading to a point in the Gulf of Siam designated 'Point G'. Here they were to rendezvous with a further convoy of seven transports which were to leave Saigon on 5 December. From 'Point G', sixteen ships were to sail for Singora and Patani in Thailand, three to Kota Bharu and the seven ships of the Saigon convoy to the Kra Isthmus. General Yamashita and his 25th Army HQ staff sailed aboard the 10 000-ton transport *Ryujo Maru* with the intention of landing at Singora shortly after the first wave of troops.

By employing the tactic of skirting the Indo-Chinese coast southwards, and later sailing back on a north-west course into the Gulf of Siam, the Japanese hoped that if detected, the British might reason that they were headed for Bangkok. But their chief hope in avoiding discovery lay with the north-east monsoon and its 'chiefly fine mornings, rainy afternoons and clear nights, with intermittent, unpredictable and violent storms and bad visibility, particularly over the sea'.[9] Any seaborne assault is aided by low cloud cover and the above weather conditions while its convoys are concentrated, before moving to their objectives. Lieutenant-Colonel Tsuji, sailing on the *Ryujo Maru*, recorded that: 'During the day, everyone from the Army Commander to the private soldiers was tense in the clear weather. Never had I wished so earnestly for heavy rain as I did then.'[10]

Those very conditions had hindered British reconnaissance sorties— the monsoonal rains had grounded all aircraft at Kota Bharu and other airfields in northern Malaya on 4 and 5 December. But the next day a flight of three Hudsons of No. 1 Squadron RAAF left Kota Bharu at 10.30 am to patrol the western area of the South China Sea. Just after midday, a Hudson commanded by Flight Lieutenant John Ramshaw identified three 10 000-ton transports and a covering cruiser around 290 kilometres east of Kota Bharu and sailing due west. A short time later Ramshaw sighted the main convoy. His crew counted one battleship, five cruisers, seven destroyers and 22 transports at around 425 kilometres from Kota Bharu and steaming due west. When the Hudson was seen by the convoy, the *Kamikawa Maru* catapulted a float plane, which prompted Ramshaw to seek cloud cover. At about

12.45 pm, the crew of a second Hudson commanded by Flight Lieutenant Jim Emerton also spotted the convoy, but their assessment was two cruisers, ten destroyers and 21 transports. Ramshaw and Emerton signalled Singapore and the former then requested permission to shadow it, which was refused, on the basis that both Hudsons were at the limit of their range. The two crews would later claim that one or both Hudsons could have maintained contact with the convoy until relieved, as they had enough fuel for a further three hours.[11]

These events caused some understandable uncertainty in Singapore. Had the two sightings identified two separate convoys or one? As the convoy sighted by Ramshaw was heading in a north-westerly direction into the Gulf of Siam, was the possible second convoy following it? Were the Japanese landings to be at Thailand or at Kota Bharu or both, or were they a feint designed to entice the British to start the war?

At 4.20 pm another Hudson commanded by Flight Lieutenant Patrick Smith took off from Kota Bharu with orders to relocate and then shadow the enemy convoy. It failed to make contact. Meanwhile, in order to deliver a potential strike, seven Vildebeestes of No. 36 Squadron RAF were armed with torpedoes and flown to Gong Kedah (not far from Kota Bharu). After the first degree of readiness was ordered, a Catalina from No. 205 Squadron RAF was despatched from Singapore to undertake a night search. When no information came from the first Catalina, a second left Singapore at 2.00 am under the command of an Australian, Flying Officer Patrick Bedell.

Early on Sunday 7 December, amidst early fog, rain and low cloud, two more Catalinas took off from Singapore and three Hudsons from No. 1 Squadron RAAF from Kota Bharu. The poor weather caused the early return of two of the Hudsons and the third failed to report a sighting. At around 8.20 am, Bedell's Catalina was detected by a Japanese float plane from the *Kamikawa Maru*. After avoiding this threat by turning to the west, Bedell was discovered by a flight of five 'Nate' Japanese Army fighters. His aircraft was shot down and its crew lost, while the first Catalina was also presumed downed.[12] Sailing aboard the *Ryujo Maru*, General Yamashita received news of Bedell's fate. From his perspective, the early detection of the convoy whilst travelling towards 'Point G' was tolerable, but as his Chief Staff Officer, Colonel Tsuji would later write: 'Everyone subconsciously held his breath.

The discovery of the convoy sailing to the north-west we could bear with patience, but from 2 o'clock in the afternoon our change of course . . . must be concealed even from the gods.'[13]

But at around 3.45 pm on 7 December more up-to-date news reached Singapore. A Hudson of No. 8 Squadron sighted a Japanese merchant ship steaming south 'with a large number of men on deck in khaki'.[14] Two Hudsons of No. 1 Squadron immediately took off to search to the north of this sighting, and just on darkness Flight Lieutenant Douglas's Hudson found four ships heading due south about 95 kilometres north of Patani near the end of the Kra Isthmus. He estimated the enemy shipping as three transports escorted by a cruiser. At 5.50 pm, the second Hudson piloted by Flight Lieutenant Lockward signalled identification of a cruiser—actually a destroyer—and a motor ship around 180 kilometres from Kota Bharu.

At midnight on 7 December 1941, the situation still seemed unclear to Air Headquarters: reconnaissance sorties which had located Japanese convoys on the 6th had failed to re-establish contact the following day; further operations had been either hampered by the poor weather conditions, or, when ships had been sighted, the limited visibility had caused varied intelligence; and it had been late evening on the 7th before four ships steaming south had been seen off Singora. By this time, the RAF's ability to contest enemy landings at Kota Bharu consisted of eleven Hudsons of No. 1 Squadron RAAF and two Buffaloes of 243 Squadron fully armed and prepared for offensive operations, while seven torpedo-armed Vildebeestes remained at Gong Kedah. Should the order be given for 'Matador' to be undertaken, the north Malayan airfield of Sungei Patani with its twelve Buffaloes of 21 Squadron RAAF and twelve Blenheims of 27 Squadron RAF were to support General Heath's III Indian Corps. At the outbreak of hostilities, there were—between Singapore Island and Northern Malaya—some 164 first-line British aircraft and around 88 in reserve. The Japanese were ready to deploy around 560 aircraft of which about 180 were fighters.[15] (The vastly differing quality of the protagonists' aircraft and pilots has been discussed.)

The Commander-in-Chief Far East, Sir Robert Brooke-Popham, had been walking on a politico–military tightrope for months. During October 1941, when intelligence sources were indicating that the Japanese were training troops in jungle warfare on the island of Hainan, that landing craft were being built in Shanghai, that shipping was being assembled in Japanese-occupied ports and that they were building airfields in southern Indo-China, Brooke-Popham had clung to the conviction that they were intent upon joining the Germans in their war upon Russia. The Japanese activities in Indo-China and their jungle training initiatives at Hainan ought to have made him sternly question this belief—even if the British War Office shared his views. Events in November 1941 should have further eroded his theory: Japanese shipping was being sent south; the landing craft constructed at Shanghai had also headed southward; and, most significantly, Japanese aircraft strength in Indo-China had increased markedly.

But Brooke-Popham did in fact react to this intelligence. On 21 November, he pressed the Chiefs of Staff for a clarification of the circumstances in which he might launch Matador, reminding them that the potential for its success hinged upon the arrival of British troops at Singora in Siam before an enemy landing. Time was the key. In the interim, he ordered General Percival to bring his army formations to the second state of readiness, and deployed a number of air force units to positions further north. Brooke-Popham would have drawn little confidence or comfort from the Chiefs of Staff's ambivalent reply four days later. Kirby has recorded that:

> They instructed him that, as soon as any situation arose which in his opinion was likely to lead to 'Matador', he should make preparations to launch the operation without delay should he be ordered to do so. The War Cabinet's decision should reach Singapore within thirty-six hours of the receipt of a report that the Japanese were on the move.[16]

Of course Brooke-Popham would 'launch the operation without delay', but how was he to interpret 'a report that the Japanese were on the move' as a basis for notifying the War Cabinet? Was Matador to be launched as soon as there was a Japanese fleet presence in the Gulf of Siam? An increasingly anxious Brooke-Popham reminded the Chiefs of Staff yet again on 27 November that Matador must have fair warning. The enemy could, he warned, stage a landing on the Kra Isthmus within 36 hours of its embarkation from Saigon. Under these circumstances, given the same time span needed by London to make its decision, and then relay it to him, the Japanese would have already landed—Matador would have thus become redundant.

Events now moved quickly. On 1 December, Brooke-Popham was informed that the Americans had been asked to commit armed support if the British contested a Japanese incursion on the Kra Isthmus. The following day, he received notification that the pro-Japanese faction of the Siamese Government had suggested to the Japanese that they invade Malaya at Kota Bharu, which would cause the British to enter Siam, and should that occur, it would declare war upon Britain. Two days later, Brooke-Popham intimated to the Chiefs of Staff that such a contingency would make the desire for the avoidance of war with Japan unnecessary, as he believed that an attack upon Kota Bharu would occur simultaneously with an assault upon Singora. Should this happen, he requested the authority to implement Matador.

On 5 December 1941, the Commander-in-Chief received a much more intelligible reply to his repeated requests—and a welcome one. The Americans, he was told, had finally made a commitment. Kirby has stated that Matador was:

> . . . conditional on the Japanese attacking British territory, or the Netherlands East Indies, or on 'Matador' being undertaken either to forestall a Japanese landing on the Isthmus of Kra or as a reply to a violation of any other part of Siamese territory. Accordingly with the approval of the War Cabinet they told him that he could order 'Matador' without reference to Whitehall, should the Japanese violate any part of Siam, or if there were good information that a Japanese expedition was advancing with the apparent intention of landing on the Isthmus of Kra.[17]

From 5 December—for two critical days—having been granted the independence to make a defining Matador decision, which he had repeatedly pleaded for, Brooke-Popham vacillated. On receipt of the telegram, his Chief of Staff reportedly stated that: 'They've made you personally responsible for declaring war upon Japan.'[18] Brooke-Popham would later state that 'I considered it my duty to be scrupulously careful in acting on the telegram of the 5th of December.'[19] The intelligence gathered and passed on to him on

6 December should have been the signal to instigate Matador. 6 December was the day—the day to move decisively. Given the time needed to move his troops into Thailand, any decision after that day would prove too late. But as Kirby has stated, Brooke-Popham demurred and 'took counsel of his fears'.[20] He signalled his recent intelligence to Admiral Phillips, who had flown to Manila to confer with Admiral Hart and General Douglas MacArthur.

Brooke-Popham's 'fears' must have been heightened on 7 December by an emphatic appeal from the British Siam Ambassador, Sir Josiah Crosby, not to violate Siamese sovereignty. Crosby maintained that Siam would remain pro-British provided the Japanese made the first move. His plea should have fallen on deaf ears. The whole concept of the British defence of Malaya lay on the assumption that the RAF would deliver a mauling of the Japanese at sea or at their landing points, and that, any enemy landings at Singora and Patani would be contested at Singora itself, and at the Ledge. In the military sense, Siamese blessings—or condemnation—meant little if the Japanese attacked first and gained their beachheads. It remains the contention of this work, however, that Matador was a poor plan because it did not allow for the below-standard training of the troops chosen to implement it; that the time factor between reconnaissance in the north-east monsoon and the arrival of a force at those places was always contingent upon an early and therefore bold decision; and, finally, that the logistical considerations and support for the exercise were beyond the capabilities of Malaya Command. But the real tragedy lay in the fact that Brooke-Popham placed Percival in a tactical halfway house. Percival had totally rejected Simson's sensible suggestions for set-piece defences at defiles right down the Malay Peninsula, and most importantly, a major defence line across the vital ground of southern Johore; he had—with Percival's concurrence—placed his faith in Matador; but when the crunch came and a brave, resolute decision was required, Brooke-Popham quite simply lacked the intestinal fortitude to take it. It had now come to pass that neither option would be enacted: there was to be no Matador, nor an in-depth set-piece defence of the peninsula or of a principal line in Johore.

Percival had regarded the cable from London on 5 December giving Brooke-Popham freedom to order Matador as 'news of the first importance'. So vital was this information that he 'decided to go to Kuala Lumpur the following day ... to discuss it with Heath'.[21] At around 3.15 pm, Percival received a message that two convoys had been sighted, and, looking at a map with his corps commander, came to the obvious conclusion that if the Japanese maintained their course, Singora must be their landing point. He wrote that: '... after all it seemed, we had got the news in time and should be able to put Matador into operation'.[22] General Heath immediately ordered the first degree of readiness for his III Indian Corps, and believing that Matador was about to be staged, further ordered Major-General Murray Lyon and his 11th Indian Division to be ready to move at short notice. Percival returned by plane to Singapore that night. Ever the gentleman and always understated, Percival, in his *The War in Malaya*, made the point that given the numbers of Japanese ships sighted he was 'a little surprised to find that Matador had not been ordered'.[23] The next few days were to be full of surprises—the 'bull' was about to instigate a war and run riot before the arrival of a feeble 'Matador'. We have outlined the air reconnaissance of 7 December and Brooke-Popham and Percival's agreement at around 10.30 pm to again not order the operation. By then it was too late.

At around midnight on 8 December 1941, three Japanese troop transports carrying 7 550 troops of the 42nd Infantry Regiment and their support units left the main convoy and, sailing on a south-eastern course in pitching seas, headed towards Pitani.

At 2.00 am the main Japanese convoy carrying the 25th Army's forward operational HQ and its 5th Division—less the Patani detachment and the 21st Regiment—and numbering around 13 500 troops dropped anchor opposite Singora beach. The first intimation the Japanese had as to the accuracy of their arrival was the intermittent flashing of Singora's lighthouse. Lieutenant-Colonel Tsuji remembered that: 'The seas were at least three metres high—possibly higher. In peacetime manoeuvres men would not have been exposed to the danger of transhipment in such circumstances. It seemed that the boats would be swamped as they lay alongside.' And then later: 'In the dim moonlight the launching of the boats had somehow proved easier than had been thought possible. Soon the next signal light appeared. "Commence transhipment."'[24]

Tsuji landed at 4.00 am. Siamese resistance ended within a matter of hours. Although Ambassador Crosby's plea for a Japanese instigation

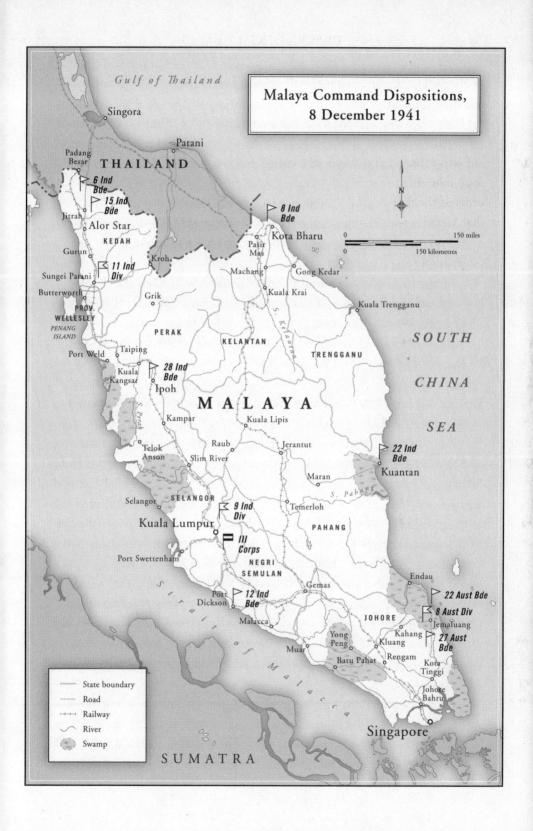

Malaya Command Dispositions,
8 December 1941

of hostilities in Siam had come to pass, it would prove a most empty and costly concession.

Further down the coast at the market town of Patani, the Japanese 5th Division's 42nd Infantry Regiment (with artillery and engineers in support) landed at dawn on 8 December. Lieutenant-Colonel Tsuji would later write that:

> . . . the men of the detachment began to disembark on the beach at Patani, from which they had to drive the Thai Army, which resisted strongly . . .
>
> Once ashore it was found that the roads were bad and the mountains precipitous. Progress was slow, for determined resistance had to be broken down. The results of this assault were however remarkable; it drove a powerful wedge into the enemy's flank and made the operations on the main front much easier.[25]

Despite this initial stiff resistance, the Japanese operation was a resounding success, and the Patani airfield was captured quite quickly.

Thirty minutes prior to Tsuji's landing at Singora, radar at Mersing and then Changi identified planes at a range of about 220 kilometres from Singapore Town. This gave a thirty-minute warning to the city. The three services reacted to the warning, but Singapore's lights were still glowing as nine Japanese bombers, flying at 12 000 feet, made a pass over the city to draw anti-aircraft fire away from eight others that bombed the town from about 5000 feet.[26] 'Little or no damage' was done during an attack on Seletar airfield, while three of No. 34 Squadron's Blenheim bombers on Tengah were damaged and the runway cratered.[27] Three Buffalo fighters, ready to engage the Japanese, were denied permission to take off for fear of friendly anti-aircraft fire.[28] Around 200 civilian casualties were caused by the bombing of Raffles Place and Chinatown, of which around 60 were fatalities.

There is some conjecture as to why Singapore Town was not blacked out during the raid. Two theories are offered. The first is that the Air Raid Precautions HQ was not manned, while the second states that this HQ was indeed manned, but that the head warden—the only person with the key—had gone out to a late-night movie. Thompson, in his *The Battle for Singapore*, seems to offer credible evidence as to the latter theory.[29] Brooke-Popham would claim in his postwar despatch that the absence of a blackout had little bearing on the Japanese bombing of Singapore owing to a full moon that night which assisted the Japanese pilots' identification of both the coast and town. The reader is left to ponder the political and military reaction had a head warden failed in his duty, or an Air Raid Precautions HQ been unmanned, during air raids over London or Coventry. The truth is that the civil authorities in Singapore—and the military—were still, on 8 December 1941, doing their 'la-di-da'. The next morning, the authorities in Singapore reacted to the bombing by rounding up and interning all Japanese civilians in Malaya and Singapore. Two days later, Duff Cooper assumed the lofty title of Resident Minister for Far Eastern Affairs, which had as its brief, political advice for military commanders; the settling of emergency matters on the spot; the power under emergency circumstances to authorise departmental heads to spend monies without permission from London; and lastly, to preside over the War Council.

Lying approximately eight kilometres from the coast on the Kelantan River, and only about 20 kilometres from the Siamese border, Kota Bharu was, in December 1941, of critical importance to the air defence of Malaya. About two-and-a-half kilometres behind the town lay the main airfield from which the twelve Hudsons of No. 1 Squadron RAAF and six Vildebeestes of 36 Squadron RAF were stationed. The airfield at Gong Kedah with its Vildebeestes of 100 Squadron RAF was a mere 40 kilometres to the south-east of Kota Bharu, while the unoccupied Machang airfield was about 28 kilometres to the west of Gong Kedah.

Brigadier William Key's 8th Indian Brigade (of Major-General Barstow's 9th Indian Division) was charged with the defence of Kota Bharu. Key had deployed his brigade along 48 kilometres of beach front. His 3/17th Dogras occupied a sixteen-kilometre front south of the Kelantan River, of which the area between the beaches of Badang and Sabak was considered his vital ground. Each of these beaches was manned by a company of the Dogras and consisted of lines of concrete pillboxes, wire entanglements, machine

gun posts, both anti-tank and anti-personnel mines, and some dug-in
artillery support. Key's 2/10th Baluchis—charged with the defence of
the Gong Kedah and Machang airfields—occupied a far longer stretch
of beach which was not fortified to anything like the standard of the 3/17th
Dogras' vital ground. One sixteen-kilometre area contained nothing more
than dummy pillboxes. Brigadier Key also had the 1st Hyderabads and
1st Mysore State Force Infantry to further safeguard the three airfields,
while the 2/12th Frontier Force (detached from the 22nd Brigade) and the
1/13th Frontier Force Rifles acted as his reserve.

At about 11.45 pm on 7 December 1941—only an hour before Admiral
Nagumo's carrier task force aircraft initiated their attack upon Pearl
Harbor—the transports *Awagisan Maru*, *Ayatosan Maru* and *Sakura Maru*
carrying Major-General Hiroshi Takumi's 5300 soldiers of the 56th Regiment,
18th Division (and supporting units) anchored about three kilometres off
Sabang and Badang beaches. The three transports were escorted by two
cruisers and four destroyers. If Key regarded this beach frontage as his vital
ground, the Japanese prized it no less. They regarded the Kota Bharu airfield
just to the rear of the beaches as the major potential obstacle to a successful
landing.

As had occurred at Singora heavy seas made the task of loading the troops
into their barges a difficult one. At 12.45 am, as the barges began their trip in
under a barrage from the Japanese warships, they were met by a combination
of shell fire from the dug-in eighteen-pounders and machine gun fire from
the Indian pillboxes. Although some barges were either sunk or damaged
and casualties taken, the death toll was greatest on the beaches as the troops
landed. Here, amidst the wire entanglements, concentrated machine gun fire
and mines—and lack of cover—the Japanese sustained heavy losses. But a
number of barges were steered through the creek mouth between the two
beaches, and it was through this passage, that the Japanese were able to eventually gain the rear of the pillboxes. Eventually, as enemy soldiers both in the
front and in the rear intensified their assaults and gained ground through the
Indians' minefield, hand-to-hand fighting ensued. Lieutenant-Colonel Tsuji:
'Hand-grenades flew and bayonets flashed, and amid the sound of warcries
and calls of distress, in a cloud of black smoke the enemy's front line was
captured.'[30]

Lieutenant-General Sir William Dobbie (centre) when Governor of Malta. (AWM MED0411)

Lieutenant-General Bond (AWM 007912)

Major-General Keith Simmons (left) and Air Chief Marshal Sir Robert Brooke-Popham.
(AWM 134879)

Lieutenant-General A.E. Percival (left) (AWM 134877)

The Governor of Singapore (left), Sir Shenton Thomas, and Lady Thomas (centre) welcome the 22nd Brigade AIF to Singapore. Lieutenant-General Bond is behind Lady Shenton. (AWM 005908)

Major-General Gordon Bennett, GOC 8th Division AIF. (AWM 003616)

Brigadier H.B. Taylor, OC 22nd Brigade AIF. (AWM 005512)

Lieutenant-Colonel H. Rourke, 8th Division HQ. (AWM 001507)

Lieutenant-Colonel Broadbent (left) and Lieutenant-Colonel J.E. Thyer, 8th Divisions HQ. (AWM 005516)

Major-General Gordon Bennett (left) and Major-General Murray Lyon, GOC 11th Indian Division. (AWM 005954)

Lieutenant-General Tomoyuki Yamashita, GOC 25th Japanese Army. (AWM 127911)

Colonel Masanobu Tsuji, Chief of Operations and Planning, 25th Japanese Army.

Colonel (later Brigadier) I. Simson, Chief Engineer, Malaya Command, in 1938. (AWM 145317)

Lieutenant-Colonel Frederick 'Black Jack' Galleghan, CO 2/30th Battalion, with Sergeant Heckendorf (left). (AWM 011304/04)

Lieutenant-Colonel J. Robertson, CO 2/29th Battalion. (Courtesy Andrew Warland)

Lieutenant-Colonel Robertson and his senior officers: (left to right back) Captain Sumner, Major Olliff; (left to right front) Captain Bowring, Robertson, Captain Morgan, unknown, Captain Maher. (Courtesy Andrew Warland)

Sergeant Charlie Parson's gun in action at Bakri. (AWM 068592)

Bakri—the devastation in the cutting. (AWM 011301)

WO Bert Mettam, 2/29th Battalion. (Courtesy Ric Mettam)

Corporal Bob Christie, 2/29th Battalion. (Courtesy 2/29th Battalion Association)

Corporal Jim Kennedy (back) and Corporal John Roxburgh, 2/29th Battalion. (Courtesy 2/29th Battalion Association)

Private Jim Kerr, 4th Anti-tank Regiment. (Courtesy Jim Kerr)

Lieutenant-Colonel C. Anderson VC, CO 2/19th Battalion. (AWM 012562)

Lieutenant Jim Howard, 2/19th Battalion. (Courtesy Jim Howard)

Private Gus Halloran, 2/19th Battalion. (Courtesy Mrs J. Halloran)

Private Jim Stewart, 2/19th Battalion. (Courtesy Leanne Kerschler)

Lieutenant-Colonel A. Boyes, 2/26th Battalion. (Courtesy Mrs V. Linton-Smith)

Lieutenant-Colonel A. Varley, CO 2/18th Battalion. (AWM 005515)

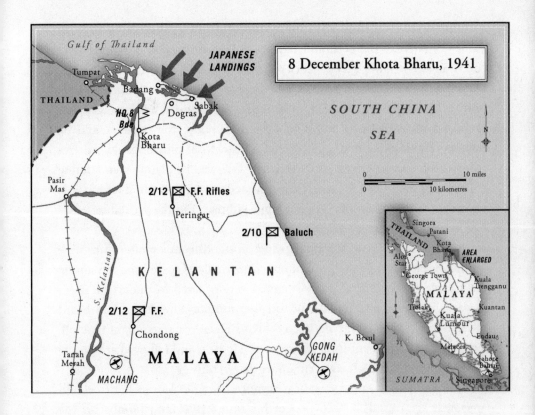

Not long after midnight, while these events were unfolding, Wing Commander Davis, the RAAF on-duty controller at Kota Bharu, received a call from Brigadier Key's HQ alerting him to the sighting of three small vessels moving slowly just off shore. At about 12.30 am, just as he received authority from Singapore to stage a reconnaissance of the area, Davis heard the Japanese shelling of the Dogras' beach perimeter. Almost immediately, the enemy shelling was confirmed by Key's HQ and Davis was further told that transports 'could be seen lying off shore apparently preparing to land troops'.[31] This should have been the moment for decisive action, but Davis was prohibited by an order banning offensive action without authority from Singapore—even if a convoy had been discovered. Douglas Gillison: 'In Singapore Air Chief Marshal Brooke-Popham received the news in his office at the naval base. After a hurried conference with Air Vice-Marshal Pulford he ordered an immediate offensive against the Japanese ships with all No. 1 Squadron's available Hudsons.'[32]

Many great moments in history are preceeded by a superfluous, bureaucratic conference. Davis should have been free to use his initiative—and
common sense—when both the Japanese presence and intent were so
blatantly obvious. Given that Brooke-Popham and Percival, and a whole
host of appreciations stretching over years, not months, had unanimously
predicted Kota Bharu as a Japanese landing point, the reader could be
forgiven for thinking that a shelling of a beachfront only a few kilometres
from a strategically prized airfield, closely followed by plainly seen landing
craft, might have been the catalyst for immediate action from a responsible
officer on the spot. Brooke-Popham and Pulford, and the procedures they
had in place, deserve severe censure.

Seven Hudsons were bombed up and on stand-by as a matter of routine
at this moment, while the ground crews hurriedly prepared the remaining
serviceable planes.[33] The Hudson crews were ordered to undertake independent low-level attacks. At 2.08 am—90 minutes after Davis had heard
the shell fire at the Dogras' perimeter—No 1 Squadron's first flight took off,
led by Flight Lieutenant John Lockwood's Hudson and followed at two-or-
three-minute intervals by the remaining six aircraft.

Lockwood's first target was the transport *Awagisan Maru*. On his second
approach at around 50 feet, two of his four 250-pound bombs hit the
transport amidships. During these Hudson attacks the *Awagisan Maru* was
hit again and later abandoned to sink—sustaining around 40 dead and 70
wounded—while hits were also scored upon the third transport, causing a
casualty count of three dead and sixteen wounded. The bombing and strafing
of the Japanese transports and barges continued throughout the early hours
of 8 December. When at 5.00 am, Wing Commander Davis called a break
in the operation so that his aircraft could refuel, rearm and be inspected for
damage, interrogation of his crews revealed that one of the Japanese transports had been blown up (the *Awagisan Maru*) and that 24 barges had been
either overturned or sunk.[34] Troop casualties either on the transports or in
the landing barges are not known, but must have been significant.

Alan Warren, in his *Singapore 1942*, makes the important point that the
Hudson operations on the night of 8 December 'badly disrupted the disem-
barkation of the third and final wave of infantry'.[35] He also gives an example
of how little time it took for the Hudsons to deliver their bomb loads, strafe

the enemy barges and return to Kota Bharu airfield—'in less time that it takes to smoke a cigarette'.[36] Warren is referring to an account given by Flying Officer Don Dowie, who was the only survivor of Flight Lieutenant Ramshaw's Hudson which was shot down during its second strike: 'We took off and bombed the convoy. The entire mission must have taken only a few minutes as when we landed from the first run, I realised that I was still smoking the same cigarette I had lit just before take off.'[37] If Warren is correct in his assessment that the Hudsons of No. 1 Squadron attacked the third wave of Japanese troops at Kota Bharu—and the sequence of timing between the first shelling of the beach (around midnight) and the time that the Hudsons were first airborne (at 2.08 am) would seem to support his view—then given that one sortie might be over in 'the time it takes to smoke a cigarette' what damage upon the Japanese shipping and landing infantry might have been accomplished had the Hudsons been allowed to contest the first wave of barges and their rearward transports? The time taken between Davis requesting permission to undertake the obvious, and Brooke-Popham and Pulford's permission to be given, was absolutely critical to the Japanese landing at Kota Bharu. It had been the first Japanese infantry wave that had understandably floundered on the beaches in the face of the Dogras' intense shell, machine gun fire, wire entanglements and mines, and therefore, had the first sorties of Hudsons contested the landing earlier (ideally against the first wave), far greater carnage may have been inflicted. Nonetheless, the performance of the Hudsons of No. 1 Squadron RAAF on the night of 8 December 1941 was exemplary.

At dawn the next morning, with the Japanese having driven a wedge between the Dogras on Badang and Sabak beaches, Brigadier Key tried to reinforce them with the 1/13th Frontier rifles at Badang, and the 2/12th Frontier Regiment at Sabak, with the intention of them linking and destroying the intervening enemy troops in the 'wedge'. The attacks failed, largely because the arrival of the reinforcements was delayed by several creeks behind the beaches. When a further effort later in the morning met the same fate, the situation on the coast at Kota Bharu remained obscure.

At around 6.00 am on the morning of 8 December 1941, a Hudson reconnaissance flight confirmed that the Japanese fleet, with nine bombers now screening them, was retiring from Kota Bharu. Just before it landed, the Hudson also reported that there were numerous power-driven Japanese boats off shore and further confirmed the position of a disabled and burning transport. In response to this reconnaissance, Vildebeestes from Kota Bharu and Kuantan flew off in heavy rain to attempt a torpedo attack upon the retiring Japanese ships. They were unsuccessful.

At dawn three flights of Hudsons from No. 8 Squadron RAAF and eight Blenheims of No. 60 Squadron RAF left in heavy fog from Kuantan to the Japanese landing points at Kota Bharu. A bombing of the already disabled and still blazing *Awagisan Maru* and some strafing of landing craft continued for some time before one flight picked up a message from the control room at Kota Bharu ordering that the Hudsons leave the landing sight and detect and attack the retiring Japanese convoy. But a heavy rain storm shielded the Japanese vessels and the Hudsons thereby returned to Kota Bharu to continue their attacks at the landing site.

On the morning of 8 December, the Japanese took the air war to the RAF and RAAF with an aircraft performance and a level of pilot skill that made an instant impression on their enemy. Brooke-Popham's assertion given to the Australians in Canberra in February 1941 that the Japanese were 'not air minded'—and especially against 'determined opposition'—was cruelly shattered. Kota Bharu was their first target. Just after 9.00 am, navy 'Zeros' and army 'Nates' flying in formations of five to ten fighters arrived over the airfield. Douglas Gillison:

... "peeling off" at between 5,000 and 7,000 feet, [they] dived recklessly to fire their guns from almost tree-top level. The enemy pilots left the defenders of the airfield in no doubt of their skill in handling their aircraft. The first attacks were against the anti-aircraft posts, but later they concentrated on men and aircraft on the ground. From then on, at intervals throughout the day, these raids continued and though casualties were few they greatly hampered the work of the maintainance crews and the aircrews landing and taking off.[38]

The above-described attack(s) upon Kota Bharu airfield were matched in both timing and ferocity across the main airfields of northern Malaya.

In the west the airfield of Sungei Patani was attacked with the loss of two Buffaloes destroyed and six others damaged, while at Alor Star four Blenheims were destroyed and a further five damaged. By the morning of 9 December the remaining planes and pilots of those two airfields had been understandably ordered back to Butterworth. And that evening, the total aggregate of serviceable bombers and fighters was ten. On the east coast, in addition to the attacks made at Kota Bharu, Gong Kedah and Machang were bombed and soon evacuated. At Kota Bharu the evacuation of aircraft and personnel was marked by a degree of confusion over the presence of enemy troops either at or near the airfield. Amidst some confusion, the aircraft were flown off, the buildings were set ablaze, but the station's petrol and ammunition dumps were mistakenly left for the enemy.

If there was a degree of disorder over the possible presence of enemy infantry at Kota Bharu, no such immediate threat existed at the airfields to the west. When Sungei Patani was abandoned by its ground crews on 8 December, and Kuantan two days later, the Japanese were presented with both airfields' supplies of petrol, oil and surplus stores. But at Alor Star, the denial to the enemy of the same commodities was so rigorously undertaken that the resulting explosions and dark smoke cloud caused unease amongst the troops forward of the airfield. The army now issued orders that all future destruction of petrol and oil would be undertaken by simply opening the tanks, and further, that all required demolitions must be left to them.

Within 24 hours the Japanese had crippled their enemy's ability to wage an effective air war in northern Malaya. They often coordinated their attacks with either the departure or arrival of planes at those fields, or attacked as they were on the ground being rearmed. Moreover, by employing lighter bombs loads that were effective in the destruction of aircraft and the killing and maiming of personnel, but which caused less damage to the airfields themselves, the Japanese further displayed proficiency in both the planning and execution of a modern air war. In *The War in Malaya*, General Percival best summed up the war in the air on that first fateful day:

The rapidity with which the Japanese got their attacks going against our aerodromes was quite remarkable. Practically all the aerodromes in Kelatan, Kedah, Province Wellesley, and Panang, were attacked, and in most cases the bombers were escorted by fighters.

The performance of Japanese aircraft of all types, and the accuracy of their bombing, came as an unpleasant surprise. By the evening our own air force had already been seriously weakened.[39]

To Percival, these events might well have come 'as an unpleasant surprise', but they should not have been such to the senior officers in the RAF in Singapore—nor Brooke-Popham. At the outbreak of hostilities, there were but four radar stations in operation in Malaya and Singapore, and none of these were in northern Malaya; adequate anti-aircraft guns for airfield protection had still not yet been supplied; the internal communication system was inadequate; and, when these limiting factors were allied to the poor quality and number of British aircraft, the inexperience of most aircrews when compared with the Japanese, the crushing defeat in the skies—and destruction of aircraft on the ground—on 8 December 1941 is not hard to fathom. Douglas Gillison has recorded that by the end of that first fateful day Brooke-Popham had:

... sent a telegram to the British chiefs of Staff warning them that it was unlikely that the R.A.F. air effort could be maintained as it then was for more than two or three weeks, and asking that air reinforcements should be sent urgently, particularly two squadrons of long-range bombers and two squadrons of night fighters.[40]

And all this within 24 hours.

While these events in the air war had been in train, Brigadier Key and his 8th Indian Brigade had had a testing time. General Barstow had authorised Key to withdraw from his Kota Bharu dispositions should he deem it necessary. By around 8.00 pm on 8 December, with the airfield abandoned and therefore the chief reason for his presence on and near his beaches gone, Key decided to stage a withdrawal north of the town, while his southward 2/10th Baluch were to also withdraw inland to Peringat. It was a tough movement for exhausted troops who, amidst the confusion and obstacles of heavy rain, darkness, the crossing of numerous streams and swamps, poor communications and some contact with enemy patrols, arrived at their new positions around dawn on 9 December. But when the Japanese aggressively followed up his withdrawal and began to infiltrate his new lines, Key staged a further movement in stages to the line Peringat–Mulong. There was a fortunate lull in the fighting the next day, which enabled Key to recover small parties of his troops who had been cut off or lost during the withdrawal. On this day, so as to protect his tenuous line of communication, he wisely staged a further withdrawal to a position just south of Machang, along the way having carried out demolitions at Gong Kedah and at Machang airfields and upon roads and the railway. During 11 December, this 48-kilometre withdrawal had been completed. And it had been fortunately aided by little contact with the enemy.

But while these events had been unfolding, a massive disaster had befallen the British defence of Malaya and Singapore.

9

BAD NEWS FOR
THE HOUSE

On 28 November 1941, after his arrival at Colombo aboard the *Prince of Wales*, Admiral Phillips had been ordered by the Admiralty to fly to Singapore—where he had welcomed his flagship and the *Repulse*—and subsequently to Manila on 4 December, for conferences with the American, Dominion and Dutch admirals regarding the coordination of naval forces in the Far East. But when news reached him on 6 December that reconnaissance flights that day had revealed a Japanese presence off Siam, Phillips departed by plane that night for Singapore. He arrived there on the 7th.

The events during the roughly 30-hour period from Phillips's arrival back in Singapore to his departure aboard the *Prince of Wales* during the late afternoon of 8 December are clouded in some controversy. In the British Official History, Kirby stated that:

Admiral Phillips called a meeting on board the *Prince of Wales* at 12.30 p.m. on the 8th which was attended by his Chief of Staff (Rear-Admiral A.F.E. Palliser), the Captain of the Fleet (Captain L.H. Bell), the Captains of the *Prince of Wales* (Captain J.C. Leach) and *Repulse* (Captain W.G. Tennant) and staff officers.[1]

But Brian Montgomery, in his biography of Sir Shenton Thomas, relates a claim by Lieutenant Commander J. McClelland, who was the Singapore Navy Base signals officer at the time, of a prior meeting called by Admiral Phillips. McClelland has stated that Phillips called this meeting in the War Room at the base at 2.30 am on 8 December. According to McClelland, those present were: the Commander-in-Chief, Sir Robert Brooke-Popham, and his Naval liaison officer; Phillips and two of his staff officers; Air Vice-Marshal Pulford; a brigadier and colonel from Percival's HQ; Sir Shenton Thomas and two civil servants; Commanders Goodenough and Beardsworth Royal Navy; and Commander Greening, Royal Navy, staff officer to Admiral Layton.[2]

McClelland stated that he was asked by Admiral Layton to sit in his 'signal officer's cubby-hole' at the far end of the War Room, and hopefully undetected by the participants, take notes of the meeting. Further, McClelland recorded that after the war Layton had told him that he was afraid at the time of Phillips's intention to organise a Force Z operation against the Japanese, when, in fact, Layton believed that the only sensible course of action was to have the fleet put to sea and avoid a quite likely air or naval—or both—confrontation with the Japanese. Such an operation was, he considered, doomed at the outset by the vulnerable composition of the Eastern Fleet. It had no aircraft carrier protection or strike capability and could hardly rely on the RAF in Malaya and Singapore to protect it. It is significant that Layton's tenure as the senior naval commander in Singapore had ceased at midnight, thereby now making Phillips the senior Royal Navy commander at this gathering. He had therefore called this meeting two-and-a-half hours after taking over. McClelland also stated that no minutes of the meeting were kept.

During his opening appreciation, McClelland recorded that he (Phillips) believed that the Japanese would not deploy carriers or capital ships in Malayan waters against him so long as the US Fleet remained in the region and operational. At this juncture, the news of the Japanese attack upon Pearl Harbor had not reached Singapore. Further, Phillips stated that his main concern centred upon enemy submarine attacks and aircraft assaults. Concerning the latter, he believed that high-level bombing was no great risk, given the quality and volume of his ships' anti-aircraft fire and the anticipated difficulties in enemy accuracy. Japanese dive-bombing missions did, he felt, offer a greater concern, but not debilitating enough to cripple either the *Prince of Wales* or *Repulse*. The torpedo bomber, claimed Phillips, was the principal air threat to any capital ship, and as such, his chief defence against it would have two components. The first consisted of a fighter escort that might attack torpedo aircraft at their most exposed time—during the descent to torpedo dropping height. The second was the north-east monsoon, whereby the often unpredictable and intermittent low cloud, heavy rain, storms and poor visibility—particularly over the sea—might not only make the coordination of simultaneous attacks by formations of torpedo bombers difficult, but also shield his presence, and therefore make his detection by enemy reconnaissance harder.[3]

Phillips finished by stating that if the Royal Navy's present obligation was the preservation of the fleet, then the logical course of action was to retire to the west and await reinforcements. Montgomery then quotes McClelland's record of the reactions by those present to Phillips's appreciation.

Shenton Thomas displayed his ignorance as to the original shortcomings of the composition of Force Z by stating that he did not realise that the battleships constituted nothing more than a British 'bluff', and, given the difficulties outlined by Admiral Phillips, suggested that London be contacted immediately to find out what the Admiralty thought should be done. Brooke-Popham, according to McClelland, rejected this outright and pointed out that he still believed that the Japanese had Thailand as their objective. Pulford then spoke, pointing out the deficiencies in his aircraft and the poor training of his pilots in a fighter protection role for Phillips's ships, but nonetheless pledged his support for the Admiral's plan—'whatever that might be'.[4] Pulford then left the gathering. At this point, Shenton Thomas again expressed doubt concerning any operation using the capital ships against submarines without additional destroyer support, and suggested that if air support could not be guaranteed, that the ships should not be used in any offensive capacity. With Pulford now absent, Thomas looked to Brooke-Popham for a reaction. None was forthcoming. Then, according to McClelland, the Commander-in-Chief made an extraordinary remark: 'Do you know, Admiral, that I am beginning to believe that *if* the Japanese intend to attack, your intervention is the only thing that can prevent the invasion succeeding.'[5] This was an extraordinary statement from a

Commander-in-Chief before the outbreak of hostilities. Brooke-Popham's verbose and false assessments over a considerable period of time regarding the RAF's ability to contest a Japanese invasion, and his equally flawed rating of his enemy, now appeared to evaporate behind the plans of a risky naval operation, where critical land-based fighter support for Force Z might not, therefore, be guaranteed. The meeting was soon broken up by the already discussed first Japanese air raid on Singapore.

McClelland also claimed that Phillips then cipher-telegrammed his intentions to the Admiralty at around 6.00 am on 8 December. He further asserted that London acknowledged that signal at 9.30 am. McClelland's account concludes with another interesting observation:

> Phillips must have been aware that he was taking a risk, which was impossible to calculate, with two valuable ships. He may have hoped to receive the comments of the Admiralty on his intentions, as expressed in the signal which I sent for him. But he would most certainly have wished to give the First Sea Lord time to instruct him (Phillips) NOT [sic] to take the risk, if, for reasons not known to him, Admiral Pound did not wish him to take it. But Phillips received no reaction to his signal [sic].[6]

Admiral Tom Phillips decided to put Force Z to sea late on 8 December. By then his available intelligence pointed to Singora as the main Japanese landing site. Accordingly, Phillips decided that Force Z would contest those landings, and, further believed that his enemy's fleet opposition might consist of one battleship—probably the *Kongo*—and around seven cruisers and twenty destroyers.[7] Weighing up the dangers from Japanese land-based torpedo and bombing sorties, and the ever-present possibility of submarine attacks, against the chance of Force Z being able to inflict great destruction upon the Japanese transports and their escorts, Phillips chose to take the risk. In this decision, he was supported by all the Royal Navy officers at his later naval conference. Perhaps Phillips and those officers considered that the navy should act and act decisively, and not be charged with leaving the fight to the air force and army. Such a potential charge to a man like 'the Cock-sparrow', or the 'Pocket Napoleon' would most certainly have rankled.

While Singora lies 720 kilometres by direct sea route from Singapore, Admiral Phillips's plan entailed a total sailing distance of 1120 kilometres to that destination. Leaving Singapore on the night of 8 December the *Prince of Wales*, *Repulse* and the destroyers—*Electra*, *Express*, *Tenedos* and *Vampire*— sailed eastwards and around the Anambas Islands, with the purpose of minimising contact with enemy submarines and minefields. It was also hoped that such a course might avoid aircraft reconnaissance patrols during daylight the following day. In this, Phillips hoped that the predicted north-east monsoon weather might also conceal his passage. If all went according to plan, he anticipated that his final approach to Singora would occur under the cover of darkness during the night 9–10 December, which would see him arrive at dawn with the advantage of surprise. Phillips anticipated that should all of this come to pass, his real problem would then be his escape from his area of operations under long-range bomber attacks. G. Hermon Gill has outlined Admiral Phillips's requested air support from Air Vice-Marshal Pulford for the above plan: '. . . air reconnaissance 100 miles [160 kilometres] ahead of the fleet throughout daylight on the 9th; air reconnaissance along the coast from Kota Bharu to beyond Singora from dawn on the 10th; and fighter cover over the fleet off Singora from daylight on the 10th.'[8]

The RAF replied that its reconnaissance request for 9 December would be met, but 'there was doubt as to the ability to supply it on the 10th, and greater doubt that fighter cover could be made available off Singora'.[9] But this air support was so critical to any chance that Phillips had of success that he had personally written to Pulford before sailing, strongly emphasising the importance of his Singora fighter cover. As Force Z passed the Changi signal station, the Admiral received the RAF reply: 'regret fighter protection impossible.'[10] He is reputed to have said, 'Well, we must get on without it.'

Force Z had initial good fortune on 9 December. After having successfully rounded the Anambas Islands under low cloud cover and rain, the ships turned northwards in the early afternoon, with the weather still shielding them. Later that afternoon a Japanese submarine discovered them. But Admiral Tom Phillips's luck had not deserted him yet. Either by a wrong transmission of the fleet's position or by a navigation fault, the Japanese—on this occasion also slow to receive the signal in Saigon—acted on a reported position that was some 224 kilometres off the mark. The resulting enemy strike planes in Saigon, which had hurriedly been rearmed from bombs to torpedoes, left there just before sunset, but failed to find Force Z. A further attempt by the ships *Haruna* and *Kongo* and two heavy cruisers which rendez-voused with the 7th Cruiser Squadron at around 2.30 am also failed to locate Phillips because of the faulty intelligence.

At around 7.00 pm on 9 December Force Z reached a position about 480 kilometres east of Singora. Phillips now changed course to the west, and increased his speed from around 18 knots to 20 knots with the intention of an attack upon Japanese shipping just after dawn with the *Prince of Wales* and *Repulse*. The destroyers 'would be detached to a rendezvous off the Anambas Islands at 10 pm'.[11] With no fighter cover, Admiral Phillips knew that he had but one potential operational ally: surprise. It was jeopardised just after he had steamed for Singora, when HMAS *Vampire* signalled a possible sighting of one enemy aircraft, and then that critical element of surprise was shat-tered by three enemy aircraft, which began to shadow his ships in clearing skies. Phillips knew immediately that his Singora attack was now an unwise venture, and turned away south-east at 20 knots for the Anambas Islands. He also ordered the destroyer *Tenedos* to break from the convoy and head straight for Singapore, and at 8.00 am the next morning to signal that Force Z would arrive off those islands at around 6.00 am on 11 December. During this critical time, Phillips received two signals from Singapore. The first stated that air reconnaissance had found one enemy battleship, eleven destroyers and transports off Kota Bharu, while the second signal—and a far more disturbing one—intimated that the enemy had occupied the airstrip at Kota Bharu; were bombing and strafing all northern Malayan dromes rendering them unsustainable, and that Brooke-Popham was 'hinting' that all of his air resources would henceforth be required to protect 'the Singapore area'. Further, Phillips was informed that the enemy now had the 'undisturbed' ability to attack him with land-based bombers from Saigon within five hours after any reconnaissance sighting of his ships. Within a matter of a few hours, Admiral Phillips's mission had changed from a thus far undetec-ted potential surprise attack, to a desperate escape from an area where the enemy was all-powerful, searching for him, and unhampered by a receding RAF ability to offer him support. As usual, Brooke-Popham was engaged in dithering and 'hints' rather than bold, plain dialogue and action.

We now come to 'the fog of war' in its most sinister form. At around midnight Force Z received another signal from Singapore—'enemy reported landing at Kuantan . . .'. The enemy had not landed at Kuantan. In what was later to become known in some circles as 'Blitzkrieg night', panic and resulting indiscriminate firing at a non-existent enemy had ensued. The source of such chaos would seem to have come from a Hudson's sighting of a merchant ship steaming south around 120 kilometres north of Kuantan, and a separate sighting of a group of ten barges at a similar distance to the south. After III Corps HQ had been notified of these discoveries, Brigadier Painter's 22nd Brigade's 2/18th Royal Garhwal Rifles, who were manning the beaches at Kuantan, were put on full alert. Just after dark the battalion reported barges approaching and requested artillery support, which was given. Brigadier Painter then signalled 9th Division HQ reporting that an attack was anticipated at dawn. Malaya Command responded to this news with the despatch of three Hudsons and six Vildebeestes to attack supporting Japanese ships and contest the 'landing'. The torpedo bombers arrived on the scene at around 4.00 am to find three small boats which were bombed, while the Hudsons arrived to find no targets.

But Admiral Tom Phillips assessed Kuantan in a different light. Engaged in a return passage back from a fruitless mission, he now saw a last chance to influence events. At 12.45 am he steered for Kuantan at 20 knots. In the process, Phillips made two critical errors of judgement: he ordered Force Z to observe strict radio silence and also believed that, as he was now around 720 kilometres from Japanese air bases in Indo-China, he was probably out of range of enemy land-based torpedo bombers. In his first decision, Phillips effectively cut Singapore's ability to know of, and then support, his decision to head for Kuantan, and his second mistake amounted to nothing less than total ignorance of the Japanese aircraft range from Indo-China. Alan Warren, in his *Singapore 1942*, has rightly concluded that: '. . . this calculation was based on the relatively short range of antiquated British torpedo bombers.'[12] The game was now well and truly up.

Unbeknown to Phillips, Force Z had been discovered by a Japanese submarine not long after he had altered his course for Kuantan. Lieutenant Commander Sohichi Kitamura's I–58, despite experiencing trouble with a torpedo tube, managed to get away a spread of five torpedoes which, because of the time lost while repairing the tube, caused the range to be far too great.[13] The torpedoes missed. After receipt of Force Z's new and far-distant position, Admiral Kondo realised that a fleet confrontation with Phillips was not possible, and decided to use the 22nd Air Flotilla's aircraft to stage an air attack.

At 5.00 am on 10 December in an effort to locate Force Z, nine seven-man crew Mitsubishi medium bombers ('Nells'), acting as recce planes, left Saigon, followed by two Mitsubishi reconnaissance planes ('Babs')—each with a two-man crew—which took off from Soc Trang (south of Saigon). These eleven aircraft—with ample range for their task—were ordered to fan out over the area of ocean in which the British ships were known to be sailing. The 22nd Flotilla's strike force set off between 6.30 am and 8.00 am: 25 'Nells' armed with torpedoes; 26 Mitsubishi Bombers (Bettys) also armed with torpedoes; and 34 'Nells' armed with either two 250-kg bombs or one 500-kg armour-piecing bomb.[14] The Japanese strike force flew towards their minefield which had been laid between the Tioman and Anambas Islands, and which Phillips had successfully avoided during Force Z's early passage north. The Japanese pilots hoped at best for their own contact, but failing this, a reconnaissance radio contact from the eleven recce aircraft.

The first contact came at around 8.30 am when the destroyer *Tenedos*, making its way back to Singapore, was sighted by a 'Babs' recce plane. Its two 50-kg bombs fell wide of the mark. But not long after, *Tenedos* was detected again by a much more substantial force—nine 500-kg bomb-laden 'Nells'— which also missed their prey. Not long after Phillips received the destroyer's signal that she was under attack, a 'Nell', on its return from its reconnais-sance limit, saw the much-sought after twin prize. The 'Nell' sent two signals, the first identifying a 'fleet' and its course, and the second, a change in that course; then came a third signal, bearing the electrifying news the Japanese had sought: 'Enemy force escorted by three destroyers. Sailing in regular order, the *Prince of Wales* and *Repulse*.'[15]

At 11.00 am *Repulse* became the first target. Eight 'Nells' each dropped a 250-kg bomb from around 11 500 feet, one of which was a direct hit amid-ships, while two others were 'straddling near misses'.[16] Attacks now began against the *Prince of Wales*, and consisted of waves of two and three torpedo-carrying 'Nells', which managed to score two critical hits. G. Hermon Gill

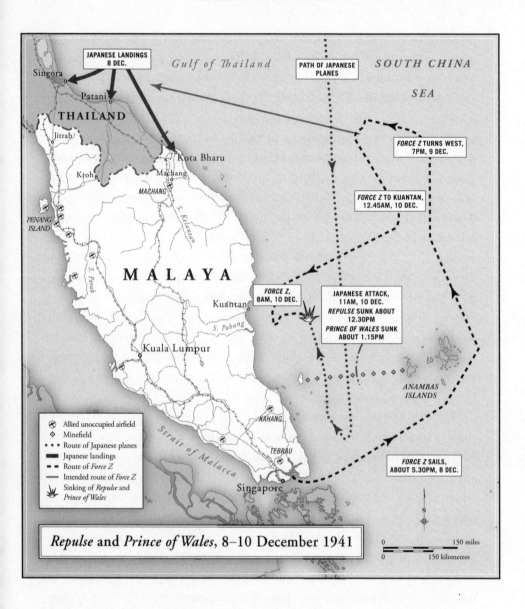

Repulse and **Prince of Wales**, 8–10 December 1941

recorded that: 'Thereafter she was never under complete control. Both port propeller shafts were stopped, reducing her speed considerably; the steering gear was affected; some machinery rooms were flooded; and she took a list to port, with increased trim aft so that the port side of her quarterdeck was soon awash.'[17]

Meanwhile *Repulse* had been attacked by eight 'Bettys' which came in at wave-top height. But Captain Tennant managed to 'comb' the torpedoes. 'Combing' was accomplished by steering the ship parallel to the advancing torpedoes and thereby narrowing their target. It was usually done by either running parallel to the sighted wakes of the torpedoes, or, if these were not visible, attempting to run parallel to the attacking enemy vessel. According to Captain Tennant's report of 11 December 1941, *Repulse* was able to 'comb' around fifteen torpedoes by identifying their wakes. Shortly after this expert effort, Tennant was able to yet again 'comb' another torpedo attack—harder this time because six 'Nells' approached from the port side, while one came in from starboard.

The final attack on Force Z was undertaken by 26 'Bettys' which arrived late over the confrontation. At this juncture *Repulse* was still able to maintain 25 knots and was also able to manoeuvre, but *Prince of Wales* was out of control and handicapped further by over half of her guns being ineffective. Christopher Shores and Brian Cull, in *Bloody Shambles*, have vividly described *Prince of Wales*' next ordeal: 'Of the first six torpedo-bombers which attacked her, four gained hits; the first torpedo struck well forward and blew a hole which erupted through the other side; the second hit just forward of the bridge, a third alongside the rear 14-inch turret while the fourth damaged the outer propeller shaft.'[18] Just before midday Captain Tennant, aware of the damage to *Prince of Wales*, broke radio silence and contacted Singapore for help.

Repulse was now attacked again. This time, at about 12.20 pm, to inhibit her ability to 'comb' their torpedoes, the 'Bettys' approached from a number of bearings. *Repulse* sustained a hit aft which jammed her rudder, and, although still able to make 20 knots, she was now sailing out of control. When she was then hit by a further three torpedoes—one on her starboard side and two on her port—she quickly listed to port and rolled over and sank. The time taken between the onset of the 'Bettys' assault and her disappearance beneath the waves was a mere thirteen minutes. After *Repulse* had capsized, Admiral Phillips ordered HMAS *Vampire* and HMS *Electra* to move in and pick up the survivors. Captain Tennant, eight other officers and 213 sailors were taken aboard *Vampire*, most of whom were suffering from either varying degrees of burns or exposure and shock.[19] *Electra* rescued a further 574 men. This left the final death toll from *Repulse* at 27 officers and 486 ratings.[20]

Meanwhile, about eight kilometres from that scene, the *Prince of Wales* had sustained a further three torpedo hits during the same attack: one aft, another amidships, and the third at the stem (the extension of the keel at the forward end of the ship). But her *coup de grace* was finally delivered by seventeen 'Nells' which, in the face of now reduced anti-aircraft battery fire, dropped their 500-kg bombs from 8500 feet. One hit was taken on the catapult deck, others straddled her, which probably caused further damage, and there were numerous near misses. Although HMS *Express* came alongside to rescue the wounded, the pride of the Royal Navy rolled over and sank in about 200 feet of water at around 1.15 pm. Admiral Sir Tom Phillips and Captain Jack Leach did not leave their ship, and, when she rolled over and sank, they were taken under with her. Later, their floating corpses were found. The *Prince of Wales* final casualty count was twenty officers and 307 ratings lost, and 90 and 1195 rescued. The whole operation had cost the Japanese but two 'Bettys' and one 'Nell' and their crews.

With Admiral Phillips gone, Admiral Layton regained his post as senior naval commander at Singapore. His response to the tragedy was ungenerous: 'I don't know exactly what's happened. But I always said he would make a balls of it, and he has.'[21] Serving in Gibraltar, Admiral Somerville caustically stated that the man he had previously referred to as 'the pocket Napoleon' had put up a 'thoroughly bad show . . . why the hell don't they send someone out there who has been through the mill and knows his stuff?'[22] But such sentiments were not universal. In a letter to Admiral Phillips's widow, the First Sea Lord, Sir Dudley Pound, wrote that: 'His death is one of the tragedies of the war—much more so, infinitely more so, than the loss of those two ships. In time we can replace the ships—we can never get another Tom.'[23] When Captain Tennant returned to Singapore he was met by Air Vice-Marshal Pulford who stated: 'My God, I hope you don't blame me for this. I had no idea where you were.'[24] The critical question is, to what extent did Admiral Phillips make 'a balls of it'?

In the tactical sense Force Z embarked on a mission against the odds. But the significance of the meeting at the Singapore Naval Base described by Lieutenant Commander J. McClelland, is important. If the meeting did in fact start at 2.30 am on 8 December, by this time the intelligence that had reached Singapore during 6 December and particularly only hours before on the 7th, was critical. On the 6th, Brooke-Popham learned of the existence of a Japanese fleet—significantly made up of transports and a cruiser—heading towards the Gulf of Siam. But by the time the meeting occurred, Brooke-Popham knew that Singora, Patani and probably Kota Bharu were enemy destinations. The significance of transports and one sighted 'with a large number of men on deck in khaki' would certainly have confirmed that this was no ruse. Appreciation after appreciation from many years previous had identified Singora, Patani and Kota Bharu as probable Japanese objectives. Brooke-Popham had been a strong advocate of the RAF's ability to either destroy a great portion of the enemy fleet at sea, or cause it great grief at its landing points. And now, when he must have been very aware that the present RAF strength was way below what was required, and also, having made the decision to not employ Matador, Phillips's operation was all that lay in the offensive cupboard. His comment, 'Do you know, Admiral, that I am beginning to believe that *if* the Japanese intend to attack, your intervention is the only thing that can prevent the invasion succeeding,' would seem to prove the point.

Given this situation, there were two obvious choices: rely immediately on an army defence of Malaya and Singapore, or initiate some sort of offensive action. No one at that meeting—other than Shenton Thomas—spoke against the operation. If, therefore, Brooke-Popham and the RAF were committed to it, their cooperation was to be critical. The days of capital ship-dominated battles at sea were over—any fleet without aircraft carrier or land-based bomber and fighter support was doomed if the enemy possessed such a capacity.

Air Vice-Marshal Pulford's commitment to the operation proved both vague and ever-changing. At the meeting he pledged his support for the operation 'whatever that might be'. As stated, Phillips asked for reconnaissance ahead of the fleet during daylight on 9 December; reconnaissance from Kota Bharu along the coast north of Singora from dawn on the 10th; and fighter cover over his fleet during daylight on that day. He was advised that his first request was granted, as to his second 'there was some doubt' and about his third there was 'greater doubt'. The fact that Phillips sent a hand-written letter to Pulford has been mentioned, and as Force Z sailed past the Changi signal centre Phillips was told, 'Regret fighter protection not possible.' The circumstances of this train of events were, to say the least, amateurish. Force Z should have known exactly what the RAF commitment was; Phillips should never have resorted to a hand-written letter and then sailed before a favourable reply; and Brooke-Popham's later decision that the air defence of Malayan airfields and of Singapore itself would, in the end, be more important than air cover for Force Z should have halted the operation. Once Brooke-Popham and Pulford had endorsed the mission, their commitment to providing air cover should have been unqualified. Alan Warren, in his *Singapore 1942*, raises a fascinating point concerning Brooke-Popham's decision to safeguard Malayan airfields and Singapore over air cover for Force Z. For 10 December he states that:

> Early in the afternoon all four of Pulford's Buffalo squadrons were still at Singapore, but only eleven Buffaloes from No. 453 Squadron were ordered to take off. There had not been any serious air attack on the island over the previous two days, nor were there any of the squadrons on the immediate verge of being transferred northwards. Apart from patrolling around Singapore, the pilots of the forty to fifty Buffaloes stationed on the island had little to do since the outbreak of war.[25]

This invites a simple question. Given their inactivity, why weren't these aircraft allotted by Pulford and Brooke-Popham to the Force Z operation as a matter of top priority? And given the previous propensity of the RAF to construct airfields over much of the Malay Peninsula, why was it not possible to have moved some of them north to maintain cover for Force Z despite enemy activity at this time?

In the end Phillips was hasty and embarked on an enormous risk without unqualified RAF support, while Brooke-Popham and Pulford had little to be proud of. They were vague and indecisive.

In simple terms, the Kuantan episode amounted to 'the fog of war'. Had it not occurred Phillips might possibly have got out of the area. But his failure to break radio silence—a costly idiosyncrasy—ruined his chances for the belated air cover he had ardently craved. Pulford's comment to Captain Tennant on his return, 'My God, I hope you don't blame me for this. I had no idea where you were', is strictly fair for the Kuantan venture, but the point is that for much of the time Force Z was at sea, he did know where it was, where it was going and what it was trying to achieve—and had endorsed the operation at the meeting. To therefore 'blame him' for the episode would be grossly unfair, but his hesitancy did not help.

In the end, had the Force Z mission been meticulously planned and implemented, and had there been a high degree of cooperation and coordination between the services, and had the 'fog of war' descended upon the Japanese rather than Phillips, the chances of its success would still have been slim. The Japanese air arm had proven itself thoroughly professional and far superior in terms of its training and equipment. And these factors told.

At the political and strategic level the British lost heavily. The First Sea Lord received the information at around 8.30 am on 10 December. A few minutes later, after composing himself, he rang the Prime Minister. Winston Churchill would later write that:

> I was opening my boxes . . . when the telephone at my bedside rang. It was the First Sea Lord. His voice sounded odd. He gave a sort of cough and gulp, and at first I could not hear quite clearly. 'Prime Minister, I have to report to you that the *Prince of Wales* and the *Repulse* have both been sunk by the Japanese—we think by aircraft. Tom Phillips is drowned.' 'Are you sure it's true?' 'There is no doubt at all.' So I put the telephone down. I was thankful to be alone. In all the war I never received a more direct shock . . .
>
> As I turned over and twisted in bed the full horror of the news sank in upon me. There were no British or American capital ships in the Indian Ocean or the Pacific except the American survivors of Pearl Harbour [*sic*], who were hastening back to California. Over all this expanse of waters Japan was supreme, and we everywhere were weak and naked.[26]

At 11.00 am that morning, Churchill faced the House of Commons and began his speech with 'I have bad news for the House . . .' When he returned to make a full statement the next day, in part he said: 'It may well be that we shall have to suffer considerable punishment, but we shall defend ourselves everywhere with the utmost vigour in close cooperation with the United States and the Netherlands.'[27] Britain and the US had already suffered considerable punishment—within a period of some six hours and 35 minutes on 7 December—Greenwich Time—the Japanese had landed in Malaya, bombed Pearl Harbor, the Philippines and Hong Kong. And now, three days later, the Prime Minister had announced the destruction of two of the nation's premier capital ships.

In Australia the news was received with dismay. The government and its people had embraced the arrival of the Eastern Fleet as a significant measure of Britain's commitment to Empire defence. Few, if any, understood the structural deficiences of that fleet, but were lost in the sheer symbolism of its arrival—and the resultant elation and propaganda. The loss of the two ships questioned the faith in, and the ability of, Britain to protect her empire. Events in 'the near north' were becoming uncomfortably 'near'.

The sinking of the *Prince of Wales* and *Repulse* sent shock waves through the English civil community in Singapore and Malaya. It was incomprehensible that such all-powerful symbols of the very pride of the Royal Navy, which had majestically glided into Singapore with their decks lined with the pomp and ceremony of white uniforms and stirring brass band anthems, could meet their doom within a paltry six days. It was not, therefore, merely a matter of two ships going to the bottom, but rather the cruel, sudden intimation that the old and privileged world was under immediate threat. The Governor, Sir Shenton Thomas, on hearing of the Japanese arrival at Kota Bharu, had simply stated: 'Well, I suppose you'll shove the little men off.' The 'little men' bombed Singapore, and on 8 December 1941, when the pride of the British Navy had gone to deal with these upstarts, disaster had ensued. If the magnitiude of these events was catastrophic, then the sheer speed of their unfolding seemed unreal. A sense of bewilderment now began to take seed in the British consciousness—one which would flourish, not fade.

For most Chinese the news was particularly frightening. There was a cold realisation of the consequences of a possible Japanese victory. Years of suffering and torment in the home country, such as had occurred in Nanking, might now await them. The Malay and Tamil workers, while apprehensive, saw the whole episode more in terms of a struggle between their present masters and fellow Asians, which might constitute a changing of the guard.

Within 48 hours of the outbreak of hostilities, the Japanese had rendered the British naval and air forces' ability to defend Malaya and Singapore utterly impotent. The army had always been their poor relation. For years it had been seen as a mere garrison force deployed to protect a £60 000 000 naval base, which was built to accommodate a fleet that would arrive when needed. In the end, Churchill's 'deterrent' became engaged in an operation for which it was not structured or intended. The very ship in which he had sailed to the Atlantic conference now lay at the bottom of the South China Sea with *Repulse*. And when the RAF had boldly asserted that it could destroy 40 per cent of a potential enemy invasion force at sea, or significantly maul it on its invasion beaches, airfields had sprung up over the Malay Peninsula like mushrooms after a spring rain. The army, not consulted as to the location of these airfields, could do nothing but disperse and therefore dilute its strength guarding them. Poorly trained, ill-equipped and under-resourced, General Percival's army was now Singapore's last hope.

10

THE JITRA LINE

———>•<———

The failure to immediately implement Matador when the Japanese appeared in the Gulf of Siam caused a strained relationship between General Percival and his III Corps Commander, General Heath. After the war, when interviewed by the British Official Historians, Heath rightly asserted that Matador's only chance for success lay with a decision on 6 December. When Matador was not enacted, he further claimed that General Percival ought to have occupied the Jitra Line earlier. In Heath's eyes Brooke-Popham 'couldn't make up his mind' and Percival 'was no commander'.[1]

There would seem some basis for Heath's views. His III Corps HQ was told that Percival—a keen supporter of Matador—hoped to have a decision by 11.00 pm on 7 December; at 11.30 pm Heath was told that the issue was still undecided, and that he should stand by in case the order was given in the morning; and, finally, during the early morning of the 8th Percival's staff contacted Brooke-Popham for a decision and were told 'Do not act', which was passed on at 8.20 am. But worse was to follow. Percival's biographer, Clifford Kinvig, has claimed that Percival contacted III Corps at 9.30 am on 8 December and:

> ...told them of the reports indicating that the Japanese were already at Singora and Patani and authorised Heath to operate the

prearranged harassing and demolition activities and to 'watch northern frontier'. This was the clearest message that MATADOR [*sic*] was not to take place. The cancellation decision by Far East Command appears to have been passed to Percival's headquarters shortly before 10 am. By this time the GOC had gone off to report the outbreak of hostilities and the emergency measures taken to the Straits Settlements Legislative Council which met that morning.[2]

This is an extraordinary revelation. Military orders require clear, firm statements, and should not be couched in vagueness, apparent in Kinvig's comment above. Further, the reader might be entitled to wonder why a GOC was appearing before a Legislative Council giving a necessarily incomplete summation of the general picture, while matters of critical importance were occurring within his command. Kinvig then mentions that while Percival was away Brooke-Popham's response came in, 'formally releasing the 11th Division from MATADOR [*sic*] and authorising Percival to send forces to occupy the Ledge position'.[3] He then states that those orders were passed on to Heath at around 11.00 am with a suggestion that a covering force be despatched over the border to delay the enemy, thus giving the 11th Division more time to prepare its positions at Jitra. An extraordinary aspect of this episode was that when Heath had rung Percival's HQ, he had been 'fobbed off' by Brigadier Torrance, Percival's BGS or Chief Staff Officer, with the news that Percival was at the Legislative Council.[4] The reader will recall that Torrance was the learned gentleman who had referred to Lieutenant-Colonel Stewart of the Argylls as being a 'crank' for embarking on a realistic and, as history shows, competent program of training for his troops. Kinvig quotes Heath as later reacting to the news of Percival's appearance before the Council with the term 'Ye Gods'. He then records that: 'In fact, for some reason which has never been made fully clear, the vital message 'MATADOR off, man Jitra' was not received by 11th Division until 1.30 pm on 8 December, despite Percival's telephone call to Heath over two hours earlier.'[5] The Japanese had been given a ten-hour start in the race—and they used it with great enterprise.

We have recorded Brooke-Popham's pathetic dithering over Matador, but Heath's criticism of Percival's role in these proceedings would seem justified.

Kinvig rightly claims that the decision was Brooke-Popham's, and goes on to imply that Admiral Phillips may also have had an influence. The fact is that there is no evidence that Percival insisted on a definitive reply within a reasonable time frame.

—————

The alternative plan to Matador was undertaken on 8 December. It will be remembered that two mobile columns were to cross the border: one code-named Krohcol was to occupy the Ledge on the Patani–Kroh Road and thus delay the enemy advance from its landing at Patani, and the other was codenamed Laycol, which was to perform the same task against Yamashita's force moving from its landing at Singora, along the Singora–Alor Star Road. Lionel Wigmore:

> The main defensive line to be held, running from east of Jitra to the west coast, was in the state of Kedah, astride the main road and railway from Malaya into Thailand. Its right flank rested on jungle-clad hills which had been considered by the planners of Malaya's defence system to be militarily impenetrable. Selected for the protection of the airfield at Alor Star and others south of it, the line was the only so-called prepared position of such extent on the Malayan mainland.[6]

Major-General Murray-Lyon's 11th Indian Division, with the 28th Brigade as its reserve, were to implement these plans.

When Operation Krohcol began, nearly everything that could go wrong, did. As stated, the mission's objective was a defile known as the Ledge—about halfway between Patani and the Siam–Malayan border. The Ledge was so named because at this point the Patani–Kroh road was cut into the side of a hill. It was anticipated that demolitions at the Ledge and a set-piece defence of the area might forestall the Japanese—mainly their armour, artillery and supply—for a number of days or at best weeks. This operation was critical for the long-term defence of the Jitra Line. Should the enemy move down the Patani–Kroh road and reach the coastal Trunk Road kilometres to the south of Jitra, that position might quickly become outflanked and possibly cut off.

But poor staff work saw the Penang based 5/14th Punjabis and a mountain battery fail to arrive at Kroh on time. And time was at a premium. The lorries of the Australian 2/3rd Reserve Motor Transport Company, carrying Lieutenant-Colonel Henry Moorhead's 3/16th Punjabis, crossed the Siamese border at about 3.00 pm on 8 December. Josiah Crosby's suggestion that the Siamese would side with the British if the Japanese committed the first act of aggression on Siamese soil, was shattered when an Indian soldier was almost immediately killed passing through the customs barrier at the border. Three hundred Siamese police were able to contest the advance until their enthusiasm for the fight ran out during the late afternoon of 9 December. The problem was that mere police officers had cost Moorhead's soldiers just over 24 hours of time for a paltry advance of eight kilometres to the town of Betong—hardly an inspiring effort given the circumstances.

Now, a catastrophic combination of Brooke-Popham's indecisiveness, appalling communication between Malaya Command and its III Corps HQ, abominable staff work in ordering and then moving a half of Krohcol and a pedestrian 'battle' with the Siamese constabulary—all conspired to produce the Ledge calamity. About nine kilometres short of his objective, Moorhead was confronted by fire from a Japanese regiment with light tank and artillery support, which had landed at Patani at around 3.00 am on 8 December, and with great haste had travelled some 120 kilometres in just on 60 hours. And as disciplined, highly trained infantry are apt to do—however tired they might be—they then proceeded to rapidly overrun and cut off the leading two Punjabi companies. On 11 December, one of the two missing companies regained their lines, but the majority of the second remained lost. During the evening of the 11th, Moorhead requested permission to withdraw his now badly battered formation to Kroh. This was granted. But the persistent Japanese had pressed their advantage, outflanked the Punjabis during the night, and then proceeded to maul them again in the morning.

By late on 12 December, Moorhead had withdrawn his now half-strength force to a position astride the Kroh–Sungei Patani Road. Krohcol's belated attempt to occupy the Ledge had been an ill-timed and costly disaster. The Japanese speed of movement, their ability to make rapid contact, maintain that contact, systematically outflank the Indians when necessary, repair demolished bridges, and always, therefore, maintain the initiative, were

admirable traits of a highly trained and well-led army—qualities they were
to employ throughout the campaign.

Having described the attempt to obstruct the Japanese 42nd Regiment's
advance along the Patani–Kroh Road at the Ledge, we now turn to operation
Laycol along the Singora–Alor Star Road. This force consisted of a carrier
platoon of the 1/8th Punjabis, a portion of the 273rd Anti-tank Battery
and some artillery and engineers. A third movement into Siam was undertaken by an armoured train at Padang Besar in the state of Perlis, carrying
a platoon of the 2/16th Punjab and engineers. The train travelled as far as
Khlaung Ngae, about 25 kilometres into Siam, and was able to demolish a
60-metre railway bridge on the Singora line before withdrawing uncontested
back across the border.

By dusk on 9 December, Laycol had advanced about sixteen kilometres
inside Siam along the Alor Star–Singora Road to the village of Sadeo. It
occupied a position just north of the village. At around 9.00 pm on 9 December, a Japanese column of about 30 trucks and headed by tanks with
headlights on, approached the Indians. Two of the three advance guard
Japanese tanks were hit by anti-tank guns. Lieutenant-Colonel Tsuji vividly
recalled the well-drilled and instant Japanese response:

> Jumping from their lorries two companies of our men, like hunting
> dogs, swiftly dispersed into the rubber plantation on both sides of the
> road and our field gun opened fire on the enemy front. After fighting
> for about an hour the British weakly crumbled to pieces and retreated
> to the south, leaving a blood-stained armoured car and sidecar . . . we
> discovered a blood-smeared map in the armoured car . . . it . . . showed
> clearly the enemy fortifications and dispositions around Changlun
> and Jitra.[7]

Tsuji was not alone in his admiration of the Japanese infantry near Sadeo
on 9 December. The first British company commander to witness their drill
agreed with his observations, but added a haunting perspective on these
Japanese tactics: '. . . the British and Indian soldier had no answer—and
indeed for a time simply could not comprehend.'[8] We now turn to the main
Kedah British defensive position on the Jitra Line.

While the muddled and lengthy deliberations over Matador were occurring in Singapore, the 11th Indian Division troops assigned to either implement that contentious operation, or man the Jitra Line, were in a state of flux—both physically and mentally. Percival's biographer, Clifford Kinvig, has stated that: 'To keep such a large invasion force "cruising around", as General Brooke put it, for so long for such a negligible purpose made little strategic sense.'[9] To refer to the 11th Indian Division's plight at this time as 'cruising around' is misleading.

When news of the Japanese landings came, two of the 11th Division battalions were standing by at Anak Bukit Railway Station ready; another two had their trucks loaded and were in camp ready to advance into Siam by road; and the remaining two were deployed near the frontier. All were awaiting the result of Brooke-Popham's deliberations. The 1st Leicestershire Battalion's experience would seem typical:

At 0300 hours on the 9th . . . the Battalion moved on bicycles to Anak Bukit Station and entrained for the move into Thailand . . .

Orders, however, were not received for the train to move, and at about 0800 hours twenty-seven enemy aircraft arrived and bombed Alor Star airfield and more passed over towards Penang. The Battalion detrained and waited in the fields near the station until 1500 hours, when it was ordered to return to man the Jitra Line. The sudden change from the offensive to the defensive caused the spirits of the whole division to drop considerably. For the next three days the Battalion worked night and day to complete the defensive position, especially erecting wire, of which there was, up till then, none in place; camouflaging and the laying of anti-tank mines also took place. The rain was almost continuous, mud was everywhere and, as all tents had been struck, the men were lying in the open with never a chance to get their boots, socks and feet really dry.[10]

According to the Leicesters' historian, the defences at Jitra had begun in June, but progress had been slow due to 'frequent change in the layout of the line and to the marshy ground, which had necessitated breastworks in many places'.[11] It is extraordinary to record that he also mentioned wheelbarrows being unavailable and that wiring was forbidden owing to a fear of the wooden stakes rotting.[12] The Chief Engineer, Brigadier Simson, has recorded that he saw Major-General Murray-Lyon as late as 1–2 December 1941 at Jitra—nine days before the fighting there—and saw no defences of any sort, other than the anti-tank ditch still under construction by the Public Works Department. Murray-Lyon explained that as he was on call to move off for Matador he was 'reluctant to . . . risk any delay in unpacking tools and carrying out the work'.[13]

The 11th Indian Division's Jitra Line extended over about nineteen kilometres of ground, running from just east of Jitra, to the coast. Brigadier Garrett's 15th Brigade was deployed on the right sector, responsible for the defence of Jitra itself and around five kilometres of rubber plantations, rice fields, jungle and swamp. Hills bordered the eastern side of this right flank. The 2/9th Jats occupied the right flank of this 15th Brigade perimeter—around 3600 metres in length—from the eastern hills to the main Singora Road. To the Jats' left were the 1st Leicesters, whose perimeter contained a portion of both the Trunk Road and its branch road which ran through Kodiang to the railway line situated at Kangar in Perlis. The Leicesters' main responsibility was the security of the two roads.

Brigadier Lay's 6th Brigade left sector perimeter was far larger, about 16 000 metres, with the 2nd East Surrey on the right and the 2/16th Punjab on the left. It was larger because 'with the exception of the sector given to 2nd East Surrey and a belt of cultivated country on either side of the main railway line, the greater part of this wide front consisted of swamp'.[14] Brigadier Carpendale's 28th Brigade was in reserve. Support for the Jitra perimeter was to be given by two batteries of the 155th Field Regiment, one battery of the 22nd Mountain Regiment and three batteries of the 80th Anti-tank Regiment.

To provide both a covering screen and to create more time for the construction of the Jitra perimeter, Brigadier Garrett was allocated a part of the 1/14th Punjabis and the 2/1st Gurkhas to man outposts. By the evening of 10 December, the Punjabis were deployed about nine kilometres from the frontier on the Trunk Road at Changlun, while the latter were deployed behind a stream just north of Asun. Two further outposts, separated by six kilometres of thick jungle, were astride the branch road at Imam, and

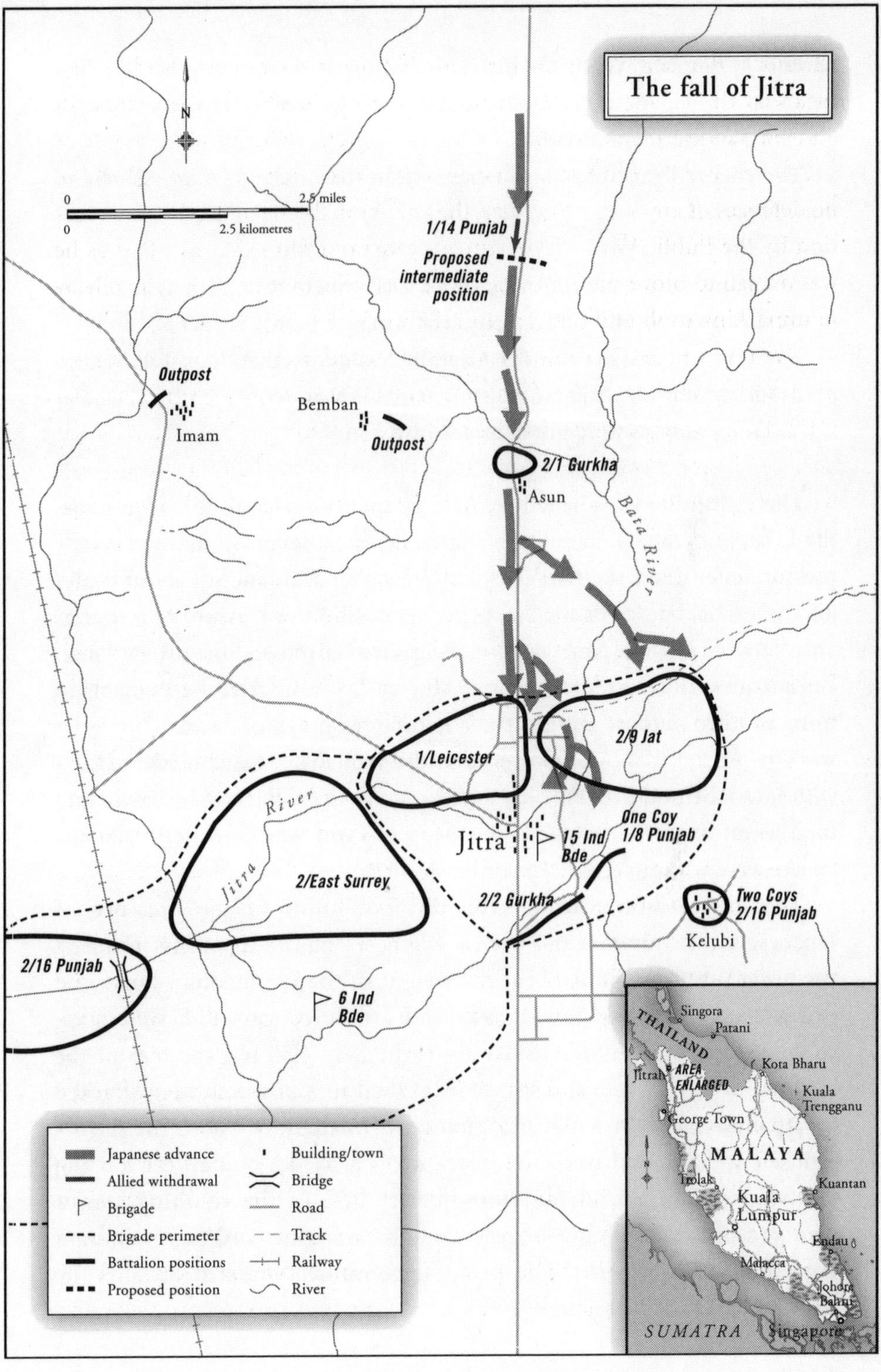

The fall of Jitra
N
0
2.5 miles
0
2.5 kilometres
1/14 Punjab
Proposed intermediate position
Outpost
Imam
Bemban
Outpost
2/1 Gurkha
Asun
Bata River
1/Leicester
2/9 Jat
River
Jitra
2/East Surrey
Jitra
15 Ind Bde
One Coy 1/8 Punjab
2/2 Gurkha
Two Coys 2/16 Punjab
Kelubi
2/16 Punjab
6 Ind Bde
Japanese advance
Allied withdrawal
Brigade
Brigade perimeter
Battalion positions
Proposed position
Building/town
Bridge
Road
Track
Railway
River
Singora
Patani
THAILAND
Jitra
AREA ENLARGED
Kota Bharu
Kuala Trengganu
George Town
MALAYA
Trolak
Kuantan
Kuala Lumpur
Endau
Malacca
Johore Bahru
SUMATRA
Singapore

another at Bemban. While the Jitra Line occupants were strengthening their defences, the Japanese had spent much of 10 December repairing bridges and parts of the Trunk Road.

The enemy thrust began in earnest again the next day. Alan Warren, in *Singapore 1942*:

> At Changlun on the morning of 11 December the 1/14th Punjabis were dug in behind the Sungei [river] Laka. A patrol of two platoons was sent out at dawn under Captain Mohammed Akham but was never seen again. A Japanese spotter plane was soon seen overhead and the Punjabis were under attack by 8 a.m.[15]

The 1/14th Punjabis halted the first Japanese attack on the bridge across the Laka, but when a demolition charge failed to destroy it and the enemy pressure intensified, the Battalion withdrew over a distance of about twelve kilometres back towards the 2/1st Gurkha position near Asun. At a conference between General Murray-Lyon, Brigadier Garrett and the two battalion commanders during the afternoon, Murray-Lyon ordered the Punjabis to form another outpost around three kilometres north of Asun. This order was against the wishes of Garrett and the Punjabis' CO, who advocated a withdrawal behind the causeway at Asun, so as to enable it to be blown and used as an anti-tank obstacle. But Murray-Lyon was convinced that the enemy were without tanks. The order stood.[16]

The only reason Murray-Lyon did not know of the presence of Japanese tanks was that the enemy engineers had been busily repairing the bridge at Changlun to bear the weight of the ten medium tanks and a mixture of reconnaissance tanks and armoured cars that were soon to descend upon the Indians. At approximately 4.30 pm the rear of the column, in driving rain and still short of their new position, were attacked by Japanese medium tanks and motorised infantry. Many of the terror-stricken Indians had never laid eyes on a tank, let alone been on the receiving end of its intense close-quarter fire. In the resulting confusion and panic, the Punjabis lost two anti-tank guns and two mountain guns and were scattered. The Japanese continued onwards towards the Gurkhas' perimeter at Asun.[17]

Aggression and speed of movement by the Japanese, and a lack of depth in the Indian defences, now caused pandemonium. When enemy tanks were seen approaching the bridge, the Gurkhas made two attempts to blow it up, but the charge failed. When the leading tank was then halted by an anti-tank rifle, the Japanese maintained the momentum of the assault by crossing the river and immediately conducted a frontal and flank attack. The tanks then resumed their progress. By 6.45 pm on 11 December, aggressively maintaining their momentum along the road, the Japanese had by-passed the Gurkhas behind the swamp and proceeded to overrun their battalion HQ, which fell within a half hour. Alan Warren has left us with a tragic summary of the plight of the Punjabis and Gurkhas during their barely ten-and-three-quarter hour nightmare:

> Of 550 Gurkhas to go into action, only two hundred made their way back to British lines. Of the 350 missing, perhaps twenty to thirty were killed in the fighting and the rest were eventually rounded up and taken prisoner. Of the Punjabis, around 270 were led southwards by Garrett and other officers to escape capture.[18]

Back at Jitra, the 1st Leicesters had a standing patrol beyond the bridge in front of their right flank. At around 8.30 pm on 11 December, approaching lights were spotted. When a flare was fired from the standing patrol the enemy tanks stopped and turned off their lights. Heavy fire now ensued. In a disturbing repetition of past attempts, a charge on the bridge failed to explode and the tanks came on. The first two were stopped by anti-tank guns and stalled on an embankment, blocking the rest of the column. The Leicesters had also hastily prepared a nearby roadblock the night before, consisting of tree trunks, wire and some mines. Meanwhile, north of the Leicesters' perimeter on the Kodiang Road, troops moving back from an outpost were mistaken for the enemy, causing a bridge to be blown—this time the charge worked. Lost on the far side of the stream were 'the trucks and carriers of the covering and outpost troops, four mountain guns, and seven anti-tank guns'.[19]

With Brigadier Garrett still missing, command of the 15th Brigade was given to Brigadier Carpendale, and, as the 1/14th Punjabis were still scattered, the 2/2nd Gurhkas became the brigade reserve. At dawn on 12 December, it was discovered that the Japanese had penetrated the Leicesters' C Company perimeter and a small area to the east (the Jats' side) of the road. A counter-attack by C Company, which was strengthened by elements of A Company and a number of carriers, eventually drove the enemy from the area. But the real threat seemed to be further to the east in the Jats' perimeter.

Although the Leicesters managed to secure the right flank of their peri-meter, the Japanese did make some progress between them and the Jats to their east (the right flank). During the night misleading reports came in from the far eastern boundary of the Jats' perimeter claiming that the enemy were infil-trating between their eastern extremity and the jungle-clad hills. The reports were misleading because the phone contact to that company had failed. But an anxious Brigadier Carpendale, after contacting Brigadier Lay, managed to procure two companies from each of the 2/16th and 1/8th Punjabis to be deployed well to the south of the perceived gap. This measure would, it was hoped, prevent the Japanese from a wide encircling movement around the eastern boundary of the Jitra Line. The four-company reinforcement of the Jats had been done without the knowledge or consent of Murray-Lyon.

At around 9.00 am on 12 December, Murray-Lyon arrived at 15th Brigade HQ. Two issues dominated his thoughts. The first was the disturbing news concerning the rapid Japanese progress from Patani towards Kroh against Lieutenant-Colonel Moorhead's Krohcol—already examined by us—which if sustained at its present pace, would gravely threaten his 11th Division's line of communication. The second, and more immediate, was the situation at Jitra. All his reserves had been committed; a worrying Japanese penetration of his right flank had occurred; there had already been significant losses in men and material; and he noticed the debilitated condition of his troops. He therefore asked permission for his 11th Division to stage a 49-kilometre withdrawal to Gurun.

Lieutenant-General Heath was in no position to consider Murray-Lyon's request. At this very time, he was on a train to Singapore to demand permis-sion for Brigadier Key to be allowed to withdraw his brigade from Kelantan State. It will be remembered that Key's 8th Indian Brigade had, at this juncture, withdrawn south of Machang, having abandoned the defence of the Kota Bharu and Gong Kedah airfields. Heath has received criticism for his journey to Singapore. Kirby has referred to it as 'an apparently unneces-sary journey'.[20]

In his postwar despatch, General Percival explained his reasons for disal-lowing Murray-Lyon's request for the withdrawal to Gurun:

> Such a long withdrawal had not been considered in our prewar discus-sions of war plans and it would immediately have prejudiced our chances of denying the west coast aerodromes to the enemy. Moreover I felt that such a withdrawal would have a most demoralising effect on both the troops and on the civil population. This view was endorsed by the War Council which was sitting at the time. I therefore replied to the effect that pending further orders the battle was to be fought out on the Jitra position. At that time, the Jats were, in point of fact, the only battalion which had incurred serious losses although two battal-ions had, as already recorded, been rendered ineffective the previous day.[21]

This passage deserves close scrutiny. First, the fact that the current state of affairs had not existed in prewar discussions of war plans defies reality— nor had the RAF being virtually destroyed on the first day, and two Royal Navy capital ships sunk, been considered in prewar war plans. Second, with regards to Percival's claim that a withdrawal would 'have prejudiced our chances of denying the west coast aerodromes to the enemy', it should have been obvious to him that the airfields in northern Malaya were already lost; that should his three brigades in contact with the enemy suffer extreme casualties, and/or lose their line of communication—which was a possibil-ity at this critical time—then the airfields in western Malaya would have no chance—all would be definitely lost. Third, the notion that a withdrawal at this time would have a demoralising effect upon both the troops and the civil population is a feeble assessment. The morale of the 11th Division was already floundering. What condition would it have deteriorated into had further heavy casualties and a possible rout have occurred? Last, his last sentence above is a contradiction in terms. How could the Jats have been the only battalion to have incurred 'serious losses' when, in the same sentence he states that two others had been rendered ineffective the previous day?

The truth is that there were three battalions engaged in operations at this time that had had the 'stuffing' knocked out of them, and, to compound Murray-Lyon's problems, his reserve had been eaten away to virtually nothing.

Malaya Command's prime mission had fundamentally changed within a mere 48 hours of the enemy landings with the almost total ruination of the RAF in Malaya. What mattered now was blatantly obvious. They must delay the enemy by a fighting withdrawal into Malaya and Singapore's vital ground: southern Johore. Lose that and lose the war. At this exact time, the RAF was no longer the prime defensive weapon in Malaya and Singapore—if it ever had been—and the *Prince of Wales* and *Repulse* lay at the bottom of the South China Sea. Airfields were no longer the vital ground. When any air force is outnumbered and outgunned then all does not augur well for the future. Moreover, the notion that an 11th Division withdrawal would have a demoralising effect upon the civil population borders on the comical. Any competent commander will put the morale of his fighting troops first. The civil population had, within a few days, suffered the shock of the Royal Navy being humiliated and of having Singapore being bombed on the first night of the war. The potential shock to the civil community of the loss of the Jitra Line should always have come a very poor second to keeping the 11th Division intact and able to fight another day.

Meanwhile, back on the Jitra Line at about noon on 12 December, the commander of the Japanese 9th Infantry Brigade, Major-General Kawamura, arrived at the front to take over from the advance guard. Kawamura then ordered his 41st Infantry Regiment to reinforce the advance guard and attack the British east of the main road. Clearly, he wished to exploit the weakness between the Leicesters' and the Jats' positions. But the enthusiasm of the advanced guard had not waned, and before the fresh troops could be committed, it put in a battalion strength attack just to the east of the road. The sheer concentration and aggression of the attack drove a deep wedge through the Jats' left forward company, which then forced a with-drawal of the rearward company to the south-east. The advanced guard then attacked the right flank of the Leicesters and also penetrated the British perimeter further south to make contact with the 2/2nd Gurkhas on the line of the River Bata. Despite the fact that this Japanese attack punched a wedge of some 1600 metres between the Leicesters and the 2/2nd Gurkhas, both battalions held firm. A counterattack by the East Surrey carrier platoon stabilised the front and at least 'temporarily checked the enemy's attempt to envelop the Leicesters' right. By 3 p.m. all was quiet.'[22]

Perhaps this lull in the fighting bolstered Brigadier Carpendale's confidence, for he now planned a tightening of his perimeter and a counterattack. To plug the gap between the Jats and the Leicesters, he ordered the Jats to pull back and occupy the ground between the village of Kelubi and the right of the Punjabis, while the Leicesters were to concentrate west of the Trunk Road and just north of the river—these moves would then enable the Leicesters to counterattack to the east the next morning. But Carpendale quickly lost his enthusiasm for the notion of a Leicesters' counterattack. Instead, he now ordered the Battalion to swing its line using its established western or left flank point at Rimba, and pivot in an south-eastern arc back along the River Jitra, to Padang, and thence to the River Bata. The Leicesters protested to Carpendale, pointing out that they had not lost ground, had suffered only minor casualties, and had not recced their proposed positions. The Battalion was ordered to move at 4.00 pm and had settled into its new perimeter by 7.30 pm. Although the British Battalion found the move hard enough, the Jats displayed their lack of training and sound staff work by failing to notify the right forward company of the withdrawal—it was incorrectly believed that they had been overrun.

We now arrive at the point where all the characteristics of untrained, exhausted and indeed demoralised troops cause them to finally crack—through no fault of their own. Alan Warren has quoted the Leicesters' unit diarist:

The scene at the Bata [river] Bridge and for two hundred yards south of it from 5 p.m. onwards, was one of indescribable confusion. Indians and Gurkhas were firing in most directions, but chiefly to the north east, from both sides of the main road and, as far as could be seen, into the backs of elements of the 2/9th Jats and one of the Gurkha battalions. Several men were seen to be shot dead by their comrades at a range of less than the road's breadth.[23]

Amidst this panic, which was compounded by the Japanese mortaring Jitra village and the nearby battalion perimeters, an Indian non-commissioned officer (Halvidar) of the Royal Engineers asked for permission to blow the Bata Bridge—before all of the transport and anti-tank guns had been recovered from the far side.

Major-General Murray-Lyon had witnessed aspects of this panic when forward at around 6.00 pm. On arriving at his HQ thirty minutes later, he was informed that 'the Leicesters had been attacked as they were withdrawing, that the Jats had been overrun and that the enemy was attacking 2/16th Punjab at Kelubi'[24]—all of which was untrue. To add to his dismay, he now learnt that Krohcol had arrived at Kroh with a strength of only 350.

Murray-Lyon had known that the game was up before his first request to withdraw. The panic he witnessed whilst forward, the disturbing Krohcol news and the potential for the Japanese to employ a fresh tank assault against his disorganised dispositions and troops—which were lacking in tank defences—all demanded another plea to Percival to allow him a withdrawal to a position covering Gurun during the night. Percival's biographer Clifford Kinvig:

> . . . his [Murray-Lyon's] message was again relayed to Singapore where Heath and Percival were still conferring. This time they let him go, confirming that his task was to fight for the security of North Kedah and suggesting that he should dispose his force in depth on the axis of the north/south roads and based on good tank obstacles.[25]

It would seem 'conferring' is a soft term for Heath and Percival's Singapore meeting. For Heath to have left his HQ when he did was, in some ways, 'inopportune' as Kirby has put it, but it might well have been that Heath had had enough of the lack of purpose—of the weak-minded dithering—which was causing a deterioration of his 11th Division's physical and mental energy reserves. In the end, Heath had been earlier advocating either a decisive order for Matador, or a similar order to occupy the Jitra Line. For critical hours his 11th Division were empowered to do neither—it was unforgivable. While it is easy for the historian or the reader to allow Percival to hide behind Brooke-Popham's weakness, there is no evidence that he aggressively supported his Corps Commander, nor the soldiers for whom he bore the ultimate responsibility. Prewar war plans, civilian morale, the protection of a now redundant collection of Malayan airfields and an air arm that was already confined to night fighter operations and the protection of convoys were largely irrelevant issues that simply shrouded his real challenge.

At 10.00 pm on 12 December 1941, Major-General Murray-Lyon issued the order for his troops to stage a withdrawal from the ill-fated Jitra Line beginning at midnight. When given permission by Percival and Heath to withdraw from the line, he had also been informed that the command of Krohcol was to be now taken back by III Corps HQ as from midnight. The first phase of Murray-Lyon's 11th Indian Division's withdrawal to Gurun was to the south bank of the Kedah River at Alor Star. It was an understandable disaster.

The Kedah River lay some 24 kilometres to the south; the main line of communication along that withdrawal was a single road; there were no vehicles available for the movement, requiring the troops to march back; communications within the perimeter were threadbare and, in places, non-existent; units were dispersed over difficult ground, thereby making that communication, and the coordination of movement, difficult; and the withdrawal was staged in darkness and at times in heavy rain. To break contact with one's enemy and then perform such a withdrawal under these conditions is no mean feat for well-trained, well-led, highly experienced and tough infantry. It almost becomes 'mission impossible' for the novice. While the 6th Brigade, under the least amount of contact and pressure, made a relatively clean break from its perimeter, the units of the 15th Brigade floundered.

The first problem was communication. Two companies of the Leicesters, one company of the 2/9th Jats and a detachment of the 2/1st Gurkhas failed to receive the withdrawal order and remained in their perimeters until the next morning.[26] Events like this do not merely dent morale, they are more likely to destroy it. The consequence was a fragmentation into sub-units which, while most escaped, were forced to leave their equipment. Many of those who did receive the order reasoned that the single escape road might be crammed, and worse, used by enemy tanks, and therefore made their way out across country, or along the railway to Alor Star, or made for the coast in anticipation of movement south by boat. One small party's enthusiasm for the withdrawal saw them reach Sumatra.

An example of the nature of the withdrawal is provided by the 1st Leicesters' historian who has described the CO and his main group's move:

> After a very arduous march through swamps and paddy this party reached the railway line and turned south down it, and finally reached Alor Star at 1400 hours in a very exhausted condition. It was here found that the only bridge across the river had been blown some hours before. The party was engaged by Japanese in the town and was split in two. Some forty other ranks with the C.O. and R.S.M. managed to get across the river with the help of some friendly Chinese boatmen, but the remaining seventy-odd, under Captain Burder, were mostly never seen again.[27]

The CO's party then undertook a sixteen-kilometre forced march, after which they were picked up by motor transport and taken to a position two kilometres south of Gurun early on 14 December—'for the time being reduced to a mere handful of utterly exhausted men'.[28]

While the fighting at Jitra had been a disaster for the British, Lieutenant-Colonel Tsuji was full of praise for his troops' efforts:

> . . . each man had moved to the front with dry bread and rice sufficient for only a few days in accordance with the plan: 'depend upon the enemy for rations.'
>
> We had to be grateful to General Percival, not only for provisions for the men, but also for cars and gasolene abandoned in abundance. If such tactics as these could be kept up then our fighting officers and men would not go hungry. Speaking to an English engineer taken prisoner, I asked, 'How long did you think this fortified position would hold out?'
>
> He replied, 'Held by the full strength of the 11th Division I believed it would hold out for three months at the least.'[29]

And later during the conversation: 'What was the reason for the feeble break-down?' I asked. 'God alone knows,' he answered.[30]

God should not have been the only one who knew. The fighting at Jitra really constituted nothing more than pronounced bungling at the highest levels of command. It tragically impacted upon the largely ill-trained, inexperienced and therefore vulnerable soldiers who had to pay a severe price for it.

From a high command perspective, the first failure was the whole concept of Matador. We have stated that staff plans are one thing, but having trained troops to implement them is fundamental to operational success. The fact that Matador was beyond the ability of the troops chosen to embark upon it was amply demonstrated. When a force cannot deal with 300 Siamese police without military training and military support, and is restricted to an eight-kilometre gain in 24 hours, one is entitled to question its prowess. Infantry companies which are continuously overrun or by-passed and scattered merely show the worth of their training and experience. The fact that General Percival believed in Matador merely shows that he lacked the essential ability to translate a war plan into action. In short, Matador was a plan always doomed to fail its practical test.

The 11th Indian Division's defence of the Jitra Line is undeniable proof that its training was barely adequate for the most basic of tasks. If the line was to have had any hope at all, a set-piece defence of a first-class perimeter would have had to have been enacted. It wasn't, because its soldiers were preparing its defences at the last possible minute—exhausted, wet and with minimal equipment. We have outlined Brigadier Simson's top class training in Scotland and his sound strategies for set defences at defiles down the Malay Peninsula and on Singapore Island. It would seem curious that much has been made—justifiably—of Malaya Command's lack of trained specialists, of the number and quality of its soldiers, and its support. And yet Simson was arguably amongst the best in his field and much of the equipment he needed was at hand. He was made to sit idly by and watch tragic events unfold.

At the tactical level, Major-General Murray-Lyon's defensive perimeter lacked depth at its vital ground: the Trunk Road through Jitra itself. Once the Japanese had penetrated the vital ground between the Leicesters and the

Jats, that lack of depth told. In hindsight, he might have chosen his troops for this key ground more carefully. He could have left the Leicesters where they were, but deployed the Surreys to the right side of the road. However much that idea might have split brigade battalions, had the Surreys been able to hold in the same manner as the Leicesters, a more efficient defence of that road might have occurred. Despite the fact that the breakdown in communication across the perimeter was partly caused by the last minute laying of exposed cable on swampy ground, there can be no excuse for companies failing to receive orders to withdraw, however late those orders might arrive. Jumpy, inexperienced soldiers should never be left high and dry when those around them are withdrawn. Also, the notion that local commanders are able to request and receive reinforcements without the knowledge and approval of the divisional commander can only lead to a confusion of plan and purpose. In fairness to Major-General Murray-Lyon, his withdrawal from the Jitra Line should have been allowed when first requested. After the war, he told Kirby that 'the reluctance to face facts which caused the delay in granting permission to withdraw, was undoubtedly an important contributory cause of the difficulty and costliness of the withdrawal'.[31] Heath concurred. It would seem that Percival made his initial decision based on his 'pre-war war plans' and the morale of the army as a whole and the civil population, rather than placing his trust in his commanders on the spot. If Heath was criticised by Kirby for embarking on his train journey to Singapore, and therefore being too-distant from his III Corps battles, then Percival made a fundamentally flawed decision from as great a distance.

But the startling revelation from the battle at Jitra came after the war. At the time, Murray-Lyon believed that he had been assailed by at least two brigades, while Percival believed that the enemy column was at divisional strength. The truth is that the 11th Indian Division at Jitra was mauled by an advanced guard force consisting of only two battalions.

The battle at Jitra broke the 11th Indian Division. Lionel Wigmore has recorded that:

The 15th Brigade emerged from the battle barely 600 strong, and the 1/Leicester alone of all its units had any carriers or mortars left. The 6th fared less badly, but had suffered serious losses in men and equipment. The 2/1st Gurkha had been reduced to one company, and other units of the 28th Brigade had suffered substantial casualties. Two commanding officers and twenty-five other officers had been killed or lost. Losses of guns, vehicles, and signalling equipment were heavy, and particularly serious in some instances owing to lack of sufficient reserves in Malaya from which to replace them. Many of the men who remained with or later rejoined the division were badly affected by their experiences and unfit for further action in the near future.[32]

11

THE DEFENCE OF GURUN

———✦———

By 13 December 1941, only five days after their landings at Singora, Patani and Kota Bharu, the Japanese had made substantial progress along all three axes of advance. It will be remembered that General Heath's original purpose in visiting General Percival in Singapore had been to request permission for Brigadier Key and his 8th Indian Brigade—which had conducted the defence of Kota Bharu—to withdraw altogether from the State of Kelantan to the railhead at Kuala Lipis. Given that the main enemy thrust appeared to be in the west from Singora and Patani, that the three airfields which Key's brigade had been protecting were now not in use by the RAF and, in view of events at Jitra, this request was granted on the 12th. After repulsing two heavy attacks near Machang on the 12th and 13th, Key was able to withdraw his brigade to Kuala Krai without much difficulty. All stores were evacuated by 15 December, bridges just south of that town were blown, and on the 19th the railhead was evacuated. The withdrawal also saw the despatch of the 4/19th Hyderabads to rejoin their 12th Brigade on the west coast. By 22 December Key's movement had been completed and his 8th Brigade now occupied the area of Kuala Lipis–Jerantut.

The operations conducted by the 8th Indian Brigade at Kota Bharu and subsequently at Machang deserve high praise. Although it had suffered casualties of 553 killed, wounded or missing, and had lost a number of vehicles, machine guns, mortars and anti-tank rifles, Key's leadership and the efforts of his troops had preserved their formation intact and ready for further action. We now rejoin Krohcol on the Patani–Kroh Road.

At midnight on 12 December, when General Heath had taken over command of Krohcol, General Percival had decided to reinforce the 11th Division with the 12th Indian Brigade: the 4/19th Hyderabads, the 2nd Argyll and Sutherland Highlanders, and the 5/2nd Punjab. With the Hyderabads still fighting under Brigadier Key's command in Kelantan, and not destined to rejoin their brigade for some days, Lieutenant-Colonel Stewart's Argylls arrived by rail at Kroh at 4.00 pm on 13 December, to be followed by the 5/2nd Punjab the day after.

During the night 12–13 December, the Japanese continued their advance along the Patani–Kroh Road by making contact with the 5/14th Punjab. Kirby has recorded that:

> To avoid becoming too heavily engaged this battalion withdrew about noon on the 13th to Betong, from where, after destroying the road bridge, it moved to join 3/16th Punjab in the defensive position west of Kroh. This withdrawal uncovered the road running south from the village of Kroh through Grik to link with the main west coast road at Kuala Kangsar. North of Grik, it was little more than a narrow unmetalled track fit for use by light motor vehicles in dry weather.[1]

During the afternoon of 13 December, General Heath ordered one company of the Argylls and some armoured cars to Grik to secure this road, while the remainder of the battalion was sent to Balang to form a defensive perimeter. It arrived at around 4.00 pm on the 14th. Command of Krohcol now passed to the 12th Brigade's Brigadier Paris, who sent his 5/2nd Punjab to Merban Pulas to occupy and protect his left flank. Krohcol passed through the Argylls' perimeter at 3.00 am on the 15th having blown parts of the road as they withdrew.

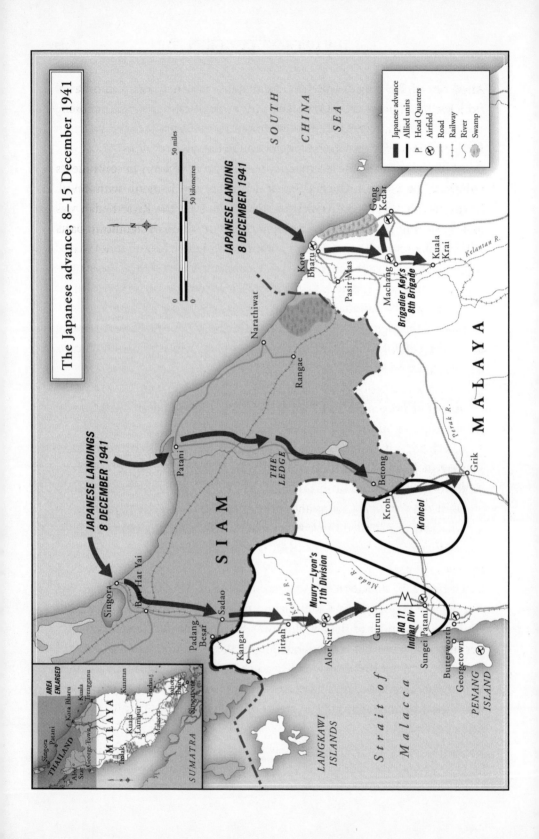

The Japanese advance, 8–15 December 1941

50 miles

50 kilometres

Legend
- Japanese advance
- Allied units
- Head Quarters
- Airfield
- Road
- Railway
- River
- Swamp

SOUTH CHINA SEA

JAPANESE LANDING 8 DECEMBER 1941

JAPANESE LANDINGS 8 DECEMBER 1941

Gong Kedar

Kota Bharu

Pasir Mas

Machang

Kuala Krai

Kelantan R.

Brigadier Key's 8th Brigade

Narathiwat

Rangae

Patani

THE LEDGE

Betong

Perak R.

Grik

M A L A Y A

Kroh

Krohcol

Hat Yai

S I A M

Singora

Sadao

Padang Besar

Kangar

Jitrah

Alor Star

Muary–Lyon's 11th Division

Kedah R.

Gurun

Muda R.

Sungei Patani

HQ 11 Indian Div

Butterworth

Georgetown

PENANG ISLAND

Strait of Malacca

LANGKAWI ISLANDS

SUMATRA

AREA ENLARGED

Singora
Patani
Alor Star
George Town

THAILAND

Kota Bharu
Kuala Trengganu

M A L A Y A

Kuala Lumpur

Malacca

Kuantan
Endau
Kluang
Johore Bahru
Singapore

After the 11th Division staged their fragmented and utterly weary withdrawal from the Jitra Line to the southern side of the River Kedah by mid-morning on 13 December, it immediately became clear to Major-General Murray-Lyon that, should the Japanese mount a concerted attack upon his troops, disaster might well result. He therefore ordered the division to continue its retirement to Gurun, which entailed a further 32-kilometre withdrawal. It was an astute decision. When the main bridge on the River Kedah was blown, Murray-Lyon was given a graphic demonstration of significant parts of his 11th Division's mental and physical state. He would later recall that:

> When the bridge went up . . . the 1/8th Punjab which was sitting down in a palm grove about six hundred yards from the bridge rose as one man and started to run down the road in panic. Two companies of the 2/16th Punjab did the same . . . it was only by getting in my car and getting ahead of them that I managed to stop them and turn them back. In the case of the 2/16th Punjab Companies I actually had to threaten some men with my pistol before they would stop.[2]

The dispirited withdrawal was staged in driving rain along a single congested road during the night of 14/15 December.

When Murray-Lyon arrived at Gurun he was presented with a number of critical problems. The first was the now greatly reduced strength of his division. His 15th Brigade—now commanded again by Brigadier Garrett—was virtually worn out by their fighting at Jitra and numbered a mere 600: the Leicesters were reduced to about ten officers and 130 other ranks; the Jats to four officers and 187; and the 1/14th Punjabis could muster only two companies. Although the 6th Brigade had not been exposed to the same intensity of fighting at Jitra as had the 15th Brigade, it too was down on strength at Gurun. The Surreys had lost a company during the retreat and the 1/8th Punjab was reorganised into three rifle companies. The 2/16th Punjab Battalion was still missing after being shot up during their movement into a perimeter at Jitra and in the confusion of the withdrawal from it. After Garrett's return to his 15th Brigade, Brigadier Carpendale resumed command of the 28th. Two of his battalions, the 2/2nd and 2/9th Gurkhas, had lost a little over a company between them, but the 2/1st had taken heavy casualties during its battle at Asun. Murray-Lyon's 11th Indian Division was thus critically understrength.

The extreme fatigue of his troops was his second problem. Severe casualties and exhaustion, followed by a testing and disjointed withdrawal, constitute a tough test for seasoned troops, but it must have been a shattering experience for the ill-trained 11th Division to arrive at Gurun to discover that there were no prepared defensive positions. General Percival, in *The War in Malaya*:

> Most of them had had no rest for a week and were to have none now, for the position had to be prepared for defence. As soon as war broke out, orders had been issued for a large civilian working party to be assembled to work on the Gurun position under the supervision of military officers, but no work had been done and there were no labourers there. Whether they had assembled and dispersed or never assembled at all I cannot say as reports on this point are conflicting.[3]

This is an appalling piece of self-indictment. Given the fighting prowess of the 11th Indian Division, and their extreme fatigue at this time, to subject them to the immediate construction of their defences a second time within days was inexcusable. Percival had previously denied the division permission to withdraw on the grounds of the adverse effect upon the morale of the army as a whole and the civilian population. The lack of prepared positions at Jitra and Gurun was hardly good for morale for the personnel who really mattered: the 11th Division. But the most damning admission in Percival's above quoted passage is surely that he waited for war to break out before ordering the construction of defensive positions. Further, the admission that orders for work had been issued, but no work had eventuated, constitutes nothing more than slack command. Also, Percival's statement that the defences were to be undertaken 'under the supervision of military officers' is vague. The 'military officers' surely should have been engineers and, critically, all personnel should have been under the supervision of the Chief Engineer, Brigadier Simson, who had arrived at Singapore on 5 August—four months before the war began. In the end, Percival must bear the ultimate responsibility for this failure. Given his twenty-month period of time as General

Dobbie's chief staff officer which ended in 1937, and Dobbie's desire to build a defensive line in southern Johore, it is strange that Percival did not perceive the need for any form of fortifications along the Malay Peninsula. Stranger still that he employed schemes such as Matador, given the training of his Indians. And the 11th Division was about to pay for this sin a second time.

Gurun was regarded by Percival as 'perhaps the best natural defensive position in Malaya'.[4] The village, nestled between rubber estates, lay where the Trunk Road and the railway converged. To the west of Gurun, through about one-and-a-half kilometres of rubber, stretched the formidable 1200-metre-high and thickly wooded Kedah Peak, which ran almost to the coast. Away to the east of the village, and through an extensive rubber belt containing numerous estate roads, lay the jungle-covered beginning of Malaya's central mountain range. Chempedak Railway Station was found just north of Gurun. Here a lateral road ran to the west and just north of Kedah Peak to the coastal location of Yen. The ground to the north of the railway station consisted of rubber, rice paddy and swamp.

Major-General Murray-Lyon deployed Brigadier Lay's 6th Brigade where the Japanese might be expected to attack: astride the Trunk Road and railway line. The most northern part of the perimeter was around the Chempedak Railway Station and was manned by a company of the 2/16th Punjab and its HQ. The 2nd East Surreys, less one company and to the south-east of the Punjabis, occupied the roughly one-and-a-half kilometre gap between the railway and the Trunk Road. On their left flank and astride the Trunk Road were the 1/8th Punjab and one company of the Surreys. To the east of the railway Brigadier Carpendale's 28th Brigade occupied the right flank. The 2/9th, 2/1st and 2/2nd Gurkhas occupied positions along an eastward rubber estate road. The 6th Brigade HQ was situated in a hut in the village and on the western side of the railway, while the 28th Brigade HQ was located in the village to the east of the rail. Murray-Lyon placed his worn and greatly diminished 15th Brigade just south of Gurun at around the 23-mile peg, astride the Trunk Road and railway.

If Murray-Lyon had expected to buy some much-needed time for his exhausted troops by blowing up the bridges across the River Kedah and withdrawing virtually straight to Gurun, then a combination of very poor British demolition work and skilled repairs by the enemy engineers saw the

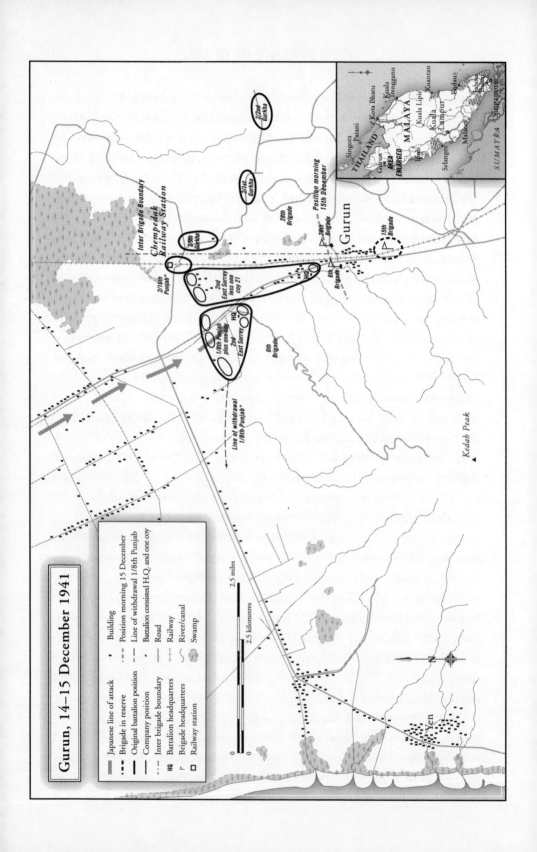

Gurun, 14–15 December 1941

Legend:

- ▬ Japanese line of attack
- ⁚⁚ Brigade in reserve
- ▬ Original battalion position
- ▬ Company position
- ⊣⊢ Inter brigade boundary
- HQ Battalion headquarters
- ⊿ Brigade headquarters
- ◻ Railway station
- ▪ Building
- ⁵ ᵐ Position morning 15 December
- ⁻⁻ Line of withdrawal 1/8th Punjab
- ✝ Battalion consisted H.Q. and one coy
- ⌒ Road
- ⊢⊣ Railway
- ⌇ River/canal
- ▩ Swamp

0   2.5 miles

0   2.5 kilometres

22nd Gurkha

21st Gurkha

Inter Brigade Boundary

Chempedak Railway Station

29th Gurkha

28th Brigade

Position morning 15th December

28th Brigade

Gurun

15th Brigade

2/16th Punjab*

2nd East Surrey *less one coy 21*

HQ

6th Brigade

1/8th Punjab *plus one coy*

HQ

2nd East Surrey

6th Brigade

Line of withdrawal 1/8th Punjab

Kedah Peak ▲

N

Inset map:

Singora
Patani
THAILAND
MALAYA
Kota Bharu
Kuala Trengganu
Kuala Lipis
Ipoh
Kuala Lumpur
Selangor
Gurun
AREA ENLARGED
Malacca
Kuantan
Endau
Johore Bahru
Singapore
SUMATRA

11th Indian Division followed up quite rapidly. By dawn on 14 December the enemy had secured heavy vehicle access across the River Kedah, and around noon Japanese patrols were in contact with the forward elements of the 11th Division at the intersection of the Chempedak–Yen and Trunk Roads. At 2.00 pm twelve Japanese trucks headed by three tanks approached the crossroads. When immediately engaged by artillery and one anti-tank gun, the Japanese column moved back with damage to the leading tank. The speedy arrival of enemy tanks came as a monumental shock, for it had been expected that the demolition of the bridges over the Kedah River would keep them out of the battle for a number of days. Clifford Kinvig, has stated that: 'There was no natural tank obstacle at Gurun and there had been no time to construct one.'[5] No troops are able to construct tank obstacles as they arrive on a battlefield with the enemy in hot pursuit—such endeavours are best undertaken with a degree of forward planning. The truth is that a number of the 11th Division units' poor training, physical condition and morale had all conspired to reduce its slim chances of success, and these grave handicaps were dramatically compounded by an almost total lack of High Command forward planning and by unrealistic expectations.

By 3.00 pm, within an hour of this first contact, the rearward Japanese infantry had sprung from their trucks and swept the Indians from their forward posts and caused their retirement back into the main perimeter. Kirby has recorded that within a further hour the now reinforced Japanese had 'succeeded in penetrating the position held by the 1/8th Punjab whose morale was by this time shaky, and some retrograde movement began'.[6] This is a terribly polite way of stating that the 1/8th Punjab panicked and began to 'shoot through' in much the same manner as they had done only hours before at the Alor Star bridge. And given their training and recent experience, who could blame them? The interesting question that might be asked is why that formation was deployed on the vital forward ground covering the Trunk Road. There may have been few alternatives, but it would seem that just about any other choice might have been a better one. Common sense suggests that a stiffer defence of the vital ground at both Jitra and Gurun might have occurred had the Surreys and Leicesters occupied such positions.

When the 1/8th Punjab had begun its 'withdrawal' Brigadier Lay sent elements of the 3rd Cavalry to deal with the enemy penetration. They too were shot up and hastily withdrew. We now come to a piece of inspired leadership. Brigadier Lay hurriedly collected a group of about 50 soldiers and moved forward. Alan Warren has recorded that a lieutenant from the Surreys saw:

> The brigade Commander ... pipe in his mouth, a cheery grin on his face, and he is waving his walking stick at us. He even has his battered old red hat on! As he goes by, he calls out to us: 'Come along, you fellows, we've got to push them back, they say there're hundreds of the blighters, all the more to kill!'[7]

Lay, by his very presence and guile, directed his soldiers to 'get around the bastards and push 'em out'.[8] Although the post at the crossroads remained in enemy hands, the immediate perimeter was restored.

During the afternoon of 14 December, General Heath visited Murray-Lyon at 11th Division HQ, about six-and-a-half kilometres south of Gurun. Kirby has recorded that Murray-Lyon 'urged that the time had come to concentrate in order to avoid defeat in detail and explained that his troops were quite unfit for a series of dogfights at frequent intervals'.[9] Two thoughts dominated his appreciation. The first was that, in essential terms, the fighting withdrawal was not working. The British were giving ground but not buying time. The enemy was, through poor demolition of key features and equally poor defences at the chosen sites, not being checked for acceptable periods of time. Further, as had occurred at Jitra and, he feared, would also happen at Gurun, a comprehensive mauling of his division would transpire. Murray-Lyon was now sensibly advocating a far more pronounced withdrawal by either road or rail or both to allow for a concentration of his force and time to prepare dispositions. His second assessment constituted the age-old commander's fear when committed to a withdrawal along more than one axis: an enemy outflanking movement, encirclement and annihilation. He told Heath that he saw the present Japanese thrust down the Grik Road in this light.

Heath told Murray-Lyon that he had sent the 12th Brigade to bolster the defence along the Kroh and Grik Roads, and pointed out that Kuala Kangsar—the main line of communication—should be safe for some time.

He ordered Murray-Lyon to hold Gurun for as long as possible and then, when Kuala Kangsar was so threatened, he saw a withdrawal across the Perak River as the best option. When Heath contacted Percival that night, he told him that:

> ... if the 11th Division was to be reconstituted, it would be wrong to fight at Gurun; the plan should be to go right back to the Perak River, the enemy's advance being delayed by demolitions and a temporary stand on the Muda River in order to give time for Penang to be evacuated. Percival replied that III Corps was to continue to cover Penang and was not to withdraw further than the line of the Muda River without his permission.[10]

When the three commanders' perspectives are examined, the immediacy of Murray-Lyon's dilemma—and its validity—is not hard to fathom. Heath's response was realistic but was fortified by the anticipation of 12th Brigade being able to slow down the Japanese advance along the Kroh and Grik Roads. It also displays Heath's ability to see the need for his III Corps to be given a chance to concentrate and, critically, to rest and construct, or at least gain, a realistic defensive position. Percival's response was academic, in that there seems no evidence of a realistic grasp of 11th Division's plight. It was fighting a first-class enemy who had displayed a masterly ability to concentrate his force, to employ tanks against few anti-tank weapons, to probe aggressively, to rapidly outflank and to maintain the initiative by keeping his line of communication intact, and moving at great speed. As a result, the 11th Indian Division was demoralised, exhausted, panic-stricken and a spent force. Another Jitra simply re-enacted at Gurun, followed by further failed demolitions, and another rushed, disorganised and exhausting flight to the next disaster, could only repeat the humiliation. And it began within hours of Murray-Lyon and Heath's meeting.

Brigadier Lay had planned a counterattack at around dawn on 15 December. The Japanese quite simply maintained the initiative by attacking at 1.30 am. Preceded by a concentrated mortaring of the Punjabis, they attacked straight down the Truck Road and managed to not only burst through that battalion's right flank, but to overrun the Surreys' depleted A Company and then Battalion HQ. The CO and five other officers were killed. But worse was to follow. Following up their success, the Japanese advance guard descended upon 6th Brigade HQ where a further slaughter took place. Fortunately, Brigadier Lay and his intelligence officer were on other business and escaped the fate of some of their colleagues. Lay then reported to Brigadier Carpendale that his HQ had been eliminated. When Brigadier Lay ran into the CO of the Leicesters on his way to report to Murray-Lyon, their short conversation aptly described the tragic chain of events at Gurun. Lay: 'I've just lost my brigade.' Lieutenant-Colonel Morrison: 'And I, Sir, have just lost my battalion.'[11]

During this mayhem, the CO of the forward Punjabis, believing that the Surreys on his right flank had been overrun, ordered a withdrawal of his battalion and the company of Surreys under his command to the west towards Yen, in the hope that his force could come around the coast and rejoin the division. With the Trunk Road and virtually the whole western side of the perimeter now in Japanese hands, it was left to Brigadier Carpendale and his 28th Brigade and elements of the 15th Brigade to attempt to hold the Japanese around Gurun.

On the morning of 15 December, Murray-Lyon was forced to order a general withdrawal. There are few more tragic sights than a demoralised army in retreat. By the morning of 16 December, preceded by the now familiar and premature demolitions, the exhausted remnants of 11th Division had withdrawn behind the Muda River. It was fortunate indeed that the Japanese did not follow this withdrawal up with their characteristic speed and aggression. It may well have been that as they had achieved this startling success by employing not two battalions as at Jitra, but only one at Gurun, that they might have felt the need to consolidate their gains and concentrate their force. Gurun, no less than Jitra, was ample testimony to their considerable military prowess.

On 14 December, near the 'important crossroad', Lieutenant-Colonel Tsuji noted the 'vast quantities of munitions' which were 'piled up like a mountain' by the road. He saw trucks containing yet more 'Churchill supplies' which he felt had been left 'to welcome our army'.

———————

The rapid loss of Jitra and Gurun now constituted a direct threat to the security of the island of Penang. Lying about four kilometres to the west of the town of Butterworth on the west coast of Malaya, and a mere twelve kilometres south-west from the new 11th Division lines at the Muda River, Penang's prime military significance lay in its port facilities, its two telegraph cables connecting Malaya with Ceylon and India, and its fixed defences. Also, the island had extensive dumps of military hardware and stores, and handing over further 'Churchill supplies' to the enemy was not to be countenanced. It had been decided that two infantry battalions and their supporting units would be deployed from the mainland to secure the above-mentioned facilities if it were necessary. The rapid deterioration in events, however, had frustrated this plan.

The reality of war descended upon an unprepared Penang on 11 December 1941. During the morning Georgetown received an extensive bombing of its harbour and districts by 41 'Sally' bombers of the Japanese Army Air Force. Escorted by 'Oscar' fighters, and untroubled by British planes and non-existent anti-aircraft guns the Japanese bombers inflicted over 2000 civilian casualties. Because there were no air raid shelters the ignorant and helpless native population had eagerly occupied places such as Bishop Street and the busy market in Penang Road to witness dogfights and the bombing raid. They became terrified participants both during the bombing, and shortly after, when the Japanese began strafing the city. To add to the human cost, the city's fire station suffered a direct hit and was powerless to respond. In some quarters 11 December 1941 became known as 'Black Thursday'.

The next day, Japanese air raids began at around 9.00 am and continued during the day. They concentrated on Georgetown's harbour, the Penang Channel and nearby fishing villages. On the 13th came the belated entry of eight Buffalo fighters of No. 453 Squadron which had flown up from Singapore to Ipoh and Butterworth. Although five unescorted bombers were shot down, the destruction continued. By 15 December the Japanese air raids had achieved their purpose and the carnage stopped. But the damage had been done.

Such a shameful episode clearly indicated how empty were the claims of Brooke-Popham, the civil administration and Malaya Command concerning civilian morale. The initial rampant destruction and the lack of any form of an early civil or military response crushed the morale of the native population. The first obvious indication was a direct hit and obliteration of Police HQ on Penang Road, which caused the death of a number of Sikh police officers. This in turn led to the desertion of many of the local constabulary who took to the hinterland with great speed. In the absence of law and order, and with a breakdown of the town's water supply and other utilities, looting and the potential for disease now became the chief concerns. The scale of looting, the number of disfigured corpses in varying states of decay and uncontrolled fires around the city all conspired to force the authorities to evacuate the European women, children and the wounded service population from the island. In his postwar despatch, Percival was to state that: 'Lack of transport would have made it quite out of the question to evacuate large numbers of the Asiatics. Moreover it was undesirable at that stage to increase the population of Singapore.'[12] By this decision, the Asian population, and particularly the Chinese, were left in little doubt as to their place in the scheme of things. As Peter Thompson has astutely pointed out: 'Considering that 24 self-propelled vessels, several dozen junks, private yachts and a collection of sampans, barges and rafts—all later found to be capable of ferrying Japanese soldiers—were left bobbing at anchor in Penang Harbour, this was one of Percival's more disingenuous statements.'[13]

Here, surely, was a concrete chance to show some genuine concern for the morale of the civilian population, and for that matter, to create a permanent labour supply—however limited—that might have begun some belated work upon defensive positions at any desired point along the Malay Peninsula and/or on Singapore Island. In blunt terms, the civilians evacuated from Penang could have been literally press-ganged into construction work in exchange for their freedom, and the Chinese especially might well have been keen to contribute to the war effort. Brooke-Popham, Percival and the civil administration had become nothing more than masters of empty rhetoric. To variously complain about 'civilian morale' or the lack of a 'labour construction force' and be seen to be doing little to address either issue smacks of incompetent leadership. Peter Thompson in *The Battle For Singapore* provides us with a stinging rebuttal to such behaviour:

Shenton Thomas broadcast an appeal for volunteers to provide temporary shelter for the trainload of Penang evacuees expected to cross
the Causeway early on 15 December. He went to Singapore Railway
Station himself to greet the refugees. Many Chinese families who had
gathered at the station expecting to find relatives on the train were
shocked to discover that only Europeans had been evacuated.[14]

Duff Cooper went one better—or worse. In a broadcast to the people of
Singapore, he stated that many of the citizens of Penang had been evacuated,
but then proceeded to insert his foot fairly and squarely in his mouth by
pointing out that Singaporeans could feel thankful that so many people had
been rescued. The small percentage of the population who were in fact white
must have indeed felt relieved, but the Chinese, Indian and Malay reaction
can be well imagined. Penang was occupied by the Japanese on 19 December
1941, and with the circumstances of its occupation, the integrity of British
rule lay in tatters.

By the morning of 16 December 1941, the 11th Indian Division—against
the background disasters of Gurun and Penang Island—had retreated to the
south side of the Muda River. In the tactical sense nothing had changed.
Lionel Wigmore, in *The Japanese Thrust*:

> The road from Kroh through Balang linked with the road system in
> the Muda area; and the route from Kroh southward through Grik
> reached the Trunk Road and the railway west of Kuala Kangsar. How
> long could the enemy force which had captured Kroh be kept from the
> division's present right flank and rear? How long was it safe to keep
> the division west of the Perak in all the circumstances?[15]

Early on 16 December—with the above issues in mind—General Heath
decided to deploy the 11th Division behind the River Krian, which, flanked
by swamps, constituted the best natural tank obstacle between the Perak and
Muda Rivers. He ordered the 28th Brigade to cover a roughly four-kilometre
line stretching from the rail bridge and road at Nibong Tebal westwards to

the sea; to his eastward or right flank at the River Krian centre of Selama, he deployed the 3/16th Punjab and the 10th Mountain Battery; his exhausted and diminished 6th and 15th Brigades were sited between the River Krian and the key junction of Kuala Kangsar at Taiping to recover and reorganise; and to protect this critical move, he ordered Brigadier Paris's 12th Brigade to conduct a rearguard action through Titi Karangan 'where the Balang road linked with the road system south of the Muda, to Selama'.[16] From Selama, the 12th Brigade was to move through the 3/16th Punjab to Taiping.

Brigadier Paris had decided to concentrate his 12th Brigade on 15 December. The 5/2nd Punjab was ordered to hold the bridge on the Muda River at Batu Pekaku while the Argylls were sent to Titi Karangan. On 16 December, Japanese infantry dressed as natives, and led by a 'European in plain clothes',[17] tried to storm the Batu Pekaku bridge. The ruse failed and the bridge was demolished. The next day Brigadier Paris withdrew his 5/2nd Punjab from Batu Pekaku, and following up closely, the Japanese encountered the Argylls at Titi Karangan.

It will be remembered that the Argylls were commanded by Lieutenant-Colonel Stewart—a 'crank' according to Percival's chief staff officer, Brigadier Torrance. Titi Karangan was a poor defensive locality. Stewart has recorded that:

There was no natural obstacle across the front, for the line of the Muda was being given up. The country is not jungle, but rubber, thus giving the attacker the advantages not only of easy cross country movement but of concealment, the perfect conditions for encircling attack. The only counter under these circumstances is to fight a battle of manoeuvre, but even this was precluded by the orders to the 93rd [the Argylls] rigidly laying down a particular line to be denied till 12.00 hours.[18]

The Argylls' dispositions and drill at Titi Karangan relied upon companies being able to fight as self-contained, dispersed groups. These were composed of carriers, armoured cars, mortars and operated with armoured car contact between companies and with the battalion's transport 'four miles to the south well clear of interference'.[19] All companies were to operate with both a tactical attack and withdrawal plan. Stewart deployed his A Company just north of Titi Karangan in an ambush position with his B Company poised to then encircle and attack. In addition, his armoured cars were to remain hidden from the enemy until the attack, so as to 'come as a moral and tactical surprise'.[20]

At 10.00 am on 17 December the Japanese made contact with the Argylls' A Company. Stewart later claimed that the ambush failed because the Japanese opened fire first and that they 'surprised our men by appearing in native dress and not in uniform'.[21] But the enemy certainly did not have it all his own way. When around 200 Japanese infantry subsequently attempted to outflank the Argylls by a movement off the road and through the rubber-covered hillside, they were confronted by two light machine guns and two 2-inch mortars, which had been positioned 'forward on the edge of the jungle strip'.[22] Lieutenant-Colonel Stewart would later write that: 'They were in close order and the perfect answer to a machine-gunner's prayer. Our fire completely surprised them, and at 75 yards' range was devastating. They ran around in all directions in a bewildered way, making no response. A European amongst them was shot.'[23]

In response to this carnage, at around 10.45 am the Japanese brought telling mortar fire to bear and knocked out the Argylls' mortars, in unison with frontal attacks and rapid attempts to outflank them. Stewart determined that he stood little chance of delaying the enemy until midday without much of his unit becoming encircled, and therefore decided to attack. In so doing, he would have denied the enemy the ground he was expected to hold until midday, but the cost would have been horrendous—he estimated his losses might have been the greater part of his two forward companies.

In the event, the decision was made for him when, just as the bugler was about to sound the call for an attack, a despatch rider from Brigadier Paris gave Stewart permission to 'withdraw any time at your discretion'.[24] The Argylls withdrew in an efficient, professional manner, and after marching to their rearward transport arrived at a disused hospital about sixteen kilometres to the rear. During its first action, the Argylls lost eleven soldiers but inflicted at least 200 casualties upon their enemy. Stewart would later note that the '200' rapidly became '500' when the news reached the media in Singapore.[25] By midnight on 17 December 1941, Paris's 12th

Brigade had arrived at Selama and had come under the command of the 11th Division. By sunrise the next day, Murray-Lyon's force was south of the River Krian.

Meanwhile, a detached company of the Argylls and a number of their armoured cars which had occupied a position on the Kroh–Kuala Kangsar road were attacked by the Japanese on 16 December just north of Grik. As a consequence they were forced to withdraw towards Kuala Kenering and subsequently to Sumpitan on the 17th. Although the potential use of this road by the Japanese had been foreseen—despite its poor condition for motor transport—the sheer speed of the enemy's use of it had prohibited the necessary charges being laid for its demolition. The Japanese intent had been to reach Kuala Kangsar via a southward thrust through Grik instead of a westward movement through Balang. Thus they sought to cut the 11th Indian Division's line of communication. But unable to employ their light tank battalion because of the poor condition of the road and heavy rain, the Japanese advance had been slowed.

General Heath, aware of the danger, had previously sent the 1st Independent Company to Lenggong to reinforce the Argylls' company and its armoured cars. However, on 17 December, with their now customary speed and momentum, the Japanese forced him to take the 12th Brigade under his command and deploy it at Kuala Kangsar to block the enemy advance along the Grik Road. And he was also aware that as the Perak River ran north–south—and therefore not across the enemy line of advance—he might soon be forced to withdraw as far south as the road and rail junction of Kampar.

———◆———

Against the background of the crushing defeats of his 11th Indian Division in Kedah State—primarily at Jitra and Gurun—General Percival reassessed his strategic position in mid-December. Although his prime piece of military real estate was the Singapore Naval Base, that defence hinged upon the retention of Johore—lose Johore and lose the war. His intelligence was poor: the Japanese force was estimated at a division on the Trunk Road; there was, it was claimed, one on the Patani–Kroh–Grik road; a third on the east coast axis in Kelantan; Percival was informed that the Japanese 'had already landed further forces at least equal to those in the front line'; and in Indo-China, that the Japanese 'undoubtedly held reserves, which he could either use to reinforce those formations which he had already landed or for fresh enterprises'.[26] The truth is that the 11th Division had been ejected from Kedah State by an enemy force *half* the strength of his assessment.

To counter this Japanese advance, Percival had about a division on the west coast and two brigades to the east. In his postwar despatch, he pointed out that though the 11th Division's morale 'was not broken it could not be regarded as being as high as one would have wished'.[27] He gave three reasons for this state of affairs: the Division's poor physical condition after continuous fighting and 'movement by both day and night'; the overwhelming Japanese air superiority; and the absence of British tanks. He further mentioned that the last two Japanese advantages—air superiority and tanks—'could not but have the most adverse affect [*sic*] upon the trust of the Indian troops in the might of the British Empire'.[28]

In assessing future enemy options, Percival considered that it was now obvious that their main thrust would continue along the west coast 'with a view of attacking Singapore from the north'. But he also foresaw the possibility of an enemy thrust down the east coast being complemented by possible seaborne landings. Such landings might allow the Japanese to cut the British line of communication to their northern forces. It was this concern that prompted Percival to leave the Australian 8th Division in Johore rather than employ it to replace the 11th Division in the north. Such a relief, he thought, would temporarily leave the defences in Johore very weak. He decided that if the exhausted 11th Division manned those former Australian defensive positions, the issue of time in transfer and the Indian ignorance of the ground would be negative factors. He also felt it was 'undesirable to break up the A.I.F. organisation'.[29]

Given that Percival—and Brooke-Popham—believed that the aim of operations should be to keep the Japanese as far north as possible to deny them airfields and large quantities of tin and rubber in the central states, it was decided that the 11th Indian Division must continue the fight.

In view of the above appreciation, late on 17 December 1941, Percival decided to travel to Ipoh to confer with General Heath. The next day, after a 'reconnaissance of the area and a visit to the forward troops',[30] he made a number of important decisions. The first three were that:

(a) While adhering to the general policy of withdrawal behind the
     River Perak, the enemy would be held west of the river as long
     as possible without permitting our forces to become inextricably
     committed.

(b) The Commander 3 Indian Corps [Heath] would select and
     have prepared a series of positions between Ipoh and Tanjong
     Malim.

(c) The immediate role of 9 Division [Barstow] would be (i) to
     continue to deny the Kuantan aerodrome to the enemy, (ii)
     to secure the 11 Indian Division and its communications against
     attack from the east coast.[31]

Percival's other initiatives included the use of the Perak Flotilla to counter
Japanese landings along the west coast; the formation of Roseforce—
50 Australian soldiers based at Port Sweetenham—to disrupt enemy communications west of the River Perak; the allocation of labour supply was to
be the responsibility of the RAF for the maintenance of new air strips on
Singapore Island and in southern Johore; and the amalgamation of the
greatly diminished 6th and 15th Brigades to form the 6th/15th Brigade.

There are a number of noteworthy points concerning Percival's appreciation. His comment concerning the morale of the Indians of the 11th Division
is bland. When companies of troops run from a position at the sound of a
bridge being blown, it is clearly evident that such troops' morale is in fact
broken and that the situation is far, far more serious than 'not . . . being as
high as one would have wished'. Percival's reluctance to 'break up the A.I.F.
organization' would seem to indicate that he was aware of General Gordon
Bennett's charter. Bennett's diary, 14 December: 'General Percival called &
asked what would be the position if Singapore was attacked and help from
A.I.F. were required. I said if troops on the island failed I would have to move
to help as we are here to defend this island.'[32]

Percival's order to Heath on 18 December that 'The Commander 3 Indian
Corps would select and have prepared a series of positions between Ipoh and
Tanjong Malim' demonstrates yet again that for some unexplained reason
Brigadier Simson was still—after the defeats of Jitra, Gurun and the loss

of Penang—a redundant resource in the preparation of set-piece, in-depth, and above all, tank defence positions along the III Corps withdrawal route. By obvious extension, there was the need to create a firm base in depth at or near General Dobbie's suggested line in Johore. By this time it was late, and it was becoming very late—but it was most certainly not too late.

But his order that 'labour supply priority was to be allotted to the RAF for the maintenance of new air strips on Singapore Island and in southern Johore' shows all the characteristics of a general who has lost touch with military reality. It is well worth mentioning the state of the RAF at this time. Douglas Gillison, in his *Royal Australian Airforce, 1939–1942*, quotes a memorandum issued by Brooke-Popham on Christmas Eve:

There have been many cases of gallantry and devotion on the part of individual officers and airmen but there have also been instances where aerodromes appear to have been abandoned in a state of approaching panic. Stores that will assist the enemy in his further advance have been left behind, material that is urgently required has been abandoned and a general state of chaos has been evident.[33]

After quoting Brooke-Popham, Gillison then states that:

In these depressing circumstances the air force in Malaya had a serviceable strength of only 146 aircraft—40 bombers, 34 torpedo bombers, 38 fighters, 17 general reconnaissance and 17 miscellaneous. Of these only 74 (including the Glenn Martin and Blenheim bombers which could be called scarcely be termed "modern") could be regarded as current types and even these were no match for the types the Japanese could bring against them in vastly superior numbers.[34]

But in a chilling footnote to this observation, Gillison pointed out that on 7 December the strength of the RAF was 164, but of the now available 146 aircraft, 52 had been flown in since the outbreak of hostilities: 24 Dutch Martin bombers, nine Dutch Buffaloes, six Wirraways, five Albatrosses, four Swordfish and four Sharks. He then stated that 'many replacement aircraft had been destroyed by enemy action' and that 'nor of course, was the combat efficiency of the aircraft then available nearly as high as at the outbreak of war'.[35]

Thus, although Percival and Brooke-Popham were loath to see the Japanese acquire airfields in central Malaya, and thereby enhance their ability to attack potential troop reinforcements to Singapore, the stark truth was that such reinforcements of soldiers and material could not, by Percival's own admission, arrive by sea until mid-January 1942 at the earliest. Given the ground already lost by the 11th Indian Division in just over two weeks, all available labour should have been placed under the Chief Engineer's control for the preservation of the vital ground—the ground that was always going to decide Singapore's fate, and that was Johore. The plain truth is that at this critical stage of the fight for Singapore, the army had become the prime force that would determine success or failure, and that while the decision to employ the very limited and obsolete RAF primarily for patrolling and future convoy protection was pragmatic, to deny the army—which was fighting for the very survival of Singapore—much-needed labour was foolhardy. Further, not a syllable of Percival's appreciation appears to have addressed any of the ingredients of such recent disasters. In short, he expected Heath and his III Corps to carry on the same fight with the same lack of expertise and materials which had delivered nothing more than demoralisation and disaster.

On 12 December 1941, Prime Minister Winston Churchill sailed to the United States aboard HMS *Duke of York* to confer with President Roosevelt, with a view to reaching fundamental decisions regarding the future direction of the war. While at sea, Churchill wrote that he 'had clear convictions which I regret it was not in my power to enforce from mid-ocean'.[36]

Prime Minister to General Ismay, for C.O.S. [Chiefs of Staff] 15 Dec 41

Beware lest [that] troops required for ultimate defence Singapore Island and fortress are not used up or cut off in Malay peninsula. Nothing compares in importance with the fortress. Are you sure we shall have enough troops for prolonged defence? Consider with Auchinleck and Commonwealth Government moving 1st Australian

Division [*sic* should be 'corps'] from Palestine to Singapore. Report action.[37]

After a conference in Singapore on 18 December 1941, attended by representatives from Great Britain, the United States, Holland, Australia and New Zealand, a report was sent to the British Chiefs of Staff. In essence the report requested planes to complete the strength of existing squadrons in Singapore and Malaya, a further four bomber and four fighter squadrons, a new division and a brigade group of infantry, reinforcements for Heath's III Corps, three light and two heavy anti-aircraft regiments, an anti-tank regiment and 50 light tanks. The conference also approved 'Percival's policy of holding the enemy as far north as possible'.[38] Churchill was more specific—'as far north as possible' meant 'Johore'.

Prime Minister to General Ismay, for C.O.S. Committee 19 Dec 41

Duff Cooper expresses the same anxieties as I conveyed to you in my message beginning 'Beware'. Duff Cooper's proposal to concentrate on defence of Johore for the purpose of holding Singapore conforms exactly to view taken by Dill here.

2. After naval disasters to British and American sea-power in Pacific and Indian Oceans we have no means of preventing continuous landings by Japanese in great strength in Siam and Malay peninsula. It is therefore impossible to defend, other than by demolitions and delaying action, anything north of the defensive line in Johore, and this line itself can only be defended as part of the final defence of Singapore Island fortress and the naval base.

3. The Commander-in-Chief should now be told to confine himself to defence of Johore and Singapore. This should not preclude his employing delaying tactics and demolitions on the way south and making an orderly retreat.[39]

In *The Japanese Thrust*, Lionel Wigmore quoted parts of the above Churchill cables. But the fascinating point that Wigmore did not pursue was

the Prime Minister's reference to 'the defensive line in Johore'. Two points are
critical: the first is that there was no prepared line in southern Johore. Was
Churchill referring to a line on a map? A geographical line only? Surely he
was referring to a set-piece defensive line, or in other words, a line of fortifications. Further, Churchill's reference that such a line 'conforms exactly to
view taken by Dill here' is significant. Percival was a protégé of Dill's and had
been appointed by him to GOC Malaya. He would surely have been aware of
Dobbie's proposed 1937 line across southern Johore. It will be remembered
that Dill was Chief of the Imperial General Staff when Brigadier Simson was
appointed to the position of Chief Engineer, Malaya Command, and that,
according to Simson, a letter outlining his (Simson's) position and responsibilities was to have been despatched to Percival pending Simson's arrival in
Singapore. No such letter had been despatched. Wigmore also states that on
15 December Duff Cooper had:

> . . . disclosed to Mr Bowden, Australia's representative in Singapore,
> misgivings about the military situation, and said he saw the prob-
> ability of a gradual withdrawal to a line approximately covering the
> southern half of Johore, to be held pending arrival of reinforcements
> about a month hence.[40]

Duff Cooper was no military genius, but his above point merely repeats
what Dobbie had advocated in 1937—along with his GSO1, Colonel Arthur
Percival. And it supports what Churchill, Dill and Brigadier Ivan Simson
were now proposing as the only realistic plan for the defence of Singapore.

Pleas for reinforcements to Singapore were not confined to the British.
General Northcott, who was visiting General Bennett while passing
through Singapore after a visit to the Middle East, cabled the Australian
Chiefs of Staff on 18 December suggesting all possible reinforcements, and
that a machine gun battalion should be sent immediately. General Gordon
Bennett had been, through December 1941, communicating with the
Australian Chiefs of Staff and the Minister for the Army. On 13 December
he told Army HQ that: 'There is insufficient cover in the air to enable the
Army to carry out its role without molestation from the enemy's Air Force.
I fear another Crete.'[41] On the same day Bennett told the Minister that:

'Naturally, our line is thin. The 3rd Brigade of my division would have been a godsend to us now. As you know, it has been repeatedly asked for, and my requests have been repeatedly refused.'[42] On 17 December Bennett cabled Army HQ in Melbourne:

> I have seen a total absence of the offensive spirit, which after all, is the one great remedy for the methods adopted by the Japanese. Counter attacks would put a stop to this penetration . . .
>
> The position has arrived when something must be done—urgently. I strongly urge that, should the request be made, at least one division of the A.I.F. from the Middle East be transferred to Malaya . . . [43]

Bennett's cable merely reflects his utter ignorance of the Indian Army's training. It was all very well to advocate an 'offensive spirit' and that 'counter-attacks would put a stop to this penetration', but the prerequisites for success in war are surely training and equipment and support. And training is surely the first requirement.

On 19 December, the Australian Department of External Affairs cabled Mr Vivian Bowden, its Singapore representative, for a report on the state of defences in Singapore. It stated that: 'This government is far from satisfied with the results of the policy of subordinating requirements of this theatre of war' and that 'Brooke-Popham gave us assurances that all was well with Malayan defences . . .'.[44] Bowden's reply, given late on the same day, was to prove prophetic:

> I feel strongly that before further Australian troops are commit-ted every possible guarantee should be taken that they will not be abandoned with those already here. In my view real defence strength in Malaya falls far short of previous publicity and I feel assurances should be sought immediately from United Kingdom Government that Malaya will not continue to be regarded as secondary theatre of war and that reinforcements and supplies of modern arms and equip-ment will be rushed here even at cost of slowing down African offen-sive. Am convinced that unless reinforcements of modern aircraft and

operationally trained personnel are sent immediately Singapore will
before long be in gravest danger.[45]

Prime Minister John Curtin cabled Churchill the next day:

Army authorities are in receipt of disturbing report from Bennett
regarding gravity of position and request by him for dispatch of one
Australian Division from Middle East. He also refers to inadequate air
support . . .
    I shall be glad to receive most immediate reply as to military
position, the strength of your forces, and measures in hand for reinforcements, if such are required. It would be appreciated if brief report
on military situation could be cabled to me say three times a week or
more frequently if developments require it.[46]

On 23 December, Bowden cabled Curtin again:

Expected arrival of modern fighter planes in boxes requiring weeks
to assemble under the danger of destruction by bombing cannot save
the position.
    . . . Reinforcements of troops should not be in brigades but in divi-
sions . . . Anything that is not powerful modern and immediate is
futile.[47]

Bowden's words 'anything that is not powerful modern and immediate is
futile' deserve close scrutiny in light of events that were occurring in Washington, London and Canberra at this time. The first consideration is the
priority given at the strategic level to the Far East.
    Winston Churchill's trip to Washington aboard the *Duke of York* to meet
with Roosevelt and his advisors in Washington was dominated by his desire
to settle arguably the greatest strategic issue of the Second World War: the
'defeat Hitler first' proposition. Churchill has stated that:

We were conscious of a serious danger that the United States might
pursue the war against Japan in the Pacific and leave us to fight
Germany and Italy in Europe, Africa, and in the Middle East . . .

Should we be able to persuade the President and the American Service chiefs that the defeat of Japan would not spell the defeat of Hitler, but that the defeat of Hitler made the finishing off of Japan merely a matter of time and trouble?[48]

Churchill need not have worried, as Roosevelt and his advisors were of the same mind. The 'defeat Hitler first' strategy and the 'Grand Alliance' were born of that period in Washington. The consequences of that decision were simple: win the battle of the Atlantic to facilitate the build-up of immediate material supplies and eventual troop concentrations; bomb Germany to cause the eventual ruination of its capacity to wage war; win the battle for North Africa; and provide all possible material assistance to the Soviet Union to continue its war on the Eastern Front. The Far East was a subordinate and distant priority. On 17 December, Churchill had said that: 'The Japanese must be expected to establish themselves on both sides of the Straits of Malacca and in the Straits of Sunda . . . we expect, however, that Singapore island and fortress will stand an attack for at least six months . . .'[49]

Shortly after Christmas 1941, Churchill perceived that 'the question of forming a supreme Allied command in South-East Asia and drawing boundary lines was approaching'.[50] He was right. The Americans suggested that that commander should be British, and their choice was General Wavell, who had been sacked by Churchill in the Middle East, replaced by General Auchinleck, and was now ensconced in New Delhi as Commander of the Indian Army. Churchill, ever the shrewd politician—and strategist—thought that:

I was complimented by the choice of a British commander, but it seemed to me that the theatre in which he would act would soon be overrun and the forces which could be placed at his disposal would be destroyed by the Japanese onslaught. I found that the British Chiefs of Staff, when appraised [sic], had the same reaction.[51]

It is clear from the above that both Churchill and his Chiefs of Staff knew that the chances of Singapore holding out were, in the long term, slim, but as has also been intimated, the Prime Minister saw 'at least six months' as a survival time frame. A further change to the command structure in the Far East had come on 23 December when Lieutenant-General Sir Henry Pownall arrived in Singapore to take over from Brooke-Popham. This change of command reflected the fact that the Chiefs of Staff had realised that the army was now the chief service for the defence of Malaya and Singapore. Pownall formally assumed command on 27 December, while Brooke-Popham departed Singapore four days later.

The second consideration when assessing Bowden's 'anything that is not powerful modern and immediate is futile', is an assessment of the army reinforcements and the support for them in Malaya and Singapore. On Christmas Day 1941, the War Office in London ordered the 53rd Brigade of the 18th Division to Singapore and a week later the remainder of that division to the Far East. It will be remembered that the 44th Indian Brigade had already been committed.

The reinforcement formations designated for Malaya and Singapore in late 1941 constituted nothing more than a distant exercise in military expediency. At the staff level, it was all too easy to commit the 18th Division and the 44th Indian Brigade to Malaya and Singapore. But in practice, those formations were not in any way ready for war—especially against an enemy as proficient as the Japanese.

In an extraordinary appendix to the British Official History, Kirby has quoted an account made by Brigadier Ballentine, who commanded the 44th Indian Infantry Brigade. He (Kirby) has also asserted that the following observations applied equally to the 45th Indian Brigade, which will later enter our story fighting alongside the Australians at Muar. Brigadier Ballentine:

> The battalions were raised in the autumn of 1940, and the brigade was formed in Poona in July 1941. All battalions arrived in Poona under strength, consisting of equal proportions of trained regular soldiers, reservists and drafts straight from the Regimental Training Centres ...
>
> Excellent progress in all branches of training, designed solely for Middle East conditions, was made in Poona, but this was largely negatived [sic] by the appalling milking inherent in the large-scale Indian Army expansion. During the six months July to December 1941, each battalion threw off some 250 men ...

During the last month in India, each battalion took in some 250 recruits to replace wastage, many of whom had only 4 or 5 months service and were under 18 years of age.[52]

The tale of woe did not end there. The consequence of the above was that many of the recruits had been with their battalions for less than three months and a number had joined their units during their travel to the point of embarkation; the strength of experienced VCOs (holding a Viceroy's commission and therefore junior to all officers with a King's or Indian unit's officer's commission) and NCOs were few to begin with, and had been greatly reduced by the milking process. Ballentine also stated that after the milking process, there remained, on average, around three British officers per battalion. The remainder were Emergency Commissioned Officers who were 'drawn from outside India with, at the most, twelve months experience of Indian troops, their ways and their language'. Before the expansion—and the consequent milking—of the Indian Army, the number of British senior officers in an Indian battalion was between twelve and sixteen.[53]

On Christmas Day, the British War Office ordered that the British 18th Division's 53rd Brigade was to sail from Cape Town straight to Singapore, and by the onset of the New Year, the whole Division was committed to sail from Bombay as reinforcements. But there were problems with the deployment of the British 18th Division to Singapore, just as there had been with the Indian reinforcements. The 18th Division had been earmarked for the Middle East and it was anticipated that its training would be completed there. However, because both its task and destination had been changed, the 18th Division was to leave for Singapore without transport and supporting arms. Moreover, to compound these problems, its soldiers would face the inevitable problem of being inactive during weeks at sea and then face the additional challenge of acclimatisation.

In addition to these troop reinforcements, Middle East Command was ordered to send the 7th Armoured Brigade and the Australian Government was asked to approve the despatch of the I Australian Corps—the 6th and 7th Divisions—to the Dutch East Indies. The truth is that the Australian Corps and the 7th Armoured Brigade were the only proficiently trained and battle-hardened formations chosen for Malaya and Singapore's reinforcement—and yet they were the last to be moved. In all this, Kirby has made a most critical point: 'The difficulties of finding shipping and the need for speed . . . led the Chiefs of Staff to select those formations which were immediately available and nearest to the scene of operations, regardless of their fighting value.'[54]

If serious mistakes were made by the British War Office with regard to the standard of reinforcements, the Australian Army stands even more culpable. Its response to the plea for a further commitment would be the deployment of the 4th Machine Gun Battalion and about 1800 infantry reinforcements. Both parties were destined to arrive in Singapore on 24 January 1942.

The 2/4th Machine Gun Battalion was raised in Western Australia in November 1940 and had been trained there and in South Australia before being posted to Darwin. Thus, when it arrived in Singapore in late January 1942, the Battalion had received around fourteen months' training, which was comparable with units throughout the AIF. But the quality of many of the roughly 1800 infantry reinforcements sent with the machine gunners was a disgrace. Major Wilfred Kent Hughes, HQ, 8th Division AIF:

A very large number of these reinforcements were entirely untrained, had never fired a rifle, and many of their rifles had burred ejectors, which jammed after the first shot. The fault in the rifles was discovered during an inspection shortly after their arrival and a team of fourteen armourers working without ceasing for 48 hrs remedied the defect. The lack of training of the men could not be overcome in the few days before they were under fire. The fault lay not in the material, but in those responsible for sending such raw material.[55]

Lionel Wigmore has made an attempt to explain this terrible blunder by stating that 'the practice had developed of sending raw recruits to the Middle East where they received their basic training under expert instructors in the excellent training organization established there'.[56] Army HQ in Australia knew very well that there were no 'expert instructors' nor 'training organization' in Malaya. Brigadier Rowell had passed through Singapore in August 1941 on his way home from the Middle East to become Deputy Chief of the General Staff. He had suggested at the time that 'candidates from the 8th Division be sent to Australian schools in the Middle East'.[57]

This suggetion might have provided a more proficient pool of officers to command reinforcements and to replace casualties in the division. As for the standard of training of the reinforcement other ranks, Wigmore has asserted that:

> Even if there was a shortage of adequately trained reinforcements in Australia early in December, the needs of the 8th Division could have been foreseen. If necessary a shipload of reinforcements could have been sent from the Middle East where, in mid-December, after all units had been filled, there were 16,600 in the reinforcement pool (including 10,000 recently arrived), and whither, in 1941, a percentage of the men in some 8th Division units in Australia had been sent as reinforcements. In Australia on 8th December there were also 87,000 militiamen on full-time duty, many thousands of whom had already received months of training. Soon after war with Japan broke out these were debarred from enlisting in the AIF lest their units be unduly depleted by a large number of such transfers. Even so, these militiamen constituted a pool from which fairly well-trained volunteers might have been sought.[58]

For the Australian Government and Australian Army to complain at the time—and after the campaign—that Britain's response to the reinforcement of Malaya was feeble, and subsequently that the fall of Singapore was 'a great betrayal', has less credibility when their own efforts to provide quality reinforcements were so pitiable.

The last point concerning Bowden's statement is the question of RAF reinforcements. It will be remembered that Brooke-Popham had urgently requested RAF reinforcements upon the outbreak of hostilities. The first effort came on 19 December, when Australian crews flew from Singapore to Darwin to collect and deliver eight Hudsons, which arrived in Singapore on 23 December. The period 12–14 December saw twelve Blenheim planes fly from Egypt by the long and tedious air reinforcement route. Any aircraft crews flying from the United Kingdom as reinforcements were facing up to 60 hours' flying time spread over fifteen to 21 days. The crated Hurricanes already mentioned—and numbering 51—had left Cape Town by ship on

17 December. The trouble with this arrangement was time: time to arrive by sea and further time to assemble and then test the new aircraft.

Vivian Bowden contended that any reinforcement of men and material for Malaya and Singapore 'that is not powerful modern and immediate is futile'. By Christmas 1941 he would, tragically, be vindicated. To add further gloom to the rapidly deteriorating situation in Malaya, Hong Kong fell to the Japanese on Boxing Day 1941, and in the Philippines the Japanese were quickly forcing the Filipino and American Armies into the confines of the Bataan Peninsula.

12

THE WITHDRAWAL
FROM KAMPAR

It will be remembered that by 19 December 1941, Brigadier Paris, who had been given orders to defend the Grik Road, had sent the remainder of the Argylls and a troop of field guns to Lenggong, approximately halfway between Grik and Kuala Kangsar, to reinforce the existing Argylls' company and the Malayan Independent Company already deployed there. To their rear, at Kota Tampan where the River Perak ran close to the road, Paris deployed a company of the 5/2 Punjab.

After arriving in Lenggong at 7.00 am on the 19th and joined by the remainder of his battalion an hour-and-half later, Lieutenant-Colonel Stewart was told that the Malayan Independent Company 'reported its patrols as being still on the other side of Sumpitan, four miles ahead'.[1] Beyond that patrol limit, the road passed into a jungle defile. Stewart decided to take the defence of the road to the enemy by ordering the Malayan Independent Company to advance and seize the defile pending the arrival of the Argylls' D Company. In keeping with his philosophy of defence of roads in depth, he planned that the following Argyll companies were to hold the road to a distance of three kilometres against enemy outflanking efforts and to provide a firm base for his advance. His armoured cars constituted 'mobile forts' between companies and were to facilitate company manoeuvre.

Stewart later recorded that the Independent Company patrols were not in fact holding Sumpitan. When the company subsequently debussed at Sumpitan they were ambushed by the Japanese. But all was far from lost. Stewart would later recall that: '... shortly the Argyll armoured cars of D Company Group arrived, and in turn smashed into and surprised the Japs in close order, in large numbers, and at short range. Under such circumstances the fire of well-served machine guns is devastating.'[2] After an artillery barrage along the road, which unfortunately failed to hit the most forward elements of the enemy force because of their nearness, D Company attacked along it with their armoured cars and infantry.

Although the Argylls were later withdrawn, they took but three casualties, lost an armoured car, but gained precious time—and the Japanese 'made no further aggressive move throughout the day even by patrols'.[3] At dusk on 19 December, Stewart withdrew his battalion back about three kilometres to avoid the risk of an enemy outflanking movement.

There was a welcome lull in the fighting on 20 December—and with good reason. At around 4.30 pm a Chinese man reported to Stewart that at midday he had observed a Japanese force moving down the River Perak in boats and along its banks. He further reported that local labour was being forced to carry their mortars and to guide them to Kota Tampan. Should this force gain a causeway which crossed a swamp south of that venue, Stewart believed that: '... it was the end, not only for the Argylls but of Kuala Kangsar and much of the 11th Division as well.'[4]

In an immediate response to this threat, the rear Battalion HQ, a part of C Company (which had been originally deployed in the rear of the Argylls), two armoured cars, a section of carriers and two mortars were hastily loaded and transported by the 2/3rd Australian Motor Transport Company to a track junction near the 57-mile peg to keep open the approach to the causeway. The Japanese thrust was repulsed. The Argylls then withdrew to Kota Tampan at around 10.00 pm—they had been ordered to hold it till dark.

On the morning of 21 December, the Japanese attacked again. They were repulsed. Orders were then received for the Battalion to withdraw that night through the 5/2nd Punjab, which was then moving up to cover the southern and western shores of Chenderoh Lake. Stewart's Battalion subsequently passed south-west through the Indians at Sauk, which was about sixteen

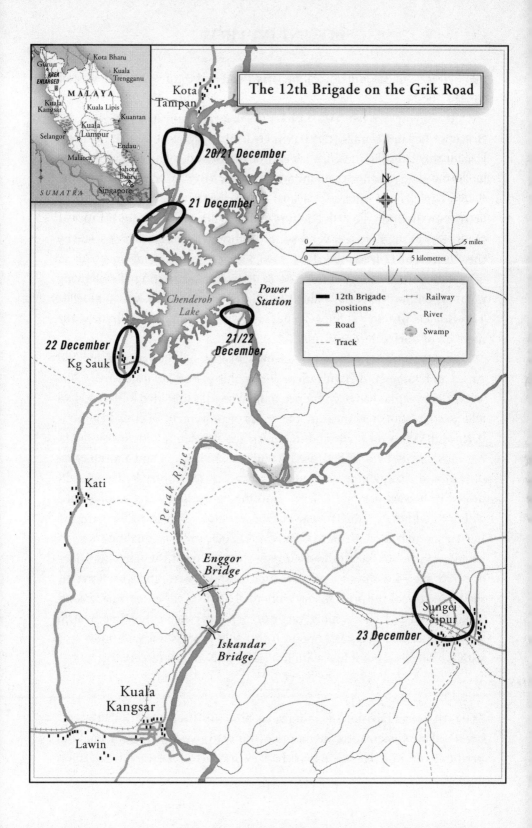

The 12th Brigade on the Grik Road

MALAYA

Gurun
AREA
ENLARGED
Kota Bharu
Kuala Trengganu
Kuala Kangsar
Kuala Lipis
Kuantan
Kuala Lumpur
Selangor
Endau
Malacca
Johore Bahru
SUMATRA
Singapore

Kota Tampan

20/21 December

21 December

Chenderoh Lake

Power Station

21/22 December

22 December
Kg Sauk

N

0 ——————— 5 miles
0 ——————— 5 kilometres

12th Brigade positions
Road
Track
Railway
River
Swamp

Kati

Perak River

Enggor Bridge

Iskandar Bridge

Sungei Sipur

23 December

Kuala Kangsar

Lawin

kilometres from the junction of the Grik Road and the Trunk Road, west of Kuala Kangsar.

After having arrived back to its 12th Brigade from its fighting under Brigadier Key in Kelantan, the 4/19th Hyderabad was sent to hold the main road at the River Siput, which lay east of the Iskandor and Enggor bridges where the main road and the railway crossed the River Perak. Even though the 3/16th Punjab had beaten back a Japanese attempt to cross the River Krian at Selama on the 20th, the 11th Division and the 12th Brigade were, because of the threats to the River Perak crossings, withdrawn behind that obstacle by the morning of 23 December 1941. Lionel Wigmore, in *The Japanese Thrust*: 'The Iskandor and Enggor bridges were destroyed, and during the following night a pontoon bridge at Blanja, south of Kuala Kangsar, was sunk. The 12th Brigade was now at Sungei Siput, and the 28th Brigade at Siputeh, at a junction of the road from Blanja.'[5]

The operations conducted by Lieutenant-Colonel Stewart and his 2nd Argyll and Sutherland Highlanders during this period are noteworthy. The Argylls' companies had been trained to fight as self-contained units, and had addressed in some real measure the issues of movement in closed country; defence in depth on roads and in defiles; the problem of enemy outflanking movements by a skilled use of both machine guns and mortars; the difficulty of maintaining communications in close country by being well-drilled in both attack and defence; and they possessed a well-coordinated ability to withdraw using transport that was close enough to their troops, but far enough away to be relatively safe. Such military qualities are not gained readily, but are acquired through rigorous prior thought and extensive training—and this process takes time. Mistakes were, and will always be, made, and out of the prior theory and initial battle experience come lessons, re-evaluation and a developing jungle or, as it was called at the time, a 'bush warfare' doctrine. The salient point is that that process was well under way with the Argylls—but it had, with few exceptions, not begun elsewhere.

The 11th Indian Division's withdrawal behind the River Perak by 23 December 1941 gave General Percival the opportunity to assess the senior command positions within it. He made four changes of which three were forced upon him. As all three of the division's brigade commanders had become casualties, Lieutenant-Colonel Moorhead was appointed to command the newly amalgamated 15th Brigade, Lieutenant-Colonel Stewart of the Argylls was promoted to command the 12th and Lieutenant-Colonel Selby was assigned to the 28th Brigade. In *The War in Malaya*, Percival wrote that:

> Then there was the question of the divisional commander. I felt that an officer with the widest possible experience of bush warfare was required to lead the 11th Division in future and suggested that Brigadier Paris, the commander of the 12th Indian Brigade, should succeed Murray-Lyon who, undoubtedly a brave and tireless leader, had had limited experience in that particular type of warfare.[6]

This is a curious statement. There was in fact no such creature. The desire for 'an officer with the widest possible knowledge of bush warfare' was nothing more than Percival's vague attempt to explain away Malaya Command's abject failure, since his arrival in Malaya, to have made any effort to address the issue of 'bush warfare'. There was in fact no developed jungle fighting doctrine. Lieutenant-Colonel—now Brigadier—Stewart had made a most impressive effort to do so. In fact his rapid escalation from 'crank' to brigadier was, in the space of a mere month, quite remarkable. Two fair criticisms of Murray-Lyon's command of the 11th Division might be made. The first was that his dispositions lacked depth—particularly on roads. The second was that his selection of units to man forward parts of his perimeters was often questionable, although, in fairness to him, such decisions are normally made at the brigade leadership level. But with respect to Murray-Lyon, almost all the prerequisites for success—even partial success—were denied him. Further, there seems little or no evidence that Paris had made any great study or had become 'experienced' in 'bush warfare'. That credit would seem to belong to Stewart, and would seem peculiar to the Argylls. The wisdom of Percival's decision to promote Paris should be judged against the fortunes of the 11th Indian Division over the following weeks.

There was already friction between Percival and Heath. The delays in the implementation of Matador, and Heath's desire on a number of occasions to withdraw the 11th Division earlier and further than Percival wished, would seem to be the prime issues. Heath wanted to promote Brigadier Key, an Indian Army officer who had performed admirably at Kota Bharu, to the command of the 11th Indian Division. Percival's promotion of Paris to that position and Stewart to command the 12th Brigade therefore saw two British Army commanders placed in command of two Indian Army formations. Nonetheless, Paris was an impressive commander. Brigadier Stewart described him as:

> A wise and sympathetic leader, with an understanding of the factors that make for morale, he never aimed off, but asked of his units only the irreducible minimum necessary to his purpose. This, combined with his sense of close timing and of realism, enabled the Battalion [the Argylls] to avoid destruction on a number of occasions . . . I personally have never known a commander who gave greater moral support to his subordinates in battle, or one in whose judgment I had greater confidence, whether it was as Brigade or . . . as Divisional Commander.[7]

At no point in his book does Stewart make mention of any great mastery or competence by Paris in 'bush warfare'.

On the early morning of 22 December 1941, elements of the 5th Japanese Division rushed into Kuala Kangsar. Lieutenant-Colonel Tsuji recorded that after viewing the ruins of the Iskandor and Enggor bridges and the pontoon bridge at Blanja they were filled with 'anger and disappointment'.[8] To compound this frustration, Tsuji noticed that within the troops of his 5th Division 'signs of exhaustion could be seen'.[9] And little wonder. However, the successful demolition of the three bridges over the River Perak also enabled General Yamashita to concentrate his force for the crossing of that obstacle and offer his 5th Division soldiers a much deserved respite.

Lieutenant-General Nishimura's Imperial Guards Division had originally been placed on 25th Army's order of battle for the occupation of Bangkok, but after the 'cooperation' of the Siamese authorities, Yamashita determined that Lieutenant-General Matsui's 5th Division spearhead should be reinforced by it. He ordered the Perak to be crossed at 10.00 pm on 26 December with the 5th Division to cross at Blanja and the Guards at Kuala Kangsar. To traverse the Perak the Japanese used boats brought overland from their Singora landings and a number of collapsible motor launches.

General Percival meanwhile had rightly concluded that although the road system on which the campaign was being fought was beginning to converge—and thus enable him to minimise the chances of having his line of communication put in jeopardy—he was now confronted with the challenge of holding the lateral road stretching from Jerantut through Kuala Lipis, westward to Raub and thence to Kuala Kubu. This road was the main link between east and west Malaya. Therefore, should the Japanese push him beyond Kuala Kubu, the only road from the east coast would be severed. He determined that 'we should withdraw the Kuantan garrison at a time to be decided later in accordance with the development of the situation'.[10]

In compliance with these orders, General Heath chose two prime defensive positions behind Ipoh. The first was some 32 kilometres south at Kampar, and the second, designed to shield the vital road junction at Kuala Kubu, was just north of Tanjong Malim. To provide defence in depth along the Trunk Road between Kampar and Tanjong Malim, he selected three further locations: Tapah, Bidor and 'in the Slim River area'.[11] To delay the enemy on the main road through and behind Ipoh, Heath chose Brigadier Stewart's 12th Brigade, while Brigadier Selby's 28th Brigade was given the same task from Blanja. For his first set-piece defensive position at Kampar, Heath deployed Brigadier Moorhead's 15th Brigade. This formation had been reconstituted by amalgamating the 1st Leicesters and the Surreys to form the 'British Battalion' and included the composite Jat/Punjab Battalion, the 1/14th Punjab, the 2/16th Punjab and the 3/16th Punjab. Heath's choice of the 15th Brigade for the Kampar position was astute given the circumstances: it had had a rest and was partially re-equipped. On 23 December, the 15th Brigade began the task of preparing its positions.

We now come to a critical train of events which yet again demonstrate a totally inexcusable blunder on the part of both General Heath and General Percival. Kirby has stated that: 'On the same day [23 December] Heath had sent a message to Percival asking that steps should be taken to construct a series of defensive positions south of Kampar on which troops could retire,

for he was unable both to fight the Japanese and to prepare rearward positions.'[12] Heath's request was entirely reasonable. However, the circumstances
behind that request are intriguing. In his book *Too Little Too Late*, Brigadier
Ivan Simson described a meeting he had with General Heath at his advanced
HQ at Ipoh on 22 December. During a conversation with Heath after dinner
that night, Simson recorded that he discussed the defences 'between Ipoh
and Singapore'.[13] He claimed that Heath 'thought I over estimated the tank
danger'. Simson then gave Heath two rather pertinent examples disputing that
view: '. . . his own success with tanks against the Italians at Keren in Abyssinia
in 1940; and the defeat in which General Percival had been involved with the
German panzer break-through in France earlier in the same year.'[14] Simson
also claimed that during their meeting, he pointed out that the Japanese had
tanks and that his Indian soldiers had had neither training or experience
in dealing with them. Further, he reminded Heath that his III Corps had
no tanks and 'few anti-tank weapons and mines'. Simson then gave Heath
the obvious solution: 'I did not see how he could stop a determined tank
thrust down the road against tired troops unless he had anti-tank defences
in depth . . .'[15]

When, on the following day (23 December), Heath and Simson inspected
the defences at Kampar, they noted that these were merely hastily dug and
that there was no sign of civilian labour to assist them. Although there were
no anti-tank cylinders at Kampar, Simson told Heath that he had supervised
the dumping of numbers of them on his way forward two days previous. It
would seem that their visit to Kampar had made some impact upon Heath,
for that night he raised the subject of anti-tank defences with Simson. It
was during that conversation that Heath framed the message to Percival
that Kirby mentions above. Incredibly, when Simson asked Heath to sign it,
Heath refused. Simson then claims that he asked Heath to send the message
to Percival. It would seem, given the passage from Kirby above, that Heath
did so. We now return to an extraordinary statement made by Kirby in the
British Official History:

Percival arranged in the following week that surplus officers from the
Public Works Department should be organized into works groups in
selected areas under the State Engineers. He informed both Heath

and Bennett of these arrangements on the 29th and said that the State
Engineers would report to them for orders, the object being to prepare
a series of obstacles, especially anti-tank obstacles, in great depth on
probable lines of enemy advance. Since III Corps staff was too much
occupied to give time to the construction of such defences well in rear
of the fighting line and the P.W.D. officers could not provide sufficient
labour, this effort produced little result.[16]

Kirby follows this revelation with the comment that had Brigadier Simson
been placed in charge of all rearward defence works, 'something useful might
have been accomplished'.[17]

The evidence would seem overwhelming that General Arthur Percival was
a very slow learner. It will be recalled that he had, at the outbreak of hostilities only a few short weeks before, ordered defensive positions prepared at
Gurun. However, the allotted civilian labourers had failed to turn up. But
surely the real indictment is that Percival failed to constructively employ
a highly trained professional military engineer under his very nose—and
under his command.

After his time with Heath, Simson drove back to Gemas, where he
made detailed notes of all available stocks of the 'more important items
we would need for defensive work'.[18] He found that there were ample
supplies and that these should be employed before stocks further south
were used. Simson reached Singapore at around 11.30 pm on Boxing Day
1941 and made straight for Percival's HQ. He was only too well aware of
the importance of his mission. During the following two-and-a-half hours
Simson reiterated the arguments he had given Percival on his arrival in
Singapore in August. They fell on deaf ears. Simson quoted Percival yet
again as claiming that, 'defences are bad for morale—for both troops and
civilians'.[19] But, according to Simson, Percival did make one concession.
If General Keith Simmons, the Commander of the Singapore Fortress
agreed, Percival said he would have no objection to Simson's proposals
for defensive fortifications on the north shore of Singapore Island. Buoyed
by Percival's compromise, Simson yet again broached the subject of such
fortifications through Johore—and Percival once again declined. Simson
left him at 2.00 am on 27 December.

Only hours later, Simson contacted General Keith Simmons and was invited to breakfast to discuss Percival's 'concession'. During the course of their conversation, Simson pointed out that the Japanese would attack the Island through the 'backdoor' or northern coast; that the seaward side or 'frontdoor' was effectively 'bolted' by Singapore's large guns, well-prepared infantry positions and the soon-to-be-erected tubular scaffolding to prevent landings by small craft. Simson argued that similar scaffolding on the north shore would serve the same purpose. After giving essentially the same argument to Simmons as he had to Percival, the Chief Engineer was given precisely the same answer. Simmons left the meeting convinced that 'Singapore was as good as lost'.[20]

Two questions should be asked concerning Simson's proposals to Heath, Percival and Simmons. The first is the obvious one: why were they rejected? Simson's opinion is interesting:

> ... all the senior commanders in Malaya ... had been taught to mistrust defences because they could become a danger for winning a war. To win a war, a commander must attack, and his troops must be willing to attack ...
>
> I thought that this doctrine had been misapplied in Malaya where it always appeared prior to the war—and very soon became obvious during it—that the problem was going to be one of 'survival' with no question as yet of 'winning'. Defences are essential for survival of fortresses when fighting a better equipped and trained enemy.[21]

The second is to what extent Simson's ideas were in accordance with Brigadier Stewart's. It should be restated that there were two near perfect static defensive positions in Malaya: General Dobbie's proposed defence line in Johore and the north shore of Singapore Island. Both, bordered by the sea, thus restricted the enemy potential for outflanking. But with regards to other roads and defiles along the Malay Peninsula, Simson's proposals were in fact designed to facilitate Stewart's ideas. By employing anti-tank obstacles—particularly when the British did not possess tanks and sufficient anti-tank guns—the initial enemy advance and rapid movement down a given road could be stopped, or at least stalled. Stewart's attack drills would therefore have been facilitated, and not retarded, by Simson's proposals.

By 26 December 1941, in compliance with his orders to fight a delaying action north of Ipoh, Brigadier Stewart had deployed his 12th Brigade in depth along the Trunk Road covering Chemor. During the brief respite around Christmas Day, he had hatched a plan to put his Argylls into a position to attempt a counterattack. He deployed the 4/19th Hyderabads to the left of the road, the Argylls on and to the right of it and the 5/2nd Punjabs around six kilometres ahead with orders to provide 'maximum delay subject to not being committed'.[22] Stewart had 24 guns of the 137th Field Regiment under his command. Given that the area around Chemor was relatively open tin mining ground with some rubber, and therefore offered some artillery observation, the plan was that the 5/2nd Punjabs would withdraw during the night of 26/27 December and then attempt to hold the Japanese astride a track junction. The Argylls, using their practised drill, were to then move through the Punjabs and attack on a two-platoon front. The remainder of the Battalion were to follow up in depth using their well-rehearsed procedure of armoured cars and carriers with their infantry companies. One company of the Hyderabads were to attempt an encircling movement from the east or right flank. The counterattack was timed to coincide with the artillery barrage, which was further timed to begin when the enemy had 'closed up in strength'[23] against the 5/2nd Punjabs. The plan was, therefore, that when the Japanese were temporarily stalled against the Punjabs, the artillery—having registered on the 26th—would maul the enemy whilst the Hyderabads attacked their flank.

Alan Warren, in his *Singapore 1942*, records that: 'At divisional headquarters Lieutenant-Colonel Harrison told General Paris that Stewart's plan "ought to work well, Sir, provided Stewart has taken the Japanese into his confidence and obtained confirmation that they'll play their part".'[24] The Japanese didn't. As had happened so often during the 11th Indian Division's campaigning in Malaya, the newly arrived Imperial Guards made the first move by attacking the Punjabs at around 7.00 am. With the 12th Brigade attack timed for 9.00 am and the Argylls engaged in their move to their start line, at 8.00 am the Punjabs were forced back about 700 metres. With the planned artillery barrage and the Argylls' attack now redundant, the attack was called off. This action brought into focus a recurring jungle or 'bush warfare' battle problem of the time: communication. While the Hyderabads and Argylls were able to stage a successful withdrawal, the company of the former which had been moving forward for its encircling attack could not be contacted. It was taken by surprise, and in the subsequent action, savagely mauled. Its commanding officer and most of his company were annihilated. In all, the 12th Brigade lost about 200 casualties during this engagement.

General Paris was now faced with the very same problems that had so beset his predecessor: the fatigue of his forward 12th Brigade and the continuous challenge of a fluid withdrawal. The recent, if short, respite given him by the obstacle of the River Perak, and General Yamashita's decision to briefly rest his 5th Division and bring forward the Imperial Guards, had not solved these issues. On the night of 26/27 December, General Paris ordered Brigadier Selby's 28th Brigade and Stewart's 12th Brigade to withdraw south of Ipoh. In an attempt to keep it as fresh as possible, Paris ordered the 28th Brigade to the right flank Kampar position of Sahum, while Stewart's exhausted brigade was charged with the task of occupying covering positions from Gopeng to Dipang. Like Murray-Lyon before him, General Paris was attempting to apply the basic principle of the fighting withdrawal: to trade space for time. But during the afternoon of 28 December, the enemy followed up with his usual speed and efficiency. Through that night and the next morning, the Japanese employed both a heavy artillery barrage and low level bombing, which at around noon forced the 12th Brigade to withdraw to within five kilometres of Dipang. General Paris subsequently ordered Brigadier Selby to hold the bridge across the River Kampar pending 12th Brigade's withdrawal across it at 7.00 pm.

But the fatigued Argylls' ordeal was far from over. Kirby has recorded that:

At 3 p.m. the Japanese, supported by about eight tanks, launched a strong attack on the . . . Argylls who for the second time that day were in an unprepared position without any effective anti-tank support, since owing to a misunderstanding of orders 2nd Anti-Tank Battery had failed to take its allotted position. The tanks failed to break through, but the Argylls were forced back on to 5/2nd Punjab.[25]

Stewart would later record that while the Argylls' anti-tank rifles made no impression upon the enemy tanks, 'their 38 millimetre guns, and indeed their small arms armour-piercing ammunition, went through our armour like paper'.[26] Disaster was averted only by Lieutenant-Colonel Deakin and elements of his Punjabis who, with a troop of the 2nd Anti-Tank Battery, finally hit the leading tank about a kilometre north of Dipang. This action allowed the 12th Brigade to make good its withdrawal over the bridge, which was later blown.

It will be remembered that General Heath had selected two vital points on the Trunk Road south of Ipoh for a prolonged defence of the key town of Kuala Kubu. This was the place where the lateral road stretching eastwards to Raub, Kuala Lipis and finally Jerantut concluded. The first was Kampar and the second was a position just north of Tanjong Malim.

The Kampar area was dominated by a steep jungle-covered hill called Bujang Melaka. This substantial feature, fourteen kilometres long and nine-and-a-half kilometres wide, rose rapidly to a height of about 1240 metres. After reaching Dipang, the Trunk Road ran alongside the western side of Bujang Melaka, while the railway line ran into Kampar from the north-west. Another road ran from Dipang eastwards around the northern extremity of the hill through Sungei Siput, Sahum and southwards to Kinjang. The ground to the north and due west of Kampar was essentially an open tin mining area interspersed with small pockets of rubber. But away to the south-west lay the extensive Cicely Rubber Estate, where there were fields of fire extending up to a kilometre. Bujang Melaka offered excellent artillery observation over the approaches from the Trunk Road, railway and away to the west. Any attempt to outflank the 11th Division's occupation of Kampar would most likely come via Teluk Anson from a Japanese movement down the River Perak or by sea.

To give depth to his defence of the Trunk Road and also cover the railway, General Paris deployed Brigadier Moorhead's 15th Brigade with the British Battalion—the amalgamated 1st Leicesters and the Surreys—about one-and-a-half kilometres north of Kampar village. The battalion's left flank was held by one company, with three ridges to the east of the Trunk Road each held by the remaining companies. These were named Thompson's Ridge, Green Ridge and Cemetery Ridge. To the British Battalion's rear, stretching from Kampar village to the Trunk Road and railway junction, were the Punjabis: the 1/14th, 3/16th and 2/16th. The now amalgamated 1/8th Punjab and the Jats—now named the Jat/Punjab Battalion—were deployed as the brigade reserve to the east of the Trunk Road and opposite the 3/16th Punjab. Brigade HQ was sited in Kampar village. Brigadier Moorhead had the 273rd Anti-Tank Battery and 88th Field Regiment in support.

To cover the road from Dipang around the eastern side of Bujang Melaka to Sahum, Paris deployed Brigadier Selby's 28th Brigade. It initially had the dual roles of primarily blocking enemy penetration and attacking the Japanese line of communication once it had become established along the Trunk Road, towards Kampar village. The Brigade's 2/9th Gurkhas were deployed in depth along the road from Sungei Siput towards Dipang; the 2/2nd Gurkhas were astride the road about midway between Sahum and Sungei Siput; and the 2/1st Gurkhas were stationed astride the road about five kilometres south of Sahum. Selby's HQ was located at that village. The 28th Brigade had the 155th Field Regiment and the 215th Anti-Tank Battery in support.

To cover possible Japanese outflanking attempts via the sea or the River Perak, Paris deployed Brigadier Stewart's worn 12th Brigade at Bidor, while the 1st Independent Company and 3rd Cavalry were ordered to guard the approaches to Teluk Anson. Brigadier Stewart's support consisted of the 137th Field Regiment and two troops of the 215th Anti-Tank Battery. At Temor, General Paris held the 5/14th Punjab, a mountain battery and an anti-tank battery as his divisional reserve.

The Japanese plan to capture Kampar involved three thrusts. The first was a direct attack down the Trunk Road at Kampar, to be undertaken by the 5th Division's 41st Regiment (Colonel Okabe). The second was an encircling movement from the west against the 11th Indian Division's

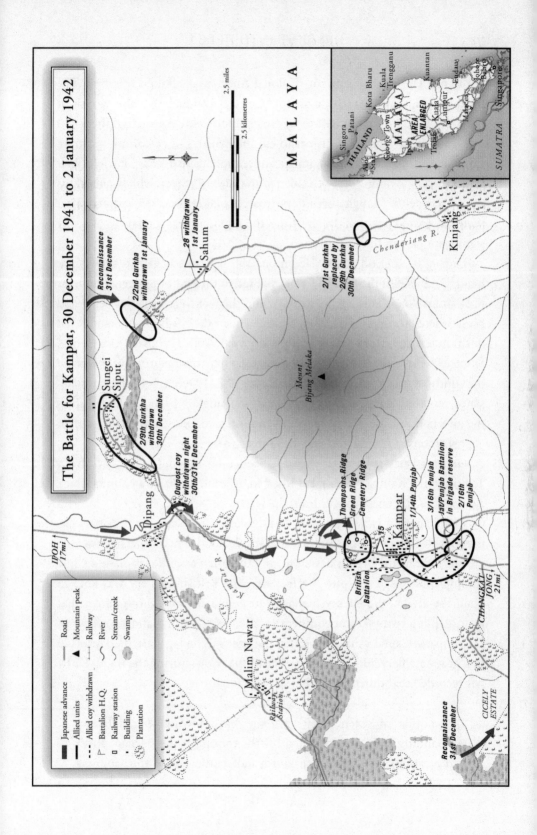

The Battle for Kampar, 30 December 1941 to 2 January 1942

MALAYA

2.5 miles

2.5 kilometres

Reconnaissance
31st December

2/2nd Gurkha
withdrawn 1st January

28 withdrawn
1st January

Sahum

2/1st Gurkha
replaced by
2/9th Gurkha
30th December

Chenderiang R.

Kinjang

Sungei
Siput

2/9th Gurkha
withdrawn
30th December

Mount
Bujang Melaka

Dipang

Outpost coy
withdrawn night
30th/31st December

IPOH
17mi

Thompsons Ridge
Green Ridge
Cemetery Ridge

1/14th Punjab

3/16th Punjab

Jat/Punjab Battalion
in Brigade reserve

2/16th
Punjab

Kampar

British
Battalion

CHANGKAT
JONG
21mi

Kampar R.

Malim Nawar

Railway
Station

CICELY
ESTATE

Reconnaissance
31st December

Legend

- Japanese advance
- Allied units
- Allied coy withdrawn
- Battalion H.Q.
- Railway station
- Building
- Plantation
- Road
- ▲ Mountain peak
- Railway
- River
- Stream/creek
- Swamp

Inset map (MALAYA)

THAILAND

Singora
Patani

Kota Bharu
Kuala
Trengganu

AREA
ENLARGED

Ipoh

Kuantan

George Town

Kuala
Lumpur

Endau

Johore
Bahru

Malacca

Singapore

SUMATRA

left flank. The 42nd Regiment (Colonel Ando) was allotted this task. The third was to land the 11th Regiment (Colonel Watanabe) at the mouth of the River Bernam subsequent to an attack upon Teluk Anson and thence to the Trunk Road south of Kampar to cut the British line of communication. In the event, Ando's 42nd Regiment's operation against Kampar's left flank was stalled by swamps on both sides of the River Kampar, which caused his troops to spend a tough three days' 'march' before their belated arrival at their designated position. By this time, the regiment was too late to play any significant part in the operation.

During the period 30–31 December, the Japanese began to show their hand. On the 30th their patrols were sighted to the east of Sungei Siput near the Sahum Road. This enemy activity, and the fact that Brigadier Selby had been ordered to remove his 2/1st Gurkhas from their Sahum–Kinjang Road position, caused him to now pull his exposed 2/9th Gurkhas from Sungei Siput to replace the 2/1st. The following day Japanese patrols were seen to the south-west in the Cicely Rubber Estate. On 31 December, air reconnaissance reported 'small convoys of boats off Pangkor Island'.[27] And during the afternoon of the 31st, a patrol of the Independent Company identified enemy troops at Lumut and east of Simpang Ampat.

General Paris reacted to this intelligence by moving his reserve from Temoh to the Kampar–Changkat Road in order to facilitate a counterattack against these Japanese moves from the west.

At 7.00 am on New Year's Day 1942, following a heavy artillery barrage, the 41st Regiment attacked down the Trunk Road. Their objective was the ground held by the British Battalion, and their first assault was made against Thompson's Ridge. Despite the fact that the British artillery was able to maul the attack, the enemy managed to gain a tenuous foothold on that feature. But a two-platoon counterattack led by the commanding officer of D Company, Captain Vickers, ejected the enemy. The Japanese then resorted to a heavy artillery and mortar barrage of that ridge during the night. Kirby has recorded that during the evening of 1 January:

> ... a flotilla of seven small steamers, each towing several barges and landing craft, was reported off the mouth of the Bernam River and at about 7.30 p.m., one and a half battalions of the Japanese

11th Infantry Regiment, which had embarked at Port Weld, began landing at Utan Melintang. Driving back a patrol of 3rd Cavalry, the enemy had by 8 p.m. gained possession of the village and of the cross-roads about half a mile north.[28]

Late on 1 January, with no enemy activity on the right flank at Kampar along the Sahum Road, Paris decided to withdraw his 28th Brigade's 2/2nd Gurkhas to the Slim River area to further bolster his rear against the building enemy threat to his line of communication. But this threat also prompted him to ask Heath for permission to withdraw 'at his discretion'.[29] At this juncture, Heath and Percival were together at Kuala Lumpur, the latter having decided to tour both the 9th and 11th Indian Divisions to assess their condition. In assessing Paris's request, Percival still saw his prime objective as the retention of the Kuantan airfield in the east until at least 10 January. After that date, he could withdraw his 9th Indian Division westwards from Jerantut along the vital Jerantut–Kuala Kubu Road. But to accomplish this, General Paris would have to hold Kuala Kubu until the 15th. Given that his 11th Indian Division's line of withdrawal from Kampar to that centre still stretched over some 110 kilometres—and that the road passed through a defile south of Kampar—Percival granted Paris his request. Uppermost in Percival's mind was also the necessity of not allowing his 11th Division to become encircled and all but annihilated at any given place along that 110-kilometre line of communication.

At daybreak on 2 January 1942, the Japanese again attacked the British Battalion at Thompson's Ridge. After being initially halted by artillery fire, they managed to overrun a British Battalion platoon and gain another tenuous foothold on the extreme right of the ridge. Lieutenant-Colonel Morrison immediately requested a 15th Brigade counterattack. The first attempt was made by a company of Jats from the Brigade's reserve Jat/Punjab Battalion, but faltered in the face of heavy enemy machine gun fire. But the second, led by the Battalion second in command, Captain Graham, who was in charge of the Sikhs and Gujars from the 1/8th Punjab component of the Jat/Punjab Battalion, first gained a foothold and then, with a last desperate effort, drove the Japanese off the ridge. Alan Warren in *Singapore 1942*, has left us with the triumphant, yet tragic, account of that attack: 'The assault had been expensive, and there were only thirty unwounded men in the company. Captain Graham lost both legs when a mortar bomb was lobbed at his feet. He died on a stretcher as he was being carried to the rear.'[30]

No praise can be too high for the exploits of the British Battalion on their ridges at Kampar—particularly Thompson's Ridge—during the first two days of January 1942. Such exploits bear fair testimony to the need for thorough basic training, inspired leadership, *esprit de corps* and steadfastness in order to defeat an enemy as formidable as the Japanese. The high quality of the Battalion's artillery support is also noteworthy. And such exploits contrasted markedly with a number of other units in the 11th Indian Division which had been 'milked'—or 'gutted' as this work has preferred to call it—at both the junior leadership level and amongst its other ranks.

But despite the British Battalion's resolute stand at Kampar, events near the west coast caused General Paris to exercise his option to withdraw 'at his discretion'. On 2 January, the Japanese who had landed on the coast were reinforced by elements of the Imperial Guards Division. They landed at Teluk Anson and immediately engaged the 1st Independent Company. Brigadier Stewart's 12th Brigade had, meanwhile, occupied the road in depth commencing with the Argylls about six kilometres outside Teluk Anson. By mid-afternoon, the Japanese had made contact with that unit, and by nightfall the Brigade was occupying a position about eleven kilometres from the town.

Under the circumstances, the withdrawal of the 11th Indian Division from Kampar went smoothly. While Stewart's 12th Brigade continued to block the Japanese near the west coast, the 28th Brigade, followed by the 15th, withdrew to the Slim River.

General Yamashita had originally planned that two battalions of his 55th Infantry Regiment were to stage a surprise seaborne landing at Kuantan and capture its prized airfield on 28 December. But in the belief that the RAF had not been sufficiently negated, he cancelled that operation on 23 December. By this time, the 56th Regiment, having occupied Kuala Krai on the 19th, had moved south along the coast and established contact with patrols of

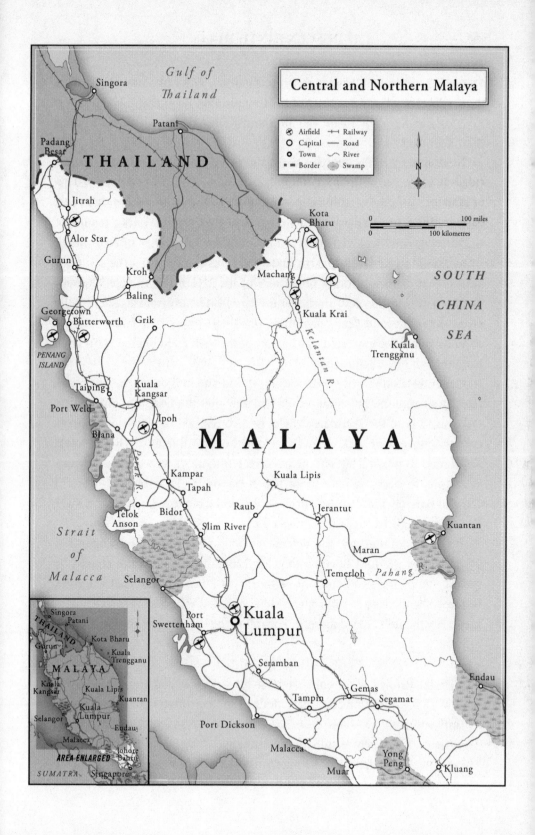

Central and Northern Malaya

Airfield   Railway
Capital   Road
Town   River
Border   Swamp

0   100 miles
0   100 kilometres

N

Gulf of
Thailand

Singora

Patani

THAILAND

Padang
Besar

Jitrah

Alor Star

Gurun

Kroh

Baling

Georgetown
Butterworth   Grik

PENANG
ISLAND

Taiping

Port Weld

Blana

Kuala
Kangsar

Ipoh

Kampar
Tapah

Telok
Anson   Bidor

Strait

of

Malacca   Selangor

Port
Swettenham

Raub

Slim River

Kota
Bharu

Machang

Kuala Krai

Kuala
Trengganu

SOUTH

CHINA

SEA

Kelantan R.

MALAYA

Perak R.

Kuala Lipis

Jerantut

Maran

Temerloh   Pahang R.

Kuantan

Kuala
Lumpur

Seremban

Tampin

Port Dickson

Malacca

Gemas

Segamat

Muar

Yong
Peng

Endau

Kluang

SINGORA
Patani

THAILAND   Kota Bharu

Gurun   Kuala
Trengganu

MALAYA

Kuala
Kangsar   Kuala Lipis   Kuantan

Selangor   Kuala
Lumpur

Malacca   Endau

Johore
Bahru

AREA ENLARGED
SUMATRA   Singapore

Painter's 22nd Indian Brigade north of Kuantan. Yamashita now decided on an overland attack, and instead of landing his 55th Regiment there, ordered it to land at Kota Bharu on the 30th and follow up the already advanced 56th Regiment.

In his defence of the Kuantan airfield, which lay about fourteen kilometres from the coast and to the west of the river, Brigadier Painter had deployed his brigade in anticipation of an enemy amphibious landing. Accordingly, he had his 2/18th Garhwal Rifles with a company of the 2/12th Frontier Regiment under command deployed along about seventeen kilometres of coast north of the Kuantan River; his 5/11th Sikhs were positioned along the southern side of that feature; and the remainder of his 2/12th was in reserve about 24 kilometres to the west on the Jerantut road. The only passage across the river—a tedious and time-consuming one—was by a single ferry. Painter's 22nd Brigade was supported by a battery of the 88th Field Regiment and two from the 5th Field Regiment.

General Heath saw two roles for his 9th Indian Division on the east coast: one actual and one potential. While he knew that the Division's immediate task was to hold the Kuantan airfield, he also realised the Division's potential for a movement back westwards along the critical Jerantut–Raub–Kuala Kubu road to possibly attack the enemy's left flank of its west coast thrust. Therefore, to best facilitate those two roles, on 27 December Heath told General Barstow that Painter's brigade should be deployed behind the River Kuantan as soon as Yamashita attacked from the north.

Brigadier Painter saw the defence of Kuantan in a different light. On 28 December, he told Barstow that his 22nd Brigade's defence should be fought east of the river, and not behind it, as he considered that extensive feature to be too easy to infiltrate. If General Barstow backed Painter's judgement, Heath and Percival did not. The following day, Heath sent Barstow his orders:

General Percival is in entire agreement with me that the preservation of the entity of 22nd Brigade is of greater importance than the imposition of two days' delay upon the enemy advance to Kuantan airfield . . . I therefore still adhere to the view that, from the strategical aspect, it is definitely wrong to risk the loss of a large number of

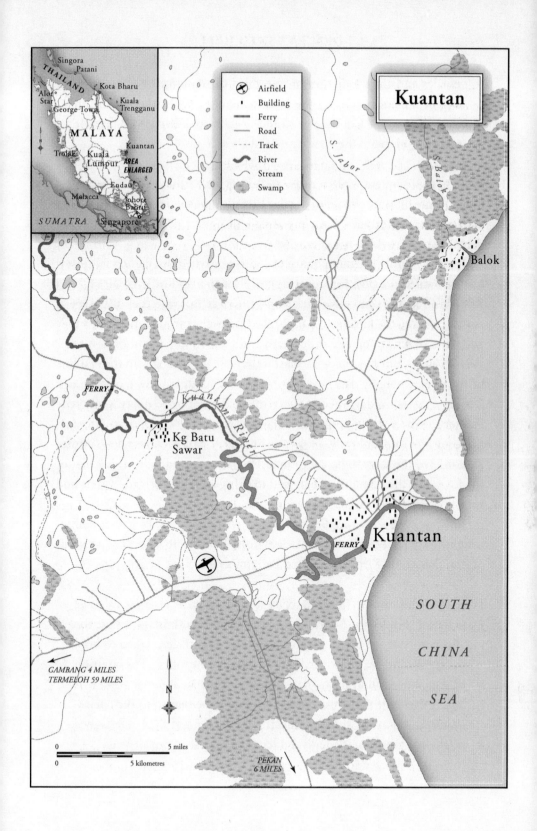

Kuantan

Airfield
Building
Ferry
Road
Track
River
Stream
Swamp

THAILAND

Singora
Patani

Kota Bharu

Alor
Star

Kuala
Trengganu

George Town

MALAYA

Trolak

Kuala
Lumpur

Kuantan

AREA
ENLARGED

Malacca

Endau

Johore
Bahru

SUMATRA

Singapore

S. Jabor

S. Balok

Balok

FERRY

Kuantan River

Kg Batu
Sawar

FERRY

Kuantan

SOUTH

CHINA

SEA

GAMBANG 4 MILES
TERMELOH 59 MILES

N

0   5 miles
0   5 kilometres

PEKAN
6 MILES

vehicles and the mutilation of one-third of the force by attempting
to fight the enemy east of the river. I therefore wish you to issue an
instruction to the Commander 22nd Brigade to redispose his brigade
in accordance with the view expressed above.[31]

Barstow's subsequent written order to Painter stated that: 'The preservation
of the future fighting efficiency of your brigade under existing circumstances
is of greater importance than imposing a delay of a few more days in the
denial of the airfield to the enemy.'[32]

On 30 December, in compliance with these instructions, Painter withdrew
his Garhwalis to a position covering the river line and ordered all of 22nd
Brigade's transport and guns back across the river. But with their usual speed
and aggression, the Japanese attacked the Garhwalis through the Jabor valley
and, after overrunning one of its companies, proceeded to cut off a further
two. Severely undermanned, the Garhwalis were pushed back to the east line
of the river, where by darkness that night they occupied a line of outposts.
During that same day, the Japanese made determined efforts to impede
Painter's withdrawal of equipment across the river, by continuous attempts
to bomb the one and only ferry. But one ferry had become two—Painter
had ordered the ferry to be cut in half. The Japanese did indeed sink half of
the ferry, but the remainder managed to bring all of the brigade's guns and
transport across the river during darkness.

In what he saw as compliance with his written orders, Brigadier Painter
sought, on 31 December, permission from Barstow to withdraw towards
Maran that night. Kirby has quoted Barstow's reply:

It is of the utmost importance that your brigade with its valuable
material should not be jeopardized. Within the limitations that the
above imposes, you will ensure that every advantage is taken to hold
the enemy and deal him such blows as opportunity offers. The question
of denial of ground particularly applies to the Kuantan airfield. It is
highly desirable that this should continue to be denied to the enemy.
Reinforcements are shortly expected in Malaya and their safe arrival
might be hampered if enemy fighters had the use of the airfield.[33]

That night Brigadier Painter therefore ordered the Garhwalis to withdraw west of the river and join the 2/12th in a perimeter defence of the airfield, after which the ferry was to be destroyed. Before their crossing of the river, the Garhwalis had lost contact with two of their companies, and with a company of the Frontier Force also lost, Painter's Brigade was severely reduced in number. On New Year's Day, his orders were again given new emphasis. Painter was now told to hold the airfield for five days—until 6 January.

By 2 January, the Japanese had crossed the river and were moving towards the airfield. It was now crystal clear that Painter could not fulfil all of his ever-changing orders. If, as now ordered, he was to hold the airfield for a further four days, he would have to commit his force to battle—not minor delaying actions or skirmishes, but a set-piece defence of that area. After the war, Percival claimed that 'Heath must have misunderstood him, for his policy throughout was to give first priority to denying the enemy the use of Kuantan airfield'.[34] Given this revelation, Painter would have surely argued that his original plan to contest the Japanese advance upon the airfield might have been adopted. In the period 29 December until 2 January, it would seem that Percival and Heath were asking Painter for the impossible: he was to hold Kuantan airfield for five days but not commit his forces to a heavy loss of both men and material.

In the event, this conundrum was solved by the Japanese at Kampar. General Paris's 11th Indian Division, forced to stage a withdrawal from that Trunk Road town on the night of 2/3 January, now caused Barstow's 9th Division to be ordered to quickly concentrate in the Kuala Lipis–Jerantut–Raub area in anticipation of a withdrawal from the State of Pahang. During the night of 3 January, the Kuantan airfield buildings and installations were demolished and that evening, the Sikhs, the brigade's transport, its sappers and most of the artillery withdrew. But at 8.00 pm, the Japanese attacked the two companies of the 2/12th who were acting as the brigade rearguard. In the ensuing fighting, much of it hand-to-hand, Lieutenant-Colonel Cumming was bayoneted, but managed to fight his way back to safety. About 40 soldiers escaped that confrontation. Some of the remainder of the two-company rearguard eventually found their way back. For his bravery at Kuantan, Lieutenant-Colonel Cumming was awarded the Victoria Cross.

On 4 January, 22nd Brigade's withdrawal passed through Maran, and by the early hours of 7 January it reached the Raub area. The fighting in the Kuantan area cost Brigadier Painter's 22nd Brigade a third of its strength. The Garhwalis had sustained losses in excess of 250 killed, wounded or missing, while the 2/12th now numbered a mere 220.

The enemy landings on the west coast of Malaya around Teluk Anson had compelled General Paris to withdraw from his Kampar perimeter—despite the fact that the British Battalion had staged such a commendable 48-hour defence of it—and thereby diminish the threat to his line of communication. By 4 January 1942, therefore, Paris had concentrated his division in the Sungkai–Slim River area.

General Percival, his mind still dominated by the desire to protect the arrival of his reinforcements—the first of which, the Indian 45th Brigade, arrived on 3 January—ordered General Heath to hold the airfields at Port Swettenham and Kuala Lumpur until at least 14 January. Kirby has recorded that he (Percival) 'had urged him to take every opportunity of imposing delay by attacking the enemy's flanks and rear'.[35] This 'urge' constituted nothing more than an unrealistic dream. By this time Paris's 11th Division was exhausted, well below strength, lacking in key support and, according to Percival, its task was to deny airfields in central Malaya to the enemy. Previous attempts at this tactic had met with failure. And it was arguably the best trained and best drilled battalion in the Division for this kind of operation which had failed: the Argylls.

Alan Warren, in his *Singapore 1942*, has succinctly summed up Heath's dilemma:

[He] was concerned . . . that the Japanese would again hook around his left flank from the sea. South of Teluk Anson and the mouth of the Perak River a forty mile [64 kilometre] stretch of swampy jungle effectively covered the coastal flank of the division, but further south at Kuala Selangor and Port Swettenham troops landed on the coast could cut inland to reach the Trunk Road and Kuala Lumpur far behind the Slim River and Tanjong Malim.[36]

Heath had anticipated General Yamashita's intention: a two-pronged assault upon Kuala Lumpur. Yamashita planned that his 5th Division's 42nd Regiment (Colonel Ando) and an attached tank battalion were to pursue the 11th Division from Kampar along the Trunk Road direct to Kuala Lumpur, while the 11th Infantry Regiment—less one battalion—was to strike through this force as soon as the British had been defeated north of that objective. The coastal prong was to be undertaken by 111/11th Battalion followed by the 4th Guards Regiment, which were to secure Kuala Selangor and Port Swettenham before advancing on Kuala Lumpur from the west.

On New Year's Day 1942, Heath had transferred his 3rd Cavalry from the 11th Division and Brigadier Key's 8th Brigade's 3/17th Dogras and the 73rd Field battery to the command of Brigadier Moir, with the instruction to deny the enemy Kuala Selangor. Turning to the Trunk Road, on the night of 4/5 January, Heath ordered General Paris to deploy his 15th Brigade at Tanjong Malim, the 3/16th Punjab to Rawang, and to position the rest of his 11th Indian Division in the Trolak–Slim River area covering the river crossings. These changes in dispositions were made with the intention of holding the Japanese from Tanjong Malim for a minimum of four days.

On 2 January, Heath's predicted enemy landing attempt at Kuala Selangor materialised. During that afternoon, a steamer, about a dozen sampans and motor launches were sighted. When the sampans and motor launches began their passage to shore, the British artillery opened fire at about a one-kilometre range. After two sampans were sunk and a number of the other vessels damaged, a Japanese withdrawal was staged to the steamer, which in turn suffered a number of hits. The Japanese attempted another approach during the early hours of the next morning, but another withdrawal was necessary when the Japanese learnt that the British were still waiting for them. However, if the landing by sea had come to grief, the coastal track advance by the 4th Guards Regiment proved successful. When a battalion of the 4th Guards Regiment arrived at the River Selangor they turned inland and, moving along its northern bank, approached the bridges at Batang Berjuntai. This battalion was now only eighteen kilometres from the Trunk Road at Rawang—and a staggering 48 kilometres south of Slim River.

Heath reacted to this critical threat by despatching the Jat/Punjab Battalion and the 1st Independent Company to reinforce Brigadier Moir's force.

When the Japanese pushed elements of Moir's force back, Lieutenant-Colonel Moorhead was put in command. A successful counterattack put in by the Dogras on the night 5/6 January drove the enemy back, which allowed Moorhead to withdraw behind the river and blow the bridges. A lull now ensued along the barrier of the River Selangor.

———

After the recent victorious Japanese entry into Ipoh, and 'thinking back over the military operations which had so far overwhelmed the northern part of Malaya', Lieutenant-Colonel Tsuji observed that:

> If it was considered that the enemy would rely on Singapore Fortress, and hold out there to the last man, then the military strength that had been poured in north of the Perak River was excessive . . .
>
> Viewing the war from the standpoint of the British Empire at that time it appeared that in North Africa the British Army was in the midst of a life-and-death struggle with Rommel's German Army advancing on the Canal. The defence of Suez would be considered to take precedence over the defence of Singapore. If this was accepted as a natural war principle, then in Malaya the British would have to conserve their forces. It appeared a mistake for them to exhaust successively their military strength in the unprepared fighting zone of northern Malaya . . .
>
> Pouring in fresh reinforcements to support the forces destroyed in the opening battles was like pouring water on thirsty soil. While this continued there was reasonable hope for our success.[37]

While Tsuji was in fact guessing that Percival would soon commit substantial reinforcements to the battle, these too would suffer the same fate as had the 11th Indian Division. Paris's formation had been 'poured' and 'poured' into that very highly trained, well-led and aggressive Japanese 'thirsty soil'. Soon, all of the British military sins previously committed were about to be exposed on a scale that Tsuji could not have contemplated: at Slim River.

13

SLIM RIVER

⟨✦⟩

While the Japanese advance on the west coast was being contested, General Paris's 11th Indian Division had fallen back to the next delaying position on the Trunk Road between Kampar and Kuala Kubu: the Slim River crossings.

To provide depth to his defence of that locality, Paris had divided it into two distinct sectors. The northern, or Trolak sector, stretched from a point about five-and-a-half kilometres north of that village, down through it and to a position about one-and-a-half kilometres north of Slim village. The 12th Brigade was assigned the Trolak sector. Brigadier Stewart disposed his brigade with his usual emphasis on depth along the road and railway. His most forward perimeter, which stretched for about a kilometre, was occupied by the 4/19th Hyderabads. Reduced now to three companies, the first was astride the railway and behind two bridges, the second was forward on the road and manned a roadblock, and the last lay behind both on the road. The 5/2nd Punjab occupied an area stretching roughly from just forward of the 61-mile peg back to just beyond the 62-mile peg—one company was astride the railway and three were along the road. The Argylls formed the rear of the sector from Trolak village to a position of some considerable width bordering the Punjabs. At the northern end of their perimeter, the Argylls manned a second roadblock. Stewart's brigade HQ was situated about a kilometre behind his left company on a rearward plantation road. For added security and depth, a check position was chosen adjacent to the 65-mile peg, and the 5/14th Punjab was on short notice to man it if required. In the meantime, that unit was deployed just north of Slim village to rest.

The second sector in the defence of the Slim River crossings was allotted to Brigadier Selby's 28th Brigade. This sector stretched from the Slim River railway station around eleven kilometres eastward to the Slim River bridge. In an effort to provide 28th Brigade with a much-needed break, General Paris, after having had dispositions on the railway and road near Slim village and in the Cluny Rubber Estate reconnoitred, rested the Brigade in the village, with orders for a speedy occupation of their perimeters when needed. Selby's HQ was situated on the eastern edge of Slim village.

Infantry support for Brigadier Stewart's 12th Brigade Trolak sector was provided by one squadron of the 3rd Cavalry (located in the Tilau Rubber Estate) and the 5/14th Punjab, while further support consisted of the 137th Field Regiment, the 3rd Field Company and one troop of the 215th Anti-Tank Battery. The support for the Slim River sector consisted of the 155th Field Regiment, the 23rd Field Company and one troop of the 215th Anti-Tank Battery.

By the morning of 5 January 1942, after two days' strenuous work, these formations and dispositions were in place at the Slim River and the 15th Brigade had been disposed at the rear of Tanjong Malim.

At face value, the 11th Indian Division dispositions appeared sound. The road and railway ran through a narrow corridor and were a mere few hundred metres apart; the ground to the west of Trolak was essentially kilo-metres of marshy jungle; to the east lay dense jungle rising to, and onto, the mountain barrier; unlike a number of earlier engagements, the defence was in considerable depth; and the dispositions in the second, or rearward, Slim River sector were well-placed to counter Japanese attempts at encirclement.

But three absolutely critical factors for disaster lay dormant at Slim River: tank defence, communication and the physical condition and morale of the defenders.

Any fair examination of the 11th Division's potential for adequate tank defence comes back again to the employment—or lack of employment—of the Chief Engineer, Brigadier Simson. In late November 1941, Simson

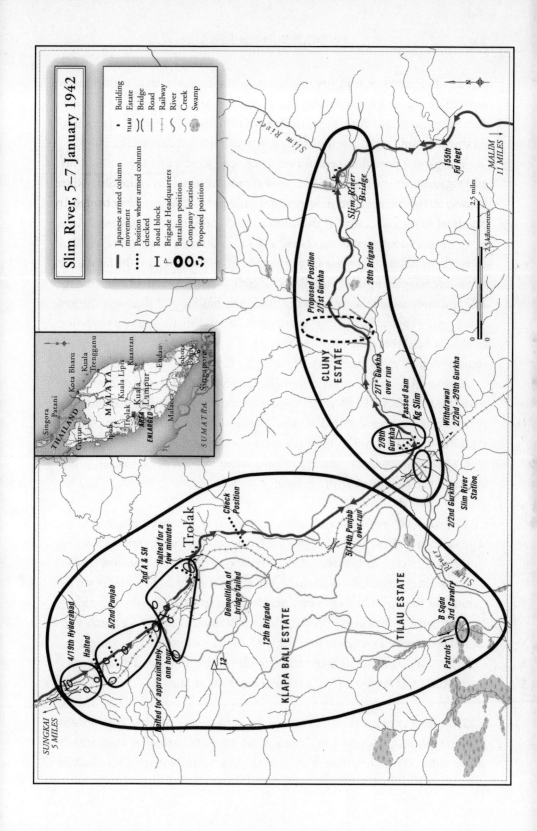

Slim River, 5–7 January 1942

Japanese armed column movement
Position where armed column checked
Road block
Brigade Headquarters
Battalion position
Company location
Proposed position

Building
Estate
Bridge
Road
Railway
River
Creek
Swamp

THAILAND
MALAYA
Singora
Patani
Gurun
Kota Bharu
Kuala Trengganu
Kuala Lipis
Ipoh
Trolak
Kuala Lumpur
AREA ENLARGED
Malacca
Endau
Mersing
Johore Bahru
Singapore
SUMATRA

N

2.5 miles

0   2.5 Kilometres

MALIM
11 MILES

Slim River

155th Fd Regt

Slim River Bridge

28th Brigade

Proposed Position
2/1st Gurkha

CLUNY ESTATE

2/1st Gurkha over run

Passed 8am
Kg Slim

2/9th Gurkha

Withdrawal
2/2nd – 2/9th Gurkha

2/2nd Gurkha
Slim River Station

5/14th Punjab over-run

SUNGKAI
5 MILES

4/19th Hyderabad
Halted

5/2nd Punjab

2nd A & SH

Halted for a few minutes

Kg. Trolak

Halted for approximately one hour

Check Position

Demolition of bridge failed

12th Brigade

KLAPA BALI ESTATE

J2

TILAU ESTATE

Slim River

B Sqdn
3rd Cavalry

Patrols

had discovered that War Office pamphlets on defence methods against tanks were still lying, in unopened bundles, in the General Staff cupboards where they must have been for several months, if not years. Simson had hurriedly produced a condensed pamphlet for distribution to all commanders. Given its timing—the pamphlet was not ready until 6 December 1941— it is quite understandable that this information was never digested by them. But as we have observed, Simson could have, and should have, been placed in complete charge of the construction of the fortifications along the Trunk Road.

In his book, *Singapore: Too Little, Too Late*, Simson revealed that he had correctly anticipated the use by the enemy of medium and light tanks. He advocated the placing of obstacles to stop tanks and thus render them vulnerable to close-range fire. He recommended the building of drainage ditches along roads to discourage the tanks from leaving them and thus evading established gun sites. He favoured the use of field guns against enemy tanks when anti-tank guns were in short supply.

Almost all of the necessary elements for anti-tank defence at Slim River were absent, because of an understandable lack of training and imagination. Local commanders and Public Works Department officials were poor substitutes for a Chief Engineer and his expert staff. Brigadier Simson has left us with a cutting summary, which not only addresses the anti-tank issue, but also the ongoing difficulty of bridge demolition:

Had the Engineers from Command Headquarters been allowed to prepare anti-tank obstacles, mine chambers, etc., for the really effective demolition of major bridges, in peace or early war time—as had been often suggested—it seems certain that much of the pressure on units of the Third Indian Corps, as also their resulting casualties, could have been materially reduced during the retreat. In fact it is probably not too strong a criticism to say that Malaya provides a good example of how the Army's engineer arm should not be used—nearly always too little and far too late, when they were used at all.[1]

The second critical problem confronting the defenders at Slim River was how to maintain effective communication. The 108 radio set, used mainly at the company and battalion level, had been a major disappointment in closed country. Weighing around 11 kilograms, the set was cumbersome to carry on the signaller's back, and required a line of sight—rarely available in Malaya—for reliable transmission. The radio used at the brigade and division level was far bigger and required a truck for its use and storage. It was vulnerable to air attack and also proved unreliable. The chief methods of communication at battalion and brigade level were signal cable, despatch riders and, where possible, the local civilian telephone facilities. The need for defence in depth along roads and in general perimeters, therefore, compounded these communication problems.

The third factor was the physical condition and morale of the defenders. Colonel Deakin, the CO of the 5/2nd Punjab, noticed the condition of his men just prior to the action at Slim River:

> The battalion was dead tired; most of all the Commanders, whose responsibilities prevented them from snatching even a little fitful sleep. The battalion had withdrawn 176 miles in three weeks and had had only three days rest. It had suffered 250 casualties of which a high proportion had been killed. The spirit of the men was low and the battalion had lost 50 per cent of its fighting efficiency. During the 5th January, I found a most lethargic lot of men who seemed to want to do nothing but sit in slit trenches.[2]

It was all very fine, therefore, for General Percival to advocate that the 11th Indian Division should 'take every opportunity of imposing delay by attacking the enemy's flanks and rear', but given Deakin's assessment of his men—in the front line of the Trolak sector—those soldiers were in questionable physical and mental condition to defend a given locality, let alone attack the enemy.

The first attack by the Japanese at Slim River was inauspicious. Preceded by a mortar barrage during the late afternoon of 5 January, two companies of infantry came onto the Hyderabads via the railway. The Indians held their fire until the enemy were almost onto their wire, with the result that the attack was quickly broken up, and some 60 Japanese were left dead or dying near that obstacle, for little loss to the Indians. The next day was unusually quiet apart from minor patrol activity. General Paris decided to leave his still tired and worn 28th Brigade in their rest positions at the village, with the idea of positioning them in their Slim River sector at around midday on the 7th. It would prove a fateful decision.

Alan Warren has recorded that late on 6 December, an Asian refugee arrived in the 12th Brigade's perimeter with information. He 'claimed that he had seen a column of "iron land-ships" at Sungkai',[3] about thirteen kilometres north of Trolak, and that the blown bridge there had been repaired. Alan Warren:

> Stewart concluded that the vehicles were only lorries. As Stewart would not permit Deakin's Punjabis to damage the road in their area, Deakin ordered his sepoys to lay anti-tank mines on the Trunk Road in a narrow cutting. Old loop roads in the Punjabis' sector were left open for the Hyderabads' vehicles.[4]

Two points above are of critical importance. First, Stewart's assumption that the 'iron land ships' were lorries would seem wishful thinking. In fact, it was an assumption he could not really afford to make. The second revelation is the fact that there were three loop roads in the Punjab perimeter. Small loop roads were used to minimise or straighten out bends on roads, particularly for convenience near rubber plantations, with the result that while such old sections of road were disused and partly grown over, they were in fact accessible—particularly by tanks. The first was about 650 metres south of the 60-mile peg, the second just north of peg 61 and the last at about peg 62. It is hard to credit that a military engineer of the seniority and standard of Brigadier Simson would have left three loop roads within the prime defensive perimeter 'uncovered' by concrete obstacles, mines or anti-tank guns.

The forestalled frontal movement along the railway on 5 January against the Hyderabads had caused Colonel Ando to change his plan for his 42nd Regiment's capture of Trolak on the night of the 6/7th. He now decided to stage an attack down the Trunk Road with tank support in unison with an outflanking movement through the jungle. But his tank commander convinced him to allow a tank thrust down the main road, arguing that if this failed, his original plan could still be implemented without affecting his timetable. The Japanese attack was to constitute what Colonel Tsuji would later call a 'thoroughly consolidated fighting force'.[5] And it was. The column was headed by a tank company, closely followed by an infantry company and engineers. Behind them came a concentrated column of tanks and infantry in lorries. This magnificently balanced and potent Japanese force was, by its very composition, set to exploit the three weaknesses that have previously been discussed.

Supported by an artillery barrage from guns near the railway and on the east of the road, and assisted by 'brilliant moonlight',[6] the Japanese attacked straight down the Trunk Road at around 3.30 am on 7 January. Concentrated artillery and tank fire enabled a rapid clearing of the Hyderabads' first roadblock and a consequent overunning of their forward company. The Japanese now used the first loop road to create utter confusion and a consequent withdrawal of the Hyderabads along the railway.

While this mayhem was in train the tank column pushed on. At around 4.30 am its leading tank reached a cutting near the 61-mile peg at the front of the Punjabis' perimeter and struck a mine. While the enemy initially lost three tanks, and close quarter fighting broke out, they now employed the loop roads to encircle the defenders and destroy or scatter them. Barely 800 metres further along the road, the tanks and infantry easily repeated their success by overrunning the next Punjab position, which possessed no anti-tank defences. Within a further hour the advance had travelled a further 750 metres before it was temporarily halted by an anti-tank mine in front of the Punjabis' reserve company. For the young Indians, exhausted, dispirited and attempting to defend their perimeters with such poor support, the experience must have been terrifying. Kirby has quoted Colonel Deakin's vivid description of their plight:

The din ... baffles description. The tanks were head to tail, engines roaring, crews screaming, machine-guns spitting tracer, and mortars and cannon firing all out. The platoon astride the cutting threw grenades, and one tank had its track smashed by an anti-tank rifle. The two anti-tank guns fired two rounds, one of which scored a bull, and then retired to the Argylls area. One more tank wrecked itself on the mines.[7]

Although they incurred heavy casualties, the Punjabis' reserve company and headquarters gamely inflicted an hour's delay upon the Japanese column. At this time, however, another undefended loop road came into play. When the Japanese discovered it, they promptly surrounded the Punjabis and by around 6.30 am—with daylight looming—moved on. The survivors of this party made their way back towards the Slim River bridge, with intelligence gained the hard way: they had counted 30 tanks and, amidst the din described by Lieutenant-Colonel Deakin, identified the sound of further tanks to the rear. Now, when such information was critical to the erection of further anti-tank obstacles down the Trunk Road, the poor communications of the perimeter came tragically into play. The local telephone system had been cut by the enemy. Brigadier Stewart, trying to make sense of these rapidly unfolding events, guessed that while the Japanese had pushed through the Hyderabads, they had been stopped by the foremost Punjab company. To stabilise his perimeter, he now ordered the reserve 5/14th Punjab to deploy at the brigade check position at the 65-mile peg, the Argylls to hurriedly construct roadblocks covering Trolak, and, critically, he ordered Deakin to hold his position regardless of whether the enemy broke through.

The Argylls quickly placed two roadblocks within their rearward 12th Brigade perimeter: the first on the Trunk Road at the northern edge of the Klapa Bali Rubber Estate (the extreme northern edge of their perimeter); and the second at its southern extremity, just forward of Trolak. At approximately 6.30 am, and now in full daylight, four medium tanks smashed through the first obstacle and within a half-an-hour ran into the second. Here they were stopped for a short time by the Argylls' armoured cars and anti-tank rifles. This was a brave action but a futile one. The two armoured cars which contested the advance were very quickly, and understandably, knocked out, and the anti-tank rifles proved worthless.

We now come to another recurring 11th Indian Division, and indeed III Corps, failure: the consistent inability to blow bridges promptly. Although the Trolak bridge had been wired for demolition, all went astray. Brigadier Stewart would later record that:

But the demolition, the cause for which the sacrifice was made, failed. No sappers were to be found, and the wires had been cut by retreating traffic. Captain Turner, the able leader of the carriers, and armoured cars, gallantly pushed one of the knocked-out armoured cars on to the bridge under the continuous fire of the tanks. But it sufficed for only a few minutes' delay. The tanks came up, pushed it cautiously aside, and continued down the road.[8]

The repeated, inept performance in demolition of bridges by both divisional and brigade engineers must have infuriated Brigader Simson. The fault should not be attributed to the former, but to the complete failure by General Percival to employ the expertise at hand. And it would seem that the lessons were not recent, but had been learnt during the First World War and implemented in British Field Service Regulations as early as 1922. Simson would later write that mine chambers should have been built for future use and further: '... small demolition squads should actually live in dugouts at those bridges ...'[9] The notion that local engineers might lay a charge and then remain at the desired bridge to ensure its successful demolition would seem a basic one.

The Argylls were now capable of doing nothing other than watch a stream of enemy tanks file past them. When further Japanese tanks arrived at the Trolak bridge, all that could be accomplished by the by-passed right forward Argyll company, and its overrun road remnant, was to destroy their remaining armoured cars and carriers, and set off through the jungle in an attempt to reach the Slim River bridge before the enemy.

The 12th Brigade and 11th Division's primitive communications caused their commanders to be virtually out of touch with tragic events. For his part, at 6.30 am, General Paris was informed that 'there had been some sort of breakthrough', when in fact two of his battalions had been overrun. He reacted to this news by ordering Brigadier Selby to immediately occupy his positions in the Slim River sector. Even Stewart, whose HQ was on a side road in the Tilau Rubber Estate, remained ill informed. He told Selby that he thought the situation was serious rather than critical, which must have given the latter a false sense of security. Stewart now only had contact with his company on the Estate Road and a remnant of the Hyderabads. At 9.00 am, he ordered both to delay any further Japanese movement down the Estate Road, and began a 12th Brigade HQ withdrawal to Slim village. The Argylls and Hyderabads who had been cut off were all later either annihilated or captured—and the wounded were slaughtered by the Japanese.

The audacious Japanese tank commander, with further bridge objectives in mind, continued his rapid advance forward of Trolak without his infantry support. At about 7.30 am, while the 5/14th Punjabis were moving along the Trunk Road to occupy their checkpoint at the 65-mile peg, they were surprised—understandably so, given they were nearly five kilometres short of their objective—by the enemy tank advance guard. Moving in company line of column, the front company was hit and scattered, the following severely mauled and left with only twenty unwounded soldiers, and the remaining two quickly melted into the rubber to eventually occupy a point on the road. They too fell foul of supporting tanks and infantry. So fast and concentrated was the Japanese vanguard that it quickly encountered the 28th Brigade troop of anti-tank guns—a rare commodity at Slim River—and proceeded to overrun it before it could deploy for action.

Paris's decision to allow his 28th Brigade to bivouack in Slim village to rest now came home to haunt him. At around 8.00 am, the 2/9th Gurhkas were only just beginning to occupy their perimeter just out of Slim village when the enemy tanks swept past them. About five minutes later, and moving in a column of companies down the Trunk Road towards their Cluny Rubber Estate perimeter, the 2/1st Gurkhas were taken completely by surprise when they, too, were confronted by the leading tanks. Understandably, they were completely overrun and scattered. Two batteries of the 137th Field Regiment were next. Deployed beside the road in the Cluny Estate, they were given a short but comprehensive spraying of both cannon and machine gun fire, before the enemy's urgent dash to the Slim River bridge continued. When the bridge was reached at about 8.40 am, the Japanese had only to contend with one troop of light anti-aircraft Bofors guns which, despite the fact that they fired at a mere 100 metres, did no damage. The soldiers manning these guns, unprotected by infantry, were soon scattered; and the tanks, leaving one of their number to guard their prize, soon made off. They made a further three kilometres before being confronted by the 155th Field Regiment, which was proceeding north to its task of support for the 28th Brigade.

It should be conceded that any support unit which encounters an advanced enemy tank column about 30 kilometres from what it considers to be the front line will be somewhat horrified by the experience. Kirby has recorded that:

> Although the tanks overran the regimental headquarters, one detachment managed to get its 4.5-inch howitzer into action and, despite being under heavy fire, hit and stopped the leading tank at a range of about thirty yards . . .
>
> The tanks patrolled for a short distance south of the river during the remainder of the day but, harassed by hastily formed tank-hunting parties, withdrew later in the afternoon to the bridge . . .[10]

It must have been disturbing news for General Paris, when at 8.30 am he learnt that the Trolak sector had been pierced. But he would surely have been devastated 90 minutes later when told that the Japanese tank spearhead had captured the Slim River bridge. He immediately despatched an anti-tank battery north of Tanjong Malim, alerted his remaining formations to be prepared for tank contact and informed General Heath of the breakthrough. Heath responded by sending the 15th Brigade's 2/16th Punjab, which was disposed at Rawang, to hurriedly reinforce Tanjong Malim.

Late on the morning of 7 January 1942, Brigadiers Selby and Stewart had a joint HQ established east of Slim village. They knew that the four Battalions of 12th Brigade and the 28th Brigade's 2/1st Gurkhas were at worst destroyed or at best, dispersed. Selby now decided to stay in the area with his two remaining 28th Brigade Battalions until dusk, to allow for the collection of the maximum number of stragglers, and then, after the last of his transport had been destroyed, to move his Slim River survivors back along the railway to Tanjong Malim. This was accomplished by around 3.00 am on the 8th.

The Battle of the Slim River constituted the final destruction of an already debilitated 11th Indian Division. On 8 January 1942, barely a month after the outbreak of hostilities, it lay in tatters: the 4/19th Hyderabads could muster but three officers and 110 other ranks; the 5/2nd Punjab one and 80; the Argylls four and 90; the 5/14th Punjab six and 129; the 2/2nd Gurkhas 400 all told; the 2/9th Gurkhas 350 all told; and the 2/1st Gurkhas, none.[11]

In his postwar despatch, General Percival inadvertently included an appalling piece of self-indictment:

It would be easy, but unprofitable, to attribute the defeat at the Slim River Battle to the inadequacy of the anti-tank defences, the failure to blow the bridges or to a variety of other causes. The real cause lay in the utter weariness of the troops, both officers and men. They had been fighting and moving by day and by night for a month, and few of them had had any proper rest or relief.[12]

All troops engaged in any prolonged fighting withdrawal become weary—and extremely so. But Percival's inability to facilitate adequate defensive locations compounded this problem. Further, given his description of the 11th Indian Division's physical and mental state, the sensible course of action would have been to relieve it. Percival repeatedly stated that the Division was to fight, withdraw, but at all costs, stay intact. In the end it failed, and by any sensible evaluation, it failed in no small measure because of his mistakes.

Kirby, belatedly in his 1971 book, *The Chain of Disaster*, has pointed out that such a relief might well have been made by transferring General Barstow's 9th Indian Division from its eastern front where he claimed 'it had been kept idle in Pahang except for the futile and unnecessary effort to hold the Kuantan airfield'.[13] Kirby's point has merit. The 8th Indian Brigade had been stationed in Kuala Lipis since 22 December, and it was possible that its fellow 9th Division's 22nd Brigade could have joined it there by the end of December. Thus both brigades could have fought in the Slim River–Tanjong Malim area by early January 1942. A further point not mentioned by Kirby is that Percival's obsession with the central Malayan airfields would appear to have been an over emphasis. The forecasted reinforcement convoys directed to Singapore in mid-January and early February could have approached their final destination under darkness—as was the case during the seige of Tobruk. In the end, all reinforcements reached Singapore without loss, and the destruction of his 11th Indian Division, therefore, was not an acceptable price to pay for possible attacks on convoys, or the so-called 'administrative problems' of relieving it.

All such decisions assume varying degrees of risk, but, in the end, Percival lacked what Montgomery called a 'grip' of his campaign.

———— ✦ ————

At first light on 7 January 1942—as Japanese tanks were ravaging the 11th Indian Division's perimeter at Slim River—General Wavell landed in a Catalina on Singapore Harbour. He was on his way to Java to assume supreme command of the newly created ABDA (American–British–Dutch–Australian) Command. Wavell had determined that, in broad terms, his task was to hold both naval and air bases stretching through a line from Singapore to Sumatra, Java, Timor and finally to Darwin.

With regards to the retention of Singapore, Wavell realised that Johore was the vital ground, and that time must be bought north of this state until the arrival of reinforcements. In the short term, he saw the despatch of the British 18th Division as a means of stabilising the front, and, eventually, he anticipated that the proposed deployment of the 1st Australian Corps might facilitate a counterstroke. Those reinforcements would then allow him to send the Indian divisions to the Netherlands East Indies. His trip to Singapore was thus planned for meetings with the commanders of Malaya Command, to assess the condition and morale of its troops, and, importantly, to attempt to form a time frame for these objectives. Wavell was due to arrive at Batavia on 15 January to open his HQ.

That day, Wavell met with Duff Cooper, the Resident Minister for Far Eastern Affairs, General Pownall and Percival. General Wavell had now become Percival's third commander in as many weeks. Wavell flew to Kuala Lumpur the following day. During the early morning of 8 January, he met 'a disconsolate Heath' followed by a journey forward to confer with Paris, Stewart, Selby and Barstow. All were understandably exhausted. In view of the fact that Wavell was to later order Stewart out of Singapore before its fall, to employ his knowledge of the campaign, Wavell's first impression of the 12th Brigade commander was not favourable: 'Well, I've never listened to a more garbled account of an operation.'[14] It is possible that Pownall had again influenced his perceptions. On 27 December—eleven days before Wavell's arrival—Major-General Gordon Bennett had recorded in his diary that: 'Pownall came in. Had been to the front and accurately sized up personalities. Was not sure of Heath or Paris. He is full of fire & demands commanders also with fire. I like him . . .'[15]

Upon his arrival back in Singapore Wavell sent for Percival. After keeping him 'waiting in an ante-room for a considerable time',[16] he presented him with a written plan which he was to implement without delay. Wavell had decided that Major-General Gordon Bennett would be placed in command of north-west Johore, with the 9th Indian Division under command. Heath's III Corps HQ and his 11th Indian Division were to be rested and refitted in southern Johore, and III Corps was also to be responsible for eastern Johore and its south-west coast. The AIF 8th Division's 27th Brigade (Brigadier Maxwell) was to come under Bennett's command forthwith, while its 22nd Brigade (Brigadier Taylor) was to be moved from Mersing on the east coast as soon as possible. In addition, the newly arrived—if poorly trained—Indian Army's 45th Brigade (Brigadier Duncan) was to also come under Bennett's command. Wavell's plan thus embodied a decisive break to a line Muar–Segamat–Mersing and, therefore, the virtual abandonment of the provinces of Selangor, Negri Sembilan and Malacca, where it was considered the road system would make delaying tactics quite difficult. He was well aware that his plan presented the Japanese with three provinces at little cost, and that the relief of the Australian 22nd Brigade on the east coast would risk deploying troops there who had 'less knowledge of [the] ground in that area'.[17] The salient point is surely that for the first time decisive action was being taken to buy real time to rest and refit III Corps; that fresh formations were being committed, if belatedly; and that, while calculated risks were involved, they were being taken.

According to Kirby, Wavell added another critical order to those already given:

> . . . finding that, although reconnaissance had begun, no defences had been constructed or even planned in detail on the north shore of Singapore Island, he ordered these to be put in hand at once in case a withdrawal to the island became necessary.[18]

Simson, of course, had made a personal plea to Percival late on the night of 26 December 1941 for defences to be built on the north shore of the island forthwith, but Percival was not to be convinced. Early on the morning of 27 December, Simson had breakfast with General Simmons. Once again his basic, common sense advice was rejected. Even after Percival's new commander had ordered him to undertake those very constructions, that order failed to be executed. There can be no excuse offered for either Percival or Simmons for this chain of events. Further, it would seem a contradiction in terms for General Keith Simmons to have held the title 'Commander, Singapore Fortress'. What fortress?

The notion that Wavell was attracted to the idea of Bennett assuming a major role in the defence of Johore certainly made sense. The 8th Division was well-trained both prior to leaving Australia, and in Malaya; its 22nd Brigade had been there for a year, while the 27th had arrived in August 1941; and, above all, it was fresh and ready to fight.

On 10 January, another conference was called at Segamat between Percival, Heath and Bennett to arrange the handover between Heath's III Corps and the AIF. Bennett was now to command 'Westforce': the 27th Brigade AIF; the 8th and 22nd Brigades of the 9th Indian Division, reinforced by Singapore Fortress's 2nd Loyals (less one company); and the newly arrived 45th Indian Brigade. Bennett's Westforce was to hold the line Batu Anam–Muar. Heath's III Corps, meanwhile, was to assume responsibility for the line in Johore from the lateral road Endau–Kluang–Batu Pahat southwards. He was to command the 22nd Brigade AIF in the Mersing area, while his 11th Indian Division's 15th and 28th Brigades were rested and refitted in Johore. His 12th Brigade was sent to Singapore Island for the same purpose.

The time was now near when Major-General Gordon Bennett's 8th Australian Division was to be given its baptism of fire. Bennett had been open in his criticism of others and had not missed an opportunity to publicise the AIF in Malaya. He was now itching to show the worth of both his 8th Division and its commander.

14

GEMAS

—————

While Generals Wavell, Percival, Heath and Bennett were planning Malaya Command's defence of Johore, General Yamashita's 25th Army was reinforcing its forward troops and preparing plans for the final capture of Malaya. On 8 January 1942, the 5th Division's 21st Regiment (Colonel Harada), accompanied by a large contingent of support units, reached Singora. Two days later, the 5th Guards Regiment (Colonel Iwaguro), followed by Guards Divisional troops, reached Ipoh. By this time the Japanese were acutely aware of their long line of communication, which began at Singora. Accordingly, they earmarked the 18th Division's 114th Regiment, one battalion of the 55th Regiment and divisional troops for a landing at Endau during late January. Not only would this operation shorten that line of communication, but they anticipated that it might allow them to outflank the British retreat through northern Johore.

—————

After their disaster at the Slim River, the 11th Indian Division's greatly weakened 12th and 28th Brigades, although reinforced by the 2/16th Punjab, still retained the task of defending the Trunk Road. On 8 January General Heath, only too well aware that the division was in no condition to offer a sustained resistance, ordered General Paris to hold Kuala Lumpur until midnight on 10 January, and then retire about 50 kilometres to the vicinity of Seremban.

Paris knew that the mountain barrier to his immediate east was essentially safe, and therefore looked to defend his northern Trunk Road approach and the western coastal area. To this end he deployed his formations in three key sectors. The first was a defence of the Trunk Road, where he posted the 28th Brigade, reinforced by two companies of the 3/17th Dogras. The second area was essentially the section of road between Batang Berjuntai and Rawang, where he deployed his 15th Brigade—reinforced by Brigadier Painter's 22nd Brigade's 5/11th Sikhs. The coastal sector was his last, and was covered by the Jat/Punjab Battalion and the 3rd Cavalry. Paris withdrew command of this area from the 15th Brigade and placed it under Brigadier Moir. As a timetable for withdrawal, he ordered that Rawang, the River Buloh and Klang were to be held until 4.00 pm on 10 January, and subsequently, either the 15th or 28th Brigade was to then hold Kuala Lumpur, while Brigadier Moir's coastal force was to defend Batu Tiga until midnight on the 10th.

Despite the fact that the 15th and 28th Brigades were able to hold their areas in the face of repeated and concentrated enemy attacks, the price was heavy. By the time the 28th Brigade had broken contact and withdrawn, the two companies of Dogras, including its HQ and CO, were overrun and lost. And the 15th Brigade fared worse—the whole of the 1/14th Punjab suffered the same fate.

On the coastal sector, the Japanese crossed the river at Kuala Selangor and made contact with the Jat/Punjab Battalion, the 3rd Cavalry and the 73rd Field Battery, which were covering the approach to the bridge at Klang. Alan Warren, in *Singapore 1942*, has recorded that:

At 6.30 p.m. the British–Indian force withdrew from Klang as planned and headed east along the road to Kuala Lumpur. About 10 p.m., amid a rain shower, the 3rd Cavalry and the Jat/Punjab Battalion were ambushed and disintegrated. Only two hundred survivors were gathered together at Batu Tiga to continue the retreat southwards.[1]

An additional Japanese attempt to cut off Kuala Lumpur was staged by a Guards battalion which, after having landed at Port Swettenham on the 10th, by-passed Klang and headed for the Trunk Road, which was reached the next day. It was a near thing—the last truck convoys had passed only hours before.

Japanese troops entered Kuala Lumpur at around 8.00 pm on 11 January 1942 and 'took over the civil administration and quickly enforced law and order'.[2] In a sign of things to come, law and order were certainly 'quickly' enforced. The heads of likely anti-Nippon locals or of those who had looted were displayed on poles in public.[3]

The sheer speed of the Japanese victory at the Slim River had caused a less than satisfactory British destruction of military stores at Kuala Lumpur and Port Swettenham. Although Kuala Lumpur's airfield buildings were fired and the runways cratered, the Japanese were quick to repair much of the damage. Heath's 11th Division reached Tampin on the 13th and during that night withdrew through Westforce to the Kluang–Rengam area, while his 9th Division's 8th Brigade reached Batu Anam on the 11th. On 13 January 1942, the 9th Indian Division came under command of Major-General Gordon Bennett's recently constituted Westforce, and occupied its new dispositions as a part of the defence of Johore. Shortly after the III Corps withdrawal, Percival made further command changes. He would later write:

> At the request of the Commander 3 Indian Corps I appointed Brigadier Key to command the 11 Indian Division in place of Major-General Paris. The reason for this was that we considered that an Indian Army Officer was now required to pull together and re-establish confidence in what remained of the 11 Indian Division. Brigadier Lay, who had now returned to duty, was appointed to command the 8 Indian Brigade and Col. Challen took over command of the 6/15 Indian Infantry Brigade in lieu of Brigadier Moorhead.[4]

Heath finally had his way with regard to the command of Indian formations by Indian Army officers. General Paris was sacked and returned to his 12th Brigade. Percival, ever the gentleman, would write in *The War in Malaya*, that he 'took pains to explain to Paris that the change by no means indicated loss of confidence in him'.[5]

Despite these gloomy events, 13 January saw the much welcomed arrival at Singapore of the British 18th Division's 53rd Brigade; one heavy and one light British anti-aircraft regiment; one British anti-tank regiment; and, most importantly, 50 crated Hurricanes, 24 pilots and ground crew personnel.

Two significant characters now enter our story. The 27th Brigade AIF was commanded by Brigadier Duncan Maxwell. In keeping with Brigadier Taylor's prewar decision to appoint veterans of the First World War to the original commands of his 22nd Brigade, Maxwell had become the original commander of the 2/19th Battalion. Lionel Wigmore:

> Maxwell, six feet three inches in height, was the shorter of two sons of a Tasmanian bank manager. Both had given distinguished service in 1914–1918 when they were affectionately known as 'Big' and 'Little' Maxwell. They served as troopers in the light horse on Gallipoli, and later were commissioned in the infantry. In France, each was decorated for his exploits at Mouquet Farm.[6]

After the First World War, Maxwell had graduated in medicine at Sydney University and had gone into private practice at Cootamundra in NSW. It was not until August 1939 that he returned to soldiering as second-in-command of the 56th Militia Battalion. His interwar training and experience were thus limited.

Bennett chose the 27th Brigade's 2/30th Battalion from NSW as the first unit to confront the Japanese. It was commanded by Frederick 'Black Jack' Galleghan, who was senior to all of the infantry battalion COs in the 8th Division, and had commanded three militia battalions in succession since 1932. Following the First World War, Galleghan had been a public servant in the Newcastle area of NSW until 1936, after which he worked for the Commonwealth Investigation Service in Sydney. Wigmore: 'Tall, dark-visaged, possessed of drive and determination, he tended to ride roughshod over the opinions of others, and had won a reputation as a disciplinarian

which preceded him to his new battalion.'[7] When training the 2/30th Battalion Galleghan had expected it to get up earlier and march further than other
battalions. He was tough in the extreme towards all within it: officers and
other ranks alike. Any form of debate or initiative was not encouraged—
all that mattered was unquestioning loyalty from anyone and everyone.
The Battalion, according to 'Black Jack', was going to be the finest unit in
the 2nd AIF. Captain Ron Maston, 2/30th Battalion: 'He was a very strong
determined bloke . . . he set out to make we [*sic*] officers and NCOs capable
leaders . . . [and how] caustically he dealt with us at times . . .'[8]

Lieutenant Bert Farr, Signals Officer, 2/30th Battalion:

> His insistence on discipline . . . everybody knew exactly where they
> stood as far as the old man was concerned . . . [at Bathurst] he would
> say to the fellows going on leave, 'OK, you've got five days leave, and
> for every day you're late coming back it's going to cost you a pound a
> day.' One of the fellows was a bit of a keen punter, and when he came
> back a few days late the old man said to him, 'Well, three days late, it's
> going to cost you three quid. How did you go at the races?' And Bill
> said, 'Oh, I won a bit.' And he [Galleghan] said, 'In that case, it'll cost
> you five quid!'. . . He could have a battalion parade, with the officers
> in front of their particular companies and troops and so forth, and he
> wouldn't hesitate to tick off an officer in front of his troops because
> he argued that that bonded the officer to the troops . . . in other
> words, they weren't a separate race and they weren't immune from
> his discipline. But everything he did in the disciplinary sense was very
> fair, absolutely fair.[9]

But it would seem that not everyone was intimidated by Galleghan's
authoritarian style of leadership. Captain Rowley Richards, RMO, 2/15th
Field Regiment:

> . . . we saw him as very much a bully, and a classic example, shortly
> after we arrived in Malaya . . . we were invited to Black Jack's Mess for
> lunch one day. 'We', being the CO, the Adjutant, and myself. During
> the course of lunch, all of Black Jack's officers were 'Yes Sir, No Sir,'

all of that sort of stuff. He had 'em all absolutely bluffed . . . Our original CO, John O'Neill, he was a magnificent man. He was a bloody larrikin, brought up in the pool rooms of Melbourne, he was a man's man . . .

And during the course of the proceedings one of them said something the other disagreed with. There was a little bit of an argument going on between John O'Neill and Black Jack. And google eyes all around the place, all these officers, 'Nobody talks to our CO like that!' And then finally, John O'Neill said, 'Fred, I'm a guest in your Mess, I can say what I like, you can go and get fucked!' And Black Jack just backed off.[10]

The fact remains, however, that both Galleghan and his 2/30th Battalion performed admirably during the fighting on both the Malay Peninsula and on Singapore Island. Lieutenant-Colonel 'Black Jack' Galleghan will feature prominently in our story—and at times controversially—both during the fighting and in Changi.

Galleghan held little respect and less affection for Maxwell. When the original 27th Brigade commander, Brigadier Marshall, was forced to relinquish his command through ill-health, Bennett chose the 2/19th's CO, Maxwell, as his replacement, even though Galleghan was the senior battalion commander in the division. When the 27th Brigade arrived in Singapore, Galleghan is alleged to have greeted his new brigade commander with, 'Well, you need not expect me to congratulate you on the red flannel you're wearing![11] Galleghan's attitude did not augur well for their future relationship.

———

Because the foremost Japanese thrust had been along the Trunk Road, and with his 22nd Brigade AIF still committed to the Endau and Mersing area, Major-General Gordon Bennett placed his 27th Brigade as the foremost Westforce formation on that axis. The Brigade's leading unit on the Trunk Road was the 2/30th Battalion, which was deployed nearly five kilometres west of the River Gemas. The rearward town of the same name, where the railway ran from the east coast and met the Trunk Road and railway from the west, was critical to the defence of Johore. Lieutenant-Colonel Galleghan had a battery of the 2/15th Field Regiment and the 16th Anti-Tank Battery, less one troop, in support. Behind the 2/30th was the 2/26th Battalion AIF (Lieutenant-Colonel Boyes). It was positioned between Gemas and Batu Anam, in the Paya Lang Estate, just north of the Trunk Road. Support for the 2/26th was provided by the 29th Field Battery. Behind that battalion was the 2/29th (Lieutenant-Colonel Robertson)—between Batu Anam and Segamat—at Buloh Kasap. Brigadier Maxwell's 27th Brigade HQ and that of the 2/15th Field Regiment were stationed near Segamat, while Bennett's advanced Westforce HQ was located at Labis.

The remaining perimeters of the Westforce defence of the Trunk Road were occupied by the 9th Indian Division, which 'were allotted various responsibilities from Segamat to Batu Anam, and westward of the main road to guard approaches through Jementah, on a road from Malacca to the west coast'.[12]

It is hard to offer any real criticism of Bennett's Westforce dispositions along the Trunk Road. They had suitable depth and were occupied by fresh, trained and motivated troops whose support was at least adequate. But West-force did have one major problem: the coastal flank in north-west Johore. Bennett decided to post the inexperienced 45th Indian Brigade, which had only recently arrived in Malaya at Muar. But the Muar River was Westforce's weakness. However, Percival agreed with Bennett's deployment of the 45th Brigade because he believed that, as previous enemy attempts to conduct coastal operations had been on a small scale, the main Japanese thrust would continue to be along the Trunk Road. It was therefore anticipated that the 45th Brigade would be capable of dealing with such limited operations. Bennett had been a strong advocate for counterattacks, ambushes and all-round defence. The word 'withdrawal' was an abomination to him. He now had his chance to put this conviction into practice. By the employment of an ambush, he believed he could check the Japanese advance and provide the opportunity for a potential offensive.

The site chosen for the Gemas ambush was in the vicinity of a wooden bridge spanning the Gemencheh River. This location was about eleven kilometres west of that town. The main road from Tampin—the direction from which

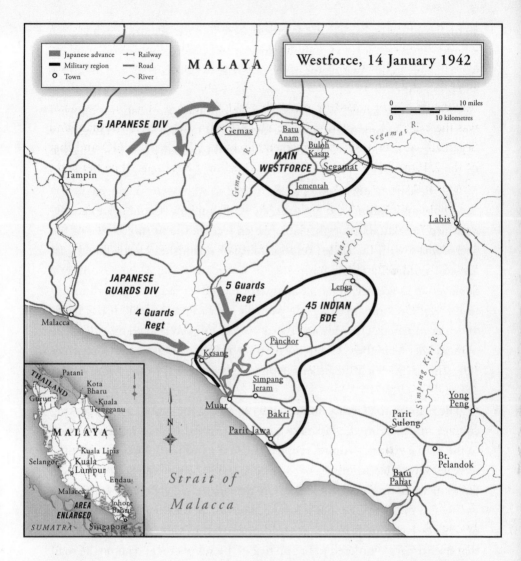

Westforce, 14 January 1942

the Japanese would come—took a bend about 220 metres before leading onto the wooden bridge, which was about fifteen metres long. The ground on that side of the bridge was relatively open. Since the Japanese were expected to arrive in a truck convoy, the bridge would have been visible to them for only a short period of time before they crossed it.

After crossing the bridge, the Japanese were to travel along about 50 metres of road running through 'low scrub and offering little conceal-ment'.[13] But the actual ambush position was ideal. After covering that first

50 metres after the bridge, the Japanese were to enter a cutting, which was around 40 metres long and about three metres high. Ample concealment was available to the Australians in the jungle above the cutting and for about 350 metres after it.

As Galleghan could not deploy a full battalion ambush, he allowed his company commanders to draw lots for the honour of Australia's first engagement in Malaya. Captain Duffy won; B Company was to spring the trap.

The remaining three companies of the 2/30th were deployed nearly five kilometres behind the ambush site. C Company (Captain Lamacraft) occupied the Battalion's right flank, which was on the northern side of the Trunk Road, with the added responsibility of establishing a roadblock just forward of the Battalion perimeter. A Company (Major Anderson) was deployed in the centre, adjacent to and south of the road, with Battalion HQ to its rear. D Company (Captain Melville) occupied the 2/30th left flank, which terminated at the railway. Two anti-tank guns were sited on either side of the road: one in the C Company perimeter, and the other on A Company's side. The 2/15th Field Regiment deployed its guns just to the south of the railway.[14]

The plan for the Gemas ambush envisaged the III Indian Corps breaking contact and allowing the Japanese an uninterrupted 48-kilometre approach to the killing ground—uninterrupted because a number of wooden bridges were left intact to encourage over-confidence and complacency. But a critical component of the plan hinged upon the artillery's ability to plaster the enemy side of the bridge after it had been blown. In the inevitable congestion of vehicles, equipment and troops leading up to the bridge, it was anticipated that the artillery—ordered to fire up to 270 metres over it and along the road and to either side of it, should cause utter carnage. To this end, two signal lines were laid from Duffy's ambush site: one to Battalion HQ, and the other to the rearward artillery.

Galleghan made a number of further decisions which were to prove significant. The first concerned anti-tank defence in his main perimeter. Since Galleghan did not believe the enemy would employ tanks against him, he regarded the anti-tank guns as an encumbrance. He even sent a third one back that had arrived later that day.

In an effort to thoroughly conceal his main perimeter dispositions from air observation, Galleghan also forbade his troops to dig in.[15] However, infantry in a defensive position—exposed to potential enemy machine gun, tank, artillery fire and air bombardment—should always be dug in.

<hr />

At around 4.30 pm on 13 January 1942, and in driving rain, Captain Duffy led his B Company forward to its ambush position. The last of his troops arrived at dusk. Duffy disposed Lieutenant Head's 12 Platoon on both sides of, and at the head, of the cutting. This was the closest position to the bridge. B Company HQ was slightly to the rear on its southern side. Head's platoon had two Bren guns sited to sweep the relatively open ground on the far side of the bridge and a liberal supply of grenades, which would be used to target the anticipated Japanese truck convoy. Lieutenant Geike's 10 Platoon was stretched along the road on its northern side, while Lieutenant Jones's 11 Platoon was similarly deployed on the southern side. To secure and hold the company's Quarry Road withdrawal route, a small detachment was posted near the Trunk Road–Quarry Road junction. The bridge was wired for demolition by engineers of the 2/12th Field Company.

Captain Duffy's instructions were clear: he was to let the first column of trucks over the bridge, through the cutting, and up to the Quarry Road junction. This was the time to then blow the bridge, allow his 12 Platoon to hit vehicles and troops on the far side, and signal back to the Battalion perimeter for concentrated artillery fire on the far side of the blown bridge. Concealment, silence and great fire discipline were the keynotes of B Company's ambush. However, there was one grave error in the preparation of the ambush. On two occasions artillery signal wire was noticed beside the road. Twice orders were given to conceal it, but the orders were not carried out.

At around 4.00 pm on 14 January 1942, the action began. Private Ray Brown, 12 Platoon, 2/30th Battalion: 'Brown and Smith were the foremost troops at the ambush, 80 feet [about 24 metres] from the bridge we were going to blow. Our task was to take out the second truck. All the way down the ambush site, each section had a certain truck to take out. We expected them to come on in trucks.'[16] Corporal Harry Holden, D Company, 2/30th Battalion:

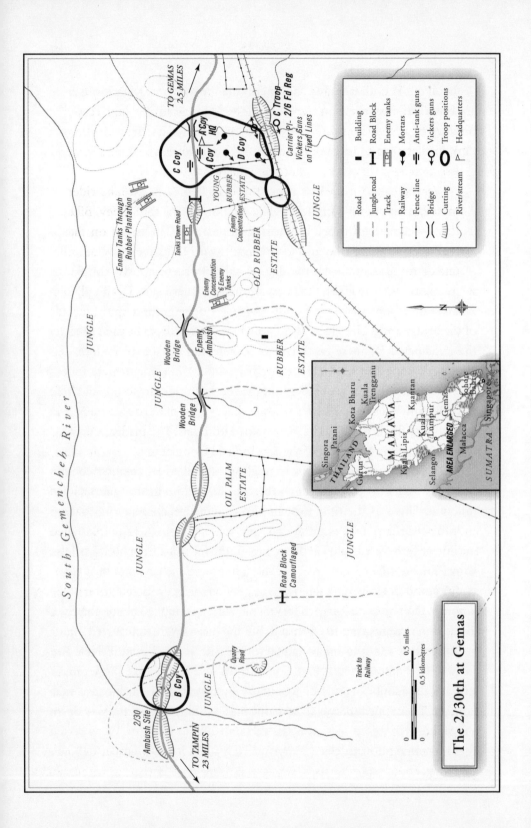

The 2/30th at Gemas

We were not to take any prisoners and we were to abandon our wounded. They were straight out orders. Eventually the Japs came. Now the first one through, was a scout on a motor bike. He pulled up and cut the wire. I had a bead on him . . . I could have shot him, he was less than 30 yards away . . . that was a major blue.

Very shortly the cyclists came through. Being an old bike rider myself, I thought, 'This looks like the Goulburn to Sydney Bike Race—so many of them, hundreds! Thick as they could get on the road . . . chattering away and skylarking . . . we didn't have any weapon pits or anything, we were just hiding in the bushes . . . After a while, they seemed to be going through, too many of them for us to handle. Of course Captain Duffy, he was waiting for the mechanized transport . . . anyway, the bridge went up. Did it ever go up! . . . there were bits of bikes and Japs and debris . . . all around us.[17]

The Japanese in the main column had no chance. The road was narrow; the Australians were only metres from them; and the Japanese had their rifles strapped to their bikes. In fact so close was the enemy, Corporal Holden found himself unable to risk using his extensive supply of grenades, and instead concentrated on rapid rifle fire, while the Bren gunner alongside him used five magazines. Private Ray Brown used his 'cup discharger (E.Y. Rifle) with "68" anti-tank bombs from the shoulder',[18] to telling effect across the river. Corporal Holden: 'There was some plain and fancy shooting there for a while, and a terrible noise . . . we were making all the noise.'[19]

Immediately after the bridge went up, Captain Duffy ordered the artillery forward observation officer (FOO) to signal back for the barrage to begin. Faint calls, 'Robert Charlie, Robert Charlie' were heard from the rearward perimeter—the artillery were trying to reach their FOO—before the line went dead.[20] Galleghan was now in an awkward position. Although all ears strained for telltale sounds of an explosion, nothing was heard over that distance. The artillery barrage that could have caused such devastation never happened.

The incredible slaughter at and near the Gemencheh River bridge was all over in about ten minutes. Duffy now ordered his company to withdraw.

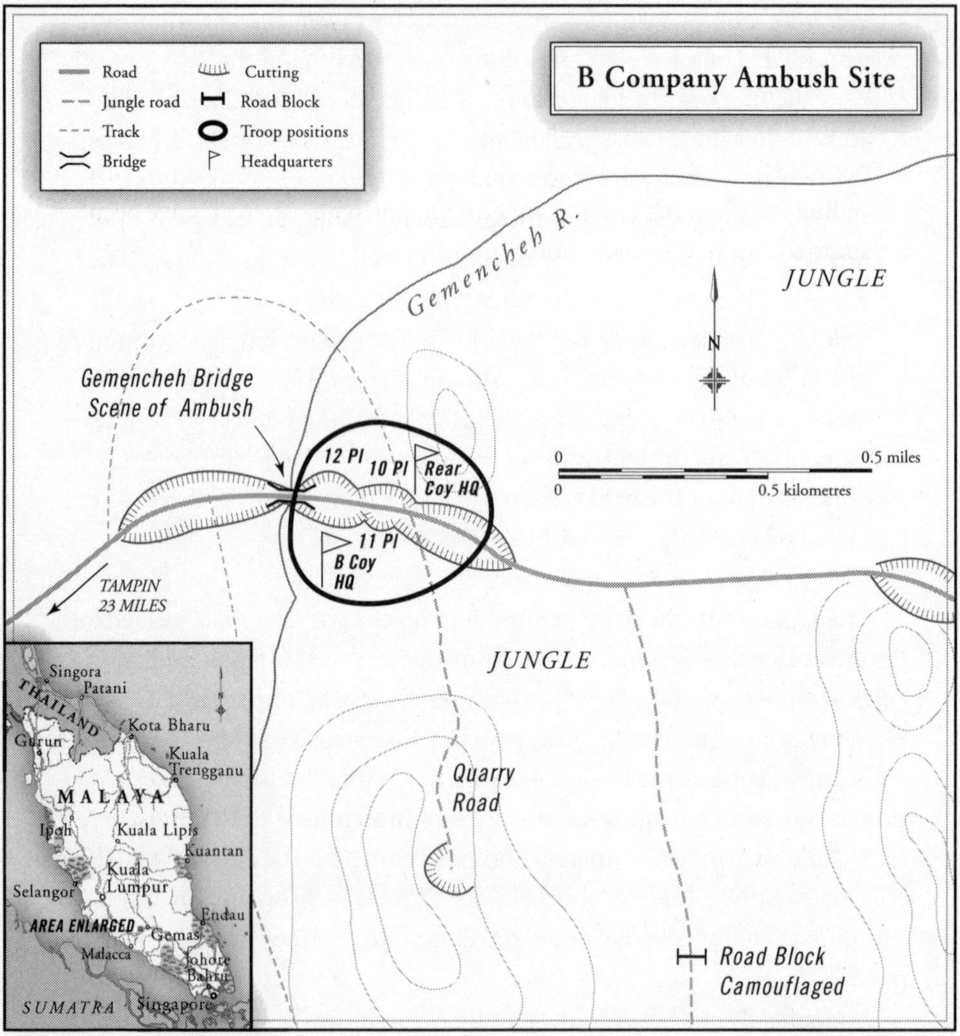
B Company Ambush Site
Road
Jungle road
Track
Bridge
Cutting
Road Block
Troop positions
Headquarters
Gemencheh R.
JUNGLE
N
0
0.5 miles
0
0.5 kilometres
Gemencheh Bridge
Scene of Ambush
12 Pl
10 Pl
Rear
Coy HQ
11 Pl
B Coy
HQ
TAMPIN
23 MILES
JUNGLE
Quarry
Road
Road Block
Camouflaged
Singora
Patani
THAILAND
Kota Bharu
Gurun
Kuala
Trengganu
MALAYA
Ipoh
Kuala Lipis
Kuantan
Kuala
Lumpur
Selangor
AREA ENLARGED
Endau
Gemas
Malacca
Johore
Bahru
SUMATRA
Singapore

When some of them crossed the road, the scale of the massacre became evident. Private Ray Brown:

> [Lieutenant] Harry Head said, 'We're moving out now and we're going down the road to mop up anyone who's still alive . . . so we moved along the road walking over the bodies—600 blokes, you could hardly walk between them. There's bikes through people, people without heads, a hell of a mess. I never saw anyone alive actually—if they were alive, they kidded dead.[21]

Corporal Harry Holden:

> One thing I do recall, I can't account for it, the psychologists
> could ... after everything went quite, my fellas, we came out with
> our rifles and bayonets at the high port, yelling our heads off! Just
> yelling ... we weren't saying anything in particular. It must have been
> some sort of nervous reaction or something.[22]

Captain Duffy now ordered a company withdrawal to the Quarry
Road rendezvous point. Lieutenant Jones's 11 Platoon, sited adjacent to
Quarry Road, was to act as the rearguard. During the withdrawal, a small
number of Japanese who had either been just forward of the ambush and
had turned back, or had survived the slaughter, stirred to action. When
Lieutenant Head and members of his 12 Platoon began to withdraw,
they were attacked by the enemy near a bend in the road, and Head, after
shooting an enemy officer, became a casualty. Geike's 10 Platoon also
ran into small numbers of Japanese who were killed or scattered by the
bayonet. In this action, Geike was also wounded. Jones's 11 Platoon, having
held their position until the others had gained the Quarry Road exit, then
made their way out. After having taken to the jungle, Duffy's B Company
became separated into two groups, both of which returned to their Battalion
lines during 15–16 January.

Late on the night of 14 January, Lieutenant-Colonel Galleghan sent
volunteers out in an attempt to repair the signal lines—to no avail. He later
sent three patrols out to ascertain Duffy's B Company whereabouts and to
gather intelligence as to the position(s) and size of the enemy force in the
area. The first was led by Sergeants Arneil and Hall. At around 11.35 pm
they encountered a Japanese patrol estimated at platoon strength, on which
they inflicted heavy casualties. The second, under Lance-Corporal Heckendorf,
left the Battalion lines at 2.10 am on the 15th in search of B Company,
and, although contact was not made with Duffy, this patrol was able to
establish that the Japanese had repaired the ambush bridge, and were
advancing on the 2/30th perimeter in force accompanied by tanks. Unfortunately,
Heckendorf's patrol did not return to the Battalion lines until
6.00 pm on 16 January—far too late for its information to be of value.

The third was a fighting patrol from A Company. Lieutenant Lyn Booth, A Company, 2/30th Battalion:

> The fighting patrol was to go out, make contact with B Company if possible and also find out where the enemy was situated, and if we found them, to attack them ... at 4.15 we set out across the open ground in front of us with two guides from the Intelligence Section ... the night was a particularly black night, heavy cloud, it had been raining, there was no moon, and we were in dense rubber ... the only way we could maintain contact with each other was by ... each man holding the bayonet scabbard of the man in front ... I had decided to ... do a detour and swing around to come in behind where we suspected the enemy were ... by the time dawn arrived ... we had found no sign of any B Company forces or of the enemy ... we pressed on, and at about 8 o'clock we heard chattering in front of us and also the dropping of tail boards of motor vehicles ... coming up and discharging men. At the same time my leading section came under fire from Japanese who were in position on top of the rise which we were coming up ... it was a fairly large debussing point and assembly point ... [the Japanese] appeared to be massing for an attack on the Battalion positions ... also at the time four tanks came into the area which no one was expecting ... the best thing to do for us was to get out ... return to the Battalion and warn them of the situation which was developing.[23]

The 2/30th Battalion patrols on 14 and in the early hours of 15 January are noteworthy. First, they demonstrate the extreme difficulty of communication in the Malayan environment at this time. Signal cable was inclined to deteriorate in that moist, humid environment; its repair—especially at night—was both difficult and hazardous; and it required a reasonably static and prolonged use to be effective. It was not a satisfactory means of communication during a fluid withdrawal. Second, movement over any significant distance was hard in that environment. Heckendorf's patrol gathered useful information, but was too distant from its base to be able to convey it in time to be of any great use. Even Lieutenant Booth's fighting patrol—however well executed—was only able to bring in its information virtually as the enemy were about to attack the 2/30th.

But the real observation to be made from the ambush at Gemas concerns the Japanese. Although badly mauled at the ambush site, within a mere 28 hours they had repaired the bridge, concentrated their force—supported by tanks—and had attacked the 2/30th Battalion. Their infantry's ability to assault their enemy with tremendous initial power and aggression, their employment of their tanks and, critically, their magnificent engineering skills always enabled them to maintain the initiative. They never seemed to allow their enemy to adequately stabilise his front.

At around 9.00 am on 15 January, the Japanese began their assault upon the 2/30th Battalion's main perimeter. A reconnaissance tank appeared, moving cautiously down the cutting with only its turret and cannon visible. On the right or northern side of the road was Sergeant Charlie Parson's two-pounder anti-tank gun, and, just to its rear on the other side of the road, was Sergeant Ken Harrison's gun. The remarkable thing about the 4th Anti-Tank Regiment's Gemas performance—and others during the campaign— was their remarkable success given their equally notable lack of training and experience. Ken Harrison: 'Compared with these [Japanese] battle-tested veterans, we were babies. Apart from firing six shots out to sea from a few old French 75s, none of us had ever handled an artillery gun since we enlisted. We were going into action with a two-pounder gun we had never fired, except in theory.'[24]

The first effort of the 'babies' showed their inexperience. Both guns immediately fired at the only partly revealed reconnaissance tank, and thereby disclosed the number of guns and their positions. Minutes later a light tank, very soon followed by a medium tank, came around the slight bend into the cutting, and then slowly moved towards the roadblock. Just before gaining that feature, Parsons and Harrison—this time displaying much more patience—opened fire.

Parson's first shot hit the medium tank, while Harrison's second turned the light tank into a 'sheet of flame' whereupon its crew 'attempted to escape from their burning coffin'.[25] During the ensuing action the Japanese committed two more groups of tanks against Parson's and Harrison's guns. The first consisted of two medium and one light. Using a combination of

armour-piercing and high-explosive shells, the Australians were able to set
the first on fire, disable the second and cause the last to be towed from the
action. The second attempt was made by four tanks, which used the previously disabled and blazing tank as cover, and were supported by infantry
mortar fire and machine guns. But the two Australian guns and mortar fire
from the 2/30th were more than equal to the task. The first tank 'was hit, the
second disabled, the third set on fire and the fourth wrecked by a mortar
bomb which exploded after entering the turret'.[26]

During what the diarist of the 2/30th Battalion was to call, 'General
battle—sustained firing on both sides',[27] the Japanese made about an hour-
long attempt to pierce the Australians' perimeter, but were forced to withdraw
in the face of concentrated artillery and infantry fire. At around 11.15 am
the Battalion's spirits received a fillip with the return of the bulk of Duffy's
B Company and news of their ambush success.[28]

By early afternoon on 15 January, Galleghan knew that the Japanese
had repaired the Gemencheh River bridge with astonishing speed, and, as
a consequence, were already concentrating their infantry and support for
further and stronger attacks. The isolated nature of his advanced position
therefore caused him to make two decisions. The first was to counterattack and therefore hinder the enemy build-up, and the second was to
immediately recce a fall-back position behind the Gemas River that evening.
Galleghan therefore ordered his just-returned and worn B Company to
occupy D Company's perimeter and thereby release it for the counterattack. Captain Melville's attack was timed for 11.45 am and was to be given
supporting fire by A Company. Its objective was a hill about 900 metres in
front of its perimeter. Melville was ordered to hold it until dusk if possible,
and then retire back through B Company.[29]

But the impending D Company attack was to be postponed twice within
an hour when Japanese aircraft—which had been busy bombing the town of
Gemas—suddenly attacked the 2/30th perimeter. Battalion HQ was the first
target. After describing the many measures taken to disguise that HQ from
air observation, and therefore expressing surprise that the HQ could have
become a target, the 2/30th Unit History claimed that:

Whether the enemy's efficiency in pin-pointing a wireless transmit-
ting set is over estimated or not it was subsequently accepted in the

Battalion that the enemy had ascertained the location of Battalion
H.Q. by the operation of the wireless telegraphy during the morning.
(This was confirmed, after the capitulation of Singapore, by a Japanese
officer ...)[30]

In the event, the bombing was close to rather than on the HQ, but this
proved of little consolation to the troops who had been ordered not to dig
in. Casualties were taken.

Captain Melville's D Company attack went in at 12.45 pm on 15 January
1942. Expecting their enemy to be somewhere around 900 metres on or
near their hill objective, the company was rapidly placed under intense fire
from only about 270 metres. Despite the additional handicap of the artillery
firing beyond the enemy's advanced position, D Company managed to move
forward. It was assisted greatly by A Company's covering fire and accurate
mortar fire. The Japanese took significant casualties and lost two guns and
their crews. However, as 16 and 17 Platoons came to the fence separating the
'young rubber' and 'old rubber' sections of the plantation, they came under
enfiladed Japanese machine gun fire, which slowed them down and caused
them casualties. It was at this time that elements of 18 Platoon encountered
what was to become a common Japanese ploy: they were subjected to sniper
fire from nearby trees. Although most Japanese engaged in this practice were
usually eliminated in time, casualties and a loss of momentum were the
usual by-products.

It was at about this time that enemy tanks now became a grave problem.
It will be remembered that Galleghan had sent the third anti-tank gun
'packing' as not required after Harrison and Parsons had sited their guns.
He must have deeply regretted his decision when Japanese tanks appeared
to the right of the road and began to rake the 2/30th positions with concentrated fire—against soldiers who were not dug in. Harrison and Parsons,
whose vision was obstructed by the lines and obstacles of rubber trees,
could do nothing to assist them. Harrison claimed that that very side of
the road was where Lieutenant Peck had planned to deploy the third anti-
tank gun.

While the anti-tank gunners' splendid support was now at an end, Major
Ball and a troop of 25-pounders from the 30th Battery joined the fray. Firing

over open sights, they were able, with added assistance from the mortars, to keep the tanks at bay while the 2/30th began its withdrawal. During that process, both two-pounder anti-tank guns and all but one field gun had to be abandoned on that boggy ground.

At around 2.45 pm, and in the face of 'further enemy air activity',[31] more of the Battalion's trucks made their exit from the perimeter, while the forward troops, moving through the HQ area, started to concentrate on a hill to the rear as a prelude to a withdrawal along the railway and through the rubber to Gemas. At about 3.15 pm, the 2/30th was able to successfully break contact with the Japanese and two-and-a-half hours later the Battalion less its A Company had arrived at Fort Rose Estate, where it formed a night perimeter.

The 2/30th Battalion's fighting forward of Gemas during the two-day period 14–15 January 1942 deserves high praise. A. W. Penfold in *Galleghan's Greyhounds*:

> Under the circumstances, the unit's casualties for the two days were very light: 1 officer and 16 other ranks killed, 9 other ranks missing and 55 wounded (including 4 officers) . . .
> Enemy casualties were conservatively estimated at 800 on the first day (ambush), and an additional 200 in the later action. Against the enemy's certain loss of six tanks, the Battalion lost three 25 pounder guns, two anti-tank guns and 10 vehicles, besides some equipment.[32]

The ambush at the River Gemencheh was brilliantly conceived. The decision to leave unexploded bridges leading up to Captain Duffy's B Company positions appears to have lulled the enemy into a false sense of security. The choice of the ambush site was astute, because the narrow, jungle-topped cutting and the subsequent thick vegetation on each side of the road extending for some considerable distance proved both an extensive and intensive killing ground. Moreover, the escape route was well planned and essentially well used. Above all, Duffy's B Company demon-strated exceptional fire discipline. But the failure to cover the signal cables constituted a major mistake and cost the unit a chance to inflict far greater Japanese casualties by means of the planned artillery barrage.

In the rearward 2/30th perimeter, the dispositions were sound and occupied by disciplined troops whose fire and movement during the counterattack were well rehearsed. The standard of patrolling by the Battalion also reflects its high standard of training. The 2/30th Battalion's performance at Gemas must reflect upon the excellent training and leadership of Lieutenant-Colonel Galleghan and his officers. But Galleghan's decision not to order his troops to dig in was a mistake, and, above all, his failure to embrace his anti-tank capacity demonstrated that he did not fully appreciate the tactical use of this critical support—which was an error destined to be repeated only days later.

Any estimate of the combined Japanese losses at the ambush site and at the rear of the 2/30th perimeter is difficult. However, it is quite possible that some 400 to 500 enemy troops were caught in that first hail of fire. A total Japanese casualty count of around 600 to 700 would thus seem fair. The Australian war correspondent Ian Morrison recorded that Gemas: '... was a triumphant beginning. It set all of the Australians cock-a-hoop. It had a tonic effect on all the British forces.'[33] Unfortunately, the 'tonic effect' was not to last long.

15

THE BATTLE OF MUAR

On 14 January 1942, while the 2/30th Battalion ambush was under way on the Trunk Road near Gemas, General Nishimura's Imperial Guards Division had occupied the west coast port of Malacca. Nishimura's next task was to cross the Muar River and then move in two columns: one along the coast road to seize Batu Pahat, and the other to capture Yong Peng via the inland road. The Muar River was a formidable military obstacle and the town of Muar, which lay on the southern bank near its mouth, was accessible only by ferry. Given that he had no landing craft with which to cross it, and the British had moved all existing vessels to the southern bank, Nishimura ordered his 4th Guards Regiment (Colonel Kunishi) to contain the enemy at Muar while his 5th Guards Regiment (Colonel Iwaguro) crossed the river upstream under the cover of darkness. Once across, the 5th Guards were to attack Muar from the east and then move on Yong Peng, while the 4th Guards were to take the coastal axis. In order to cut off the subsequent Westforce retreat along the coast road, Nishimura ordered the 1/4th Guards Battalion to move by sea and land between Batu Pahat and Senggarang, where it was to lay in waiting pending the rest of the regiment's thrust along the coastal road.

The defence of the Muar River had been entrusted to Brigadier Duncan's newly arrived 45th Indian Brigade, which had arrived in the area on 12 January. In compliance with General Bennett's orders, Duncan deployed his 7/6th Rajputana Rifles on his left flank between Muar and Jorak, thereby occupying fourteen kilometres of ground. His right flank was held by the 4/9th Jats, who were disposed along some 24 kilometres to cover the river crossings of Grisek and Lenga. Bennett ordered both battalions to place two companies across the river for ambush roles. Brigadier Duncan held his 5/18th Royal Garhwal Rifles in reserve near Bakri, with one of its companies forward at Simpang Jeram, and a small detachment stationed on the coast south of Parit Jawa. The 65th Battery of the AIF 2/15th Field Regiment (Major Julius) was allotted as his support. Kirby has stated that:

> General Bennett appears to have lost sight of the main reason for placing the 45th Brigade in the Muar area—to protect the direct route from Muar to Yong Peng and so secure his line of communications— and to have attempted to cover all possible routes from the Sungei [River] Muar towards Segamat and Labis as well as southwards.[1]

While Kirby's assertion is valid, three points should be raised. First, given the training of the 45th Brigade, Bennett's decision to order Brigadier Duncan to deploy two ambush companies from both battalions across the northern side of the river was foolhardy. Second, Bennett—and Percival— grossly underestimated the size of the Japanese force against them in the Muar area. This was certainly nothing new as Malaya Command's intelligence was abysmal throughout the campaign. Third, we have noted Percival's failure to allow Bennett to conduct his Westforce operation with both brigades of his 8th Division. It is worth remembering that the 22nd Brigade AIF was arguably the best trained brigade in Malaya Command. It is therefore intriguing to contemplate how the operation might have unfolded had the complete 22nd Brigade been at Bennett's disposal.

The Japanese bombed Muar repeatedly during the four-day period 11–15 January. On the 15th, while the fighting was in progress at Gemas, the Japanese surprised and overran the two forward companies of the Rajputana Rifles on the northern side of the Muar River. Incredibly, its Battalion HQ was none the wiser. Late that morning, Japanese infantry were seen opposite Muar and were shelled by the Australian artillery. And during that afternoon enemy boats were seen off the mouth of the river and small parties of Japanese were identified landing between the town and Batu Pahat. However, it was during the night 15/16 January that the great speed and purpose of the Japanese, and the utter inexperience of the 45th Brigade, were amply demonstrated.

Scrounging a few small boats in adjacent fields, the 111/5th Guards Battalion was able to cross the river and then return with native craft moored on the southern bank. Within a short time the Japanese possessed a bridgehead over the Muar River. Kirby has described their only contact with the Indians as being 'a brush' with a patrol which 'hastily withdrew', and that this 'brush' on the south side of the river was not reported.[2] Having crossed in large numbers by daylight, the Japanese quickly moved south and fell upon and eliminated a company of the 7/6th Rajputana Rifles. This force then proceeded to attack the advance company of the Garhwalis at Simpang Jeram and a company of the Rajputana Rifles which had been sent forward to protect Muar from the east. Further chaos ensued when Brigadier Duncan ordered a Garhwali company to reinforce the town. It got lost, failed to reach its objective and later returned to Bakri. Alan Warren, in his *Singapore 1942*, has recorded the next Indian 45th Brigade tragedy for 16 January:

> The company of the 5/18th Garhwal Rifles at Simpang Jeram had been joined by the battalion's advance headquarters the previous evening. About 6.30 a.m. on 16 January the Garhwalis' Lieutenant-Colonel James Wooldridge had visited Muar. He was killed when his party was ambushed on the return journey to Simpang Jeram. A Garhwali patrol was also ambushed forward of the village. The company's commander was among the dead.[3]

At Simpang Jeram, the Garhwalis attempted a counterattack at around 1.00 pm, which was repulsed with heavy casualties. They were forced to retire to Bakri. The only positive event for the day occurred when the Japanese attempted to cross the Muar River opposite the town and were fired on over open sights by the 65th Australian Battery. A small number of boats were sunk and the remainder retired. Late on the afternoon of 16 January, the remainder of the Rajputana Rifles in occupation of the Muar township were overrun by a Japanese assault from the east. In the process, the CO, Lieutenant-Colonel Lewis, and his second-in-command, Captain Alderman, were killed. The 65th Australian Battery and what was left of the Rajputana Rifles then withdrew to Parit Jawa.

In an action-packed and disastrous 36 hours, Brigadier Duncan's 45th Brigade had been put to the sword. The Garhwalis had lost their CO and around a company of infantry and the Rajputana Rifles could now muster a mere two officers and 120 other ranks. The Muar River was, apart from the Jats' tenuous positions, now in Japanese hands and the Indians had fallen back towards Bakri. If the Japanese thrust through Muar—already unfolding at a frightening pace—enabled them to gain the Trunk Road at Yong Peng far to the rear of the remainder of Westforce, then the defence of Johore would lay in tatters.

In response, during the evening of 16 January, Bennett decided to send his reserve 27th Brigade's 2/29th Battalion (less one company and a platoon) to Muar. In support of the 2/29th he assigned a troop from the 4th Anti-Tank Regiment and a number of armoured cars. Still unaware of the enemy strength, he ordered the 2/29th to counter-attack and remove a Japanese force which he considered to be around 200 strong. If the enemy were in strength, however, the 45th Brigade and its attached 2/29th were to hold the Muar–Yong Peng Road for seven days to allow Westforce's withdrawal along the Trunk Road.

The 2/29th Battalion had been raised in Victoria and was commanded by Lieutenant-Colonel John Robertson. It arrived at Bakri at around 3.00 pm on 17 January. Brigadier Duncan had planned that defensive perimeters would be manned on both the Muar and Parit Jawa Roads, and, pending the arrival of his 4/9th Jats from their Muar River dispositions, the 2/29th was to then stage a counterattack and capture Simpang Jeram. Lieutenant-Colonel Robertson envisaged an occupation of a night perimeter on the Muar Road about two-and-a-half kilometres forward of the Bakri crossroads, then a movement forward during the early hours of 18 January, and a counter-attack at daylight.

C Company (Captain Bowring) was sited forward near a bend to the left of the road in a rubber plantation, which then gave way to jungle to the west; B Company (Captain Maher) was to the right of the road also in rubber with jungle and swamp further east. Just behind those two forward companies lay a six-metre-high cutting through which the road narrowed. To the right rear was Captain Sumner's A Company. It was also in the rubber, which in turn was bordered by swamp. Because the Battalion's D Company was left out of battle, Headquarter Company (Captain Olliff) occupied the left rear part of the perimeter. Many of its specialist soldiers were now employed as riflemen.

At 6.00 pm an armoured car which had travelled about three kilometres forward of the Battalion's perimeter down the Muar Road came under fire from an enemy roadblock. An hour later a C Company patrol clashed with the enemy. The Japanese quickly followed up with a concentrated mortar barrage of the 2/29th perimeter and a probing of its C Company front. Corporal Bob Christie, Signals, 2/29th Battalion:

> Their mortars . . . they decided to do a block mortaring. So, in other words, they'd drop their mortars along that line, and they might drop four or six shells . . . and then they'd come to the next lot . . . and we'd see them do that lot and we'd get out . . . and go back to the ones they'd just done.[4]

When the Japanese moved up onto C Company, firing broke out, which caused the Australians to learn their first lesson in fire discipline within a night perimeter. Captain Victor Brand, RMO, 2/29th Battalion: 'It was night time and you weren't able to shine lights. I was feeling their wounds and trying to dress them with a syringe [grasped in his mouth] that I would use to give morphine. Clive Bowen [his Sergeant and a pharmacist] had made up a lot of morphine solution that I could use.'[5] Brand discovered that six of the eight gunshot wounds he treated were caused by Australian .303 bullets. Orders were later given for only grenade and bayonet use during darkness.[6]

As the retreating Garhwalis neared Parit Jawa village, they were ambushed and scattered. When only about 400 of them subsequently joined a detachment of the 7/6th Rajputana Rifles deployed one-and-a-half kilometres on the Parit Jawa Road outside of Bakri, Major Julius's 65th Battery became vulnerable. At midnight he asked Lieutenant-Colonel Robertson for protection for his guns. By 1.30 am on 18 January, Captain

Sumner's A Company had left its 2/29th perimeter and was in position for this task. Both the 2/29th Battalion's forward perimeter, and the Bakri crossroads itself, were now under threat of being cut off.

Meanwhile, on 16 January General Percival had realised the potential threat of the enemy activity at Muar and of their landings on the west coast. Westforce's line of communication was vulnerable. He therefore 'adjusted the boundary' between Bennett's Westforce and Heath's III Corps so as to give Heath the responsibility of securing these communications. Percival ordered the very recently arrived 53rd Brigade (Brigadier Duke) to move forthwith to Ayer Hitam to come under Heath's command.

At noon on 17 January, Percival, Bennett and Key held a conference at Westforce Rear HQ. During the course of their conversation, they discussed the option—if events at Muar continued to deteriorate—of whether to stage a withdrawal on the Trunk Road from Segamat. Yet again, and seemingly obsessed with the effect such a decision might have upon morale, Percival decided to further reinforce Muar and attempt to hold it. He now ordered one battalion of the 22nd Brigade AIF to journey to Muar to further bolster Brigadier Duncan's 45th Brigade. The 2/19th Battalion AIF was now ordered to move from Mersing on 18 January and be replaced at Jemaluang by the 5th Norfolk Battalion of the 53rd Brigade. Yet again Bennett registered his desire to have his complete 22nd Brigade sent to him rather than the piecemeal offering proposed by Percival. Percival held that there was 'not time in the existing situation to carry out the relief'.[7]

The 4th Anti-Tank Regiment sent four guns under the command of Lieutenant Bill McCure to Bakri in support of the 2/29th. Two were from its 16th Battery (Sergeants Harrison and Parsons) and two were from its 13th Battery (Sergeants Thornton and Peake). McCure decided to deploy two guns forward and two in reserve near Bakri. His choice of positions for his two forward guns would prove to be decisive. Just forward of C Company's front, and about 350 metres from, and directly in line with, a bend to the right in the road, McCure placed Sergeant Clarrie Thornton's gun. This position was far enough off the road to provide excellent camouflage and yet it had a long-range view of approaching tanks. It was here that Clarrie Thornton added a further refinement to the siting of his gun. Sergeant Harrison had told him that at Gemas the Japanese tanks had 'aimed low so that the shells would explode underneath the guns'.[8] Observing an extensive mound near his position, Thornton heeded Harrison's advice and manhandled his gun behind it. Sergeant Charley Parson's second gun was positioned in the cutting—around 450 metres from Thornton—and sited to give enemy tanks little time to react to its presence. Lieutenant Bill McCure's base was sited in C Company's perimeter about 350 metres behind Thornton and in line with the front of the cutting.

At 6.45 am on 18 January, five Japanese light tanks made their move. Corporal Jim Kennedy, Signals, 2/29th Battalion: '...a noise, a clank, clank, clank, and then there was cannon fire, and somebody yelled out, "tanks!"...and then all hell broke loose!'[9] As at Gemas, the gunners of the 4th Anti-Tank Regiment showed a remarkable fire discipline. Thornton waited for the first two tanks—travelling at about twenty kilometres an hour[10]—to be side-on and then opened fire with armour piercing (AP) shells. But the shells 'seemed to go straight through them'.[11]

Although hit and damaged, the first two tanks continued slowly down towards the entrance to the cutting. Meanwhile Thornton now opened up on the fourth and fifth tanks, which stopped them in their tracks. An urgent request was then placed with McCure to send high-explosive (HE) shells forward. Parson's gun now came into play with HE shells which set the leading tanks ablaze. When the third tank became jammed between these stationary infernos a 2/29th officer dropped grenades through its turret and blew it up. Thornton now completed the demise of the Japanese tanks by hitting the fourth and fifth tanks with HE shells. Captain Victor Brand, RMO, 2/29th Battalion: '...what a racket these guns made. What a racket!...It was the noise of this gun that was most impressive.'[12]

But the 'racket' was far from over. At around 7.15 am Thornton, although having sustained a shrapnel wound to a hip, was now confronted by three more Japanese tanks.[13] The first approached the bend cautiously before shelling his position. It was at this time that the mound in front of his gun came into play—the shells either whizzed past or landed on that obstacle

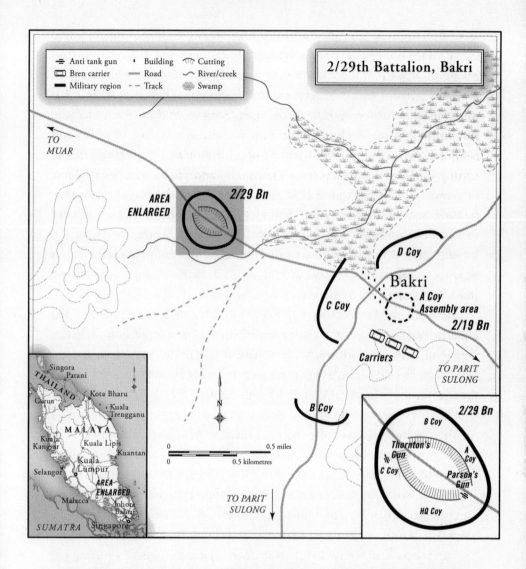

rather than beneath his gun. Thornton replied with a burst of HE shells. 'The tank stopped dead in its tracks, burning furiously and billowing a trail of smoke.'[14] One of the remaining two tanks remained behind the blazing tank, while the third took to the jungle and came into a position about 180 metres in front of Thornton and C Company. In an extraordinary display of speed and precision, Thornton turned his gun on the tank in the jungle and scored multiple hits, which stopped it. If the Australians were proving brave and well drilled, then the Japanese infantry were no less so.

Not once, but twice, Japanese infantry manned the crippled tank and fired upon Thornton. Now receiving fire from both tanks, the Australian turned his attention back to the tank on the road, and despite shells 'whizzing past', finally crippled it and then set it on fire. Thornton would later record that his crew then 'turned quickly on the tank firing at us from the jungle and silenced it, this time for keeps'.[15]

The Japanese lost all eight tanks during that brief but intense engagement with Thornton's and Parson's guns. The former had wreaked his share of the havoc by firing around 70 shells. Later that day, and during a lull in the fighting, Sergeant Ken Harrison went forward to view the carnage. Harrison, in *The Brave Japanese*: 'The officer in the front tank had committed *hara-kiri* by stopping a direct hit from a two-pound shell. In another tank the driver was still seated at the controls with an air of determination, but he had no head. And there were numerous charred bodies.'[16]

Although the tank action was followed by an understandable lull, the Japanese resumed their attack upon the 2/29th's C Company around 8.30 am. Not long after daylight, movement within the Battalion perimeter had become most hazardous, as Japanese snipers had infiltrated the area during the night. Lance-Corporal John Roxburgh, Signals, 2/29th Battalion:

There were Japs up in the trees ... There were officers being potted off ... and some bloke said, 'There's the bastard up a tree.' They opened up with their machine guns, and this little tiny Jap fell out of the tree, as dead as a door nail, and we looked at him, little rubber boots and underneath his shirt, in a little bag around his middle, he had a little pouch of food ... [he was] more towards C Coy than us ...[17]

Roxburgh's observation is astute. The officers were 'being potted off' for a number of reasons. First, most of them were wearing their insignia; unlike the other ranks, most were carrying pistols; gestures of command and body language tended to give their rank away; and at times they were prone to underestimate the close proximity and cunning of the enemy sniper. The lessons of jungle warfare were coming thick and fast. Private John Boehm, B Company: '11 Platoon was just near us, and they were saying, "There's a sniper firing.... Clark [Lieutenant] is going to draw his fire." I could hear this in the background. He got it right between the eyes . . . he was only in his twenties.'[18]

By 9.30 am the Japanese, in addition to their sniping just outside and inside the 2/29th perimeter, had set up machine guns in front of C Company. Three Bren gun carriers were sent to deal with this threat, and, although all three sustained wounded, the machine guns were either eliminated or forced to move. The Japanese infantry to their rear were unable to pierce the Australians' perimeter. With the enemy tank assault defeated, and his Battalion more than holding its own against Japanese artillery, mortar fire, and infantry attacks, Lieutenant-Colonel Robertson left for 45th Brigade HQ on the back of a motor cycle driven by a despatch rider named Baulkham.

The conference at Bakri was attended by Brigadier Duncan; General Bennett's GSO1, Colonel Thyer; Lieutenant-Colonel Robertson; and the newly arrived Lieutenant-Colonel Anderson, CO 2/19th Battalion. Robertson was able to inform the gathering that his 2/29th had been fighting troops from the Imperial Guards Division and that he had patrols out to contact the Jats and bring them into Bakri. Still seemingly unaware of the enemy strength—and events towards the coast—Duncan decided to deploy the now arriving 2/19th Battalion at and around the Bakri crossroads, leave the 2/29th in its current positions, and, after recovering the Jats, to attack and drive the enemy back. It was to prove wishful thinking.

As Baulkham and Robertson were returning to the 2/29th perimeter, they ran headlong into a Japanese roadblock. In the ensuing burst of fire both were hit. Despite their wounding, Baulkham managed to drive on and Robertson managed to hang on, until, some relatively short distance from the 2/29th, the CO fell off the motor bike. Captain Victor Brand, RMO, 2/29th Battalion:

> He [Baulkham] just fell off the bike and I was attending to someone . . . and he collapsed the bike quite close to me. And I don't know who said, or who knew, that Robertson had fallen off the bike a couple of hundred yards back there, so . . . Neil Gahan took a carrier and went down the road and lifted him into the carrier and brought him back to where we were . . . I helped lift him out; we laid him on the ground . . .[19]

Baulkham had been hit in the arm. Captain Brand: 'It ripped all his nerves and vessels; that's why it was amputated later on . . . so I sent him back with the first load of wounded . . . he got back to Australia.'[20] The CO was in a far worse state. Brand: 'He [Robertson] obviously had a head injury and he had some bullet wounds. I didn't take much notice of it, because he was obviously mortally wounded.'[21]

Lieutenant-Colonel John Robertson had been examined by a medical board weeks before, but had pleaded with General Bennett to be allowed to command the Battalion he had raised, in its first action. Bennett had granted him his wish on the condition that he be sent home after the first few days of that fight. The 2/29th felt his loss keenly and when detailed to dig his CO's grave, 'the sergeant in charge burst into tears and most of the men were visibly affected'.[22] It is a popularly believed story that before his death, Robertson summoned the 4th Anti-Tank Regiment's Lieutenant McCure to offer him an apology for reputedly reacting to the presence of the regiment in much the same way as Lieutenant-Colonel Galleghan had at Gemas. During an interview with the author Brand maintained that he was with the CO for the full 30 minutes before he died; that no such meeting took place; and that Robertson's head injuries were so severe that he would have been in no position to have had such a discussion.[23]

When Lieutenant-Colonel Duncan Maxwell was promoted to command the 27th Brigade AIF, Major Charles Anderson, his second-in-command, assumed command of the 2/19th Battalion. Anderson was 43 years of age when he arrived at Bakri. Born in Cape Town, South Africa, he had seen action with the King's East African Rifles during the First World War and had been awarded a Military Cross. He had subsequently married an Australian, emigrated to Australia and had settled on a property at Crowther in New South Wales. After having joined the 56th Militia Battalion in 1938, Anderson had enlisted in the AIF and was posted as second-in-command of the 2/19th at its inception. Lieutenant Jim Howard, Carrier Platoon, 2/19th Battalion:

Appearance wise, he probably looked like a country Parson: horn rimmed glasses; five-ten, maybe six feet [height]; quick-speaking;

inquisitive mind; a master of quick decision exercise . . . a quiet sort of man . . . tended to be a bit of a loner . . . but the Battalion practically worshipped him. He was an inspiration.

His tone of voice wouldn't change. He didn't have what I would describe as a good speaking voice . . . a quiet sort of bloke by nature.[24]

Private Gus Halloran, 2/19th Battalion:

A very quiet, very unassuming bloke. You would almost say gentle. A tremendous walker, he had legs like a mallee bull—he was over 40 years of age—and if you could keep him in sight, you were doing extremely well. He never conveyed the impression of being hard but he was determined, very resolute. Everyone liked him and respected him.[25]

Private Jim Stewart, Signals, 2/19th Battalion:

He was a great leader . . . a very quiet voice. As a matter of fact his voice was almost effeminate. But he had instilled in the whole of the Battalion a great faith in him. He did simple things that gave everyone confidence, like we had a bloke called Ted Donnelly, who was a bloody problem, he was always drunk and always fighting and always getting into trouble. Anderson made him his personal body guard, he changed like that [click of the fingers] he was completely devoted to Anderson. Wherever Anderson was, Donnelly was behind him with his Tommy gun . . . he [Anderson] instilled this sort of confidence . . . Unobtrusive, but he didn't have to discipline people because people did as he said. He had a good lot of other officers. Most stuff didn't get to the Battalion orderly room . . . it usually got to the company orderly room.[26]

On 18 January 1942, having left two platoons of his D Company out of battle—one of them was guarding the concrete bridge at Parit Sulong—Lieutenant-Colonel Anderson deployed his B Company on his left flank, about 1300 metres down the Parit Jawa Road. He ordered Captain Keegan to patrol aggressively down that road given the uncertain whereabouts of both the Indians and Japanese. Anderson sited Captain Beverley's A Company to the left of the road to link up with B Company and the one available platoon of Captain Westbrook's D Company. C Company (Captain Snelling) was stationed astride and to the left of the Muar Road, forward of Bakri village. The Battalion's carriers, pioneer platoon and mortars were positioned near Battalion HQ. A and B Echelon (Captain Newton) were around one-and-a-half kilometres to the rear of 45th Brigade HQ. The 2/19th had occupied their perimeter at Bakri by approximately 12.30 pm.

At about midday a 2/19th armoured car patrol which had been sent down the Muar Road to make contact with the 2/29th met an enemy road-block. As Brigadier Duncan had decided to send the 2/29th Battalion's A Company back to its Battalion perimeter, it was sent back down the Muar Road with a carrier, an armoured car and mortar support to destroy the roadblock and rejoin the Battalion. Although the attack failed, A Company ascertained that the enemy road obstacle was covered by infantry on both sides of the road, and was able to estimate their numbers and firepower. The roadblock itself consisted of a burnt out truck and a number of rubber trees laid over and around it.

Anderson now sent A Company 2/29th Battalion, two platoons of his C Company and carriers and mortars to attack and clear the obstacle. The 2/19th were well drilled in their use of carriers. Lieutenant Jim Howard:

> We converted them to mobile machine gun nests within our own infantry. They proved effective. We were attached to a company. You were within their ranks, any enemy would have to come through them to get at you, to get close enough to lob a grenade . . . and the infantry knew that you needed their protection . . . and they were getting protected, because they could go down on their bellies and we could sit up, and shoot the shit out of people 50 or 60 yards away.[27]

With the carriers providing covering fire, and an accurate mortar barrage, the roadblock was cleared. The 2/29th's A Company then reoccupied their perimeter and Lieutenant Howard's carriers returned with the 2/29th's Captain Gibson and various correspondents and cameramen who had filmed Thornton and Parson's 4th Anti-Tank Regiment's action that morning. Their film footage and stills remain some of the most graphic and detailed of the fighting in Malaya.[28] A number of trucks containing 2/29th wounded also passed through to the 2/19th area.

When a Jats officer reached Bakri at 4.00 pm with news that his Battalion remnants were about nine kilometres north-west of Bakri village, and further, when that location and the 2/19th's perimeter came under concentrated shell fire an hour later, Lieutenant-Colonel Anderson knew that any thought of offensive action was lost for the day. That night Brigadier Duncan ordered the remaining elements of the Garhwalis and Rajputs back into the 45th Brigade perimeter.

During the night of 18 January, the Japanese continued to exert pressure upon the 2/29th. At about 8.00 pm they again attacked C Company with an estimated force of 100 to 150 who advanced 'shouting and clashing their weapons together and generally working themselves up into a frenzy'.[29] Employing their enemies' shouts and other forms of noise as a guide to their location, the soldiers of C Company inflicted telling losses upon the Japanese, who were followed up and pushed well back from the Australian perimeter. Another enemy attempt at the same locality, this time with 40 men, met the same fate. Throughout its fighting forward of Bakri, the Japanese were unable to penetrate the 2/29th perimeter, and were, on all occasions, beaten back with substantial losses. The Battalion's constant patrolling forward of their perimeter, their aggression and superb use of the bayonet were the keynotes of their success.

Brigadier Duncan had planned a 2/19th company attack along the Muar Road for the morning of 19 January. Its purpose was to facilitate the recovery of the long-lost Jats, and to 'test the strength of the enemy'.[30] Lieutenant-Colonel Anderson now adjusted his Battalion dispositions: during the night of 18/19 January, a section of carriers relieved Beverley's A Company and occupied a rubber-covered ridge within the former A Company perimeter; A Company then left and assembled behind Bakri village ready for a 7.30 am attack the next morning; the remaining remnants of the Garhwalis and Rajputs were sent to their former position in front of B Company; and, last, Captain Keegan's B Company remained in their overnight position. Captain Snelling's C Company remained at the

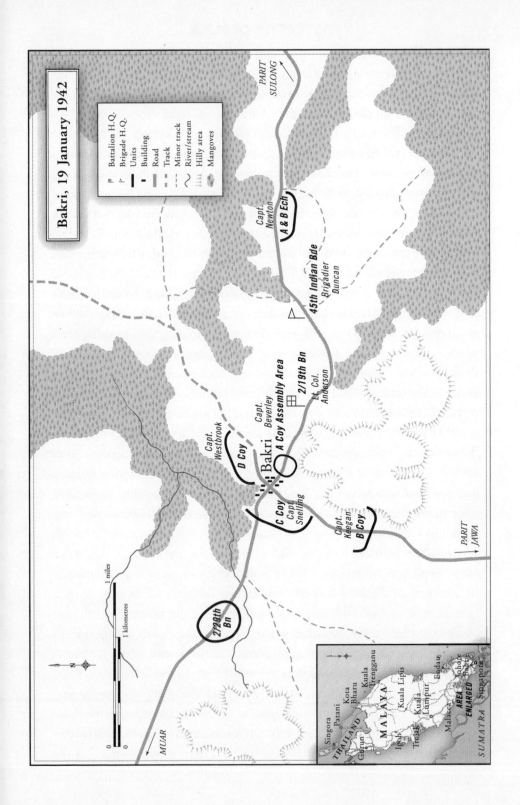

Bakri, 19 January 1942

Battalion H.Q.
Brigade H.Q.
Units
Building
Road
Track
Minor track
River/stream
Hilly area
Mangoves

PARIT SULONG

Capt. Newton
A & B Ech
45th Indian Bde
Brigadier Duncan

2/19th Bn
Lt. Col. Anderson

Capt. Beverley
A Coy Assembly Area

Capt. Westbrook
D Coy

Bakri

C Coy
Capt. Snelling

Capt. Keegan
B Coy

PARIT JAWA

2/29th Bn

1 miles
1 kilometres

N

MUAR

AREA ENLARGED

Singora Patani
THAILAND
Kota Bharu
Kuala Trengganu
Kuala Lipis
Kuantan
Ipoh Kuala Lumpur
Trolak Endau
Gemas Johore Bahru
Malacca Singapore
MALAYA
SUMATRA

Bakri crossroads with a platoon of D Company to their right. In his deployment of B Company, Anderson was astute, as he had created a reserve and also tightened his perimeter.

Beverley's 7.30 am departure did not eventuate owing to the British anti-tank support's failure to arrive at the designated time. But at 8.00 am a Japanese force of around 300—which despite 2/19th patrolling at dawn that day was not detected in its movement from east of the Parit Jawa Road— attacked the carrier-occupied ridge, which forced the carriers off that feature. Lieutenant-Colonel Anderson reacted swiftly. He ordered Captain Beverley's assembled troops to immediately stage a two-platoon attack upon this enemy force and retake the ridge. Lieutenant Weily's platoon put in a frontal attack, while Lieutenant Crawford's platoon moved along the ridge astride the Japanese right flank. Sergeant Christie's section of three carriers moved in support of this counterattack. Anderson waited for the attack to begin and then sent orders by carrier for Captain Keegan to move his B Company about 360 metres eastwards to cut off the Japanese force south of the ridge. To cover B Company's absence from their line Anderson ordered Captain Snelling's C Company to hold the Indians at Bakri village and plug that gap.

If Lieutenant-Colonel Anderson's reaction to the Japanese attack was both decisive and astute, then the implementation of his orders by his A and B Companies was equally impressive. Lieutenant Weily's A Company platoon put in their frontal attack with great gusto, and when Lieutenant Crawford's platoon attacked along the ridge on the enemy's right flank, the Japanese were halted and eventually forced to withdraw. And then came a new Malayan Campaign experience for the Japanese: they ran headlong into Captain Keegan's waiting B Company. The experience of 11 Platoon is an example of the B Company experience. Lieutenant Pat Reynolds, OC 11 Platoon:

After emerging from the defile where visibility was about 10 yards, our field of vision was enlarged to 40 yards, but only at five feet above the ground, which was densely covered with young rubber.

After 150 to 200 yards, my leading section topped a rise and saw Japs about 60 yards away. The section commander, Corporal Turner, kept going for another 20 yards before ordering the men to open fire. The Japs literally ran around in circles.[31]

When two of his sections became bogged down, Reynolds was able to employ his men's excellent fire and movement training, by moving one section to enfilade the enemy positions. Under a shower of grenades the platoon put in a spirited bayonet charge and routed the enemy. After the fighting had concluded, the Japanese resorted to old tricks. As various members of A and B Companies went 'back over the battle area to make sure that all the Japanese were dead and to establish a quick count'[32] a number of the 'corpses' came to life. Despite some anxious moments these were eliminated.

The duration of this 2/19th counterattack lasted a mere 90 minutes but cost the Japanese some 140 dead at a cost to the Australians of ten killed and fifteen wounded. As had happened along the 2/29th front, not only were the enemy forced to pay a severe price for their attacks, but they were unable to capture and hold any part of the 2/29th or 2/19th perimeters. The Australians retained their ground.

If the 2/19th felt an unrestrained euphoria at the Battalion's first engagement, a sobering piece of news reached Anderson during that fight, when he learned that Captain Newton's rear transport location had been attacked by some 400 to 500 Japanese who had come from the direction of Parit Jawa. Anderson immediately ordered a section of carriers to destroy the enemy roadblocks and force a passage through to Newton. This failed. To compound a rapidly deteriorating chain of events, the Japanese bombed the area at 10.00 am and scored a direct hit on 45th Brigade HQ. Lieutenant Ben Hackney, 2/29th Battalion, who had been one of the wounded evacuated from that forward battalion's perimeter, witnessed the devastation:

Outside the brigade headquarters was an ugly sight ... men's bodies lying everywhere ... portions of soldiers' stomachs hanging on limbs amongst the leaves of the trees—torn bloodstained limbs scattered about with only a lump of bloody meat hanging to them to indicate the body from which they were torn—just beside the road a naked waist with two twisted legs lay about two yards from a scarred bleeding head with a neck, half a chest and one arm ... There were some still alive but bent over, and others crawling, with every manner of injury.[33]

Amongst the victims of this carnage was Major Julius of the Australian 65th Battery, 2/15th Field Artillery, who was mortally wounded; all of Brigadier Duncan's staff, except his Brigade Major were killed; and the Brigadier himself was stunned to the point of being unable to continue his command. The human cost of this bombing was horrific, but the destruction of all of the copies of Westforce signals cipher meant that communication with the rear would be delayed for some critical time. The 45th Brigade Major immediately asked Lieutenant-Colonel Anderson to assume command of the Brigade.

In the early afternoon of 19 January 1942, Lieutenant-Colonel Charles Anderson was faced with a command consisting of the forward and isolated 2/29th Battalion, which had already been cut off by roadblocks twice, but had tenaciously held its ground; with continuing pressure upon his own 2/19th perimeter at Bakri; with a grievously threatened line of communication that had seen his A and B Echelon attacked and cut off; with a considerable remnant of the Jats still stranded and all but lost outside of his perimeter; and with the cruel prospect that if he should fail to extricate this force, the Japanese might capture the rearward prize of Parit Sulong and destroy Westforce.

The mild-mannered, softly spoken commander of the 2/19th Battalion was about to lead his mixed force through one of the most tragic, yet inspiring, confrontations in the Australian story.

16

TO PARIT SULONG

The Japanese pressure upon the 2/29th and 2/19th Battalions intensified as 19 January wore on. During the afternoon about 200 of the long-awaited Jats moved into the 2/29th A Company perimeter from the adjacent jungle and swamp. In consequence, the enemy immediately began a concentrated shelling of that area. Utter pandemonium ensued. Sergeant Bert Mettam, Mortar Platoon, 2/29th Battalion:

> They'd become a rabble. They'd lost almost all their officers and NCOs ... they were in our lines ... they [the Japanese] started this shelling, and it was very intense ... these Indians, when the shelling started, they were being told to take cover or get down, but they were running around like chooks ...[1]

And 'running around like chooks' had ramifications for others. The Japanese artillery, using a 'spotter' plane which could clearly see the Jats, was able to bring down accurate fire onto the exposed Indians—and the dug-in Australians. Lance-Corporal John Roxburgh, HQ Company, 2/29th Battalion:

> If the approaching scream continued on over our heads we knew we were safe but when it stopped in front of us we copped it. Limbs of

trees began crashing down on top of us, men with huge chunks of flesh ripped away from their bodies began moving back to the RAP while those unable to walk were carried back by their comrades. The Indians in front of us instead of lying flat on the ground panicked and began rushing madly through our position. The result was absolute carnage, those that lived were frightfully torn by shrapnel and those that died were blown to bits.[2]

When the artillery barrage lifted, the Japanese mounted attacks under mortar fire across the forward C and B Company fronts. B Company repulsed theirs and inflicted telling casualties, and although one C Company platoon was forced back about 40 metres, a counterattack eventually saw the Japanese driven back some 500 metres.[3]

While the 2/29th was thus occupied, pressure had mounted upon Captain Keegan's 2/19th B Company perimeter. At about 3.00 pm, a Japanese force estimated to be at three-company strength, and supported by heavy machine gun fire, placed severe pressure upon Keegan's front. As the afternoon progressed, the 2/19th deployed four of its carriers and its 3-inch mortars, while the 65th Battery personnel joined the fray with additional mortars borrowed from the Indians. The Battalion Unit History would later record that with B Company's platoon commanders directing and controlling the mortar fire from forward positions, coupled with the infantry and carrier firepower, the Japanese had sustained at least 300 casualties.[4]

Late that afternoon, Major Olliff received orders from Lieutenant-Colonel Anderson that his 2/29th was 'to cut its way back to 2/19th travelling east side of the road'.[5] The order of withdrawal was A Company, Battalion HQ, HQ Company, C Company and B Company. Last were a number of trucks in which about 40 or 50 wounded had been placed. The anti-tank guns and a small rifle detachment formed a rearguard. The companies were to move out at ten-minute intervals and an artillery barrage was timed to assist their withdrawal.

By this time the Japanese had a number of machine gun positions behind the 2/29th—a notable one being in a small brick dwelling positioned just off the road—and when A Company began its withdrawal it was brought under raking fire from both sides of it. Small numbers of its soldiers were ordered to silence these posts, but it was a forlorn hope, and all perished. In preparing for his withdrawal, Olliff now made a critical error in judgement in that he decided not to employ his mortars and anti-tank guns against the enemy positions.

A Company was cut to shreds first in attempting to attack and clear the Japanese positions, and subsequently, in trying to cross an open patch of ground near their original perimeter between the road and jungle. Hours later at Bakri it would number a mere 45 to 50 soldiers—no officers and at half of its original strength.

It will be remembered that the men of HQ Company were deployed on the western side of the road. They were next out and were to face that same open patch of ground twice. Major Olliff, who had taken over command after Robertson's death, was amongst the first hit. Bob Christie, Signals, 2/29th Battalion: 'and suddenly he [Olliff] said, "They got me, they got me in the hand!" He turned around and they shot him down the belly. I'd say it was a machine gun bullet . . . very close to where we were.'[6] Lance-Corporal John Roxburgh, HQ Company:

> The . . . side of the road was continually raked with machine gun fire so in single file with bayonets fixed we began this mad dash for freedom. The whole road was littered with dead and dying Indians, several hundred more who had endeavoured to reach us by coming up the road had obviously been ambushed and wiped out by the Japs . . .
>
> The track we moved along ran parallel to the road and some five feet below this level the road forming a natural protection for us from enemy concentrations on the right. To our left was jungle and swamp so our only outlet was this all too narrow path we moved along.
>
> At last there came a halt for in front of us lay an open stretch of some twenty yards which had to be crossed at top speed.
>
> Several men already lay dead in that open space and it was a gamble between life and death when your turn came to make the dash. Our sig officer who was in front of us [Lieutenant Arthur Sheldon] went down but the rest of us made the grade . . .
>
> So our retreat continued only to be halted a few moments later.

Word was sent back from A Company that the Japs had consolidated in front . . .

Orders came back to turn in our tracks and go back along that never to be forgotten path.[7]

But worse was to follow. Corporal Bob Christie: 'When Jock Olliff got shot and Sheldon got shot, and other blokes got shot, we then went straight into the rubber on the left . . . and we ran into our own artillery fire . . . it was a tremendous amount, a lot of our blokes got killed . . .'[8] In their desperate flight, they missed a small track which some of the Jats had used for a passage through to the 2/19th earlier in the day. Both B and C Companies found that narrow exit and returned to the 2/19th lines that night.

When the 2/29th were ordered to pull out of their perimeter, their medical officer, Captain Victor Brand, had decided that if the rearward Japanese roadblocks could not be broken, he should stay behind with the trucks holding his wounded. When that attempt failed Brand was ordered out. Captain Brand:

I was going to stay. It was [Lieutenant] Neil Gahan who said, 'Come on you've got to go!' I said, 'I can't leave the wounded.' He said, 'Don't be silly. You've got to come!' I was going to say to the Japs, 'These men are under the control of the Red Cross.' I wouldn't have been able to get a word out.[9]

And the Battalion doctor wasn't the only one who sensed the fate of anyone who fell into Japanese hands. The wounded must have felt totally helpless. Sergeant Bert Mettam, HQ Company:

The trucks were lined along the road, and as I walked out, I remember I was walking down the side of the trucks and more or less on the road, and this chap called me, and I went over to him . . . and he said, 'Bert, please don't leave me here, don't leave me here!' And I said, 'Where are you wounded Allan?' He pointed down into his groin . . . And I said, 'Don't worry about it Allan, you'll be alright. The trucks'll be taking off shortly, as soon as the carriers clear the road.' And then I went on.[10]

Shortly after, as Captain Brand and his walking wounded made good
their escape with elements of B Company, they heard 'yelling and screaming coming from the direction of the trucks'.[11] The details of the massacre
of those 40 to 50 members of the 2/29th Battalion were never recorded—
despite there being an eyewitness—nor does any form of official documen-
tation exist.[12] At around 8.30 pm on 19 January 1942, about 190 men from
the 2/29th who had escaped from their forward Bakri perimeter arrived in
the 2/19th lines. A Company had around 45 to 50 all told; B Company about
100; C Company about 45; and there were seven officers.[13]

Meanwhile, Headquarter Company, having been driven into the swamp
and jungle by the artillery barrage, was to spend a miserable night. And in
that darkness and despair came one of the horrors of war: the mercy bullet.
Sergeant Bert Mettam:

> I heard it; I heard the whole thing. I know who the chap was who
> gave him the mercy bullet . . . it was his mate. Every time that poor
> old _____ made a moan . . . the Japs had a machine gun lined on
> us, and they were firing . . . and by that time I'd moved over onto a
> bank . . . they were firing tracers . . . and every time there was a noise—
> moaning or calling out, the machine gun would open up. One bloke
> got hit in the neck . . .[14]

Lance-Corporal John Roxburgh, 2/29th Battalion: '. . . I can still remember
someone saying, 'For God's sake kill me, shoot me!' And I heard a gun go off,
and the next thing there's this bloody silence. It was right in the middle of
this swamp at about two o'clock in the morning.'[15]

After three days of trekking through jungle and rubber in its attempt
to reach Yong Peng, the HQ Company Group found the enemy had beaten
them to it. What then transpired would create great antipathy between some
of the Battalion's officers and its other ranks, both at the time and after the
war. Sergeant Bert Mettam:

> I think it was about the third day. We started off, and after we'd
> been walking for perhaps an hour, two hours, a road appeared
> on our left. And coming down it were bloody Malays and Chinese

and Indians . . . rubber tappers. They were all fleeing down this
road . . . where we were heading for, this kampong, the Japs had been
in there that morning . . . and they [the tappers] were all fleeing.
They told the officers this, so they had a conference . . . they called
me up . . . they said to me, 'We've got to split up, split up into small
groups.' . . . I didn't like the sound of that. I thought, two hundred of
us, all armed, that we could go on. Anyhow, they were the instructions,
so I asked them for a compass—didn't have any to spare! And I asked
them for a map—same answer, didn't have any to spare. They said, 'All
we can tell you is that Singapore is in a general southeasterly direction.' Then they started to tell me how to tell north by your watch. The
officers all went together they didn't split . . . some [of the officers]
said they were heading north; they were going to hide away until the
Jap forces had gone through, and then they were going to make their
way back to Singapore. And I thought, 'Well, that's a silly bloody idea,
you're in front of the Japs now, you might as well keep going and stay
in front!'[16]

Corporal Bob Christie:

That's something I don't want to talk about. I can still see them, the
officers . . . Gibson, Morgan, McGlinn . . . discussing it . . . and saying,
'Now we'll split up into groups of six.' . . . Sumner [Captain] was with
us at the start. We had no compass, we had no map. All we went by
was the sun.[17]

Corporal Jim Kennedy, 2/29th Battalion, had joined the Battalion with
his Albury mate, John Roxburgh:

And they split us up into small parties and they took the compasses!
Bob Christie was with us; Jackie Cowell, Strahan White, and Alec Ross
and us [Roxburgh and Kennedy] . . . no compass; no map; no food;
limited ammunition . . . they [the Japs] didn't know we were there,
and we didn't want them to know we were there, we weren't heroes
who were going to take on the Jap army, so what we wanted to do

was to get back to Singapore to reform the Battalion . . . the Malayans were on the side of the Japs because they were getting paid . . . and at one stage, one was leading us into a Jap camp, and we had to do away with him . . . bayoneted him. Green pineapple is not recommended for your gums and teeth, I can tell you that now, but it helps if you're hungry . . . that's why now, I won't go camping anymore—I'm a great believer in motels. The point is, we were just lucky, we finally got to a Pommy camp . . . and they fed us . . .[18]

The fate of those numerous groups varied enormously. Some have quite simply never been seen or heard of since. It is highly likely that many were executed on the spot by their Japanese captors. Others, including a number of the officers, were captured and sent to Pudu Prison in Kuala Lumpur. As stated, Mettam's party, which included Roxburgh, Kennedy and Christie, regained their Battalion in Singapore. Another group reached Sumatra and were captured; another fought behind the Japanese lines with the Chinese communists; and one group made their escape to Australia—where they faced the accusation of desertion, although charges were not laid.[19]

While Headquarter Company of the 2/29th was enduring the misery of its swamp experience, there had been a lull in the fighting at the 2/19th Battalion area. But that lull was broken by a further demonstration of the poor training and discipline of the Indians. At about 7.40 pm a small number of them began to fire wildly—at nothing—and in the resulting panic and confusion, yet more men were wounded. Private Gus Halloran, 2/19th Battalion:

Well, apart from being completely disorganised, they moved like a patch of damp fog. There were blokes trying to keep them under control . . . they'd put them into a position, and as soon as something moved at night—we used to observe strict silence at night complete absence of gun fire or reaction—these blokes would blaze away . . .[20]

Lieutenant-Colonel Charles Anderson and his officers spent much of the night of 19/20 January preparing the structure of the 'new' force and its objectives for the withdrawal to Parit Sulong. Five companies were formed: the almost intact 2/29th Battalion's B Company (about 100 men) was left under the command of its Captain Maher; the A and C Company 2/29th remnant was allotted to Captain Westbrook's original 2/19th Battalion's 1 Platoon of D Company (the other two had been left out of battle), making a complete company; and the 2/19th Battalion's A, B and C Companies retained their establishment and commanders. The remaining Indians were designated as two groups: one consisted of two companies of Jats (Major White), and the second was a composite group of Garhwalis and Rajputs (Captain Wood).

The order of march of his force clearly demonstrates Anderson's ability— as Lieutenant Jim Howard has termed it—as 'a master of quick decision exercise'. He deployed Captain Keegan's B Company 2/19th as his advance guard; Keegan was followed by three carriers under Lieutenant Howard and two British anti-tank guns; next came Battalion HQ; this was followed by a troop of the 65th Battery, the mortars and a section of carriers (Lieutenant Pickup), and various other HQ platoons; then came the trucks carrying the wounded, Anderson's most vulnerable and cumbersome component; then the Jats, who formed a flank protection for the trucks; and, to complete the main portion of the column, Anderson deployed his last section of carriers and placed Captain Snelling's C Company 2/19th as a reserve with a counter-attack role. In order to guard his left and right flanks in as much depth as possible, Anderson placed his A Company (Captain Beverley) and his composite 2/29th–2/19th D Company (Captain Westbrook) on either side of the road, and roughly in line with the main column of trucks. The 2/19th adjutant, Captain Hughes, was given command of the rearguard, which consisted of Captain Maher's B Company 2/29th Battalion, the Jats, one section of the 65th Battery, the last section of carriers and two 4th Anti-Tank Regiment guns.[21]

Lieutenant-Colonel Anderson set the eight kilometres of road to the 95-mile peg as his first objective for 20 January. He wanted to get there before nightfall. It was imperative that that objective be gained, since the ground from Bakri to it consisted of some cover. But from that peg onwards, the ground around the road was composed of swamp and rice paddies, which would leave his force open to daylight air bombardment. Therefore, should he fail to move forward of the 95-mile peg during darkness, his column could be comprehensively mauled.

Anderson and his officers worked through the night before issuing their orders just before dawn. All trucks were assessed for use, the wounded were loaded into those selected vehicles, ammunition was distributed, all non-essential material was discarded, and the padre and Pioneers dug graves for a dawn burial service. At around 7.00 am on 20 January, Anderson's column left Bakri.

At 8.00 am Captain Keegan's B Company advance guard struck a road-block not far out of Bakri, and about 800 metres in front of Captain Newton's old A and B Echelon harbour. The Japanese selection of their block was astute, as it was sited on a rise south of the road; its approach was bordered by swamp which ran right up to the road on the enemy right flank; it possessed a further swamp area to the Japanese left flank which also covered access to its rubber approach; and, to its rear, lay a belt of further swamp north of the road.[22] Keegan attacked almost immediately. Employing their now standard drill, the carriers and machine guns provided strong supporting fire, but the B Company attack faltered at about 40 metres from the enemy. Anderson reacted swiftly by ordering Captain Beverley's A Company into the fray to attack the Japanese left, or southern flank. In an extraordinary addition to his orders to Beverley, Anderson told him to tell his men to sing. A Company responded with 'Waltzing Matilda' as they went into battle. In their book, *Did Singapore Have to Fall?*, Karl Hack and Kevin Blackburn claim that Lionel Wigmore had 'waxed lyrical' when making the claim.[23] Wigmore had not 'waxed lyrical'. Private Gus Halloran, 2/19th Battalion: 'We were on the left of the road . . . the road blocks were put in up the road. I heard the song and dance, the Waltzing Matilda . . . as they went in, and they did a remark-able job! . . . the hair used to stand up when I heard Waltzing Matilda for a long time after!'[24] Obviously Anderson wanted to raise the spirits of the participants, as they became engaged in an attack from which all knew there would be significant casualties. Newton in *The Grim Glory* referred to it as an attempt to 'relieve the tension'.[25]

And Lieutenant-Colonel Charles Anderson played no small part in this victory. When Keegan's B Company went in the second time, Anderson personally destroyed two enemy machine gun posts with grenades and shot two Japanese occupants with his pistol. Further, he was constantly among his troops, and his unshakable demeanour inspired them. Private Jim Stewart, Signals, 2/19th Battalion: 'I can remember Anderson walking around saying, "Now keep down chaps, keep down, don't put your heads up too high." But he's walking! Absolutely, completely unperturbed!'[26]

As the embattled convoy then moved on, with Captain Beverley's A Company now the advance guard, Anderson faced two critical problems. The first was the need to enable his line to gain some momentum, as it was still too contracted, and therefore most susceptible to artillery and air bombardment—particularly the trucks carrying the wounded and the convoy's supplies. The second was that the trucks were rapidly filling with further casualties. The first roadblock had cost B Company one of its three platoon commanders killed, one badly wounded, and fourteen other ranks dead and nineteen wounded. As the column moved through the former 2/19th A and B Echelon harbour, they witnessed evidence of a savage and costly fight. Amidst the burnt-out trucks and bodies of both Australians and Japanese lay priceless rations and ammunition which were gratefully retrieved by the column. The whereabouts of Newton and any other survivors could only be guessed.

At 12.30 pm on 20 January, Anderson's column came to a second major roadblock, which consisted of a number of abandoned A and B Echelon trucks and stacked tree trunks. It was manned by numerous dug-in infantry and about six machine gun posts. The enemy had again chosen his site well, as its approaches from either side of the road were covered by tree-ridden swamp. To compound this problem at the front of the column, the Japanese now increased their pressure on its rear—four of the rearward column trucks were lost and the Jats 'had become difficult to control'.[27] As the column rearguard lost ground, Brigadier Duncan personally led a counterattack of a mixed group of Australians and Jats and, although it cost him his life, restored the situation.

Lieutenant-Colonel Anderson once again reacted quickly to the front roadblock. In an effort to strengthen Beverley's A Company advance guard attack, he sent in Westbrook's composite 2/29th–2/19th D Company, on Beverley's left flank, or left-hand side of the road. Private Gus Halloran's experience as a part of its 2/19th Platoon during that attack clearly demonstrates that not all ventures by the soldiers of the column were clear-cut victories, and that on occasions, confusion reigned:

> We were on the left of the Battalion . . . We put in an attack on a hill . . . a platoon strength attack. We wouldn't really know what we were going up against, because there were Japanese there and they were in trees and in a variety of places . . . it was an abortive attack, anyhow. We got done. We did a bayonet charge . . . we didn't know what we were charging at really . . . and they were shooting at us in large quantities. And they were hitting some, and they hit me in the elbow. It didn't do me any harm, it just went through and through . . . it wasn't impeding me at all really, I could still run, I had my legs.[28]

Westbrook's second platoon was from the 2/29th and was led by Lieutenant Cootes. Its task was to test the enemy's strength by a wide movement around this left flank. Gunner Jim Kerr, who had been a member of Sergeant Ken Harrison's reserve 4th Anti-Tank Regiment gun crew at Bakri, had been posted to Cootes's platoon for the withdrawal:

> . . . and the Japs were entrenched on this slight hill . . . so we had to go through the jungle—I mean jungle—around the back of this hill . . . the Japs saw us and started firing, because they were on top of this hill . . . a couple got to the top I think but not too many . . . when we broke off the action there was only nineteen of us . . . when we were finished, we didn't get back to the main body again . . . and then we wandered around these nineteen of us . . .[29]

Kerr's subsequent experience clearly demonstrates the influence of sheer luck when soldiers were cut off. Wigmore cites Cootes's fate as being 'Killed in action 12 March 1942 (after capture)'.[30] The truth is that the Japanese executed Cootes and a companion swiftly after their capture because they were covered in sores and were in very poor physical condition.[31] Wigmore states that the survivors eventually reached Yong Peng. Some did, but a number of these men (including Kerr), after having separated into small groups, were captured and placed in Pudu Prison in Kuala Lumpur. (It is extraordinary to contemplate that Jim Kerr had joined the army at fifteen years of age, had had his seventeenth birthday while engaged in avoiding the Japanese in the jungle, would later slave on the Thai–Burma Railway, and, was destined to celebrate his 21st birthday back in Australia in 1946.) Westbrook's third platoon was also a 2/29th component, and was led by Lieutenant Carr. It too attacked along this left flank, with little success, and Carr was killed in the process.

Lieutenant-Colonel Anderson now deployed his reserve C Company 2/19th (Captain Snelling) through Beverley's company on the right flank. Yet again Anderson stamped himself on events by personally addressing Snelling's soldiers. It must have been quite a speech. The 2/19th Unit Diary recorded the men's response:

> ... every man was fighting mad. Mortar shells were directed on to targets by Infantry men just a few yards from the target (voice relayed back) gunners were fighting with rifles, bayonets and axes (range too short for 25 pdrs. except to Jap rear areas west). A gun crew pushed its 25 pdr. round a cutting and blew out the first road blocks (vehicles) at 75 yds range. Carriers pushed within 5 yds of Jap M.G.'s and blew them out. Two carriers [attacked a] concrete house ... House contained 3 Jap M.G.'s and about 60 men. Men went forward under heavy M.G. fire and chopped road blocks to pieces with axes. About 1830 hrs the Japs had had enough and cleared out ...[32]

Lieutenant Jim Howard, 2/19th Carrier Platoon:

> People got carried away ... they were going to get through—win, lose or draw ... I can remember the 25 pounder over open sites straight across the road with a high explosive shell. It lifted bloody bodies and trucks up and put them down again ... that was the afternoon I got hit.[33]

Although Captain Snelling was badly wounded with a shattered thigh, and Westbrook's attack was both fruitless and costly on the left flank, the C Company success demonstrates the Australians' excellent use of their carrier and artillery support, and their recurring ability to mount very successful close quarter bayonet charges. Yet again, Lieutenant-Colonel Anderson demonstrated his tactical excellence and inspirational leadership. After two savage roadblock confrontations in daylight, the column now successfully moved over the open ground it had sought to cross during darkness, and all within its ranks might have been excused for thinking that their objective lay near. But at midnight on 20 January, an Indian soldier informed the column that the bridge at Parit Sulong lay in Japanese hands. Anderson immediately sent two despatch riders, who confirmed the news.

At around 2.30 am on the morning of 21 January 1942, Anderson moved his exhausted column out of the last section of open country, to occupy about one-and-a-half kilometres of rubber-covered road. Two hours later he sent a recce patrol under Sergeant Lloyd Davies, C Company 2/19th Battalion, towards the Parit Sulong bridge. Davies returned at about 7.30 am to report that it was in enemy hands. The column, now about five kilometres out from the bridge, came under an early morning Japanese attack upon both its front and rear. A Japanese attack of company strength at the front was beaten back when Anderson sent his B Company (Captain Keegan) around his left flank to swing in behind the enemy. Anderson then sent his carriers down the right side of the road. The Japanese were between Keegan's soldiers on the left and the carriers on the right, and were subjected to telling fire and took heavy casualties and withdrew. At the rear of the column, the 65th Battery artillery brought down accurate fire upon an enemy tank attempt to pierce their lines. Anderson's column moved on, and at around mid-morning its A and B Companies 2/19th Battalion reached the outskirts of Parit Sulong. It was here, so close to their goal, that the advance guard found the Japanese had set up numerous machine gun nests in depth around the bridge and village. But when wireless communications were briefly re-established, Anderson learnt that General Bennett had a relief force on its way. When artillery fire was heard in the distance, the men's spirits rose. Courage feeds on hope.

Anderson's column faced three enormous problems as 21 January 1942 wore on. The first was the extreme pressure again placed upon both its front and rear. As his manpower resources were now stretched to breaking point, he was forced to employ soldiers from his transport, artillery, and even those wounded who could make a contribution, to protect the main body of the column. The infantry companies were concentrated at the back and front. His second difficulty was the wretched condition of his wounded. During the late afternoon the enemy intensified his air bombing of the convoy, which resulted in a further loss of vehicles and often the death of some of the wounded. His third dilemma was the inevitable dwindling of his resources: small arms ammunition, mortar and artillery shells, and importantly, medical supplies.

Two thrusts were made towards Parit Sulong and the river late that morning and early afternoon. At around 11.00 am, Indian troops attacked from the west and actually gained the bank of the river, while later Captain Beverley's A Company and Captain Keegan's B Company were also able— with the decisive support yet again of the 2/19th Carriers—to reach the river bank. But when Beverley's Company reconnoitered the bridge with a view to an attack upon it, they soon discovered that the enemy strength there precluded their chances of success. Anderson would have been still clinging to the hope of a breakthrough from the other side of the Parit Sulong bridge.

As further casualties were taken throughout that afternoon, the two doctors suggested that the Japanese be approached to allow a number of trucks over the bridge carrying the most seriously wounded. Captain Victor Brand, Medical Officer, 2/29th Battalion: 'It was my idea. I went to Anderson and he said, "Well, you discuss it with Lloyd Cahill [Regimental Medical Officer, 2/19th]." Which he did . . . Anderson agreed . . . so we spent a lot of time getting wounded into trucks. And then Anderson changed his mind. He said, "No, only one or two [ambulances] with the worst wounded." '[34]

During the late afternoon and into the night the Japanese exerted further tank pressure upon the rear of the column. A little after 8.00 pm Lieutenant Ross (65th Battery) and Sergeant Tate realised that the enemy tanks had made an entry into the perimeter. This assault was first met by grenades—lobbed into the leading tank's turret when an enemy soldier opened it—which caused the tank to grind to a halt. The anti-tank gun then scored a direct hit on that vehicle and set it ablaze, causing a roadblock. By a combination of that gun, anti-tank rifles and grenades, the Japanese were held back. In a rare piece of good fortune, the 8th Division wireless truck managed to send General Bennett a message asking for ammunition, food and morphia. Because the cipher books had been long destroyed, Colonel Jim Thyer (Bennett's GSO1) replied with a message that only an Australian might have understood: 'Look up at sparrow fart.'

The intervening hours of darkness before dawn on 22 January 1942 were a misery for the exhausted soldiers and the wounded. Private Jim Stewart, 2/19th Battalion:

> The shelling on the last night was just unbelievable ... I was so completely exhausted, I was actually asleep during the bombardment, in the drain [running alongside the road] that was my cover. And it blew me out [of the drain], and woke me up. And I saw all these flashes going on and I thought I better get back in. Yeah, it was a very heavy night ... you can imagine being in those trucks on the open road ... there was just a line of trucks and the shells were coming everywhere.[35]

The wounded suffered horribly, caused in part by their original wounds, often compounded by additional injury sustained in their exposed trucks, and then cruelly exacerbated by the paucity of morphia. The fate of Captain Maher, B Company 2/29th Battalion, was a case in point. Wounded by shrapnel during the night, he was later killed when the car in which he was placed received a direct hit—there was absolutely no respite for anyone, anywhere in that embattled column. At around 10.00 pm Anderson received word from one of the ambulance drivers that the Japanese commander at the bridge had refused to either let the ambulances through, or treat the wounded within them, but had ordered their deployment on the bridge as a roadblock. His ultimatum was clear: Anderson was to surrender; his wounded would then be looked after; but, should he not comply, the two ambulances on the bridge were to remain as a roadblock and fired on if they tried to move. Anderson knew that those in the bridge ambulances had not long to live and that there was still a slender chance of a relief column breaking through to him. In those circumstances surrender was out of the question. Later, as a result of an extraordinary lack of Japanese security on the bridge, Lieutenant Austin, who had been wounded in the neck and shoulder, and another wounded driver managed to release the brakes of the two ambulances and 'rolled them down the slope of the bridge'. Then amidst the din and confusion of battle, they proceeded to start the engines and drive back to Anderson's lines.

At dawn on 22 January 1942, two Albacores escorted by three Buffalo fighters flew over the beleaguered column and dropped a number of canisters: three contained food and another quantities of priceless shell dressings and morphia. Those obsolete but welcomed aircraft banked and flew in for a second passing, this time to bomb the Japanese positions, and, unfortunately, also the Australian. Gunner Russell Braddon reported that: 'Three rubber trees lay up-rooted: a huge crater gaped like a burst boil; and, of the group of men who had stood there, all that could be discovered was one boot, one shoulder blade and one tin hat . . .'[36] And as if enemy tanks, artillery, mortars, infantry, and air strafing and bombardment were not enough, daylight brought enemy sniping. Lieutenant Jim Howard, Carrier Platoon, 2/19th Battalion had already been wounded:

It got full light, and I'm starting to move around a bit . . . and that's when . . . this bastard up a tree saw me and took a couple of shots at me, while I was lying in the truck [the bullets creased Howard's neck] . . . they frightened the shit out of me but didn't hurt me . . . so I called out to a stretcher bearer and he dropped the tail board of the truck, and I moved as quickly as I could, and dropped on the lee side of the truck . . . there was a dead Indian . . . so I grabbed his rifle and got over to the drain, it was a big drain . . . and I got down the lee of the drain, and watched the trees on the other side of the road. And I got two of these bastards that were up there, sniping. They were firing at other targets. I saw one body drop out of a tree, and I suspect that the other bloke was caught, because his weapon dropped out of a tree.

And that's where Anderson found me and said, 'Jim, can you walk?' And I said, 'With assistance yes.'[37]

Anderson's enquiry as to Howard's ability to walk was pertinent. Between dawn and 9.00 am Anderson came to the painful realisation that the game was up. With ammunition stocks rapidly dwindling, casualties mounting at an alarming rate and with an enemy tank breakthrough a real possibility, he knew the column faced extermination. And, cruelly, the distant sounds of support from his rear had not become louder. Help was not on its way. The 2/19th Unit Diary would later record Lieutenant-Colonel Charles Anderson's last order:

> ... decided to leave M.T. [motor transport] Guns, and wounded and withdrew [*sic*] North, then East to Yong Peng. Orders were given for the force to withdraw to the North (Bearing 340 degrees), then East 'B' Coy, then 'C' Coy, then 'A' Coy, then 2/29th Bn., then 'D' Coy (who covered the withdrawal) at five minute intervals.[38]

As often happens during withdrawals under intense pressure—and with poor communications—not everyone received the order out. The experience of Private Charles Edwards, 2/19th Battalion, is an example:

> He [Major Vincent] called up his Sergeant-Major to make a reconnaissance of the perimeter and report back to him. His name was Sonny Loy . . . he was so shot up around the jaw, . . . he had his head bandaged . . . He made his reconnaissance and he came back and said, 'There's a gap over on the west side of the road . . . about a hundred yards . . . with not a single man in it.' So he [Vincent] said, 'Get ten men and fill the gap.' And Sonny said, 'Where am I going to get ten men?' And Vincent said, 'Take Edwards!' . . . And his batman was there, and his batman's name was Lenny Harrison. Len's nickname was 'Crow' and if you didn't call him 'Crow' he wouldn't answer you. So he said, 'Take Crow . . .'
>
> He found eight others who I didn't know. The ten of us trooped off, positioned ourselves along this hundred yards . . . we were on the western side of the road. Crow was on the river, then me, I suppose about three or four metres apart, then the rest of them . . . we spent the night, slept fitfully, next morning we woke up and Crow . . . said, 'Edwards, can you swim? Would you swap places with me, I can't swim, and if things get tough here . . . I'd drown.' So we swapped places. Now within 30 seconds of that change, a Jap tank broke through the jungle about a hundred yards away, and machine gunned down that line.

When I looked round at Crow, what was left of him you could have put in a plastic bucket . . . from then on I thought I had a guardian angel. I waited four or five minutes, nothing further happened, so I walked back up . . . there had been about 30 of us over that side of the road, and there were eleven of us left. We sent a man over to the east side . . . to see what was going on there and he came back and said, 'There's not a single man left'. They had gone up river and forded the river . . . I don't know whether they either forgot about us, or sent a man over to get us and he didn't get there . . . well, we had two badly wounded men with us . . . I met Clarrie Thornton there [of 4th Anti-Tank Regiment fame] . . .[39]

Edwards did not make good his escape. He and Thornton were destined to be later captured and placed in Pudu Prison.

When the remnants of Anderson's column reached the Base Depot at Johore Bahru the true cost of their gallant fight became apparent. Lionel Wigmore:

The 45th Brigade now had no commander or headquarters, no battalion commanders or officers second-in-command, and only one of its adjutants. Only two or three of its remaining British officers had had more than a few months' experience. Anderson had 271 left in his battalion, including fifty-two wounded who made their way back. Of the 2/29th Battalion, which had first taken the weight of the main Japanese advance near Bakri, only 130 mustered at Yong Peng. Its commander and most of its officers had been killed or were missing. The 65th Battery numbered 98 at this stage, including 24 wounded who had made their way from Parit Sulong.[40]

The Japanese had a dreadful reputation for extreme brutality towards a defeated foe. There were massacres of not only enemy troops but of women and children (around 3000 of them) in Port Arthur in 1904; there was the Rape of Nanking in 1937; and there were many examples of the Japanese demonstrating vindictiveness towards any unit or formations that had caused them high casualties. In other words, fight well against them, inflict heavy casualties upon them, and their unrestrained fury and inhumanity knew no bounds. The fate of the wounded left behind in the trucks at the rear of the 2/29th perimeter forward of Bakri is testament to that characteristic. Now, on 22 January 1942, the wounded at Parit Sulong were about to suffer the penalty for Anderson column's heroic fight.

Perhaps many of the wounded who were to be left behind, as well as a number of the impending 'leaving', must have had more than an inkling of what might lay ahead. Lieutenant Jim Howard, 2/19th Battalion:

> Snelling was a bloke I knew ... he administered C Company ... Snelling was in the wounded on the road [to Parit Sulong], I knew his wife, I knew his two kids. We went back a fair way, to the Scottish Regiment ... I was conscience stricken, I said, 'I can't leave you here like this.' And he said, 'You piss off, and do as you're told!' You've been told what to do, now do it!' And so I did.[41]

The wounded comprised 110 Australians and 35 Indians. A large number of the critically sick and immobilised wounded were in the trucks; a small number—probably anticipating their fate—were engaged in attempting to crawl away from the truck column; others more recently wounded were seeking to drag themselves off the exposed road and gain the shelter of the vehicles; and, others still, such as the 2/29th's Lieutenants Hackney and Tibbitts, lay underneath a truck firing in the general direction of the enemy, hoping to delay them and allow extra time for their comrades to escape. Captain Ray Snelling, his thigh shattered, lay against a truck wheel.[42]

Having also suffered heavy casualties, the Japanese must have been eager to claim victory. Perhaps a small number of them saw Captain Snelling waving a crude white flag, which caused them and others to grow in confidence. Lynette Ramsay Silver, in her *The Bridge at Parit Sulong*:

> The Japanese were soldiers of 2 Battalion, 5 Infantry Regiment, Imperial Guards Division ... under the command of Lieutenant-Colonel Kojima Yoshinori. With a great deal of unintelligible yelling, vigorous arm waving and forceful, painful persuasion, they made

it clear that all those still in the trucks, as well as those lying on the ground, were to assemble in front of a single-storey building, set on metre-high concrete stumps on the western side of the road.[43]

Many of the wounded, incapable of movement or requiring the assistance of others, struggled pitifully to fulfil the command and were beaten severely—on their wounds by preference. And in some cases, when their captors' patience ran out, death by the bayonet followed quickly.

The prisoners were then made to strip to just their socks and boots, and pile their clothes and belongings in a heap. As more substantial numbers of Japanese troops moved through the area, Lynette Ramsay Silver has recorded that the sight of '100 nude bodies, unshaven and filthy, their unattended wounds dirty and clotted with blood or, in many cases, freely bleeding from the effects of recent blows and kicks[44] was too good an opportunity to miss. The passing 'visitors' set to work on anyone within reach—repeated blows, bayoneting, rifle butt strikes and, as had occurred from the start, a demented preference for targeting existing wounds and thereby maximising the prisoners' pain and misery. While these events were in train, an English-speaking Caucasian officer dressed in British uniform examined the clothing, then systematically collected valuables, money and pay books, after which the Australians and Indians were ordered to dress. The prisoners were then herded into a nearby shed where, crammed beyond the capacity of that dwelling, the worst wounded suffered dreadfully, crying out for water, a smoke, some form of medical attention. When a Japanese officer appeared and instructed troops to provide water and cigarettes, some of the wounded must have thought that a reprieve was near. After photos were taken of this 'humanitarian' act, the water and smokes which had been tantalisingly close were withdrawn.

At sunset on 22 January 1942, the prisoners were tied together with rope or wire and some bayoneted, some shot and still others remained alive. Petrol from the Australian transport was used to douse the corpses—and a small number still alive—and soon the sickly sweet smell of burning flesh was punctuated by a small number of screams. Despite the fact that a Japanese officer walked around the scene shooting anyone showing signs of life, the suffering must have been beyond description.

The 2/29th Battalion's Lieutenant Ben Hackney, who had been left for dead, miraculously survived after having his boots removed, and his body checked for signs of life by numerous prods with the bayonet. After roaming the jungle for 36 days he was captured, returned to Parit Sulong, and then sent to Pudu Prison in Kuala Lumpur. Hackney and a young soldier named Wharton were to be the only survivors of the massacre.

———◆———

The Battle of Muar is noteworthy for a number of reasons. General Percival would later write that it:

> ... was one of the epics of the Malayan campaign. Our little force by dogged resistance had held up a division of the Japanese Imperial Guards attacking with all the advantages of air and tank support for nearly a week, and in doing so had saved the Segamat force from encirclement and probable annihilation.[45]

The sad truth is that serious mistakes were made at the top levels of command. Percival's deployment of the 45th Indian Brigade at Muar was, yet again, another instance of him allotting tasks to formations that were simply beyond them. Whilst it should be acknowledged that Malaya Command's intelligence was abysmal throughout the campaign, there can be no excuse for him refusing to follow General Wavell's order to concentrate the 22nd Brigade AIF under General Bennett's command. Percival's excuse, as so often given, was the administrative difficulties of such a move.

At the local command level, the performance of the 2/29th and 2/19th Battalions forward of Bakri and around the crossroads was first class. The 2/29th Battalion did not lose ground at any time during its fighting. The Battalion's patrolling forward of its perimeter, its fire and movement, counterattacks, the use of mortars, and its leadership were all impressive. But, in hindsight, the unit did pay a heavy price because of two decisions. The first was the failure to withdraw it sooner from its forward position. First Brigadier Duncan, and later Lieutenant-Colonel Anderson, succumbed to the understandable desire to retrieve the Indians. But with the 2/19th Battalion already roadblocked to its rear, and the potential of the Japanese to block the passage between the two battalions, a speedier withdrawal by the 2/29th back to Bakri might have been desirable. The Indians would have had to trek only another two-and-half kilometres. The second mistake was Major Olliff's failure to employ his mortars and anti-tank guns to assist in a roadblock breakthrough. The consequent cutting off of a significant part of the 2/29th was the penalty.

The 2/19th Battalion performed brilliantly at Bakri and during the withdrawal. Its early training in Australia and Malaya under Lieutenant-Colonel (later Brigadier) Maxwell had given it a solid basis for its prolonged training in Malaya. Its junior officers were well trained and led with great tactical competence and command skills; the Battalion's ability to coordinate the use of its carriers and mortars was also impressive; and its performance in counterattack—particularly during the withdrawal—was most notable.

A key component of the two infantry battalions' success during the Battle of Muar was the quality of their support. The 4th Anti-Tank Regiment's destruction of the enemy tanks near and at the cutting within the 2/29th Battalion's perimeter showed an ability to site and camouflage its guns well; its crews' fire discipline was superb, and its ability to slow and then destroy enemy tanks at the front and rear of their column was astute—especially under concentrated enemy fire. Throughout the Muar operation the 2/15th Field Regiment's 65th Battery also provided strong support providing barrages, or destroying roadblocks and tanks.

But underpinning the accomplishments of the battle at Bakri and the subsequent fighting withdrawal of the 45th Brigade remnant, the 2/29th and 2/19th Battalions, and the support units, was surely the expertise and inspirational leadership of Lieutenant-Colonel Charles Anderson. His ability to think quickly and decisively was critical; when events of high drama and import were constantly in train, Anderson's calm, measured and seemingly unrushed command style impressed all around him; and his personal bravery in eliminating two Japanese machine gun posts was a stirring example to his soldiers. The demonstration of competent, calm and inspiring leadership travels like wildfire throughout any army unit. For his exploits during the Battle of Muar Lieutenant-Colonel Anderson was awarded the Victoria Cross.

However, the failure of the feeble British attempt to recapture the bridge at Parit Sulong, which could have rescued the cut-off forces and prevented a massacre, caused a great resentment, and indeed bad blood, between the Australians and the British.

17

A GREAT SCANDAL

Events elsewhere in Johore, leading up to and during the Australians' defence of Bakri and their consequent withdrawal to Parit Sulong, deserve close scrutiny.

On 16 January 1942, General Percival had anticipated the impending Japanese threat to his line of communication at Muar and on the west coast. Accordingly, he had adjusted the boundary between Major-General Bennett's Westforce and General Heath's III Corps, so as to give Heath the added responsibility of securing those communications—to which were now added the Trunk Road from Ayer Hitam to Yong Peng and westward to Batu Pahat. To bolster Heath's resources for this additional III Corps task, Percival sent him the British 18th Division's 53rd Infantry Brigade (Brigadier Duke), which consisted of the 2nd Cambridgeshire, the 5th Norfolk and 6th Norfolk Battalions. The Brigade came under the operational command of the Indian 11th Division (General Key). We have noted that the 53rd Brigade had arrived at Singapore only four days earlier. On 17 January, the Brigade was given three roles. The first was to relieve the British Battalion at Batu Pahat, which was accomplished by the 2nd Cambridgeshire. The second was to protect Yong Peng, by an occupation of a defile near the 78-mile peg on the Yong Peng–Muar road, which was undertaken by the 6th Norfolk.

Kirby has recorded that: 'the inexperienced Norfolks occupied Bukit [Hill] Pelandok and Bukit Belah early on the 18th and sent two platoons forward, one to patrol the road to Parit Sulong and the other to guard the bridge there.'[1] The relief of Lieutenant-Colonel Charles Anderson's 2/19th Battalion at Jemaluang—to allow it to join the 2/29th Battalion at Bakri—was the 53rd Brigade's third task. This was undertaken by the 5th Norfolk Battalion.

Whilst these changes were occurring on the Trunk Road and west coast, on 14 January patrols of Brigadier Taylor's 22nd Brigade AIF had made contact with the Japanese north of Endau on the east coast. When the enemy bombed Mersing and Endau on 16 and 17 January, and therefore seemed to be preparing for an attack on that east coast, Brigadier Taylor withdrew his brigade—less his 2/19th Battalion—to Mersing. Kirby has recorded that during the morning of 18 January:

> ... Heath visited Mersing and told Taylor that as from 6 a.m. on the 19th a new force, named 'Eastforce', would be formed under his command and that his task had been changed to that of protecting the Jemaluang–Kota Tinggi road instead of holding Mersing. 'Eastforce' would consist of 22nd Australian Brigade (less one battalion), 5th Norfolk and all other troops in the area.[2]

Early on 19 January—while Lieutenant-Colonel Anderson's 2/19th Battalion was under attack at the Bakri crossroads—General Key reacted to two threats: one at Batu Pahat and the other at the critical defile at Bukit Pelandok. To hold the former, he deployed the 15th Brigade to occupy the town and the British Battalion as a reinforcement. Because he had already sent the 2nd Cambridgeshire to Batu Pahat and the 5th Norfolk to Jemaluang, Key found that he was now holding the critical Bukit Pelandok defile with only the 6th Norfolks. He now sent the 3/16th Punjab to reinforce it. At a conference on the afternoon of 19 January—attended by Generals Percival, Key, Bennett and Brigadier Duke—Percival decided to further reinforce the 53rd Brigade with the 2nd Loyals from the 9th Indian Division; and he ordered that Brigadier Duncan's embattled 45th Brigade (and the Australian 2/29th and 2/19th Battalions) should be withdrawn through the 53rd Brigade west of Yong Peng and Bennett's 'Westforce' to the Trunk Road town of Labis. This was typical of Percival's recurring habit of splitting brigades and often selecting the most inexperienced formations to undertake the most demanding tasks. While his best trained 22nd Brigade AIF was, as late as 19 January, engaged in spasmodic patrol contact with the enemy outside of Endau before a movement back to 'protect' the line Jemaluang–Kota Tinggi, Percival had—against Wavell's orders—left it there and then despatched its 2/19th Battalion to Bakri. He could have, and indeed should have, sent the 53rd Brigade to conduct this static task, thereby releasing the whole of General Bennett's two-brigade 8th Division for operations on the Trunk Road and the west coast. Months before, Bennett had been allotted the defence of Johore, and when that task had become a reality, the two best trained brigades in Malaya were split and either thrown into piecemeal tasks or left virtually idle—and all because of 'administrative' difficulties. An administrative difficulty is surely a much more palatable problem to deal with than the recurring slaughter of untrained troops. The 53rd Brigade had been, until literally five days previous, completing an eleven-week journey by sea to Singapore, and was therefore unfit and not acclimatised for immediate operations in Malaya.

During the afternoon of 19 January, a company of the 6th Norfolks occupying the Bukit Pelandok defile was attacked by elements of the Japanese 1/5th Battalion, and evicted from its position. After having crossed the road, the enemy occupied the slopes of Bukit Belah, which cut off access to the road to Bakri. Late that same day Brigadier Duke made plans to recapture the defile. He ordered Lieutenant-Colonel Moorhead's 3/16th Punjabis to reinforce a company of the 6th Norfolk, which was still in occupation of a location on the northern slopes of Bukit Belah, overlooking the Parit Sulong Road. He further ordered Moorhead to send a second company to a position about 450 metres further north. Once the two 3/16th Punjab companies were in position, Duke planned that the Norfolks, under covering fire from the Punjabis, were to attack and recapture Bukit Pelandok.

The operation was a disaster. Moorhead's first company set out at 4.00 am on 20 January to reinforce the Norfolks. In the darkness the approaching Punjabis were mistaken for Japanese and fired upon. Although this 'friendly' fire was soon halted, the well-concealed Japanese then proceeded to riddle the defenders with close-quarter fire which drove all and sundry off the feature. In the process, the brave Moorhead, who had voluntarily relinquished his brigade command to return to his 3/16th Punjab Battalion, was killed and his unit took heavy casualties. The Japanese remained in possession of the defile. Lionel Wigmore:

> So serious were the losses that despite the urgent need to clear the road to Bakri, Brigadier Duke decided that he would have to await the arrival of the Loyals before making a further endeavour. It later transpired that a Norfolk detachment which had relieved Lieutenant Varley's platoon at the Parit Sulong bridge, having been without rations since the 18th, and thinking that it had been cut off, had left its vital post during the morning of the 20th and set off across country to Batu Pahat.[3]

Lieutenant-Colonel Anderson's escape route via the bridge at Parit Sulong would soon lay in enemy hands.

There is much controversy surrounding the events that were to ensue. On the late morning of 20 January, General Key visited General Bennett's headquarters. It is critical to realise that at this juncture the 53rd Brigade was under the command of General Key. Colonel Thyer (Bennett's GSO1) has stated that Bennett 'requested'[4] that Key send his 53rd Brigade to capture the defile and push on to occupy the bridge at Parit Sulong (and thereby facilitate Anderson column's escape). Wigmore, using Thyer's account of the campaign and the 8th Division War Diary, has carefully stated that Key 'feared'[5] that 'the brigade [the 53rd], or a substantial part of it, might find itself cut off in attempting such an operation, thus adding to the already heavy losses and further endangering Yong Peng.'[6] But the 8th Division Diary states that: 'The commander 11 Div [Key] replied that although he would like to do this by so doing he would uncover the approaches to the main north road and Yong Peng, and the general safety of the force must take priority.'[7] There is a significant difference between a 'fear' or concern, and an outright refusal. Bennett was 'far from satisfied'[8] and referred the matter to Percival.

In his book *The War In Malaya*, Percival claimed that he reacted to Bennett's request 'early on the morning of the twenty-first'.[9] It was very early, as Thyer would later record that:

Gen Percival agreed and ordered 11 Div to place 53 Inf Bde at the disposal of Westforce forthwith. He instructed GOC Westforce to withdraw 27 Aust Inf Bde (less 2/29 Bn) straight back to Yong Peng cross roads instead of halting them South of Labis as was originally intended. This would ensure the protection of the withdrawal of 9 Ind Div and free 53rd Inf Bde from its role of protection of Yong Peng.[10]

The 8th Division Diary records that the order to move the 27th Brigade AIF to Yong Peng was received at 1.00 am.[11]

At 9.00 am on 21 January, General Key arrived at Westforce HQ and now told Bennett that if the 53rd Brigade was ordered to attack Bukit Payong 'he would personally assist in the issue of the orders'.[12] Bennett told him that he 'intended to employ the 53rd Brigade 'in the manner he had already suggested, and that the attack should be launched at 1400 hours'.[13] Key now sent his GSO2 (Major Parker) to inform Brigadier Duke that the Loyals were to stage the attack. On his way to Duke, Parker called in at the HQ of the Loyals and gave a warning order for the attack and made arrangements for transport. To save further time, he also instructed the Loyals to send forward a reconnaissance group at once.[14] The train of events that now ensued are extraordinary.

Parker and Thyer met the Loyals' CO, Lieutenant-Colonel Elrington, and the three officers then went forward at noon to join Brigadier Duke at the far end of the causeway. An amazed Thyer witnessed:

> ... the reconnaissance for the attack and the issue of the plan being made completely in the open, in full view of the defile only a thousand yards away. When it was suggested that this was an unsound and risky manner in which to conduct the preparations for an attack, GSO1 Westforce [Thyer] was informed by the Bde Comd [Duke] that he was convinced that there were no troops on the hill feature. It was then suggested that if this were the case, the forward Bn, the Punjabs, should be sent forward to occupy the hill immediately instead of waiting for a set-piece attack by the Loyals. Failing this, at least, fighting patrols should be sent forward to probe the position and locate enemy localities.[15]

An anxious Thyer then journeyed to Bennett's HQ to inform him of these events. He returned to Duke at around 4.30 pm with orders from Bennett that the attack was to go in immediately. Duke informed Thyer that the artillery was not yet in a position to give accurate fire support and that the Loyals had not been able to conduct a proper reconnaissance. The truth was that the Loyals had not even arrived.[16]

Despite the fact that the 53rd Brigade had had six hours' warning for the attack, and, according to Thyer, the Loyals only slightly less time, the operation was rescheduled for 5.00 pm. Further delays now occurred. Although the artillery registration had begun at 2.00 pm it was slow and its results were 'unsatisfactory', and when a company of the Loyals took over an hour to embus, it became apparent that the Battalion would not be concentrated in the area before 6.00 pm at the earliest. Duke now cancelled the attack until 6.00 am the next morning (22 January). Thyer would later write that: '53rd Inf Bde claim that the 11 Div [Key] had stated that arty support was a pre-requisite for any attack on this defile, and since the support available was limited, it was necessary that it should be accurate.'[17] Fair point. But despite the fact that the artillery had had nearly all of the afternoon in which to register its guns, Duke ordered that 'it would be necessary to fire testing rounds at dawn to ensure the accuracy of the supporting fire'.[18] It is therefore critical to record that at around 9.00 pm on the night of 21 January 1942, the Australians offered Duke additional artillery support, which was refused. Despite the abject failure of the support both in terms of time and accuracy, Duke believed that the existing battery 'could adequately fulfill the task'.[19] On the morning of 22 January, Duke yet again postponed the attack until 9.00 am because once again the artillery registration took too long. And when at daylight the Loyals were found by Japanese aircraft and bombed, Duke cancelled the attack altogether, and resumed his former defensive positions. The Loyals sustained six soldiers killed and another six wounded—hardly crushing casualties that might cause an attack to be cancelled. Anderson column's already slim chances of rescue were now dashed.

After the war, Percival made two insipid attempts to both explain away and avoid any form of accountability for 53rd Brigade's failure to even attempt to recapture the defile and occupy the bridge at Parit Sulong. In 1949 in *The War In Malaya*, he stated that: 'For various reasons, in no way due to

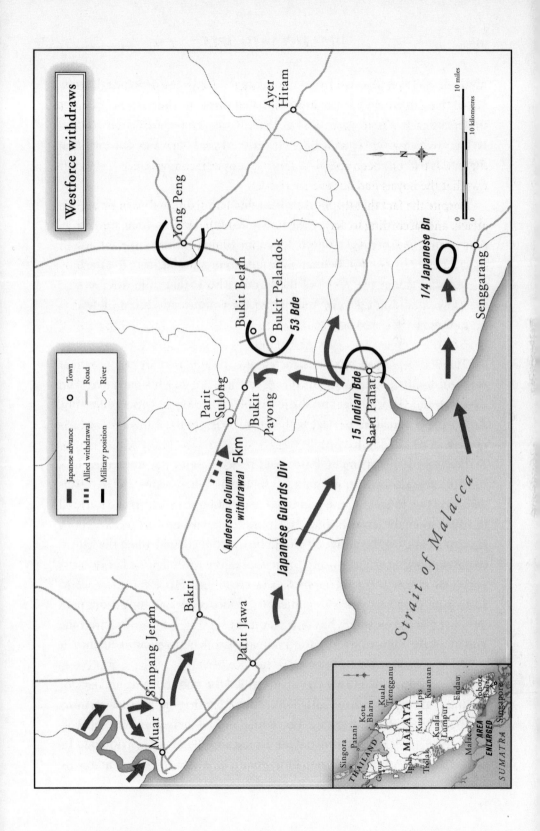

Westforce withdraws

Ayer Hitam

Yong Peng

10 miles

10 kilometres

N

Bukit Belah

Bukit Pelandok
53 Bde

Senggarang

1/4 Japanese Bn

Parit Sulong

Bukit Payong

5km

15 Indian Bde

Batu Pahat

(Anderson Column withdrawal)

Japanese Guards Div

Bakri

Simpang Jeram

Parit Jawa

Strait of Malacca

Muar

Town
○ Town
Road
River

Japanese advance
Allied withdrawal
Military position

SUMATRA

THAILAND

MALAYA

Singora
Patani
Kota Bharu
Kuala Trengganu
Kuala Lipis
Kuantan
Ipoh
Tapah
Kuala Lumpur
Endau
Mersing
Johore Bahru
Singapore
Guru
Malacca

AREA ENLARGED

any lack of effort, this attack never got going.'[20] And a few sentences later he stated that: 'It should be remembered that at this time the 53rd Brigade was under orders of Westforce.'[21] And in 1954 he made an equally poor attempt to lay the blame on General Bennett's shoulders. Lodge has recorded that Percival wrote:

> I have recently had an opportunity of discussing this with Col. Elring-ton. He was very upset by what I told him. He has documentary evidence to prove, as I suspected, that the timing of the counter-attack as ordered by Gordon Bennett was quite impracticable from the start. In fact, I gather that some of the Loyals, who at that time were very scattered, did not get any warning of the counter-attack until a few minutes before zero hour.[22]

The above passage was constructed as a response to an early draft of the British Official History, which caused Kirby to alter his narrative. And alter it he did. After a brief and shallow explaining away of Duke's dithering, Kirby simply ended his passage with 'Duke, owing to the difficulties already described, was unable to comply.'[23]

Percival's 1949 statement 'for various reasons, in no way due to any lack of effort, this attack never got going', is shameful. When a company of troops takes an hour to embus, one is entitled to question their commander's level of effort; when the circumstances of Duke's reconnaissance are recalled, both his competency and endeavour should be questioned; and when the 'effort' of the supporting artillery—and the refusal of the Australians' offer of assistance—is assessed, Percival's point lacks credibility. His 1954 utterance to Kirby regarding Elrington's 'documentary evidence' was nothing more than a thin smokescreen which has never seen the light of day. Surely, given the gravity of the failure, if Elrington had had such 'documentary evidence' it would have been publicly disclosed. It has not been.

But while historians have rightly identified the poor training and lack of acclimatisation of the three battalions of the 53rd Brigade, no such scrutiny has been given the 2nd Loyals. The Battalion had arrived in Singapore in April 1938 under the command of Lieutenant-Colonel G. Williams. Its second-in-command was Major Elrington, who assumed command of the unit in September 1940. Wigmore has claimed that the Loyals had not left Singapore Island during their service.[24] But the unit historian has recorded that after having served in a number of roles in the defence of Singapore Island, the Battalion became a part of Malaya Command's mobile reserve. As such, in March 1941, it had a week's training at Kluang, and most significantly, at Yong Peng; during late April it moved to Mersing, where it was in training until August when relieved by the 22nd Brigade AIF; and, from then on, it had been part of the Singapore 'Fortress' under the command of Major-General Simmons.[25] The 2nd Loyals, therefore, did not suffer from a lack of acclimatisation; they—and Elrington—were surely well versed with Yong Peng and Mersing, and could therefore have rendered valuable service with the 53rd Brigade at Mersing which would have allowed Brigadier Taylor's 22nd Brigade AIF to have served with Bennett on the Trunk Road and/or at Muar. Further, given that the Battalion had seen service in Singapore and Malaya since April 1938, there can be absolutely no excuse for its slack efforts in movement and its poor reconnaissance procedures.

Given the background of the Loyals, the training and condition of the 53rd Brigade, and the command decisions of Brigadier Duke, it becomes apparent that probably General Key, but most definitely Duke and Elrington, never had any real intention of staging their ordered attack to recapture the Bukit Pelandok defile or to subsequently secure the bridge at Parit Sulong. For Percival to therefore state that every effort had been made, and that because Bennett was in overall command, that he was therefore culpable for the failure to attack and secure the bridge at Parit Sulong, holds absolutely no credibility—in fact the whole episode is a sad reflection upon his own poor handling of his resources. General Bennett's diary, 22 January 1942:

> W/T signals from party v. [very] faint. Loyals attack timed for 1400 yesterday postponed till 1730, then f [first] light today, then 0930, then abandoned. Sent message to Anderson to escape. Very very sad & upset. Told press story. Then 53 Bde was told to hold on 48 hours to enable escape. Later 53 Bde decided to withdraw & thus abandon these men. Ordered them to stay put till ordered to move & told Percival.[26]

Given Anderson's determination to recover the 45th Brigade soldiers into his Bakri perimeter and the dogged fighting of the Australians at that location, and then along the perilous escape route to the bridge at Parit Sulong, Bennett's angst is entirely fair and reasonable. The dithering performance of Key, Duke and Elrington deserve strong condemnation.

Whilst the desperate fighting at and around Bakri was unfolding, General Wavell had become increasingly uneasy about the defence of Singapore Island. On 19 January 1942, Wavell signalled Percival. It was an extraordinary communication, and, while both the Australian and British Official Historians later quoted it, they both omitted the first paragraph:

A. P. Wavell to General Percival   19 January 1942

Have seen Dobbin [Wavell's Liaison Officer to Percival] and learnt that no detailed scheme exists for withdrawal to island and defence of it if Johore is lost. Sincerely trust it will never come to this but you must have scheme prepared. You are in better position than I am to judge what troops are likely to be available at any given time, if I can give you none except those arriving by convoys of which you are aware.[27]

The fact that the GOC Malaya Command was, at that time, becoming aware of a major battle unfolding in the Muar area, and, given that his III Corps had been evicted from northern Malaya in such a short and costly campaign, would seem to constitute more than enough motivation for a contingency withdrawal plan to Singapore Island—and for a rapid digging and wiring and mining of all of its possible approaches. After the first paragraph cited above, and not quoted by Kirby and Wigmore, Wavell's signal of 19 January continued with:

You must think out problem of how to withdraw from mainland should withdrawal become necessary and how to prolong resistance on the island ...

Will it be any use holding troops on southern beaches if attack is coming from north? Let me have your plans as soon as possible.

Your preparations must of course be *entirely secret*. Battle is to be fought out in Johore till reinforcements arrive and troops must not be allowed to look over shoulders. Under cover of selecting positions for garrison of island to prevent infiltration of small parties you can work out scheme for larger force and undertake some preparation such as obstacles or clearances but make it clear to everyone that battle is to be fought out in Johore without thought of retreat. Keep going and make everyone fight the Jap hard, every day brings reinforcements closer.[28]

On the same day Wavell signalled Churchill:

Officer whom I had sent to Singapore for plans of defence of island has now returned. Schemes are now being prepared for defence of northern part of island. Number of troops required to hold island effectively probably as great or greater than numbers required to hold up enemy in Johore. I have ordered Percival to fight out the battle in Johore but to work out plans to prolong resistance on island as long as possible should he lose Johore battle. I must warn you however that I doubt whether island can be held for long once Johore is lost ...

Part of garrison has already been sent into Johore and many of troops remaining are of doubtful value. I am sorry to give you depressing picture but do not want you to have false picture of island fortress. Singapore defences were constructed entirely to meet seaward attack. I still hope Johore may be held until next convoy arrives.[29]

And in an effort to assist Percival, Wavell offered late the same day to fly from Java to Singapore. His offer was accepted.

During Wavell's seven-hour visit, he discussed with Percival a plan for further fighting in Johore, a withdrawal plan to Singapore Island should Johore be lost, and a plan for the defence of the Island. Wavell believed that the Japanese would land on the north-west coast, whereas Percival thought they would land on the north-east shoreline. The Supreme Commander did not interfere in Percival's appreciation, bowing to the judgement of the responsible commander on the spot. It was agreed that the soon-to-arrive British 18th Division and the Australian 8th Division were to occupy the two most likely landing areas. According to Wavell's biographer, 'then, with Wavell sitting beside him, Percival drafted a new batch of orders for Heath, Gordon Bennett and Keith Simmons'.[30]

In essence those orders envisaged a new defensive line from Mersing on the east coast (Brigadier Taylor's Eastforce) to Kluang (9th Indian Division), then to Ayer Hitam (27th Brigade AIF) and on to Batu Pahat on the west coast (11th Indian Division). There was to be no withdrawal from any part of this line without the express orders of General Percival, and in the event of a general withdrawal to the Island, the three main roads which converged on Johore Bahru were to be used, facilitated by suitable demolitions and anti-tank obstacles. When Percival had finished writing these orders, his Supreme Commander witnessed his signature, placed a copy in his briefcase and promptly flew back to Java.[31]

Given that Wavell had ordered Percival to fortify Singapore's defences weeks earlier, and that he had discovered through his liaison officer that Percival had, as late as 19 January, not framed a withdrawal plan from Johore to the Island, and worse, had still not addressed the issue of fortifying the 'fortress', his trip to Singapore and his signed copy of Percival's belated new orders would seem to suggest that Wavell was covering himself against future criticism. And in the light of Churchill's very recent and forthcoming signals to him, such behaviour is understandable.

Churchill had begun to ask pertinent questions while in Washington on 15 January, and the day after, Wavell had begun to answer them. The news that nothing had been done to fortify the northern side of Singapore Island profoundly shocked the Prime Minister:

So there were no permanent fortifications covering the landward side of the naval base and of the city! Moreover, even more astounding, no measures worth speaking of had been taken by any of the commanders since the war began, and more especially since the Japanese had established themselves in Indo-China, to construct field defences . . .

Now, suddenly ... I saw before me the hideous spectacle of the almost naked island and of the wearied, if not exhausted, troops retreating upon it.

I do not write this in any way to excuse myself. I ought to have known. My advisors ought to have known and I ought to have been told, and I ought to have asked. The reason I had not asked about this matter, amid the thousands of questions I put, was that the possibility of Singapore having no landward defences no more entered my head than that of a battleship being launched without a bottom.[32]

On 19 January, in a minute to General Ismay for the Chiefs of Staff Committee, Churchill was under no illusion as to the possible political ramifications: 'I warn you this will be one of the greatest scandals that could possibly be exposed.'[33]

And what would Churchill have thought if he had known that a highly trained chief engineer had arrived in Singapore on 5 August 1941 with express orders to construct the very fortress that he, Churchill, was advocating and had taken for granted? What would the Prime Minister have thought had he known that that appointment had been made without Simson having written orders? It is suggested that if such revelations might have caused an outburst, then Churchill's rage might have known no limits had he then been told that the Chief Engineer had made a detailed reconnaissance of the Malay Peninsula, suggested the implementation of a series of defences down that feature, had endorsed General Dobbie's line of fortifications planned in 1938, had a detailed plan for fortifications for Singapore Island, and, critically, had discovered that the materials for the task lay readily at hand. And what scandal might have followed if the final lesson in the Prime Minister's education had contained the knowledge that Generals Percival, Heath and Simmons had all personally rejected Simsons' expert and practical plans, and in the case of Percival, had not carried out an order from Wavell to fortify the Island?

We now return to the defence of southern Johore and the subsequent withdrawal to Singapore Island during the period 24–31 January 1942.

While Lieutenant-Colonel Anderson's column was involved in its fighting withdrawal from Bakri, events at the west coast town of Batu Pahat were delicately poised. Three key roads ran from Batu Pahat: one to Yong Peng, one to Ayer Hitam and the third along the coast through Senggarang, Rengit, Benut and Pontian Besar before reaching Pontian Kechil, where it then turned inland to join the Trunk Road near Skudai. Batu Pahat, with its rubber plantations and mines, was far from an ideal defensive locality, and lent itself to potential Japanese encirclement.

General Nishimura saw two options for the future employment of his Imperial Guards Division. The first was a thrust upon Yong Peng, and the second was a southward advance along the coast road to cut off the British force at Batu Pahat. With the 5th Division already at Labis on the Trunk Road, he decided to head southwards. To this end he ordered his Guards Reconnaissance Battalion to attack Batu Pahat from the north-east while his 4th Guards Regiment moved south to link up with the battalion which he had deployed earlier near Senggarang. This would see the south road cut and the British at Batu Pahat encircled. At the same time, by sending his 5th Guards Regiment to cut the Ayer Hitam–Batu Pahat road, any British attempt to rescue the besieged defenders at Batu Pahat would be forestalled.

Brigadier Challen wanted to withdraw from Batu Pahat. Percival refused the request on 23 January, probably believing that the 5th Norfolks, due to arrive the next day, would strengthen Challen's force sufficiently to hold the town. And in a further endeavour to reinforce the west coast, the 53rd Brigade (the 3/16th Punjab and 6th Norfolks) was extricated from the Bukit Pelandok area—after having a costly encounter with Japanese tanks in the process—and sent westwards to Skudai and then to Benut. The Loyals were sent to reinforce the 27th Brigade AIF on the Trunk Road.

On 25 January, Brigadier Challen again sought permission to withdraw his 15th Brigade from Batu Pahat. At a conference that day, with intelligence indicating that the Japanese were now near Sengarrang, Percival issued orders for Challen to withdraw to the Sengarrang area and that a staged withdrawal to Singapore Island be planned. The final crossing to the Island was scheduled for 31 January 1942.

The 15th Brigade—the 2nd Cambridgeshire, the British Battalion, the 5th Norfolks and a portion of the 6th Norfolks—withdrew from Batu Bahat during the night of the 25th/26th. But about six-and-a-half kilometres short of their Sengarrang objective they ran into an enemy roadblock. As Anderson and his column had found on the road to Parit Sulong, the block was well sited, amidst 'close and swampy country'[34] which made passage around it by vehicle impossible, and by infantry difficult. In an effort to clear the 15th Brigade's escape route, General Key ordered Brigadier Duke to send his newly arrived 53rd Brigade from Benut northwards along the road to Challen. Just after midday, Duke despatched a column consisting of about 100 men of the 6th Norfolks, armoured cars, carriers and artillery, and commanded by a gunner, Major Banham, to occupy Rengit. But when that column—having made the critical error of moving in close formation—reached a Japanese roadblock just north of the village, it was all but annihilated.[35] Banham, in a noteworthy individual performance, occupied the only carrier to reach Sengarrang. Given that the relief column had been reduced to a single carrier, and that Barham informed him that he had passed through six roadblocks, Challen did not need much convincing as to his next move, and immediately ordered the destruction of his guns and vehicles, that the wounded were to be left under the care of the Red Cross and Padre Duckworth, and finally, that two parties of infantry were to make good their cross-country escape to Benut. On this occasion there was no massacre of the wounded.

While the Japanese captured Rengit on the night of 26/27 January, the two parties left Sengarrang. The first, numbering around 1200 men, travelled east or inland from the coast road, and were guided by a Malayan police officer. Those exhausted soldiers reached Benut during the afternoon of 27 January. Brigadier Challen, meanwhile, led the second party which moved westwards between the road and coast. When Challen's group struck a river obstacle that night, the brigadier attempted to reconnoitre a crossing and was captured. Colonel Morrison now led the party to the coast and concealed it on ground consisting of swamp and coconut trees, while his Brigade Major journeyed by boat to Pontian Kechil to report to 11th Indian Division HQ.

The sad and sorry plight of the west coast force ended over the next three nights when around 2700 soldiers were evacuated by sea to Singapore Island.[36] And as a result of that evacuation, Heath now realised that with this force cut off and eliminated from the fighting, he could now only look to the greatly understrength 53rd and 28th Brigades to hold the coastal road. Accordingly, he now ordered Key's 11th Division to withdraw to Skudai on the Trunk Road and cover Westforce's eventual withdrawal, which was timed for 31 January–1 February 1942.

General Nishimura's Imperial Guards Division had staged a brilliant west coast offensive which had all but dismembered the Indian, Australian and British force opposing it, and in so doing, had gravely threatened the security of the Trunk Road. And for all those great gains, the cost had been around the equivalent of a battalion of his division.

We now cross to the east coast and Brigadier Taylor's 'Eastforce' during this same period.

On 22 January 1942, and in compliance with the withdrawal timetable ordered by General Heath, Brigadier Taylor had withdrawn his 22nd Brigade HQ and the 2/18th Battalion (less one company) to the Nithsdale Estate, around seventeen kilometres north of Jemaluang. While this move was undertaken, his 2/20th Battalion was left to cover the approach to Mersing. Lionel Wigmore:

> During the afternoon of the 25th, Brigadier Taylor held a conference of his commanding officers. The day before, when Kluang airfield was endangered and he was ordered to destroy Kahang airfield, he had moved his headquarters to a point east of Jemaluang. He now issued orders for his headquarters to be established on the Kota Tinggi road south of Jemaluang, and for the 2/20th Battalion to withdraw from its strongly prepared positions to Jemaluang crossroads that night.[37]

Although Taylor's Eastforce was rightly withdrawing to conform to the general defensive line planned by Percival and Heath, the Australians were still keen to take the fight to their enemy. It would seem that the use of ambushes as a means of inflicting telling casualties upon the Japanese was not confined to General Gordon Bennett and Lieutenant-Colonel Galleghan, but was universal within the 8th Division AIF. The 2/18th Unit Diary, 23 January 1942:

Knowing that the 2/20 Bn would be withdrawing through the 2/18 Bn this evening the C.O. submitted a proposal to the Bde Comd for Bn offensive operation against the enemy force in this area. This was approved, plans made and B and D Coy Comdrs with Pl. Comds and NCOs inspected the area. Mersing Bridge blown by 2/10 Fd Coy Engrs 2300 hrs.[38]

The 'offensive operation' was, in fact, a large-scale ambush.

The Nithsdale and Joo Lye rubber estates lay alongside the western side of the road between Mersing and Jemaluang. The 2/18th area stretched from a

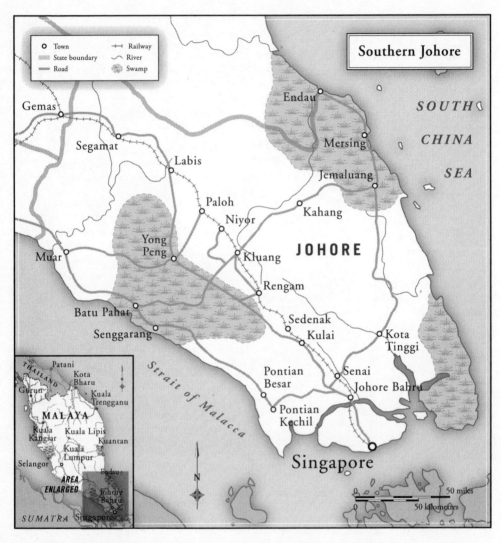

bridge to the north, and just east of Gibraltar Hill, running about three-and-a-half kilometres southwards along the road, and past both rubber estates. Along the western or left side of the ambush area, was the high ground, with the estates nestled on relatively level ground amongst the hills. On the eastern or right hand side of the road the ground was essentially flat except for one hill which lay about halfway between the two rubber estates. The ground then fell away eastwards into swamp land.

The 2/18th Battalion's use of this ground was shrewd. D Company (Captain Edgley) was disposed astride an estate road on the left side of the

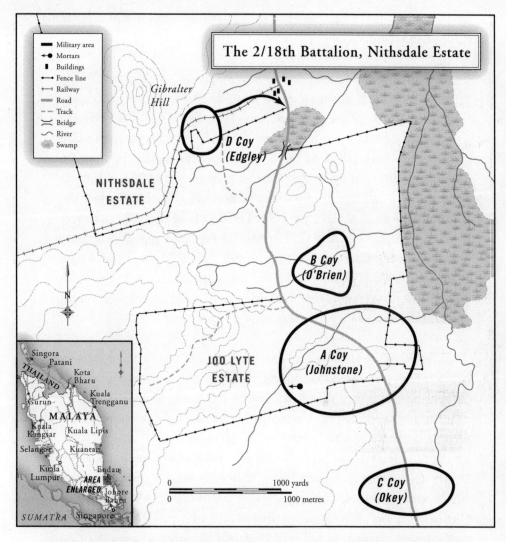

The 2/18th Battalion, Nithsdale Estate

main road; B Company (Captain O'Brien) was some 900 metres south of D Company, and on the eastern or right hand side of the road; A Company (Captain Johnstone) lay astride the road about 500 metres behind B Company, and just after a bend and directly opposite the Joo Lye Estate; and C Company (Captain Okey) was also astride the main road and was disposed about 450 metres to A Company's rear.

In laying his 2/18th Battalion ambush, Lieutenant-Colonel Varley was anticipating that an enemy force which was reported to be moving from Endau to Mersing would not arrive upon his ambush ground 'until after daylight 27 Jan 42'.[39] The 2/18th Battalion Diary reveals the detail of planning involved in the operation:

> . . . telephone communication to be installed to all Coys and D Coy to have 1000 yds of wire forward in attack. It was proposed to allow approx. one Bn of the enemy to pass D Coy and B Coy in ambush, to be blocked by A Coy with C Coy in reserve. Then, with the application of an Arty barrage lasting up to 7 minutes plus similar fire from Bn Mortars, followed by an Arty barrage moving at the rate of 100 yds in [every] 2 minutes, the attacking Coys [D and B] were to attack the enemy north of A Coy's position. The details of the Arty plan were given to Maj. Kerr, Actg C.O. 2/10th Fd Regt and approved by him. Mortars were placed in position behind Hill 167, JooLye [sic] Estate and four Vickers placed on Hill 167 for supporting defensive task. An Arty C.P. [Command Post] was also to be established on Hill 167 with a commanding view over the proposed battle area.[40]

All appeared ready. But the Japanese battalion which had been sighted between Endau and Mersing and which had been anticipated to arrive about daylight on the 27th was not the first to arrive. There was another much closer and it was closing in. The well-conceived daylight ambush was now to become a desperate battle in pitch-black darkness.

The first clue as to the possible nearness of the enemy came at 6.00 pm on 26 January, when a recce patrol from each of A and B Companies encountered an enemy patrol. The second came not long after when the foremost northern section of D Company first identified a patrol moving through the Nithsdale Homestead followed by 'Japanese troops in column of route, by pls marching south past their position . . .'[41] At about 2.00 am a section of Lieutenant Warden's 9 Platoon, A Company, was assailed by a Japanese platoon. Warden and two of his soldiers were killed during the action and when, at 3.00 am, A Company came under a company strength attack and enemy troops in numbers were noted northwards in D Company's perimeter, Varley decided to instigate the artillery and mortar support plan, which was the agreed prelude to the Battalion operation.

At 3.15 am the artillery opened fire which was followed 30 minutes later

by Captain Edgley's D Company advance. To the amazement of the Australians, they encountered anything but a stiff fight, as the Japanese had, on the
commencement of the barrage, scurried up onto the hill on the eastern side
of the road between the forward 2/18th D and B Companies, and as well-
drilled troops are liable to do, had furiously dug and scraped small pits into
which they withstood much of the barrage. When Edgley reported to Varley
that he now intended to withdraw to B Company's lines, he was informed
by the CO that he could expect a strong Japanese presence between him and
that company. This was the last contact with Captain Edgley. It transpired
that between the artillery barrage and the efforts of the two forward companies, the Japanese both inflicted, and took, heavy casualties.

At 4.15 am the artillery barrage stopped and D Company, now in the
vicinity of the Nithsdale Homestead, moved south along the road. When
they arrived adjacent to the hill on its eastern side—and about halfway back
to B Company—they came under concentrated Japanese machine gun fire
from both sides of the road. Edgley now ordered a two-platoon attack with
the third moving around the left flank. The fighting during that night and
into the next morning became a series of isolated, confused and desperate
hand-to-hand battles, which saw neither side give ground. It transpired that
many of D Company were overwhelmed, but its soldiers all fought to the
last, and took an equally heavy toll of the Japanese. Sometime during that
night and early morning Captain Edgley was killed. While this battle raged,
B Company had also been attacked, but facing a smaller enemy force, had
repulsed it.

When daylight came B Company advanced to render assistance to
D Company. It too ran into strong enemy positions and heavy fire. But
at 7.30 am, Varley had some critical intelligence, which came from the
Intelligence Section's Sergeant Wagner, who had miraculously moved from
A Company's perimeter through enemy lines and contacted B Company's
11 Platoon and Lieutenant Simmons's platoon of A Company. The 2/18th
Unit Diary recorded that:

This information gave the C.O. the dispositions of B Coy, one pl of
D Coy, and approximate location of balance of D Coy and also positions thickly held by the enemy including Machine Gun and mortar

positions. With this information the Arty were given tasks . . . and the
resultant fire produced excellent results.[42]

With B Company in the process of assisting the forward D Company,
Varley now planned to send Captain Johnstone's A Company to stage a
counterattack to aid them, but, just as this plan was about to be implemented, Brigadier Taylor contacted him. When Taylor had endorsed Varley's
ambush plan four days previous, he had stipulated that General Heath had
made it absolutely clear that the withdrawal timetable to Kota Tinggi and
thence to Johore Bahru must be strictly adhered to, and that, any attacking 2/18th Battalion companies must be prepared to withdraw immediately.
Varley had no alternative. D and B Companies would have to make their own
way out. The 2/18th withdrawal to Jemaluang was essentially uneventful—
the Japanese did not follow up.

During their fighting at Nithsdale and Joo Lye Estates, the 2/18th Battalion lost six officers and 92 other ranks killed or missing.[43] The Battalion's
Unit diarist would later claim an enemy casualty count of 600, while the
2/10th Field Regiment's Unit History would claim 1000. Both estimates
would seem to be highly inflated and cloud the real achievement of the
Australian performance.

Alan Warren in his *Singapore 1942*, has claimed that:

> The ambush had certainly been a disappointment for Varley. Despite
> months of training in the jungle, the battalion had been taken by
> surprise in dispositions quite inappropriate for a night battle. There
> was a good deal of ill-feeling within the battalion over the perceived
> abandonment of D Company.[44]

There can be no doubt that Lieutenant-Colonel Varley would have felt a
sense of disappointment over his ambush. While Warren's point that Varley's
dispositions were unsuitable for a night battle is fair, the fact remains that
his available intelligence—the Battalion did conduct recce patrolling in its
vicinity—was forecasting a Japanese arrival on the morning of 27 January.
His dispositions for the ambush, his employment of his artillery support, his
use of the unit's mortars, his communication, and, above all, the magnificent

performance of his troops (particularly his two forward companies) were first class, and must therefore reflect upon his command performance and the training of his Battalion.

Lieutenant-Colonel Varley's 2/18th Battalion's fighting at Nithsdale and Joo Lye Estates did once again demonstrate that well-led, well-trained and adequately equipped and supported Australian troops were more than a match for the much-vaunted Japanese. Much the same could be said of the exploits of the Argylls, the Leicestershires and the East Surreys.

A Japanese source later described the fighting against the 2/18th Battalion as 'an appalling hand-to-hand battle'.[45] The fact that Jemaluang was not occupied by them until 29 January, and, significantly, that Eastforce was essentially left unmolested before retiring to Singapore Island is ample proof of the intensity of the engagement—and the Japanese losses—at the Nithsdale and Joo Lye Estates.

With the Eastforce front stabilised, and the withdrawal of forces on the west coast complete by late January 1942, the Trunk Road and railway remained the critical sites of battle.

18

TO THE CAUSEWAY

The plan for the withdrawal of Westforce in the central sector required that the 27th Brigade AIF (the 2/26th, 2/30th and the Loyals) was to withdraw down the Trunk Road, while the 9th Indian Division (General Barstow) was to move down the railway. On 24 January 1942, the 2/30th Battalion and the Loyals occupied a perimeter about five kilometres north of the vital road junction at Ayer Hitam—vital because the eastward road from Kluang, the northern road from Yong Peng and the western road from Batu Pahat converged there.

Lieutenant-Colonel 'Black Jack' Galleghan had chosen his ground well. At the 61-mile peg and to the right of the road, he deployed his A Company (Captain Anderson), one platoon of B Company and a detachment of mortars on 'Bare Lalang Hill', which dominated the area. To the extreme north of this A Company perimeter, Galleghan sited his mortar observation post, which had a far-reaching view of the forward ground. Away to the east he sited a small standing patrol to observe any enemy attempt to move around his right flank. His left flank, to the left of the road, was occupied by the Loyals' A Company, also on a hill. The forward perimeter was 'devoid of vegetation excepting bracken and lalang (long grass)',[1] which therefore offered excellent fields of fire. To the rear of these dispositions lay an extensive area of swamp and bog on either side of the road which ran up to, and past the River Sembrong, and eventually gave way to jungle to the south. The swamp and bog area also provided a substantial natural tank obstacle. About two-and-a-half kilometres behind the forward perimeter, and around 800 metres north of Ayer Hitam, Galleghan sited his B Company to the right of the road with his D and C Companies to the rear on the left and right sides respectively.[2] While the 2/30th forward perimeter offered excellent surveillance over the potential enemy approaches, its one major drawback was the fact that it was susceptible to observation from the air. To counter this, Galleghan issued orders for no digging in, and limited movement during daylight, other than to pass dry rations forward from soldier to soldier.

The 2/26th Battalion (Lieutenant-Colonel Boyes) was disposed to the rear to cover the westward approach along the Batu Pahat road, while one of its companies was deployed to the east to cover the Kluang Road. To conform to the general peninsula withdrawal plan, the 27th Brigade was required to hold their line for 48 hours.

The Japanese began to press the Australians early on 25 January. *Galleghan's Greyhounds*:

> In the morning rain set in and continued during the day. Conditions deteriorated, rest was impossible in the wet and mud and emergency rations were drawn, as others could not be brought up from the rear. Enemy planes were active throughout the day attempting to destroy the bridge over the Sembrong, without success, and often flying low in their search for movement and artillery positions.[3]

Beginning at dawn, aggressive and sustained 2/30th Battalion patrolling detected enemy activity on the right flank. At about 8.00 am, a fighting patrol led by Sergeant Russell found an enemy officer and three other ranks in trees, engaged in spotting for their artillery and mortars. All four were killed. About 450 metres further on Russell discovered a large formation of Japanese forming up for an attack and promptly sent a warning back to A Company HQ. Shortly after, the patrol came across another six of the enemy and killed four. It would appear that these Japanese patrols were engaged in attempting to draw the Australians' fire prior to concentrated attacks. The ploy failed as the 2/30th continued to respond by sending out numerous fighting patrols to take the fight to the enemy, whilst still holding fire within their forward perimeter.[4]

During the remainder of the morning and early afternoon the Japanese attempted to destroy the bridge by artillery fire, to hit the 2/30th Battalion mortars and to form up for early probing attacks. But their endeavours were frustrated. At 10.00 am a platoon was scattered by accurate 2/30th mortar fire, which was directed by Sergeant McAlister's observation post in A Company's perimeter. An hour later when the Japanese mortared Lalang Hill and were seen forming up again at about company strength, McAlister's work again saw them take casualties and disperse. And when the intrepid Sergeant Russell yet again moved forward and identified the position of the Japanese guns, an artillery dual ensued. A forward enemy party attempting to determine the Australian positions and draw their fire was eliminated by this bombardment. As the afternoon wore on the Japanese continued their efforts to locate the Australian positions and to hit the bridge and the 2/30th mortars—to no avail.

During the late afternoon they mounted three concentrated attacks. The first was against the ground from the road eastwards along the 8 and 9 Platoon positions of A Company's right flank.[5] Curiously, this initial attack was preceded by a subaltern 'carrying a large Japanese flag'.[6] His demise did not dampen the enemy's enthusiasm, as a second officer, then a third, were mown down before the flag was left on the battlefield. The resulting attack was beaten back by the defenders' small arms fire with the usual accurate assistance of mortars. A two-company enemy assault further to the east on A Company's perimeter was staged at 4.00 pm but, although the forward standing patrol was forced back to its 12 Platoon position, the enemy yet again received a severe mauling, which saw them stopped about 70 metres from the Australian lines. Leaving half of their number dead on that ground, the Japanese withdrew to re-form on a wooded ridge to the rear, but when hit by yet further 2/30th Battalion mortar fire, further casualties caused them to flee.

Unable to pierce the right flank, the Japanese now directed their attention to the western side of the road, through a covered jungle approach onto the Loyals' A Company. At around dusk they launched a strong assault upon

those rearward positions as well as on the front of the perimeter. The Loyals'
company commander led a spirited counterattack with the bayonet which,
although failing to dislodge the enemy from a portion of that high ground,
did prevent encirclement. But the cost was heavy. During that hand-to-hand
fight the Loyals took heavy casualties. The Japanese now attempted to exploit
their high ground advantage by moving along and across the road. In this
they were thwarted yet again by the 2/30th Battalion's A Company mortar
and machine gun fire.

Knowing that the 27th Brigade was due to withdraw that night, and
with his forward left flank perimeter having been penetrated, Lieutenant-
Colonel Galleghan decided to withdraw at the same time as his rearward
2/26th Battalion. With the Japanese now in possession of a part of the road
and in occupation of the high ground on the front left flank, that withdrawal
was made through the swamp and bog back to the bridge on the River
Sembrong. Whilst darkness most certainly offered relative concealment, the
roughly 800-metre journey through often waist deep swamp with enemy
tracer and machine gun fire just overhead, made for tough travel, especially
for the stretcher bearers and mortar crews.

The 2/30th Adjutant, Captain Peach, had gone forward with the withdrawal orders. The Loyals were his last point of call:

> ...but enemy machine guns, traversing the road, forced him to
> remain in the swamps, in mud often four to five feet deep. He eventu-
> ally accomplished his mission, a most hazardous one, and returned to
> the demolition point, bruised, scratched and almost unrecognizable,
> due to the mud. A party of Engineers was there, and, on being assured
> that the last man was over the bridge, Capt. Peach gave orders for its
> demolition. It was then approximately 9 o'clock.[7]

While Captain Duffy's B Company and some of the Loyals provided a rearguard under covering fire from the 30th Battery of the 2/15th Field Regiment,
the 2/30th and the Loyals made good their withdrawal and reached the 54-mile
peg at 11.00 pm.[8] The 2/26th Battalion then passed through their lines and
the Loyals returned to Singapore to rest and refit. They were replaced by the

2nd Gordon Highlanders, who had been posted from Singapore. At around 2.30 am, the 2/30th embussed at the 52-mile peg and reached the 41-mile peg at 4.00 am, about eight kilometres south of Simpang Rengam.[9]

The action fought just north of Ayer Hitam caused the Japanese an estimated 250 casualties at a cost to the 2/30th of four killed and twelve wounded or missing. It was, yet again, testimony to the excellent training of the 2/30th Battalion and also to the outstanding leadership of Lieutenant-Colonel 'Black Jack' Galleghan and his officers.

On 26 January 1942, the leading positions in the defence of the Trunk Road fell to the Gordons at the 48-mile peg, the 2/26th Battalion at the 44-mile peg and the 2/30th in reserve at the 41-mile peg. During that morning the Japanese kept strafing the road and the lines of the Gordons and the 2/26th Battalion, which was a prelude to infantry pressure upon the Gordons along the road during the afternoon. This Japanese advance was halted by artillery and mortar fire. But late that day, when the Gordons were placed under more intense pressure, they withdrew. Wigmore has claimed the reason given was that they 'had run out of food and water and their ammunition was running short'.[10] Kirby asserted that they were 'short of ammunition'.[11] Thyer, General Bennett's GSO1:

> . . . an enemy force was seen moving down the edges of the road. These were engaged by 25-prs and mortars which inflicted heavy casualties. It was just prior to this that Brig Maxwell had gone forward to discuss the question of future withdrawals and the probability of the Gordons withdrawing to the 42 mile post position alongside 2/30 Bn the following day. Lt-Col Stitt, CO of the Gordons, must have misunderstood the Bde Comd's intention, for at 1830 hours he ordered the withdrawal of his Bn to the 41½ mile post.
>
> By 1730 hours, the Gordons had reported that they were running out of ammunition and that the men had not been fed, nor was any drinking water available. On enquiries being made, it was discovered that the Bn carried no reserve of rations, and that the water supply had not been replenished since the day before. The location of the ammunition point at the 35-mile post had been notified.[12]

Wigmore placed the second paragraph from the above Thyer quote in a footnote,[13] but decided that Thyer's first and next paragraphs might best be passed over:

At 1900 hours, Comd Gordons reported that the enemy was still pressing and that the unit was withdrawing. On being ordered to remain in position he stated that the move was already under way. The CO was then sent forward to halt the Bn at once, and to take up a position immediately in rear of the 2/26th Bn.[14]

Kirby would later write that the Gordons withdrew 'with the Brigade Commander's permission through 2/26th Battalion to Milestone 42½'.[15] It would seem that the 'permission' came after the withdrawal had already begun, and that the paucity of rations, water and ammunition was used as an excuse. This was a clear example of substandard staff work.

On 27 January, the Japanese made several low-level strafing attacks upon the 27th Brigade, and at 3.00 pm the enemy opened fire on the 2/26th Battalion front with light machine guns and small arms fire.[16] The Battalion Diary observed that: 'All parties of enemy observed were engaged by our tps. Enemy also using rifle grenades, Chinese crackers. Enemy personnel were dressed as "Indian troops".'[17] And if the enemy air attacks were unpleasant, at least their regular timing gave the Australians a chance to prepare for the onslaughts. The unit diarist recorded that the Japanese 'planes work "union" hrs—0830–1200, 1400–1700: their appearance is most regular'.[18] At 5.00 pm the 2/26th were ordered to withdraw, and with its forward companies keeping the enemy at arm's length by frequent patrolling and superb support from the 30th Battery 2/15th Field Regiment, the Battalion successfully broke contact. By 11.00 pm the 2/26th had begun the task of digging in at its new positions near the 42-mile peg, which covered a road leading into the Namazie Estate. The Gordons were deployed just ahead of them astride the Trunk Road.

The defensive perimeter occupied by the Gordons, the 2/26th and 2/30th Battalions at the Namazie Rubber Estate on 28 January 1942 was not an ideal one. Enemy attacks along the left flank or western side of the Trunk Road were unlikely, as the ground consisted of jungle-ridden hills interspersed with swamp, which ran right up to the road. But the extensive

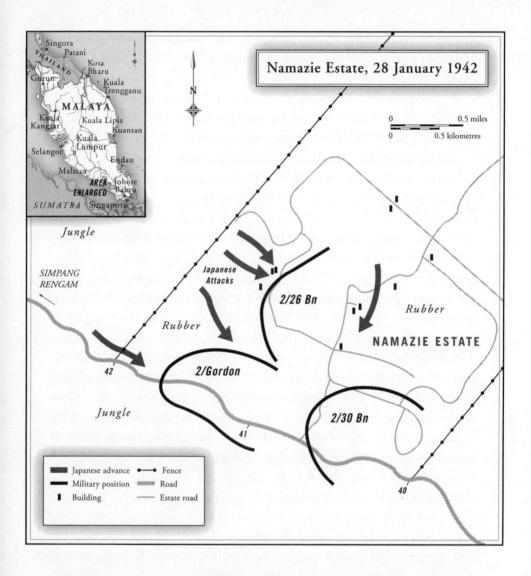

rubber plantation ground to the east of the Trunk Road offered the Japanese the chance to outflank the Australians. There were a number of estate roads and an extensive area of high ground with its contour drainage ditches, which they could use. This sort of rubber country also offered limited defensive observation and thus restricted the Australians' use of their mortars. Should the Japanese manage to penetrate that right flank and gain the cover of the jungle on both sides of the rear portion of the Trunk Road—a jungle defile—the 27th Brigade would be cut off.[19] Brigadier Maxwell and

Lieutenant-Colonel Galleghan discussed a large-scale 2/30th ambush at this defile, but the concept was abandoned because 'reconnaissance was made almost impossible by air activity'[20] and the worn condition of the troops.

With the obvious security of the western side of the Trunk Road seemingly assured, and knowing the Japanese would almost certainly attempt initial frontal assaults and a wide outflanking movement through the eastern or right rubber estate flank, the 27th Brigade perimeter was planned accordingly. The Gordons were deployed astride the Trunk Road and stretching just eastward, with the 2/26th Battalion's B, A and D Companies occupying ground further east. Its C Company added depth to the Battalion's perimeter, being deployed just to the rear of D Company. Galleghan's 2/30th Battalion had two critical roles. Positioned just forward of the junction of an estate road and the Trunk Road, it was perfectly placed to either reinforce the forward perimeter, or protect the right flank against an outflanking Japanese movement—or both. Galleghan immediately instigated a detailed patrol program for his Battalion through this extensive right flank.

The Japanese attacked A Company's left flank of the 2/26th perimeter at around 7.00 am on 28 January. When they were met by determined opposition they started to feel for the extent of the Battalion's eastward perimeter along the C and D Company front. The fact that the enemy were 'moving back and forward across front and right flank',[21] whilst their planes bombed and strafed the general area, would seem to suggest that they were engaged in their usual activity of feeling for a point of weakness in the forward defences, with the intention of allowing themselves time to pin down that forward perimeter and outflank it.

Just after midday, a recce patrol from the 2/30th Battalion's D Company encountered a small enemy patrol about 300 metres east of its position. When a two-section 2/30th fighting patrol was sent out to eliminate those Japanese it came under intense fire. Galleghan's prediction of an enemy outflanking movement to cut the Trunk Road was rapidly coming to pass. He now acted decisively. Lionel Wigmore:

> Three more platoons, two armoured cars and a section of mortars were moved to the area, and the forward units were told of the situation. At Galleghan's request Boyes sent him a company of

the 2/26th Battalion [his B Company, closest to the Trunk Road] to come under command and reinforce his right flank. Three platoons, covered by two others, were ordered to attack under Captain Duffy's direction the high ground occupied by the Japanese, and a strong out-flanking attack was to be made.[22]

At 4.40 pm on 28 January 1942, the 2/30th Battalion yet again showed its fighting prowess. While two platoons produced a terrific din of small arms covering fire, the three attacking platoons advanced steadily towards the enemy. The two armoured cars engaged Japanese light machine gun posi-tions with their Vickers machine guns, and, when an additional enemy force in close formation was spotted forming up on a ridge it too came under armoured car fire. As the 2/30th soldiers closed on the enemy, the bayonet was used with telling effect, and the Japanese withdrew in disorder. Such exposed enemy movement invited further devastating armoured car fire. But the Japanese employed an unusual weapon to cover their withdrawal. The 2/30th War Diary recorded that the enemy retreated 'under cover of [a] type of toxic smoke bombs . . . effect of gas prevented further exploitation of enemy retreat'.[23] The anguish of soldiers caught in that 'toxic smoke' without respirators can be imagined, but it later transpired that the gas was 'found to lose effect quickly on gaining fresh air'.[24]

With Brigadier Maxwell's Brigade HQ about eighteen kilometres to the rear, Galleghan had assumed command of the Brigade operation at Namazie Estate. We have noted Galleghan's lack of professional respect for his briga-dier, and, through the intense pressure of recent events on the Trunk Road, Bennett too had become increasingly disenchanted with his 27th Brigade commander. Maxwell had repeatedly requested withdrawals before their planned timings, and had previously wrongly assumed that the Gordons had taken heavy casualties. Bennett's diary for 28 January summed up a number of his repeated concerns: 'Maxwell again full of flap messages. Fearful for his men's comfort. Makes wild statements.'[25]

At 6.00 pm on 28 January, Galleghan ordered a withdrawal to commence at 7.00 pm. To his great credit, the withdrawal proceeded as had his handling of the brigade at the Namazie Estate—flawlessly. The exhausted 27th Brigade soldiers withdrew in darkness, trekked over nineteen kilometres to their transport and arrived just north of Ayer Bembam in the early hours of 29 January. Wigmore has recorded that Lieutenant-Colonel Boyes 'set aside standing orders' to use his A Echelon transport to ferry a number of his troops back, and also employed a water cart for the same purpose as well as handing out water.[26] 'Black Jack' Galleghan's compassion was no less impressive: 'The highlight of the day had been the sight of the C.O. giving a nip of whisky to the men as they passed him standing by the roadside—a present from Padre Polain.'[27]

The Japanese followed up the 27th Brigade withdrawal with their usual speed. Daylight on 29 January found the 2/26th Battalion deployed as the forward unit near the 31-mile peg on the Trunk Road. To its rear, the Gordons occupied a position astride the road near the 29-mile peg, while the 2/30th was deployed at the junction of the Trunk Road and the road leading eastwards to Sedenak on the railway.

Lieutenant-Colonel Boyes's dispositions made maximum use of his ground. The Battalion perimeter was nestled in amongst rubber and ran off into jungle and swamp. He sited his A Company to the right of the road, with C Company to the immediate left of it, and partly on a raised contour. To C Company's left, he deployed his D Company, on 'the reverse slope of a hill, while covered with lalang on the crest, offered good cover on its rear slopes, and only maintained a sec [sic 'section'] on the fwd slopes as a standing patrol . . .'[28] B Company occupied a 'kidney shaped' contour on the left flank, which dominated the open country from the left forward portion of the perimeter right around to the left rear. Boyes took full advantage of the excellent fields of fire offered in front of his forward B and D Company positions by dismounting machine guns from his carriers and allotting a section to each.[29] Despite there being a shortage of entrenching tools, the 2/26th 'took advantage of rubber drains that were fairly plentiful in the area'.[30]

The first enemy incursion into the 2/26th perimeter occurred shortly after 8.00 am and bordered on the comical:

. . . a cyclist patrol of about thirty dressed in Japanese, British and native clothing were observed moving down the rd. Fire was withheld until the party stopped and dismounted between A & C Coys area

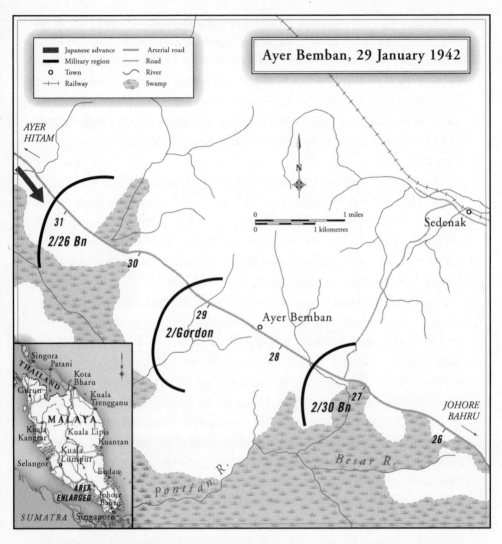

then while they offered a good target at close range the nearer secs of both coys opened fire and wiped them out to a man.[31]

An hour later the 'comedy' was over. The D Company standing patrol on the forward slope of its hill was confronted by a battalion strength assault coming up that feature. After inflicting around 50 casualties upon the enemy who had 'bunched up' before attacking, the standing patrol withdrew in great haste. Their flight was followed by a concentrated enemy mortaring and shelling. The 2/26th Battalion replied with accurate mortar fire.

When the Japanese failed to follow up their artillery and mortar fire, the commanding officer of D Company, Captain Treacy, rightly assumed that they were engaged in an outflanking movement. Accordingly, he sent a patrol out to assess the enemy's strength and intent, which discovered that they were in great strength on the hill. Treacy now ordered a strong platoon attack on the western flank, which was covered by supporting fire from HQ Company and a further platoon. The attack went in with grenades and bayonets to the fore, and the platoon returned to its lines with three captured light machine guns, boxes of ammunition and a number of rifles, at a cost of six of its B Company soldiers wounded.[32]

The Japanese responded with heavy artillery and mortar fire, and when enemy aircraft appeared, the newly won but exposed lalang grass position was abandoned for the security of the original perimeter. To add to the enemy's frustration in forming up and moving forward, the 2/26th's dismounted armoured car machine guns took a heavy and continuous toll. The Battalion Diarist noted that the Japanese 'did not seem disheartened by the heavy casualties they were suffering'.[33] Late that morning sustained fighting broke out across the entire front, but the Japanese were still frustrated in their attempts to gain ground, mainly because of the Australians' excellent observation and resulting supporting fire. A notable example occurred at around 2.00 pm when a large enemy force was seen by D Company forming up in front of its neighbouring C Company. The resulting 2/15th Field Regiment's fire was most accurate—and was supplemented by high-explosive 2/26th mortar fire.

During the mid-afternoon a number of enemy in front of A Company on the right flank emerged and planted a white flag and signal on the road. They were killed, but succeeded in guiding a flight of Japanese bombers. A Company took casualties, which reduced its strength to 57 all ranks.

At 7.15 pm the 2/26th Battalion withdrew from its perimeter to the 21½-mile peg forward of Kulai. This was a significant location, as it marked the convergence of the railway and Trunk Road. Throughout its fighting on 30 January, the Battalion gave no ground and inflicted, for the loss of twelve killed and 51 wounded 'or shocked', heavy enemy losses. The 2/26th Unit Diarist estimated that the Battalion had killed approximately 500 Japanese, without taking into account the highly effective artillery

support. It would seem that a total enemy casualty figure of 500 is conservative. Wigmore quoted a captured Japanese account of the action, which
supports the statement:

> ... the frontal resistance was so powerful that a pincer movement
> was attempted, but 'the warriors continued their suicidal resist-
> ance like wounded boars'. Near the end of the battle 'the enemy,
> defying death, strangely and impudently counter-attacked with
> bayonets along the whole line'. The force which had detoured to the
> right flank made a fierce attack, but was repelled, and 'finally, one
> severely wounded soldier was the sole survivor of the rosy-cheeked
> commander's unit.'[34]

Thursday, 29 January 1942, marked the end of the 27th Brigade AIF's
campaigning on the Malay Peninsula. Through a fortnight's tough fighting
countering the Japanese axis of advance along the Trunk Road, it had repeatedly shown its enduring fighting qualities, its professional use of artillery
and mortar support, its magnificent mastery of minor infantry tactics both
in defence and attack, and the great skill and elan of its officers. When the
achievement of its detached 2/29th Battalion's defiant performance at Bakri
and its participation in Anderson's column's epic fight to Parit Sulong are
added to the 2/30th and 2/26th Battalions' fighting withdrawal along the
Trunk Road, the 27th Brigade amply demonstrated its right to be awarded
no less praise and respect than any other formation in the AIF.

Having covered General Bennett's Westforce operation (27th Brigade AIF)
along the Trunk Road during the period 24–30 January 1942, we now turn
to Westforce's other task: the parallel withdrawal along the nearby railway
by the 9th Indian Division (General Barstow) during the same period.
At this time the Division was composed of two brigades. The first was the
8th Indian Brigade (Brigadier Lay), which consisted of the 1/13th Frontier
Rifles and the 2/10th Baluch (plus one company of the 3/17th Dogras). The
22nd Indian Brigade (Brigadier Painter) was the second, and was composed
of the 5/11th Sikhs and an amalgamated battalion consisting of one com-

pany of the 2/12th Frontier Force Regiment and the 2/18th Garhwalis.

On 23 January, the 22nd Indian Brigade had been deployed to guard the Kluang airfield, with its 2/18th Garhwal to the north at Paloh, where a road ran westwards to join the Trunk Road near Yong Peng. When the Japanese attacked, the Garhwalis withdrew and during that process, its HQ lost contact with its four rifle companies. Lionel Wigmore:

> Lacking this contact, the companies continued their withdrawal and reached Kluang that night—by which time the Kluang airfield also had been abandoned by the air force. The 8th Indian Brigade, on the main road covering the approach from the north, held off the enemy during the day and at night passed through Yong Peng. It was then transported to the Rengam area, on the railway line south of Kluang.[35]

The withdrawal by the Garhwalis created an opportunity for the Japanese to gain ground. As a consequence, the 22nd Brigade was ordered to stage a counterattack (by the 5/11th Sikhs), which was to be facilitated by the rearward 8th Brigade moving forward from Rengam. After spending the night three kilometres south of Niyor, the 5/11th Sikhs put in a spirited action against a Japanese force forming up on their front, and then withdrew. During the night of 25/26 January, the 22nd Brigade pulled out to Rengam, to be joined by the Sikhs the next morning, and the 8th Brigade arrived at Sayong Halt that same night.

The following afternoon (26 January), General Heath held another conference to formulate a timetable for the complete withdrawal to Singapore Island on the night 31 January/1 February 1942. That timetable saw General Bennett issue his Westforce schedule at 12.20 am on the 27th. His orders for the 27th Brigade (Brigadier Maxwell) on the Trunk Road and the 9th Indian Division (General Barstow) on the railway were to hold their present positions that night. On the second night (27/28 January), the 27th Brigade was to withdraw to the 44-mile peg and the 9th Division to railway mile 440. On the third night, 27th Brigade was to withdraw to the 32-mile peg. On the fourth night, they were to reach road mile 25 and railway mile 450 respectively. And on the fifth night (31 January/1st February), both formations were to cross the causeway to Singapore Island.[36]

We now come to a tragic train of events. When the above Westforce time-table was released it contained a mistake for the night 27/28 January. In the text of the orders the 9th Indian Division was given railway mile 440 as its destination, while in the appendix that destination was given as railway mile 438½. The intended position was that quoted in the text (440), because the ground between 430 and 440 consisted of extensive rubber estate ground and its inevitable estate roads would present the Japanese with numerous and speedy avenues for outflanking any force on the railway adjacent to that ground.

After visiting Bennett early on 27 January, General Barstow returned to his HQ at Rengam and summoned Brigadiers Painter and Lay, where he issued verbal orders to them: Painter's 22nd Brigade was to hold the area from railway mile 437 to 432, while Lay's 8th Brigade was to occupy a rearward position to defend a section of the railway leading to Sedenak. Predictably, Painter protested for the reasons just described, but Barstow was adamant. The order stood.

Later, Brigadier Painter did not help matters by deploying his battal-ions behind each other along the railway, and thereby further enhancing his chances of being cut off. And when Lieutenant-Colonel Parkin of the 5/11th Sikhs subsequently asked him twice for permission to both widen his peri-meter and place a 'linking' company to the rear between the two brigades to offset this risk, Painter refused.

During the late afternoon of 27 January Barstow again went forward to visit Brigadier Lay and ordered him to occupy a ridge about one-and-a-half kilometres south of Layang Layang. Lay's Brigade passed through the 22nd Brigade at around 4.00 pm that afternoon. In his withdrawal along the railway, Barstow was to be handicapped by the fact that there was no road between a point just south of Layang Layang and Sedenak, a distance of some sixteen kilometres. All 9th Division artillery and transport had therefore to be sent from Rengam along estate roads to the 40½ mile peg on the Trunk Road, and as a consequence, all infantry would be required to travel by foot. To compound this vehicle problem, wireless communication (carried in trucks) was thus unavailable, and therefore messages had to be sent via the railway telephone line. When Barstow left late on 27 January for his HQ, he knew that wireless communication from his HQ forward was not possible, and therefore told his two brigadiers to 'coordinate their movements by mutual agreement'.[37]

At about 10.00 pm Lay told Painter that his 8th Brigade was moving just south of Layang Layang and that he would call again later. Then disaster struck. For not the first time during the Indian Army's campaigning in Malaya, a railway bridge just south of Layang Layang was 'accidentally' demolished. This had two tragic consequences. The first was that the 22nd Brigade was now out of touch with the 8th Brigade, because the railway telephone was destroyed with the blown bridge. The second was that the stream now became an obstacle, if a fairly shallow one, to the withdrawal of the 22nd Brigade. And to compound these catastrophic events, Brigadier Lay's 8th Brigade did not occupy the ridge as ordered by Barstow, but one 1500 metres further back, thereby increasing the gap between the two formations. Incredibly, 'no attempt was made either to repair the telegraph line or inform 22nd Brigade that the bridge had been blown'.[38] Moreover, Lay did not make any attempt to inform Painter of his new dispositions. Kirby described the blowing of the bridge and Lay's failure to occupy the ridge selected by Barstow as 'two unfortunate events'.[39] When elements of the 22nd Brigade heard Japanese movement around their flank during the early hours of 28 January, and after Painter yet again refused a plea from Parkin to withdraw, the whole brigade was about to feel desperately 'unfortunate'. At 10.15 am Brigadier Painter finally decided to pull back down the western side of the railway.

At daylight on 28 January, General Barstow set out from his Sedenak HQ to visit his Brigades. With him were a 9th Indian Division staff officer, Colonel Trott (an Australian) and Major Charles Moses, an 8th Division AIF liaison officer. The Moses papers contain a vivid account by both men of what then transpired.

Lieutenant-Colonel Trott:

On the morning of the 28th January, 1942, Major General Barstow, Comd. 9th Ind Div set out to visit his two Brigades which lay one in rear of the other astride the railway. The 22nd Ind Inf Bde, the leading Bde, being in the vicinity of Layang Layang ... We proceeded forward in a small rail inspection car driven by an Indian military driver.

The General first contacted the Comd. 8th Bde (the rear brigade.) [Brigadier Lay] Here he discovered that a gap between the Bdes existed, and that, in error, a railway bridge had been destroyed by the 8th Bde in their withdrawal during the night before, which demolition the Bde was not covering. The destruction of the bridge had severed signal communications with 22 Inf Bde and these had not been re-established.

Having ordered the leading Bn [the 2/10th Buluch] to move forward and cover the demolition the General with Major Moses and myself then proceeded forward in the rail car, until further progress was stopped by the demolished bridge. We got out of the car, crossed the damaged bridge and walked forward along a high railway embankment towards Layang Layang station, which station was visible in the distance. The General and Major Moses walked along the eastern side of the embankment and I, some little distance in the rear, was walking along the western side of the embankment. We had proceeded about 300 yards when suddenly from half right in the high grass on the eastern side, a Japanese appeared about 30–40 yards away and yelled: almost simultaneously with his appearance fire was opened by concealed enemy with light automatics and rifles.

My immediate reaction was to leap down the embankment on the side nearest me [the western side] into the long grass. I made two ineffectual efforts to get back over the railway embankment but the volume of fire made this impracticable, so that I made my way into the jungle about 50 feet from the railway ... [40]

In the confusion of the moment, Major Charles Moses had gone the way of General Barstow down the eastern side of the embankment. Major Moses:

When General Barstow and I were about three-quarters of the way down the embankment, I realized we were on the same side as the enemy and said to the General: 'Come on Sir, we can't stay here, let's go back over the top.' I scrambled under fire up the embankment which had long grass to about 15 ft. of the top, and glanced back to

Westforce, the 9th Indian Div., 24–30 January 1942

see the General sliding downwards into the high grass. He appeared unhurt and I thought he had in mind making his way back on the eastern side of the embankment. I told Col. Trott this when I later joined him on the other side . . .

When I last saw General Barstow sliding into the high grass he did not appear to be wounded. It was only after some hours, when he had not returned to the 8th Inf. Bde. that we realized he might have been wounded and perhaps taken prisoner.[41]

General Barstow was dead. His loss was felt very keenly both within the Indian Army and the AIF. Gordon Bennett would later write that Barstow was 'a popular officer, particularly amongst the Australians', and that he was 'fearless' and 'inspiring', but that he was 'hampered by some very weak officers under his command'.[42]

The leading battalion of 22nd Brigade ran into Japanese blocking the railway at about midday on the 28th. Although the Sikhs managed to clear this initial Japanese force they suffered ten of their number killed and 35 wounded. Painter was now faced with a cruel decision. He could maintain his effort to clear a way through to the 8th Brigade by a single or series of railway attacks, or he could attempt an encircling movement around the enemy and hope to regain his lines. In choosing the latter option, he faced a number of challenges. The first was the fact that he would have to carry his wounded through tough terrain; second, that poor speed of movement through the rubber, jungle and possible swamp might cause him to fail to reach Lay in time; and third, that he possessed no artillery support to assist him in a railway breakthrough—and thus the associated risk of further casualties. In the end, he chose a jungle exit. But after following a track through the jungle shown on his map, that passage abruptly ended, and 22nd Brigade were brutally condemned to a jungle trek by compass that would see it take 48 hours to gain a position still three kilometres north of Sedenak. On 31 January, Brigadier Painter was forced to leave his wounded behind at a rubber plantation, and on 1 February with only 400 of his number left, he ordered a surrender. Less than a quarter of that number escaped to Singapore.

Major Moses:

It would be correct to say that the responsibility for the loss of the 22nd Indian Bde. was Brig. Lay's: he made the elementary error, apart from not following the specific order given by his Divisional Commander, of not occupying the ridge intended which was an excellent defensive position covering a natural obstacle (i.e. the river) and having a clear view of the intervening country west of the railway right up to Layang Layang and about 300 yards to the river on the west. As soon as Col. Trott and I reported the situation to Col. Coates (G1 of the 9th Indian Div.) and to General Bennett, steps were taken immediately to relieve

Brig. Lay of his command, which was taken over by Co. [*sic* 'Col.']
Trott.[43]

Brigadier Lay's performance was indeed poor. In addition to Moses's
criticism, it should be stated that when an effort to bridge the gap between
the two brigades was later made it was—not unlike the weak effort to assist
Anderson at Parit Sulong—half-hearted. But there were other contributing
factors in the debacle on the railway sector. The two conflicting railway mile
points issued in the original 8th Division (Westforce) timetable was the first
error. The second was Barstow's apparent attempt to prove to Bennett that
the Indian Army was indeed capable of sterner stuff, but in the end, such a
demonstration was at the expense of basic local judgement. Although Brigadier Painter was placed in an appalling situation by a number of blunders
on the part of Brigadier Lay, he too erred badly. When faced with a Japanese
occupation of the railway behind him, he should have opted for a further
determined attempt to breach the line. It seems inexcusable for a full brigade
movement to have petered out in thick jungle because a track ceased to exist.
Such an escape route should have been explored—time spent on reconnaissance is never wasted. On the 28 January, before it was discovered that
the 22nd Indian Brigade was missing, General Percival decided to shorten the
withdrawal timetable by 24 hours. In this decision, he was guided by the fear
that the 11th Indian Division could not hold the western sector and thereby
deny Skudai to the enemy for much longer. Faced with 'mission impossible',
Painter's effort to regain his lines was thus unwittingly reduced by a day.

On the night of 30/31 January 1942, Brigadier Taylor's Eastforce passed
through the outer bridgehead and crossed the causeway, followed by Bennett's
Westforce, and finally General Key's 11th Indian Division's force which had
been holding off the Imperial Guards near Skudai. An inner bridgehead
through which all forces passed was manned by the Argylls.

This Argylls' remnant marched last across the causeway at 7.00 am on
31 January with its two pipers resolutely playing 'Hielan' Laddie'. The causeway
was then blown. The AIF's Captain Wyett crossed with Colonel Stewart, and
when he enquired as to why the regiment had been piped across, Stewart
replied: 'You know, Wyett, the trouble with you Australians is that you have
no sense of history. When the story of the Argylls is written you will find that

they go down in history as the last unit to cross the causeway and were piped across by their pipers.'[44] All 'terribly British'. Stewart's own sense of history was somewhat limited. His pipers were in fact playing a lament for an empire on which the sun was setting. It might have been truer to the brutal reality of the moment to have piped 'Flowers of the Forest', which is usually played at funerals. The days of the white master ensconced in his luxurious Malayan plantation bungalow, complete with servants and sipping on his gin sling, were over. British Singapore, the great commercial crossroads of an empire, had but a fortnight to live. And an adolescent and naïve Australia was to soon learn its own tough lessons.

19

'COMETH THE HOUR . . .'

On the first day of February 1942, General Percival spoke to Singaporeans from the radio studios at Caldecott Hill:

> Our task has been both to impose losses on the enemy and to gain time to enable the forces of the Allies to be concentrated for this struggle in the Far East. Today we stand beleaguered in our island fortress.
>
> Our task is to hold this fortress until help can come—as assuredly it will come. This we are determined to do.
>
> In carrying out this task we want the help of every man and woman in the fortress. There is work for all to do. Any of the enemy who sets foot in the fortress must be dealt with immediately. The enemy within our gates must be ruthlessly weeded out. There must be no loose talk or rumour mongering. Our duty is clear. With firm resolve and fixed determination we shall win through.[1]

Within a few days he also faced the press. Amongst a host of British editors, censors, broadcasters and members of the Ministry of Information was the Australian war correspondent Ian Morrison. Reading from notes, Percival made 'an attempt to plead'[2] for the cooperation of the civil population, explained the reasons for most of the remaining aircraft being withdrawn to Sumatra, elaborated on the difficult issue of labour supply and asked for the support of the press. He ended his statement with a final appeal for successful resistance which 'would depend on whole-hearted cooperation between the military and civilian elements'.[3] Morrison was not impressed:

> Much of what the general said was sensible. But never have I heard a message put across with less conviction, with less force. Afterwards there were questions, and long agonizing silences before the next question was put. It was embarrassing as well as uninspiring. I felt that the general not only did not know how to deal with a group of pressmen, but that he did not know how to deal with any group of men.[4]

It will be remembered that Duff Cooper had been appointed Resident Commissioner for Far Eastern Affairs with Cabinet rank on 10 December 1941, and that he was also to preside over the War Council in Singapore. It had not taken Cooper long to identify the petty bungling and inefficiency of the civil authorities. He informed Churchill of the problem only eight days after his arrival, and three days later he cabled the same concerns to the Secretary of State for the Colonies. On 11 January, just prior to his return to the United Kingdom, he suggested the introduction of martial law and the appointment of a military governor.[5]

The issues of poor rates of pay for coolie labourers and their failure to turn up to dig critically important defensive dispositions on the Malay Peninsula have been previously identified. These problems were repeated in Singapore. It would seem strange for Percival to state that: '. . . not only was there no civil labour available for work on our own land defences of the island, but there was very often no military labour available either',[6] when Singapore's population had been listed as 900 000 at the time when ration cards had been introduced[7] and had swollen 'to more than a million Asians'[8] during the withdrawal from Malaya. The labour in both Malaya and Singapore *was* there. However, Percival believed that 'we were likely to get better service by the voluntary system, provided we could get the support of influential leaders . . .'[9] But his very next sentence is an admission of his own poor judgement and lack of drive:

As the difficulties increased, there was a growing demand in some service quarters for compulsion to be applied. It was in answer to this demand, and when the volunteer system had failed to produce the required results, that a measure was passed on 20 January to introduce compulsion. It came too late for its value to be disclosed.[10]

The supply of civilian labour was not the only problem. In time of war it must be put to highly prioritised tasks, organised efficiently, and supervised competently—and if necessary, ruthlessly. When such leadership is lacking, chaos is the end result. An example is the order in December that trenches be dug across sports fields in Singapore to prevent enemy landings. After the deputy municipal engineer had dutifully put coolies to work digging straight trenches, another official—pointing out that the trenches would also be used for shelters—demanded that they be redug in a zigzag pattern to counter air strafing. But after the work was completed, a third official demanded that the trenches be refilled owing to the potential health problems caused by mosquitoes breeding in them. The solution? The already shallow one-metre trenches were half filled.[11]

On 31 December, the long overdue expertise needed in Singapore was provided by the appointment by Duff Cooper of the Chief Engineer Brigadier Ivan Simson as Director General Civil Defence. For all intents and purposes, Simson was still an unused commodity in the military sphere, and now, as the enemy were at Singapore's causeway, he was asked to achieve the impossible. There was a lack of air raid shelters, poor protection for the docks and key buildings, substandard fire protection measures and, yet again, the unnecessary hindrance of the civil administration when Simson discovered that his deputy, Mr Bisseker, was actively thwarted in his attempts to administer efficient civil labour and transport.[12]

———

It will be remembered that when Wavell had visited Percival in Singapore during 7–8 January 1942, he had asked for plans for the defence of the north

shore of Singapore Island. There were none. On the 9th Percival ordered
Major-General Keith Simmons to undertake a preliminary reconnaissance of
the north coast. When Wavell instructed Percival on 20 January to prepare a
withdrawal timetable from Johore, and yet again, enquired into the defences
on the north coast, Percival belatedly released a plan on the 23rd. It was
undertaken by Major-General Keith Simmons, Brigadier Paris and officers
of his 12th Brigade, and others representing III Corps and the Australian 8th
Division. Major Dawkins, Bennett's GSO2 was the Australian representative.
Neither Brigadier Simson nor any of his Chief Engineer Staff were present or
were consulted during this planning.[13]

In defending Singapore, Malaya Command was faced with two challenges. The first was to contest and hopefully defeat any Japanese attempt
to invade the Island's north coast, whilst the second was to protect the
perceived vital ground: the central strip of land starting along a north–south
line running from the River Kranji to the River Jurong, and stretching eastwards to the north–south line of the River Seletar through Paya Lebar and
on to a point a few kilometres east of Kallang airfield. Within this central
portion of the Island was to be found Singapore Town, with most of the
population, its wharves, food stocks and a significant concentration of fixed
defences. This central area also contained three vital reservoirs—the water
supply from Johore had been cut off—a pumping station and pipelines, and
in the vicinity of Bukit Timah lay further extensive ammunition and food
dumps (and the always coveted high ground). Added to these features was
the fact that this central area also contained the Island's hospitals and oil
storage tanks.

In an effort to strengthen the western and eastern ends of this central
area, two defensive lines were envisaged. The first, the Jurong Line, was on
the western extremity and was to have stretched from the lower waters of
the River Kranji southwards to the upper waters of the River Jurong. On the
eastern side the Serangoon Line extended from the lower reaches of the river
of the same name, southwards towards the coast. In an extraordinary revelation, Kirby has recorded that:

These [lines] had been reconnoitred before the outbreak of war and a
layout of the defences prepared, but no works had been constructed or

trenches dug. During January, on the Jurong Line an anti-tank ditch had been partially dug, a few section posts had been constructed and some clearing had been undertaken to provide a field of fire, but no other preparations had been made by the time the troops were withdrawn from Johore.[14]

The two lines were known as 'switch lines' because they 'offered means of switching forces between east and west and of shortening the front and reducing the area to be defended if this became necessary'.[15]

There is no shortage of inconsistency about how the north shore of Singapore Island was to be defended. Kirby in the Official British History (1957) states that Percival's instructions were: '. . . the whole coastline had to be defended on the beaches'.[16] In *The Chain of Disaster* written thirteen years later, Kirby provided a different perspective:

He [Percival] told Keith Simmons that, as the coasts were unsuitable for the normal form of beach defence, the plan in each brigade area was to be based on small defended localities covering approaches to the coast, such as rivers, creeks, road and tracks. These defended posts were to be supported by mobile reserves located so that they could operate against Japanese parties seeking to infiltrate through or around the forward posts.[17]

'Small defended localities' do not constitute 'the whole coastline' being defended on the beaches. In *The War in Malaya* (1949), Percival, in hindsight, took an each way bet: 'The basis of the defence was that the enemy must be prevented from landing or, if he succeeded in landing, that he must be stopped near the beaches and destroyed or driven out by counter attack.'[18] Warren (2002) had written that 'Malaya Command's defence policy was to defend the coast with posts prepared for prolonged resistance. If the posts were surrounded they were to hang on and wait for relief by a counter-attacking force.'[19] In the end none of the above objectives would be satisfied, because put simply, the plan was beyond the capabilities of the available men and material.

The defence of Singapore was organised in four areas: Northern, Western, Southern and Command Reserve. The Southern Area extended from the

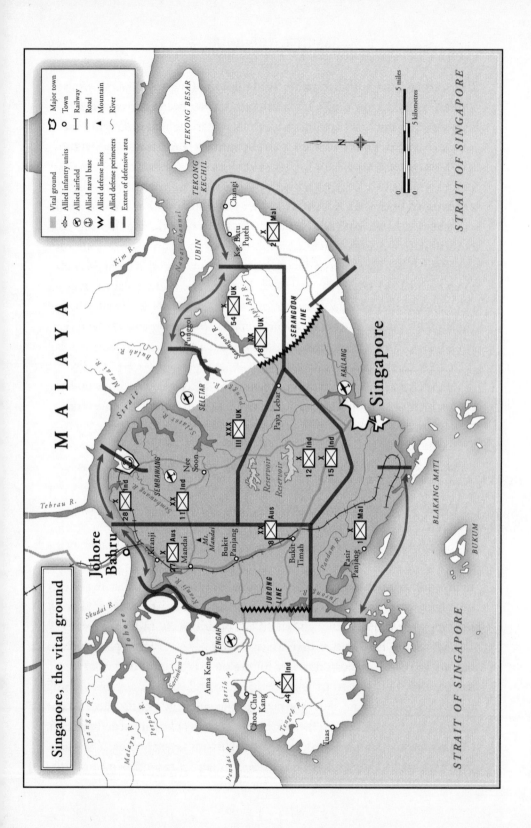

Singapore, the vital ground

River Jurong eastwards around the coast and up to Changi. This sector was manned by the 1st and 2nd Malaya Brigades, the Straits Settlement Volunteer Force Brigade and Fortress Troops. It was under the command of Major-General Keith Simmons. The Northern Area stretched from Changi around the north-eastern coast to the pipeline near Woodlands. This III Corps sector was held by the British 18th Division and the 11th Indian Division, and was commanded by General Heath. The Western Area was under the command of General Bennett, and was manned by the 8th Australian Division and the 44th Indian Brigade. The Reserve Area was roughly bounded from west to east by Bukit Timah and Paya Lebar, and from Seletar Reservoir in the north to around Holland Road in the south. This central area was well sited but woefully undermanned, and consisted of the 12th and 15th Indian Brigades. Brigadier Paris's 12th Brigade was in fact at roughly battalion strength—250 of the Argylls, 150 attached marines and about 500 of the 4/19th Hyderabads.[20]

Percival always believed that the Japanese would attack Singapore on the north-east coast, but in his postwar despatch and *The War in Malaya*, he made poor attempts to deny this fact:

This was the danger area [the AIF's west coast] and I had specially selected for it the Australian Imperial Force under command of Maj.-Gen. Gordon Bennett because I thought that, of the troops which had had experience of fighting on the mainland, it was the freshest and the most likely to give a good account of itself.[21]

In a postwar letter to Kirby, Percival admitted that the above statement was 'incorrect' and 'based on hindsight'.[22] Of course it was. The allocation of resources confirms this fact. It will be remembered that Wavell and Percival had differed on this point. They had agreed that the soon-to-arrive British 18th Division should occupy the area most likely to be attacked, and that the AIF should occupy the second most vulnerable location. Wavell had forecast Bennett's area as that locality, while Percival had chosen Heath's. The Northern Area subsequently received five brigades to defend a 24-kilometre coastline, while Bennett possessed three to cover a coastline stretching for 32 kilometres. The artillery support was therefore in that

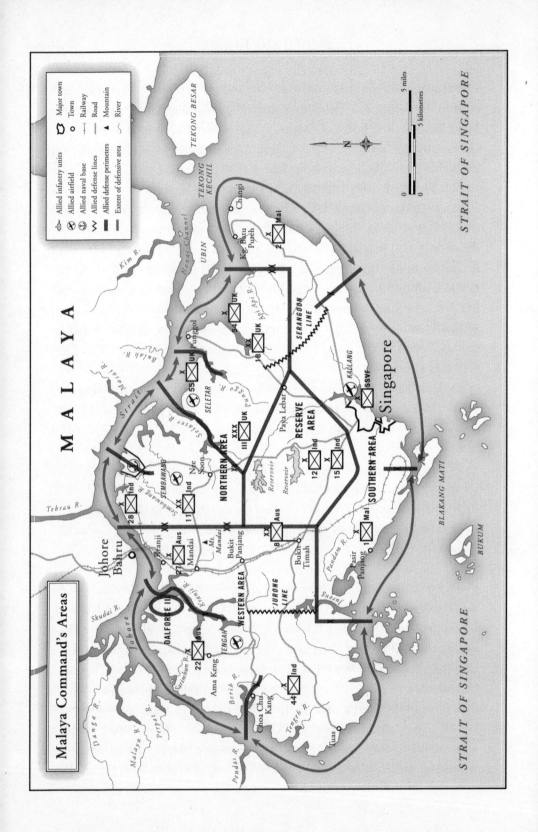

Malaya Command's Areas

MALAYA

STRAIT OF SINGAPORE

STRAIT OF SINGAPORE

Major town
Town
Allied airfield
Allied naval base
Allied infantry units
Allied defense lines
Allied defense perimeters
Extent of defensive area
Railway
Road
Mountain
River

5 miles
5 kilometres
N

TEKONG BESAR
TEKONG KECHIL
UBIN
Nanai Channel

Kim R.
Butah R.
Masai R.
Strait
Seletar R.
Tebrau R.
Skudai R.
Johore R.
Danga R.
Perpat R.
Malayu R.
Pendas R.
Berih R.
Serimbun R.
Tengeh R.
Kranji R.
Sungei R.
Pandam R.
Ayer Api R.
Punggol R.
Serangoon R.

Johore Bahru

Changi
Kg Batu Puteh
X 2 Mal
X 54 UK
X 18 UK
XX UK
X 55 UK
SELETAR
Punggol
XXX III UK
NORTHERN AREA
Ne Soon
Sembawang R.
XX 11 Ind
X 28 Ind
SEMBAWANG
Mt. Mandai
Kranji
X 27 Aus
Mandai
Bukit Panjang
Paya Lebar
RESERVE AREA
X 12 Ind
X 15 Ind
Reservoir
SERANGOON LINE
KALLANG
X SSVF
Singapore
SOUTHERN AREA
X 1 Mal
Pasir Panjang
Bukit Timah
XX 8 Aus
WESTERN AREA
JURONG LINE
DALFORCE II
X 22 Aus
Ama Keng
TENGAH
Choa Chu Kang
X 44 Ind
Tuas
BLAKANG MATI
BUKUM

proportion. The fact that Major-General Simmons had allocated the newly arrived Australian 4th Machine Gun Battalion to dig a part of Heath's area just prior to the withdrawal from the mainland—against the understandable protests of Bennett—would seem yet more evidence of Percival and Simmons's assessment.

The frontages of all brigades on the Island's coast were allocated by Major-General Simmons and his staff subsequent to their recent reconnaissance and planning.[23] In the Australian sector the plan contained a significant flaw which the Japanese were destined to fully exploit. Brigadier Maxwell's 27th Brigade front stretched from just east of the causeway to the Kranji River, a length of around 3.6 kilometres, whereas Brigadier Taylor's 22nd Brigade coastline sector was just over 14.6 kilometres. The last, and least vulnerable portion of the AIF coast, was manned by Brigadier Ballentine's 44th Indian Brigade.

In the end, Percival's plan to defend Singapore Island bore little relationship to reality. Four constructive criticisms should be made. First, it was based on the notion that the Japanese were to be stopped on the beaches, and yet the defenders (most notably Taylor's 22nd Brigade) were hopelessly dispersed. Second, Taylor was forced to deploy all three of his battalions across his extensive coastline, which prevented him from using one battalion as a reserve. In an attempt to create a reserve he ordered each battalion to deploy one company at Battalion HQ. In so doing, he was forced to further weaken an already thin coastal defence. Third, we have noted that Malaya Command's central reserve area was manned by a threadbare force which might at best have offered weak counterattacks. Last, when examining Percival's army on Singapore Island, it should be remembered that the terms 'battalion' (and therefore equally 'division' and 'brigade') are misleading. Lionel Wigmore has left us with a realistic if depressing summary:

> . . . the battalions varied widely in quality, condition, and equipment. Only one of the Indian battalions was up to numerical strength, three (in the 44th Brigade) had recently arrived in a semi-trained condition, nine had been hastily reorganized with a large intake of raw recruits, and four were being re-formed but were far from being fit for action. Six of the United Kingdom battalions (in the 54th and 55th Brigades

of the 18th Division) had only just landed . . . and the other seven battalions were under-manned. Of the Australian battalions, three had drawn heavily upon the recently-arrived, practically-untrained recruits. The Malay battalions had not been in action, and the Straits Settlements Volunteers were only sketchily trained. Further, losses on the mainland had resulted in a general shortage of equipment. The experiences of the troops had affected their morale in varying degree. The general effect was bad.[24]

From an Australian perspective, the problem of reinforcements was much more serious than 'recently-arrived, practically untrained troops'. The battle at Bakri and the subsequent withdrawal of Anderson's column to Parit Sulong had virtually gutted the 2/19th and 2/29th Battalions. Wigmore has claimed that the 2/19th received 370 reinforcements, while the Battalion Unit Diary and its Unit History put the figure at 630—100 from the General Base Depot and 530 from the recently arrived 'untrained' reinforcements.[25] The 2/29th received around 500. One reinforcement officer posted to the 2/29th recalled that when some married men were refused as reinforcements, 'they filled up the platoon with men out of Bendigo jail'.[26] The same officer also noted that many had just entered training camp, that a significant number later attempted to jump ship at Fremantle, and that such disillusionment continued on the way to Singapore with 'a bit of physical violence aboard . . . with officers and so on'.[27]

The problem was not confined to the other ranks. Some of the nineteen reinforcement officers were also of poor quality. One 'new' platoon commander had to be taught by a few of his 'veterans' not to order his troops to run off towards bushes during an air raid, but to simply hit the ground. After having seen numerous Indians running around under an artillery barrage forward of Bakri only a few weeks before—with horrendous results—such behaviour did not inspire the men's confidence in a number of officers. Any battalion which receives a new CO, second-in-command, three new company commanders and about 480 virtually untrained and often disgruntled troops will struggle in battle. And to compound this state of affairs, the 2/29th also had to cope with a severe lack of specialists in its HQ Company. Corporal Jim Kennedy, Signals 2/29th Battalion: '. . . and these reinforcements didn't have a clue about signals . . . or anything. They got them in the mortar platoon, they got them in the carrier platoon, and the transport . . . you had to make up the numbers and that's what they made them up with.'[28]

The 2/29th Battalion was deployed in the Causeway Sector as 8th Division reserve. Given its just mentioned problems of training, leadership and specialist expertise, the chances of it being able to assume a mobile reserve role were slim.

In an effort to augment his meagre reserve General Bennett raised two additional battalions. On 3 February, he promoted Major Robertson (2/20th Battalion) to command a Special Reserve Battalion which consisted of 'surplus Army Service Corps and ordnance men and 2/4th Machine Gun Battalion reinforcements'.[29] The quality of this unit can be imagined— the Army Service Corps were known as 'the Galloping Grocers'.[30] Two days later Bennett raised 'X' Battalion, also manned by 'spare men and reinforcements'.[31]

The Australians complained to Malaya Command concerning the allotment of artillery rounds. The daily expenditure of ammunition was restricted to twelve rounds for each 25-pounder gun, 29 per 4.5-inch howitzer, and 25 for each eighteen-pounder gun.[32] Colonel Thyer, Bennett's GSO1, would later record that:

Representations were made to HQ Malaya Command that these allotments were inadequate. However, the instructions were repeated and further restrictions imposed to the extent that the allotment only applied to guns actually fired during the 24 hour period, allotments were not transferable from gun to gun within a regiment and were not cumulative. A 'silent' policy which provided that guns were not to fire from their main positions except in the event of an attack, meant that the daily expenditure of ammunition on the front of any sector was again drastically reduced.[33]

The employment of the artillery support for the defence of the north shore would prove a controversial one, particularly in light of the fact that General Yamashita's 25th Army actually possessed less artillery than Malaya

Command. Further, those guns were restricted to 1000 rounds per field gun and 500 for each heavy gun—less than Singapore's stocks.[34]

With the resources at his disposal, General Percival's plan for the defence of Singapore Island was severely flawed. In effect, he sought to cover all contingencies and in the end covered none. Wavell would later tell General Brooke that the defence of Singapore required a leader who was a 'really vigorous, ruthless personality . . .' and that he had sought one 'but could not see him'.[35] What would this 'vigorous, ruthless personality' have done?

First he would not have needed Wavell to repeatedly order him to fortify the north shore of Singapore Island. We have discussed the complete and utter failure by Percival to employ the Chief Engineer during the fighting in Malaya. There can be no excuse for Simson not having been rapidly employed on the north shore of Singapore Island from late December 1941 onwards. Any defensive locality needs depth, secure flanks, a mobile reserve, and critically, a forward killing ground. The geography of the Island presented the commander with relatively secure flanks (the eastern and western coastline) and the Johore Strait was a natural killing ground. The Chief Engineer had proposed 'underwater obstacles, mines, petrol fire traps, anchored but floating barbed wire, and methods of illuminating the water at night'.[36] Simson has recorded that the necessary barbed wire and mines were available, and there was no shortage of abandoned petrol supplies at the naval base or airfields. To provide depth to the defences, he had advocated mutually supporting wired trenches, switch lines and pillboxes. We have already discussed the labour supply problems on the Malay Peninsula and the Island. The complete incompetence in marshalling, prioritising and supervising that labour is best illustrated by Colonel Thyer's description of events on the Jurong Line as late as February 1942:

> . . . it was ascertained that a plan for the construction of a series of defence works on this line had been produced and a contract had been let to a Chinese contractor. Work was proceeding in a leisurely peacetime manner. Some difficulties were being encountered in providing the coolies with meals, but the greatest problem was to keep them at work. At the first sight of a group of enemy aircraft, the gangs would disperse, some returned hours later, some not at all.[37]

A really 'ruthless, vigorous' commander would not have 'tendered' work to contractors—he would have quite simply declared martial law and press-ganged a labour supply; he would not have tolerated work at 'a leisurely' pace; he would not have endured difficulties with meal supplies, and his orders for the military supervision of labour would have been totally unforgiving.

The second critical question was the numerical paucity of defenders across the north coast—particularly Taylor's 22nd Brigade front—and the threadbare reserve. Warren (2002) has provided us with the simple answer: Percival was 'unwilling to take a risk in any sector . . .'[38] Wavell's 'vigorous' commander would have denuded his southern area of at least its British battalions (the Loyals, the Manchesters and the Gordons) and used them to strengthen his north coast and reserve. Further, as the Manchesters were a machine gun battalion, their firepower across the Johore Strait killing ground might have proved invaluable. Whilst splitting formations is always undesirable, Percival had done it repeatedly during the Malayan Campaign. Although ABDA Command Intelligence had discovered a Japanese convoy en route to the Anambas Islands on 4 February, and Percival had worried whether it might be eventually heading for Singapore, intelligence soon correctly ascertained that this convoy was Sumatra bound. There are always calculated risks involved in high command decisions, but the 'ruthless, vigorous' commander takes them. Malaya Command's only chance to induce a prolonged siege relied on its ability to inflict telling casualties on the enemy as he formed up to attack, then as he crossed the Johore Strait killing ground and, finally, to be able to withdraw to strong defensive positions in depth. Percival had a capable chief engineer and yet again had failed to employ him.

'Cometh the hour cometh the man.' The hour had long been predicted and had now come—but a 'really vigorous, ruthless personality' had not.

———⊷⊶———

Before the war the Japanese had identified the north-west coast of Singapore as the best landing site. They had done so for three reasons. The first was that the mangrove-covered western coastline concealed the rubber estate and river assembly areas for troops, landing craft and artillery. Second, the Johore Strait was at its narrowest along this western side and therefore diminished the British killing ground and, hopefully, as a consequence, heavy Japanese casualties in its crossing. Third, the Japanese believed that Malaya Command would use the Jurong Line as its prime defensive locality and, because of the multitude of rivers and mangroves in the area, it would only man the north-west coast with small outposts.

General Yamashita allowed a mere week for his concentration of men and material for the attack upon Singapore. He planned that his 18th and 5th Divisions were to concentrate at the River Skudai and commit sixteen of their battalions to the main attack with a further five in reserve. This highly trained, aggressive and well-led striking force was to be faced by Brigadier Taylor's 22nd Brigade AIF, hopelessly dispersed and, in the case of the 2/19th Battalion, way below its former fighting proficiency. Yamashita deployed his Guards Division to the east of the causeway at the River Tebrau, where it was to stage a feint, to be followed by a secondary attack. The feint involved the occupation of the island of Pulau Ubin, constant vehicle activity in the area and concentrated artillery fire upon Heath's east coast positions. This ruse would have fortified Percival's conviction that the attack was to be staged on the north-east coast.

On 4 February 1942, the Japanese began artillery barrages upon the Island. Any chance Malaya Command had of contesting the enemy build-up was hampered by a decided lack of decent intelligence and the stringent ration-ing of the defenders' artillery ammunition. But on the night of 6 February, two patrols departed from Brigadier Taylor's west coast sector. The first was undertaken by the 2/19th's Lieutenant Dal Ottley, Sergeant Dempsey and Corporal Donnelly of B Company, who left at around 10.30 pm in a canoe, each armed only with a revolver and six rounds, one tin of bully beef and biscuits, and wearing sandshoes. Ottley's mission was ambitious, and in essence required him to reconnoitre from Kampong (village) Bahru, which lay directly across from the 2/19th perimeter, inland and then travel east-wards as far as the River Malayu. This stretch of the mainland coast covered the region opposite the 2/19th and 2/18th perimeters. In the process, his eastward inland recce was to involve a passage through four large estates to ascertain any enemy assembly areas and numbers of landing craft.[39] At about the same time, Lieutenant Homer and four men of the 2/20th Battalion also paddled across the Strait and performed the same task as Ottley from the

River Malayu eastwards to the River Skudai, thereby completing the stretch of coast opposite Taylor's Brigade.[40]

The results of the two patrols were impressive. Ottley reported large concentrations of enemy troops in three of the estates, provided map references of numerous gun emplacements, but saw only a few landing craft on the River Malayu. Homer's patrol likewise reported heavy rubber estate troop concentrations, gun emplacements, but, as Ottley had found, 'only moderate boat concentrations'.[41] It would seem that the two patrols' information was slowly absorbed and hardly acted upon. The 8th Division Diary records that it received 22nd Brigade's report at 11.50 pm on 7 February,[42] whilst Kirby claimed that Malaya Command did not receive this intelligence until 3.30 pm on the 8th[43]—nearly sixteen hours later. Warren (2002) has claimed that the intelligence 'was not adjudged to be of any special significance',[44] and quotes Thyer as stating postwar that: 'It did not, however, enter anybody's head to order harassing fire.'[45] Yet in his own report on operations Thyer wrote that:

> The gist of these reports [Ottley's and Homer's] were passed by 22 Bde to Western Area and by 2/15 Fd Regt to the CRA [Commander Royal Artillery]. The latter ordered the regiment to put down fire in the areas indicated. Later the CO 2/15 Regt reported back that the targets had been engaged to the satisfaction of 22 Bde.[46]

In the event, the response to the intelligence gathered by the two patrols would seem to have been poor—and no effort was made to tighten the pathetically thin 22nd Brigade defensive line. Within 24 hours, Lieutenant Ottley, the members of his patrol and Lieutenant Homer were killed in action. At around 10.00 am on 8 February 1942, the Japanese began a concentrated shelling of the 22nd Brigade's perimeter, which did not ease until 6.00 pm. The defenders might have expected that lull to have been followed by comparative quiet, but the Japanese launched a further barrage after sunset, the intensity of which was far greater than its predecessor. The invasion of Singapore was just hours away.

20

'I DREW MY MEN BACK . . .'

We have noted that in order to defend Singapore's north-west coast, Brigadier Taylor was forced to deploy each of his three 22nd Brigade battalions across a front approximately 4.8 kilometres wide, each with a platoon from the 4th Machine Gun Battalion in support. The 2/20th Battalion (Lieutenant-Colonel Assheton) was placed between the Rivers Kranji and Sarimbun with a company of Dalforce on its right flank; the 2/18th Battalion (Lieutenant-Colonel Varley) was deployed between the Rivers Sarimbun and Murai; and the 2/19th (Lieutenant-Colonel Anderson) was sited from the River Murai to the River Berih. Taylor's 22nd Brigade HQ was well placed just south of Ama Keng village.

General Yamashita chose the coastline between Cape Buloh and Cape Murai for his landings on the north-west coast. That he adhered to the principle of 'concentration of force' is an understatement. On his left flank, he planned to attack Lieutenant-Colonel Assheton's 2/20th Battalion with almost all of the nine battalions of his 5th Division. Of those nine battalions, six were to land around the River Sarimbun area. Yamashita ordered his 18th Division to land on the 2/18th and 2/19th fronts with a three-battalion left flank, and a four-battalion right flank attack.

It will be remembered that while Lieutenant Ottley's 2/19th and

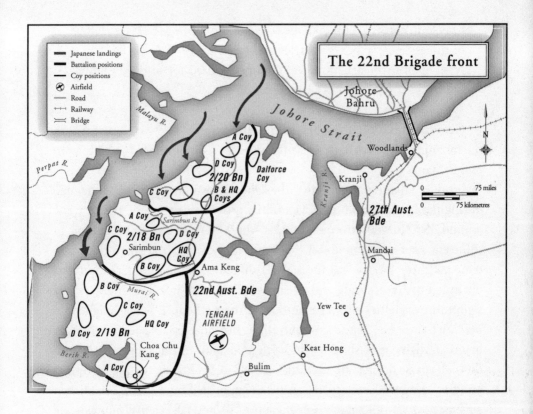

Lieutenant Homer's 2/20th recce patrols had identified numerous enemy assembly points and gun emplacements in the area opposite 22nd Brigade's coastline, they had not found extensive landing craft concentrations. In an effort to avoid detection, their likely landing points and therefore exposure to artillery fire, the Japanese 5th and 18th Divisions did not move their landing craft to the coast until 24 hours before the assault. Around 300 vessels, which consisted of motor launches, collapsible boats and pontoons, were to carry four waves of troops across the Strait. Lionel Wigmore:

> The collapsible boats, constructed of plywood with rubber joints and built in two sections, were capable of being assembled by one man in two minutes. Propelled by a 30 horsepower 2-cylinder outboard motor, each could carry twelve fully-equipped troops with a four man crew; linked together in threes they were capable of carrying field artillery pieces. Two types of pontoons were used. One, similar to but

heavier in construction than the collapsible boats, was linked together in threes to carry heavy vehicles and tanks up to 16 tons. The other type, of steel construction, was commonly used for bridge building, but could also be used as a landing craft.[1]

General Yamashita's two initial objectives were the Tengah airfield on the morning of 9 February, to be followed by a line extending south from Hill Panjang.

From a Japanese perspective the landings would be most vulnerable during the first critical hours. The initial problem was for the first wave—around 3500 to 4000 troops—to cross the Johore Strait killing ground in sufficient strength to establish a beachhead. Australian artillery fire upon their assembly points was the second difficulty. If that embarkation was disrupted by an accurate and intense shelling, the Japanese might expect significant casualties and a disruption to their schedule, which might well prejudice their beachhead concentration. But once established in strength before daylight, Yamashita would be in a position to stage a rapid advance through sparse defences to his initial Tengah airfield objective. A consequent build-up of tanks, artillery and vehicles, supported by his long-established air superiority, would surely see Singapore fall, and fall relatively quickly.

We now come to a tragic train of events. The potential for the Australians to contest the enemy crossing of the Johore Strait killing ground is the first issue. That defence hinged on three factors: the ability to provide obstacles on the Strait; the capability to illuminate the Strait so as to enfilade it with telling machine gun fire; and the artillery potential to disrupt the succeeding waves of invaders at their assembly and landing points.

The failure to utilise the Chief Engineer's expertise and available resources has been discussed. However, in a last-ditch effort to assist the north-west shore defences, Brigadier Simson had sent barrels of petrol to be used on the mangrove coastline and at river and creek mouths, which could be set off electronically or by tracer fire. In addition, he had sent 'underwater obstacles, floating logs with barbed wire and car headlamps to illuminate the shore . . .'.[2]. When Malaya Command discovered Simson's initiative, orders were given for the transfer of those commodities to the north-east coast where they were 'only partially installed'.[3] Ever the masters of knee-jerk, belated and piecemeal response, Malaya Command, 'at the last moment',[4] ordered them moved back to Taylor's sector. In the end, those measures were successfully employed in neither sector.

The ability to see the enemy during his approach, and therefore employ accurate machine gun fire across the Strait and also to exploit the limited water obstacles, was dependent upon the available searchlights, headlights, artillery star shells and flares. Brigadier Taylor's available searchlights were manned by the British 5th Searchlight Regiment. He delegated the authorisation for their use to the battalion commanders on each sector of his front, but in so doing, ordered that it would be 'better to reserve their use for actual emergency, when they should operate, as would artillery, on the signal for defensive fire being given'.[5] Taylor's reasons for this decision were that sufficient time had not been given for their protection, and that in due course, they would be shot out. Despite the fact that only one light was destroyed by enemy fire before the landings, the remainder failed to be employed, 'perhaps' Wigmore thought, 'because of misunderstanding or confusion . . .'.[6]. Further, the problem of illuminating the Strait was compounded by the fact that the 2/15th Field Regiment would later record that there was an absence of star shells.[7] Searchlights that fail to be used due to 'misunderstanding or confusion' and a lack of artillery star shells seem poor excuses for such a critical failure. Surely any heavy enemy artillery fire might have caused the lights to be switched on—at any price. Further, there seems little evidence as to why more flares were not used along that coastline, as any form of illumination would have greatly aided the machine gunners of the 2/4th Machine Gun Battalion and those of individual units. Warren has claimed that '. . . the idea that a handful of searchlights could have been profitably exposed in the face of the automatic weapons of a two division assault was always fanciful'.[8] The fact remains that some light for some time from a unit stationed along the coast for that very purpose would have been of assistance in killing the enemy at his most vulnerable time: crossing the Johore Strait. When a significant defensive tool is available it should be used.

If the 22nd Brigade's massive front was hopelessly undermanned, if its intelligence was both poor and late, if its artillery was foolishly rationed, if its water obstacles were almost non-existent and the attempts to light the Strait pitiable, then the recurring problem of communication experienced on the mainland was beyond description. Although the Brigade's wireless sets had just been returned after servicing, they yet again failed to work, especially during darkness. As on the Malay Peninsula, the dense vegetation prevented signallers having a clear line of sight and without it the sets were of little use. Communication between companies, to Battalion HQ, and then to Brigadier Taylor's HQ was by signal cable, runner, and further back, by motor cycle. Lieutenant-Colonel Varley, CO, 2/18th Battalion:

> Despite the abnormally high rate of shelling the casualties in the Bn were light due to the fact that it had been impressed on all ranks the necessity for the construction of slit trenches holding one or two men and all ranks provided themselves with this cover . . . Signal comn was severed, faithfully repaired by linesmen and severed again . . .[9]

Varley recorded that the Japanese artillery barrage during 8 February was heavier than any he had experienced during his entire First World War experience—including Pozieres. But while that barrage caused few casualties (probably because of the soft soil in which the mangroves grew), it continuously disrupted communications and added to Taylor and his battalion commanders' 'fog of war'.

If the above-mentioned defensive deficiencies were critical, then General Bennett compounded the problem by a poor command decision just prior to the Japanese landings. At 7.30 am on the morning of 8 February 1942, the 2/19th's CO, Lieutenant-Colonel Charles Anderson, was ordered to hospital suffering from acute dysentery. General Bennett replaced Anderson, against the latter's advice, with Lieutenant-Colonel Robertson (the former second-in-command of the 2/20th), who had only recently been promoted to command the newly formed Special Reserve Battalion. The 2/19th Unit History:

> Why was not Tom Vincent [the 2/19th Battalion 2/ic] given command of the Battalion? He knew all and everything about the Battalion defensive position; he knew of Colonel Anderson's plans and methods and was highly respected and known by all ranks, and had proved himself capable of fighting and handling the Battalion at Muar . . .

This was not meant to be against Lieut. Col. Robertson, but in all fairness he did not know the area; he did not know the Battalion, and above all the members of the Battalion knew this.[10]

Although Lieutenant-Colonel Robertson was senior to Major Vincent, Bennett had previously promoted Maxwell to command the 27th Brigade despite the fact that Galleghan was his senior—seniority should not have been an issue.

In the event of a Japanese breakthrough at any given 22nd Brigade Battalion perimeter, Taylor had ordered that platoons cut off should withdraw to their company HQ, and if necessary, cut-off companies to their Battalion HQ. The relevant HQ locations were known and the moves had been rehearsed, particularly at night. Kirby has criticised Taylor for this decision,[11] but in the absence of a series of prepared withdrawal lines (a Malaya Command bungle), it was a fair plan. Percival's edict that cut-off formations, however small, were to fight on and await reserve counterattack(s) was fanciful. Senior Australian commanders pondered the obvious: what reserve, in what strength and from where?

Given the above withdrawal tactic, Robertson committed a terrible error on the very day of the Japanese landing. After a recce of the 2/19th perimeter, and during a heavy enemy bombardment of the battalion area (particularly Battalion HQ), he was of the opinion that 'it would be best to move the Battalion HQ later in the day in the darkness in order to obtain some relief and to retain some control'.[12] Despite the fact that the 2/19th's senior officers 'heatedly and vehemently'[13] protested, Robertson confirmed his order. The move of Battalion HQ—and the consequent drain upon the signals' personnel, and their time and equipment—was destined to be undertaken only hours before the enemy landing. Both the duration and intensity of the enemy shelling and bombing should have been reason enough for Robertson to have realised that this was no time to be making such a move—an enemy landing must be close.

———— ⋙⋘ ————

The Japanese soldiers who came in that first wave across the Johore Strait must have felt extremely vulnerable travelling in collapsible plywood boats

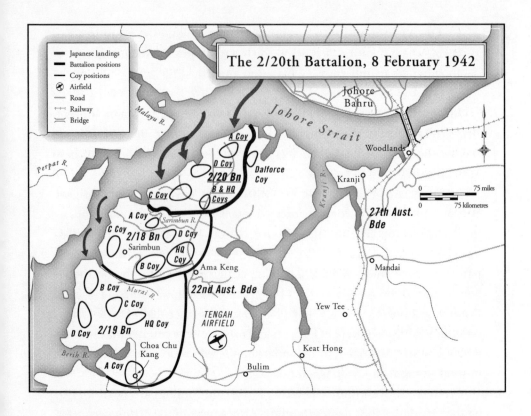

The 2/20th Battalion, 8 February 1942

across what they believed would be an illuminated killing ground into a withering hail of machine gun and artillery fire.

D and C Companies of the 2/20th Battalion occupied key positions at, and around, the two branches of the Lim Chu Kang Road, which ran almost to the coast. Captain Richardson's D Company was supported at the eastern track shoreline by three guns of Lieutenant Eric Wankey's 13 Platoon, 2/4th Machine Gun Battalion. The guns were sited along a 100-metre stone retaining wall, which had a small jetty and sun shelter at its end. Apart from the machine gun pits, the soldiers of the 2/4th had buckets of grenades in anticipation of any enemy concentration at and around the jetty.[14]

At about 10.30 pm, soldiers of Richardson's D Company and Wankey's machine gunners, peering through 'a little light coming from the reflection of the burning oil tanks at Kranji',[15] saw the dark shapes of incoming barges. Wankey counted at least twenty craft approaching the jetty area. The Australians waited until the barges were within about 40 metres.

Caught in that intense fire a number were sunk, others capsized, and their former occupants subjected to a further hail of machine gun and small arms fire as they floundered in the water. As the Japanese gained the jetty and shore around the embankment they were met by a stream of grenades lobbed into their craft and along the beach. Those enemy losses were quickly increased when a barge carrying explosives caught fire and illuminated other approaching craft. But the Japanese barges kept coming, and when they tethered one of their number to a fish trap off shore and set up a mortar, telling fire was returned onto the machine gunners, who began to take casualties.

About 30 minutes into the battle Lieutenant Wankey and Private Loller took over one of the guns amidst that enemy mortar fire. Soon after, both men had one of their legs wounded by a mortar. Wankey refused to be evacuated and, propped up against a tree, continued to direct the three guns' fire.[16] Both Wankey and Loller later had their wounded leg amputated. Although the fighting often became hand-to-hand, Richardson's D Company soldiers, ably assisted by the machine gunners, gamely held their ground during the ensuing three hours' fighting. But while that dim light and then the hit to the explosives barge had provided an effective localised killing ground, successive craft were eventually able to pinpoint gaps in the coastline from which fire was not forthcoming and, landing virtually unopposed at these points, the attackers began to infiltrate inland.

By around 1.30 am Lieutenant Wankey's machine gunners had expended about 10 000 rounds from each machine gun and, nearly out of ammunition and with clear evidence of having been outflanked, they destroyed their guns, were reorganised into a rifle platoon and withdrew. They managed to carry Wankey, Loller and their remaining wounded out to a truck.[17]

Others in that perimeter were less fortunate. When his soldiers' ammunition began to dwindle Richardson withdrew them to the airstrip behind his perimeter. That withdrawal became a series of confused hand-to-hand struggles conducted with the grenade, rifle and bayonet. Those of D Company and the machine gunners who had survived that ordeal arrived at the airstrip to be reinforced by three carriers and a reserve platoon. At around 5.30 am Lieutenant-Colonel Assheton ordered the reinforcements to withdraw to help form a battalion perimeter. That order did not reach Richardson.

Away to the west C Company occupied about 1800 metres of coastline running up to the River Sarimbun, the boundary between the 2/20th and 2/18th Battalions. The great distances between platoons, the enemy mortar fire brought down on them from nearby Sarimbun Island and limited visibility and fields of fire in that thick vegetation enabled the Japanese to rapidly infiltrate the perimeter. When contact was lost with company HQ, the withdrawal of the C Company platoons became a scattered collection of soldiers each making their way back to Battalion HQ by 'God and by compass'.

While the fighting along that lengthy D and C Company coastline had been intense, confused, and had then caused the Australians to be broken up into isolated groups, Captain Merritt's A Company and the Dalforce Company away to the east had had a relatively quiet time. When Assheton ordered the withdrawal of his D and C Companies, Merritt was also ordered to move back to the Battalion perimeter. An example of such a movement and its ensuing confusion in that terrain and darkness—which must surely have been repeated elsewhere—occurred when some A Company troops encountered a number of Chinese soldiers from Dalforce. These men, unable to converse in English, were shot.[18]

If any evidence as to the success, size and rapid build-up of the Japanese landing and resultant infiltration of the 2/20th perimeter was needed, it came with the experience of Sergeant Shelly's reserve B Company patrol which moved to the gap between the forward D and A Companies. Sergeant Shelly would later recall that: 'There must have been a couple of battalions, landing craft were locked together and the men were jumping from barge to barge and forming up in company groups on the shore.'[19]

During the early hours of 9 February 1942, the exhausted 2/20th Battalion and its Dalforce remnant—less Richardson's D Company—made their way back to Assheton's Battalion perimeter, which was located about one and a half kilometres inland astride the Lim Chu Kang Road. Richardson's men stayed until about 10.30 am on the 9th, before finally receiving the order to withdraw to the Battalion HQ perimeter. We shall return to their fate.

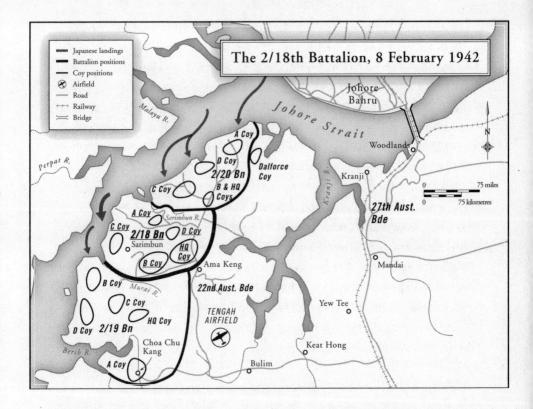

The central sector of the 22nd Brigade's front was held by Lieutenant-Colonel Varley's 2/18th Battalion. Two of Varley's companies each with two platoons forward on the coast, and one in reserve, were deployed across this vital coastal ground. Captain Johnstone's A Company was sited on the right flank just west of the River Sarimbun, while Captain Okey's C Company formed the left flank. Both forward positions were on difficult ground. Two of Johnstones platoons occupied the 'high ground'—'high' when tidal islands were caused by each incoming tide. Okey's ground was a maze of rises and tidal inlets. Varley deployed Major O'Brien's B Company to the rear to guard a road junction that led both into the 2/18th perimeter to the north-east and into the left flank of the 2/19th perimeter. Captain Chisholm's D Company was deployed at Battalion HQ as the unit reserve. The inhibiting common denominator throughout Varley's ground was the vegetation, which consisted of a mixture of rubber, tidal mangrove and scrub. In the 2/18th perimeter therefore, the defenders were handicapped by poor vision across a very wide but thinly held perimeter, while the Japanese were in a position to use the numerous inlets and cover. Varley's C Company in particular was always going to be heavily reliant upon accurate artillery support.

At about 10.30 pm A Company's 7 and 8 Platoons, each sited on a tidal island, were assaulted. When two enemy motor launches landed around 80 men onto Lieutenant Vernon's 8 Platoon 'island' position the Australians either killed or dispersed them. Lieutenant-Colonel Varley:

> They were then subjected to heavy mortar fire which caused thirteen casualties in the platoon and were again attacked by a fresh force ... eventually under weight of numbers [they] were forced to withdraw over the River Hantu and mangrove marshes on its banks while the river was at high tide. Some men were unable to swim and wounded men were on their hands, however by joining rifle slings they managed to get across and take their wounded with them, several trips being made by the platoon commander [Lieutenant Vernon] with the wounded.[20]

Lieutenant Richardson's 7 Platoon (no relation to Captain Richardson in the 2/20th), which was deployed on the second tidal island, was bypassed on both flanks, but remained in its perimeter during that night and the following day. When the defenders withdrew at daybreak, the battle had swept well past them and only small parties managed to regain their lines.[21]

On Varley's C Company front the Japanese, although taking heavy casualties in front of 15 Platoon's hill position, were able to both infiltrate around, and bring repeated pressure upon, the Australians' posts. As that pressure intensified Captain Okey gave the order to withdraw. During that movement 15 Platoon remained relatively intact, and later made the reserve lines of Captain Chisholm's D Company near Battalion HQ, but the remaining members of the company became 'split up in the darkness, amid hills, swamp and jungle, and under attack'.[22] Despite the fact that the soldiers of the 2/18th fought with great courage and persistence that night, the darkness, the difficulty of movement in that vegetation, and most of all, the isolated nature of the Battalion platoons and sections made it impossible to prevent outflanking and eventual withdrawal. And in that darkness, with the enemy on their heels, platoons became splintered and disorientated, and command control impossible. During the early hours of 9 February Varley withdrew his 2/18th Battalion into a defensive perimeter around the village of Ama Keng. When the remnants of A and C Companies reached his HQ—now numbering seven officers and 81 other ranks between them— Varley immediately deployed them 'on a rise west of the Lim Chu Kang road',[23] while D Company was sited to cover the northern approach to Ama Keng. O'Brien's B Company had been broken up during its movement back from the Battalion's left flank. In a stroke of luck, the greatly diminished 2/18th Battalion's perimeter was strengthened by the employment of around 200 engineers from the 2/10th Field Company.

Of the three 22nd Brigade battalions defending that north-west coast, the 2/19th was now, without doubt, the least qualified. With its dynamic commander hospitalised on 8 February, and both its other ranks and officer establishment massively reinforced by often ill-trained and therefore inexperienced soldiers, that magnificent battalion of Bakri and Muar fame was now the same unit in name only.

Captain Keegan's B Company and a HQ Platoon were disposed on the right flank on the coast near the River Murai, which separated the 2/19th and 2/18th Battalion perimeters. The right flank was manned by Captain Vincent's D Company, while Captain Thomas and his C Company formed the Battalion reserve just west of Lieutenant-Colonel Robertson's Battalion HQ. The 2/19th's left flank bordered the River Berih, which also separated the 22nd Brigade sector from Brigadier Ballentine's 44th Indian Brigade. That river was an obvious Japanese landing site, since from the village of Choa Chu Kang, which lay behind it, an enemy force might use the road from the village to gain access to the Tengah airfield. From that feature, the same road would provide speedy access to the villages of Bulim and Keat Hong, and then the vital causeway road at Panjang village. It will be remembered that the airfield and a line extending south-west from Panjang village were Yamashita's first two objectives. As a response to this threat, Anderson had deployed Captain Cousens's A Company at Choa Chu Kang village. To further bolster this crucial 2/19th sector, the 2/15th Field Regiment

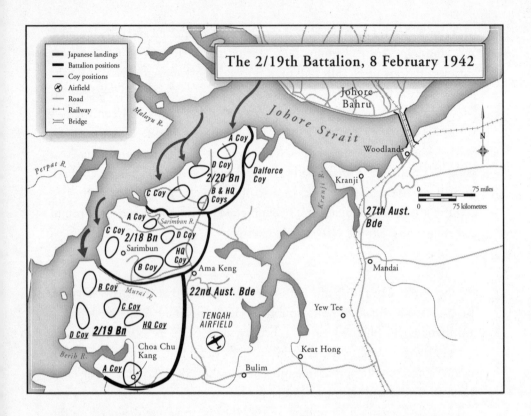

The 2/19th Battalion, 8 February 1942

Legend:
- Japanese landings
- Battalion positions
- Coy positions
- Airfield
- Road
- Railway
- Bridge

had registered the area and it contained more machine guns than any other 22nd Brigade perimeter.

As had occurred elsewhere along the north-west coast that night, the Japanese landed in great force at their chosen locations. In the case of the 2/19th, a promontory in the northern part of Captain Keegan's B Company was the chosen point. At around 10.30 pm, Keegan's soldiers saw many 'little dots'[24] heading towards them which gradually materialised into 50 barges, some driven by chugging engines, some in tow, and others being rowed.[25] Keegan's men shot red Verey flares requesting artillery support and white flares to illuminate the enemy approach. The former were not seen at the rearward relay point, but the latter must have been of some use, however temporary.

When the enemy landed close to the B Company defenders and were therefore seen, they took heavy casualties, but a systematic bypassing of the Australians transpired over their long and thinly held perimeter. Although

Keegan's company managed to hold its ground, the Japanese moved down the River Murai in strength. In an effort to contest that thrust, most of Captain Thomas's C Company were ordered to move up to its headwaters. Thomas's patrols soon reported that the enemy were outflanking the Battalion and moving in strength on Ama Keng. Private Ron Stanton was a reinforcement with C Company:

> When we went forward we went through rubber and then scrub . . . the Japs were coming through and they were making a hell of a noise. You see most of the problem was, you'd be holding the Japs and then you'd find that they'd gone around you somewhere . . . we were cut off, cut off a few times.[26]

At around 3.00 am on the 9th, with his company still under attack and having taken heavy casualties, Keegan ordered it to withdraw to the Battalion HQ perimeter. Thomas's C Company was also ordered out. While B and C Companies had been thus heavily engaged, Captain Vincent's D Company had experienced a relatively quiet time. But when it too was ordered to withdraw, two of its platoons were cut off on their way back to the Battalion perimeter. In an interview with the author, Sergeant Bert Donaldson, an original of D Company, noted the confusion of the withdrawal in that pitch-black darkness, and the lack of training of some of the reinforcement officers:

> . . . I didn't see them [the Japanese] coming, or landing, they'd already landed . . . we were told to withdraw and we were heading back to Company HQ . . . I got to company HQ and there were four or five blokes including Lieutenant Furner standing in a group, no doubt discussing the situation, what they had to do. And the bullets were starting to fly around, this is how much they knew . . . and I came along and said, 'Don't just bloody stand there keep moving!' . . . as soon as I sang out, bang I got hit and they opened up on these blokes that were standing in a group . . . I brought Lieutenant Furner out who was also wounded . . . through the chest and he was spitting blood.[27]

By the onset of daylight on 9 February 1942, Brigadier Taylor's 22nd Brigade had been subjected to a crushing assault in overwhelming strength on the north-west coast, which had seen it rapidly infiltrated and dispersed into often confused, scattered parties.

We left Lieutenant-Colonel Assheton's 2/20th Battalion remnant in its Battalion HQ perimeter about one and a half kilometres inland astride the Lim Chu Kang Road. At daylight its soldiers saw Japanese forward of their perimeter moving across that road in strength towards the east. In an effort to assist Captain Richardson's D Company to regain the perimeter, Assheton ordered a mortar barrage and a platoon-strength attack. But by around 9.15 am, with a further enemy crossing of the road south of his perimeter and also with their strength increasing, Assheton ordered his men to withdraw to Ama Keng village, with the intent of linking up with Varley and his 2/18th Battalion.

While moving to a position on the 2/20th's left flank, Captain Ewart's B Company was ambushed, which saw the Battalion intelligence officer killed and Ewart wounded. After Lieutenant Cornforth's A Company platoon had attacked and eliminated those Japanese, Cornforth's men and the B Company remnant pressed on only to find themselves immersed in another fight against the Japanese occupying their objective. The Australians took further casualties. In the confused and desperate fighting which then ensued, Major Merritt's A Company rearguard (less Cornforth's platoon) held its ground until around 10.00 am, when as last out, it came under intense enemy machine gun fire from its rear, which caused it to break up into small parties. Cornforth's platoon meanwhile was joined by Lieutenant-Colonel Assheton and also withdrew. This 2/20th remnant was now ordered by the CO to traverse the swamp country around the River Kranji and attempt to gain Australian lines. In that process, Lieutenant-Colonel Assheton was killed and the party were broken up and scattered, eventually reaching Bukit Panjang village.

We left Captain Richardson's D Company, 2/20th Battalion still in its positions after having failed to receive Assheton's earlier order to withdraw to Battalion HQ. When Richardson finally received the order at around 10.30 am on 9 February, his men, accompanied by Lieutenant Wankey's machine gunners, did in fact gain that perimeter only to find its only occupants long dead. Moving southwards, Richardson's men reached the River Kankar 'and ran into a party of Japs who were up trees and lying in the undergrowth'.[28] The resulting fight saw the party split into two groups, one consisting of Captain Richardson, his HQ and a part of a platoon which went to the west, while the other (without officers) broke to the east. Richardson's soldiers crossed the river at its shallow point, despite taking casualties in the process, while the second party suffered the mixed fortune of the strong swimmers assisting the less competent (one or two still drowned), while others had to abandon their packs and weapons to cross.

The 2/20th Battalion's fighting on its north-west coast perimeter had been against impossible odds, as the greatest concentration of enemy troops had landed on their perimeter. After inflicting telling casualties upon the Japanese—with the sterling assistance of the 2/4th Machine Gun detachment—the 2/20th had been broken up, had lost its command control and had been forced to traverse country that caused many within it to have great difficulties in navigation.

While the 2/20th were thus engaged during the early hours of 9 February, it will be recalled that Lieutenant-Colonel Varley's 2/18th Battalion had formed a partially occupied battalion perimeter north of Ama Keng to offer a staging point for its incoming troops. Varley then gave orders for his second-in-command to withdraw his HQ to the southern outskirts of Ama Keng, while he went to Taylor's Brigade HQ to report in. Lieutenant-Colonel Varley:

It was after . . . returning to Bn HQ position, about 20 minutes later, that firing was heard where the enemy had made contact with A Coy and this firing increased as time went on. Simultaneously Major Davis who was acting as Bn 2/ic . . . with Captain Hence, Adjutant, contacted [the] Brigade Commander while establishing Battalion HQ and in the subsequent discussion understood that he was ordered . . . to move Battalion HQ and its personnel . . . to the NW corner of Tengah Aerodrome about 2000 yds further back. This plan was carried out unbeknown to me. I was at this time at Ama Keng village. There was apparently a misunderstanding of the Brigade Commander's instructions and orders . . . I found myself . . . with about 25 men . . . and therefore not sufficient men to hold this portion of the perimeter should an attack against us be made.[29]

Varley's B Company, now greatly under strength, found itself repeatedly in contact with enemy parties. It was unable to reach Battalion HQ, moved off and reached Bukit Timah village without contacting any 22nd Brigade personnel. Incredibly, those luckless soldiers were then gathered in by 'Admin personnel' and driven by truck convoy to the General Base Depot. The remainder of the Battalion were then ordered by Brigadier Taylor back to Tengah airfield and thence to the village of Bulim. In this move the 2/10th Field Company performed magnificently in an infantry support role, which facilitated the 2/18th's withdrawal. Varley's exhausted Battalion had paid a horrendous price for its unequal battle. After less than 24 hours' fighting it now numbered slightly less than half its original strength in both officers and other ranks.

The story of the 2/20th and 2/18th Battalions' withdrawal from Singapore's north-west coast is tragic enough, but the 2/19th's passage out was also a terrible ordeal. We left those soldiers in a battalion perimeter in the early hours of 9 February.

When Captain Vincent's D Company had made its way out of its left flank perimeter to join the remainder of the Battalion at its HQ, its attached 16 Platoon of the 2/4th Machine Gun Battalion, deployed at the water's edge, had great difficulty withdrawing. After destroying their guns they found Vincent's Company HQ deserted and set off through enemy-held territory in small groups. Of the 25 members of the platoon, ten were later listed as killed or missing, and six of the remaining fifteen were wounded.[30]

At around daylight it became clear to Lieutenant-Colonel Robertson that the new Battalion perimeter around his HQ was surrounded. He determined that the only chance the Battalion had was to force a breakthrough towards Tengah. He hoped to achieve this by infantry attacks to the north, east and west sides of the perimeter to gain time and space for his carriers to force an escape route. This would be used by four trucks and two ambulances carrying the critically wounded. It was a forlorn hope—the Japanese had aircraft support, were in strength on an extended ridge covering the main track to the road to Tengah and had concentrated artillery and mortar fire

cover of that feature. Robertson hoped that once the pressure upon the perimeter had been eased by the infantry attacks and a penetration of the main enemy ridge position was completed, the carriers and trucks would be able to burst through any further 'isolated' enemy positions. The folly of Lieutenant-Colonel Robertson's earlier move to shift his Battalion HQ just before the enemy landing was now cruelly exposed—the very ridge occupied by the Japanese was, in fact, the site of Anderson's original Battalion HQ. Anderson had chosen it carefully because it dominated the area, and as such was ideally suited as the Battalion rendezvous point, and as the obvious line of withdrawal. Anderson had chosen it for all the right reasons, and Robertson had abandoned it for all the wrong ones.

The attack went in at about 7.00 am. Although the infantry gained some ground the cost was high. And when the vehicle column moved out, Japanese air strafing, artillery, mortar and small arms fire disabled the lead carrier just as it reached the crest of the ridge, and its occupants were unable to make ground. In scenes reminiscent of Anderson column's withdrawal to Parit Sulong, the trucks were hit, and a number of their wounded occupants, keen to assist, took up arms and joined in. Amongst them was Lieutenant Dal Ottley, who had undertaken the recce of the mainland on 7 January. His body and many of the wounded from the trucks were found a month later by work parties of Australian POWs. Despite the fact that Sergeant Parramore in the disabled lead carrier continued to fire onto the enemy ridge positions, the Japanese set up a series of roadblocks to the 2/19th rear, and with Parramore now cut off at the front, the position was hopeless. When Major Lloyd Hughes saw Parramore and his carrier troops become pinned down and cut off, he gathered twenty men from HQ Company and attacked. After gaining the ridge he was 'struck by a machine gun burst, killing him instantly'.[31] The 2/19th had lost one of its favourite sons.

Within an hour of that brave but futile action, and with the enemy in such strength to the front on the ridges and in possession of the rear tracks, Robertson decided to attempt to force an escape passage along the rearward swamp line, cross the River Berih and push through to Brigade HQ. Just as this movement was under way, around 50 Japanese broke through the perimeter. Although most were eliminated, a couple found cover and poured telling fire at the Australians. The 2/19th Unit History would later record that:

Major Tom Vincent had about twenty men with him nearby, and they immediately rushed towards the Japanese. They had to cross a small rise in the ground, and as they went forward Major Vincent caught a full blast from one of the enemy light automatics and fell. The remainder of the Japanese were speedily disposed of, but it was one of our worst moments to see Tom Vincent fall.[32]

The story of those 2/19th Battalion parties that were able to escape their perimeter during the morning of 9 February is one of a slow, laborious passage through the swamp line, assisting their walking wounded, and in the process, being further broken up and scattered. Sergeant Parramore and a couple of his comrades, still cut off at the front stayed, fought, and perished. About a hundred of the Battalion's badly wounded and those unable to walk were left in the care of the Battalion doctor, Captain Shale and two orderlies. They were not seen again. The 2/19th Battalion estimated its losses at ten officers and 259 other ranks 'plus the many wounded never recorded, and the missing'.[33] Given that Captain Cousens's A Company had only sustained eight wounded during the Japanese air and artillery bombardments at their Choa Chu Kang village perimeter and had made good their withdrawal from that venue, the 2/19th losses on the coast were very heavy for the three companies committed.

In about twelve hours Brigadier Taylor's 22nd Brigade AIF had been cut to ribbons and virtually destroyed as a cohesive fighting force.

We now come to the onset of arguably the most controversial issue in the fall of Singapore: stragglers. In his *Operations of 8 Australian Division in Malaya, 1941–1942*, Colonel Jim Thyer, Bennett's GSO1, wrote that:

It is important to record that about this time [during the morning of 9 February] a most disturbing report was received at HQ Malaya Command to the effect that there were 2000 AIF troops in Singapore. The Staff Captain of 22 Australian Infantry Brigade was dispatched with transport to collect these men and transfer them to their units. Some stragglers were found, but the number originally stated seems an exaggeration. A check of units ascertained that all the artillery, signals and engineers were still at their posts, the 27 Brigade was intact,

Brigadier Taylor still had 300 men of his Brigade with him and 700 men driven out at the landings were at the base depot being re-clothed and re-armed. Some of these had in the first instance been collected in the streets of the city. Nevertheless, there were many fighting men, Australians, British and Indians wandering around the docks attempting to board ships, when their place was at the front.

It was subsequently learnt from the Provost Marshal at Singapore that although there were many troops seeking safety and means of escape, the bulk of the men were stragglers who had come back looking for food and rest.[34]

The term 'straggler' is an ambiguous one, because it is used to describe four distinctly different types of soldiers not with their unit. The first is the soldier genuinely lost and attempting to rejoin his formation; the second applies to wounded men making their way to the rear; the third refers to a soldier who is separated from his unit and cannot be returned to it because of his mental rather than physical condition; but the term also includes a soldier who has no legitimate reason for being absent. In blunt terms, the last is a deserter.

Lieutenant-Colonel Pond had been the 27th Brigade's Brigade Major. Promoted to command of the 2/29th Battalion after Muar, he observed first hand this last category of 'stragglers':

... Indians and Australian tps [troops] were moving back through Bn position thus attracting attention from the air. These troops were quite out of control and leaderless and stated that they had had enough. CO [Pond] called on several parties to stop and occupy the line but they would not do so. Men were mainly from 2/19th and 2/20th Bns. One party of about 50 from 2/19th Bn was halted by the CO and it was found that an Offr [sic 'officer'] (whose name was not taken) was included in it. After great difficulty the party was persuaded to occupy a position but it ultimately vacated it.[35]

We have noted the tremendous performance of the 2/19th's survivors of Bakri and Parit Sulong only hours before on that north-west coast.

The men described above were obviously untrained reinforcements. And Pond's observation of 'Indians' as well as Australians is also significant. The Indians must have been 'stragglers' from the adjoining 44th Indian Brigade, who had seen very little action the previous night. It will be recalled that Brigadier Ballentine's very poorly trained 44th Indian Brigade had arrived at Singapore on 22 January, and the Australian reinforcements two days later. Further, although Lieutenant Wankey's machine gunners had fought bravely on Richardson's D Company 2/20th shoreline when the withdrawal to the airstrip occurred, six of their number 'became detached'.[36] Major Cough, 2/4th Machine Gun Battalion: 'In my opinion, becoming detached is a nice way of saying "they shot thru" . . .'[37] The point is that the six men described were members of Wankey's 13 Platoon who had fought tenaciously at the shoreline.[38] Clearly, they were not deserters. Here we have an example of the 'fog of war' in which there is a tendency to brand anyone who is lost, or cannot find a withdrawal point as a 'deserter'. In many instances, therefore, the term can constitute an unfair slight upon soldiers who are guilty of being nothing more than utterly confused. And Pond's 2/29th Battalion was soon to endure its own difficulties due to its massive reinforcements.

As the fighting on Singapore Island becomes ever more desperate over the next few days, the issue of 'stragglers' will become more pronounced and controversial.

It was not until around midnight on 8 February that Brigadier Taylor began to receive some idea of the magnitude, and success of, the Japanese landings on his 22nd Brigade front. He immediately contacted Bennett and requested fresh reserves to enable him to counterattack at dawn. Shortly after, Bennett ordered Lieutenant-Colonel Pond's 2/29th Battalion to move to Tengah airfield and placed it under Taylor's command; he further ordered the 2/10th Field Regiment to shell the obvious Japanese assembly point across the Strait at the River Skudai; he asked Malaya Command for air support at dawn; and, after ordering the Special Reserve Battalion—formed the day before and now under the command of Major Saggers—and the reserve company of the 2/4th Machine Gun Battalion to 'stand to' at 3.00 am on 9 February, he ordered both formations forward to Tengah airfield just over an hour later.

General Percival reacted to the extensive Japanese landings across Taylor's front at 8.30 am on 9 February. When he discovered that General Heath's Northern Area had not been attacked, he ordered Brigadier Paris's 12th Indian Brigade forward to the village of Keat Hong to come under Bennett's command. As had applied so often during the campaign the term 'brigade' is misleading. Percival was, in fact, committing little more than a battalion to the fight. After its dreadful losses at Slim River, the 5/2nd Punjabis had not yet rejoined their Brigade, and the Argylls and Hyderabads could muster but 900 officers and other ranks between them. Further, the 12th Indian Brigade was to be committed as the Malaya Command reserve without its standard artillery support.

Percival's infantry reserve was threadbare and the available air support was meagre. Early that morning, in response to Bennett's request, eight Hurricanes intercepted a force of around 80 enemy aircraft which were engaged in bombing and strafing over the Strait. After a hurried landing and refuelling, a second sortie was flown which resulted in Japanese losses of 'four destroyed, three probably destroyed and 13 damaged in the two flights',[39] for the loss of one plane. Although there was a desperate war being waged on the north-west coast and in the air, it appears that some personnel to the rear clung to old habits. One of the pilots recalled: 'We landed by a low-level run into the aerodrome at about 1150, and were rewarded by a severe warning from HQ for low flying during siesta period!'[40]

As the plight of his Brigade became clearer during the early morning of 9 February, Brigadier Taylor sought to establish a stop-line extending from the northern end of Tengah airfield to the village of Choa Chu Kang, where he might stabilise his front and subsequently stage a counterattack. With communication between himself and Western Area HQ sporadic, it was not until 9.30 am that a liaison officer from Bennett reached him with orders to counterattack and retake Ama Keng village, using Pond's 2/29th Battalion. Although Taylor, the 2/15th Field Regiment's Lieutenant-Colonel Wright and Pond went forward to plan that operation, it became impossible to implement when it was discovered that the Japanese were moving east of Tengah airfield. Wigmore has left us with a succinct summation of Taylor's plight:

... his two main problems were now to prevent the Japanese from getting around the airfield towards the Kranji-Jurong area, as yet unmanned; and to protect the right flank of the 44th Indian Brigade. He estimated that the Japanese could have landed twelve battalions. To meet such a situation he had at his disposal some 500 men of his own brigade; Pond's and Saggers' battalions; the Jind Battalion and the reserve company of the 2/4th Machine Gun Battalion—a force small in comparison, and one comprising units either hastily organized, in process of reorganization, or, in the case of the Jind, trained solely for airfield defence.[41]

At about 11.00 am Taylor decided to cancel the counterattack and form a westward line running from east of Tengah airfield through the village of Bulim and extending towards the Jurong Road. He sent his Brigade Major to inform both General Bennett and Brigadier Ballentine of his decision. Taylor's new line was in fact only just forward of the previously selected Jurong Line. We have noted that this line stretched from the lower waters of the River Kranji, southwards to the upper waters of the River Jurong, and therefore offered a shortened front with relatively secure flanks for any defensive operation. However, the point is that the Jurong Line was nothing more than a line on a map. It had not been prepared in any real way for defensive operations.

General Gordon Bennett did not go forward to Taylor nor any part of his front during 9 February. At around 2.30 pm his 8th Division staff suggested that the 22nd and 44th Brigades be withdrawn onto the Jurong Line before dark. Bennett refused. Not long afterwards when communications were restored to 22nd Brigade HQ, Bennett was informed by Taylor that he (Taylor) had ordered his Brigade to fall back to his chosen line running east of Tengah airfield through the village of Bulim and extending towards the Jurong Road. Bennett, according to Taylor, told him 'that I had acted without orders, that what I had done was quite wrong, and that all I could think of was withdrawing'.[42] Bennett was out of touch with Taylor's plight. Clearly he had two alternatives for effective command. The first was to go forward and communicate directly with Taylor and then issue orders, or to place his trust in him as the local commander on the spot. Having an aggressive attitude is one thing, but a part of the art of war is surely knowing when to instigate a sensible withdrawal, stabilise one's front and then counterattack if possible. Taylor was not at fault.

On the afternoon of 9 February, Percival further reacted to events in Taylor's sector by committing the 15th Indian Brigade (Colonel Coates) from the Northern Sector to Bennett's Western Area. He then ordered Bennett to occupy the roughly five-kilometre-long Jurong Line by withdrawing Ballentine's 44th Indian Brigade to its southern end and deploying Taylor's 22nd Brigade and the 12th and 15th Indian Brigades along it. Bennett would now have four brigades under command. Brigadier Taylor was instructed to hold Bulim until 6.00 am on the 10th and then withdraw to the central part of the Jurong Line. Percival further ordered Brigadier Maxwell's 27th Brigade AIF—where no landings had occurred—to stay put on the Western Area's vital Causeway Sector.

Brigadier Duncan Maxwell's 27th Brigade AIF had been deployed along the vital Causeway Sector of General Bennett's Western Area. The River Kranji— about 1100 metres wide at its mouth on the Johore Strait—formed a natural boundary between Maxwell's 27th Brigade and Taylor's 22nd, while a point about 800 metres east of the causeway separated Maxwell's perimeter from General Heath's Northern Area. The 27th Brigade, therefore, occupied a perimeter some three and a half kilometres long, which was roughly a quarter of the frontage of Taylor's coastline.

Maxwell had deployed his 2/26th Battalion running from a point approximately 900 metres north of Mandai village along the River Kranji and stretching eastwards about halfway along the coast towards the causeway. To counter the vast swamp areas within his perimeter, Lieutenant-Colonel Boyes sited his companies on patches of high ground 'with standing patrols and listening posts forward',[43] and put in train a coordinated plan for mutually supporting machine gun, mortar and artillery fire. The soldiers of the 2/26th were unable to dig trenches as 'any hole more than six inches deep filled with water'.[44] Their only means of protection, therefore, was the building of breastworks 'constructed of "sandbags" or any other type of suitable material available'.[45] Maxwell deployed his 2/30th Battalion at

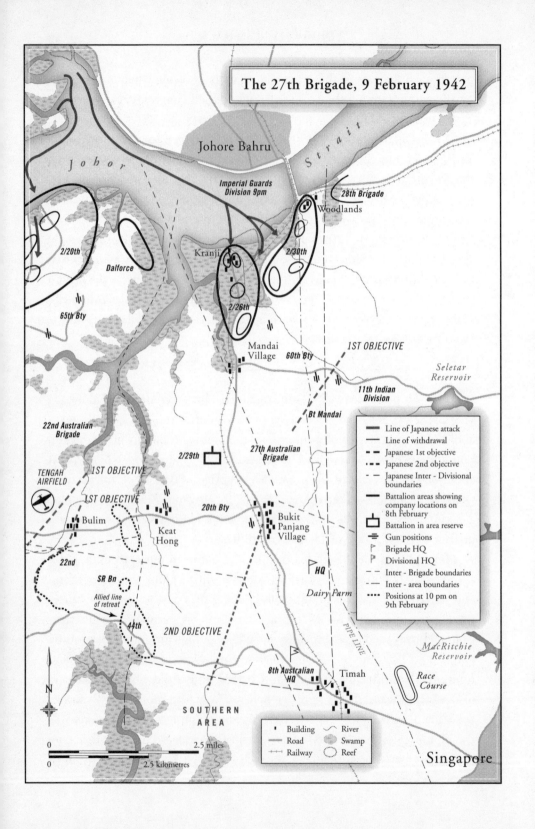

The 27th Brigade, 9 February 1942

Johor Strait

Johore Bahru

Imperial Guards
Division 9pm

28th Brigade

Woodlands

Kranji

2/30th

2/20th

Dalforce

2/26th

65th Bty

Mandai
Village

60th Bty

1ST OBJECTIVE

Seletar
Reservoir

11th Indian
Division

Bt Mandai

22nd Australian
Brigade

2/29th

27th Australian
Brigade

TENGAH
AIRFIELD

1ST OBJECTIVE

1ST OBJECTIVE

Bulim

Keat
Hong

20th Bty

Bukit
Panjang
Village

22nd

SR Bn

Allied line
of retreat

44th

2ND OBJECTIVE

HQ

Dairy Farm

PIPE LINE

MacRitchie
Reservoir

8th Australian
HQ

Timah

Race
Course

N

SOUTHERN
AREA

Singapore

Legend	
▬▬▬	Line of Japanese attack
───	Line of withdrawal
▬ ▬ ▬	Japanese 1st objective
▪▪ ▪▪	Japanese 2nd objective
─ ─ ─	Japanese Inter - Divisional boundaries
▬	Battalion areas showing company locations on 8th February
⊓	Battalion in area reserve
≡	Gun positions
⚑	Brigade HQ
⚑	Divisional HQ
·─·─·	Inter - Brigade boundaries
─·─·─	Inter - area boundaries
▪▪▪▪	Positions at 10 pm on 9th February

▪	Building
───	Road
┼┼┼┼	Railway
⌒	River
◯	Swamp
⬭	Reef

0 ————————— 2.5 miles

0 ————————— 2.5 kilometres

and around the causeway, and stretching back along the main road to link with the 2/26th Battalion. It will be recalled that Lieutenant-Colonel Pond's 2/29th Battalion had originally been deployed between Mandai village and the Choa Chu Kang Road as the 8th Division reserve. Maxwell placed his Brigade HQ eleven kilometres south of the causeway at the Singapore Dairy Farm (and close to Bennett's HQ). In view of the fact that Japanese bombing and artillery fire had, and would continue, to disrupt communications, this location was far too remote from his battalions.

Early on the morning of 9 February when news reached 27th Brigade HQ that the Japanese had broken through Taylor's 22nd Brigade front, Brigadier Maxwell, not for the first time during the campaign, became anxious and thought more about withdrawal than defence. Despite the fact that the River Kranji and its swamps extended nearly five kilometres inland and therefore offered his Brigade a relatively secure left flank, Maxwell became deeply concerned that the Japanese might attack towards the area containing the headwaters of the Kranji and the Choa Chu Kang Road, which could result in his Brigade being cut off. At 11.00 am therefore, he asked Bennett to allow him to withdraw the 2/26th to form a line running from the Woodlands–Kranji Road junction southwards to the twelve-mile peg, about three kilometres north of Bukit Panjang village. Given that the Causeway Sector was vital ground, that the 27th Brigade had not as yet been attacked and that steps were being taken by Percival and Bennett to strengthen the Jurong Line, Bennett rightly refused this request. However, in an effort to assist Maxwell, permission was given to form a 2/26th composite company composed of the newly created fourth platoon of each company. This scratch force was given to D Company to hold an approximately kilometre-long perimeter facing the eastern side of the River Kranji. We now come to an extraordinary train of events.

On the morning of 9 February 1942, Maxwell removed Lieutenant-Colonel Boyes as commander of the 2/26th Battalion. According to the 27th Brigade War Diary, Maxwell visited Taylor's 22 Brigade HQ at 11.00 am on 6 February to request that Major Oakes—the second-in-command of his old 2/19th Battalion—be released to command the 2/26th Battalion as soon as possible.[46] Presumably he had already discussed this matter with Bennett, or alternatively, was about to. Oakes's appointment was recorded in the 2/19th War Diary on 7 February.[47] Maxwell would claim postwar that, 'Boyes had not been a satisfactory battalion commander.'[48] His assertion has no basis for two reasons. First, Lieutenant-Colonel Boyes's command of his 2/26th Battalion on the Malay Peninsula cannot be fairly criticised. We have noted that Battalion's sterling service, which must reflect favourably upon him. Second, there is ample evidence that the 2/26th Battalion held its CO in high regard.[49] While Galleghan's lack of professional respect for Maxwell has been recorded, there is evidence that Boyes also had little admiration for his Brigade Commander. Lieutenant-Colonel Arthur 'Sapper' Boyes was a permanent soldier who had experienced exchange duty with a British regiment, had raised and trained his Battalion with zeal and competence, and had led it with distinction. His soon-to-be-recorded fate is tragic.

At around midday, as the volume of enemy artillery fire and bombing of his Causeway Sector increased, Maxwell again asked for permission to withdraw. Wigmore, writing in 1957, and understandably under very close participant scrutiny, apparently decided to take an each way bet on what then occurred: 'This [Maxwell's request] appears to have been granted, conditionally upon the withdrawal of the brigade not being commenced before the oil tanks near the Causeway, in the 2/30th's sector, had been demolished.'[50] But after the word 'demolished' above, Wigmore added a footnote: 'General Bennett said after the war that he himself did not give permission for any withdrawal from the Causeway.'[51] Given that the very word 'withdrawal', let alone its implementation, was an anathema to General Gordon Bennett, and that he had, that very morning, admonished Taylor for rightly withdrawing, it would seem to be a fair assumption that Bennett did not grant Maxwell his second request to withdraw—the second request in the space of but a few hours. After the war, Thyer also denied any prior knowledge of Maxwell's intent to withdraw and was equally certain that Bennett had not granted permission. In an interview with Wigmore and Kirby in January 1953, the historians recorded that: 'Thyer said the withdrawal from the Causeway was contrary to Bennett's character. Whenever withdrawal was suggested Bennett more or less flew off the handle.'[52]

Barely an hour and a half later, at about 2.00 pm on the 9th, during a conference at his HQ, Maxwell replaced Galleghan with the 2/30th Battalion's second-in-command, Major George Ramsay. The 27th Brigade War

Diary recorded that Galleghan was 'ordered' by Maxwell 'to report to AGH [Advanced General Hospital] for a medical examination', because he did 'not consider him fit to carry on his duties due to an ear condition'.[53] There is no evidence that Galleghan requested his evacuation. With the former COs of the 2/26th and 2/30th Battalions now gone, Maxwell ordered both battalions to prepare to withdraw from their Causeway Sector perimeters that night. Further, he placed the onerous task of coordinating that two-battalion operation to Oakes, while he, Maxwell, remained at his far distant Brigade HQ—still a full eleven kilometres from the causeway.

In a letter to the Official Historian in March 1954 Galleghan posed an intriguing question: 'Should a historian raise the question why Maxwell had two COs moved, one to hospital and one relieved of command at such a vital period[?]'[54] A historian should. In an interview with Wigmore and Kirby in Adelaide on 19 January 1953, Thyer stated that Maxwell came to the forward 8th Division HQ on 9 February at 9.00 pm.[55] Thyer:

He told me (he was very tired) that he was a doctor in civil life and his function was to save life. Maxwell considered that what was going on on Singapore Island after the Japanese landings was senseless slaughter. Maxwell was going back to Percival to urge him to surrender.[56]

The Official Historians recorded that: 'Thyer urged him not to do this but to go to Bennett.' We do not know whether Maxwell actually visited Percival and stated his case.

Pratten (2009) has raised the issue of whether Maxwell's action in removing Boyes and Galleghan was 'premeditated'.[57] It would seem that it was. Brigadier Maxwell's choice of Major Roland Oakes as a replacement for Boyes is questionable. Oakes had been left out of battle when his 2/19th Battalion had served at Bakri and during the withdrawal to Parit Sulong. He therefore had had no operational command experience in Malaya, and now, the very morning after the enemy landings on Taylor's front, Oakes was sent to command a battalion he did not know and on ground and dispositions of which he was unfamiliar. Further, incredibly, Maxwell placed him in overall command of any withdrawal that the two battalions were to undertake—

a far from satisfactory command decision, as Oakes knew as much about the 2/30th Battalion and its ground as he did about the 2/26th. It is worth recording that Oakes and Maxwell were old friends from the 2/19th Battalion. In a postwar interview with the Official Historians, Galleghan said: 'There was no brigade control and Oakes was inefficient. To let him determine when my battalion would go out was a mistake.'[58]

In appointing Oakes and Ramsay to their commands, Maxwell could undoubtedly count on the loyalty of the former, and the compliance of the latter, since Ramsay was to be under Oakes's command decision if and when a withdrawal was to occur. The reader might contemplate the reaction(s) of Galleghan and Boyes to a withdrawal from the vital Causeway Sector before an enemy landing had even occurred. Maxwell was removing two forthright, aggressive commanders, and replacing them with two others whose compliance he could count on.

This question becomes even more interesting when we examine a comment made by Brigadier Arthur Blackburn VC in his diary during captivity in Formosa (Taiwan) with Brigadiers Maxwell and Taylor in 1943. Blackburn had told 'an 8th Division Brigadier' that he could not fathom how the Japanese had managed to cross the Johore Strait. The 'Australian Brigadier' could only have been Taylor or Maxwell, who were both in captivity with Blackburn. The reply astounded him: 'Look here Arthur, I'll tell you what happened. I knew it was hopeless so I drew my men back from the beaches and let the Japs through.'[59] It would seem that Maxwell was the brigadier in question. If all this was poor enough, as the afternoon of 9 February wore on, the volume of Japanese shelling of the Causeway Sector increased preparatory to General Takumo Nishimura's Imperial Guards Division's landings on Maxwell's front. Obsessed with a withdrawal, Maxwell was about to have a war of his own.

General Yamashita had two prime reasons for mounting landings on the Causeway Sector. The first was the acquisition of the vital main road running straight across the Island from Singapore Town to Woodlands and thence across the causeway to Johore Bahru. Capture that route and dominate the Island. The second was that, while achieving this key first objective, he would also frustrate any British attempt to use troops in this area to assist Taylor's hard-pressed soldiers across the River Kranji. But those two benefits came with two distinct hazards. The first was the narrow front between the River Kranji and the causeway—around four kilometres of shoreline—which would limit the concentration of his force in the initial wave. Therefore, the Guards Division would not enjoy the same advantage as had the 5th and 18th Divisions landing along Taylor's massive front. The second problem compounded the first. Not only was the Causeway Sector front relatively narrow, but landing sites along that shore were limited. Along the western 2/26th front lay extensive and therefore slow-to-cross mangroves. The only region where the mangroves lacked depth was in front of Kranji village. On the 2/30th's eastern side, the defenders would have the advantage of the occupation of the high ground—just behind the road and overlooking the shore. Yamashita opted to attack.

At about 8.30 pm on 9 February 1942, as the 2/26th was engaged in extending its left flank, the enemy barrage stopped and barges carrying the 4th Guards Regiment began to appear. A half an hour later the main Japanese assault landed on the 2/26th Battalion's perimeter at and around the pier in front of Kranji village. Subsidiary landings were attempted along the Battalion's swamp shoreline, and others in the 2/30th sector at the Rivers Mandai and Mandai Kechil.

As had occurred on Brigadier Taylor's 22nd Brigade front the previous night, enemy shelling of the sector cut communications, and the lights on the 2/26th front did not operate. Moreover, numerous flares requesting artillery support and machine gun fire were not initially seen. It would be twenty critical minutes before the 2/4th Machine Gunners opened fire. But for all this, the advanced A and B Companies of the 2/26th—the former to the left of the road and facing the pier, and the latter to the right—held their ground. The 2/26th Battalion Unit Diary recorded that:

Hand to hand fighting became general with the forward platoons of both Coys [A and B] ... Infiltration around the left flank of A Coy forced the forward platoons to withdraw and a line was re-established 300 yds south of the waters edge on the only high ground in the area. Despite casualties that had reduced A Coy to

100 and B Coy to less than 60 the two Coys held firm and no further penetration took place. The enemy persevered by sending barges up the S. [River] Mandai where heavy casualties were inflicted by MGs and Mortars.[60]

The invaders fared poorly in attempting less concentrated landings on the mudflats on the 2/30th Battalion sector. The Australians were dug in on the high ground just behind the causeway road, and covering access to the streams, their intense fire denied the Japanese any chance of landing barges at or near that vital feature.

Thus, although the 2/26th Battalion had taken significant casualties, the Japanese had failed to pierce the 27th Brigade perimeter to any great extent. But Maxwell was still committed to his withdrawal. When communications were briefly re-established between himself and Oakes at around midnight on 9–10 February, he ordered Oakes to withdraw as soon as the Shell Depot oil tanks—holding about 2 000 000 gallons of fuel—were destroyed. That demolition did not, at first, go according to plan because the truck carrying the equipment and explosives was hit by a shell. However, Lieutenant Watchorn joined his sappers and 'coolly set the charges within earshot of the enemy'.[61] When the tanks exploded at around 4.30 am Oakes led the two battalions out. We now come to more controversy and differing accounts.

Earlier that day Ramsay had agonised over the decision to withdraw. Lionel Wigmore has shed some light on his predicament:

> Ramsay, concerned at leaving a position which he considered his battalion capable of holding, [and which the 2/30th did indeed hold] subsequently discussed the plan with Oakes. The two agreed that having regard to the tactical position generally, and their lack of adequate knowledge of what was happening on the 22nd Brigade front, they would not be justified in asking their brigade headquarters to reconsider the order.[62]

Two points should be made. First, 'their [Ramsay and Oakes's] lack of adequate knowledge of what was happening on the 22nd Brigade front' was quite simply not their—or Maxwell's—concern. That issue was one for Bennett to consider. Battalion commanders and a brigadier on one brigade front are not responsible for events and decisions on another. Second, although conjecture, both the historian and the reader could be forgiven for pondering how Boyes and most certainly Galleghan might have reacted to Maxwell's orders, which would seem precisely why they were no longer with their battalions. We have noted Galleghan's pertinent question to the Official Historian after the war. Ramsay and Oakes had been in command of their battalions for only hours. Their acquiescence is understandable.

Oakes then proceeded to lead the two battalions further back than Maxwell had planned. The 2/26th War Diary provides us with a damning indictment of Brigadier Maxwell's decision:

> The fault of handing over control to a C.O. who had not been in the area for a day and lacked local knowledge became apparent when at 4.30 hrs . . . A & B Coys broke contact and moving through C Coy made for their respective positions without knowing the location of Bn H.Q. or the other coys. The Composite Coy had been ordered to pass on the withdrawal order to D Coy before it withdrew but failed to do so with the result that at 1000 hrs the battalion was occupying its new area with D Coy still in position on the Kranji.
>
> The Bn was disposed on a frontage of 4000 yds in impossible country. Each Coy occupied a steep hill feature in gaps of 1000 yds of heavily scrub-covered country between and in most cases failed to establish contact with Bn and one another until late in the afternoon.[63]

During the morning of 10 February therefore—and with the 11th Indian Division completely unaware of the 27th Brigade withdrawal—the 2/30th Battalion occupied a perimeter behind Mandai Road and nearly five kilometres inland from the causeway shore, while the 2/26th was deployed south of it along the Woodlands Road. There was now a sizable gap between the 27th Brigade perimeter and General Key's 11th Indian Division's eastward dispositions.

From a Japanese perspective the attack on the Causeway Sector was a near-run thing. When Yamashita had planned the landings on Taylor's 22nd Brigade front General Nishimura had protested concerning the preference given to the 5th and 18th Divisions. He had 'emphatically demanded' that his Imperial Guards Division fight 'shoulder to shoulder' with those divisions.[64] It would therefore appear that the landings on the 27th Brigade Causeway Sector were in part a concession to Nishimura's demands.

General Yamashita had crossed the Johore Strait at sunset on the 9th and set up a command post at Tengah airfield. The bulk of the 25th Army staff remained on the mainland to organise the logistical requirements for operations on Singapore. Early the following morning, Yamashita was breakfasting on dry bread in his tent when a officer arrived with the news that a staff officer of the Imperial Guards had angrily protested that the leading battalion had been all but annihilated in a sea of fire while trying to land.[65] According to Lieutenant-Colonel Tsuji, he, and then Yamashita, admonished Nishimura's failure to send a staff officer along with the leading troops to gauge the success of the landings. There had been no love lost between Nishimura and Yamashita over the years and, after the latter ordered that further reports be made concerning the progress on the causeway, it transpired that the initial report had been a mistake. Tusji would later write:

> During the afternoon of that day [10 February] there came a tele-
> phone call from Headquarters . . . 'The Konoe Division's report this
> morning was a mistake. At the time we verified the situation, the
> division's front line, after trifling losses, was in the midst of an attack
> on the enemy's position on the southern side of the Causeway. The
> division commander reports to the Army Commander that he will
> this evening carry out a further advance on the Causeway Sector.'[66]

Tsuji maintained that this episode constituted the 'only mistake throughout the Malayan Campaign'.[67] If the Japanese had made one mistake—and not a great one at that—during the first critical hours of the Battle for Singapore Island, then Malaya Command and the Australians in their Western Area had committed a multitude of sins.

General Percival made two key decisions during the early hours of 10 February. We have noted his two obvious choices in defending Singapore Island: cover the north coast adequately, or provide a powerful reserve capable of holding the Jurong Line and capable also of conducting a potent counterattack. And now, on the early morning of 10 February 1942 when Yamashita had shown his hand, Percival refused to create that reserve by denuding other areas of their strength. He considered that the deployment of his 12th and 15th Indian Brigades to the Jurong Line would stabilise his front. Given Taylor's massive losses and the fact that Yamashita would be busily building up his beachhead both in terms of men and material, now was the time to take a calculated risk and both man that Jurong Line with the best available formations on the Island and counterattack in strength. The identity of those units was obvious: elements of the 18th Division from his North-Eastern Sector and English battalions from his Southern Area.

Major-General Keith Simmons had been the 'Fortress Commander' in title only. He still, at this late hour, possessed fresh troops who might have been committed to the battle. For months beforehand, and now during the critical first days of the Battle for Singapore Island, the reader is entitled to ponder what it was that the Fortress Commander and his troops ever did to defend the Island. In blunt terms, many of Simmons's troops had been slack for years, and now when the long-awaited war had erupted, those soldiers were still not making a significant contribution. What price now for Simmons's edict that 'fortifications are bad for morale', and for his hopelessly dispersed dispositions on the north-west shore? Malaya Command was, yet again, attempting to cover every contingency, and in the end, adequately covering none.

After having visited Bennett's Western Area during the afternoon of 9 February, Percival devised a plan to cover a possible Japanese breakthrough along the Bukit Timah Road, which would necessitate a final defensive perimeter on the Island. The only effective option for such a plan was to safeguard his supply dumps, depots and hospital facilities leading into, and at, Singapore Town. Further, such a defence hinged upon his ability to hold the reservoirs and pipeline water supply to the Town. During that afternoon Percival verbally outlined a new defensive perimeter to Heath and Simmons—Bennett was not present.

At around 12.50 am on 10 February, Percival issued his order for the final perimeter in writing as a 'secret and personal instruction for the information of his three senior commanders and senior members of his own staff'.[68] According to Wigmore, Percival issued this order 'so that responsible senior officers might know his intentions in case the situation developed too rapidly for further orders to be issued'.[69] The plan, marked 'secret and personal', was to be shown to area commanders only. The train of events that were destined to unfold within hours of Percival's order would be catastrophic.

While Percival and Simmons were excessively cautious, the Australians must also be criticised for their poor performance during those first critical hours. General Gordon Bennett, as ever obsessed with offensive action, failed to go forward and take a grip of his operation. Instead, he admonished Taylor for conducting a withdrawal during terribly difficult circumstances, where the 'fog of war' was as much an enemy as the Japanese. Lacking a reserve worthy of the name, Taylor was, and would be forced, to stem an enemy advance that had developed into a gaping military wound with significant numbers of untrained and untried reinforcements who were incapable of holding their extensive ground. And as that problem was to magnify, the Australians were forced to deploy dubious formations such as X Battalion to fill the gaps.

However, transcending all of these difficulties was a brigadier who did have a potent, well-trained, motivated and well-led force. *Galleghan's Greyhounds*:

> ... the withdrawal from the Causeway ... was disliked strongly, by both Command and troops [of the 2/30th]. The men, in particular, felt that for the first time they were facing the enemy in positions nearer to approximate equality than ever before and they looked forward to a clash with confidence and almost professional interest. The 2/4th Machine-gunners, recent arrivals, had yet to meet the Japanese in open combat and had no hesitation in expressing their reluctance to withdraw before coming to closer grips.[70]

To Brigadier Maxwell's shame, he declined to allow his well-trained and experienced Brigade to fight the Japanese when there was a reasonable prospect of their holding their ground and inflicting serious losses on the enemy.

By the early morning of 10 February 1942, the defence of Singapore lay in tatters. Ahead lay nothing but more tragedy and controversy.

21

FURTHER RETREATS

For war correspondents such as Ian Morrison of *The Times* newspaper, there were no shortage of stories to gather in Singapore during the morning of 10 February 1942. Against a seemingly all-encompassing, depressing background of black smoke from the still-burning oil tanks, he rode a bike out into Singapore's western suburbs and noted the intermittent sounds of artillery, machine gun and small arms fire from the not-too-distant battle. Morrison also observed the troops in the town: 'Some, with full battle-kit and an air of purpose, were moving to take up new battle stations. Others were wandering, grimy, lost, leaderless, without orders.'[1]

In times of terror and uncertainty rumours flourish. Singapore, according to Morrison, was 'buzzing' with both the positive and negative variety: the Japanese had 'been pushed back into the sea', and the Americans had 'landed in Penang', while others had heard that the enemy were only five kilometres outside of the Town and that 'parachutists had tried to seize the broadcasting station . . .'[2].

At midday, the Governor delivered the most inane statement yet promulgated by officialdom. 'We are all in the hands of God,' Sir Shenton [Thomas] declared, 'from Whom we can get comfort in our anxieties and strength to play the man and help one another in all the ordeals which are to come.'[3]

God was destined to provide little comfort, and had the citizens of Singapore known of the military blunders that had been committed during the first 36 hours of the defence of the Island—and those that were to occur that very day—the true hopelessness of their plight might have been apparent. On the basis of what he saw that morning Morrison gave the British fortress 36 hours before a capitulation.

At around 3.10 am on 10 February Bennett's HQ signalled Malaya Command that all was quiet on the Causeway Sector. Two hours later news reached it that the Japanese had landed at Kranji, and just ten minutes later still came the news that Maxwell had withdrawn his 27th Brigade. At around 5.30 am Bennett's HQ informed Malaya Command of these events.

Brigadier Maxwell's withdrawal from his vital Causeway Sector during the early hours of 10 February was not well received by General Key, the GOC of troops in the Northern Area. He learnt of the move at around 6.30 am and immediately contacted Bennett's HQ asking that the 27th Brigade immediately reoccupy its former perimeter. The Australians replied that they possessed 'insufficient troops to do this'.[4] In response to this refusal, and in an attempt to secure his now vacant left flank, Key immediately committed his 8th Indian Brigade reserve (Brigadier Trott) to recapture three key high-ground positions just south of the Australians' former perimeter.

Although two of Trott's objectives were secured without great loss, the Garhwal Rifles Composite Battalion took heavy casualties attacking the third and failed in their attempt. In the process they lost their CO and six of their British officers. When Key reached Trott's forward position on the afternoon of the 10th, he ordered him to secure the gap between the 27th Brigade and the Garhwalis at dawn on the 11th by deploying the 2/10th Bulach at Point 130.

In view of Maxwell's withdrawal during the early morning of 10 February, Percival decided to place the 27th Brigade under Key's command. At 11.00 am Key requested—understandably—that Ramsay despatch a 2/30th Battalion detachment to occupy the road junction at Mandai village. The 2/30th Unit Diary would later record that the Battalion: '. . . was still under orders 27 Aus Inf Bde and it was not until 1700 hrs that evening that the position was fully clarified and the attachment to 11 Ind Div confirmed.'[5] Maxwell was advised of the order at 3.00 pm and must have journeyed to Key's HQ at 6.30 pm with great apprehension. It is not known what transpired at the meeting, but in a feeble attempt to whitewash his withdrawal Maxwell was to later supervise the writing of 'Appendix C' to the 27th Brigade Diary, claiming that after he and Key had later met in Changi to discuss a number of 'misunderstandings or doubts as to the relative qualities of formations which may have existed before the discussion', they had 'been settled'.[6] In a letter to Kirby on 19 November 1952, Key's GSO1, Colonel Harrison, held a different view:

> As regards Brigadier Maxwell's observations that 'General Key expressed regret at having misjudged the Bde.' and that 'both Comds. expressed their satisfaction at having clarified the situation' I can say that, to my knowledge, General Key has never changed his original opinion, which he expressed to me on 11 Feb., that Brigadier Maxwell was guilty of grave dereliction of duty. On 11 Feb. he said to me: 'If Maxwell was a British officer, I would place him under arrest.'[7]

General Gordon Bennett should have at the very least relieved Maxwell of his command.

It will be remembered that on the evening of 9 February Bennett had ordered Brigadier Taylor to hold Bulim until 6.00 am on the 10th and then move back—over a short distance—to occupy the central portion of the Jurong Line between the 12th and 44th Brigades. At around 9.00 am Bennett made a further adjustment to the line by deploying his reserve (Brigadier Coates's 15th Brigade) to the left of Taylor's 22nd Brigade between the Jurong Road and Point 117. Further, he altered the 44th Brigade's perimeter to stretch from the Jurong Road southwards to link up with the 1st Malaya Brigade on the southern coast. In occupying his sector of the line, Brigadier Taylor deployed the 2/29th Battalion to the right in contact with the 12th Brigade, his Special Reserve Battalion (Major Saggers) on the left in touch with 15th Brigade and, finally, the remnant of his 22nd Brigade in reserve near the village of Keat Hong. When, at daybreak, the 2/18th Battalion's carriers observed a Japanese force at about two-company strength advancing eastwards along the main road, they took such a heavy toll of them that Taylor's withdrawal was accomplished with little hindrance from the enemy.

We now come to a train of events where the recurring problems of poor communication and inept command decisions spread like a malignancy through the final defence of Singapore.

General Percival had issued Malaya Command Operation Instruction No. 40 during the evening of 9 February for a final perimeter defence of Singapore should the Jurong Line be lost. Paragraphs 3 and 7 deserve scrutiny:

> 3. Should it be impossible to hold the enemy on the line mentioned in para 2 above [the line Kranji River–Bulim Village–Jurong River], the G.O.C. Malaya intends to withdraw to an inner posn on which the final battle for Singapore will be fought.

> 7. Recces of areas will be carried out at once and the plans for the movement of formations into the areas allotted to them will be prepared. Formations will arrange to move back and locate in their new areas units located in their present areas which are under comd of H.Q. Malaya Comd.[8]

Paragraph 7 clearly implies that the said recces would need to be undertaken by the units themselves, and that, in addition, such units would also be responsible for the movement of additional units in their areas 'which are under the command of HQ Malaya Command'. Such plans would therefore require some reasonable notice and time to plan and implement. Upon receipt of this order, Bennett—quite understandably—passed it on to his commanders at 7.30 am on 10 February as an initial warning. Lionel Wigmore:

> When Brigadier Taylor read the order its limited nature escaped him, and he interpreted it as requiring the new positions to be manned forthwith. He accordingly ordered the units under his command— other than the 2/29th Battalion and the Special Reserve Battalion,

which were committed to the Kranji–Jurong line—to positions along the line of Reformatory road, in the sector provisionally allotted to his brigade.[9]

Kappe and Thyer, writing in their *Operations of 8 Division in Malaya 1941–1942*, which was produced in Changi during imprisonment, were under no illusions as to where the blame lay:

> The portions [of Bennett's relayed order] stating that no action except reconnaissance was to be taken, were repeated. Copies typed at Div HQ were delivered by DR [motor cycle rider] to recipients, so that mutilation in transmission cannot be pleaded . . .
> This order was clearly understood by all commanders except Brigadier Taylor who obviously misread it, for immediately on its receipt he promulgated orders for the occupation of the position on Reformatory Road.[10]

Brigadier Taylor's behaviour during the morning of 10 February 1942 portrays a commander who was near to breaking point both physically and mentally. Two of his actions that morning would seem to support this view. His 'misreading' of Bennett's orders was the first. Kappe and Thyer's evidence cited above would seem to indicate that Taylor's interpretation of Bennett's relayed message from Percival was the by-product of a muddled, exhausted commander. His second supports the thrust of the first. After ordering the withdrawal of the bulk of his Brigade, Taylor undertook the reconnaissance of his new positions near Reformatory Road. Warren (2002) rightly claims that: 'Taylor's units still holding the front line were thus deprived of the presence of their brigadier and supporting troops during a vital period.'[11] Taylor should never have undertaken such a recce during critical operations on his front. That exercise should most definitely have been assigned to a battalion commander or staff officer. Within 48 hours Brigadier Harold Taylor's mental and physical reserves of energy were to reach breaking point.

On the way to recce his new positions, Taylor called on Bennett. He would later claim that: 'He [Bennett] . . . made some disparaging remarks in relation to my handling of the situation and about the Brigade. He stated that it was not his intention that the order I had received should be put into operation forthwith, but only under certain circumstances.'[12] The extraordinary outcome of what must have been a stormy meeting was that, firstly, Bennett allowed Taylor's error to stand, and secondly, after Taylor left Bennett's HQ, he still proceeded to undertake the recce.

While these events were in train, the Japanese had began to move around the right flank perimeter of the 12th Indian Brigade (Brigadier Paris), which was deployed at the northern end of the Jurong Line. In response, Paris withdrew his Brigade about 900 metres to a position just to the west of Keat Hong village. The Australian 2/29th Battalion—less one company and the CO who had lost contact with the rest of the Battalion during the withdrawal from Bulim—now formed the front on the Choa Chu Kang Road. When Paris learnt that Brigadier Maxwell's 27th Brigade withdrawal had left the Woodlands Road unoccupied to the vicinity of Mandai village, he withdrew his Argylls and the 2/29th to Bukit Panjang village which lay at the intersection of the Woodlands and Choa Chu Kang Roads. Thus Maxwell's unauthorised withdrawal had become a precedent for others—all wrong, all undisciplined, and all based upon a lack of fortitude when an enemy threat materialised at any point along a neighbouring front.

Early on 10 February, the 15th and 44th Brigades had deployed on the southern end of the Jurong Line. At around 1.30 pm, the Japanese began to move down the Jurong Road. In response the 6/1st Punjabis (44th Brigade) and elements of the 15th Brigade's British Battalion undertook a limited withdrawal. When Brigadier Ballentine was inaccurately informed that the 15th Brigade was withdrawing, he reacted to a perceived threat of being outflanked by instigating a movement into his allotted area as per Percival's final perimeter. Late on the afternoon of the 10th, therefore, Brigadier Ballentine's 44th Brigade had withdrawn a number of kilometres to Pasir Panjang village. This farcical chain of events continued when Brigadier Coates discovered that, with Ballentine's Brigade gone, he was exposed on his left flank. Consequently, he too withdrew eastwards to a perimeter which was only about three kilometres outside of Bukit Timah village. In turn, this movement left Major Saggers and his Special Reserve Battalion exposed on both flanks and it too withdrew to join the 15th Brigade south of Jurong Road.

By the early afternoon of 10 February, therefore, the mythical Jurong Line had been abandoned to a foe who had done next to nothing to acquire it. From a psychological perspective, a strongly fortified Jurong Line manned by a fresh, motivated force would have very much forestalled panicky, precipitant and poorly executed withdrawals. A line on a map was cold comfort for inexperienced, poorly equipped and exhausted troops who, in numerous cases, were commanded by senior officers who looked back rather than forward.

General Wavell's last visit to Singapore on the morning of 10 February 1942 was opportune. Accompanied by three staff, he joined Percival at Sime Road and then visited each of the Area Commanders. Bennett was his first port of call, then Heath followed by Key. It was at this time, having been told by Key that the Trunk Road lay exposed after Maxwell's withdrawal, that Percival placed the Australian 27th Brigade under Key's command. He also ordered Heath to furnish three battalions from his yet unused 18th Division to form a reserve for Bennett for a defence of the key Bukit Timah area. Under the command of Lieutenant-Colonel Thomas, this reserve was to be codenamed Tomforce. Finally, belatedly, and a full 36 hours after Yamashita's landings on the north-west coast, Percival was creating a *fresh* reserve.

During the early afternoon of the 10th, Wavell and Percival visited Bennett a second time. It was during this meeting they learnt that the Jurong Line was lost. Wavell was adamant that the Line be recaptured. After having visited General Simmons, Wavell and Percival then journeyed to the latter's residence at Flagstaff House, where Percival showed Wavell his written orders to Bennett for the counterattack. It was during this time that Wavell received a cable from Churchill:

Prime Minister to General Wavell   10 Feb 42
I think you ought to realise the way we view the situation in Singapore. It is reported to the Cabinet by the C.I.G.S. that Percival has over 100,000 men, whom 33,000 are British and 17,000 Australian. It is doubtful whether the Japanese have as many in the whole Malay peninsula, namely, five divisions forward and a sixth coming up. In

these circumstances the defenders must greatly outnumber Japanese forces who have crossed the straits, and in a well-contested battle they should destroy them. There must at this stage be no thought of saving the troops or sparing the population. The battle must be fought to the bitter end at all costs. The 18th Division has a chance to make its name in history. Commanders and senior officers should die with their troops. The honour of the British Empire and of the British Army is at stake. I rely on you to show no mercy to weakness in any form. With the Russians fighting as they are and the Americans so stubborn at Luzon, the whole reputation of our country and our race is involved. It is expected that every unit will be brought into close contact with the enemy and fight it out. I feel sure these words express your own feeling, and only send them to you in order to share your burdens.[13]

Percival's biographer, Clifford Kinvig recounted:

Wavell then retired to a separate room and drafted in pencil on the back of a naval message form a similar exhortation which he signed and passed to Percival. The tone was the same . . . It is difficult to decide which message was more discreditable, the Prime Minister's or Wavell's.[14]

Whilst Kinvig's comment is entirely fair, Churchill's cable was, and remains, the most inept document of the two. In modern warfare, battles are not decided purely in terms of numbers. The prerequisites for a competent fight, let alone victory, are more often than not air superiority or at least air parity; a naval presence worthy of the name; some half-reasonable support in terms of artillery, tanks and anti-aircraft batteries; and most of all, well-led, trained, seasoned, and motivated infantry. A number of the above-mentioned military requirements for success—as we have chronicled—had been denied Percival by Winston Churchill. His last sentence to Wavell, 'I feel sure these words express your own feeling, and only send them to you in order to share your burdens', is trite.

It can be imagined what Percival must have thought of Churchill's cable and Wavell's equally poor effort for the troops—which were deeply resented

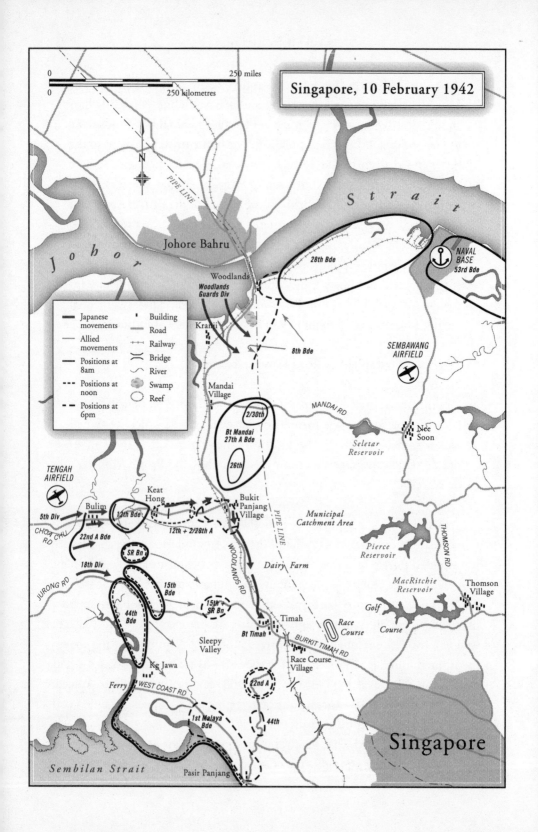

by all and sundry. The following day, with an order to read Wavell's message to the troops, came Percival's own message:

> In some units the troops have not shown the fighting spirit expected of men of the British Empire.
>
> It will be a lasting disgrace if we are defeated by an enemy of clever gangsters many times inferior in numbers to our men. The spirit of aggression and determination to stick it out must be inculcated in all ranks. There must be no further withdrawals without orders. There are too many fighting men in the back areas.
>
> Every available man who is not doing essential work, must be used to stop the invader.[15]

By the afternoon of 10 February, despite the belated creation of a fresh reserve and a counterattack being planned, it was to require a lot more than 'Boy's Own Annual' messages from the Prime Minister and senior commanders to forestall the 'clever gangsters'.

General Bennett's 8th Division HQ issued his orders for the recapture of the Jurong Line at around 4.00 pm on the 10th. The attack was to consist of three brigades with a further two in reserve. The right flank attack was to be undertaken by the 12th Indian Brigade with 2/29th attached (Brigadier Paris); the 15th Indian Brigade were in the centre; and Brigadier Taylor's 22nd Brigade was deployed on the left flank. Brigadier Ballentine's 44th Indian Brigade and the newly constituted Tomforce were assigned as the reserve formations. Bennett planned three phases or objectives. The first phase envisaged the occupation of a line extending from Point 138 in the south, northwards to Milestone 9 on the Jurong Road, and thence to Milestone 11 on the Choa Chu Kang Road. That first objective was to be taken by 6.00 pm that day. Phase two was designed to gain about a further 1100 metres of ground westwards by 9.00 am the next morning (11 February). The third and final phase was the complete occupation of the Jurong Line by 9.00 pm that day. Bennett assigned the Australian 2/15th Field Regiment as the 22nd Brigade's artillery support, and the 44th Brigade's 5th Field Regiment for the 15th and 44th Brigades.

Bennett's plan was flawed in three key areas. The first was time—particularly in terms of hours of daylight. Although the 15th and 12th Brigades were somewhere close to their startlines, Taylor's 22nd Brigade was not. Therefore an order given at 4.00 pm for an attack at 6.00 pm without the chance to conduct suitable daylight reconnaissance was ambitious in the extreme. The second factor was control. Given the appalling communication network available to the force, given the fact that much of it had been engaged in heavy fighting, that much of the force was currently involved in withdrawals to new positions, and were severely diminished in strength both numerically and physically, the chances of success were slim. Third, the artillery support was placed in a most unfavourable position. The 2/15th Field Regiment had initially been assigned to support the 22nd Brigade, but at around 5.45 pm it received orders to in fact support the 12 Indian Brigade. The unit 'had already taken up battery positions on Farrer and Orchard Roads to support the Aus Bde [sic] and therefore were [sic] some 10,000 yards in rear of 12th Brigade's first objective'.[16] Bennett's three-phase operation to retake the Jurong Line would prove a disaster.

On the right, or northern flank, the Japanese pre-empted Brigadier Paris's 12th Brigade's first phase movement by attacking his Hyderabads who were deployed near Milestone 11 on the Choa Chu Kang Road. Kirby used the term 'disintegrated'[17] to describe the Hyderabad's fate, while Thyer's report would later state that the unit had suffered 'many desertions during the day', and that Paris believed that 'he could only rely on about 100 men from that Battalion'.[18] Enemy infantry followed by tanks then appeared out of the darkness and attacked the 2/29th Battalion. According to its War Diary two tanks were disabled,[19] but the strength of the enemy infantry and further tanks caused the Australians to withdraw to the pipeline and thence to the racecourse. There Lieutenant-Colonel Pond regathered his Battalion and early on 11 February deployed it to the left of Tomforce.

With the Hyderabads and the 2/29th out of action, the Argylls were now confronted by an enemy advance down the vital Woodlands Road. They reacted in their usual dogged fashion. Two roadblocks were hurriedly constructed. The Argylls used an armoured car at the first, and despite that unequal battle, valuable time was won. When the enemy encountered the second block they were confronted by an anti-tank rifle and a few mines.

At around 10.30 pm the Argylls HQ had withdrawn to a position east of the Trunk Road, while its companies had moved to the Singapore Dairy Farm. After the initial Japanese assault, however, Brigadier Paris had sent word back to Bukit Timah of the Japanese tank assault, which enabled Major Fraser, a liaison officer from Bennett's HQ, to organise a 4th Australian Anti-Tank position. Moving back about 250 metres, Fraser then organised two troops of British howitzers to offer an additional block. At midnight on 10 February a number of enemy tanks and accompanying infantry gained the road junction at Bukit Timah and thus, by occupying the eastern end of the Jurong Road, had now severed direct communication with the 15th Brigade and Taylor's troops moving forward to their phase one objective. Clearly, the tank column might have pushed on, but chose to stop. The Japanese had probably decided to consolidate their advance by bringing up additional infantry. At dawn, any hope the Argylls had for a counterattack from the dairy farm was dashed when the strength of the enemy force was realised. Paris then decided to withdraw the Argylls along the pipeline, which later saw them reach Tanglin.

Of the three brigades deployed to implement Bennett's capture of the Jurong Line, Brigadier Taylor's 22nd Brigade was given the toughest role. Taylor ordered the just-formed 'X' Battalion (Lieutenant-Colonel Boyes) to occupy a position on the right named 'Jurong I' and Merrett Force (Major Merrett) on the left flank at Point 85, which lay just west of Sleepy Valley Estate. Away to 'X' Battalion's right lay the Special Reserve Battalion (Major Saggers) and further still 15 Brigade (Brigadier Coates).

The formation of Merrett Force and 'X' Battalion deserves some scrutiny. It will be recalled that Merrett Force had been created after the fierce fighting on Taylor's front during the Japanese landings on Singapore's north-west coast. It consisted of Captain Cousens's A Company, 2/19th Battalion, which had seen little action during the enemy landings, elements of C and D Companies 2/19th Battalion, and a group of around sixty 2/20th soldiers who had managed to regain their lines under Major Merrett.

'X' Battalion (Lieutenant-Colonel Boyes) was much more of an 'odds and sods' formation. It was comprised of three companies, each manned primarily by soldiers who had survived the heavy fighting on the north-west coast only days before. Company Number One consisted of

2/18th Battalion soldiers commanded by Major O'Brien. Company Number Two was composed of 2/19th Battalion men under the command of Major Keegan and Company Number Three was Captain Richardson's D Company, 2/20th Battalion. Within each company were experienced officers and other ranks who had fought with great distinction in both Malaya and on Singapore's north-west coast. Keegan, Richardson and O'Brien are examples. But there were also reinforcement officers and other ranks within those companies, some of whom fought well, while others found the experience overwhelming. Further, there were a number of non-combatant base personnel who also found themselves assigned to the formation.

The Unit Historians of both the 2/19th and 2/20th Battalions have rightly questioned the failure of both Bennett and Taylor to send returning members of 22nd Brigade Battalions back to their units after their recovery from the front. Their argument has substance. Reg Newton, 2/19th Battalion Historian: '. . . we felt that we were the leaderless legion, and split up everywhere. The fact that Lieut. Col. Varley had kept his 2/18th Battalion survivors . . . together, and still functioning as a unit, rankled with our remnants.'[20]

Don Wall, 2/20th Battalion Historian:

There was no attempt by Staff Officers to keep Units together and there appears to be no excuse for fragmenting battalions further. The 2/20 Bn had taken the full force of the enemy onslaught, and still had the best part of two companys' strength and in the same locality and yet they remained fragmented.[21]

Late on 10 February, therefore, Brigadier Taylor was deploying two formations to spearhead his role in the recapture of the Jurong Line which were of dubious military quality and poorly outfitted. 'X' Battalion was equipped with rifles, fifteen sub-machine guns, eight light machine guns, five 2-inch mortars, and two 3-inch mortars.[22] Incredibly, according to Thyer's report, 'some men were un-armed except for a load of hand-grenades', and others were 'merely ammunition carriers with bandoliers hung about their shoulders'.[23]

'X' Battalion arrived in the vicinity of the Reformatory at around 4.00 pm. Two hours later—as darkness was approaching—Boyes received his orders to proceed to Jurong I, a kidney-shaped feature just south of the nine and a half mile post on the Jurong Road.

Lieutenant-Colonel Arthur 'Sapper' Boyes and the more experienced with him must have quickly realised that all was not well. As they moved through the burning Bukit Timah area accompanied by distant sounds of fighting to their right, British troops informed them that the enemy was just ahead. These were the sounds of the fighting on 12 Brigade's front to the north, and heading towards Bukit Timah. When 'X' Battalion came within about 500 to 600 metres of their objective, Boyes met Saggers of the Special Reserve Battalion, but was unable to make contact with the 15th Brigade's Punjabis who were to be on his right. And Merrett Force, which was supposed to be journeying to form his left flank, ran into 'bog and tangled undergrowth'[24] and subsequently formed a defensive perimeter to the rear in Sleepy Valley where Merrett intended to push on at daylight. As 'X' Battalion approached its objective, the troops saw Indian bodies—not long dead—and their transport littered around the area. Some movement was also detected in the surrounding scrub on the northern side of Jurong Road.

By around 1.00 am on the morning of 11 February, having reached his objective, Boyes had deployed Richardson's company on the left flank, O'Brien's on the right, and Keegan's near Battalion HQ to the rear. A small recce patrol journeyed ahead—and was not seen again. The exhausted 'X' Battalion soldiers rapidly fell asleep with a small number of sentries providing cover and warning of Japanese activity. According to the 2/20th Unit History, Boyes is reported to have told Richardson: 'I don't like this, we're not going to get out of this tonight, tell the men they may as well die here than back in Singapore.'[25] Richardson did not pass the message on.

Boyes had every reason to 'not like this'. The Japanese had pushed fighting patrols westwards from their captured ground near Bukit Timah and by the time 'X' Battalion gained its designated perimeter, they had virtually surrounded the Australians.

The Japanese struck at about 3.00 am. A fuel dump adjacent to Battalion HQ, which consisted of 44-gallon drums 'stacked in several layers',[26] was ignited by tracer fire. Against this brilliantly lit background, many dazed Australians were bayoneted where they lay, while others were very quickly cut down by sniper, automatic and small arms fire. Both Lieutenant-Colonel

Arthur Boyes and Major Dick Keegan died early during the assault. Very little counter fire could be employed because the battle in many places was hand-to-hand and extremely confused. During that mass slaughter at Jurong I that night, 'X' Battalion lost somewhere between 100 and 150 of its men. The few survivors—in small groups ranging from two or three to section-strength—were those who chanced their fortunes by either seeking cover and waiting for their opportunity to move out, or others who made a desperate dash for freedom via a journey southwards towards Pasir Panjang.

Away to the south-east, in their perimeter at Sleepy Valley, Merrett's 200-strong Force saw tracer fire and heard 'X' Battalion's battle erupting at 3.00 am. Their turn came at dawn when the Japanese, who had occupied the surrounding high ground during darkness, wrought concentrated machine gun fire upon them. After bitter and yet again confused fighting, Merrett's men withdrew in two groups to the 2/18th area near Reformatory Road. Major Merrett was wounded during this action and evacuated to hospital. His force had suffered around 50 casualties during the early morning of 11 February.

In a statement in his later report, Thyer would claim that:

. . . Merrett Force had demonstrated clearly that if given resolute leadership, stray parties from disintegrated battalions could be welded into an efficient fighting detachment capable of engaging superior forces. The end of this Force was far from being an inglorious one.[27]

This superficial statement merely masks the truth. Merrett Force's action just after dawn on 11 February was no more than a brave and fortuitous escape from annihilation by capable officers and other ranks. The real issue on Brigadier Taylor's Brigade front from the moment of its fighting on 8–9th until 11 February was simple. The formations had, right from the start, been allotted impossible tactical tasks and were manned by a combination of exhausted veterans and untrained and untried reinforcements. Trained, tried and seasoned officers such as Lieutenant-Colonel Arthur Boyes and Major Dick Keegan deserved better.

Having described the fate of Paris's 12th Indian Brigade and Taylor's 22nd Australian Brigade in their attempts to recapture the Jurong Line, we now turn to Brigadier Coates and his 15th Indian Brigade. Coates was only required to move his battalions a little forward to reach his phase one positions on the night of 10 February. By 11.00 pm his British Battalion constituted his left flank, astride the Jurong Road at Milestone 9 with the Special Reserve Battalion to its left; the 3/16th Punjab occupied a ridge just north of the road; and to the right of the Punjabis were the Jats. Coates intended to move on his phase two objective at daylight on the 11th. In a prelude to impending disaster, Kirby has stated that, 'The Jats on the right reported—somewhat naturally—that they were unable to make contact with 12th Brigade.'[28] 'Somewhat naturally', because the 12th Brigade unit they attempted to make contact with were the Hyderabads who, as we have recorded, had suffered 'many desertions during the day'. Paris believed that 'he could only rely on about 100 men from that Battalion'.[29]

As the tragedy that befell Paris's 12th Indian Brigade, Taylor's 'X' Battalion and Merrett Force began to unfold during the night of 10/11 February—witnessed only vaguely in terms of various illuminations on the horizon and distant noises of battle by Saggers's Special Reserve Battalion and Coates's soldiers—Coates sent a liaison officer back at around 2.30 am to report in. By 5.30 am he realised that his Brigade had lost communications and, with firing heard from his rear, he knew he was cut off. Orders were sent cancelling the dawn attack, but were not received by the Jats, who duly attacked at dawn and according to Kirby 'were never seen again'.[30] Wigmore was more revealing: 'The Battalion remained in the locality, unable to make its way back, until the fall of Singapore, then it broke up. Its commander, Lieut-Col Cummings, and some of his British and Indian officers eventually made their way to Sumatra, and were transported to India.'[31]

After having withdrawn about 350 metres during the last hours of darkness, dawn brought fierce Japanese fire upon the forward Special Reserve and the British Battalion. The Brigade HQ was attacked by an enemy force which had moved from Bukit Timah village. Coates was forced to move forward to the British Battalion lines, where he subsequently ordered a general brigade withdrawal to Reformatory Road. Only a determined counterattack by elements of both battalions allowed the 15th Brigade to withdraw in three groups: one British, one Indian and the last Australian.

After gaining about 900 metres through good cover, the three columns were forced to cross an open depression and were caught in a hail of fire which inflicted severe casualties and caused them to become dispersed. When, after heavy fighting, the remnant reached Reformatory Road, they were mauled again before forming up on the eastern side of that feature.

By the early morning of 11 February 1942, General Bennett's counter-attack to retake the Jurong Line had been a costly disaster. In a number of cases, units failed to gain their phase one startlines, while others, already close to their initial objective, reached it but made no ground in attempting to occupy their phase two lines. And in the process, the 12th and 15th Indian Brigades—two reserve formations—were savaged to such an extent that they ceased to exist as formations. On that fateful morning, the Special Reserve Battalion could muster a mere 80 of its soldiers, while the combined survivors of Coates's Brigade now stood (with the Jats missing) at 400—little more than half-battalion strength. Taylor's 22nd Brigade, already decimated by its fighting on the north-west coast, had had its newly formed 'X' Battalion all but annihilated, and Merrett Force had also suffered heavy losses. Brigadier Taylor now possessed nothing more than a threadbare force to hold the Japanese advance along Reformatory Road and into Singapore Town.

When, during the early hours of 11 February, General Bennett became aware of the magnitude of the losses to Brigadier Paris's 12th Indian Brigade, and, most of all, the loss of Bukit Timah and its associated stores of food, ammunition and petrol, he ordered his newly acquired 18th British Division's Tomforce reserve to recapture Bukit Timah and then Bukit Panjang village. It was a tall order given that by the time Tomforce attacked, it was faced by the 18th and 5th Japanese Divisions, each with two regiments forward and one in reserve, and in possession of the high ground. While the defenders had committed their scant, and tired reserves piecemeal, Yamashita had paused after his capture of Bukit Timah, consolidated and was now in a strong position to either blunt counterattacks, or resume his advance.

Against a depressing background of a still-smouldering Bukit Timah, and the ever present black clouds of burning oil, Lieutenant-Colonel Thomas sent in his Tomforce 1/5th Sherwood Foresters along the left of the road, the 4th Norfolks on the right of it and the 18th Reconnaissance Battalion along it. However, the recurring problems of movement through a maze of jungle, scrub and plantations, and the very steep nature of the country, not only caused a loss of contact within units, but slowed their progress. Those difficulties were compounded by the fact that the 4th Norfolks, although gaining two of their high-ground objectives, were then pushed off them, and in the case of the Foresters, one of its company's progress was retarded by a movement through its path by elements of the retreating 15th Brigade. Scattered, and therefore vulnerable to any concerted Japanese attacks during the night, Major-General Beckworth-Smith ordered Tomforce to withdraw to the racecourse. These events then impacted upon the neighbouring 2/29th Battalion, which in turn also withdrew. This unit, now manned by very inexperienced reinforcement junior officers and other ranks, was widely dispersed by spasmodic skirmishes during the night, which later saw only Lieutenant-Colonel Pond and elements of his Headquarter Company arrive at Bennett's HQ at Tanglin Barracks at first light.

Fighting at and near the Jurong Line and Trunk Road during the period 10–11 February had seen unit after unit belatedly committed, torn to shreds, demoralised and then scattered.

With the dimensions of his Singapore perimeter diminishing rapidly on the early morning of 11 February 1942, General Percival moved his HQ from Sime Road to Fort Canning. Not long after, the main petrol depot just east of the racecourse caught fire, which thickened the dull, black blanket that had enveloped the Island. Percival now made three key decisions. He assigned all operations east of the racecourse to General Heath; bolstered General Bennett's Western Command by moving the 2nd Gordons from Changi to it; and created a unit composed of base reinforcements and deployed it at the eastern end of the racecourse.

Aware that the Imperial Japanese Guards Division might well attack southwards towards the reservoirs from their landing points on the Causeway Sector, and that Yamashita might also thrust eastwards from Bukit Timah through the gap between the reservoirs, Heath created another new brigade formation called Massy Force (Brigadier Massy-Beresford), which was to hold a line extending from just east of the MacRitchie Reservoir to Thompson village and thence to the Woodleigh pumping station—all vital

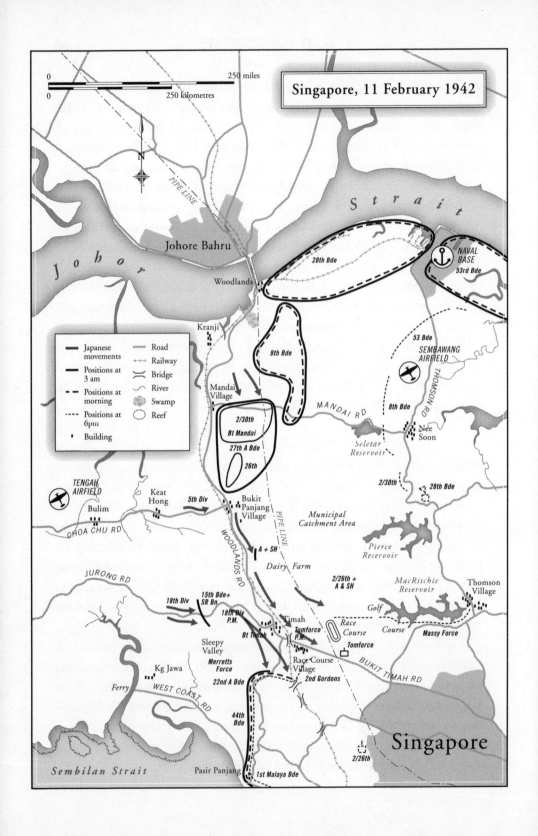

Singapore, 11 February 1942

0 ——————— 250 miles
0 ——————— 250 kilometres

Japanese movements
Positions at 3 am
Positions at morning
Positions at 6pm
Building
Road
Railway
Bridge
River
Swamp
Reef

Johor

Strait

Johore Bahru

NAVAL BASE

28th Bde

53rd Bde

Woodlands

Kranji

8th Bde

53 Bde

SEMBAWANG AIRFIELD

Mandai Village

MANDAI RD

8th Bde

Nee Soon

2/30th
Bt Mandai

27th A Bde

26th

Seletar Reservoir

TENGAH AIRFIELD

Keat Hong

5th Div

Bukit Panjang Village

2/30th

28th Bde

Bulim

CHOA CHU RD

PIPE LINE

Municipal Catchment Area

Pierce Reservoir

A + SH

Dairy Farm

2/26th + A & SH

MacRitchie Reservoir

Thomson Village

JURONG RD

18th Div

15th Bde+ SR Bn

18th Div P.M.

Timah

Tomforce P.M.

Race Course

Golf
Course

Massy Force

Bt Timah

Sleepy Valley

Merretts Force

Race Course Village

Tomforce

22nd A Bde

2nd Gordons

BUKIT TIMAH RD

Kg Jawa

Ferry

WEST COAST RD

44th Bde

Singapore

Sembilan Strait

Pasir Panjang

1st Malaya Bde

2/26th

PIPE LINE

THOMSON RD

WOODLANDS RD

locations to be held. Massy Force was also created in part to bridge the gap between Tomforce and the reservoirs. Wigmore has recorded that Massy Force:

> ... comprised the 1/Cambridgeshire, from the 55th Brigade, the 4/Suffolk (54th Brigade), the 5/11th Sikh (from the Southern Area), a detachment of the 3rd Cavalry, one field battery, and eighteen obsolescent light tanks recently landed, and manned by a detachment of the 100th Light Tank Squadron.[32]

When Percival visited Massy-Beresford on the afternoon of 11 February he now considered Massy Force's main priority was to bridge the gap between Tomforce and the reservoirs. To this end he ordered him to capture a locality named Point 300, which was the high ground just north-west of the racecourse. But before the operation could be executed, the Japanese occupied that feature. In the interim, however, the 18th Division's Major-General Beckwith-Smith had visited both his Massy and Tomforce HQ and decided that the ground occupied by both forces was unsuitable for defence and, with Heath's approval, withdrew both to a new defensive position along a line extending from MacRitchie Reservoir to the racecourse and then to the racecourse village.

By the morning of 12 February, the critical Malaya Command western front—facing Yamashita's 18th and 5th Divisions—now consisted of Southern Command's 1st Malaya Brigade, which occupied a line extending from just west of the coastal village of Pasir Panjang, northwards to a line just west of the Reformatory Road–Raja Road junction; its 44th Brigade was deployed from that junction to the Ulu Pandan Road junction; Bennett's Western Area now consisted of Taylor's 22nd Brigade's front which swung in an eastwards arc from the Ulu Pandan Road–Reformatory Road junction to the railway and Holland Road junction, where the 2nd Gordons continued that arc to link up with Tomforce and Massy Force. Alan Warren has left us with a succinct and damning sentence which describes Malaya Command's delayed and fragmented attempts to hold Singapore: 'It had taken Percival almost three days to get the main body of the 18th Division actively involved in the defence of Singapore.'[33]

While General Yamashita's 5th and 18th Divisions had attacked aggressively and won substantial objectives on Bennett's Western Area perimeter,
the Imperial Guards Division had continued to play a less formidable role.
It will be recalled that Brigadier Maxwell's premature 27th Brigade withdrawal from his Causeway Sector during the early hours of 10 February had
laid General Key's 11th Division's left flank bare. In response to Maxwell's
withdrawal, it will also be remembered that Key had ordered Brigadier
Trott to secure three high ground positions to the immediate rear of the
27th Brigade's former perimeter. When only two of those three objectives
were gained, Key had ordered the 2/10th Bulach to secure the gap between
his left flank and the 27th Brigade early on the 11th.

Now, on the early morning of that day, we come to more controversy
and varying accounts of disjointed and confused actions by commanders.
Kirby, the British Official Historian, has claimed that at around 7.30 am
on the 11th, Maxwell informed Key that his Brigade was no longer under
Heath's command, and that he had been ordered to 'occupy and hold Bukit
Panjang Village'.[34] Warren states that Maxwell told Key that he was 'going to
move southwards towards Bukit Panjang', and that Maxwell 'later claimed
that he was acting on the orders of Malaya Command'.[35] The Australian
Official Historian, Lionel Wigmore, states that 'Heath's anxieties grew when
he learned early on 11th February that the 27th Australian Brigade had been
ordered to recapture Bukit Panjang'.[36] Wigmore, not for the first time when
dealing with controversy, then gives us critical evidence which is relegated to
the obscurity of a footnote:

> No conclusive evidence has come to light as to who issued the order,
> although an attack on the enemy rear supplementary to a frontal
> attack by Tomforce would have been a logical move to retrieve
> the situation in this most critical area. According to General Key
> (11th Division) and his senior staff officers Brigadier Maxwell told
> them at the time that it came from General Bennett, but General
> Bennett has denied having given it. Brigadier Maxwell has recorded
> emphatically that it came from General Percival. It would have been
> contrary to military practice for either Percival or Bennett to issue it
> direct to the 27th Brigade while the brigade was under Key's command.

However, in the confusion of the time the chain of command might have become somewhat dislocated.[37]

Thyer, in his voluminous record of the campaign, made no mention of 27th Brigade being transferred back to Bennett, or of the consequences for Key. We will probably never know who issued that critical order, but, yet again, we note Brigadier Maxwell's distant, uncoordinated and seemingly contradictory accounts of his actions.

The critical issue concerning Brigadier Maxwell's command of his Brigade at this juncture is the fact that his HQ was now around 7.25 kilometres east of Mandai village, which, given the poor communications throughout the campaign, was foolhardy in the extreme. The time taken for his orders for the attack on Bukit Panjang to reach his 2/30th and 2/26th Battalions demonstrate the point. Incredibly, in the case of the 2/26th Battalion, those orders were taken by one of its officers (Captain Anderssen), returning to his unit from hospital. He was forced to travel on a motor cycle, then by foot, and did not reach 2/26th Battalion HQ until 10.30 am, where he found that Oakes and all but C Company had moved. Oakes, who had realised that the Japanese had captured Bukit Panjang, had instigated his Battalion's move to the previously ordered rendezvous along the pipeline to the racecourse. This move began fifteen minutes before Maxwell's planned attack on Bukit Panjang—which Oakes was completely unaware of. In his movement out, Oakes ordered his 2/26th companies to move independently if the enemy attacked. The enemy did. Eventually, three companies found their way back to the Singapore Golf Club and the last to the General Base Depot.

Meanwhile, when Lieutenant-Colonel Ramsay received his orders for the Bukit Panjang attack, his 2/30th Battalion had had no contact with either the Baluchis nor the 2/26th. Ramsay was now being pressured by the enemy to his rear, was still out of contact with the 2/26th and also with Maxwell, and had no idea of the enemy strength at Bukit Panjang. As a consequence he wisely decided to withdraw. During the afternoon, he was able to talk with Maxwell after making contact with a Brigade signals party which was laying a line at the proposed Bukit Panjang attack assembly point. Ramsay was then ordered to occupy a position between the Peirce Reservoir and the Seletar Rifle Range.

Brigadier Maxwell had yet again failed to exercise effective command over his Brigade. He had yet again placed the inexperienced Oakes and Ramsay—whom he had appointed for dubious reasons—under incredible strain. By the morning of 12 February 1942, Maxwell had again compromised the potentially beneficial deployment of two of the best and still intact battalions in Malaya Command.

General Heath reacted to Maxwell's second withdrawal from his Northern Area left flank by ordering the evacuation of the naval base and its demolition. By about 6.00 pm the base had been evacuated; his 53rd Brigade had formed an arc facing north-west and extending from the River Simpang southwards to shield the Sembawang airfield; Trott's 8th Brigade had extended the arc to a point a little west of the Nee Soon road junction; and the 28th Brigade was deployed south as a reserve.

To add further misery to a disastrous day, 11 February saw Japanese aircraft drop numerous copies of a demand from Yamashita for Singapore's surrender.

The Japanese had accomplished a series of most impressive landings along the north-west shore of Singapore Island during the night of 8/9 February. During the next two days, that initial success had been spectacularly exploited, culminating in the capture of the critical high ground at the centre of the Island: Bukit Timah. On 12 February, General Yamashita now sought to complete the concentration of his force, hurriedly finish his repair of the causeway, and thereby increase his artillery gun numbers and ammunition supply.

Early on the morning of the 12th, the Japanese attacked Massy Force, which was deployed astride and just north of Bukit Timah Road. By 8.30 am a number of enemy tanks had reached the racecourse village before they were checked by a troop of the British 45th Anti-Tank Battery. But to the north of the road, the enemy infantry were able to infiltrate Massy Force (now fighting with Tomforce attached), which caused Lieutenant-Colonel Massy-Beresford to order a withdrawal to the junction of Bukit Timah and Adam and Farrer Roads. The move was completed by late afternoon and, as the Japanese now paused and did not attack again that day, the 18th Division's

Massy Force and Tomforce remnant were able to dig in, and further anti-tank guns and reinforcements were used to bolster this vital main road into Singapore Town.

It will be remembered that on the previous day in the Northern Area, General Heath had abandoned the naval base and had moved his 53rd and 8th Brigades into an arc facing north-west and extending from the River Simpang southwards to a point a little west of the Nee Soon road junction, and had sited his 28th Brigade further south in reserve. At daybreak, the Japanese attacked the 8th Brigade near Nee Soon along the southern portion of that newly occupied arc. This attack was directed at the 2/10th Baluch, which was astride the Mandai Road, and the 1/8th Punjab, which was on its right flank. When the Punjabis 'began to disintegrate'[38]—the term used by Kirby to describe a panic-stricken flight from the area—there was a very real chance that the 53rd Brigade to the north would be cut off. Key immediately sent elements of his reserve 28th Brigade to fill the gap.

During the morning of the 12th, Percival visited Massy Force HQ and Bennett's Western Area and became very conscious of the possibility of a Japanese breakthrough down the Bukit Timah Road and into the heart of Singapore Town. Aware of his heavy losses in men and material during the previous day, and the fact that only scant defences in depth lay along that vital Bukit Timah axis, he now, in consultation with Heath, determined that the continued occupation of the northern and eastern shores of the Island was a redundant measure given the Town's vulnerability.

Percival would later write that:

> ... the time had come to take up a perimeter defence round the town. Such a perimeter defence must of course include the water supply. So I instructed Heath to withdraw his troops from the northern beaches and to select and occupy a position covering the water supply and linking up on the right with Southern Area which would be holding the Kallang aerodrome.[39]

Malaya Command's final perimeter was to be occupied during that night (12/13 February) and was to extend from Buona Vista on the south-west coast inland to Tanglin Halt (1st Malayan and 44th Brigades); from Tanglin

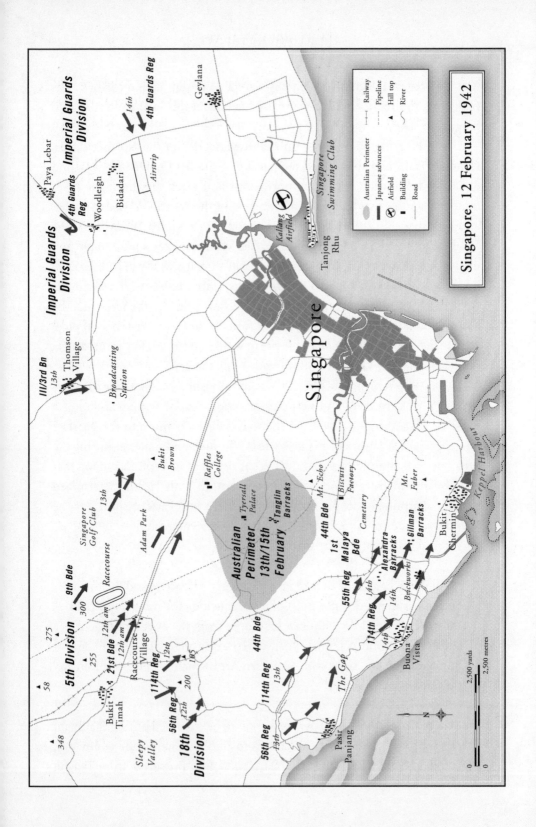

Singapore, 12 February 1942

Halt to near the Bukit Timah–Farrer Road junction (8th Division and 2nd Gordons); from Bukit Timah Road–Adam Road to MacRitchie Reservoir, Thomson village, Woodleigh crossroads (Massy Force and Tomforce and the 18th Division); from Woodleigh crossroads to Paya Lebar airstrip (11th Indian Division); and from that airstrip to Kallang airfield (2nd Malaya Brigade).

After his orders were given for the final Singapore perimeter, Percival called on the Governor, who soon gave instructions for the destruction of the Broadcasting Station which was only about a kilometre inside the new perimeter, and for the burning of the remaining currency notes at the Treasury. By this time, the war had come to Government House in the form of enemy shelling. On 12 February, Sir Shenton Thomas recorded the effects of a blast on his back verandah under which 'many of our boys were sheltering'.[40] 'During a lull I crawled under the House with Dawson and Simson and found several bodies . . . No signs of wounds, and death must have been instantaneous from blast—all covered with yellow dust and almost unrecognisable.'[41]

The 12th also saw another significant casualty. By the early morning of that day, the pressure had got the better of Brigadier Taylor:

Tired though I was, I could not sleep, and about 0700 hrs I realised that I would have to get a few hours rest in a quiet spot; my brain refused to work and I was afraid that if I carried on without rest the Bde would suffer. I accordingly sent for Lt Col Varley, who had been in reserve with the 2/18 Bn since 1800 hrs the previous day. Shortly after he arrived everything went black and my legs gave way.[42]

Before being sent to hospital Taylor called on Bennett. It was an acrimonious conversation which saw Bennett relieve Taylor of his command of the 22nd Brigade. The 2/18th Battalion's Lieutenant-Colonel Varley was promoted and replaced him.

The fight for the Island had rapidly degenerated into a last-ditch stand for Singapore Town itself. By Friday 13 February 1942, however, the issue of stragglers and the associated problems of drunkeness, looting and lawlessness at the docks had reached alarming proportions.

22

FINAL DAYS

The defence of Singapore Island during the period 9–12 February 1942 on the north-west coast, around the Jurong Line and Bukit Timah had been nothing short of a military disaster, and the consequences for Singapore Town itself were no less catastrophic. We have noted that a great many stragglers had been created by that desperate, confused fighting, and caused in no small measure by the often disjointed and piecemeal senior command response to the enemy advance.

According to the 8th Division Provost Company Unit Diary, the Australian Military Police problems began as early as 4 February:

> Reports coming in that Australian soldiers are causing disturbances in Singapore. Capt Menz, in company with Major Thompson of HQ AIF., visited all Hotels, Bars, and places where soldiers foregather in Singapore, but could only find two AIF soldiers in the town, and they were sober, but British troops were plentiful. Nearly all British troops are wearing Aust. style slouch hats, which apparently is why AIF troops have been blamed for all disturbances involving troops.[1]

It is easy to examine the problem merely in terms of 'stragglers', and perhaps, in terms of the nationality of those stragglers. But in the final days leading up to the Japanese landings, disorder and panic had begun to permeate both the base troops' behaviour and to a lesser extent, the civilian population. On 6 February the provosts reported: 'Very heavy shelling also Air bombing in Bukit Timah and Bukit Panjang areas, owing to which W/shop Units and Vehicle Reception Park moved their locations, but left behind a great many serviceable vehicles of all types.'[2]

On 8 February the provosts recorded: 'Civilian and military traffic on Bukit Timah and other main roads very heavy, and difficulty experienced in handling owing to civilian vehicles being so numerous, and desiring to go in so many directions.'[3] The following day, as news came of the enemy landings and heavy fighting, the panic increased. Jurong Road became jammed with vehicles, and the provosts discovered that a five-kilometre journey took four hours, and as a consequence reinforcements 'that should have arrived could not get through'.[4]

The number of stragglers in Singapore rapidly increased on 10 February as the full effects of the coastal fighting were felt. Lieutenant Hector Chambers, an 8th Division Provost Officer during those last action-packed days, wrote a revealing account of his observations that day:

Owing to the fact that twenty-six Australians preferred being drunk and shooting up civilians and native police to being with their units at battle stations, I and my small unit were tied to the unsavoury job of looking after them . . .

Stragglers were beginning to filter in, wandering along with a bewildered, completely lost look, singly and in twos and threes. A larger number arrived from the by-ways and alleys of the city where they had been rounded up by the Provost patrols who were quartering the whole of the rear area. Our work began in ernest [sic] then. Trucks had to be found, scrounged or just lifted without the owners' permission, and brought along to our depot; drivers obtained much in the same manner, and the stragglers herded aboard and sent off along the shell bespattered road towards the Botanical Gardens . . .

Let me say here that the accumulation of troops in the city was not confined alone to AIF troops. There were more British troops there, and an infinitely larger number of Indians. I say this, not as an excuse, but by way of explanation. Regiments and battalions which had been fighting on the coast had . . . lost all unity. Officers and NCOs had lost control, and the obvious and natural result was that men would drift back towards the only kind of solidarity and reality they knew . . .

I emphasize this aspect of the situation so that it may be clearly understood that the confidence of the troops in their military leaders was waning rapidly and that their morale was deteriorating with every gloomy day that passed. This state of affairs became more and more evident as the enemy closed in on the city.[5]

By this time the rapid increase in the number of stragglers was compounded by a tragic but virtually uncontrollable 'snowball' effect. We have observed that those stragglers were composed of a mixture of soldiers who were genuinely looking for their withdrawn and scattered units; others who were either totally exhausted or wounded; some 'shell-shocked'; and others still, who were undoubtedly deserters, fleeing the battle. Of the last category, it would seem beyond doubt that the vast majority of the Australian variety were untrained and untried reinforcements. But it mattered little as these troops wove their way through the countryside or through frequent traffic jams caused by the 'narrowness of road, bad driving and bad convoy discipline'.[6] Kirby called the process 'disintegration', while others more bluntly referred to these men simply as 'deserters'. But the truth is that many undisciplined base personnel who saw the front line troops moving back simply followed suit, or indeed in some cases, after the fate of some of their comrades in dubious formations such as 'X' Battalion, had no intention of doing anything other than avoiding action. As the battle raged ever closer to Singapore Town, many resorted to alcohol and looting, while others saw another possible solution to their despair: the wharves and a chance to escape by ship or small boat.

The 17 000 tonne *Empire Star* was one such prize. On the 11th that vessel was busy embarking women and children, nursing sisters and RAF personnel. After an aggressive, armed group of Australians were cleared from the gangway, and after it had been raised only with the assistance of military police that evening, it was discovered at sea that a number of Australian troops had managed to board the vessel, including a captain. It would transpire that the *Empire Star* and around eleven other ships disembarked about 175 other ranks and that captain at Java. The overwhelming majority of them were Australian Army Service Corps personnel—base troops.

As dawn broke on the morning of Friday 13 February 1942, it was crystal clear that Singapore's final demise was near. The military perimeter lacked depth, both in numbers and equipment; the morale of many of the defenders was at breaking point; significant numbers of them and those to their rear had given up the fight; the critical loss of the Bukit Timah food depots had reduced supplies—other than those still held by individual units and the civil administration—to a paltry seven days; petrol supplies were running very low; and, most obvious to all, was the horrific plight of the civilian population which had swelled to around a million, and who were being mercilessly bombed from the air and shelled from the ground. Wigmore has recorded an officer's account of the aftermath of one such bombing:

> Buildings on both sides of the road went up in smoke . . . soldiers and civilians suddenly appeared staggering through clouds of debris; some got on the road, others stumbled and dropped in their tracks, others shrieked as they ran for safety . . . we pulled up near a building which had collapsed onto the road—it looked like a caved-in slaughter house. Blood splashed what was left of the lower rooms; chunks of human beings—men, women and children—littered the place. Everywhere bits of steaming flesh, smoldering [sic] rags, clouds of dust—and the shriek and groan of those who still survived.[7]

The Japanese chose to attack but one portion of Malaya Command's perimeter on 13 February. During the early morning the 18th Division's 56th Regiment, supported by a concentrated two-hour artillery barrage,

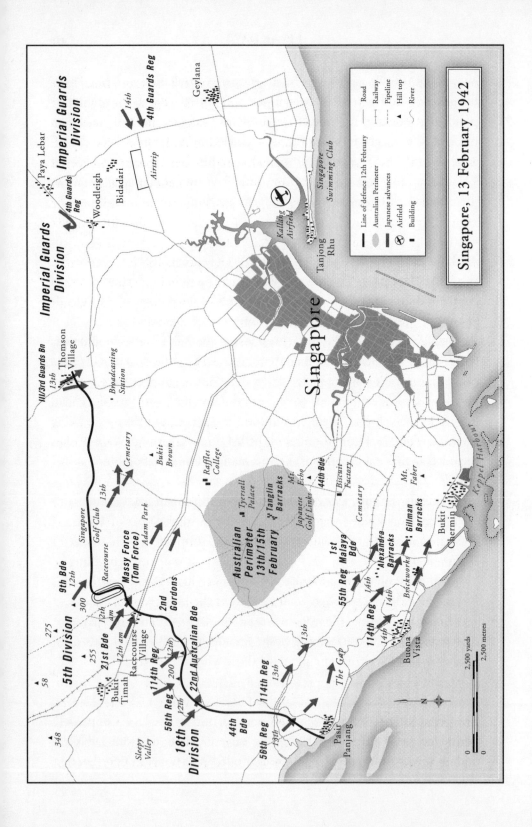

Singapore, 13 February 1942

Legend:
- Line of defence 12th February
- Australian Perimeter
- Japanese advances
- Airfield
- Building
- Road
- Railway
- Pipeline
- Hill top
- River

Imperial Guards Division

Paya Lebar

14th

4th Guards Reg

Geylana

Woodleigh

Bidadari

Airstrip

4th Guards Reg

Imperial Guards Division

Singapore Swimming Club

Tanjong Rhu

Kallang Airfield

III/3rd Guards Bn

13th

Thomson Village

Broadcasting Station

Singapore

Cemetary

Bukit Brown

Raffles College

13th

Singapore Golf Club

9th Bde

12th

Racecourse

300

Massy Force (Tom Force)

Adam Park

Tyersall Palace

Tanglin Barracks

Australian Perimeter 13th/15th February

Mt. Echo

Japanese Golf Links

44th Bde

Biscuit Factory

275

255

5th Division

21st Bde

12th am

Racecourse Village

114th Reg

12th

200

2nd Gordons

22nd Australian Bde

Cemetary

Mt. Faber

Bukit Chermin

Keppel Harbour

58

Bukit Timah

56th Reg

12th

18th Division

114th Reg

13th

44th Bde

114th Reg

13th

The Gap

13th

1st Malaya Bde

55th Reg

13th

Alexandra Barracks

114th Reg

14th

Brickworks

Gillman Barracks

348

Sleepy Valley

56th Reg

13th

Pasir Panjang

55th Reg

14th

114th Reg

14th

Buona Vista

0   2,500 yards

0   2,500 metres

N

assaulted the 1st Malaya Brigade's coastal area, which stretched from Pasir Panjang village (1st Malays), along the Pasir Panjang ridge to the Raja Road (the 2nd Malays and 2nd Loyals). Despite stiff resistance, the Japanese broke through and travelled some distance eastwards towards Buona Vista Road. After dark, the 1st Malaya Brigade and the 44th Indian Brigade were forced to withdraw to a line running from just east of Buona Vista village northeast to the junction of Depot and Raja Roads, and then to a position near Mount Echo to link with Bennett's 22nd Brigade. Whilst the 44th Brigade had withdrawn to conform to 1st Malaya Brigade's withdrawal, Bennett's 8th Division—bolstered by the arrival during the afternoon of Brigadier Maxwell's 27th Brigade and with the 2nd Gordons still attached—did not withdraw, which left a large AIF bulge on the western Malaya Command perimeter. This did not seem to bother either Bennett or the Japanese.

When Percival had planned his last Singapore perimeter the day before, General Bennett had reacted to it by the formation of a final AIF perimeter which was to be manned by nearly all units of his Division. The exceptions to this order were the staffs of a number of hospitals and medical units. By concentrating most of his formations, Bennett was able to provide an all-round defence of his perimeter, and when the Tanglin swimming pool was filled with fresh water and his reserve food stocks were also concentrated, he prepared for a last stand. Brigadier Taylor, now out of hospital, was given the task of forming this new AIF perimeter, which Thyer later recorded, 'assumed the shape of an ellipse 7 miles [about eleven kilometres] in circumference with Holland Road as the main axis and Div HQ at Tanglin as the centre'.[8]

While the fighting on 1st Malaya Brigade's front was in progress, General Percival had called a meeting of both Area and Divisional commanders, and a number of his senior staff officers at Fort Canning for 2.00 pm. What must have started out as a rather gloomy affair later degenerated into a personal attack upon Percival.

Heath, citing the poor physical and mental condition of the troops, strongly advocated an immediate capitulation, which was endorsed by Bennett and all senior commanders present. In answer to them, Percival stated that not only should the fight be maintained as long as possible, but that he was considering a counterattack to retake the critically important

Bukit Timah area. Percival's stance—however futile—was probably driven by a telegram received from Wavell that day.

> General Wavell to General Percival   13 Feb 42
> You must fight it out to the end as you are doing. But when everything humanly possible has been done some bold and determined person-nel may be able to escape by small craft and find their way south to Sumatra through the islands.[9]

After replying that such a counterattack had already failed, and that a fresh reserve was not available, Heath again advocated capitulation, and for a second time the senior commanders present endorsed him. According to Percival's biographer, Clifford Kinvig, Percival then stated: 'I have my honour to consider and there is also the question of what posterity will think of us if we surrender this large army and valuable fortress.' Heath's insubordinate reply brought with it a brief awkwardness and resulting wall of silence: 'You need not bother about your honour. You lost that a long time ago up in the north.' Percival finally replied with two calm sentences. 'I cannot accept your proposal that we should surrender. We will go on fighting as long as we can.'[10] Kinvig has described Heath's slur as 'cruel, insolent and public . . .'[11] He was right. Despite other failings, Lieutenant-General Arthur Percival's honour should never have been questioned.

In *The War In Malaya*, Percival also stated that the conference members expressed concern for the civil population of Singapore should Japanese troops become involved in street fighting inside the town.[12] He might have added that if British prestige had already suffered greatly after the loss of Penang, and then during the sustained Japanese bombing of the Town, then a wholesale slaughter of innocent civilians—and soldiers untrained for such skilled street fighting—would have further eroded that already fragile status. And, given the military performance of his army, that agony would have been short-lived and therefore futile. After the conference, Percival rightly decided that he should contact Wavell.

> General Percival to General Wavell   13 Feb 42
> Enemy now within 5,000 yards of sea-front, which brings whole of

Singapore town within field artillery range. We are also in danger of being driven off water and food supplies. In opinion of commanders troops already committed are too exhausted either to withstand strong attack or to launch counter-attack . . .

There must come a stage when in the interests of the troops and the civil population further bloodshed will serve no useful purpose. Your instructions of February 10 are being carried out, but in above circumstances would you consider giving me wider discretionary powers?[13]

In his usual docile, diplomatic manner, Percival was in fact merely asking for the proper right to capitulate when he—the man on the spot—realised that it was appropriate. One suspects that he agreed with his commanders, but was attempting to satisfy all and sundry.

Wavell's reply came the next day:

General Wavell to General Percival   14 Feb 42
You must continue to inflict maximum damage on enemy for as long as possible by house-to-house fighting if necessary. Your action in tying down enemy and inflicting casualties may have vital influence in other theatres. Fully appreciate your situation, but continued action essential.[14]

That same day, a weak Wavell had an each way bet with the Prime Minister in an insipid telegram:

General Wavell to Prime Minister   14 Feb 42
Have received telegram from Percival that enemy are close to town and that his troops are incapable of further counter-attack. Have ordered him to continue inflict maximum damage to enemy by house-to-house fighting if necessary. Fear however that resistance not likely to be very prolonged.[15]

In view of his own very recent visit, and Percival's telegram to him the previous day, Wavell must have known that Singapore was on its very last gasp, and that all would be lost in a matter of a few days if not hours. So much for Percival's chances of achieving a 'vital influence in other theatres'. The last outcome of the conference at Fort Canning on 13 February was the decision to evacuate all female nurses, certain staff officers and technicians. That evacuation was to be undertaken on the night of 13/14 February using all of the remaining small ships in Singapore Harbour. Around 3000 persons were to be selected, and of that number, 1800 positions were allotted to the army. The AIF received an allocation of one hundred. Bennett decided that Colonel Broadbent, his chief administration officer, would head the AIF group.

Meanwhile, in the streets of Singapore Town, the issue of stragglers was reaching alarming proportions. On 13 February, Lieutenant 'Hec' Chambers recorded:

Captain Menz had patrols out through the streets, directing all Australians to report at the Anzac Club. We set up a kitchen and fed as many as possible before loading them into trucks and sending them on to their distribution centre at the Botanical Gardens. We fed nearly two thousand men during the day.[16]

But whilst in the majority, the Australians were by no means the only stragglers. On 13 February the 8th Division Provost Company Unit Diary recorded: 'British and Indian troops wandering aimlessly about. Representations made to APM [Assistant Provost Marshal] Malaya Command to provide directional information for British troops, but with no result.'[17] And 14 February brought even less pleasure to Chambers and his fellow MPs:

The fourteenth was a wicked day. More and more troops had poured into Singapore during the night . . .
   Men were straggling in from the front line continuously now. Some of them were 'bomb happy'—that apt name for shell shock—and fine physical specimens sat on the grass and wept, others, whenever a plane was heard, cowered trembling behind the slightest shelter. Most of them were dirty and bedraggled, carrying many days growth of beard. Some had rifles and 'tommy guns', others had thrown their arms away; all of them were hungry.[18]

On 14 February 1942, Yamashita found himself with only one operational handicap in his final advance on Singapore Town: he needed more artillery guns and ammunition. Colonel Tsuji would later write:

> On the evening of the 14th February the Kanoe [Imperial Guards] Division completed repairs to the Causeway and pushed forward. Our heavy guns moved in rapid succession to positions on the heights to the east of the reservoir. For the first time our whole army was across the Johore Strait and concentrated on Singapore Island.[19]

Given that the build-up described above would probably take a further 24 hours to complete, the Japanese chose to attack along the south-west coast, where they had achieved some measure of success the previous day, on the north near the MacRitchie Reservoir and on the eastern side of the British perimeter just south of the airfield at Paya Lebar.

At about 8.30 am a number of thrusts were made against the 1st Malaya Brigade between the south coast and Raja Road. After attacking for most of the morning, during which both sides took heavy casualties, the afternoon saw a renewed enemy thrust reach a line extending from Bukit Chermin, along the canal to the brickworks, and thence to the Depot Road–Raja Road junction. During their movement along Raja Road, elements of the Japanese 18th Division reached Alexandra Hospital during that afternoon. It was here, on the afternoon of 14 February, that the Japanese added to their long, infamous catalogue of indiscriminate slaughter against defenceless non-combatants. After having been fired on by retreating Indian troops on their approach to the hospital, they entered it and proceeded to bayonet staff and patients, 'including a patient lying on an operating table'.[20] Their next act was more premeditated and therefore more shameful. After securing around 150 hospital occupants in a bungalow that afternoon, they proceeded to execute them on the morning of the 15th.

As on the previous day, Yamashita chose to leave Bennett's 8th Division's bulge-like perimeter alone, other than to subject it to periodic but concentrated artillery fire. Bennett would not have endeared himself to 1st Malaya Brigade's defenders on his left flank when it was discovered that Australian artillery support was not forthcoming—support that could have operated with superb observation over the area of fighting. Having heard that Malaya Command's artillery ammunition stocks were very low indeed, Bennett had ordered the previous day that the Australian artillery was to fire only in defence of its own perimeter, and even then, only upon 'observed targets'. In a further twist of fate, elements of the Australian 2/4th Machine Gun Battalion were also frustrated witnesses to that Japanese advance, but could not offer machine gun fire because they had been rearmed as infantry in the AIF perimeter.

On the Northern Area front on the 14th, the Japanese gained additional ground. The first attacks occurred along Thomson Road and resulted in an enemy capture of Point 105. This movement created a gap between the 18th Division's 55th and 53rd Brigades. Although the 11th Division despatched one of its battalions to plug the gap, a further attack in the afternoon along Sime Road, which was spearheaded by medium tanks, broke through and reached the outer limits of residential Mount Pleasant. Although a counterattack was planned, it did not materialise, and by dark the 18th Division had given ground and now occupied a 'U shaped' loop in its line extending from the MacRitchie Reservoir pier, southwards to Mount Pleasant Road, along that feature westwards to a point south of Bukit Brown, and then north to the original perimeter line west of Adam Road. On their eastern front, the enemy attacked around midday, and achieved some initial success before the 11th Division again managed to stabilise the front by the onset of darkness.

During that fateful day, Percival received two reports—one in the morning and the second during the late afternoon—which gave him a slim but forlorn hope that the water supply to the Town might still last for some time. During the morning, after being told that at best that supply might last for two days, he assigned 100 of the Royal Engineers to attempt to repair leaks in the pipeline. At the second meeting, Percival was informed that the water supply to the Town had slightly improved. He then asked the Director General of Civil Defence (Brigadier Simson) for an update at 7.00 am the next day (15 February).

If various units in Malaya Command had 'disintegrated' or were 'not seen again' along a rapidly diminishing defensive perimeter, then the term 'disintegration' was an apt title for the continuing destruction of Singapore Town and its inhabitants. The 8th Division Provost Company Unit Diary, 15 February 1942:

Enemy air and artillery action on Singapore greatly increased. Water mains severed, electricity cut off, and town very badly battered. Soldiers everywhere. Daily requests to Malaya Command to collect and direct British soldiers, but nothing done. AIF soldiers collected by this unit and transported to Botanical Gdns, but morale shocking. A lot of men hid themselves to prevent and avoid return to the line. Very heavy air raids and shelling about 1600 hrs. Fires in several parts of the town, vehicles on fire along the whole length of streets, general pandemonium and confusion.[21]

Captain Alf Menz, 8th Division Provost Company, diary 15 February:

As we drove around I found streets impassable. Blocked with burning vehicles, (S'pore was full of Army vehicles), debris everywhere, corpses all over the place. You could smell death, confusion abounding, trolley bus wires telephone & electric wires all over the road, electricity off, gas off. Telephones out of action and a good part of the town without water . . .[22]

Brigadier Simson's morning report to Percival on the 15th was not encouraging. The constant bombing and shelling of the water pipes towards, and in the Town, was continuing to create more breaks than could be repaired. To compound the problem, the increasing debris and human cluttering of roads made the engineers' tasks more time-consuming and labour intensive. At a commanders' meeting at Fort Canning at 9.30 am, Simson now went further than his earlier report, by stating that Singapore's water supplies could now be expected to last no longer than another day.

Percival now gave an appreciation. Although Malaya Command's food supplies were rapidly diminishing, there were still significant civil food stocks. However, whilst small arms ammunition supplies were still considerable, artillery shell supplies were very low indeed, and anti-aircraft ammunition stocks were threadbare. He then declared that petrol supplies were almost down to those presently held in vehicle tanks—there was no real reserve of petrol. And underpinning this state of affairs remained Simson's just mentioned report of a rapidly failing water supply.

In summary Percival stated the obvious: a maintenance of the present defensive perimeter could only end in the just-described administrative problems forcing a surrender, or worse, that a concentrated Japanese attack would more than likely gain them the confines of the Town and a needless slaughter of innocent civilians would result. He identified two alternatives. The first was a counterattack to restore the Town's water supply and food dumps. Clearly, those objectives would entail attacks upon the reservoirs and an attack in the Bukit Timah area where most of the food dumps had been lost. The second alternative was capitulation.

It is little wonder that the commanders' unanimous response was capitulation. Given the appalling supply problems outlined by Percival, the notion that any counterattack would constitute anything other than a token gesture—and further senseless killing—was fanciful.

Percival finally faced the inevitable. A belated telegram from Wavell that morning probably fortified his decision:

General Wavell to General Percival   15 Feb 42
So long as you are in position to inflict losses and damage to enemy and your troops are physically capable of doing so you must fight on. Time gained and damage to enemy are of vital importance at this crisis. [and then the key sentence] When you are fully satisfied that this is no longer possible I give you discretion to cease resistance.[23]

At 11.30 am on the 15th a delegation of three—Brigadier Newbigging, Major Wild and the Straits Settlement's Colonial Secretary—left Fort Canning by car and after reaching a part of the 18th Division's perimeter at the junction of Bukit Timah and Adam Roads, proceeded on by foot for another 500 metres before they were met by a Japanese staff officer. The three men returned to Percival with a Japanese flag that was to be flown over the Cathay Building as a recognition of Percival's intent to meet Yamashita at 4.00 pm to officially surrender. Later that afternoon, a Japanese officer observed a 'pale and thin and ill' Percival arrive at the Ford Motor Factory to formally capitulate.[24] The surrender document was signed at around 6.10 pm.

And so on 15 February 1942, on what General Percival would later describe as 'Black Sunday', the biggest military capitulation in the history of British Arms occurred. In a mere 70 days Lieutenant-General Tomoyuki Yamashita and his 25th Army had swept through Malaya and captured the prized jewel of Singapore: the gateway to Britain's commercial and colonial influence in the Pacific.

The reactions of the soldiers on that day were many and varied. Private Gus Halloran, 2/19th Battalion, a veteran of Muar: '...we believed that a decent fight could have been made of it, and hadn't been. So we felt really frustrated by that.'[25] And then there is the age-old humiliation every soldier in history has felt when forced to surrender. Private Paddy O'Toole, 2/29th Battalion: 'Oh Jesus Christ! I was devastated! I was just bloody rat shit! ... that was the most humiliating day, I think, in my whole life, when they said, "Lay down your arms."'[26] For others there was another more immediate fear. Sergeant Frank Baker, 2/20th Battalion, distinctly remembered the thought of possible mass executions: 'Oh yes! We had worries about that! We just didn't know what they'd do! ... Not a very good feeling!'[27]

But for most Australians there was a chance to eat a decent meal, drink their sorrows away, and to finally sleep. Sergeant Stan Arneil, 2/30th Battalion:

The odd types of food, at least odd from an army point of view, came from the buildings within the perimeter we were holding.

Our particular area included the French Consulate. It was to our eyes the ultimate in luxury and included an enormous wine cellar ...

About 5 p.m. all firing ceased. It was uncanny, one could almost hear the silence.

We saw no Japanese that night and spent hours talking about the prospects for the morning. Some men got drunk on French wine whilst others were so shocked they could hardly speak.[28]

The thoughts expressed above on that fateful day did not apply to a significant number of soldiers who sought a final, desperate escape from capture. General Gordon Bennett was the most senior of them, and would prove the most controversial. He had, since Malaya Command's withdrawal to Singapore Island, been thinking of his means of leaving. Late on 15 February, Bennett, his ADC Lieutenant Gordon Walker, and one of his liaison officers, Major Charles Moses, made good their escape to Sumatra. Bennett subsequently landed at Broome at 5.00 pm on 27 February 1942. He had escaped without informing General Percival, or indeed, without seeking his permission. In his stead he appointed Brigadier Callaghan to assume command of the 8th Australian Division.

———

At war's end and for many years to come, there would be a reckoning. General Bennett would face the final wrath of the Staff Corps after his escape, and most significantly, a final all-consuming confrontation with his old arch enemy: General Blamey. There would be bad blood and accusations between British senior commanders and between their Australian counterparts. In 1957 the Official Histories of both Britain and Australia would be completed; Kirby and Wigmore would 'cooperate' in a large measure as to what was said, and how it was said, culminating in both books being published on the same day. Over the next 35 to 40 years the controversy would not go away. In 1993 previously classified documents would unearth new evidence and new controversy.

But on or before Sunday 15 February 1942, those who had been incarcerated by the Japanese were faced with a far more immediate challenge: survival. Gunner Richard Haynes, 2/10th Field Regiment:

We had yet to learn that pride may be carried to the grave, unsullied, but it must humble itself at the gates of a prison camp.[29]

PART III
PUDU AND CHANGI PRISONS

. . . purgatory

———⊰●⊱———

Of all the inhabitants of the inferno, none but Lucifer knows
that hell is hell, and the secret function of purgatory is to
make of heaven an effective reality.

Arnold Bennett

23

'ROARING REGGIE'

———————

It has been said that war consists of prolonged periods of boredom punctuated by the most intense and horrifying moments in a soldier's life. The prisoner of war experience is very different. With either a mass capitulation, or the isolated local engagement that brings capture or surrender, comes the realisation that the primary function of one's existence—to fight and defeat the enemy—is gone. There is a certain humiliation, a sense of hopelessness, and above all, the awareness that one's destiny is no longer in the hands of one's commander or oneself. And then there is the new master. The treatment meted out to the captive is determined by a number of factors, some of which are ideological, religious or cultural, but critically, at the personal level, the character traits of the immediate master at any given place or time is paramount. An example is the experience of British and Australians captured by the Germans in North Africa compared to the fate of Russians who were captured by them on the Eastern Front. In short, through German eyes, there was an immense difference between a fellow Aryan and a Slav.

During the Second World War 8174 Australians were captured during the campaigns in North Africa, Europe and the Middle East. Of those some 265 died in captivity—around three per cent. Within a mere three months of the Japanese bombing of Pearl Harbor and their landings in Thailand

and Malaya, around 22 000 Australians became prisoners of war. In August 1945, three years and five months later, one in every three lay buried or their ashes scattered across an appalling trail of slavery, deprivation and torment which extended from Timor to Java, to Ambon, Sumatra, Singapore, Malaya, Borneo and later to Formosa (Taiwan), Korea, Manchuria and finally to Japan itself. The cost would constitute nearly half of the Australian nation's Pacific sacrifice. Our story will examine two of those camps, Pudu Prison in Kuala Lumpur and Changi on Singapore Island. Both were to generate new leaders and to cause others to flounder in captivity.

The Japanese term for officer is *shoko*. In an interview with the author in Singapore on 4 January 2008, Private Charles Letts of the Malay Volunteers would claim that one's chances of survival as a prisoner of war—particularly on the notorious Thai–Burma Railway—would depend on one's *shoko*.[1] And Letts was referring to Australian and British officers—not Japanese.

⸺⸱⸱⸺

We have noted that the breakneck speed of the Japanese advance down the Malay Peninsula had caused no small number of Indian Army, British and Australian troops to have been cut off and captured. The fate of those groups—some large and others small—had been a lottery of life and death according to the whim of Japanese senior commanders responding to stubborn resistance and heavy casualties (as at Parit Sulong), or at other times, the totally erratic behaviour of junior commanders or other ranks. Many of those fugitives were simply never seen again. Any British or Australian soldier endeavouring to make good his escape was also faced with the problem of being a conspicuous Caucasian in the midst of an Asian population, and with the fact that the Malays often cooperated most keenly with the Japanese for a monetary reward for information leading to their capture. As the tide of battle swept past them, parties of prisoners were placed in a string of regional gaols. When those became full, they were transferred by road and rail to Kuala Lumpur's Pudu Prison.

Completed in 1895, Pudu was built to accommodate 'all medium and long term prisoners'[2] in Malaya. Sited on a triangular, open tract of land in the very heart of Kuala Lumpur, its dull-grey concrete wall was about eight metres high and ran roughly 274 by 228 metres. The wall was topped

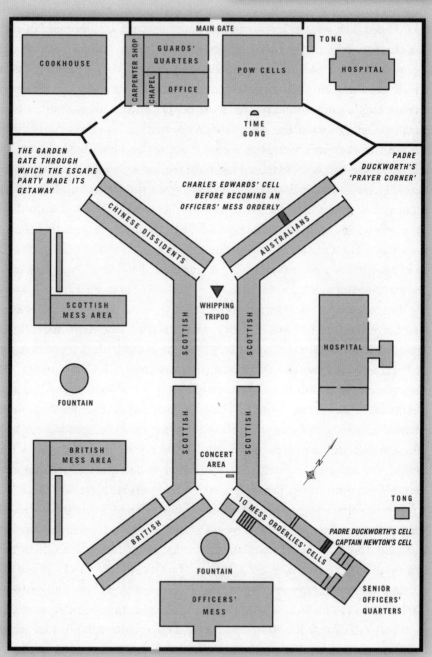

Copy of Pudu Gaol, drawn by CHARLES EDWARDS, 2/19th Battalion

with embedded broken glass and contained a number of observation towers. After entering the main gate, the prisoner was confronted with two entrance buildings each of two floors. This then led to the main gaol building which was shaped 'like a huge X with an elongated centre'.[3] At either end of this X-shaped gaol block lay two three-storey wings. The ground floor of the elongated central portion commenced with a gruesome whipping tripod which led along an open air courtyard and thence to a stage. A fountain was situated on the southern side of the prison, and another on its eastern perimeter. Also within the compound were further buildings comprising administrative offices, workshops, guards' rooms and hard labour lines. In all, the prison had been designed to house around a thousand civilian prisoners. In late January 1942, the Japanese forced the civilian authorities to remove their inmates, and began to concentrate their British and Australian prisoners in Pudu. In *The Naked Island*, Russell Braddon stated that, 'Padu Gaol was a place of fascinating stories. Every man in it had been captured in extraordinary circumstances . . .'[4] A number of familiar characters now re-enter our story.

The majority of the Australians in Pudu were survivors of Lieutenant-Colonel Anderson's 2/19th, 2/29th, 4th Anti-Tank Regiment and 2/15th Field Regiment soldiers who had fought so tenaciously during the defence of Bakri and Anderson's column's fighting withdrawal to Parit Sulong. Of the eventual 70 2/19th Battalion inmates many were survivors of Captain Newton's HQ Company A and B Echelon, which had been deployed around one and a half kilometres to the rear of 45th Brigade HQ. The Japanese had attacked and dispersed Newton's rearward force prior to Anderson's withdrawal. Others, such as Private Charles Edwards, had been left behind and eventually captured after fleeing the Parit Sulong Bridge area.

After his epic anti-tank gun demolition of the Japanese tanks forward of the 2/29th's cutting near Bakri, Sergeant Clarrie Thornton also found himself in Pudu. Thornton 'hadn't washed for weeks', other than his 'wash' in the swamp during his exit with the 2/29th, and with his hip wound still oozing 'a vile pus', was hungry and smelt 'like a pole cat'.[5] Upon arrival, or soon after it, he was to find ten other members of his unit, including Sergeant Ken Harrison and Private Jim Kerr, who had had his seventeenth birthday while cut off in the jungle with members of the 2/29th Battalion.

The 2/29th members of Pudu were to eventually number some five officers—including one company commander and the adjutant—and 44 other ranks. It is ironic that a number of these officers had been amongst those who had kept the few available compasses and maps to themselves in the swamp near Bakri, and yet had still been captured, while a substantial number of their mapless other ranks had regained their freedom. It is not surprising to record, therefore, that some of these officers were not respected by their men and thus could not perform as leaders in either Pudu or later on the Thai–Burma Railway.

Notable among the 2/29th Battalion inmates were Lieutenant Ben Hackney and Private Reg Wharton, survivors of the massacre at Parit Sulong. Hackney had suffered a broken leg and numerous bayonet wounds but, according to the 4th Anti-Tank Regiment's Sergeant Ken Harrison, his horrific physical and mental experience had 'seemed only to make him grim and unyielding to the guards'.[6] But eighteen-year-old Private Reg Wharton was a different story. Harrison observed that, 'his physical wounds had healed but his eyes were sick and he trembled and the colour drained from his face at the sound of a Japanese voice or shout'.[7] In Pudu, Hackney became Wharton's self-appointed guardian.

Russell Braddon was one of twenty gunners captured and sent to Pudu from the 2/15th Field Regiment; there were four 2/30th Battalion men from the rearguard party captured after the Gemas ambush; two 8th Division signallers were present; in all, there were five pilots; and, of critical importance to the prisoners of Pudu, were two officers from the Straits Settlements Volunteer Force and Lieutenant Ken Archer and six other ranks from the Federated Malay Straits Volunteer Force. However, the bulk of the occupants of the prison were British soldiers from such units as the Argylls, the Loyals, East Surreys and the Leicesters. During the early weeks of incarceration the morale of some of these troops was poor. As new groups arrived some of the Argylls were prone to demand any of their food supplies; stealing was rife, and most of the 'good jobs' had been taken by them.[8]

The reader will recall that the commander of the 15th Indian Brigade, Brigadier Challen, had been captured by the Japanese attempting to withdraw from Sengarrang on the west coast of Johore on 27 January. And during that withdrawal, Challen had left Padre Duckworth behind in charge of the wounded. Five days later, it will be further recalled that amidst some controversy, the commander of the 22nd Indian Brigade, Brigadier Painter, had been forced to surrender his force near Sedenak, during fighting along the Trunk Road and railway. Brigadiers Challen and Painter, and Padre Duckworth, also found themselves in Pudu.

It would seem that the strenuous withdrawals conducted by both brigadiers had taken their toll. The 2/19th Unit History would simply record their names and state that they were 'isolated' from their fellow Pudu inmates in a cell 'in with the Japanese Headquarters'.[9] Private Charles Edwards would remember seeing them together in a single cell.[10] Russell Braddon was more forthright and would claim that:

> There was also one small room in which dwelt two British Brigadiers who seemed to hate all men of rank lower than Brigadier and who asserted their now non-existent authority by urinating anywhere except in urinals . . . and by demanding larger rations than anyone else because of their seniority.[11]

If Padre Noel Duckworth had shown great courage and fortitude in his care and protection of the wounded before capture, then Pudu Prison was to prove his finest hour. A 'rosy-cheeked little man'[12] who had been the cox of the Cambridge Rowing Eight, Duckworth was to prove both the outstanding character and inspiration to all within the prison.

The first weeks in Pudu may have been tough and humiliating, but they gave an immediate insight into present and future Japanese behaviour. To begin with, around 600 prisoners were crammed into the women's civilian prison area—600 soldiers into a two-storey building built for twenty women internees in peacetime. The 2/19th's Private Charles Edwards was amongst the first to arrive:

> We were given an area along the top . . . there were 22 steps up to it. It was sort of a verandah. And we laid shoulder to shoulder . . . and there was a guard at the top. By now you haven't had a shave for weeks,

your hair's grown, your finger nails grow, dirt gets under your finger nails, you're filthy, lousy . . . you stink, and you're sweaty. It was just utter chaos . . . the benjos [Japanese term for toilet] were . . . about two metres away with a messing point—the area was so small. Flies, absolutely open to disease . . . We all had diarrhoea or dysentery. We had to bow to the guard and say, 'benjo' . . .

Anyway, I came to my turn to go to the benjo, and I bowed—wouldn't let me go. Bowed again, said, 'benjo.' 'No!' Three times I bowed. In the meantime I'd pooed my pants. So I went down to the benjo . . . I couldn't wash them so I washed them off in the dust. The benjos were just roughly dug trenches. You'd do your benjo and just kick a bit of dirt over it. This awful smell . . . came back up, and I was embarrassed as could be about this stink, so I took my shirt off, and wrapped my pants in it, and lay down. Here's where the good humour started. I was laying there for a few minutes, and one of the fellows put his head up and said, 'Edwards, I know why you joined the army—for the glamour of the uniform!'[13]

Private Edwards again:

They had a cook house. They had got cooks, mainly I think from the 2/29th Battalion . . . I would say I was one of the first thirty [Australians] taken prisoner. I got there in time to get two prison dishes . . . they were like sponge cake dishes and the idea was that when the jail was a jail for civilian prisoners, they had a little slot under the door, that the warders slid this little dish in. I was lucky enough to get two of those. But some of the men were eating out of hub caps, coconut shells . . . it was just an absolute rabble—no discipline, no organization, nothing. You'd just go and get fed, and we Australians anyway, would just go and lie down, because the rations were so light, to conserve our energy, we'd just go and lie down.[14]

On 14 February 1942, the 2/19th Battalion's Captain Reg Newton arrived at Pudu with about 30 other prisoners from Malacca. His arrival triggered something in him that defies any adequate explanation. It was as if fate had decreed that a previously unpopular soldier and man had been made for the Pudu, Changi and Thai–Burma Railway experience—for this moment in time. Private Gus Halloran, Signals 2/19th Battalion:

> Frankly, initially, I used to hate his guts. He was full of pompos- ity . . . but I came to accept Newton as being a pretty good soldier. He'd been in the business a long time . . . he wasn't terribly popular initially . . . he was bombastic in the extreme . . . a big bloke . . . good build, big voice . . .[15]

Sergeant Jack de Loas, HQ Company, 2/19th Battalion:

> He was a very pig-headed man. He liked to have his own way, and everything he said, he thought was right, and he didn't like anyone else's opinion about anything, and this is how he conducted his company actually . . . a very hard man to get on with.[16]

Both of these soldiers had served with Newton in his HQ Company since the Battalion's inception. And both are amongst no small sample of the Battalion during interviews with the author who witnessed that transformation in Pudu, or Changi, on the Railway, or during all three experiences. Sergeant Jack de Loas: '. . . he went from a bum to a gun [*sic*] . . . a different man altogether. He became quite servile; someone you could talk to . . . he had two different personalities. Something brought it out of him . . .'[17]

After having endured a rough interrogation at the hands of the Kempeitai (the Japanese secret police) at Malacca, Newton took little time to impose his personality upon both the Japanese and the Argylls upon his arrival at Pudu. As he and his party entered the crowded area Charles Edwards observed that: 'the Argylls wanted to take their stuff off them [and] Newton said, "And who the bloody hell are you!"'[18] According to Newton, he demanded and received the Argylls' names and further 'asked them how long they had been in the Japanese Army'.[19] The Argylls backed off, but the Japanese did not—the newly arrived Australian was compre- hensively beaten.

Newton made two fundamental changes almost straightaway. The first was organisation. Private Charles Edwards:

By now, there were two or three Australian officers in there—probably more. But they just didn't do anything. Within one day, Reg said, 'I'm your senior officer . . .' And he organized the officers and men into platoons . . . if he gave an order, that was it! And that was the reason why he got Pudu Jail into control . . . 'we don't want these bloody Japs to see us without some sort of discipline and order'. And he did it, and the men responded.[20]

The second was respect from all ranks. From the time of his arrival, all prisoners were given an equal share of the meagre ration—totally without prejudice and with all meals served in public—with officers served last. Russell Braddon noted that this was 'a point of etiquette which I saw in no other camp . . .'[21] If Braddon had served later in Newton's 'U' Battalion on the Thai–Burma Railway, or with Anderson Force in Burma, he would have noted the phenomenon again.

The prisoners' diet took only a matter of weeks to affect their already fragile health. It consisted of rice and 'cabbage water', referred to in some accounts as 'rice and vegetable stew', and occasional sparse amounts of dried fish. This diet lacked the vitamins B1 and B2, which caused two afflictions: 'rice balls' and 'happy feet'. 'Rice balls' began as an uncomfortable chafing of the genitals and scrotum which then often spread down the thighs. After some time, this discomfort led to a splitting of the skin, weeping and rawness of the flesh. Private Charles Edwards remembered putting 'coconut oil on it, but it used to itch like anything, and the more you scratched it the worse it got, and we walked around with our legs spread'.[22] 'Happy feet' was another condition caused by the same lack of B2. The prisoner experienced sharp, excruciating stabbing pains in the soles of his feet which denied him sleep, caused him to wander around endlessly seeking relief that rarely came, and eventually caused weight loss, sometimes blindness, and in many cases, he seemed to age. Braddon recalled young soldiers who 'became suddenly, in physique and expression, old men—shrunken and desperate'.[23]

The senior medical officer in Pudu was Captain Collins of the Indian Medical Service. To assist him he had but two British medical officers and a few of his own staff. Their equipment was negligible and drugs non-existent. The period spent by the inmates in the women's prison area was dominated by widespread dysentery, which was caused predominantly by the closeness of the latrines, the multitude of flies, and the enforced poor hygiene of the horribly inadequate 'hospital area'—the concrete floor of the former kitchen. Here the patients lay shoulder to shoulder, suffering from their stinking, infected wounds or the passing of frequent, loose and blood stained stools that caused the Japanese to make great haste through the area.

The truth is that this shameful state of affairs was utterly unnecessary. The prisoners' lack of the vitamins B1 and B2 could have been easily averted by a small ration of bran, unpolished rice, yeast, or small doses of marmite—all readily available. And there existed no small supplies of the miracle cure for dysentery, which was the drug emetine hydrochloride. It could be taken either orally by tablet or by injection, and later it was to be procured only on the black market with large sums of money and entailing incredible risk-taking. The Japanese were to condemn hundreds and hundreds of POWs to death by withholding it in a whole host of camps. Faced with this multitude of ills, the medical staff in Pudu could only crudely scrape wounds of their infection and, as frequently as possible, wash their patients' bodies of their filth. For the killer called dysentery, they could only prescribe limited courses of Epsom salts, which, it was hoped, would literally flush the germ out of an intestine already heaving its contents through almost non-stop bowel motions. The deaths in Pudu mounted. On 20 March 1942 alone, twenty men died.

Despite repeated requests for medicines, improved rations and the right to occupy the remainder of the empty prison, the Japanese steadfastly refused all pleas. However, Pudu's commandant did eventually grant one concession. In a cruel response to repeated demands for meat, he allowed Captain Collins and ten on-duty Australians to travel by truck to gather, as Newton recorded, 'all the meat you want'.[24] They drove to Port Sweetenham where the Australian Government had built an elaborate and expensive cold store for the AIF. As they approached the building the stench of rotten meat dashed their hopes. The refrigeration plant had been destroyed by the British and the doors left open. Newton would later record that: 'Colonel Collins had a few mutton carcasses, all in cheese cloth, brought out and found that the bones were covered with a thin sliver of meat and the bulk of the carcass a greyish green decomposed mess.'[25] Taking the dictum 'waste not want not' to its extreme, Collins had a number of carcasses taken back to Pudu where the foul meat was scrapped off, and, knowing full well that the remaining meat around the bone would more than likely induce vomiting, still fed it to his patients. After a number of 'stews' some men managed to keep small amounts of the vile meal down.

Two events then radically changed the fortunes of all 'Puduites'. The first was the eventual employment of work parties in Kuala Lumpur, and the second was the opening of the gaol proper to inmates on 20 April 1942.

Soon after the fall of Singapore on 15 February 1942, the Japanese realised—as they did all over their conquered lands—that they possessed a ready-made and cheap labour force. In their eyes it was also disposable. They now utilised it by sending work parties out for labouring tasks such as clearing debris around Kuala Lumpur and undertaking menial tasks normally assigned to Japanese other ranks. The Australians proved most proficient—in all POW situations—in what was termed 'scrounging'. Across a multitude of interviews, the term 'stealing' was almost resented by veterans, particularly with regards to work parties in Singapore. The act of 'scrounging' was merely the taking back of goods that were considered 'British' property, or the just and proper procurement of rations and equipment that any decent master would have granted his captives—it was always 'scrounging', never stealing.

If the Australians displayed a talent for scrounging, then a number of British subjects who had resided in prewar Malaya and Singapore perhaps as planters, engineers or businessmen were to prove invaluable. Pudu's Lieutenant Ken Archer was an example. While on a work party in Kuala Lumpur, Archer made contact with a former Indian employee named Paddy Martin, who in turn met with a Dr Gomez, a friend of Archer's. The resulting trickle of drugs from Gomez to Martin were handed over to Archer's men at the Central Market, which was about three kilometres from Pudu. When you walk through that market in Kuala Lumpur, it becomes immediately obvious as to how easy such a handover would have been. And then there was the opportunity to buy and sell goods. The original building still exists with its multitude of busy and compact stalls. But the problem was not the receiving of goods but their passage through searches at the Pudu gates. Archer would later observe that:

> Looking back on all the happenings of that period strikes me forcibly how incredibly lucky we were to get away with as much as we did over such an extended period. We would not have been able to get anything in at all only for my four lads . . . who took all the risks in getting the medicines etc into the jail . . .[26]

The prisoners of Pudu were finally allowed to occupy the whole of the main gaol on 20 April 1942. This move saw the Australians assigned to the north-eastern wing; the Chinese dissidents the north-western; the Scots the 'elongated centre' portion of the gaol; the other British troops in the south-eastern wing; and the officers occupied the south-western wing, with the senior officers housed in the condemned cells at the end. Initially there were six men to a cell but after further requests, the Japanese allowed all of the cells to be occupied on all floors, which allowed for three men per cell. The hospital patients were now transferred from the cramped and filthy kitchen floor in the female section—and its accompanying latrines—to the workshop building on the eastern side of Pudu between the Scottish and Australian wings. Still without such rudimentary items as instruments and beds, the doctors could now at least enhance the comfort and basic hygiene of their patients.

For officers such as Reg Newton, the Australian occupation of the wing opposite the Chinese brought with it both an immediate and stark lesson: the Japanese Kempeitai would stop at absolutely nothing to gain intelligence, and when that intelligence was acquired, retribution of the cruelest kind ensued. Private Charles Edwards:

> Up the front . . . near the front door was the whipping tripod . . . it's three poles. About half way down there was a big, wide belt. They lay the prisoner in it to be whipped and they'd put the belt over to cover his kidneys and they'd belt him around the shoulders. When we first went

in there they'd have the Chinese dissidents in a wing, and they used
to belt them to try to get out of them their confederates outside . . .
I for one used to peek around and have a look . . . they brought in the
woman with the cat of nine tails . . . she would walk down, and after
a while we'd hear the screams. We used to call it, 'They're giving them
a stripy shirt.' Then the next day they'd carry them out—they'd just
died. They were already half starved . . .[27]

It wasn't always a 'stripy shirt'. Sometimes a piece of rubber hose or a
bar would induce broken bones, and, with the torment of time and acute
discomfort and lack of water, punishment on the tripod became a virtual
crucifixion. The body was taken down the next morning and buried, or
perhaps another impaled Chinese head would testify to the barbaric behaviour of the Japanese. Newton would later also record: 'skin torn off the torso,
eyelids cut off and the rays of the sun reflected into the open eye with magni-
fying glasses', and that the screams were 'a hideous nightmare'.[28] Water torture
added further to the Kempeitei's cruelty. The prisoner's body was filled and
then jumped on until the mouth, eyes and nose became painful and repugnant water exits. Others were hung upside down with a cloth placed over the
mouth and eyes. Water or urine or iodine was then poured into the nose and
mouth to induce a sense of drowning. And the 'hideous nightmare' could
be as much psychologically as physically induced. A group of six Chinese
prisoners might be informed that one of them was to die the following
morning. The Australians were the captive witnesses to a night full of the
wailing and grief of the despairing Chinese, and the morning brought death
for one, and relief, silence and temporary hope for the other five.[29]

If the Japanese had shown themselves to be excellent soldiers in battle,
and calculating and cruel masters, then in other ways they often displayed
an almost child-like naivety when dealing with the European mind. Three
examples demonstrate the point. At around the time of the occupation of the
whole gaol, an almost comical figure descended upon the camp: a Japanese
intelligence officer named Watanabe. His physical appearance hardly helped
his cause. He wore a civilian shirt, coat, tie and hat, but army breeches, boots
and leggings. While others bashed, tortured and deprived their prisoners of
food and drugs, this quaint creature proceeded to hand out cigarettes and

ask the Australians questions—in fluent English—about northern Australia.
But when Watanabe's questioning turned one day to whether or not the
Australians possessed any survivors of the fighting at Parit Sulong, Newton
knew that the slightest slip of the tongue would spell a death sentence for
Hackney and Wharton. Further, upon capture, the 4th Anti-Tank Regiment's
Sergeant Clarrie Thornton had claimed that he was a reinforcement to the
2/29th. Anyone who had caused the Japanese severe casualties in battle was
forever a target of retribution.

The second was the fact that their procedures for prison security were
far inferior to their battle performance and their 'creativity' in cruelty. On
29 May 1942, a British prisoner returned early from a work party pleading
'serious' illness. He warned Newton that when the work party returned, to
be ready to create a diversion to allow the passage of a box into the prison.
To frustrate the Japanese search party, Newton organised a thronging mass
of prisoners detailed to carry the incoming rations into the gaol, and, in the
confusion, a box of 'eggs' was rushed away. The box contained an electric
radio. Newton then offered the Japanese the chance to have electricity
laid on throughout the prison in the hope that they had tired of 'kerosene
lamps, candles and oil lamps'. The offer was gratefully accepted. Within a
matter of days the 2/29th's Lieutenant McQueen and two British assistants
had restored power to the prison. Whilst Newton's new radio was only able
to provide news—and biased at that—from Singapore and Kuala Lumpur, it
was at least in English and did cover some overseas news. The third example
also came in April with the demand that all prisoners record their occupations for possible later deployment as 'specialists' in far-flung parts of the
'Greater Asian Co-Prosperity Sphere'. The Japanese must have been totally
non-plussed by the response: 'beer tester', 'brothel inspector' and 'wrapper-
uppers' were but a few of the creative replies.

In early June 1942, the Japanese introduced pay for officers and 'work pay'
for other ranks: NCOs received the equivalent of fifteen cents a day, other
ranks ten cents per day, lieutenants $15 per month, and senior officers
$25 per month.[30] The above sentence seems innocuous enough, but the
importance of money in a prisoner of war situation is critical. We shall

discover that in Changi a number of captives entered that prison with significant sums of it; that in many POW situations there were a limited number of financial 'haves' and a great majority of 'have nots'; and critically, there were others who knew not only how to acquire money, but how to 'invest' it. These soldiers often understandably used their financial position for their own good, but also to help their mates. In addition, we shall learn of some who engaged in corruption and exploitation. And contrary to popular belief some of these were officers.

Pay brought with it privileges for some and work opportunities for others. Private Charles Edwards:

At this stage they also formed an officers' mess. Now Sam Cameron was the only other member of my company, D Company of the 2/19th, in the camp. He'd been captured with Newton . . . Sam came down to my cell . . . He said that they were going to form an officers' mess, and they wanted ten mess orderlies. Reg Newton always said whatever proportion of the camp the Australians are, we have that proportion of the good jobs. There were 100 officers in the camp, ten of whom were Australian, and so one of the ten [mess orderlies] had to be an Australian.[31]

Although Edwards had to be ordered to do the job, he soon realised its potential:

I always reckoned that the Japs were a little bit dim—two men could have done this job, but they accepted ten men. Now I was working seven days a week [on work parties and as an orderly] . . . further to that there were some officers without a batman. 'Will you wash me a shirt Edwards?' 'Yes Sir, it's five cents to wash a shirt and one cent to sew on a button.' [Edwards had 'scrounged' khaki thread and needles whilst on a working party assembling Singer sewing machines.] I was getting about 70 cents a week pay and about two dollars from washing shirts. And so I became what I call, 'a Pudu millionaire'. All I had to do was buy tobacco, and I didn't smoke a good deal of that because now my rations were better, and I only smoked to cut the pain of appetite ... when I went into being that mess orderly, my life took a dramatic change. We had to walk from the officers' mess ... to the kitchen, get their rations and their tea, carry it back, serve it out to them, wait on them ... we got to know all the officers, all the civilian prisoners in there, and we got first hand, all the news. Everything else I got I shared with my mates, but not my money, it was too damn hard to get. I had a money belt which never left my body. Then came rumours that we were going down to Changi, and I thought now, I'll take a punt on this and I'll buy up as much tobacco as I could ... and I rolled up all my possessions in this sack, that was my bed, and when I got down to Changi I was proved right. I made 500% on that tobacco. And I had much more money—I was never short of money.[32]

Throughout their newly acquired 'Empire', the Japanese refused to pay the sick—no work, no pay. In response to this, Newton and an officers' committee ordered that two-thirds of officers' pay and a half of the other ranks' daily rate was to go towards the purchase of eggs and tinned meat (protein and fat) for hospital patients. It should be realised that such meagre purchases would never have restored anything like satisfactory health to the inmates of Pudu, but rather, in some cases, could have forestalled death and in others perhaps facilitated a recovery—for the time being. A number of 'Puduites' initially refused to pay their way and did so only after pressure from Newton. It would take time before some POWs were to learn a critical lesson: you might work today; you might even glean a little extra food; but tomorrow a whole host of afflictions might see you in 'hospital'. The frugal supplies of food and medicines for the hospital, therefore, would become everyone's concern, because for the vast majority of prisoners, life itself was to prove nothing more than a day-to-day proposition.

———————

June 1942 was a fortuitous month for those in Pudu. On the 12th around 150 soldiers from the Argylls and other British units arrived from the northern Taiping and Ipoh gaols. Amongst them were the Argylls' Captain David Boyle and Lieutenant Ian Primrose. The advent of those two officers saw a similar swing to massed unit pride and organisation as Newton had

brought to the Australians. And fifteen days later the morale of the prisoners received a decisive boost when three gunners from the 2/15th Field
Regiment boldly smuggled a chaff bag holding a cumbersome short-wave
transceiver 'across the quadrangle to the jail, and across the 100 yards open
space under the eyes of the guards . . .'[33] The success of this audacious mission
may have been attributed to the gunners showing the Japanese a number of
nude calendars acquired at the markets the same day. Subsequently, the BBC
night-time news from New Delhi was received by Newton and Archer and
later relayed to the troops by an ingenious method.

Padre Duckworth had spent months selling watches, pens, lighters and
all manner of items of dubious quality to the Japanese. The money from
his bartering in food and goods had always gone to Archer and his outside
contacts for the immediate benefit of the struggling 'Puduites'. Along with
his black market endeavours had come an always aggressive manner in
dealing with the Japanese. And now, with authentic news finally available
through the newly acquired transceiver, Duckworth became the purveyor of
both real and morale-raising news. Private Charles Edwards: 'So they gave
the news to Chaplain Duckworth. Now every evening, in a little corner of
the jail, he'd have a religious service—we called it "prayer corner".'[34] As the
men gathered in this north-eastern corner of the gaol, two sentries called
'cockatoos' would be posted to warn of approaching guards. If those sentries
broke into a whistling rendition of 'Mother McCree', Duckworth's sermon
would quickly become 'The Lord's Prayer'. Edwards:

> This is the way he gave out the news: '. . . under thee dear Lord, our
> brother Winston who has today dropped three thousand golden eggs
> on Wilhelmshaven, Bremen, Hamburg . . . and under thee dear Lord,
> our brother Douglas has vowed that he will return.' [Then comes the
> sound of 'Mother McCree'] . . . 'Now gentlemen, we'll all rise and
> have the Lord's Prayer.' The guard would look in through the gate,
> hear we all were deep in prayer, 'Our Father which aren't in heaven . . .'
> I call him 'The hero of Pudu'.[35]

July 1942 brought with it the opportunity for those in Pudu to notify
the outside world of their existence. When on the 7th a 2/29th soldier died,

Captain Reg Newton was approached by a Chinese man after the funeral at the Cheras Road Cemetery, who informed him that he was about to journey to Singapore with a consignment of Japanese stores. Asked 'if there was anything he could do for us in Singapore',[36] Newton promptly had a nominal roll typed and placed in the centre of a toilet roll which was duly delivered to Changi. The roll exists to this day in the Imperial War Museum. Later, Sergeant Ken Harrison was able to smuggle a similar 'document' through to Changi with the names of the 4th Anti-Tank gunners recorded. Sergeant Harrison:

> As it happened, our friends in Singapore had heard vague rumours of a camp on the mainland, but had long since dismissed them as wishful thinking. We had all been listed as 'Missing believed killed.' So my message, when it reached Major Quick, came like a voice from the grave.[37]

In mid-July a message was received from Paddy Martin via the Kuala Lumpur market for two of Pudu's inmates. From late March and through early April, a number of civilian prewar planters had trickled into Pudu, among them Frank Van Renan and Bill Harvey. Both had been involved in 'stay behind' operations behind the Japanese lines under the command of one Spencer Chapman during the fighting on the Malay Peninsula up to the fall of Singapore. Paddy Martin's message was sent by Chapman to inform Van Renan and Harvey that the time had come when they could escape and rejoin him, as Japanese pressure on the guerrilla movement in Malaya had died down to some degree. Van Renan and Harvey needed little prompting, and immediately sought permission to escape from the British CO of Pudu, Colonel Guy Hartigan. When approached, Colonel Hartigan and Lieutenant Ken Archer were pessimistic. Archer, through his knowledge and contacts outside Pudu, warned the men that the Japanese had now employed a new grid system throughout Malaya. This system was cunning and comprehensive, and relied upon a simple principle: intimidation. Each local community leader or leaders within their portion of the grid who failed to identify 'foreign' movement were to be executed. And in true Kempeitai style, such executions would be preceded by torture for intelligence and/or reprisals against all and sundry. Coupled with the bounty paid by the Japanese for the capture of, or information leading to the capture of any fugitives, the chances of success were slim indeed. But Van Renan and Harvey argued that they had extensive knowledge of the country, had various contacts and would move only by night. They also informed Hartigan that their party would consist of five: Van Renan, Harvey and two planters named Graham and Morrison, who had extensive local knowledge and could speak the native tongue. The fifth member was Major David Nugent of the 2/18th Garhwal Rifles, who seemed to have no other qualification for the party other than being a personal friend of Van Renan's. What they asked of Hartigan and Newton was a head start, an initial distraction to delay the Japanese search for them. The escape was timed for the night of 14 August 1942.

Despite the grid system, the bounty on any escapee's head and the fact that the party was required to travel around 150 kilometres to reach Chapman's HQ, few escape plans stood a better chance of success because of the men's local knowledge, contacts and linguistic skills. In addition, Hartigan and Newton had arranged for keys to be procured to two gates; they could keep an ear on the radio for possible contact from Chapman; they allowed Van Renan and Harvey to exit the camp to gather arms and ammunition; they arranged for the power to 'fail' on the night; and, critically, they were to stage a cover-up at successive *tenkos* (Japanese parades for roll counts), for the next morning and the following two days.

Unfortunately, one official and planned escape for 14 August became two, the very night before Van Renan's group was due to leave. After returning from a work party late on the afternoon of the 13th, the 4th Anti-Tank Regiment's Sergeant Ken Bell requested that Newton grant him permission to escape in a party of four led by Captain Mick MacDonald, a local Australian planter, a Dutch pilot named Jan Van Crevald and the 4th Anti-Tank Regiment's Sergeant Clarrie Thornton. But when Thornton succumbed to an attack of dysentery, the first three still requested permission to escape.

After having informed Hartigan of his plan, an acrimonious and fiery confrontation then ensued between Hartigan, Newton, Archer and Van Renan and the second escape group led by MacDonald and Bell. It must have been very 'fiery' as Newton was not universally known as 'Roaring Reggie' for nothing. Newton has left us with an account of the 'discussion' that began at around 6.00 pm and finished at midnight:

MacDonald would not budge and all he kept saying was that he had arranged to go out that night. When told about the grid system he said that this was mentioned just to stop him from going out and that he did not believe Ken Archer . . . Van Renan pointed out that if he was determined to go out then he should wait one more day to give Van Renan's party a chance for they were well organized and they were an official party, and MacDonald was not. But to no avail and despite all entreaties and protests Sgt. Bell refused to listen . . .[38]

Initially, all went according to plan. Both parties made good their escape after passing through the gates and gaining time through the staged *tenkos*.

In the end, however, both escape attempts failed dismally. The Japanese grid system that MacDonald had dismissed as a ploy by Archer to prevent his escape was in fact the very reason for the failures. The 'unofficial' party of three fared poorly: Bell and Van Cevald were in Japanese hands and back in Pudu at around midday on 16 August, and MacDonald made his eventual return to Pudu on 4 September. Two Malays were given $2 each and the local police corporal $10 as a bounty for his capture.[39] After a number of skirmishes with local Malays, Van Renan's party was also rounded up. In the process, Nugent was badly wounded and, after the 'official' party arrived back in Pudu on 7 September, Nugent died there on the 13th.[40]

The Japanese reacted swiftly to the escapes. Searches occurred and, as they would demand in Sandakan in Borneo and Changi in Singapore, on 27 August prisoners were ordered to sign a form: 'I, the undersigned, hereby solemnly swear on my honour that I will not, under any circumstances attempt escape.'[41] Colonel Hartigan refused, which caused the Japanese to place the officers six to a cell normally occupied by one prisoner. In a morale-boosting display of fortitude and solidarity, the officers endured their lack of food and water for a short period before pragmatism overruled bravery. As the paper was to be signed under duress it was not binding, but most of all, it must surely have hit home that escape was not a plausible prisoner of war pastime in Malaya. And the cost of such escape attempts was soon shown to all.

On 16 September 1942, Captain Reg Newton was finally allowed to visit Sergeant Ken Bell and Lieutenant Ken Archer was permitted to see

Van Renan and Harvey. The condemned sensed their fate. Goodbyes were said, and Newton promised that last messages would be given to next of kin. When the eight exhausted, food-deprived and shackled prisoners were put in the back of a truck, without their gear which was left lying near the vehicle, and with picks and shovels ominously stored in the back, all ranks in Pudu gathered to see them off. Ken Harrison would later record his last farewell to his 4th Anti-Tank Regiment mate:

> For a few long minutes we stood staring at the eight bound men. Twice I tried to call to Ken Bell, 'See you in Singapore, Ken,' and twice I got as far as 'See—' and I could not go on. We smiled, but our smiles were strained, and as the big gates swung open and the truck jerked forward, there was little hope in our hearts.[42]

The prisoners were driven through the streets of Kuala Lumpur to the Cherus Road Cemetery where they were made to dig their own graves and shot.

Our Pudu Prison story is crucial to the 8th Division prisoner of war journey to the Thai–Burma Railway, because it is a perfect example of how some of its leaders—and other ranks—were conditioned, prepared, or indeed shaped for leadership in an environment that would prove their ultimate and most exacting test of survival. When writing a part of the 2/19th Unit History, Captain Reg Newton actually spelt out his Pudu lessons. The Japanese, he realistically observed, were the victors, and as such, the Australians would be forced to make the best of food shortages, deprivation and cruelty. The pertinent question was how to beat the system, how to make good the lack of food and medicines and above all, how to handle 'the Jap':

> ... for at no time did they tell the truth and deliberately set out to belittle and cloud any issue ... If you were told to move at a certain time you could rest assured that there would be delays. If you were told you would go by truck the chances were you would walk.

If you were given permission to buy from canteens or on work parties you could be sure that you would lose something.[43]

But 'Roaring Reggie's' most valuable lessons concerned what we now call 'man management'. The Japanese were respectful of authority: they admired officers who ran a tight command; who interposed themselves between a mere private and his Japanese or later, Korean aggressor. Because saluting, bowing or any other mark of respect was demanded in their army—at the cost of severe corporal punishment when it was lacking—Newton quickly realised that the Japanese mind liked nothing better than an 'apparent' European display of respect; and that, from an Australian perspective, officers had the responsibility to work for the greater good of those under their command. 'This method of handling the Japanese was easy to use when it meant easing any pressures to save somebody or obtain an advantage.'[44] Newton was, of course, not the only leader to have learnt these lessons. Prior to his arrival in Changi an Australian officer named Edward 'Weary' Dunlop had learnt precisely the same lessons in Java.

We now return to the fall of Singapore on 15 February 1942 and enter Changi. It, too, would produce some outstanding leaders, but its unique POW environment would have some dire consequences for many future Thai–Burma Railway prisoners. In terms of understanding the new master, Changi was a false world.

24

LIGHT OF THE SOUTH

When hostilities ceased at 8.30 pm (British time) on Sunday 15 February 1942, 50 000 Commonwealth troops laid down their arms on Singapore Island. And of that number 14 972 were Australians. Within a few short weeks, the aggregate of Australian captives grew: Java 2736, Timor 1137, Ambon 1075 and New Britain 1049.[1] Singapore had been the commercial crossroads to the British Far Eastern Empire. Changi, situated on the eastern side of the Island on a peninsula of the same name, would become a virtual marshalling yard for the eventual collection of most British Commonwealth POWs, and then the distribution point for slave labour across much of the newly won Japanese Empire.

On 16 February, the 8th Division troops were ordered to stockpile their arms in Tanglin Square. The Australian Official Historian has stated that the Japanese sent 'only picquets' into the city that day, and those Japanese troops were 'quite friendly, refrained from looting, gave cigarettes to their prisoners, and appeared to be under perfect control'.[2] That temporary vacuum of power in Singapore Town, from the time of the capitulation until the arrival of substantial numbers of Japanese on Tuesday 17 February, is critical to any real understanding of Changi Prison. While only limited numbers of Japanese entered Singapore Town, and the vanquished congregated ready

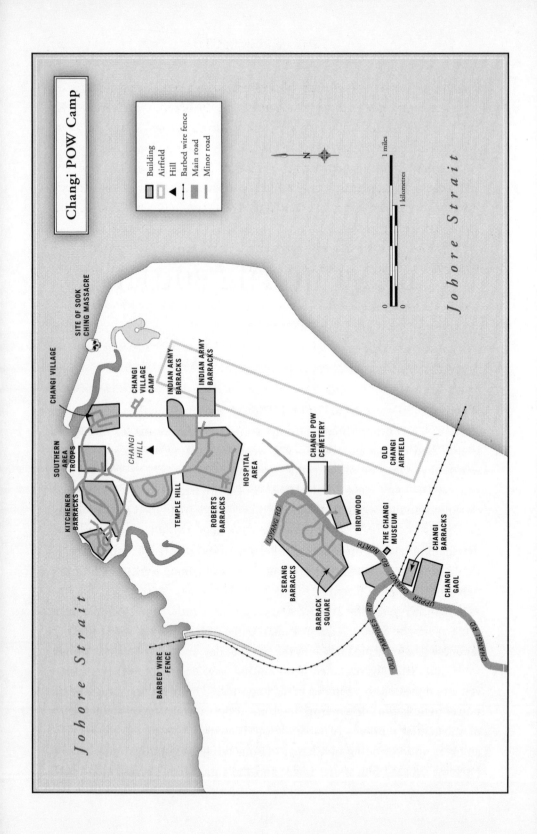

Changi POW Camp

Legend:
- Building
- Airfield
- Hill
- Barbed wire fence
- Main road
- Minor road

N

1 miles
1 kilometres

Johore Strait

Johore Strait

SITE OF SOOK CHING MASSACRE

CHANGI VILLAGE

CHANGI VILLAGE CAMP

INDIAN ARMY BARRACKS

INDIAN ARMY BARRACKS

SOUTHERN AREA TROOPS

CHANGI HILL

KITCHENER BARRACKS

TEMPLE HILL

ROBERTS BARRACKS

HOSPITAL AREA

CHANGI POW CEMETERY

OLD CHANGI AIRFIELD

LOYANG RD

SERANG BARRACKS

BARRACK SQUARE

BIRDWOOD

THE CHANGI MUSEUM

CHANGI RD NORTH

UPPER CHANGI RD

CHANGI BARRACKS

CHANGI GAOL

OLD TAMPINES RD

CHANGI RD

BARBED WIRE FENCE

for captivity, extensive numbers of the local civilian and military population were busily engaged in looting Singapore and the Island itself. Some of this was on an individual basis, but much of it was highly organised and on a very large scale. The end result was the formation—and impressive longevity— of a thriving black market both in Singapore and in Changi. The desire to participate in that market would influence the conduct of very many prisoners of war. Further, not much time would pass before the Japanese became significant participants.

In terms of its physical appearance and the manner of its administration, Changi was not an orthodox prison. There were no towers manned by armed guards, no walls illuminated by searchlights and three of its boundaries were defined by the coastline. Further, in sharp contrast to such prisons as Pudu, there was not the ever present threat of beatings, humiliation nor any other immediate or long-term Japanese presence within its extensive perimeter.

Changi had been the main peacetime base for the British Army, and contained some seven different camps in an area of about 25 square kilometres. Included in its infrastructure were 'transport lines ... workshops, various administrative buildings and parade grounds, all types of playing fields, theatres, social halls, community centres, and the many bungalows for the married quarters of various ranks'.[3] Changi's administration would also prove highly irregular. After the capitulation, both the conquerors and the conquered knew that escape was unlikely. The Japanese, therefore, did not segregate the prisoners' officers from their men but placed responsibility for the administration in their hands. The prison was to survive on its own resources for a few days and then be provided with only the most basic of supplies. Further, the Japanese warned that by April it was to be self-sufficient other than for rice supply.

To administer Changi, General Percival retained his four principal subordinate commanders: General Heath (III Indian Corps); Major-General Key (11th Indian Division); Major-General Beckwith-Smith (18th Division); and he promoted Brigadier Callaghan (CO of the 8th Division Artillery) to major-general to command the AIF in Major-General Gordon Bennett's absence. Changi was then subdivided into five basic areas to house the above commands: Southern Area (the former Singapore Fortress troops); an 18th British Division Area; an Indian Corps Area; the Australian area was Selarang

Barracks; and the nearby and centrally positioned Roberts Barracks would soon became a combined hospital.

Percival's biographer has recorded that once in Changi, the General '... could be seen sitting, head in hands, outside the married quarter he now shared with seven brigadiers, a colonel, his ADC, cook sergeant and batman'.[4] Percival was thus a lonely, forlorn figure who 'discussed his personal feelings with few', and spent a number of his first days 'walking around the extensive compound, ruminating on the reverse and what might have been ...'[5] Such a disposition—an understandable one—permeated throughout the prison. And one of its chief outcomes was an attempt by senior command to deal with apathy, low morale and initial idleness. From a senior command perspective, the answer was simple: retain a high degree of military discipline. The AIF command embraced this idea with some relish.

Captain Rowley Richards, RMO, 2/15th Field Regiment:

The next day [17 February 1942], we watched one of the British units passing by. There were numerous trucks bulging with officers' mess equipment: cane chairs, typewriters and no doubt a full set of cut glass, silver candlesticks, china and cutlery. Soon after, Lieutenant Theo Walker, the intelligence officer, brought instructions from Divisional Headquarters [8th Division] that we were to leave for Changi ... Furthermore, all food and medical supplies were to be left behind, to be transported at a later date; no vehicles other than water carts were to be taken; and each man was only to bring whatever personal belongings he could carry on his own back during the long march ahead.[6]

Understandably, Richards's CO, Lieutenant-Colonel Wright, fuming over 'the blatant arrogance of the Brits',[7] decided to ignore the order and pack trucks with supplies and drive them to Changi. The 2/15th Field Regiment left Tanglin with four supply trucks, a van loaded with food, three water carts and with Richards driving a truck full of medical supplies. Lieutenant-Colonel Wright, leading his troops, walked to Changi. Upon arrival at Birdwood Camp (located quite near Selarang Barracks), an 'incensed' 8th Division major abused Lieutenant-Colonel Wright for disobeying divisional orders, and did so in front of Wright's gunners. The supplies were handed over—other than a cache of rations and medical equipment which were hidden in a false wall and were to later prove invaluable. As our story unfolds, there will be no shortage of Australian officers—some of whom had failed in battle—who assumed privileges in Changi. Private Gus Halloran, 2/19th Battalion:

> We weren't madly enthusiastic [about them] . . . they wanted to re-establish a military discipline that reflected on them, and everyone said, 'Well you bastards made a mess of this!' . . . we were down on the beach and we lit a fire . . . and a crowd of people from Division came up . . . 'Put it out! We're not going to have that sort of conduct here!' We thought, 'Oh well they're a pack of bloody stuffed shirts.' We were going to cook something I think . . . we thought, 'Well this is typical of the sort of senior officers you have.'[8]

Gunner Richard Haynes, 2/10th Field Regiment, noted the behaviour of officers in a nearby infantry unit:

> It would seem that the two predominant things on the agenda of the indictment . . . were firstly . . . their commandeering of so great a portion of their allowed space, to be used as Mess and Quarters, that overcrowding and congestion in the ORs Lines became unbelievable. Daily, men who had spent the night virtually in the arms of their neighbours, staggered to the upper floor with wood and water for their unloved commanders. There they were greeted with the obvious fact that almost the entire floor was that untouchable of all the Holies . . . 'The Officers' Mess'. The second . . . was . . . without precedent in the Australian Lines. Whereas all other units officers were content with their portion of rations allotted by a W.O. Q.M., [these officers] apparently were not, and they had first choice of the particularly lousy rubbish that the I.J.A. was disposing of.[9]

As late as October 1942, Russell Braddon—newly arrived from a very different prison, Pudu—observed that, 'Changi was phoney not because of the mass of men in it but because of the official attitude behind its admin-istration'.[10] He noted the preferential clothing allotment to divisional officers so they might keep up appearances; the finding of menial and at times unnecessary and repetitive jobs merely designed to keep the men occupied; and, critically, that many officers ate in separate messes, kept poultry, and had numerous privileges not seen by the other ranks. For a soldier just arrived from Pudu, this unreal and privileged atmosphere did not sit well. The issue is that Changi was indeed an unreal world. And those most affected by that artificial environment were some officers who were to fail dismally on the Thai–Burma Railway. Perhaps Private Gus Halloran, 2/19th Battalion, best sums up a not uncommon POW Changi experience:

> The blokes in Changi [who were there permanently], they've always been sorry for themselves; you always get this frightful business about 'they were in Changi'. Changi I always thought was . . . a rest camp . . . you weren't doing anything serious or drastic . . . you were probably not eating terribly well, but you were not required to do anything extraordinarily energetic, at least not in the time I was there . . . we were there for about three weeks before we went to Singapore [on work parties], and we were there again when we came back . . . prior to going to Thailand. Our blokes used to maintain their interest, they used to tell lies to one another, I don't think they dwelled on the war—we'd been surrendered, as far as we were concerned we hadn't put our hands up, and we were proud of that . . . we believed that a decent fight could have been made of it, and hadn't been. So we felt really frustrated by that.[11]

The above described attitude to Changi and its administration shouldn't be interpreted as purely Australian. In his book, *Reassessing the Japanese Prisoner of War Experience*, R. P. W. Havers cites a number of British officer examples concerning the very same 'affliction'. He notes one Changi British sergeant claiming that the Brigadier's house and accompanying officers' quarters were out of bounds because 'They didn't want us to see their suckling pigs.' Further, Havers cites examples of 'our own officers [making] things worse than the Japs', and wrote that soldiers were required to 'pick up leaves from one of Changi's extensive lawn areas'.[12]

＊

While British and Australian troops were experiencing their first days in captivity small numbers of soldiers were still working in Singapore Town. Until the Japanese could arrive in sufficient numbers and take over the complete administration, elements of the Australian Provosts remained at their posts. Captain Alf Menz led them. Menz's diary:

16   February:
I was instructed by H.Q. A.I.F. that we were to retain our arms & maintain control until the Japs took over, we were the only control-ling body at the time.
    Busy all day collecting stragglers & dispatching to Tanglin Bks the assembly area for the A.I.F.

17   February:
Another busy day, stragglers still coming in but we are getting short of transport & petrol now, as Japs are taking what they want. We had to toss our pistols in today and it hurt, we have been so busy that we have not appreciated to the full the fact that we had capitulated but losing our arms brought it home to us, we feel naked.

18   February:
I have managed to retain my little truck & have done quite a few trips around town & to Tanglin with a few stragglers, nearly all drunk. I don't think I left them in any doubt as to what I thought of them. We all assembled at Newton Circus on Bukit Timah road at about 2.30 pm preparatory to marching the 16 miles to Changi to the P.O.W. Camp. We had to carry all our own gear, consequently only necessi-ties were taken, they got heavy enough. A weary march, stopping & starting all along the way, arrived about 3 am.[13]

＊

This book began with the AIF's 4th Reserve Motor Transport Company's Driver Joe Nimbs's account of the fall of Singapore, while serving as an ambulance driver based at St Andrew's Cathedral. After the capitulation he too remained on duty for about five days:

> We have had to do a lot of dirty jobs but cleaning out the morgue is the worst stinking job we have been allotted, it was chock-a-block full of bodies the dead of many nationalities. Some have been here for some time and are at various stages of decomposing all of them civilians. Many have been stripped of clothing. Most have died of wounds. The stench is overpowering. Some of the troops are sick and vomiting. It takes a lot to bring ambulance personnel to this. We will be bloody glad to get away from this lot . . .
>
> Most of the shops have been flattened. All have been stripped by looters.[14]

Particularly significant is Nimbs's description of corpses being stripped of clothing. Trade in clothing would become a thriving Singapore and Changi business. Nimbs:

> Having heard the Japs didn't search the main body of the troops when they went to Changi we [Nimbs and a mate] decided to load some pretty risky gear, a lot of watches, cameras, binoculars, and other valuables had been wrapped in torn up ground sheets and buried around the cathedral. As it now seems possible we might get them out to Changi they are being retrieved. This morning we loaded the rickshaw with all sorts of gear, a lot of which had no chance of getting past a Jap search, but we decided to take the risk. The only way we could hide the gear in the rickshaw was to put it under our ground sheet and army packs. Not much of a smother but that's all we had.[15]

For good measure, Nimbs sewed two watches in his singlet by lifting the bottom of it to sew a pocket. He also took his diary. Taking turns to pull the rickshaw along with his mate, Nimbs had an uninterrupted 'ride' to the corner of Changi and Tampines Roads:

Suddenly there is silence. A road block came into view. We could see
the armed Japs who are manning it. We pulled into some sort of Army
Unit as we got closer. We could see the road block consisted of a barb
wire fence on both sides of Changi Road with a chain across the centre
strung between two posts. Several huts with attap roofs are nearby,
a long table and some cooking gear under one of them. Many bicycles
are about the quarters . . .

As far as we could see there were about twenty Japanese guards
at the road-block. One of the Jap guards opened the road-block by
pulling the chain to one side. We walked through. Will we be searched?
I was wondering if I should have brought notes that I had written. My
friend was pulling the rickshaw. One of the guards seemed amused;
he said to him in fair English, 'You are now a Chinaman.' Unbelievable
they didn't even stop our party.

A short distance further on we turned left off the Changi road.
Here were some three storey buildings on a big square of land, mainly
asphalted. Further on there are houses set amongst lawns and gardens.
This is Selarang . . . One of the houses at the far end of the camp from
the Changi road is to be our barracks. We will share this house with
Headquarters Australian Army Service Corp . . .

It is in a setting of what would have been a beautifully kept garden
of tropical trees, shrubs and flowers . . . this is now quarters for one
hundred and ten troops. We settled in wherever we could, sheds,
garages, make shift huts. Anywhere outside would be better than the
crush in the house which is home to most.

My mate and I finished up in a hut native style with a palm leafed
thatched roof. It had a little room at one end big enough for us to
sleep in . . .

This next morning the first thing we noticed was the rickshaw had
vanished.[16]

Nimbs's experience was not unusual. He remembered a soldier with
a collection of diamond rings on 'a wire like you would see washers in a
work shop. There must be a hundred of them.'[17] Private Jim Stewart, 2/19th
Battalion: 'Well, I know one of our blokes had finished up with a beautiful

watch and ruby and everything on it that he'd pinched out of a house out of Tanglin.'[18] Thus, there would be some 'affluent' operators in Changi's black market, others who were far more modestly funded but possessed a cash flow, and yet more who were 'small time' operators. And then there were very many Changi inmates—officers and other ranks—who would consti-tute both captive and deprived customers.

The extent of such goods and funds entering Changi is hard to estimate accurately. Given Nimbs's easy passage through the Japanese picquet with such a large 'consignment', one wonders why many more soldiers did not make the most of that pause in supervision and authority during the period 15–17 February 1942. Perhaps Private Gus Halloran, 2/19th Battalion, provides us with at least a partial answer:

> You're fairly immature [Halloran was 21], and you don't realize that you should probably, when the place has been surrendered, you should immediately go and rob a bank or something. I'd have liked to pick up a couple of books. I was getting old! But you're still pretty unsophisti-cated youth . . . still pretty naive.[19]

Many of Changi's prisoners, therefore, were very much like Halloran—young and not 'street savvy' or 'street wise'. Nimbs was 33 years of age as he entered Changi; he had grown up in Fitzroy in Melbourne; had cut cane in Queensland during the Depression and sent most of his wage back to his mother, and had, therefore, become very 'street savvy'. Another character who will enter our story both in Changi and on the Railway is the 2/29th's Private Paddy O'Toole. He too will go 'under the wire' at Changi, and will find all manner of ways and means to facilitate survival in Thailand. And he grew up in Richmond in Melbourne—like Fitzroy, another tough prewar suburb—started work at thirteen, got the sack at each wage increase based on age and was thus also a 'street wise tough nut'. There were others again who like Corporal Jim Kennedy and Lance-Corporal John 'Rocca' Roxburgh, Signals, 2/29th Battalion knew of the black market but lacked the funds to participate.[20] Private Wal Williams, 2/19th Battalion: 'I would have only had the clothes I stood up in; I never had a change of clothing . . . I had a dixie, spoon and fork . . . no money.'[21] He knew about the soon-to-be thriving market, and the identity of 'about half a dozen' of his battalion who were 'going under the wire'.[22] As our Changi story unfolds, there will be victims, those willing and able to participate, but thwarted by the unscrupulous behaviour of others. This more sinister side of Changi life surfaced from day one of captivity. WO 2 Bert Mettam, 2/29th Battalion:

> What upset me, I heard before we started the march, word went round that the Japs are grabbing watches. And so plant your watch. So I got my socks and rolled them down, and put my watch around my ankle, and covered it with my sock, and marched out to Changi like that. In the morning, I got up and I was going to have a shower, so I took my blasted watch off, and put it underneath my kit . . . the water had been cut off or something, and I went back . . . and someone had seen me do it. It must have been one of our blokes . . . helped himself . . . that was about the only thing I had on me that could have earnt me a few bob on the black market.[23]

The British and Australians had suffered defeat in battle, the humiliation of surrender and were facing an uncertain future in Changi. The Chinese Singapore experience was to be far, far worse. Singapore was now to be called Syonan ('Light of the South'), and Singapore time became Tokyo time. 'Light of the South' it may have been to the Japanese, but the Chinese immediately associated the name 'Syonan' with the arrival of a new Dark Age. As the Japanese entered Singapore looters were shot on the spot, or beheaded on the spot, and a selection of decapitated heads began to appear in key places such as the railway station, where they became a grisly warning of the consequences of running foul of the new master.

The Japanese had began planning the elimination of anti-Japanese elements in the Chinese community throughout Malaya and Singapore during the Malayan Campaign. Since after the capture of Singapore, the 25th Army was required for operations elsewhere, it was deemed critical that the Chinese be purged quickly and ruthlessly. While General Yamashita issued the order, the detailed planning was undertaken by his Chief of Planning and Operations, Lieutenant-Colonel Tsuji.

Singapore Town and the Island itself were divided into a number of zones, each with a Kempeitai officer in charge. The local police, through public loudspeaker broadcasts and posters, were ordered to inform all Chinese males between the ages of eighteen and 50 to report to registration centres within each zone. These areas were fenced off with barb wire and a selection process started. The Japanese deemed that Chinese who had worked for the British in any public service role or were community leaders, who had been in the volunteer military services, who were communists, who knew members of secret societies, who were involved in the China Relief Fund, or who were criminals were to be eliminated. Using documents gained from their prewar intelligence and from raids on Chinese organisations, large numbers of Chinese were immediately detained. Those allowed to leave were 'chopped', which entailed a stamp being placed on a document or the body.

Although organised with Tsuji's usual efficiency, the recurring Japanese Army trait of units operating as separate entities—which we shall further witness on the Thai–Burma Railway—meant that the implementation of the plan differed across designated areas. Some zones took days to complete their process, others merely hours as varying standards of scrutiny were applied to the hapless, innocent victims. The selected males were bound by rope, placed in trucks and taken to a number of execution sites on the Island, in what would become known as *Sook Ching*, or 'a purge through cleansing'.

Australian POWs soon became the disgusted witnesses not to the actual executions, but to the appalling aftermath. Gunner Richard Haynes, 2/10th Field Regiment:

For days we had been watching truck after truck, loaded to the limit of its capacity with bound Chinese, disappear in the direction of Changi beach. From the rattle of MG fire we drew the natural conclusions, but they had not been verified. However a work party had been called out . . . They were coming in now. Walking through the stunted rubber by the remains of the 16 inch gun. Norley Watts . . . was in the lead. He was not talking as much as usual. He brushed one man's inquiry off. 'Just a hell of a mess, ole fellow. Just a hell of a mess.' The 19th Battery bloke came back to the attack. 'What the hell, Gee, you're not starting to get secretive are you?' Norley held his nostrils between finger and thumb. He shook his head but would not talk.[24]

On 22 February 1942, Haynes and a number of his 2/10th Field Regiment mates were part of another Australian work party sent to Changi Beach. Haynes:

We halted on the edge of the palms and surveyed the solution to our question ... They lay in silent attitudes of violent death ... They were piled in massed heaps of bloated humanity. They were strung in long lines of blackened corpses ... They had lain under a tropic sun for ... days. The flies swarmed over the stinking abattoir. A breeze from the sea blew the goulish stench up to us. The tide had moved a couple of the singly bound ones. We could see them bobbing just off shore.

It was particularly revolting, but compulsion, added to the fact that we had come a long way in the past few months made little difference to us ...

The long lines of well roped corpses gave us most trouble. We did not have a knife between us. Hammie wrested vainly with a knot gummed hard with blood ... 'Flamin rope would hold a team of bullocks.'

Digger and I left him to it and did a spell in the pit we were digging.

Eventually the untangling was complete and with the digging of the first pit, we began to carry, on make-shift stretchers, the gruesome relics up to their resting place amongst the palms. The rolling of the gentle surf upon the beach added music to our work, but it could not stifle the appalling stench of the human slaughter house. The day drew on. Any scruples we might have had were lost. The day wore away. The sun went down on the day of memory. We were still carrying the victims of barbarism to a resting place in their massed graves ... Kerplunk ... kerplunk, the pits swallowed them up symbols of the ruthlessness we were to know in years ahead. Up amongst the grass on the higher land, a couple of Japs watched us ... Our hands stank that night. We could not eat our rice.[25]

Accounts vary as to the number of *Sook Ching* victims. The Singapore Chinese community were to later estimate the slaughter at somewhere between 30 000 and 50 000, while the prosecution at the postwar War Crimes Trials would conservatively estimate 5000. A Japanese reporter attached to Yamashita's HQ would later claim that he had been told that the toll was 25 000. In the end, *Sook Ching* was yet another Japanese disgrace, another episode in a trail of infamy that had began in China at a multitude of venues such as Nanking and would continue throughout the Pacific War. But perhaps Alan Warren has best summed up another injustice:

> The British administration at Singapore made remarkably little effort after the war to determine the extent of the *Sook Ching* death toll. It was not in the interest of the returning colonial power to draw attention to its failure to protect its subjects.[26]

The Chinese took enormous risks in Singapore in both their black market 'business ventures' and their support of the British and Australian POWs. We now turn to the first fifteen months of the Australians' incarceration in Changi Prison. The reader should be aware that some mention will be made of POW work parties sent to Singapore, and also the formation of work parties sent to the Thai–Burma Railway. These two subjects will be dealt with in detail later in our story.

25

PURGATORY

———>●●<———

We now turn to an examination of Changi from the time of the capitulation until May 1943—the first fifteen months leading up to the departure of the last of the substantial forces to leave Changi for the Thai–Burma Railway.

Whilst in captivity in Changi, the 8th Division's DAQMG (Deputy Assistant Quartermaster General), Major Alan Thompson, wrote an extraordinary document. Written in a 'Log for Motor Lorry' journal (because of the acute shortage of paper in Changi), he kept a detailed day by day diary of Changi's prison existence.[1] By cross-checking this account with official records, private diaries, manuscripts and oral history interviews, a far more complete account of life in Changi emerges than ever before.

The initial problems confronting the Australians in Changi were the provision of food, water and accommodation, the maintenance of hygiene and the care of battle casualties and the sick.

Abject hunger would soon become the immediate consequence of captivity. Until 23 February—the first five days in Changi—the troops ate what was brought in with them. Such tinned supplies were sufficient, and in many cases, lasted some number of weeks as modest supplements to the Japanese ration.[2] On the 23rd the Japanese issued their first ration scale. Thompson, using the imperial system, meticulously recorded each ration item per man per day—right through Changi's existence—up to three decimal places. Such ration scales will be listed in our narrative correct to one decimal place using the metric system. The initial ration scale was: rice 500 grams per man per day; meat 50 grams; milk 15 grams; sugar 20 grams; salt, tea and cooking oil 5 grams each. In addition, each prisoner was initially to receive 40 cigarettes per month, and 100 'latrine sheets' per month.[3] Clearly, with the Australians used to a diet containing at least 4220 calories per day, their new intake was insufficient and lacking in such basic necessities as protein. The Australian Official Historian, Medical, would record that:

> From the very first the great risk of serious malnutrition was realized by the medical services in Changi . . . that unless substantial appropriate additions were made serious manifestations of deficiency diseases would quickly appear, beginning with beriberi, owing to the limited capacity of the body to store thiamin. The importance of avoiding an excess of carbohydrate in relation to thiamin in a dietary [sic] was realised . . .
>
> The early onset of the thiamin and riboflavin groups of deficiency was expected; only too soon was this prophecy fulfilled.[4]

Beriberi was a major health issue for the prisoners of Changi and would prove even more so on the Thai–Burma Railway. Caused by a deficiency of the vitamin B1, its symptoms were swelling of the legs, the abdomen and sometimes the face. Cardiac beriberi involved fluid around the heart, its effects were sudden and often meant death.

To remedy these deficiencies, a number of measures were taken, including the decision on 22 April to produce yeast as a means of combating beriberi;[5] rice polishings, which were the husks or grit from rice and taken as a bran substitute, were used 'when obtainable'; various types of grass and leaf soups were made; gardens were started; and marmite, which was held in limited supply was used very sparingly but most successfully.[6] On 6 March, the Japanese ordered that Roberts Barracks should become the combined British and Australian hospital. There had previously been a hospital in the barracks with an impressive range of medical expertise and reasonable equipment (by POW standards). It had an administration that was able to provide modest but crucial financial assistance and therefore limited extra rations and equipment. Changi had a special ward with a 'diet kitchen' known as the 'fattening pen', which was used to supply extra rations for patients who had lost much weight and required better nutrition.[7]

The death rates in Changi during its first year (February 1942–February 1943) are ample proof of the success of the administration and the medical services. The fact is that, although no POW experience under the Japanese was in any way pleasant, the survival rate in Changi compared well with other camps. Eighty-two Australians died during that first year: dysentery 29; battle wounds eleven; malaria six; beriberi four; diphtheria two; typhus one; accidents ten; and, of great interest but somewhat ambiguous, were seventeen 'miscellaneous' deaths.[8] The other interesting statistic is the death rate compared to admissions. In February 1943, for example, there were 702 admissions: dysentery 242, malaria 58, beriberi four and diphtheria seven. The deaths for that month totalled four—all from dysentery.[9] A POW admitted to Roberts Barracks, therefore, stood a strong chance of survival.

Water was another early problem. As the pipeline from Johore and the causeway had been damaged during the fighting, water was not only in short supply, but had to be boiled. At first the engineers employed 22 water carts brought in during the move into the prison, and also used 'a swimming pool in one of the ravines, a Malay school reservoir and two underground storage tanks'.[10] The early water ration stood at 2.25 litres of water per man per day and one litre for hospital patients. On 22 February, repair of the pipes commenced and six days later Selarang Square possessed a water point and, on 3 March, the pipeline supply commenced.[11]

Accommodation was very cramped but the extensive buildings, grounds and the climate allowed a number of inmates to sleep in the open, and 'many built wood and wire stretchers to lift themselves from the concrete floors'.[12]

Another immediate challenge for the AIF in Changi was sanitation. A. J. Sweeting recorded:

> In the conditions then prevailing flies—fed by corpses, offal, rotting
> garbage and unprotected latrines—bred in thousands, and outbreaks
> of diarrhoea and dysentery had begun within a fortnight of the arrival

at Changi . . . soon hundreds of men were working in shifts digging
latrines to a depth of 14 feet and boreholes to 12 feet. The Japanese
provided timber to build fly-proof structures over the latrines, and
thereafter admissions to hospital declined monthly.[13]

In a further effort to enhance basic supplies and facilities, a forestry
company was formed in March to travel out of Changi sometimes by truck,
but mostly by prisoner-drawn trailers, to supply unit cooks with firewood;
a poultry farm was begun and limited numbers of eggs (mainly for the
hospital, and medically prescribed) were provided; a fishing program began;
the few available tools were collected and placed under engineer supervision
and use; and parties were detailed to bring in sea water for salt production
when the salt ration was reduced.

The creation of an education program, to become known as 'Changi
University', and an entertainment program will not be examined in detail
here, other than to acknowledge that they contributed to the morale of
POWs. Of more interest is the work of a number of self-interested amateur
historians. Not long after arriving in Changi a vigorous and prolonged effort
was made to complete AIF unit diaries, write reports and deliver a series of
lectures from Malaya Command and AIF officers concerning the campaign
in Malaya and Singapore. Lieutenant-Colonel Kappe, 8th Division Signals,
undertook the AIF research and writing. The lectures were rather guarded
in nature, because speeches presented to both a combined and confined
British and Australian audience had to be diplomatic.[14] In terms of committing still-fresh memories of the campaign to paper, the AIF unit diaries and
reports, when concerned with the fighting, times, dispositions and tactical
outcomes were to prove of immense historical value. But, as we shall learn,
the report of Colonel Thyer and Lieutenant-Colonel Kappe's *Operations of
8 Australian Division in Malaya 1941–42* was distorted and biased. We have
already recorded Brigadier Duncan Maxwell's Changi talk with General Key
concerning his 'withdrawal' from his causeway dispositions, and Maxwell's
consequent conciliatory appendix in the 27th Brigade Unit Diary—and
Key's subsequent real thoughts.

The varying amounts of money and valuables which entered Changi upon, and soon after capitulation, have been discussed. There was also, it seems, an amount of money which came in through 'official channels'. A tracking of the 8th Division Pay Corps through its Unit Diary in the days leading up to the capitulation is instructive:

10. 2. 42.

At 0700 hrs, instructed by A.A.& Q.M.G. that the Unit must be prepared to move on foot by 0900 hours. One 30 cwt. truck was placed at the Staff Paymaster's disposal for shifting the records. Records taken were the W.F. 3A's, unposted media as far as possible, General Ledger, Journals, two typewriters, Cash Books, Advances Register and as far as possible, to ascertain all unauthorised Remittances of cash and undrawn pay. Complete stocks of Australian Stamps burnt (£8,050).

Staff proceeded to Balmoral House, Steven's Road.

12.2.42.

Majors Ferguson and Terry (O.C. 2. E.) found accommodation for both units on the 4th Floor of the Cathay Building, and by 1300 hrs the move was completed with 2 days' [sic] rations . . .

The Field Cash Office and Depot Cash were also in the Cathay Building. Command Pay Office was not functioning but the Field Cash Office were adjusting a number of advances and making a few payments.

13.2.42.

Rations very light—Capt. Watt obtained sufficient food for Pay and Echelon for 24 hours. Communicated with the A.Q. Admin. H.Q. who informed me that he could not supply rations and that we would have to fend for ourselves. . . .

Cable dispatched to the Chief Finance Officer that the Office was not functioning.

14.2.42.

. . .

The Hongkong [sic] and Shanghai Banking Corporation, Singapore, had ceased to function on the previous Wednesday, and the money held by the Div. Paymaster could not be banked [author's italics].[15]

On the same day (14 February), Warrant Officer K. Browne of Command Pay, noted:

I wandered through into the small inside room where the card school was in progress. The boys were having quite a lot of fun. Snowy was in charge, as usual when there was any gambling. The game was in full swing, money was plentiful. The boys forgot their worries for a while. I ambled around for a yarn with he [sic] and his boys, the Field Cash Office was still operating, *they were paying in fine style. I did not draw anything as I still had a few dollars.* [author's italics] They had no news.[16]

The Pay Corps Unit Diary:

15.2.42.

Was told to disarm by 3rd Indian Corps at 1600 hours—contacted H.Q. A.I.F. and was told to stand fast. H.Q. A.I.F. advised me at 2000 hrs. that the Force would capitulate at 2030 hrs. and that transport would report to me at 2030 hrs. to transfer Pay Office and 2nd Echelon to Tanglin barracks where the A.I.F was to congregate. Arrived at Tanglin 2200 hrs.[17]

Colonel Wilfred Kent Hughes recorded that the AIF Pay Command 'was still functioning when I was ordered to embark for Japan . . .'[18] [17 July 1942]. During an interview with the author, Private John Boehm, 2/29th Battalion produced his pay book to verify a withdrawal of $5 (Malay) on 25 February 1942, in Changi.[19] Although we do not know the amount of money, or the role of AIF HQ in its use, or the frequency of withdrawals transacted by Pay Command in Changi, in view of the evidence cited above a substantial amount of cash must have been taken in.

The first mention of funds made in Thompson's diary is for 11 April 1942, when he recorded that $27 000 was 'in hand to expend on food', and two days later a 'local purchase party [was] endeavouring to obtain additional vegetables'.[20] Another method of funding further purchases in April was the purchase of '$3900 worth of vegetables . . . from cash paid into soldiers' pay books'.[21] The statement seems to imply a buying of vegetables from existing cash held by units and/or individuals, which was 'honoured' by payments credited to pay books. On 30 May, Thompson would record that 'nearly all cash expended on supplementary rations' and that the decision had been made to 'keep $8000 for hospital purchases.'[22] The same day Thompson also recorded that a central canteen was to be started which would buy goods and sell them to units. When, on 6 June 1942, the Japanese agreed to pay Changi officers 25 cents per day, NCOs 15 cents per day and other ranks 10 cents, Malaya Command—the AIF had no say—had the opportunity to levy set rates from all pay, run a canteen and thereby attempt to supplement rations, purchase medicines, create a cash reserve and generally improve the lot of all Changi inmates. The first pay 'to all ranks' occurred on 13 June.[23]

The problem of overcrowding in Changi was almost immediately eased from February and throughout the following fifteen months, when the Japanese employed POWs as work parties on Singapore Island, followed by the departure of forces to the Thai–Burma Railway and Borneo. By May 1943, Changi's population dwindled to around 2000.

<hr />

An intriguing character now re-enters our story. Two of Major Alan Thompson's diary entries for July 1942 were:

18   [July]. JAPAN PARTY. All senior officers of rank of Colonel and above ordered to stand by ready to move. Engineer Officers also included in party.

21   [July]. APPOINTMENTS Lt Col Galleghan assumed command of remaining force as from 21 July 1942, Staff Officers to assist 'G' [Operations] Major Wyett, 'A' [Administration] Major Head, 'Q' [Quartermaster] Major Thompson. A.I.F to be completely re-organized

to enable it to perform any role it may be called upon to do. Conferences twice weekly. Lt Col Glyn White to be [*sic*] act as liaison Officer with I.J.A.[24]

The reader will recall the distinguished part played by Lieutenant-Colonel Frederick 'Black Jack' Galleghan and his 2/30th Battalion during the fighting in Malaya (particularly the ambush at Gemas), and the controversy surrounding his subsequent 'relinquishing' of that command on Singapore Island. In the time leading up to Galleghan's command of Changi, he had been in charge of the AIF's 'Base Depot Group', and had later commanded a work party to Mount Pleasant Estate near the MacRitchie Reservoir and then Caldicott Camp.[25]

Before leaving with the other senior officers for Formosa, Major-General Callaghan met with Galleghan on a number of occasions. With an eye to the future and a concern about how posterity should see the British/Australian relationship during the campaign, Callaghan left his successor with some clear orders. Lieutenant-Colonel 'Black Jack' Galleghan:

The following is a record of my conversations with Maj-Gen Callighan [*sic*] on taking over comd of AIF. They were recorded in a personal notebook as they occurred.

19   July 42—
Policy:- There has been too much criticism of the British—make every endeavour to stop this.

Lt-Col Kappe is to remain at Singapore or return to Singapore to meet Gen Callighan [*sic*] and Gen Percival to go into the war diaries etc. Col Kappe to continue to prepare AIF narrative of the campaign in Malaya.

Should there be any returnees to Australia prior to Gen Callighan's [*sic*] return *no* statements regarding the campaign and/or Brig Taylor are to be made.

If any orders are given regarding the return of War Diaries to Australia the following statement by the GOC was to be repeated—
'I have arranged to meet Gen Percival here after the war and go into

the details of records. They cannot be completed because there are no records of the Army Comd's conferences, orders and instructions and until such details are received from the Army Comd all AIF records are incomplete. Should you be pressed to return the diaries and other records you are to arrange with Col Kappe to return duplicates.'[26]

Galleghan's style of command has been discussed. In Changi his authoritarian manner would continue. Discipline was to be tightened, and, as had been the case from the raising of his 2/30th Battalion through to the end of the Malayan Campaign, he would display an utter determination to ride roughshod over any circumstance or individual whom he deemed to be obstructive. Such a style of leadership can have the advantage of swift, decisive actions and positive outcomes—unless the commander is wrong. Further, when a commander of this type encounters others who possess a similar 'strength of personality', the confrontation can become both acrimonious and destructive. As events in Changi unfolded, there would be a number of such incidents.

One of Galleghan's first decisions was identified by Thompson on 19 July 1942. The AIF was 'to be completely re-organized to enable it to perform any role it may be called upon to do'. 'Any role,' really referred to 'Black Jack's' determination to have elements of his Changi command ready to stage an uprising, or support in any way a future British invasion of Singapore. As early as August 1942 (a month after he had assumed command), unarmed combat classes were organised; area commanders were ordered to supply the names of majors and captains who 'were physically fit for field officer duty'; an officer training syllabus was designed; and, to further facilitate his plan, officers might be required to swap formations in order to structure the 'force'.[27]

Essentially, the troops chosen were the 27th Brigade—Galleghan's old brigade—and its commander was to be Lieutenant-Colonel Kappe. To many in Changi this concept was little more than an absurd determination to preserve a parade ground polish and strict regimental behaviour. Warrant-Officer 2 Bert Mettam, 2/29th Battalion: 'There were some that had thoughts that we could rise up and run over the top of the garrison troops . . . where the hell we were going to get the arms from I don't know.'[28] Private Gus Halloran, 2/19th Battalion, was blunter:

> ... when 'Black Jack' became part of it, [he staged] a march past in a review order. The 30th Battalion trained, and everyone was wearing their boots out ... but as with officers, he said it was good for morale.
>
> I was aware that ... the purported reason for having parades of this sort and also for the unarmed combat ... we'd rise and throw off our shackles. And everyone thought, 'Crap!'[29]

This issue seems almost trivial when examined in isolation—certain commanders and units 'playing soldiers'. The point is that when a certain force was later raised for the Thai–Burma Railway, this philosophy, this structure, and it will be seen, the selection of officers to administer command of it, would have tragic consequences.

In the administration of Changi, Major-General Callaghan and from July 1942, Lieutenant-Colonel Galleghan, faced three challenges (other than the Japanese): pilfering, gambling and, most importantly, the black market. 'Discipline' is a loose term in its Changi context. We have discussed the at times pompous behaviour of a number of 8th Division HQ and reinforcement officers when they created, and appeared to relish, their undeserved privileges. The discipline of troops, or lack of it, will be examined in the context of these three challenges.

Pilfering began almost immediately in Changi. As early as 28 February 1942, Thompson would record that: 'Morale low—pilfering continues—coconut trees and papaya trees receiving special attention. Slackness in obeying Camp Orders.'[30] Coconuts and papaya trees are one thing, but clothing is another. On 9 April, the Japanese granted permission for Major Alan Thompson and a party to go into Singapore and pack and transport the AIF clothing supplies at the Base Kit Store—and personal trunks, kitbags and clothing—back to Changi for storage and use for all personnel in the AIF. In other words, from this time on all clothing was to be pooled and issued to members of the AIF for the greater good, and only personal possessions were to be returned to individuals.

The party found that the Base Kit Store had been looted and was in a state of 'disorder'. In some measure, this was understandable, given the already described level of looting that had gone on between the capitulation and the arrival of Japanese troops in Singapore on 17 February. After the Japanese provided vehicles to transport clothing and personal effects back to Changi, pilfering on a large scale began—during the packing, in transit and after arrival.

Colonel Wilfred Kent Hughes's Changi diary:

13   April 1942:
Boots & clothing arriving in large lorry loads but no chance of stopping the thieving . . .

21   April 1942:
Long conference this morning. Went strolling in the afternoon & had another row over pinching clothing from trailers. 2 offs [officers] 1 NCO and 1 man under arrest. Stealing has become the general accepted practice now & will take a lot of stopping. Neither officers nor NCOs seem interested. Somebody will have their throat cut shortly. One man found his own watch—a present from his wife being auctioned recently . . . put the Black Market cigarette king under arrest this evening.[31]

On 26 April, when another thirteen loaded lorries arrived at the Changi Kit Store Kent Hughes reported that, 'the result was a flock of crows round the carcase & four of them under arrest'.[32] In his diary entry for 24 May 1942, Provost Captain Alf Menz recorded a more personal experience of such pilfering:

I have received information that the cigarette case that was given me by the Unit at Dubbo Xmas 1940, the gold mounted riding crop given me by the Corps Provost Coy at Broadmeadows Vic the same year and my Elgin gold wrist watch have been in possession of a man in this

camp who has gone away with 'A' Force. His name is_____2/29
Bn alias_____my informant was NX 30243 Moore R.J. 2/19
Bn. All these articles were stolen from my trunk, I hope to see my
friend . . . again one day.[33]

Menz was not destined to meet either his 'friend' or the informant—
the former died as a member of A Force in Burma, and the latter died
in Borneo during the infamous Sandakan death marches.[34] The theft of
clothing in Changi for both an 'inside' and 'outside' market would remain
a serious issue for the remainder of the war, and the sale of clothing by
individuals to raise funds on the Thai–Burma Railway will also assume
significant proportions. But the two most alarming Changi forms of pilfering would be of rice from Changi's already limited stocks, and priceless
drugs from Roberts Barracks.

On 11 August 1942, the 8th Division Diary recorded that 'there is evidence
that rice is being stolen and sold at the kampong outside the wire. An investigation is being carried out.'[35] Two days previously, Captain Menz and his
provosts were called in to investigate. Menz's diary for 9 August:

Have just received information that some men in the camp are selling
rice to Chinese in the Kampongs. By heavens we are going to do our
damnest to stop that, we have almost got arrangements completed
with the Japs for an increase in quantity & variety of rations and we
don't want the show busted by a few miserable selfish thieving individuals. to [sic] sell or exchange the rice they first have to steal it thereby
robbing their mates and if the Japs discover this business going on
we will find ourselves on short rations and will lose all chance of
an increase. Am going to stop up all night on the job.[36]

Two days later, on 11 August, Menz came to a staggering conclusion:

. . . apropos the rice business. So far have had no luck & I can see
now that the job is not going to be easy. Have waited up two nights
now and I find that on both occasions the culprits have been warned.
The only indication given that I was taking any action last night was

given at a conference yesterday of Area Comds & Staff Officers. I have
my suspicions of a Staff Officer, by golly if I can fit him as being in any
way connected with the business I'll push it hard. Everything comes
to those that wait. I'll keep at them & maybe land some big fish one
day (or night).[37]

On the 14th Menz wrote that: 'Have had no success with the rice
merchants although have lost a lot of sleep . . .'[38] And the next day the
8th Division HQ would record: 'Rice stealing. No further evidence was
available on the matter at last conference.'[39] It is of more than passing interest
to mention that Thompson's diary has constant references to the need for
'saluting' by the POWs of Changi, but that the above innocuous reference
marks the apparent end of a far from determined investigation of those
suspected of trading rice from the store in Changi.

On 28 December 1942, Menz encountered a further 'interesting' occurrence. His diary entry stated for that day: '. . . had to start M.P. patrols day &
night today, not very popular with the men who have to do it, but orders are
orders'. And two days later: 'My four men who were on patrol last night failed
to return for breakfast this morning. Later found that they had been picked
up by Japs . . .'[40] Corporal Warwick was one of Menz's four-man patrol
and later wrote a report of the incident:

2 a.m. Mounted Duty Area picket. Proceeded on area patrol in pairs.
3.30 Met at Con Depot as prearranged. 3.45 proceeded all together
down the hill path to Con Depot gate . . . North West Boundary.
Whilst about 30 feet from wire was challenged by Jap. Jap blew alarm
on whistle. 4 more Japs appeared. Were ordered outside of wire. Taken
to Japs guard house; could not speak English and no information
was exchanged. 5 a.m. one platoon of Japs marched us to Indian Camp
where we were put in compound. 10 a.m. escort arrived to take us
to Jap Headquarters. Interviewed . . . first question was why did
you try and escape to Singapore. Explained we had no intention of
escaping and detailed hours of duty, area of patrol and purpose. Jap
accused one man of being outside of wire. Replied no man outside
of wire and that Jap came into wire to bring us out. We immediately

produced the passes . . . Capt explained Japs knew nothing of patrol
and did not recognise passes as such.[41]

The four men were then taken to the Indian Camp and placed in
a compound. Corporal Warwick:

. . . 31st Dec 1942 saw Major Wyett proceeding to AIF Area and he
shouted it wont be long [*sic*]. 21st January sent written and verbal
message to Capt Menz per Cpl G. Sawyers [one of the party of four
Provosts] who was hospitalized. 27 February were released from
Indian Camp and allowed to proceed to our own area without guard.
On return we reported to Capt. Menz O.C.
   Patrol completed 60 days [author italics].[42]

It is of further interest to note that the author has been unable to discover
any instances of AIF soldiers being apprehended inside the wire—provost
and unit night patrols were a regular occurrence at Changi—who were
not in possession of any goods, and further, had official passes explaining
their presence. It is extraordinary to note, therefore, that an ordered provost
patrol, equipped with official passes, might spend 60 days returning from
a routine, one-night patrol within its own perimeter.

We have noted that dysentery was the most prevalent disease in
Changi—and would prove by far the biggest killer on the Railway. One
of the most important drugs in its treatment was the anti-bacterial tablet
M & B 693. Russell Braddon in his book, *The Naked Island*, claimed
that it was rumoured that there was a 'drug ring' in Roberts Barracks
and that 'an MO [medical officer] was one of its members . . .'.[43] Rumours
do not constitute evidence, but in response to reports of drug trading from
Roberts Barracks, Lieutenant-Colonel Galleghan issued the following
routine order on 19 February 1943:

No. 110—DRUGS AND MEDICAL SUPPLIES:
Except by authority of HQ AIF or ADMS, no person (*incl MO's*)
[author's italics] may be in possession of any form of sulphanilimide
M & B 693, or morphia.[44]

The order also stipulated that all drugs in possession of individuals were to be handed into that soldier's unit and a receipt given, and that the unit in turn was to receive a receipt from the hospital upon its reception of the drug(s). In April 1943, two Australian patients at Roberts Barracks were court-martialled for attempting to sell M & B 693. Both pleaded guilty and were sentenced to 120 days' detention.[45] Warrant Officer 2 Bert Mettam, 2/29th Battalion:

> Just between Selarang Barracks and Changi Jail there was one place with a big tennis court and they were using that as a compound. And any of these blokes that they picked up, they just put them into the tennis court. And they were guarding the tennis court—and they were flat out getting a drink of water from all accounts.[46]

In its yearly return (28 February 1942 to 1943), the 8th Division HQ revealed some interesting detention barracks statistics. Of the 47 units named, twelve had numbers of ten or more put in detention. The 2/29th Battalion had by far and away the highest number of detainees: 57 with a readmittancy count of seven, which amounted to 18 per cent of total detainees.[47] It would seem likely that this high rate was caused by two factors: the extremely large number of untrained reinforcements that were posted to it just prior to the capitulation; and the obvious lack of respect held by many of the other ranks towards some officers who, they believed, had failed them at Bakri, in Pudu Prison and in Changi. Despite Lieutenant-Colonel 'Black Jack' Galleghan's passion for discipline, the 2/30th Battalion had the second highest count of 30 with a readmittance of three, which represented nine per cent of all detainees.[48] It is pertinent to record that the 2/30th had had nothing like the numbers of reinforcements that the 2/29th or 2/19th had received. Two other units are of interest. The AGH (Australian General Hospital)—a far less 'populated' unit than the infantry battalions—had thirteen detainees, no readmittances and constituted three per cent of the total.[49] This might reflect three things: first, a possible degree of involvement in the drugs selling issue; second, that the pilfering of clothing was a notoriously easy task in a large hospital; and third, the fact that Roberts Barracks was an ideal venue to conduct black market activities because it was centrally located in Changi, and, above all, because it was a 'meeting place' and a 'cover' for a wide variety of units and nationalities attending, visiting and passing by it. Roberts Barracks was therefore an ideal trading point.

It is in no way a contention of this work that any unit should be judged by these figures, because in many cases there were plausible reasons for them; furthermore, in any unit there will be a few soldiers of doubtful integrity, whose behaviour should not reflect upon the entire unit; and last, it must be emphasised that the POW experience is an entirely different one to that of a combat soldier. It should also be appreciated that many detention sentences were handed out for common disciplinary matters, unconnected with trading in rice and drugs. An example was an infantry soldier who received ten days' detention for failing to perform his duty as a runner, for then saluting his NCO (a salute is not required to a non-commissioned officer) whilst in the act of bowing (obviously with a Japanese connotation), and later using insubordinate language (very insubordinate). Such transgressions were hardly new in any army.

On 4 March 1942, Major Alan Thompson recorded that: 'I.J.A. ordered that all shoulder badges to be removed. All officers to wear one star on left breast.' Three days later he wrote: 'Commenced wiring ourselves in under I.J.A. orders.'[50] Driver Joe Nimbs, 4th Reserve Motor Transport Company:

> They will be a formidable barrier. Two rolls of barbed wire six foot in diameter alongside one another and a single roll on the top where the two rolls meet make it about twelve foot across and twelve foot high in the centre. It would take a bit of scrambling through in a hurry. One of our unit Sergeants, Peter Chitty, is in charge of a gang wiring an area which runs down a gully. They have manoeuvred a section so it will be easier to get through if the need arises.[51]

It may have been a 'formidable barrier' but it was far from insurmountable. In Changi's very early days, the Chinese traders discreetly approached the wire and threw items over it, and the money was then thrown back. But the Sikh guards, who had swapped sides after the capitulation, and had also demanded that all POWs salute them, immediately proved not only brutal to the Chinese, but also to the Australians. Bitter and ongoing resentment followed. As late as 5 September 1942, Captain Alf Menz wrote of the Sikhs: 'I think a day of reckoning may one day come & if it does I want to be handy. They are building up a tidy score against themselves . . .'[52] And eight days later:

> The Indians (Sikhs) are becoming very nasty now. I think they are getting a taste of power & being fed a lot of Jap propaganda and upon the slightest provocation are knocking the soldiers about, using rifle butts in the process, by golly I'm afraid that if ever the tide turns here they are going to suffer some casualties. They are certainly asking for it and saying please into the bargain.[53]

We have examined the large amounts of money that had come into Changi. Gambling became an evening pastime and was not on a small scale. According to Joe Nimbs, the two-up game run by the engineers was 'the biggest game' and 'one of the patrons . . . has a pillow-slip nearly full of Malayan dollars and will bet the tail for any amount'.[54] Attempts were made by AIF HQ to shut down such pursuits but these were unsuccessful. According to Nimbs, provost and unit patrols either ignored the games or merely drove them to new venues. As early as 20 March, the Japanese made an attempt to limit the movement of troops both within their own wired perimeter and into other areas. Major Thompson recorded: 'A.I.F. allotted three passes and five flags for movement outside area.'[55] Such 'passes and flags' were of little use. The troops merely 'joined' water parties or work parties moving through an area and went about their trading. This practice must surely have occurred with officer compliance. And there were other ways and means of movement and therefore trading. Driver Joe Nimbs:

> On parade each group was given an imaginary area and we were told that if you went outside of our allotted boundary you were to be punished. There was little hope of this being obeyed. You couldn't

keep troops in an imaginary area . . . If they wanted to buy food elsewhere they automatically became members of the Unit that was in the area that they were in at the time, should they be challenged by an Officer or Provo. When out of our own areas we did not wear hats or shirts so we would not be picked out by our colour patches. Every evening Officers and Provos are on picquet duty.[56]

The pilfering of clothing, limited drug and rice trading, the theft of personal belongings from kits and gambling, therefore, provided the means for some POWs to participate in the black market.

It would seem that Singapore and Changi's black market had a number of levels. We have recorded Colonel Wilfred Kent Hughes's diary entry for 21 April 1942, when he 'put the Black Market cigarette king under arrest this evening'. The reference to a 'cigarette king' clearly implies that there was a large and sophisticated operation involved in cigarette dealing. In other words, we are not discussing the odd packet of cigarettes here, but a considerable and consistent supply. Another interesting point that arises from Kent Hughes's statement is the fact that just as there were a number of 'kings' in Changi, so there must have been a number of Chinese 'kings' in Singapore. The regular supply of goods into Changi and, we shall discover, to work parties outside Changi implies a very complicated, multi-tiered and efficient black market. Further, the nature of those going 'under the wire' would seem just as interesting. On 4 June 1942, Kent Hughes wrote: 'The Black Market in its hey day used to pay its "carriers" $5 a night, but now it is gradually being squeezed out by the Canteens.'[57] His statement raises two interesting points. First, he very mistakenly believed at that time that the black market was being gradually 'squeezed out' by the canteen(s) run by the 8th Division. That was not to be the case. Although, as time went on, the supply of goods would diminish, we shall see that the black market was still thriving after the return of some Thai–Burma Railway POWs to Changi. The second point is that it would seem that there were three types of traders. The term 'carriers' tells us that some POWs going under the wire were acting for a 'boss' or a 'king' and, according to Kent Hughes, were being paid about '$5 a night', which would have made them quite affluent by Changi standards. In addition, others were operating in small groups and selling on an individual 'small time' basis. And there was a third category: those acting for both themselves and a small circle of mates and/or trading to assist their units.

Gunner Richard Haynes, 2/10th Field Regiment, has left us with both a rare and vivid insight into some aspects of the black market:

A man has returned from beyond the wire . . . he has a sick mate, and a friend with a sick mate. A greater portion of the night's haul goes to them. Perhaps he has a few tins of milk left. To the man who approaches him and wishes to buy, he does not say with a trace of melodrama, 'Take it friend, your need is greater than mine.' No, the trader is no Philanthropist, he has come up through life the hard way, camped under a bridge in the Depression, seen life, bitter and mean. Laughed at that life as he now laughs at Japanese. He will stand by his mate to the end, but he says, to this man who perhaps in Australia is a 'Has' while he is a 'Has Not.' . . .

'Four dollars a tin, sport.'

'God Strewth! Four dollars is all I got.'

A lean rangy man in his late twenties surveyed the last speaker. He had spent a sleepless night, and was hoping he would not cop the barbed wire fatigue. A trace of grime showed on his cheek. He spoke again, wearily.

'That's the price mate. I'm not going through the bloody fence for bugger all, except laying in the lalang half the night.'

'You're a robber. A man should put you in, to Black Jack. I told you four dollars is all I got in the world.'

The trader looked the other over, from head to foot. Then, contempt in his voice he said, 'All you got! Well what about your two good legs? What about them? Go out and get some stuff for yourself then. I'm a loner, but come out once with me, and I'll show you the ropes . . . then you can have plenty, plenty of milk. He broke off, laughing mirthlessly, and added, 'That's if you have any guts.'

The face of the buyer grew grey beneath its tan, he stared speechlessly at the Trader. We about them . . . moved restlessly, ashamed at what we saw there in that startled countenance.

The Trader spat contemptuously . . . as if to turn away . . . Suddenly changing his mind, he dug amongst his bed roll, and produced a tin of Nestles Condensed. He tossed it to the other.

'Here ya are . . . buck shee. Now go to buggery . . . ya give me the _____'[58]

Others both knew and appreciated the work of traders going under the wire, and/or doing deals within the general Changi compound. Driver Joe Nimbs:

I am still attached to the R.A.P. and supposed to be on duty at all sick parades. Most times I make it but if I want to get away the Medical Orderlies and the Doctor don't bother to find out where I am. They know I would be out somewhere, if I did any good they would be in it so I had a free hand. The R.A.P. was over staffed so it didn't really matter.[59]

In the foreword to Nimbs's manuscript his CO, Captain Newman, apart from endorsing the accuracy of the work, stated that: 'Joe lightly refers to giving food and cigarettes to many who were in need, but his generosity went further as he constantly helped others in many ways during those years.'[60] The point is that the black market had its positive qualities.

It is also worthy of mention that despite a multitude of items coming into Changi's black market, the demand for cigarettes, tinned fish or beef, and condensed milk was high. We have cited Thompson's early mention of the Japanese allowance of 40 cigarettes per man per month. Given the obvious issue of addiction, and the fact that POWs also found that tobacco helped to quell the appetite, the trade in smokes was always going to be lucrative. And so was the paper to roll it in. According to the 2/19th Unit History, any Holy Bible printed on rice paper was worth around $1.50 to $2.00 per page.[61] Paddy O'Toole would remember that Padre McNeil had a philosophical attitude to such sacrilege: 'I don't mind you boys using the Bible for cigarette paper, but please read it before you smoke it!'[62] The desire for tinned fish and beef is self-explanatory given the lack of it in the Changi diet and the abundance of it in the traditional Australian diet, and condensed milk was widely used to flavour food, to put in tea or coffee, and in some cases, to eat by the spoonful as an 'extravagance'.

So far most of our evidence refers to enlisted men, but to what extent were officers involved? A. J. Sweeting in his POW section of Wigmore's Official History, quoted the official Changi report:

> Check and detection of operators [on the black market] was under-taken by the 'G' Staff, particularly in those cases where trading in drugs was involved. Some convictions were obtained on the evidence thus gathered, but the activities had the effect of lessening considerably the black market operations. Right from the start of our PW life, the question of the black market was regarded as serious, involving as it did the creation of a market for stolen goods, the disposal of valuable drugs, the raising of prices of foodstuffs for canteen purchases, and the security angle of illegal contacts.[63]

The 'check and detection of operators' by the 8th Division G staff would seem to have had at best a chequered career and at worst a possible sinister involvement. The reader will recall Menz's suspicions that his rice investigation had been compromised, and the curious arrest of his four-man patrol whilst inside their Changi perimeter by Japanese who entered the camp from outside the wire to effect the arrest. On 15 July Captain Adrian Curlewis, an 8th Division staff officer, also noted that the 'lack of organisation on G side staggered me. Selfishness of Staff Officers also.'[64]

The truth is that far from attempting to stamp out the black market, a large number of Changi officers were most willing participants in it. Kent Hughes's diary for 13 June 1942: 'We tried hard to pick up some cigarettes from the canteen outside the wire with the sole result that our delegates were picked up.'[65] 'Official reports' rarely cite such evidence. Further, people such as Nimbs, who were both going under the wire and using their large cash flow brought into Changi to trade widely across its unit areas—and in the outside world—usually have a fair insight into the nature of the market in which they trade. Nimbs:

Some of the troops say they have met some of our young A.I.F. Officers scrounging for goods outside the wire. There would be trouble if the Senior Officers find out or do they know? . . .

Most of them get their batmen to buy the goods they want. They could not buy from the Troops selling food, then shift them and arrest them . . .

Deals are being negotiated between these troops and dealers in the A.I.F. area it being the centre of most dealing that went on. The troops on daily working parties to Singapore are selling a lot of watches and trinkets to the Japs in the City area. It's a queer set up. Nearly all the Camp orders are about not being allowed to do this, that and the other. I am sure the A.I.F powers that be could stop the market if they were serious.[66]

In an interview with the author, Private Paddy O'Toole, 2/29th Battalion, who was regularly going under the wire at Changi 'with four-to-five' others of his unit, was more forthright: 'They [the officers] were involved in it up to their eyeballs!'[67] Further, without the author naming Nimbs, or his manuscript, O'Toole confirmed Nimbs's accounts of the market and its procedures. And O'Toole was adamant that the majority of POWs in Changi were involved in the black market in some way.[68]

We now come to the issue of money lending. The Official History has recorded that:

No attempt was made by the camp administration to suppress lending of money at reasonable rates; indeed it would have been undesirable if not impossible to do so. Nevertheless a rate of exchange was fixed and money-lenders were forbidden to accept any negotiable security, promissory note or cheque at a rate of exchange less than 8 dollars local Japanese currency to £1 sterling.[69]

It is well documented that money-lending occurred on a large scale in Changi. Very many of those early Changi loans were to be paid back after the war. Private Paddy O'Toole remembered his C Company 'SP'

bookmaker making loans to 'officers and men'.[70] Warrant Officer 2 Bert
Mettam concurred but added:

> But then the word went round [in Australia after the war] 'Don't repay
> that money that you've borrowed in Changi!' I think I may have repaid
> one but I didn't repay another. I didn't know that many [lenders] but
> I knew two or three.'[71]

Mettam also pointed out that he borrowed $25 in Changi.[72]

Three points should be made with regards to money-lending. The first
is that there was absolutely no way that the 8th Division HQ might have
stopped it. Moreover, the above accounts refer to moneys being redeemed
after the war. This tells us that the other rank borrowers—and possibly
some officers—had no real way of paying the money back whilst in captivity. It is also commonly known that a very substantial number of such
loans were never paid back. Another point is that evidence of loans made
between officers is seemingly scarce for the period in Changi before and
during the raising and despatch of the forces to the Thai–Burma Railway
and Borneo during the period February 1942 to May 1943. However,
strong evidence of widespread loans between officers on the Railway, and
in Changi after its completion, will unfold. Colonel Wilfred Kent Hughes's
Changi diary:

> 8 May 1942:
> Two supper clubs have started in 'A' mess now, & I think Alec & Co
> have one over the way, so our end of the building is the only one that
> goes to bed hungry.—[sic] but none of us have any cash. What can you
> use for money when you have none.

> 13 June 1942:
> . . . so far my friends particularly two of them have come to light so
> often that I am almost beginning to feel embarrassed.—[sic] the latest
> is three packets of cigarette papers & a half pound tin of No Name—
> Players very best. Galleghan ['Black Jack'] always brings a packet

apiece when he comes out from Thompson Rd [this is the period in time when Galleghan was commanding a work party].

19 June 1942:
Last night thirty dollars tumbled into my pocket from a good contact. Gee but I do feel sick. First a tin of 'No Name' tobacco & now thirty dollars. I am set up for at least a month.[73]

———•••———

No examination of Changi Prison during those first fifteen months would be complete without mention of the Selarang Barracks Square incident.

Initially, Changi's first Japanese commander had been Colonel Sugita, who was responsible for the military prisoners and the civilian internees in the much smaller Changi Gaol. Sugita's subordinate was Lieutenant Okazaki, who ran the military camp. From a POW perspective, the period was notable for an absence of Japanese guards within the camp. But on 16 August, Thompson recorded that: 'Major General Shimpei Fukuye Commander of all P.O.W camps in Malaya, assumed command control of P.O.W. camps at Changi and Singapore. Lt Okazaki remaining on Administration Staff.'[74] Fukuye's initial generosity knew no bounds when he made a gift—across both Malaya Command and the AIF—two days later of 6500 tins of pineapple, and promptly distributed Red Cross supplies of 36 118 lbs of mixed soup; 12 210 lbs of sweets; 85 680 lbs of maize meal; 61 056 lbs of mixed jams; and 21 240 lbs of kaffir corn [sic].[75] Thompson:

RED CROSS SUPPLIES. DISTRIBUTION.
6% to Civil Internees
1/8 to Hospital for consumption by patients
17/42 of remainder to be issued to formations
25/42 of remainder to be retained for issue to P.O.W. other camps.
ISSUES decided to issue maize meal 2 ozs a day for 1 month
A.I.F. decided to issue other goods as a daily ration[76]

One day later, on 19 August 1942, Major-General Fukuye held a parade of all troops and stated that he would 'endeavour to be as kind to P.O.W. [sic] as regulations permitted'.[77]

On 30 August, Fukuye demanded that all Changi POWs sign a statement stipulating that: 'I, the undersigned, hereby solemnly swear on my honour that I will not, under any circumstances, attempt escape.'[78] On 2 September four escapees—two of them Australians—were executed by a Sikh firing squad under Japanese supervision. British and Australian senior officers were ordered to witness the executions. When the British and Australians refused to sign the form, all 14 609 POWs (including 1897 Australians) were marched to Selarang Square, placed on one-third rations, had access to only two water taps, and were thus confined within an area of little more than eight acres (about 3.24 hectares).[79] After negotiations over whether the 'statement' might be reworded or made an order not a request, the British and Australian commanders ordered their soldiers to sign. All in Changi maintained that because the form had been signed under duress it was invalid. On 5 September, all POWs returned to their previous quarters.

Two points are of great significance with regards to Major-General Fukuye's 'gift' on assumption of his command and the ensuing Selarang Barracks Square incident.

The first was the immediate pilfering of those stocks. Thompson recorded that $686 worth of goods had disappeared before the actual camp delivery. Lieutenant-Colonel 'Black Jack' Galleghan 'expressed his regret' but soon pointed out that some of the pilfering had occurred before the AIF fatigue party could take over. In the end, the AIF paid $230 compensation out of its funds.[80] The AIF 'recompense' paid to Malaya Command was around one-third of the pilfered amount, which would seem to indicate that a very substantial, speedy—and therefore highly organised—theft was undertaken by civilians (probably criminal societies), before the AIF had access to the supplies. There was also speculation that the pilfering was partly facilitated by Japanese collusion.

But the most significant point to come out of this incident is the parallel execution of escapees and the demand of a written promise that POWs would not, in future, undertake escape attempts in Pudu Prison at around the same time. 'Black Jack' Galleghan would later write: 'The most notable feature of this incident was the cohesion and unity of British and Australian troops, and the fine morale and spirit shown.'[81] The reader will remember that when Captain 'Roaring Reggie' Newton left Pudu for

Changi, he was well aware that the Japanese expected something in return for any apparent generosity. 'If you were given permission to buy from canteens or on work parties you could be sure that you would lose something.'[82] True, Newton wrote about the lessons he had learnt in Pudu for his unit history, which was written long after the event. But the truth is that his manner of leadership in Pudu, in Changi, on a Singapore work party, and, critically, on the Thai–Burma Railway adequately demonstrated that his 'lessons' were learnt at the time. The Selarang Barracks Square incident shows us that Lieutenant-Colonel 'Black Jack' Galleghan had learnt very little from the experience. Major-General Fukuye's issue of a multitude of foodstuffs upon his arrival and his pledge 'to be as kind to P.O.W. [sic] as regulations permitted' was merely a prelude to his demand for a signing of the non-escape document and the subsequent Selarang Barracks Square detention. The whole episode had little or nothing to do with 'the fine morale and spirit shown'.

The reader will recall that Captain 'Roaring Reggie' Newton and his Pudu contingent of Australians had been ordered to be ready to move to Singapore on 30 September 1942. After five delays Newton's men made the one-day train trip '30 to a steel truck; no food and the two Jap guards taking up all the room and fresh air at the open doorway.'[83] They were then transported by truck to Changi. On 3 October, Thompson recorded the 'arrival of 161 troops from Kuala Lumpur, majority admitted to hospital'.[84] The two radio sets which had been hidden in Pudu were smuggled into Changi and handed in to Lieutenant-Colonel Kappe.

It will be remembered that Newton had sent a toilet roll to Singapore via a Chinese courier with a nominal roll of Pudu's Australians hidden inside it. When he reported to Lieutenant-Colonel Galleghan at AIF HQ, a stormy confrontation took place. Newton would later record that he: '. . . was soundly berated and ticked off for addressing the toilet roll "Dear Fred" and in future he would be court-martialled if he addressed a senior officer publicly by his christian [sic] name.'[85] Newton claimed that he then 'turned' on 'Black Jack' and in 'blunt terms' delivered a spirited lecture on security measures, on the need to protect the Chinese courier, and that Galleghan might consider going on another work party to acquaint himself with a few 'home truths'. The reader might imagine Galleghan's reaction. Soon there were to be further conflicts.

If Galleghan and Newton had clashed, then Lieutenant-Colonel Edward 'Weary' Dunlop's arrival in Singapore unleashed an everlasting antipathy between two strong, determined commanders which would continue postwar.

After its capitulation on 9 March 1942, Java became the second largest venue for Australian POWs, with around 3000 scattered inmates. The Australians on Java, like those in Pudu, had suffered a cruel initiation of life under Japanese rule. While it is not the purpose of this work to examine in detail either Dunlop's Java experience, or his subsequent exploits on the Thai–Burma Railway—they have been comprehensively recorded elsewhere—his transit through Singapore and his Railway experience will be examined briefly as they illuminate our story.

'Weary' Dunlop had joined the Australian Army Medical Corps (6th Division) in November 1939 with the rank of captain; he had subsequently been posted as the Acting Assistant Director of Medical Services at the Australian Overseas Base Jerusalem; had served in Greece and Crete; in July 1941, he became second-in-command of the 2/2nd Casualty Clearing Station and had served as its senior surgeon in Tobruk; and when the 6th and 7th Divisions were withdrawn from the Middle East, Dunlop and his 2/2nd CCS were sent to participate in the ill-fated fighting on Java. As a lieutenant-colonel, he was in command of the Number 1 Allied General Hospital at Bandung Java, when the island fell.

During the period October 1942 to January 1943, a number of Java parties entered Changi in transit to the Thai–Burma Railway—and elsewhere. Some of them were Dutch, others Australian and some were mixed. The Dutch were often christened 'Wilhelmina's wet arsed warriors' by the Australians; it was a reference to the Dutch Queen and her soldiers' habit of using a water bottle and cloth in the toilet. The term reflected a certain contempt for their military performance on Java. A number of these Dutch Java parties were briefly accommodated in the AIF perimeter in Changi, and, given their appalling physical condition and ragged and sparse clothing, some were given limited clothing from the AIF store.

Nine hundred Australians comprising Dunlop Force arrived in Singapore on 7 January 1943. With close-shaven heads, wearing ragged and tattered uniforms, some of them bootless, and all gaunt, worn and hungry, they were immediately struck by both the appearance and military demeanour of their new hosts. Dunlop's first encounter was with Malaya Command British officers. They were neatly dressed, carried canes, and were 'blowing out puffy little moustaches and talking in an "old chappy" way'.[86] When Dunlop met Galleghan the following day, all went wrong from the start. Unannounced, and wearing Changi officer armbands, Dunlop met Lieutenant-Colonel White, whom he knew, but failed to recognise Lieutenant-Colonel Galleghan. Neither Dunlop or his men saluted the party—a fatal error—because they were unaware that the Japanese had long since ordered badges of rank to be removed. It was only as the 8th Division party was leaving that 'Black Jack' introduced himself and enquired as to whether he could help Dunlop's party. Dunlop noted in his diary Galleghan's insistence on 'proper dress and smart turnout' and sarcastically described this as 'a praiseworthy achievement'.[87]

Matters now went from bad to worse when someone in 8th Division christened Dunlop Force the 'Java Rabble'. Not to be outdone, the reciprocal slogan 'the 8th Division Harriers' was coined. On 9 January 1943, Galleghan, obviously having made a hasty, ill-founded (as history shows), and egotistical decision, sent Dunlop the following memo:

To Lt-Col. Dunlop I/C AIF S. Area
From HQ AIF Q.3250 9/1
Com. AIF desires following information:
Name of senior combatant officer with party
Suggest changing O.C. party to combatant officer
Is there any reason for not making change?
1600   Alex Thompson Maj.[88]

Dunlop's reply stated that Major W. Wearne was the senior combatant officer and also explained that he, Dunlop, had commanded the force as senior officer, and that 'before making any change your further advice would therefore be appreciated'.[89]

That night Brigadier Arthur Blackburn, VC visited Dunlop to say farewell before his departure north. Blackburn had been Dunlop's superior in Java. 'Black Jack's' memo did not amuse him. He wrote, as Galleghan's superior, the following reply: 'I have considered this matter and desire Lt-Col. Dunlop to retain command for administrative and disciplinary purposes so long as the troops brought over by him remain together as one body.'[90] A simple point should be made. One officer (Galleghan) acted on a brief, superficial and preliminary meeting with a fellow officer and had then made a important decision based on that 'impression'. Another (Blackburn) knew Dunlop's qualities, had witnessed them and had entrusted the command and welfare of the soldiers of Dunlop Force—including a number of his (Blackburn's) former 2/3rd Machine Gun Battalion men—to Dunlop. One officer knew precisely what he was doing, and the other was behaving in an arrogant and dictatorial manner. Lieutenant-Colonel Galleghan was a man of many extremes—good and bad. We see him here at his worst.

Brigadier Blackburn had left Changi just before matters came to a head at an AIF dinner that night. When someone referred to Dunlop Force as the 'Java Rabble' within Dunlop's hearing, he rose and rattled off the exploits of the 'Java Rabble'. Amongst them were the Western Desert, Greece, Crete, Syria and Java.[91] He then reportedly rose and finished with: 'And now we, the Java Rabble, salute you, the 8th Division, who have fought so gallantly in Malaya.'[92] After dinner Galleghan again brought up the issue of command. When Dunlop produced Blackburn's 'note' Galleghan had no choice but to back down. He then asked what assistance was required, to which Dunlop requested clothing, boots, caps and rice polishings. 'Weary' Dunlop recorded that his men were to eventually receive six pairs of boots, 150 pairs of socks and 20 caps.[93] An examination of Thompson's diary regarding the clothing issued to a multitude of forces leaving Changi for 'up country' or 'overseas' destinations, reveals the simple fact that the 'Java Rabble' received an extremely frugal supply. Dunlop Force left Changi for the Railway on 20 January 1943. Seething at what he saw as Galleghan's neglect in assisting him, and equally angry at his interference in command, Dunlop left Galleghan with a stinging last word the day before his departure: 'Two weeks ago my men arrived in a pitiful condition in this camp from Java. You have done nothing to alleviate their needs. Tomorrow at

8.30 they leave in the same pitiable condition: bootless and in rags. You have done nothing.'[94]

⸻ ⬧ ⸻

Whilst fate can be a cruel master, it can also at times unwittingly assume the role of a 'guardian angel'. Those in Changi who were always optimistic about their chances of surviving captivity and returning home were often referred to as 'hopers'. Corporal Jim Kennedy, 2/29th Battalion:

> If it's not getting worse than this [Changi], we can put up with it, because we'll win in the end. It's no good crying about it . . . home for Christmas was the motto. It was true!
>   Home for Christmas 1945![95]

Driver Joe Nimbs was a 'hoper'. He had believed that A Force, the first force to leave Changi on 14 May 1942, was heading for 'a better' place: 'we all keep hearing that the Japs are going to send us to a neutral country and the limbless troops are to be sent home. We would all like to be on it . . .'[96] Having missed the first force, Nimbs went to great lengths not to be disappointed a second time:

> B-Force was about to move and five names were read out on parade . . . They were told to get their gear ready to move at short notice. Must be some mistake. They had forgotten to read my name out as I had earlier been selected as a member of the party and was breaking my neck to go. I felt some concern after I had asked to see the Orderly Room Officer. I was told I had been taken off the party as I was wanted at the R.A.P. Oh what a blow! My rickshaw mate the biggest 'hoper' of all time who I am going to miss although he often woke me up with his snoring said, 'Anyhow, I will wait till you get to Switzerland before I try to escape. I will know all the lurks by the time you get there.' I said Cheerio to my friend and the rest of the unit on the party, the Doctor and his Orderlies as they boarded the trucks to get on their way this morning the 8th of July. Gee, some have all the luck.[97]

There was to be no luck, no Switzerland, and no lurks for Joe's 'rickshaw mate'—he died during the Sandakan death marches in Borneo. Driver Joe Nimbs could not yet know that whilst life in Changi was no picnic, it was arguably one of the best places in the Greater Asian Co-Prosperity Sphere to be a prisoner of Nippon.

There is an immense difference between purgatory and hell.

26

THE SINGAPORE WORK CAMPS

During the first fifteen months of Changi's existence as a POW camp, its population was ever changing as parties of prisoners arrived from such places as Java, while many of its original occupants were sent out to a multitude of work camps on Singapore Island.

The ability of the Australians to scrounge all manner of items on the docks of Keppel Harbour and smuggle them into camp despite searches is not only well documented but has passed into Australian folklore. However, the effect on the POWs' health, the nature of some of the Australian scrounging and the manner in which some of those camps were run was to influence the chances of survival for many of them on the notorious Thai–Burma Railway.

It should be appreciated that the Japanese deployed work parties from Changi far and wide over Singapore Island. The physical conditions, the number of POWs in any given camp, the diet and the potential for scrounging and bartering—all depended on the location and the nature of the work to be done. On 31 March 1942, for example, Major Alan Thompson noted that there were 800 men at Bukit Timah engaged in building a Japanese memorial—who, it transpired, were living in abandoned civilian houses near the Singapore Golf Course—and that 56 were at Mersing clearing mines.[1] Many of the POWs at Mersing later returned to Changi suffering from malaria. For the purposes of our story, the highly populated camps which furnished a multitude of troops for work at Keppel Harbour and around Singapore Town itself will be examined, because they tell us so much about the work party experience for a great many of Changi's inmates, and the link between the work party experience and the Thai–Burma Railway.

After the capitulation, the Japanese almost immediately realised the tremendous labour potential at their disposal. Just five days after the Australians' arrival in Changi 200 men were marched into Singapore; the next day a further 550 were sent; on 12 March 3400 were despatched; and, in his monthly Changi summary for March 1942, Thompson would record that 2109 Australian POWs were residing at the Great World Amusement Park under the command of Major Schneider, and a further 1291 at River Valley Road under Major Anderson (2/30th Battalion).[2] And replacement parties of varying sizes often left Changi and others returned due to accidents, sickness, or as the Japanese demand for workers grew or subsided.

The Great World had been Singapore's most popular prewar amusement park. Situated on about 2.8 hectares in the heart of Singapore Town, it provided instant accommodation for its multitude of new inhabitants. Gunner Richard Haynes arrived there in March and fondly remembered the '. . . combination of Beer Gardens, Cabarets and Side Shows. However, now were added the words "prison camp" to the three words which had represented to us many good times, and happy memories of Singapore Leave.'[3] Some units camped in the large cabaret halls, others in the multitude of small sideshow stalls, but all made themselves relatively comfortable and relished the relative freedom of movement and the relative scarcity of Japanese guards. The Australians faced a 45-minute walk to the docks at Keppel Harbour each morning to begin work. Private Gus Halloran, 2/19th Battalion:

> You'd get up early, you'd have a breakfast of sorts . . . it'd be rice of some sort . . . there were Jap guards on the camp as a whole, but they were not living with us actually . . . they would go down with you, you'd probably have half a dozen or so guards [who] would take about a company size down to the wharf, depending on what sort of jobs you'd have. There'd be a sling party unloading

a ship or something ... you might have a sake ship, in which case you'd be unloading cases of sake or you might have a rice ship; you could be loading trains with rice or unloading, or stuff coming in from Kuala Lumpur where they had big godowns [warehouses] ... and they were bringing that down to Singapore for transportation. And we'd sometimes go to a rail siding that was back from the wharf and unload stuff there and load it into trucks usually driven by our fellows ...[4]

Sergeant Stan Arneil, 2/30th Battalion, recorded that the godowns were 'some 100 yards long. They were packed to the eaves with merchandise of every conceivable variety, from all ports of the world.'[5] As work parties began to move over much of Singapore, an 8th Division record was kept of the locations of food dumps, military supplies, wireless transmitters, anti-aircraft units and Japanese barracks. All of this intelligence was written in an exercise book complete with map grid references and or addresses, and found its way home to Australia after the war with Captain Adrian Curlewis.[6] Thirty-six godowns and their contents were listed. A sample: '13 (cloth & cotton) 14 (shirts & shorts) 15 (sox) 16 (soap & blankets) 29 (Tin baths. Torches & batteries) 34 (boot polish. Fibre, tables) 35 (Toilet paper, lamps, aspirins) 36 (Newspaper, paint)'[7]

From the time of their arrival at the Great World and the beginning of work in the godowns of Keppel Harbour, an age-old game was enacted: Sergeant Frank Baker, 2/20th Battalion:

You see what happens in prisons and prison camps ... it's another world and no matter how you police people, or incarcerate them or whatever you do, you will not stop that [scrounging and barter-ing], because they will always find a way. And no matter what sort of supervision there is or what sort of punishment is meted out, they'll find a way ... you've got to survive! ... you've got nothing to lose.[8]

Both the quality and volume of goods scrounged by the Australians on or near the docks at Keppel Harbour were dependent upon two factors: the nature of the goods stored in the godowns and the level of security enforced by the Japanese guards. Frank Baker:

Each Godown had a Jap in charge and of course you got to know which Jap was what too. There was Joe in number 46 and Mickey the Mouse was in, I think 48 . . . Mickey the Mouse, he was a quiet little bloke. All Australians! Ooooh! Ooooh! He'd just give you away! [leave you alone] You could take what you liked and do what you liked, he wasn't going to worry about you because you were going to pinch 'em anyway . . . Joe was in 46 and Joe was a bastard! . . . mostly tinned foods [in 46] . . . but Joe I think also had some connections with . . . people in Singapore. Joe had something going and if you took from there Joe didn't get it you see. Joe was a nasty person . . . he'd work with them [the Chinese traders] he'd work with anyone for a quid . . . He'd only have to walk along the wharves and he'd find a few Chinese wandering around . . . there weren't too many like Mickey the Mouse . . . But the normal bloke who had some minor thing going . . . he was alright, as long as he didn't catch you stealing anything, as long as you were doing your work, they'd just walk around, they wouldn't care. But blokes like Joe watched you, they had a hawk eye . . . but they still lost a lot of stuff because we weren't mugs, we could pinch it too![9]

The prized items to be 'pinched' were consumables and tobacco for the individual and his mates, and goods which were in demand by the Chinese. Such sales of non-consumables raised a cash flow which in turn bought food or goods which might not have been available in a particular godown at the time.

The Australian POWs on work parties in Singapore turned scrounging into an art form. Bike chains were placed in the inside of a belt or even placed inside a boot; prized sewing machine and gramophone needles were placed in the hair, or in the rim of a hat; cigarettes, tobacco and papers were similarly concealed; and when larger supplies of goods were moved, false pockets inside singlets, sleeves and pants were sewn. But perhaps the best known and most widely used container was the water bottle. Gus Halloran recalled that '. . . those big ambulance water bottles were the ideal thing. Fellows had cut the bottom out of them . . . they'd have . . . water in the top half, cut the bottom out, they'd solder them . . . they were great for pinching cigarettes.'[10] Other popular water bottle items were sewing machine oil and sugar. Inevitably, as the Japanese became familiar with scrounging methods, subtle changes would occur, or new ones invented. Gunner Richard Haynes recalled that: 'The first question going the rounds if we entered a strange place of employment, invariably was, "Do you know what rackets the Nips are a wake up to, here?"'[11]

Once scrounged, such goods were either taken back to the Great World for consumption, bartered with Chinese walking alongside the Australians back to the Great World, sold 'through' or 'over' the fences of the park, or transactions were undertaken inside the camp with Chinese manning an official canteen. Very soon after his arrival at the Great World, Haynes was most impressed with the excellent exchange rate and the variety of 'goods' available:

The first discovery of 'The World' was that to the natives, the British Malayan dollar was as good as ever. We were able, through numerous holes in the back fence, to buy anything from a Virgin [sic] to a tin of condensed milk. When I bought four tins of this latter for one dollar, the boys thought that I was kidding them. Their Changi price on March 21st was four dollars each.[12]

There were varying degrees of risk in all forms of scrounging and bartering. The punishment for being caught in the act depended on whether the miscreant was a POW or Chinese, but most of all on the whim or mood of the Japanese guard involved. If caught, a bashing was inevitable. The term 'bashing' is reminiscent of our grappling earlier in our story with the term 'straggler'. Bashing took a number of forms. Gus Halloran:

... you'd get a bit of a bashing but that was nothing ... it's a bit humiliating to have your face slapped and stood to attention and in some cases knocked down, but on the whole they were not professional punch throwers ... most blokes would be riding the punches pretty well anyhow.[13]

Sergeant Frank Baker:

I've seen a few hit with the first thing they could get hold of . . . Number 46 Godown . . . Joe would lay into you with a tin of salmon or whatever he had to his hand, then he'd take the stuff off you and go away and sulk! Mickey the Mouse never bashed you at all, just shake his head and walk away. Others would pick up anything they could find and this was the danger! They'd do it spontaneously. Pick up anything! . . .[14]

The point is that a 'bashing' might constitute a few slaps across the face, a number of punches and/or a few kicks, but, on occasions 'the Japs used to work themselves up into a terrible rage',[15] which caused an almost complete lack of self-control and dire consequences for the POW. Baker's reference to a guard 'picking up anything' might refer to a lump of wood, a rifle butt, or an all-in frenzy of punches and kicks from a number of guards. The bewildering aspect of such behaviour was that any of the above mentioned acts of violence might result from a minor issue—the punishment often did not fit the 'crime'. A POW could not, therefore, readily apply any real sense of logic or predictability to any given situation with a Japanese guard. And the final frightening aspect of this behaviour was the fact that corporal punishment was normal within the Japanese Army. From 7 December 1941, through Japanese eyes, the lowest form of life was a POW—and he was treated accordingly.

The treatment handed out to the Chinese was worse. Lance-Corporal John Roxburgh, 2/29th Battalion:

Once going in at one of the wharves, going into a warehouse, I saw a kid of about eight or nine throw a cigarette . . . and there was a high fence . . . over the fence to anyone; just a cigarette not a packet. There was a bloody Jap guard there and he got this kid and he started to belt him, fists first, hands, and then eventually the rifle butt to the back of the bloody head and on the side of the head, and that kid eventually was just lying on the ground just bleeding . . . the poor little bastard . . . unbelievable, and I thought they were just bloody animals.[16]

The Australians were witnesses to the Chinese receiving the 'water treatment' and saw the numerous impaled Chinese heads displayed at key venues such as the Singapore Railway Station. But although the scrounging and bartering might abate temporarily during and after such 'purges', it soon reappeared. Life went on.

Gunner Richard Haynes has left us with one intriguing question, and one equally succinct observation concerning the Japanese role in the black market on Singapore Island—and later by extension—the Thai–Burma Railway. 'We cannot understand the Japs yet. Are they dumb? Or are they just giving us a go?'[17] At the time, the Australians were inclined to think that 'they' were just 'dumb'. One of the most famous postwar Australian stories illustrates the point. Hank Nelson, in his book, *P.O.W. Prisoners of War, Australians Under Nippon*, recorded a speech given by a Japanese officer to a number of Australians concerning their scrounging: 'When a Japanese mounted a box to admonish an Australian work party over cigarette stealing he said: "Now you Australian soldier you think we know fuck nothing that's going on here. You are wrong, we know fuck all!"'[18]

Japanese such as 'Mickey the Mouse' probably did know 'fuck all', but the issue is that many of those guards knew and were involved in a lot more than the Australians understood at the time. 'Giving us a go' was the farthest thing from their minds. Making money—at varying levels of sophistication—was uppermost. The point is that on the Thai–Burma Railway some Australian (and British) commanders would appreciate the nature of the 'game' and the Japanese involvement in it, and one in particular would turn that knowledge and understanding into a positive and decisive method of ensuring a high survival rate in his battalion.

Gunner Haynes's observation:

The value of goods disposed of through this valuable source, cannot be estimated in dollars, but in lives that it might have helped save. Some of the proceeds found their way back to starving Changi, some were hoarded against that rainy day so soon to come, to buy those dozen eggs, that, eeked out, pulled a convalescent shadow [on the Railway] up from the depths. Only in this unknown estimate of lives can the value of the trade be appreciated, and recognition to the mercenary, ever bartering Chinese be granted.[19]

The truth is that many Australians were to later leave Changi in top physical condition because of their time at work camps on Singapore Island. Sergeant Stan Arneil, 2/30th Battalion, recorded that after being in the Great World: 'We were still in excellent condition after working hard on the wharves for months and having eaten (stolen) the very best of food.'[20] Private Wal Williams, 2/19th Battalion went further: 'At that stage we were in pretty good nick . . . at Changi we weren't getting too much food, but once we got into [the godowns], I'd say we were living better there than we were in the army.'[21] Life at the Thompson Road camp also improved Lieutenant-Colonel Pond's physical condition: 'I noted on the 29 September 1942 [he arrived there on 5 May] that my weight was 10 stone 11 lbs, the heaviest for years, and my waist was a little bigger too. It would seem that although we thought we were being badly done by in the matter of food, we were not being starved at that stage.'[22] Not unlike the troops over much of the Island, Pond's diet was therefore more than adequate. But, unlike the other ranks, he was unable to work for a degree of fitness, and so resorted to 'a plunge bath . . . after a little PT in the morning'.[23] A number of the work camps on Singapore Island, therefore, were responsible for maximising the chances of survival on the Railway.

We now come to another important work party issue. Sergeant Stan Arneil, 2/30th Battalion: 'News from Changi and from other work parties came in to us from time to time. Although we had no reliable communication with Changi we managed to send messages and occasional parcels of food to friends still in Changi.'[24] Such parcels of food and tobacco were not hard to send, as the trucks transporting POWs back and forth were driven by Australians. Jim Stewart, 2/19th Battalion, remembered receiving orders 'from Changi as to what food to send back to Changi—mainly Marmite'. He also recalled being told to watch for medicines, and that some were sent.[25] Paddy O'Toole, 2/29th Battalion, also recalled limited medicines being sent in.[26] Such movement of supplies back into Changi was both desirable and prudent. But Sergeant Frank Baker, 2/20th Battalion, despite the fact that he could not remember ever being told to scrounge medical supplies, had an eye to the future. He was to later serve with Captain Reg Newton's Battalion on the Railway as an orderly to Captain David Hinder, Newton's RMO. Baker:

... I used to carry a bag with me with a bit of medical stuff in it, not much, but I could pinch enough down there. And there was one thing you could always do and the Japs didn't object to this, if you had somebody sick, and there was some medical stuff available, you could go and get it.[27]

At the same time, Baker scrounged priceless, if limited, medical supplies:

Almost anything that you would find in a normal chemist shop ... I got some, not plenty, because those things weren't very plentiful ... there was no thought of us going back to Changi. You lived from day to day, you didn't know what you were going to do. You were in the Great World for this length of time, and then they started to chop you about, they sent us to Havelock Road, to River Valley Road, to Delta Road ...

[Baker scrounged] ... particularly stuff that wasn't necessarily medical; marmite for instance ... that was the biggest thing as far as the treatment of beri-beri was concerned and deficiency diseases ... bandages, instruments of various kinds, Doc Hinder I think got instruments from me that he wouldn't have had otherwise. Coming from those parties ... bandages, if there happened to be ointments ... for instance Tiger Balm, good stuff![28]

The quantity of drugs and general medical supplies that made their way into Changi—both brought by individuals and bought by 8th Division purchasing parties—is hard to ascertain, but Baker maintained that it must have been a significant amount.[29] What is of interest to our story is that the systematic scrounging by POWs such as Baker certainly had a pronounced influence on the survival rate for some battalions on the Railway.

The numerous work parties on Singapore Island also gives us an insight into ongoing leadership issues in Changi, and later on the Railway.

It will be recalled that Lieutenant-Colonel 'Black Jack' Galleghan had been in command of a work party to Caldicott Hill prior to assuming command back in Changi in July 1942. Lieutenant-Colonel Pond observed that:

At the Caldicott Hill POW camp—the Australian part—Lt Colonel Galleghan was the OC of No 3 Group where he & his HQ lived in some style & comfort. The Group HQ was pervaded by quite an air of self promotion for the staff called Galleghan Brigadier, Capt Dillon of the ASC was Brigade Major and Lieut Eaton was Staff Captain. In fact the ASC officer Goddard the Sergeant-Major and the Sergeant Clerk were the only ones not promoted![30]

An extraordinary event occurred during May 1942 that clearly demonstrates the compartmentalised nature of the Japanese command structure. After having said their goodbyes to the Japanese officer in charge of their camps (Abamatsu) and his 'Yokoyama unit', the Australians suddenly found themselves 'unsupervised'. Lieutenant-Colonel Pond:

> ... there was no work from 18 to 26 May both inclusive. All troops were in the lines for the first three days but then in the absence of guard started to straggle out to the Kampong & as far as Singapore. On the 22, 23 and 24 May more than a hundred troops were away from the camp in spite of parades & muster roll calls which we arranged. The Japanese did not interfere at all. Men went down the main roads, saluted Japanese & were allowed to proceed. They rode in buses and trams with the Japanese. Some were even given meals in cafes by Japanese officers. There was no set of restrictions at all on troops moving about. The Japanese were disinterested & this made discipline very difficult for us to enforce. The freedom allowed to our troops by the Japanese in this period was incredible, & bore no resemblance to the ordinary treatment of POW. Two of our officers ... went to Singapore to see what was doing and they were welcomed everywhere, even to the extent of being given a lift home by a Japanese soldier who made a special trip out to the camp with his truck.[31]

Pond recorded the inevitable, if late, Japanese response:

> ... eventually the Japanese military police became much concerned.
>   ... Colonel Galleghan—the senior of our group of parties—was

rebuked by the Japanese for lack of discipline and was told that officers would be held liable for failure of discipline.[32]

Criticism of Galleghan here would be unfair. But in the light of this incident, 'Black Jack's own treatment of officers such as 'Weary' Dunlop and 'Roaring Reggie' Newton for a supposed lack of discipline would seem hypocritical and unfair. Pond also clarifies another issue that saw a clash between Galleghan and Newton back in Changi in December 1942. Major Alan Thompson's Changi diary for 21 December: 'Return of Working Parties . . . A.I.F party of 1,200 march in. Discipline bad, party ate all its Red Cross supplies before returning.'[33]

Captain Reg Newton had commanded part of this group. According to Newton, 'another donnybrook ensued'[34] between the two headstrong commanders, with Newton claiming that the Changi units had been given their Red Cross supplies and that—pointedly—Galleghan had done the same thing when on a working party with his men. Lieutenant-Colonel Pond had also handed out his Red Cross supplies. Pond: 'Red Cross comforts were received on the 4th October 1942 . . . Distribution of the main items was arranged on a weekly basis to last six months.'[35] No commander or POW could possibly know whether he was destined to return to Changi, or whether he might be shipped and entrained elsewhere, or, for that matter, whether any issued Japanese supplies might be confiscated upon re-entry into Changi. It seems that all units in Changi and around Singapore consumed their Red Cross supplies, but that the incident was used by Galleghan to admonish only one commander: Newton.

The last issue of importance to our journey from Changi and its work parties to the Thai–Burma Railway is a brief insight into leadership in the former and how it affected the latter. We have noted Lieutenant-Colonel Galleghan's order in early August 1942 when in command of Changi that area commanders were to supply the names of majors and captains who 'were physically fit for field officer duty', and that officers might be required to swap formations in order to structure the 'force'.[36] We have also recorded his attempt(s) to remove 'Weary' Dunlop from his command because he was a 'non-combatant' officer. Further, we have identified the at times aloof, self-indulgent manner in which *some* Changi officers conducted their commands and lived. Although not applicable to all officers, Galleghan's notion that commanders chosen for Thai–Burma Railway battalions should be from field officer ranks only would prove a mistake. Lieutenant-Colonel Pond made a critically important observation as he left his work party camp: 'On the evacuation of the area camps, the Havelock Road area was left very dirty by Fairley's party and Quick's lines were shocking, so that 250 other men were requested to clean up. Indians then moved in.'[37]

The above will prove but one example of flawed command choices. If Major Quick's lines were 'shocking' on a Singapore work party, his chances of effectively commanding troops on the Thai–Burma Railway—where hygiene standards and camp organisation were to prove a matter of life and death—were slim. Another commander in identical circumstances would view the Japanese and his selection of officers for his party in an entirely different manner—with very different results.

The Australian POW experience on the Thai–Burma Railway forged many bonds. Sergeant Bert Donaldson, 2/19th Battalion: 'My POW mates are more important to me than my own siblings, my own brothers and sisters. I'm more concerned about their livelihood than I am about my brothers and sisters. Seems a bit hard doesn't it, but it's true.'[38] Most Australians have some concept of the brutality, the hunger, the slavery, the mateship and the sacrifice on the Railway. And much of this legitimate legend is embodied in the story of that great Australian 'Weary' Dunlop, and the symbolic stage or setting for that adulation has been Hellfire Pass. We now turn to a much wider Railway study, and particularly to the impact of a number of commanders upon their men's chances of survival. There are new heroes—some commanders, others doctors and their orderlies—and they figure in equally dramatic situations.

PART IV
THE THAI–BURMA RAILWAY

... the gods don't give a damn

———⊰⊱———

Human decency is not enough to provide a shield, it can
only be its own reward—the gods don't give a damn

Ian Denys Peek, *One Fourteenth of an Elephant*

27

THE KILLER CYCLE

———⸙———

'You're in this other world . . . it's not this world, it's not the world you know, or anybody who wasn't with us knows.'[1] The will to survive in Sergeant Frank Baker's 'other world' is a powerful human emotion. It inspires the very best qualities in most men, but in sheer desperation, the worst in others; but the will rarely wavers. We have seen soldiers such as Private Paddy O'Toole going under the wire at Changi and scrounging on the docks at Keppel Harbour. Scrounging and trading on the Railway would be far harder. Paddy O'Toole:

> Green stuff see! I used to eat grass . . . bloody green stuff! Horses live on it, cows live on it! It's not goin' to do me any bloody harm! Mind over matter. Think positive all the time. I always said to myself and to my mates, I said, 'Look, if there's one man going to get out of this to tell a fuckin' story, it's going to be Paddy O'Toole!'[2]

Warrant Officer Bert Mettam: 'You couldn't survive without a mate. You had to have someone there who could help you.'[3] Private Wal Williams:

> See . . . if a bloke got crook, and he just lay there, if no bastard came near him, mate, he was curtains! . . . You've gotta go and speak to him,

you've got to go and sort of buck him up. 'How [are you] going, mate? You'll be right, keep getting that bloody rice into you!' The dixie'd be there. 'Come on, get it into you!'

'Oh Jesus, I can't eat it!'

Eat it![4]

Your mates will literally force feed you your rice today, tomorrow, and the next day, and if you have dysentery they'll also try and make you comfortable by washing the shit off you, your clothes, and the bamboo floor surrounds, over and over again if necessary. When a move to another camp is on they'll help you there and carry your gear. And if a POW succumbs he will rarely die alone—there are those who perform death watches. The phenomenon of mateship played a powerful part in enhancing survival on the Thai–Burma Railway.

While there was no such thing as a good day in this 'other world,' some were better than others. Captain Adrian Curlewis, diary, 29 June 1943:

Two km again to carry vegetables and food for Nips. We still live on dry rice three times a day. Bought a cup of gula malacca [like golden syrup] with a borrowed dollar to flavour the meal. At night was given a cup of coffee by Brigade boys with gula. Heaven! A good night, feeling well in spite of everything. I volunteer for everything and simulate content [sic] and happiness.[5]

But this existence also has its sinister side. Curlewis, 30 August 1943:

God, how weary I am of squalor, mankind and illness. I live in a tattered tent with nine officers too ill to work, who talk of nothing but their illnesses (my breakfast in the dark as they lie in bed accompanied by boasts of the number of their visits to the latrines at night). My day is amongst foul-mouthed animals who have lost self respect and decency, who rob their mates, who cry to me for help on all occasions and then let me down by lying. Razors have been sold for food, brushes and combs gone, soap almost unobtainable, clothes in rags and dirty, tempers on edge and hope gone. Personally I have succeeded by weary

---

---

hours of sewing, scrubbing and will power to keep a certain amount of appearance. As I lie now in the tent five officers are sitting on their haunches just gazing at nothing or talking in faded voices—men without hope or, if they have hope, they are fighting for health to get them home. Two are cholera convalescents. Have just supervised 240 men (skeletons) drawing their lunch issue of rice; blasphemy, flies, dirt. God, how I hate it all![6]

There were many ways of dying on the Railway: dysentery, beriberi, pellagra, malaria, oedema and diarrhoea. And then there's the seemingly harmless scratch that slowly becomes a creeping, foul, pus-ridden nightmare that envelops the leg or foot, sometimes causes an amputation, and sometimes death. But the mere mention of the word 'cholera' would constitute the ultimate form of terror for both the POW and his guards. You can have a mate who is here now but soon unrecognisable and gone within hours. Sergeant Frank Baker worked in a cholera tent:

With the loss of fluid you cramp up, and they cramp and double up and their face becomes . . . this gaunt, shrunken face with their eyes sticking out, and the shuddering . . . that sets in with the limbs . . . it's cramps . . . it's serious cramps. . . .you're in pain all the time and you're exuding fluids from both ends—it's the most frightful disease! . . .

I never put my fingers in my mouth for years after I came back. I would not put my fingers in my mouth for anything . . . you knew that that finger could kill you . . . you didn't handle your food, you didn't handle anything that went into your mouth . . . habitual.[7]

For the majority of POWs, a cholera case, whether he was alive or dead, was to be avoided at all costs. Private Jack Coffee:

. . . he [an NCO] came, he says, 'Look, I want four blokes for a light duties job.' He said, 'I'll make sure you get full rations.' That sounds good, didn't have to go to work that day. He said, 'I'll see you in the morning.' The morning comes. 'What's the job?' His name was

_____ He'd died. [Coffee goes on in tears.] He says, 'Here he is over here, you've got to go and burn him.' I said, 'Jesus!' It's not something you do every day of the week. The four of us, we went out, 'What are we going to do?' So we built a pit, filled it with bamboo, and set him alight. But as the time went on, it was a bloody disgrace [the failure of the cremation] ... while I was looking at it, another bloke had just died so they cart him up and, 'One, two, three,' They threw him up on the pyre ... it was pretty horrific.[8]

At a number of camps along the Railway the cremation pyres would burn all night, during the day and all night again, and the distorted, wasted corpses would be burned in their dozens. The lingering image of *risus sardonicus*—the pre-death sardonic grin caused by spasms of the facial muscles—and those roaring infernos would haunt observers long after captivity. And today, over 70 years on, at some of the sites where those fires burnt, the ground is still discoloured.

———— ❦ ————

When the Japanese invaded British Burma in December 1941, they sought to gain access to its key raw materials of oil and wolfram (tungsten), and also to cut the road from Lashio in Burma to Kunming in Yunnan province in China, which was the only Allied supply link to Chiang Kai-shek's Chinese Army. The offensive began on 16 December 1941 from southern Thailand and had the initial objectives of the airfields at Victoria Point and Mergui. Japanese forces subsequently moved through Three Pagodas Pass and Mea Sot and pushed on to Rangoon (Yangon), which fell on 9 March 1942. The next month Lashio was captured and the Allies had thus lost the prized Burma Road. By the end of May 1942 the British had been forced back over the Indian border.

The naval battles of the Coral Sea (5–8 May 1942), and Midway (4–6 June 1942) redressed the balance of naval power in the Pacific War. The Japanese had relied chiefly on their merchant shipping to supply their Burma army via a long and tenuous line of supply down the Malay Peninsula and around the Straits of Malacca to Rangoon. Further, that shipping needed at least some naval cover. A railway from Nong Pladuk in Thailand to Thanbyuzayat in Burma would greatly alleviate the Japanese commitment to both forms of shipping.

—————

The day after the Japanese surrender, a Dutch officer, Lieutenant-Colonel Warmenhoven, assumed command of the Railway and began interviewing a number of Japanese senior officers. Warmenhoven: 'They admitted the decision that the line should be built must have been taken immediately after and maybe even before the invasion of Siam but they rather suggested all action was taken on the spur of the moment.'[9] At around the time of the fall of Singapore in February 1942, a rail route from Nong Pladuk to Thanbyuz-ayat was ordered, which was followed by Southern Region Army's Railway Control directive the next month that preparations be made for its construc-tion. The Japanese deployed two of their railway regiments—each of around 2500 officers and other ranks—to the project. The 5th Railway Regiment was given the task of constructing about 135 kilometres of rail from Thanbyuzayat to Nieke, while the 9th Railway Regiment was made respons-ible for the rail running north from Nong Pladuk Station (approximately 286 kilometres).

The building of the Thai–Burma Railway was a seemingly impossible task. It entailed carving a pathway through utterly inhospitable terrain involving the shifting of 3 000 000 cubic metres of soil and rock; the building of 4 000 000 cubic metres of embankments; and the construction of a monumental fourteen kilometres of bridges. This was to be achieved despite the lack of an immediate labour supply and the means to get the necessary heavy machinery required to build it into such inaccessible locations.[10]

The Japanese surmounted these obstacles by the employment of slave labour. Scattered across their newly acquired empire were what they consid-ered to be the lowest form of life: prisoners of war. Here was a disposable labour force: housing it, feeding it and keeping it healthy mattered not; and as one former English POW described his work capacity as 'one-fourteenth of an elephant', simple arithmetic would furnish the necessary number of POWs required to accomplish any given labouring task. The toil was back-breaking and the progress glacially slow, but there was an irresistible force

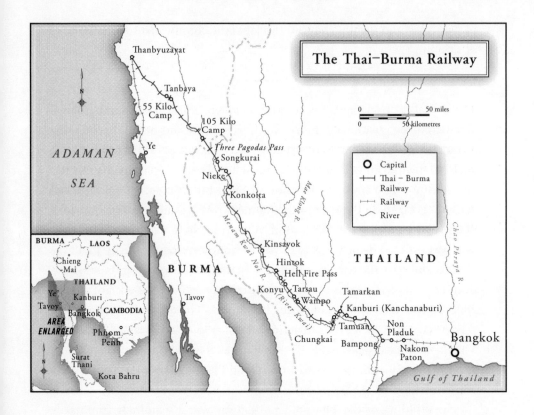

at work. The Railway would be built. The engineers on the Railway were to simply requisition their labour force in the numbers required according to the magnitude of the task at hand. Lionel Wigmore:

> The railway workers were organised by the Japanese into Groups or Branches; some branches had as few as 2,000 workers, others as many as 12,000. Two prisoner of war groups—Nos. 3 and 5—functioned on the Thanbyuzayat [Burmese] side of the railway; four—1, 2, 4 and 6, plus about 10,000 workers who came under Malayan Prisoner of War administration (as distinct from the Thai one)—worked forward from Bampong in Thailand.[11]

By examining 'A' Force in Burma and a Battalion in each of 'D' and 'F' Forces in Thailand—with pertinent digressions—we are able to tell the story of each main section of the Railway and provide three styles and standards of leadership, and the impact they had upon the prisoners' chances of survival.

———◦———

In 2007 Frank Taylor of *Kokoda Treks and Tours* and the author met Rod Beattie in Kanchanaburi in Thailand. This marked the beginning of an inspiring Thai–Burma Railway education, and a multitude of spirited discussions and research sharing. At the time of writing, Rod Beattie was the Commonwealth War Graves Commission Manager for Thailand; he was the Managing Director of the Thailand–Burma Railway Centre, Kanchanaburi; he is a civil engineer; he has served in the Australian Army; has spent over sixteen years of his life tracing, mapping and exploring the Railway in great depth; and he and his wife have also cleared the famed Hellfire Pass. Both Taylor and Beattie are extremely knowledgeable about the history and the technical aspects of the Railway.

The first lesson learnt from Beattie concerns the standard of the Japanese engineering:

> The Japanese engineering on the Railway is very, very good. I was trained as an engineer while I was working for the Queensland Main Roads Department. So my job was to design and build roads, and highways and bridges . . . and when I go out there and walk all over this Railway—beautifully built. Because you've got bigger embankments there, thirty or forty or fifty or sixty feet, and sixty-five years later, they're still perfect . . . the batters [the slopes of the embankment] are perfect; there's no soil erosion . . . [Their bridges are] technically fine! Nothing wrong with the wooden bridge! A lot of people just rubbish wooden bridges, because they're made of wood . . . so were most of ours until not that many years ago . . .[12]

And Rod knows exactly where the Japanese gained their bridge designs:

> No doubt about it whatsoever! The Japanese used the Merriman-Wiggin Engineer's handbook. That's just a standard engineers' handbook of the time, everyone was using it. If you have a look at

Railway trestle bridges in Australia . . . western Queensland, western Victoria . . . exactly the same design. That's engineers! We were taught not to memorise everything just remember where the book is.[13]

As our trip unfolded, Beattie would not hesitate to stop on a seemingly nondescript stretch of highway, order you to gather your gear and walk you through the jungle wall until another hidden world eventually opened up: embankments, cuttings and bridge sites. He would calmly machete a thin, metre-long piece of bamboo, splinter it against rock and threateningly point out what such a weapon could do to a prisoner's back—or head; and he had us scramble down an embankment, pick up a large rock and carry it up. As the research journey progressed, Beattie and Taylor would provide a number of experiences which gave us some concept of the Railway itself, and the practicalities of POW camp life.

———❧———

Late in April 1942, the Japanese informed AIF HQ Changi that 6000 of its troops would be required to 'proceed by sea to an unknown destination'.[14] When the Japanese were told that supplying this number of men would necessitate the recall of a large proportion of men on work parties on Singapore Island, that number was halved.[15] On 7 May, the Japanese issued a warning order which prompted the Australians to structure a brigade size force of 3000 POWs to be known as 'A' Force.[16]

AIF HQ was deceived from the outset. When informed by the Australians that even a force of 3000 men would be partly composed of POWs unfit for manual labour, the Japanese informed them that it would not be required as a working party; that it would be sent to one venue only; and that medical supplies, tools and cooking equipment would be supplied upon arrival at their new destination.

As the Japanese decision to remove all senior officers of the rank of colonel and above was not enacted until August 1942, Brigadier Varley was chosen as the commander of 'A' Force. The reader will recall his service as CO 2/18th Battalion and his subsequent command of 22nd Brigade on Singapore Island. Varley's second-in-command was Lieutenant-Colonel Charles Anderson, VC of 2/19th Battalion and Muar River fame, and the force was structured as three battalions: Number 1 comprised 1000 men under Lieutenant-Colonel Ramsay, 2/30th Battalion; Number 2 comprised 983 men under Major Kerr, 2/10th Field Regiment; and Number 3 comprised 1017 men under Major Green, 2/4th Machine Gun Battalion. Although about two-thirds of 'A' Force was composed of infantry personnel from the 22nd and 27th Brigades, and the artillery and engineers, there was a sprinkling of men from a diverse range of other units. Varley would record that notable amongst these were 'a number of men who had enlisted in Australia as members of Res MT units [Reserve Motor Transport Units], ages 35–45 yrs. Many are well over 50 . . .'[17] An examination of Ramsay Battalion deaths on the Railway reveal that there was a high rate amongst older men—soldiers who would surely have been subsequently weeded out of units had the capitulation not occurred.

We have established that the AIF must have entered Changi with significant funds. Grants of money for 'up-country' or 'overseas' work forces leaving Changi—as distinct from Singapore Island work parties—and how such funds were administered is critical to our understanding of command on the Railway. Changi's AIF Quartermaster, Major Alan Thompson, made no mention of money being issued to 'A' Force, but recorded funds issued to subsequent forces. Further, we shall see that such money was often spent with command consultation with the force and/or battalion doctors, who were best placed to recommend the types and quantities of food and drugs required. Whether such requests were able to be honoured was another matter, but such a liaison was critical to both the chances of survival for hospital patients, and the ability to influence the general health of those working on the Railway. Captain Rowley Richards, RMO Number 2 Battalion, and subsequently renamed Anderson Force: 'Varley and his group were with us [in Burma] . . . and we were in pretty close association, we knew what was going on, and I feel quite confident that if he'd had a significant amount of money . . . I'm sure we would have known about it . . .'[18] And surely Thompson—meticulous in his records of the administration of Changi— would have recorded such funds.

At 11.00 am on 13 May 1942, 'A' Force was inspected and staged a march past in front of the GOC Major-General Callaghan, and Brigadier Varley recorded that 'Brigs Maxwell, Taylor, Majors Maxwell, Mavor, Lt-Cols Denham, White and others came to say cheerio'.[19] 'A' Force was moved

by truck to Keppel Harbour in three 'lifts' commencing early on 14 May.
That day was marked by either a prolonged delay awaiting truck transport
or a monotonous stay at the docks. With limited water available, and no
smoking signs around the docks, the hot, stifling and prolonged wait became
too much for a number of men. When taps were approached and discreet
smoking began the guards immediately reacted. As had occurred in the past,
and would continue to happen, there was no consistency or predictability
to those responses. Some received a face-slapping, but the unlucky ones
were beaten with fists, rifle butts, logs of wood and one was strung up by
the thumbs.[20] Life under Nippon was about to take a dramatic turn for the
worse. From here on in, thousands of Australians were destined to long for
the closed, seemingly protected world of Changi. And when their mode of
transport became apparent to them, the men of 'A' Force were mortified. Two
ships lay at the wharves, the *Celebes Maru* and the *Tohohasi Maru*, each of
about 5000 tons.

The evening of 14 May 1942 was spent loading rice, aviation spirit
and other supplies aboard both ships, and late that night the men began
boarding. Two thousand and two men consisting of Force HQ, Number 2
and 3 Battalions and the engineers were placed on the *Tohohasi Maru*, whilst
Ramsay's Number 1 Battalion and the CCS staff under Lieutenant-Colonel
Hamilton boarded the *Celebes Maru*. Private Wal Williams was a member
of Ramsay Battalion: '. . . there was a bloke from Western Australia . . . he
knew the bloody ship. He said, "Christ, we used to load sheep on this bloody
thing!"'[21] Brigadier Varley immediately reacted: '. . . made several representations through interpreter, Captain Drower, for better conditions, and asked
for permission to ring Japanese HQ Singapore, but could not get permission
to do so.'[22] Any examination of Varley's diary and Ramsay's 'A' Force report
shows repeated letters of protest and representations to Japanese commanders all along the tragic path of the Force's movement to and through Burma
and into Thailand. Numerous protests—particularly in writing and kept as
evidence for later War Crimes trials—would have their use, but as a means of
changing Japanese policies and general behaviour, they were to mostly prove
worthless, and bordering on the naïve.

The Australians may as well have been sheep. The 1000 men of Ramsay
Battalion were packed into three holds on the *Celebes Maru*, each with only

enough space to lie down but not sit up between the tiers of 'bunks'; the temperature in the holds of the two ships was over 100 degrees Fahrenheit; added to this was the stench of the perspiring many in the space for a few; and critically, there were a number of men who had dysentery and others who had 'residual diarrhoea at [the] time of embarkation, and others [who] had a return of symptoms on the ship'.[23] The coming sea voyage would produce an almost indescribable stench made up of bowel movements, urine, perspiration, a lack of fresh air, and the refusal of the Japanese to allow men on deck other than in periodic groups to eventually be hosed down with salt water. The latrine facitilties for this mass of humanity were 'one three-hole at the aft and another at midships, 6 per 1000 men'.[24] The established army latrine requirements for the time were 32 per 1000 men. The inevitable fouling of latrines which were emptied but once a day, meant that boots were dirtied and then became the means for filth to be transferred back to the crammed holds where eating and sleeping occurred. And to compound this multitude of sins, the Japanese provided insufficient drinking water, no washing facilities, and only one washing-up tub for all.[25]

The two ships left Singapore at 9.30 am on 15 May 1942. Their first stop was at Medan on the east coast of Sumatra where the convoy was joined by three ships carrying British and Dutch POWs and Japanese troops. On 20 May the convoy reached Victoria Point in the extreme south of Burma, where the Japanese immediately broke their pledge that 'A' Force would not be split up. Upon arrival, Varley was ordered to have 1000 men ready to disembark. He chose Major Green's Number 3 Battalion comprising 32 officers and 803 other ranks; three officers and 128 ORs of the engineers; four HQ officers and 29 ORs; sixteen sick cases; and he entrusted the medical care of Green's men to Captain Higgin (CCS). The party therefore totalled 1016 officers and ORs.[26]

On the 22nd the convoy sailed north to Mergui. That day Varley was informed that 1000 men of Ramsay's Number 1 Battalion were to be offloaded and an additional 500 British troops picked up in Sumatra were to be added to Ramsay's command. Varley was now faced with an administrative problem, which was the balance of his now split force: 'I asked for an exchange of personnel—sending 62 engrs (including 4 pay, records and postal)—to go with Ramsay in exchange 72 CCS personnel, including

Lt-Col Hamilton join us. This will equalise engrs and also medical services, also dental.'[27]

We now come to an astounding revelation. The next day, 23 May 1942, Varley was given approval for this adjustment of his force and although his request to see Ramsay was denied, he then made an extraordinary diary entry for the 24th: '1000 hrs. 62 engrs under Lts A. Watson and L. Atyeo left for shore, and joining of No. 1 Bn. No. 1 Bn also being transhipped to shore by MLCs from their ship. Watson was given and signed for $660, being their proportion of funds given Force 'A'.'[28] We know that the Japanese had agreed to pay its Changi inmates for their labour on 6 June 1942, well after 'A' Force had departed from Singapore; we will shortly record that 'A' Force payments did not occur until after its arrival in Burma; and that the information above clearly tells us that Varley gave Lieutenant Watson '$660, being their proportion of funds given "A" Force'. It would seem that because Varley was denied permission to see Ramsay, Watson was entrusted—and therefore Varley ordered him to sign for the money—with the job of giving Ramsay the $660, which would further indicate that this was one-third of the funds allotted at Changi for 'A' Force because Ramsay Battalion was one-third of the total force and $660 was one-third of the total fund. 'A' Force therefore most likely left Changi with around $2000, entrusted to Varley's administration, since the AIF were told that the force would not be split. We should then ask why Thompson did not mention these funds in his otherwise painstaking Changi records. Although only conjecture, it might well have been that at that early stage in Changi's existence, AIF HQ was reluctant to record such matters on paper for security reasons.

On 25 May 1942, Brigadier Varley and the remainder of 'A' Force arrived at Tavoy. Over the next few months the three battalions were engaged in working on the airfields at Victoria Point (Green's Number 3 Battalion), Mergui (Ramsay's Number 1 Battalion) and Tavoy (Varley's HQ and Kerr's Number 2 Battalion). Despite the hardship of the voyage, the men's initial health was tolerable, and the work not too hard.

Ramsay Battalion (now 1500 strong) was initially housed in the local school which was built to accommodate around 600 to 800, but it later managed to move into a bamboo and attap barracks, which was far more

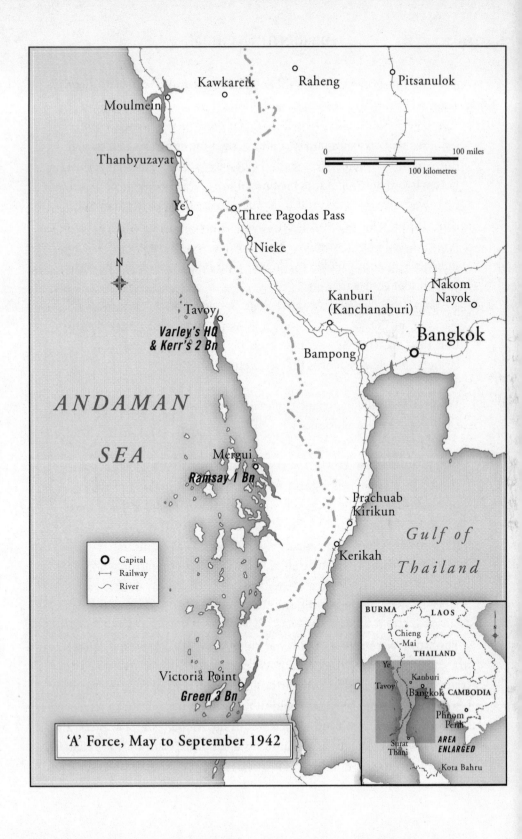

Kawkareik

Raheng

Pitsanulok

Moulmein

Thanbyuzayat

Ye

Three Pagodas Pass

Nieke

100 miles

100 kilometres

Nakom
Nayok

Kanburi
(Kanchanaburi)

Bangkok

Tavoy
*Varley's HQ
& Kerr's 2 Bn*

Bampong

ANDAMAN

SEA

Mergui
Ramsay 1 Bn

Prachuab
Kirikun

Kerikah

*Gulf of
Thailand*

O   Capital
⊢⊣   Railway
∿   River

Victoria Point
Green 3 Bn

'A' Force, May to September 1942

BURMA   LAOS

Chieng
-Mai

THAILAND

Ye
Kanburi
Tavoy   CAMBODIA
Bangkok

Phnom
Penh

*AREA
ENLARGED*

Surat
Thani

Kota Bahru

comfortable. A hospital was also established. Private Wal Williams was working on the airfield at Mergui with Ramsay Battalion:

> Oh Jesus that was a bastard of a job . . . napping stone, you used to sit down with a napping hammer and a bloody lump of granite and just boom, boom and belt it into blue metal size . . . and a couple of blokes had two bamboo poles and a couple of rice bags, or hessian bags, slung through the poles and you'd put it onto that . . . and they'd carry it out . . . and blokes would level it . . . when you've got hundreds and hundreds of bloody blokes carting the stuff it's surprising the amount of stuff that comes up.
>
> They [the Japanese] wanted their pound of flesh, there was no slacking on the job . . . the average bloke was in a lot better condition then to what he was later, and he more or less took it in his stride . . . there were blokes that were crook . . .[29]

While at Mergui, Lieutenant-Colonel Ramsay was able to obtain what he referred to as 'outside assistance':

> . . . my Adjutant and myself were permitted to visit the village accompanied by a Japanese sergeant for the purpose of making purchases of amenities for the sick, advances of approx. 4000 rupees were made available to me by one or two of the local residents without the knowledge of the Japanese. This fund was administered by Mr. K.M. Bostock, the Australian Red Cross representative, who was a P.O.W. with my force, and enabled me with his invaluable assistance to alleviate the conditions at the hospital.[30]

The word 'advances' would seem significant. We know that Brigadier Varley sent $660 with Lieutenant Watson for Ramsay's use when they arrived at Mergui. Further, when the Japanese began paying the men for their work, 50 of the 70 rupees paid to the officers per month[31] was placed in Bostock's Red Cross fund, which would have repaid the 'advances' and kept some sort of cash flow. On an individual basis, Ramsay also refers to the local Burmese—under great risk of doing so—handing his men fruit and eggs as they departed or returned to camp on work parties. He also referred to 'medical supplies' in addition to 'amenities'.[32] These commodities were sparse to say the least, but Ramsay's purchases would have been invaluable to the hospital and, in a more limited way, the men's diet. In addition, some POWs engaged in the same activities as had occurred in Changi—individual selling or trading of items for the benefit of themselves and a few mates. Any ability to supplement the poor nutritional value of the Japanese diet with fruit or vegetables was crucial to long-term survival.

While Green and Ramsay Battalions were thus engaged at Victoria Point and Mergui respectively, Brigadier Varley's HQ and Major Kerr's Number 2 Battalion had been landed at Tavoy. Originally quartered in an aircraft hangar which according to Varley, 'was covered with broken rock, apparently prepared for concreting',[33] the men initially suffered from a lack of water, no cooking utensils, and the threat of being shot should they leave the 100 metre by 100 metre hangar.[34]

On 2 June 1942, Varley recorded that eight men had attempted an escape. It is highly likely that this escape attempt was driven by the belief that the Burmese were friendly, and would not in any way hamper the effort. The eight were wrong. Although many Burmese continued to give the prisoners food, there were others who were attracted by the bounty being offered by the Japanese for information leading to the capture of fugitives. At 3.00 pm on 6 June Varley was informed that the escapees were to be shot at 5.00 pm and that he was required to witness the executions. Each time he requested permission to see the men and obtain messages for their families, he was told 'after death talk'.[35] When he further requested that the men be given their religious rites by the Church of England and Roman Catholic padres present, he was told 'after death'. Varley recorded that eight graves had been dug, that the men were blindfolded, and that sixteen guards were used—two to each prisoner—and 'death was instantaneous'. He later wrote:

Just before death the spirit of these 8 Australians was wonderful. They all spoke cheerio and good luck messages to one another and never showed any sign of fear. A truly courageous end. The 2 padres carried out the final service. Execution took place about 1840 hrs.[36]

Like Ramsay at Mergui, Brigadier Varley was eventually able to make contacts with the Burmese markets and begin to buy limited stocks of food for the hospital and vary the men's diet. On 22 June he recorded that he had 'asked several times about changing our money which we brought with us. No reply.'[37] This was the money brought with him from Changi. Five days later he recorded another request to the Japanese for an exchange of currency. But on 28 June he recorded that 1119 rupees and thirteen annas were received as the first Japanese payment for work.[38] The problem faced by Varley was that the large note denominations of pay precluded the men from receiving their share in rupees. He was conscious of what he termed as 'indiscriminant trading' which would cause prices to soar. But despite these initial problems, Varley noticed an improvement in the men's health and decreasing numbers of men on sick parade, presumably because of his purchases, the pay and therefore slightly better food.

In his efforts to enhance the quality and quantity of food for his men— particularly when his force was moved into the more remote country where the Railway was to be built—Brigadier Varley was faced with two distinct disadvantages which were not applicable to later forces in Thailand. The first was ready access to supplies. 'A' Force was not able to avail itself of the barge passage of supplies along the far-distant River Kwai and, therefore, his efforts to purchase and then transport supplies along the Railway through Burma were subject to pilfering before arrival. And that process began in earnest at Tavoy. The second disadvantage was the paucity of villages and commerce along his jungle oxcart track when compared to Thailand.

On 4 July 1942, the Japanese took Lieutenant-Colonel Hamilton (the Chief Medical Officer) and his quartermaster Captain Lee into the Tavoy market to survey the available commodities. Although very limited time was allowed to the resulting purchasing party, some goods were transported back to the camp. Seven days later, another purchasing party was told to report to the camp entrance at 9.30 am, but the Japanese guard did not arrive until two hours later. When the party arrived at the Tavoy market the best of the available goods had already been sold, and the prices of rice and, later, eggs began to rise. When the eggs were delivered the following day only half arrived. On 15 July Varley recorded that: 'Extra eggs etc. ordered from a native from the Tavoy market did not arrive today as expected. He is an

Indian trader at the market and apparently as unreliable as other branches of the species we have met elsewhere.'[39] Varley's purchasing problems would only increase later on the Railway.

Brigadier Varley had found the Japanese most difficult in terms of facilitating any sort of effort to enhance his men's food supplies and the quality of their accommodation. But then on 11 July 1942, he made an interesting observation concerning a number of his 'A' Force junior officers and NCOs:

> Necessary to speak to Maj Kerr about slackness of some officers. They have no life—no command, and show signs of slack training. This has been particularly noticeable among A.I.F this war. All junior officers, or rather a big majority, also NCOs seem to desire to curry favour with the men and are frightened to take full command. Result is that the men soon sum them up as weaklings and discipline generally is undermined. Offrs must not but do address men and NCOs by their Christian names, also use language in presence of them, thus creating undue familiarity and the second lapse lowers an officer's status . . .
>
> No army has ever achieved success without strict discipline. The A.I.F. of 1914–1918 had it, despite the exaggerated claims of some to the contrary. If Australia wants to retain an army efficient and capable very stern measures will need to be taken in the future to cut out the cancer which has entered the body of the army.[40]

In his Official History, Lionel Wigmore cites the above quote—other than the first sentence 'Necessary to speak to Maj Kerr about slackness of some officers.' The observation would at best seem far too general, and at worst quite simply unfair. Some of the soldiers Varley referred to would have surely been reinforcements; likewise, a number of the officers would have been reinforcement officers; and the environment into which all were placed was hardly a typical military one.

Captain Rowley Richards was present at that time with Major Kerr and his battalion at Tavoy, and recalled that Kerr was 'a fine soldier'.[41] That some junior officers had 'no life—no command, and show signs of slack training' was more than likely accurate for a few, but to brand the 2nd AIF in the above manner would seem an unfair exaggeration. Anderson's column at Muar, and the Australian performance at Gemas and along the Malay Peninsula would seem to contradict Varley's assertion. Given that a multitude of reinforcement officers and other ranks had only fought on Singapore Island and had therefore only been on their unit's establishment for a matter of weeks or days before the capitulation, the thrust of Varley's diary entry becomes easier to appreciate.

During August and September 1942, with the work on the airfields at Victoria Point and Mergui completed, Green and Ramsay Battalions were gradually shipped to Tavoy to join Varley and Kerr's men. On 24 August, Varley noted in his diary that Lieutenant-Colonel Ramsay gave him 200 rupees which was the 'unused portion of advance made to his force. Gave some to Paymaster, Capt Hetherington.' He also observed that Ramsay Battalion men seemed to be in poor condition when compared to his Tavoy men: 'was concerned with state and number of sick in hospital from Mergui—82 compared with 22 from this camp'.[42] By the middle of September, the work was completed at Tavoy and 'A' Force began its movement first to Moulmein and then by road and rail to Thanbyuzayat. Ramsay Battalion was the last to leave Tavoy. It was here, on that famous Tuesday in November, that the Japanese yet again showed their almost total unpredictability. Private Wal Williams:

There was some bloody Nip, and he must have been in Australia or something, because he knew that the second Tuesday [*sic*] was Melbourne Cup Day, and he declared a bloody holiday. And we couldn't get over it! . . . he said, 'All men yasumi' [stand at ease, rest, holiday].

. . . from memory it [the 'Cup'] was a polished coconut with a couple of bloody handles on it . . . it got organised then. Ramsay got into the swing of things, and he said, 'All right, we'll do it the right way, we'll have the Governor General come.' The blokes pulled a bullock cart in and it was decorated . . . Ramsay's sitting in there with Hence [the 2IC] he was his Aide-de-Camp, and he pulls up, and the Japs got into the swing of it, they thought it was fuckin' terrific! . . . they had bookmakers . . .[43]

A number of the fittest men became the 'horses'; jockeys were found (weight was not an issue); modest bets were laid; and most of the horses were named after previous Melbourne Cup winners. Wal Williams:

And Bobby Farrands from the 2/19th . . . won it and he got the trophy. At that time the bloody broadcaster of races here in Sydney was a bloke called Lachie Melville . . . and they built a thing like a big old radio cabinet and [a substitute Lachie Melville] got in behind that . . . it was a real morale lifter that![44]

After the presentation ceremony the 'stewards' staged an inquiry into the performance of one of the jockeys, his trainer and their 'connections'.[45]

After around six months variously spent at Victoria Point, Mergui, Ye and Tavoy, the fortunes of 'A' Force were about to take a decided turn for the worse.

Brigadier Varley reached Thanbyuzayat on 2 October 1942. This centre was the northern startline for the Railway and was therefore stacked with huge dumps of materials, a Japanese HQ and main camp, anti-aircraft defences and what would soon become the main POW hospital and HQ. Unlike the Thai section of the Railway, camps along its Burmese stretch would be chiefly identified by the number of kilometres each was distant from Thanbyuzayat (0 km). Varley and Major Kerr's Number 2 Battalion were deployed in a camp about 600 metres from the Thanbyuzayat Railway Station. They soon discovered that Green's Number 3 Battalion were in a camp about eight kilometres away and 'working on a new Railway line to Thailand'.

The next day—3 October 1942—Varley was ordered to Japanese HQ to meet the Commander of the Number 3 Branch of the Thailand Prisoner of War Administration, Colonel Nagatomo. It was at this meeting that Varley learnt that he was to have a HQ consisting of a 'General Affairs Department' of ten men; a 'Foodstuffs Department' of seventeen; a 'Property Department' also of seventeen; and a 'Medical Department' of twelve. In essential terms, his three-battalion structure was to remain intact.[46]

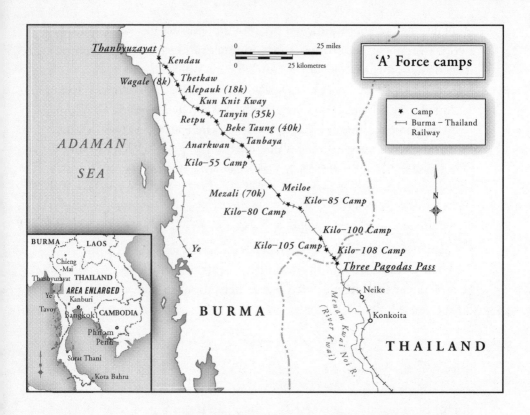

The construction of the Railway from Thanbyuzayat to about Three Pagodas Pass was mainly centred on the clearing of large trees and jungle, and the making of embankments and cuttings. In this exercise, the Japanese engineers and their POW labourers were handicapped chiefly by the absence of a parallel river—as in Thailand—and a serviceable road. The transportation of manpower and supplies would therefore prove to be time-consuming and tedious.

By the end of October, Varley's 'A' Force was expanded to include further British, Dutch, American and Australian arrivals. The Australian contingent consisted of Williams Force (Lieutenant-Colonel J. M. Williams, 2/2nd Pioneer Battalion) and Black Force (Lieutenant-Colonel C. M. Black, 2/3rd Motor Transport Company), who had travelled from Java to Singapore and then to Moulmein. As had occurred elsewhere under Japanese rule, October also saw the Japanese demand that the POWs sign a pledge not to escape. And as had also transpired elsewhere, Varley and Green were locked up under deplorable conditions until they realised that the signing of such a document made under duress was meaningless, and subsequently ordered all to sign.

During November 'A' Force was deployed in a series of camps stretching south from Thanbyuzayat: Green's Number 3 Battalion was at the 4.8 Kilo Camp (Kendau); a Dutch party was at the 8 Kilo Camp (Wagale); Lieutenant-Colonel Anderson's Battalion—Anderson had assumed command of Kerr's Number 2 Battalion—was at the 18 Kilo Camp (Alepauk); Williams Force was at the 35 Kilo (Tanyin); and Black Force was at the 40 Kilo Camp (Beke Taung). Ramsay's Number 1 Battalion arrived for work on the Railway in December and was sent to the 26 Kilo Camp (Kun Knit Kway).

November 1942 also saw the arrival of around 200 Korean guards assigned to 'A' Force. If the Japanese guards had shown a propensity for unpredictable violence and cruelty, then the Koreans were to take such behaviour to new levels. Private Wal Williams, Ramsay Battalion:

> . . . the Japanese, they disliked the bloody Koreans, no two ways about that, because they'd been under the Japanese occupation for bloody years in Korea, and they were down trodden bastards . . . and the Japs still applied it to them on the line, and the only retaliation the Koreans could get was to take it out on us, because we were the lowest of the low . . . they were brutal bastards . . .[47]

It mattered little which battalion a POW served with, or indeed, where he served with 'A' Force. All were subjected to frequent and brutal treatment that only differed according to the Korean's name and location. To Wal Williams and his mates in Ramsay Battalion, the 'Boy Bastard' and 'the BBC' (the 'Boy Bastard's Cobber') would never be forgotten. You might forget to bow; you might not be working fast enough; perhaps an instruction in Japanese was misinterpreted; but, very often, your only crime was being a Caucasian, or quite simply being in the wrong place at the wrong time and thereby being exposed to a creature who considered you the lowest of the low. Wal Williams:

> I got done in by the Boy Bastard . . . you tried to keep out of the way! As soon as you saw that bastard coming . . . you'd get out of the road

if you could. It didn't always work out that way ... they'd go round
looking for bloody trouble; they'd pick on some poor bastard for
anything really. And they'd work themselves up into this bloody
frenzy, they all seemed to do that ... a hell of a temper ... they'd do a
bloke over, they start slapping him across the dial ... and then work
themselves up and put the boot in ... they'd go for your bloody crutch
and if you avoided it well that'd make them more determined than
ever. They'd belt you till you couldn't take any more—you'd have to
drop. There was them [the Boy Bastard and the BBC], and another
bloke called Dilinger [*sic*], they were about the worst I think.[48]

Private Roy Whitecross remembered his Korean guards: there was the
short and thin 'Mickey Mouse', the short but fat 'Jeep', 'the Maggot', 'fat,
broad head, no neck', and the never-to-be-forgotten 'Storm Trooper' who
possessed a 'permanent scowl' and seemed to hit someone every half an
hour.[49] And if personal brutality was an insufficient form of entertainment,
then there was the anonymous, sudden demonstration of sadism directed to
either a POW or an innocent animal. Sergeant Jim Forbes was on Ramsay
Battalion's HQ Staff:

... you'd be talking in a hut and they'd stick a bayonet through the
attap. It didn't happen every day of every week ... I've had that
happen ... it was close enough to shut you up straight away ... the
bashing was a regular happening ... they loved this idea of bowing
to them too, as much as the Japs ... and it was easy to forget to do
so ... you got a back-hander for that ... the sadism ... the treatment
of a dog, the joy and pleasure they got from kicking a dog around. And
then you had the guardhouse situation ... yeah, that one happened to
me ... you never knew what would happen ... stand you there for a
day, a half a day. What you didn't know was what was going to happen
to you at a particular time ... when they felt like doing it ... so there
was a pressure there the whole time to sort of comply.[50]

As time went by the Australians developed a heightened instinct, an
awareness, for impending trouble. Sergeant Jim Forbes:

... you developed a sixth sense and this is not exaggeration. You developed a sense if something was about to happen ... that trouble was brewing, that something was going on, just the attitude of the guards, what was happening ... that you were going to move, that there was going to be a search ... just some action of a Japanese or the guards [Korean] ...[51]

We will never know how many POWs were exposed to a more sinister danger. Captain Rowley Richards, RMO Anderson Battalion, recalled a Korean guard christened 'Peanut' Tomoto. It seems that his nickname was derived from his poor intellect. But 'Peanut' had other qualities. Captain Richards:

In broken English he frequently talked about sex in front of us, boasting that when Japan invaded Australia they would also conquer 'Australian girls. Jiggy-jig.' His voice was effeminate and from the way he stared at some of our men, many of us soon wondered if his only, or even main, interest was in women.[52]

On Boxing Day 1942, Sergeant Ron O'Donnell and 'Peanut' were seen walking into the jungle. Shots were later heard and when Lieutenant-Colonel Anderson sent a few men out to investigate, O'Donnell's body was found; he had been shot three times, in the chest first and then twice in the head. Richards recalled that some of the men had 'speculated that Peanut may have been seeking retribution for O'Donnell rejecting sexual advances, but none of us will ever know the truth'.[53] 'Peanut' Tomoto was immediately renamed 'Dillinger'. The men were incensed. Protests brought no action. O'Donnell, the Japanese claimed, had been shot trying to escape. 'Peanut' was simply transferred to Thanbyuzayat for some time. But the salient point is that the descriptions given above of the Korean and Japanese guards' behaviour on the Railway merely served notice that life was a lottery, that in their masters' eyes a POW's life amounted to nought, and that a savage beating, prolonged pain in front of a guard house holding a rock above one's head, or other unwelcome occurrences instilled a sense of helplessness and therefore vulnerability. There was no sense of right or wrong, or the ability to protect oneself, but merely a growing resignation that one's life lay in the hands of others who possessed a completely different moral code.

———————

By the end of November 1942, Brigadier Varley was forced to take drastic action in an attempt to purchase more supplies for his rapidly increasing number of sick and dying hospital patients. On Armistice Day he ordered that all personal property of the deceased was to be collected, such as razors, pencils, watches and rings and given to Major Campbell for sale. The proceeds were then to be given to the Red Cross for such purchases. Later that very day Colonel Nagatomo ordered Varley to 'bundle' such items and that he would send them to Tokyo 'for dispatch to Australia' after the war!

Nagatomo's corrupt behaviour was not limited to trying to obtain POW possessions. On 18 November Varley recorded that: 'Evidence of over-charging of goods supplied to our canteen were accidentally discovered today by Maj Campbell, which confirmed our mind on this. By order of Lt Colonel Nagatomo camps are restricted from purchasing goods for canteens otherwise than from him.'[54] When Campbell had received the bulk purchase of supplies the previous day, he had, unbeknown to Nagatomo, examined the Burmese trader's invoice and had discovered that the Japanese paid one price for their goods and the POWs another. Varley listed the price differences in his diary and they reveal that Nagatomo was 'raking off' around 23%. Varley: 'Thus on first invoice (3 Nov) we have been overcharged $340, while on second invoice (18 Nov) the overcharge is $600 . . .'[55] In a letter of protest, Varley diplomatically accused the Burmese trader of the rort, but stated in his diary that after a meeting with Nagatomo two days later, 'very little was gained'.[56]

Apart from Nagatomo's rampant 'fundraising', Varley's plight worsened during the next few months. His force was rapidly becoming scattered along a long line of communication where getting news of his men and commu-nicating with subordinate commanders was becoming increasingly difficult. This, in turn, made the ordering, collection and distribution of critical food supplies and scant medical items for his camps almost impossible. His diary entry for Armistice Day adequately displays his frustrations. The Japanese, he claimed, always required absolute proof that any given medical condition or dietary deficiency existed, and that 'the proof lies in the burial of a number of men who could have been saved if our warnings were heeded . . .'.[57]

In December 1942, Brigadier Varley attempted to further supplement hospital rations and each battalion RAP by levying officers' pay in excess of twenty rupees per month. This money was given to Mr Murchison, the Red Cross representative, who also endeavoured to provide for those men who had chronic disabilities. The next month Group 5 arrived in Burma, which was made up chiefly of Australians, Dutch and Americans from Java. Varley requested a swap of Dutch and Australians so that nationalities, where possible, might work and live together. He made little headway.

In early January 1943, Ramsay Force was at the 26 Kilo Camp (Kun Knit Kway), Anderson Force joined Williams Force at the 35 Kilo (Tanyin), and Green Force was at the 14 Kilo Camp. Thus far, the death toll in Varley's Group 3 command had been surprisingly low: 73 in total of which 24 were Australians of 'A' Force. But events took a turn for the worse from early March when the work rate demanded by the Japanese increased, and the prolonged poor diet, the lack of decent clothing and the paucity of medical supplies began to severely impact upon the men's health.

For Australians used to hard physical labour in their civilian life, the initial demand of about one cubic metre of earth per man per day was relatively easy. For those who had come from more sedentary occupations prewar, the task was more difficult. Early on there were some who managed, when not watched, to 'lessen' the quota by moving the bamboo pegs laid down to measure the day's work. Before long however, the Japanese and Koreans demanded much more and were ruthless in their expectations. Private Wal Williams, Ramsay Force:

> When we was at Kun Knit Kway it was easy digging, it was compara-
> tively flat country . . . we started off with a metre. They conned us!
> They said, 'When you've finished you can go home.' And we did.
> We finished by bloody lunch time. Then they started putting it
> [the quota] on and bloody on. Two metres a man. People think oh
> Christ, two metres a man, you could do that on ya ear! Twelve blokes,
> and it all depends on the digging . . . the Nip would have a bamboo,
> it might be a metre long . . . here's a quota for the day, he'd peg that

out ... 24 cubic metres. It got to the stage that we were working from daylight to dark. Everybody's losing weight because everybody's starting to get malnourished ... the task's getting harder, the Japs are getting more cranky because we're not shifting the dirt, and they're keeping us out on the bloody thing longer until the quota's done ... [58]

In March 1942, the Japanese ordered the Group 3 HQ forward to the 75 Kilo Camp (Meiloe), and that Anderson Force and Williams Force were to be combined to form the 'Number 1 Mobile Force', tasked with laying the rails. The new force was to begin its work at Kun Knit Kway. For the men of 'Number 1 Mobile Force' a new sense of urgency was demanded by their captors. Teak sleepers had to be unloaded from rail bogies and then placed in position on embankments. Then gangs of spikers drilled the holes and belted the spikes in with 'poor quality four-kilogram hammers'.[59] The Japanese demanded that between one and two kilometres of rail was to be laid daily.

In April the construction of the Railway was massively reinforced with coolie labour. If the Australians, British, Dutch and American POWs suffered cruelly on the Thai–Burma Railway, then the coolie labour which consisted chiefly of Burmese, Malays (including the Malayan Tamils and Chinese), the Javanese, and the Chinese from Singapore had the odds stacked even higher against them. Specialist skills always exist within an army formation, and standards of training, discipline and hygiene are demanded and enforced. The coolies lacked the cohesion of an army unit; they lacked the specialist skills found in such units; and they lacked basic standards of hygiene. And their plight was universal along the whole line. Sergeant Frank Baker:

They lived in squalor in the cities: say they lived in Singapore or Kuala Lumpur, they'd live in the worst part of town wherever it happened to be. And they'd use the drains in those days in Singapore as latrines as well—they'd just walk out of their, whatever hovel they lived in, and squat over the drain. Of course the drain was usually about six foot deep ... so the drains were stinking, and they were living beside them ... that was parts of Singapore, parts of Singapore weren't so bad. But parts of just about every city, or even every village, or Kampongs as they called them, had that sort of person in it ...

And then taking the people out of those places, and bringing them up into the jungle with their families and putting them to work ... was the most inhumane thing you could possibly imagine. And of course they had no way of resisting it, they went [died] because they had to go ...[60]

Rod Beattie, the Commonwealth War Graves Commission Manager for Thailand, has estimated that 75 000 Malay coolies worked on the Railway and that 42 000 of them perished (56 per cent); and that 90 000 Burmese worked and 40 000 died (44 per cent).[61] Private Wal Williams:

Never saw them much, only when the poor bastards were working on the line ... you'd go into a camp that they'd been in and oh, Jesus! It was shockin' ... crap everywhere, bodies under the bloody huts, and you'd have to clean all this up before you'd even occupied it and bury them all ... the huts are all falling to bloody pieces, the attap's rotted away ...[62]

By early 1943, the tide of the Pacific War had continued to turn against the Japanese: their final defeat in Papua New Guinea had occurred on 23 January; they had suffered a major reverse during the Battle of the Bismarck Sea (2–4 March); and they had been comprehensively defeated at Guadalcanal. The Imperial Japanese Army now ordered that the completion date for the Railway was to be August 1943—the timetable was thus advanced by four months. (In the event, the Railway was finally joined on 17 October 1943.) This period of time was to be aptly referred to as the *Speedo* period. In May 1943, the complete death rate on the Railway soared to around 600; in June and July to about 1400; and with the deadline basically reached in August, the death rate reached its peak at around 1600. And the tragic consequence of this period was that the high death rate continued through to January 1944, well after the completion of the Railway.[63]

Green, Ramsay and Black Forces started the *Speedo* phase at the 75 Kilo Camp (Meiloe) and then moved to the 105 Kilo Camp. By mid-June 1943, the main 'A' Force camps were stationed just forward of the 75 Kilo Camp, and at the 105 and 108, except for the Rail laying Number 1 Mobile Force. There were four distinct 'battles' in progress during this time. The first was working during the monsoon. Wal Williams:

> See the monsoonal period mate! Rain . . . I've never seen rain like it in my bloody life! . . . up there round about the 75 or the 105, [Kilo Camps] you could stand outside mate, and the rain hit ya, and it'd be like being under a needle shower, it'd hurt ya! And if you'd had a cake of soap, you could've stood out their and lathered up and had a bloody shower! It'd rain for 72 hours non-stop! . . .
>
> Well, you'd be standin' there . . . say in the middle of the day, or maybe the evening bloody meal, it'd be raining like buggery and the bucket of rice would be swimming in water . . . you were starving mate! When you're starving you eat anything! You're always wet, you never get dry, your bloody gear would rot, and you worked in it. You'd pick up a shovel full of mud and put it in a bloody basket and lump it up a bloody embankment and tip it out and come back . . . they didn't give a stuff . . . we woke up to that early in the piece down at bloody Mergui when we jacked up when it was raining, and they put on a bloody blue and belted bloody Christ out of us . . .[64]

The second battle was between the Japanese engineers and guards. As the pressure to finish the Railway increased, the demands placed upon the latter by the former to furnish full quotas of POWs to work became relentless. In turn, the Japanese guards beat, bullied and cajoled all and sundry in the 'hospital' huts until the numbers were produced. The men of the Number 1 Mobile Force laid the rail until the day's distance was done—24 hours' continuous work if required. If a spike was bent while being hammered, and the effort slowed because of it, the engineer 'bounded along muttering or screaming abuse, and laid about him with his heavy metre stick'.[65]

———————

When you interview survivors of the Thai–Burma Railway, regardless of which force or battalion in which they served, one man will invariably be recalled with genuine respect and indeed affection by all. And terms such as 'dedication', 'selflessness', and 'compassion' will be universally applied to them. Among the many, those few were considered great Australians. These men were the force and battalion doctors. One of them would later describe the Japanese treatment of POWs as 'deliberate neglect, deprivation, starvation, denial of drugs, denial of all equipment, and denial of facilities'.[66] In an effort to overcome these seemingly insurmountable obstacles, the doctors on the Railway employed sheer determination, improvisation and efficiency to their care of literally hundreds of patients. And all of this was enacted on a daily basis. Their devotion is an inspiring chapter in the Australian story.

When 'A' Force was created its medical component was drawn mainly from officers of the 2/4th CCS. Lieutenant-Colonel Hamilton was the Senior Medical Officer. Under him were Majors Hobbs, Fisher, Chalmers, Krantz and Captains Le Gay Brereton, Higgin and White. In addition to these officers were the three battalion RMOs: Captains Cumming, Richards and Anderson. When Green's Number 3 Battalion was landed at Victoria Point, Captains Higgin and White were assigned to it as the medical officers. Cumming landed at Mergui with Ramsay Battalion and Richards was Kerr's (and later Lieutenant-Colonel Anderson's) RMO.

It will be recalled that when Lieutenant-Colonel Ramsay and his Number 1 Battalion were landed at Mergui, 500 British troops were also landed and came under his command. The doctor accompanying them was an Australian who was destined to become one of the legends of the Railway: Lieutenant-Colonel Albert 'Bertie' Coates. Captain Rowley Richards: 'Now Bertie Coates was, in my view, the most outstanding medical officer and man on the Railway. He was a man who was full of initiative . . .'[67]

Coates was born into a poor family at Ballarat on 28 January 1895 and had left school at eleven years of age. After starting work as a butcher's apprentice, and then indentured to a bookbinder, he had put himself through night lessons and passed his junior examination with distinctions in all five subjects. Coates had then decided to study medicine and despite his studies being interrupted by his service in the Great War, he came home and yet again worked night shifts—at the Postmaster General's Department—and graduated with first class honours in all subjects.

After a distinguished prewar career as a surgeon, he joined the Second AIF and was posted as a lieutenant-colonel to the 2/10th AGH at Malacca, Malaya. It was here, a full year before the outbreak of the war, that the initiative referred to by Captain Richards first materialised. Not only did Coates spend valuable time at Malacca studying all he could about tropical medicine, which had understandably been a minor part of his studies in Melbourne, but, with remarkable foresight, he realised that the day could come when Australian nurses could be evacuated from Malaya and Singapore. He therefore initiated nursing training—particularly surgical training—for orderlies. This was to prove invaluable in Changi and on the Thai–Burma Railway.

Just prior to the fall of Singapore, Coates was ordered to leave by ship for Java. The convoy left on 13 February 1942, but was bombed and Coates found himself in Tembilahan, Sumatra, where he immediately began work operating on British casualties. He declined a number of opportunities to escape from Sumatra and after arriving at Padang on 28 February, he was captured three weeks later. In May 1942, he was sent to Burma as the RMO for Williams Force.

Albert Coates's prewar surgical experience made him an invaluable medical resource on the Railway, but his personal qualities won him the trust and admiration of the diverse cross-section of humanity found in any army formation. In short, Coates had a magnificent 'bedside manner' and the common touch. 'Weary' Dunlop recalled that Coates's 'short, upright figure with a ghost of a swagger, a Burma cheroot clamped in his mouth, and his staccato flow of kindly, earthly wisdom' was to become 'the object of hero worship and inspiration'.[68] Whilst working at the 30 Kilo Camp hospital, Coates was to utter words which were to resonate across the Burmese section of the Railway:

The route home is inscribed in the bottom of every man's dixie. Every time it is filled with rice, eat it. If you vomit it up again, eat some more; even if it comes up again some good will remain. If you get a bad egg, eat it no matter how bad it may appear. An egg is only bad when the stomach will not hold it.[69]

The biggest killer on the Railway was amoebic dysentery, characterised by the growth of ulcers in the colon caused by the amoeba parasite, which produced the symptoms of inflammation of the intestine: diarrhoea and stools with blood and mucus. This condition in turn caused severe pain and dehydration. The standard treatment was the drug emetine hydrochloride. As our Railway story unfolds, we shall witness some extraordinary efforts to procure this life-saving drug. Two 'A' Force doctors, Chalmers and Cumming, had but a paltry initial supply of it, and, in contrast to other forces, the administration of 'A' Force had little or no means of procuring it on the black market. At Tavoy Coates 'performed the first ileostomy of the prison camps for this condition, with complete success, and this life saving measure was repeated in other places on a number of other patients'.[70] The procedure involved an operation which exposed the small intestine, allowed it to be drained, and thereby removed the amoeba.

When working at the 55 Kilo hospital camp Coates, still recovering from a bout of tropical typhus, was initially carried around on a stretcher to see his patients. It was during this period that he worked with a Dutch chemist, Captain Van Boxtal, who was able to make emetine from an extract of a plant called ipecacuanha, which although produced in very limited quantities, also proved priceless in the fight against dysentery.[71] Van Boxtal also distilled water from a primitive still which was used to make eye drops; he made tinea paint from sulphur and slaked lime; spinal anaesthetics were made 'by the careful evaporation and dilution of Japanese novocaine', and he 'experimented carefully with cocaine . . .'.[72] During Coates's time at the 55 Kilo Hospital his patient numbers grew to 1000 and peaked at 1800. As the demands upon both him and his staff increased, so further improvisation and initiative became the hallmark of their response. A limited number of beds for those most in need were made from bamboo and rice sacks, every available rag and piece of mosquito netting was painstakingly hoarded and used for bandages and dressings, artificial limbs were made from the ever available bamboo, and an unceasing effort was made to construct, refine and employ instruments to replace those pilfered along 'A' Force's journey to Burma. And in late 1943 at the 55 Kilo Camp Coates was able, with the rare support of a Japanese doctor, to engage in modest black market purchases of meat as a vital supplement to his critically ill patients' watery 'stews'.

Coates would later describe a typical day as 'segregating the sick from the very sick . . . curetting seventy or eighty ulcers during the morning . . . and,

in the afternoon, proceeding to amputate nine or ten legs'.[73] The daily 'curetting' and the 'amputating nine or ten legs' was the never-ending fight against
the scourge of tropical ulcers. Such ulcers spread with great speed and once
they had penetrated the connective tissue in the leg, and had entered muscles,
tendons and the lining around the bones, the severe scraping and cutting
involved led to horrible scarring at best, and often to amputations and death.
The patient's greatest chance of surviving an operation occurred when the
amputation occurred below the knee. Coates performed such procedures
under a bamboo shelter with only one knife, two pairs of artery forceps and
a saw which he was required to share with the camp carpenters and butchers.
Private Wal Williams:

> ... my ulcers were small, I mean they start off bloody small ...
> I used to go to a, like a backwater off the river, like a little tributary
> running in ... and I used to put my legs in the bloody water, and
> these little fish ... used to come along and pick all the bloody crap
> out of it. It hurt, it used to hurt like buggery ... and you've got a
> clean wound ... what they did, when they had to scrape those bloody
> things with a spoon ... that's when Coates and them [a doctor or an
> orderly], would have to come along and oh Jesus that must have been
> painful ... these blokes, ulcers from the knee down to the bloody
> ankle, all exposed, and it's all got pus ... he'd have to scrape that
> shit out every day. And the blokes would be screaming their bloody
> heads off. And the stench! The ulcer ward! Christ! You could smell
> it a hundred bloody yards away! It'd make you want to chunder! ...[74]

Coates was also an inspiration to his colleagues. Captain Rowley Richards,
RMO Anderson Force:

> He was in one of the camps ... having a bastard of a time. He'd
> had ... a fever for about a month, running at a very high temperature.
> Very crook. And I'd just finished the cholera epidemic and I was on
> my way down through to the 30 kilo where the hospital was at Retpu,
> and we called in to see him. I was uncharacteristically pessimistic
> and despondent, having been pretty bloody sick myself. As a result of

Tom Hamilton and Varley coming out to our camp Nagatomo decided that there were four of us who'd been working on the camps as distinct from the hospital group, who deserved some sort of recognition . . . And the outcome was that there were four of us; a Dutchman, Krantz, I can't think of who the other one was, and myself, and we were sent back to the 30 kilo hospital for a period, to give us a break. On the way back, we called in, saw Coates, and as I say, I was feeling a bit buggered at the time, and I said, 'You know, this is all just a waste of time, we'll never see cholera, we'll never see dysentery if we get back.' And Bertie Coates said to me, 'You have learnt something that very few doctors ever learn, and that is to know when a man is sick!' And I thought, 'Shit! How petty can you be!' When I came home, I knew what he meant . . . having that sixth sense to know when a bloke's sick.[75]

Lieutenant-Colonel Albert 'Bertie' Coates would recall after the war that his time on the Railway constituted the best work of his career. He could not have been referring to the frustrating obstacles placed in his path, nor to the many tragic and Japanese-imposed deaths he witnessed, but more to the improvisation in procedures, the design and construction of equipment against all conceivable odds, and surely, to the undeniable fact that here was a doctor's devotion to duty in its purest form—against all the odds.

The surgeons in 'A' Force—and for that matter in all subsequent forces along the Railway—were faced with large numbers of men requiring operations, and with the equally daunting care of the critically ill and dying. The RMO at a battalion or force camp bore an extremely lonely, isolated and onerous job in dealing with a multitude of ailments, and of having to determine who should go to work on a daily basis, and of having to argue with aggressive Japanese and Korean guards who demanded that the engineers' work quotas be filled.

The first quality one notices about a number of the battalion RMOs on the Railway is their extreme youth. Captain Rowley Richards was born in Sydney on 8 June 1916; he graduated in medicine from University in 1939;

had served as the 2/15th Field Regiment's RMO through its campaigning on the Malay Peninsula and on Singapore Island; and, after all this,
would 'celebrate' his 27th birthday in June 1943 with Anderson Force on
the Railway. The notion that a 27-year-old doctor might be placed in a
position of being responsible for the health of a force of 1000 men under
the conditions described would seem no small challenge. As our Railway
journey unfolds, we shall encounter other RMOs of equal youth and working
under equally daunting circumstances.

The major problem encountered by Railway RMOs was the fact that
the men suffered from a number of ailments which seemed to operate in
a regular pattern or cycle. Captain Rowley Richards:

> The thing I often talk about on the Railway was what I called the
> killer cycle. Our men in Anderson Force, over the period we were in
> Burma and down into Thailand, from May '42 to December '43, the
> men averaged 1.7 attacks of malaria per month. As soon as they had
> an attack of malaria their dysentery was stirred up; that would be
> followed by a flare-up of beriberi; and then as they were recovering
> from all that, they'd be sent out to work, and they'd get another attack
> of malaria. And you'd get this cycle that would just go on and on.[76]

Malaria, dysentery, beriberi, back to work and malaria again. The issue
was, how to treat each, how to break the cycle, and how to avoid any one—or
more—conditions being the cause of death. The heartbreaking reality of this
'killer cycle' was the fact that no surgeon or RMO had the means to break the
cycle—it could only be broken by death. If a POW was lucky, therefore,
the cycle went 'on and on and on'.

Malaria on the Railway was universal and its treatment was a calculated
game of 'cat and mouse'. Captain Rowley Richards:

> . . . from time to time, we did get quinine, the Japs supplied us with
> quinine. But then, the number of attacks that we were having in
> malaria, required a lot more quinine than we were receiving, so that
> meant that we had to make the decision—do you give a few people full
> courses or do you give them reduced courses, or what do you do? The

playing God thing. We could've chosen, perhaps, to select a few people and give them a full dosage, but that would have been not acceptable, to me anyway. We were very much on the concept established by Anderson, that we all had the same in terms of rations, accommodation, and everything else—whether we were officers or troops.[77]

Richards last sentence is very significant to our story. To it might have been added 'drugs and dosages of medicines'. We will discover that such egalitarian distribution of rations, the quality of accommodation, and most of all, the administration of drugs differed widely according to the battalion and force in question.

When a malaria attack was followed by dysentery, procedures against it varied from force to force. A relatively common approach was employed by Richards:

> ... what we did ... we had light duty blokes grinding up charcoal, with a bottle, they'd use it as a rolling pin. It gave them something to do, they felt as though they were doing something useful. And you gave it [table spoons of charcoal] to the blokes, on the basis that charcoal absorbs gases. It goes into gas masks, and it absorbs many times its volume of gas. [Did it work?] I doubt it. But the blokes felt as though something was being done for them, and they would believe that ... something was being done for them ... achieving is ninety per cent believing![78]

Elsewhere RMOs would employ Epsom salts to literally flush the system—already being 'flushed' by the dysentery condition—or, when available, Condy's crystals might be wrapped in rice paper and swallowed. But there was simply no decent substitute for drugs such as emetine hydrochloride and/or M & B 693, and they were priceless and virtually impossible to procure in Burma.

In combating beriberi and the multitude of other vitamin deficiency diseases on the Railway, the main weapon was the infrequent ability to supplement the men's diet. Such rare purchases sometimes delayed the 'cycle'. Sometimes this was done by a local or individual purchase of fruit or vegetables after receiving pay, but the limitations of the availability of canteen supplies, the individual's financial status and the sheer volume of goods needed were very prohibitive. We have noted the attempts by Brigadier Varley, Lieutenant-Colonel Ramsay and Lieutenant-Colonel Albert Coates to procure small quantities of meat and fruit and vegetables. We have also noted that the efficiency and volume of such purchases on a force level were inhibited by the rorting and pilfering conducted by local Japanese guards and the disgusting behaviour of Colonel Nagatomo 'raking fees or percentages' before the goods ever arrived.

The first three parts of the cycle—malaria, dysentery and beriberi—were terribly difficult to combat, but RMOs and their orderlies and sometimes camp officers were able to have an influence over who was sent to work and who desperately needed some respite. Captain Rowley Richards:

> I realised that we were playing God every day, all the time. 'You go to work; you can stay in today.' Playing with people's lives. At the time it did not worry me at all. I was merely doing what I saw to be my job—my duty as I saw it. Remembering that on a sick parade I'd probably spend all of fifteen seconds talking to one bloke. And you had to make instant decisions. We had these nominal rolls where we had a record of every bloke, what sickness he had, and how many days no duty . . . that was there in front of us all the time.[79]

Coates's words to Richards that 'you have learnt something that very few doctors ever learn, and that is to know when a man is sick!' become clear when the above quote is considered. The rolls were relatively detailed given the circumstances: 'Duty', 'Light duty', 'No duty', 'Hospital'. It was during the nights that Richards and his orderlies—and usually Major Kerr—would examine the notes and assign men who had been working between seven and ten continuous days a day off. Richards would record that 'it was not a matter of determining if a man was unfit or fit, but rather evaluating the relative unfitness of one man against another'.[80] Whilst the dreaded 'killer cycle' always continued to reap its tragic harvest, the initiative, devotion to duty and cunning improvisation of the battalion RMOs and their overworked orderlies produced remarkable results and saved a multitude of lives.

Driver Joe Nimbs. (Courtesy J. Nimbs Jr)

Private Paddy O'Toole, 2/29th Battalion. (Courtesy 2/29th Battalion Association)

Lieutenant-Colonel Wilfred Kent Hughes. (Courtesy Mr Sasse)

Captain Alf Menz, 8th Division Provosts. (Courtesy Geoff Menz)

Private C. Edwards, 2/19th Battalion. (Courtesy C. Edwards)

Private Wal Williams, 2/19th Battalion. (Courtesy Wal Williams)

Lieutenant-Colonel Alfred Coates, A Force.

Major Bruce Hunt, F Force. (Courtesy 2/20th Association)

Captain R. Richards, A Force. (Courtesy Dr R. Richards)

Lieutenant-Colonel D. Kerr, A Force. (Courtesy Margaret Hooper)

Captain David Hinder, U Battalion. (Courtesy Charles Edwards)

Sergeant Frank Baker, U Battalion. (Courtesy 2/20th Association)

Captain Roy Mills. (Courtesy 2/29th Battalion Association)

Lieutenant Ron Eaton, F Force. (Courtesy Catherine Goodings)

A barge transporting stores and POWs on the River Kwai, Thailand. (AWM 128451)

Bridge building, Konkoita, Thailand. (AWM P00406.002)

The Wampo viaduct, Thailand. (AWM P00761.017)

Thanbyuzayat, Burma HQ A Force. (AWM 043269)

Captain Reg Newton, CO U Battalion.
(Courtesy Reg Newton Jr)

Sergeant Jack de Loas, U Battalion.
(Courtesy Patricia Fitzpatrick)

Sergeant Bert Donaldson, U Battalion.
(Courtesy Andrew Donaldson)

Private 'Shorty' Cooper, U Battalion.
(Courtesy 2/20th Battalion Association)

Bong Pong in his store in Kanchanaburi. (AWM P00779.002)

Gunso Aitaro Hiramatsu, the infamous 'Tiger'. (Courtesy Charles Edwards)

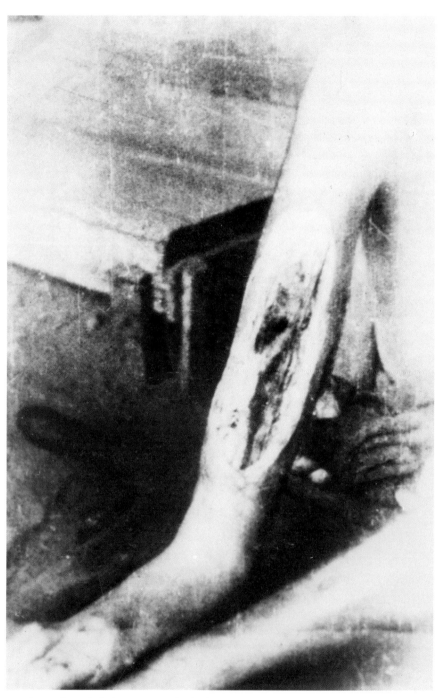

An advanced tropical ulcer, Tarsau, Thailand. (AWM P00761.010)

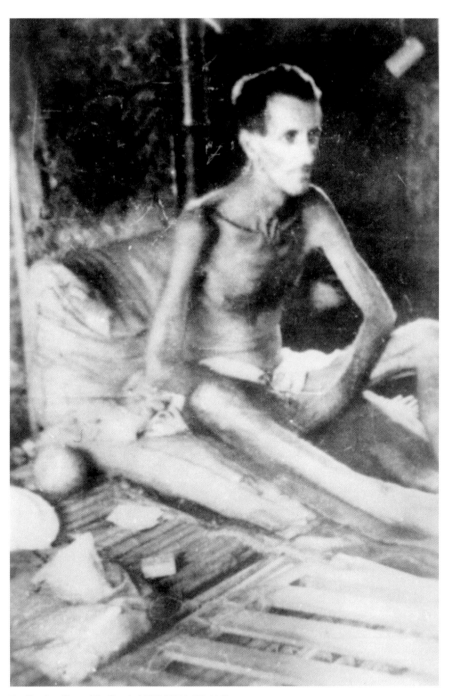

Beriberi sufferer, Thailand. (AWM P01433.020)

The 'main road' journey from Thailand to Burma. (AWM 128452)

F Force suffers dysentery at a rail siding. (AWM Aspinall Collection)

F Force Songkurai: malnutrition and beriberi. (AWM Aspinall Collection)

Cholera Hill, Songkurai. (AWM Aspinall Collection)

Lieutenant-Colonel Pond, F Force.
(Courtesy 2/29th Battalion Association)

Captain Adrian Curlewis, F Force.
(Courtesy Philippa Poole)

Lieutenant- Colonels Kappe (left), Galleghan (centre) and Johnson (right) upon liberation.
(AWM 117115)

Brigadier Varley's command of 'A' Force in Burma poses a number of fascinating questions. In the Australian Official History, Lieutenant-Colonel Charles Anderson, VC would be quoted as saying:

> During the whole of this tragic period of misery and suffering, Brig Varley's strong personality, his vigorous and fearless championship of the troops, careless of rebuffs and determined to leave no stone unturned for the better treatment of the men, won him the respect of the Japanese and I have no hesitation in saying was probably instrumental in preventing a far greater tragedy than that which took place.[81]

Further, the Official Historian identifies Varley's style of leadership as 'keeping the maximum number of people at work' while also stating that 'the best results seem to have been achieved by officers who deferred to the Japanese authority on minor matters, and concentrated on taking a definite stand on vital matters affecting the men's lives and health'.[82] Perhaps Captain Rowley Richards bests sums up this precarious situation:

> Williams and Kerr and I would argue with the Japs until decision time came. Do I feel I have reached the limit of a relatively peaceful outcome and a minimum of harm to the men, or do I run the risk of a disastrous outcome with no gain—plus a severe beating . . . for myself and the sick men? In fact there was usually no option. The exit strategy was to gain as much as possible before the Jap went berserk. Not always easy with unpredictable Japs and sometimes a bad outcome if we misjudged—as I did on one occasion! John Williams was stood bare-headed outside the guard house for 24 hours.[83]

Varley's stance on 'keeping the maximum number of people at work' is an interesting one. In most forces, commanders had the exact opposite aim. Varley's diary has registered his belief that by maximum work numbers, a corresponding maximum pay was received, which in turn meant extra food purchases for hospital patients, and to a lesser degree, the force at large. The theory had its merits, but brings into question the consequences for the men and the impact of the 'killer cycle' we have discussed. The next issue is the fate of the pay purchases. We have observed that force money brought from Changi—and not mentioned by the Official Historian with regards to 'A' Force or indeed with any other force—facilitated purchases of food. The unique problem that faced Varley was transporting those vital food supplements to his increasingly dispersed force. There was no River Kwai, no decent road (but merely a small oxcart track), and most of all, there had been a sharp escalation of prices for those stores at the purchasing points. And then there was Nagamoto's cut and persistent pilfering to contend with. Varley, therefore, worked under a rigid, difficult and corrupt system.

The Official Historian's argument that the best way of dealing with the Japanese was to defer to them on 'minor matters' but to make a 'definite stand on vital matters affecting the men's lives and health' is noteworthy. We have discussed Varley and Ramsay's voluminous verbal and written protests. The point is, surely, that such protests had little positive impact on those 'vital matters'.

In his book, *A Doctor's War*, Rowley Richards noticed the same style of command in Lieutenant-Colonel Charles Anderson. Anderson, Richards observed, 'questioned the seriousness of the medical condition of our [Anderson Force] troops, particularly in regard to pellagra, a disease he failed to understand,' and believed 'that it was better not [to] antagonise' the Japanese. In contrast, Richards noted that Lieutenant-Colonel Williams 'chose to deal with our keepers head on'.[84] Obviously personal courage was not an issue—we have noted Anderson's brilliant and brave performance at Bakri and his subsequent Victoria Cross. The point is that command in battle and command in a POW situation is an entirely different phenomenon. Varley and Ramsay and Anderson performed admirably on the Railway. The Official Historian has recorded that the 'A' Force death rate (13.06%) was the lowest of all forces.[85] This must reflect positively on Varley and the medical officers and their orderlies. But a much more accurate assessment is possible in the light of a comparison with other forces in our story. We shall return to the fate of Brigadier Varley and his 'A' Force as our Railway story concludes.

28

'U' BATTALION

We have recorded the movement of 'A' Force from Changi to Burma in May 1942 and much of its subsequent fate. One month later, the Japanese transported some 3000 British POWs by train to Nong Pladuk to commence work on the southern, or Thailand end of the line. It will be recalled that in July 1942 'B' Force was raised in Changi and subsequently sent to Borneo. On 16 August, Major Alan Thompson recorded the movement of the senior officers' party—'C' Force—from Changi. It is a reminder of the magnitude of the capitulation six months earlier:

> JAPAN PARTY. Departure of Japan Special Party 'A' 400 and Party 'B' 1000. Special Party included 6 Generals, 25 Brigadiers, 21 Colonels. AIF Special Party 13 Officers 9 O.R.s Party 'B' 6 Officers and 90 O.R.s[1]

And then on 28 November the last senior officers left Changi:

> OVERSEAS PARTY. Remaining Senior Officers Lt-Gen Heath (3 Corps). Brig Maxwell and Capt MacDonald (Cipher Officer) left Singapore on Kamakura Muru [sic] for overseas. 550 Party from Singapore travelled on same ship. Warm clothing issued to those leaving.[2]

The reader will also recall the departure from Changi to Thailand—under controversial circumstances—of Lieutenant-Colonel 'Weary' Dunlop's Force on 20 January 1943.

One of the great myths of the Railway is the notion that British POWs always lacked the standards of hygiene of the Australians; that their camps were poorly run in comparison; and that, as a consequence, their death rate was much higher. Such generalisations are misleading. While the British certainly did have a higher mortality rate, to arrive at a fair assessment one must take into account many variables: the nature of their camps and their commanders; the availability of black market food; their proximity to coolie camps; and the particular local conditions. Further, it should be recognised that some 14 000 British POWs were working on the Railway from November 1942 onwards, and exposed, therefore, to all of the rigours of labour and adversity in that severe environment, months before most of the Australians arrived. An example is the fate of the British POWs who had been with Captain Reg Newton in Pudu Prison. When Newton and his Australians were sent by train to Changi in September 1942, their British comrades were sent to Bampong to immediately begin work on the Railway. The British, therefore, journeyed straight from one environment of abject deprivation into another, while Newton's men spent months on the docks at Keppel Harbour and in Changi, and therefore in some measure at least were able to recover physically from their Pudu experience. Further, however poor the Railway camps were, it was the British who frequently arrived along the line to first clear virgin land and then live under—by Railway standards—extremely poor conditions, as they constructed the first camps. We shall witness some very poor British camps and a number of 'good' ones—the same will apply to the Australians.

At Changi on 5 March 1943, Major Alan Thompson recorded that:

> Warning order party of 5,000 to proceed up country A.I.F. allocation 2,500 including 25 officers. Only fit men capable of doing heavy manual work to be included in party. Men to be supplied from 22 Bde, L of C. [Line of Communication] RAA Bde [artillery], 27 Bde. probable date of departure 15 March 1943.[3]

Command of this new force, to be named 'D' Force, was assigned to Lieutenant-Colonel McEachern (4th Anti-tank Regiment) and was to consist of four battalions each of 555 men: 'S' Battalion (Major Gray Schneider, 2/10th Field Regiment); 'T' Battalion (Major John Quick, 4th Anti-tank Regiment); 'U' Battalion (Captain Reg Newton, 2/19th Battalion); and 'V' Battalion (Major Alf Cough, 2/4th M G Battalion). The force totalled 22 officers, 2161 ORs, seven doctors and 30 medical orderlies. Our 'D' Force case study will be Captain Reg Newton's 'U' Battalion.

We have chronicled Newton's time in Pudu Prison in Kuala Lumpur. When 'D' Force was raised, Newton drew heavily upon that experience. The selection of officers for his 'U' Battalion was his first astute decision. He was not interested in Lieutenant-Colonel 'Black Jack' Galleghan's dictum that such command appointments came down only to one's combat promotion standing. In a frank interview with Hank Nelson for his *POW Prisoners of War, Australians Under Nippon*, Newton stated that:

> I selected officers who I knew could be rough and tough, and could handle the Nips, they had proven this in Singapore work parties. I did not select anybody who had been in Changi throughout because I knew they had not had Japanese experience. But above all they had to be of the rougher and tougher type who could handle themselves and handle troops. I was determined I would only take one officer per hundred; that still left back a number of younger ones who were very good lads . . . I was determined I would not have a superabundance of officers and then be at the beck and call of all the Nips for having too many drones around the place.[4]

The reader will recall our chapter 26 criticism levelled at Major Quick's area on Singapore Island's Havelock Road camp: 'very dirty . . . and Quick's lines were shocking, so that 250 other men were requested to clean up.'[5] The notion that a commander who had failed dismally in leadership and hygiene considerations on a Singapore Island work party could be assigned a battalion command on the Railway where such standards could literally mean the difference between life and death demonstrates Changi command's ineptitude in its selection of a number of Railway commanders.

Quick's 'T' Battalion was destined to have a much more miserable, tragic time on the Railway than many other battalions. On the other hand, during interviews and in correspondence with members of the 2/19th, 2/20th and the 8th Division Ammunition Sub Park, not one veteran offered anything but a fleeting criticism of 'U' Battalion's officers on the Railway—quite the opposite. There was high praise for them and especially for Newton's selection of his leaders; there were indeed to be 'no drones around the place'.

Newton's 'U' Battalion was essentially composed of 22nd Brigade personnel. The 2/19th contingent consisted of Captains Newton, Westbrook and Harris; Lieutenants Sanderson and Weilly; the RSM WO 1 Sonny Loy; and 314 ORs. Captain Gaden, Lieutenant Ramsbotham and 198 ORs comprised the 2/20th portion, and with most of the 22nd Brigade's 2/18th Battalion in a permanent work camp on Blakang Mati, only eight other ranks from that battalion were represented. To make up the required number, Newton received 40 members of the 8th Division Ammunition Sub Park under the command of WO 2 Sid Barber.

Newton was conscious of the need for absolute cohesion within his new formation. In this, he was challenged by a strong rivalry between the NSW 2/19th and 2/20th Battalions. Sergeant Frank Baker, 2/20th Battalion and 'U' Battalion:

> . . . they used to fight in the streets and all sorts of things. When we first went over there . . . you avoided 19th blokes in groups that were around. And the same thing went the other way . . . it still exists today to a point, not nastily, but there's still this 'you and us' sort of thing.[6]

To further complicate the building of a unified battalion, Newton was faced with the small 'foreign' contingent of South Australians from the 8th Division Ammunition Sub Park. Private Walter 'Banjo' Patterson, was one of them:

> I thought he [Newton] looked a good officer, and a good chap, and when he was so concerned about us few goin' in with these New South Wales chaps, I thought, well, he's going to look after us as well as he looks after his own men. I liked him straight away really.[7]

However, such mutual respect and admiration were not always forthcoming. Sergeant Bert Donaldson, 2/19th and 'U' Battalion, recalled that:

[Newton had] . . . a very strong voice. 'Can you hear me in the rear?' And one fellow [2/20th] said to him, 'Yes, I can hear you, can you hear me?
'No, I can't hear you!'
'Well get fucked!'
It was up on the line somewhere.[8]

On 11 April 1943, the soldiers of 'D' Force received a cholera injection and were told that priority was to be afforded them in the sorting of recently arrived Red Cross mail from Australia. Small issues of clothing were given to allow all men to have one pair of boots, one pair of socks, a shirt, a pair of shorts, a hat, singlet and handkerchief. The force was also issued with '2 days reserve rations of rice, tea, sugar, preserved meat, salt and butter'.[9] It was to be a four-day trip. Although Thompson has recorded that 'only baggage which could be manhandled [was] allowed to be taken',[10] Newton and his officers 'made a few searches of the individual kit and by force lightened the load of a number of individuals'.[11] As had happened with a number of battalions, a radio was hidden in a rice container and remained undiscovered throughout.

It is of interest to note that Thompson made no mention of funds for the AIF component of 'D' Force in his diary. But Newton, in his 2/19th Battalion Unit History recorded that: 'L/Col. McEachern was handed the proportion of A.I.F. funds in hand on departure date amounting to approximately $[Malay]4 per man and he in turn would distribute to the four Battalions.'[12] Given that the AIF component of 'D' Force was 2200 officers and ORs, and the money per man was 'approximately $4' McEachern must have left Changi with around $8800. One of the universal force funding problems on the Railway was the notion that a force commander should hold his formation's money. As we have seen with 'A' Force and will soon note with 'D' Force, battalions tended to be split along the line and therefore communication between a force commander and his battalion commanders could often prove difficult.

'D' Force began leaving Singapore on 15 March 1943, in daily trainloads
of 555 men, with Newton's 'U' Battalion departing on the 18th. Newton
would recall that his men left 'thirty . . . crammed and jammed into each
steel rice truck, steaming, sticky hot by day and bitterly cold by night'.[13]
The rice trucks were about two metres wide, six metres long and a little
over two metres high. Sanitary conditions were appalling with a bucket
supplied in only some trucks, and calls of nature were often facilitated by
two men holding a man's arms whilst he performed the deed perched at
the steel door opening. Private Gus Halloran would remember having to
sleep in shifts and that the whole trip was 'bloody uncomfortable! . . . there
was no modesty in this world'.[14] Whilst soldiers lose a certain degree of
their civilian reserve during any form of military service, on the Railway
the humiliation of fouling oneself and all kinds of indignities became the
norm. Private Walter 'Banjo' Patterson, 'U' Battalion, recalled that those
Railway days were unique:

> I'll tell you how I felt! When I went into the army, we was at Wayville,
> and they got an order to take the doors off the toilets there. And
> I thought, 'What a dirty thing to do!' You're sitting there, everyone
> walking past looking at you. By the time I got [off the Railway] you
> were lonely if there wasn't a half a dozen chaps there to talk to you![15]

The above accounts of the train journey to Bampong become far more
vivid when one stands in Rod Beattie's steel railway truck at his Kanchanaburi
museum. An understanding of what lay ahead hit home in Beattie's confined
steel 'cell': the utterly confined nature of that truck with its only ventilation being a door on each side (which was often shut in transit by order
of Japanese guards); the very limited water supply; the inability to sit all at
once—much less sleep; the desire to relieve oneself; and the ever present
disturbing uncertainty of exactly where one is going and when a meal will
be provided.

After an overnight stay in a British camp at Bampong—Newton described
it as a 'typical no-hoper British camp', and a 'collection of dilapidated attap
huts, wallowing in a mess of water, filth and mud . . .'[16]—'U' Battalion was
taken by train to Kanchanaburi on 23 March 1942. It was here that two

extraordinary events took place: one a characteristic example of disjointed Japanese organisation, and the other a meeting which was to dramatically influence the men of 'U' Battalion's chances of survival.

As the men detrained at Kanchanaburi and began their march to one of the gates on the edge of that walled city, they noticed Thais waving money and goods at them, and seemingly wanting to trade. Upon arrival, the officer and guards who had brought Newton and his men from Singapore, handed them over to a new officer and departed. Newton was then stunned to see his new master wave him off and also depart with his guards. Private Charles Edwards would recall that: 'they weren't ready for us. We had a week just doing nothing.'[17] It will be recalled that Edwards had accumulated quite a stash of money whilst in Pudu, and was therefore in an excellent position to buy all manner of items.

At the 'Car Park Café', situated in one of the CBD areas of Kanchanaburi, Rod Beattie asks if we know where we are. Not a clue. It is early evening and suddenly, the vehicles depart the car park, while hordes of stall owners descend on it with plastic tables, chairs, cooking implements and all manner of other café essentials. The transformation is all over in minutes. We are standing right on what Rod calls 'the Aerodrome Camp,' where Newton and 'U' Battalion camped—totally unsupervised—for a week. This rapid transformation from car park to a thronging mass of traders and humanity must have been almost the same for 'U' Battalion in March 1943.

Some men indulged in iced coffee purchases until they found out that a number of such beverages often came from breast-feeding mothers; all manner of fruits and vegetables, eggs, ducks and fish materialised; a thriving sale of POW watches, rings and clothing ensued; and, most of all, this impromptu 'market' lasted a blissful seven days. Sometimes food is not a young man's only want. According to Private Gus Halloran, there were a limited number of POWs who successfully engaged in the pursuit of 'horizontal refreshment'.[18] It didn't take Newton and his officers long to realise the possible health pitfuls amidst this carnival atmosphere. Picquets were placed around the market, and whilst the week-long good times continued, some sense of order was restored. Captain Reg Newton in *The Grim Glory of the 2/19th Battalion AIF*:

This 'holiday' lack of control period, gave us an opportunity to check with the local store-keepers. Enquiries were made if anybody spoke English and eventually Newton was directed to a business chap in the centre of the old city. So very quietly we met Boon Pong and his wife and brother-in-law, Nai Lec.[19]

It is highly likely that Newton was again drawing on his experiences at Pudu. We have noted that when Pudu POWs were first taken out on work parties in Kuala Lumpur, British soldiers who had lived in Malaya prewar established contact with known local business people, and limited purchases of drugs and food resulted. Newton's enquiries as to whether any store owners spoke English was an attempt to make such contacts. In his chance meeting with Boon Pong, Newton established a business relationship that was destined to provide the most substantial food, drugs and trading black market network anywhere on the Railway. Boon Pong informed Newton that he had just secured the Japanese contract to provide food supplies 'to rail or barge head'. But he added that he shortly expected to gain the Japanese contract for barge supplies to be delivered directly to work camps along the River Kwai.

Captain Reg Newton was not one to think in limited terms. He told Boon Pong that:

> ... we would take barge loads which would save him time and instead of calling in at various locations and selling a bit here and a bit there, if he came straight through ... we would take the lot ... He agreed to this and said that Nai Lec looked after the river trade as a rule unless there was something important. (We did not realize the import of this remark until later.)[20]

At that fateful meeting Newton also purchased 'a small quantity of British Army medical supplies' but wisely did not ask Boon Pong his source.

But how to pay for this potential windfall? Newton drew on three sources. The first was the 'U' Battalion share of the 'D' Force funds brought from Changi. Given that we have identified this sum at about $4 per man, 'U' Battalion's portion might have been around $2200. Newton's second source of 'income' would be the Japanese payments made to his workers. Not unlike some other forces, 'U' Battalion pooled most of that money for the greater good. However, the third money source involved a touch of genius. At some point during a number of searches to lighten his men's haversacks, Newton himself, or one of his officers, discovered a Bank of New South Wales cheque book in Sergeant John French's (2/20th Battalion) haversack. Newton proceeded to cross out the Wahroonga Branch on each cheque and promptly labelled them all 'Head Office Sydney' where he (Newton) had an account. Boon Pong agreed to hold the cheques until after the war when 'Head Office' Sydney would redeem them from Newton's account.[21] Boon Pong was to be seen by the men of 'U' Battalion at various camp barge landing points along the River Kwai. Private Gus Halloran: 'Oh yes, you'd see him up the line. It was a great association. He [Newton] made the deal with Boon Pong, he was to pay him by cheque . . .'[22]

———————

At this time Newton had no real idea of the magnitude of Boon Pong's business, nor the Bangkok organisation which was the predominant source of his cash and drugs. Shortly after the war began, most British civilians were interned in the Vajiravudh College in Bangkok. Amongst them were Mr Peter Heath, the Chief Officer of the Borneo Company, which was involved in shipping and commerce; Mr K. G. Gairdner of the Siam Architects Imports Company; and Mr Dick Hempson of the Anglo–Thai Corporation (also an importing business).[23] As Gairdner's wife was a Thai citizen and had relative freedom of movement, she soon learnt through her contacts of the desperate plight of British POWs during the early stages of the Railway's construction. The first efforts by these businessmen to assist the POWs came in the form of funds essentially from their own pockets, but when the magnitude of the dilemma of the Railway camps became known, it was decided to raise funds from the general business community.[24]

Here was the beginning of the soon to be named 'V' Organisation, which was destined to become two groups, both named 'V'. Heath and Hempson would later state that: 'Money was therefore raised from persons outside the Camp under guarantee of repayment in sterling after the war. These guarantees were originally signed by persons of standing within our Camp or known to be possessed of means.'[25] Attempts were also made through the Red Cross to contact the British Government to both inform them of the POWs' plight and to obtain pledges of financial support for the reimbursement of all moneys raised after the war. An example of the size of some of these deals was the £4000 (about 68 500 ticals) received from the East Asiatic Company, which sought a guarantee from four British companies in Thailand. As an example of just four Railway camps assisted by the 'V' Organisation, Lieutenant-Colonel Alf Knights, who for some time commanded the Number 4 Group Base Hospital at Tarsau, cited the following money and medical supplies given over the Railway construction period: Tarsau £2400 (35 408 ticals); Tamarkan £2810 (42 105 ticals); Tonchan £933 (14 030 ticals); and Tamuang £1000 (15 000 ticals).[26] It will be realised that by 1943 standards these were substantial amounts of money. Whilst it will be seen that the above-mentioned camps were within reasonable proximity to Boon Pong's store at Kanchanaburi, the 'V' Organisation's exploits did in fact journey much further. In his report, Lieutenant-Colonel McEachern would cite two fascinating sums of money: 'Up River Camps' 17 400.00 ticals and 'Various' 65 236.34 ticals.[27] The 'up river' and 'various' were camps such as Tampie, Rin Tin, Takanun and as far north as Nieke. In the case of the last two, we shall scrutinise their significance when examining 'F' Force in the next chapter.

By April 1943, contacts through Boon Pong between the 'V' Organisation and the Railway camps were becoming frequent. On the 20th of that month, a letter arrived from Lieutenant-Colonel Knights at Tarsau:

As intimated in our last letter, this Camp has been turned into a base hospital and convalescent home, receiving patients from the up river Camps. At the moment there are about 4,000 sick men here of whom a number are seriously ill. Money is urgently required for food etc, to supplement the meagre Japanese rations, and the Tcs [ticals] 2,000 which is [sic] to arrive shortly will be most useful particularly as the concession whereby Officers could use their bank balances to aid the hospital has been withdrawn, and which has had the effect of depriving the hospital of about Tcs [ticals] 5,000 monthly.[28]

Knights's letter then proceeded to list the drugs required and concluded with a tragic qualification: 'Emetine and Morphia are of paramount importance as men are dying for want of the former and dying in pain for want of the latter.'[29]

In supplying the Thailand Railway camps, Boon Pong's barges therefore eventually operated from Bampong to Takanun, and during the wet season as far north as Neike. Rod Beattie:

> . . . he'd probably only own a few [barges] himself. You can put tons on these things. These old single cylinder pom pom boats, the old single cylinder diesel, would have a maximum speed of probably, four knots, that's probably only about two knots faster than the river's flowing . . . [the barges] came from Bampong . . . Boon Pong was here in Kanchanaburi . . . he was a trader. All the barges, nearly all of the supplies originated from Bampong; Kanchanaburi was a . . . little town at the time. An educated guess from here to Takanun would be about a week, because in the dry season you're having to go through sets of rapids and there were places on the river where they actually set up little satellite camps, of POWs who were towing the barges up stream through rapids . . . This doesn't apply so much during the wet season—the problem then becomes the very strong current. The Kwai Noi [River Kwai] finishes at Nieke. So your barges could only go that far . . . they could go to the Nieke camp area . . .[30]

Apart from the sheer volume of 'V' Organisation supplies for Railway camps along the River Kwai, another most impressive feature of the system was the ability of Boon Pong to hide his drug supplies from detection relatively easily. Whilst he had numerous barges in operation—either his own or others he had leased—he could always personally accompany drug and money shipments, and upon delivery, simply obtain as required by the 'V' Organisation a signed receipt from either the camp commander or the medical officer. The other striking characteristic of the barge transport system was the inability of others to significantly pilfer supplies in transit—a problem, through no fault of his own, that Brigadier Varley was repeatedly facing in Burma.

Whilst Boon Pong has received considerable praise for his constant and daring barge supply to the Railway camps, it should also be realised that he was an astute businessman. Private Jim Stewart, 'U' Battalion, would recall that watches, rings or any form of jewellery could be traded with him for cash. Stewart remembered a POW selling a ring with a gem in it to him for 'substantial cash'.[31] With the Japanese food contract, the delivery of 'V' Organisation goods and frequent trading with individuals, business must have been good.

Captain Reg Newton had certainly picked his 'U' Battalion officers with great shrewdness; had made every endeavour to unify his battalion; and, above all, had struck a mutually advantageous deal with Boon Pong in Kanchanaburi. But his relationship with his RMO provides us with a model of a commander who had realised that the one man in any unit who was pivotal to the survival of all on the Thai–Burma Railway was the unit doctor. 'U' Battalion's RMO was Captain David Hinder. Private Jim Stewart, 'U' Battalion: 'One of the quietest blokes you would ever meet . . . very retiring, very unassuming. A very plain man physically, and in features.'[32] Sergeant Frank Baker was Captain Hinder's RAP orderly:

> . . . but the background to it was Dave Hinder . . . [he] couldn't have done what Reg Newton did, he was a quiet, gentle man. He had the knowledge to impart . . . They were a team, certainly a team, because they did consult all the time . . . Hinder used to make all the rules regarding hygiene and food . . .[33]

Sergeant Bert Donaldson was more blunt: 'I think Newton fired the bullets, that our medico, Doctor Hinder made . . . and he fired them in no uncertain terms!'[34] If that meant a savage beating on occasions, then so be it. Private Charles Edwards: 'I saw Newton, when we first went to Tarsau and he refused to send men out [to work] who were sick. They belted him black and blue . . . I saw him being belted with a bamboo . . . when it was over . . . black eyes and bruises all over.'[35]

Newton did not, by any means, win every fight over the issue of sending sick men out to work. But his booming voice, his utter determination to often stand between one of his men and a beating—also expected of his fellow officers and particularly his work party NCOs—won him the unqualified respect of the other ranks. Further, the fact that officers and NCOs were never seen loafing around camps, but were always engaged in camp duties and ate exactly the same rations (after the men had been fed) instilled a sense of cohesion and lifted morale among the men. And whilst Newton administered his battalion's finances, such funds were usually handled by Captain Keith Westbrook. Private Len Gooley, 8th Division Ammunition Sub Park: 'Westbrook . . . that's what I can remember about him—he was the money man.'[36] Private Gus Halloran: 'This is the whole thing. When you have a communal sort of approach to it, you can survive an awful lot of things, by everyone pulling their weight. And it works.'[37] Halloran's comment is critical to an understanding of 'U' Battalion's exceptionally low death rate on the Railway. An examination of the structure of this unit, and the nature of 'life' or survival within it, is intriguing. We begin with the RMO and his influence upon the men's chances of survival.

During lengthy interviews over three days with the author in Sydney, Sergeant Frank Baker was able to give us an insight into 'U' Battalion's RAP. In the 2/19th Unit History, Newton recorded that Captain Hinder left Changi with a modest supply of equipment and drugs:

> . . . some mercurachrome, acraflavine, dressings and bandages, a few splints, 502 indigestion powder [a superfluous item], some mag sulph. (epsom salts), some charcoal powder and creosote pills for dysentery, 1500 atebrin tablets, 2 lbs. of quinine, 3 syringes and 3 needles, 500 M & B 693 tablets.[38]

Further, Newton recorded that Hinder had no instruments issued to him and possessed few of his own. Such a medical supply was not exceptional either in volume or content. Captain Richards of 'A' Force, however, left Changi with more. But the point is that Richards's supply was looted in transit—through no fault of his. Hinder's was not.

We have recorded Sergeant Frank Baker's initiative in scrounging medical supplies, equipment and Marmite in Singapore. Those items were to prove invaluable as a supplement to Hinder's original stocks. Frank Baker:

> I'd worked on the Godowns in Singapore and just because I knew the value of medical supplies . . . I had amassed a fair amount of stuff of different kinds—bandages, things like that . . . any medicines that I thought may have been of some good. But there weren't many medicines that were any good to you, because first of all they deteriorated if you kept them any length of time, and secondly, you didn't really know what you would treat with them. So . . . I was being practical . . . bandages, instruments . . . if I came across them, I'd hoard them. So the result was when I went up, even without knowing that I was going to be in the RAP, I took a fair amount of medical gear.[39]

That gear was not turned over to Hinder.

> No, I kept it . . . because he told me to. He'd say to me after a sick parade, 'Oh, what have you got in your box of tricks?' And I'd say, 'Well, what do you want?' Oh so-and-so. It might be 'Yes' . . . Sulphalidamide [sic] tablets for instance, I had managed to get quite a few of those . . . not at the Godowns, these came from a couple of offices in Singapore that they sent us in to clean up the furniture . . . and I got in there and looked around for anything that might be useful, and that's something I found . . . but it would be a rare occasion when you did that [hand out rare medicines].[40]

It was a 'rare occasion' because the original supplies—both Hinder's and Baker's—were sparse. And the reason Baker was told to keep his own supplies was a matter of security. Possible searches and the ever-present threat of the Kempeitai—which materialised in the base hospital camp at Tarsau—forbade central storage and widespread knowledge. The burning question then is how often did Newton receive supplies through Boon Pong and what quantities were involved. Baker: 'These are things that would have happened between Hinder and Newton. Possibly the other officers knew something about it, I don't know.'⁴¹ But Baker was aware of one fact: Hinder operated his RAP on the Railway with many more drugs than he began with. During other interviews with 'U' Battalion veterans, Baker was told that there was evidence of foodstuffs and some small quantities of drugs 'appearing' for some patients. Baker agreed:

> ... it worked because Newton had access to whatever there was. For a start, see, Newton used to just use a bulk buying system off the barges up there ... That was pretty well known! ... Newton would do any of that! Any kind of deal you like! Newton could be as unscrupulous as you like. I mean there'd be no holds barred. If it was for our benefit ... He wouldn't be worrying about who he hurt, or who he didn't hurt on the other side.⁴²

We do not, therefore, have any real idea of the exact volume of drugs that were delivered to Newton's 'U' Battalion by Boon Pong (or from other sources) or how often they were supplied. But some idea of the availability of the priceless drug emetine hydrochloride—used chiefly to combat dysentery—can be gauged from the ability of individuals to sometimes obtain it. Private Jim Stewart, 'U' Battalion:

> I remember Halloran, and he'll hate me for telling you this ... he borrowed 50 Bhat off a bloke in our battalion so that they could buy drugs for a bloke called Lindsay Robb who had amoebic dysentery ... this fella had sold a gold watch with a jewel attached to it to the Thais and had a fair bit of Thai cash ... and Halloran borrowed this on the understanding that he would give the bloke a pound a Bhat when he got home. And he did. Fifty Bhat and paid the bloke fifty pound when he got home! And the bloke took it! That was the bad part about it ... four pound a week, five pound a week was a very good wage in those days! Robbie ... had been sent back to Tarsau. Halloran got this money, gave it to Gerry Hurst who went back to Tarsau, got himself declared sick, so he could look after Robbie ... [The] drugs were available from a bloke called Boon Pong.⁴³

While the men of 'U' Battalion had a communal approach to survival, and were fortunate enough to have a strong leadership infrastructure and access to Boon Pong and his barge supplies of food and occasional drugs, further desirable commodities were obtained through the activities of small groups of men or by individuals. It has been recorded that every 'D' Force POW left Changi with a pair of shorts, shirt, boots and handkerchief. From their arrival at Kanchanaburi until the end of their time on the Railway, the sale of clothing, watches and rings allowed individuals to buy supplementary food supplies. Inevitably, as had occurred in Changi and elsewhere on Singapore Island, one often used an 'agent' for this risky venture. Sergeant Jack de Loas was one of them:

> I used to do a lot of dealing with the Thais, I used to put on about three pairs of shorts, and three shirts on the railway, and I'd sell them to a Thai, take the shirt off and he'd take it and give me the money . . . so [later] I only had what I started off on, a pair of shorts and a shirt . . .[44]

And then there were others who turned the act of scrounging into an art form, and conducted it on a most impressive scale. In all interviews with members of 'U' Battalion, one POW stands out for scrounging: Private Arthur 'Shorty' Cooper. Sergeant Bert Donaldson:

> . . . he was game, and he had a team with him. There was Arthur Cooper, Norm Crowther, Merv Alchin, Frank McKinnon and they had a cook and bottle washer, Vince Lawrence. They were in the 20th Battalion, but they were in 'U' Battalion . . . game as Ned Kelly! He'd get it from the engineers [steal through the attap in their store hut], anywhere he could scrounge it from, he'd go up the line, or they would, two or three of them, go up the line in the middle of the night to get stuff . . . he brought four gallon tins of salted pork back into the camp, a lot of it straight into the kitchen, some of it he kept himself . . . they got onto sugar, bags of sugar . . . and put some of them in the scrub . . . one or two of them back into camp . . . they were pretty heavy to carry . . . they'd be a mile or two mile away . . . they'd

spot it off in the daytime and knew what they were after, and back they'd go at night. Newton wouldn't organize that, but he knew it was going on, because it was helping the kitchen . . . that was Shorty! They'd do anything![45]

We now come to hygiene. It has been stated that dysentery—particularly the amoebic variety—was the principal cause of death on the Railway. The main cause of dysentery was the unsanitary conditions in which POWs were forced to live. Captain Rowley Richards christened the problem 'faeces, food, fingers, flies'.[46] In attempting to combat dysentery Hinder and Newton again worked closely together. Sergeant Frank Baker:

He'd [Hinder] go down to the kitchen and inspect the kitchen every day, make sure the mosquito nets were over the food, and make sure there wasn't a fly about that could get near anything, although you couldn't keep them all away . . . I had to stand at the head of the mess parade and as they went past I had to see that—we had a kerosene tin of boiling water, kept boiling all the time—they dipped their mess gear in there, and sterilized it before they went through to the mess parade. And that they washed it afterwards and that they sterilized it afterwards . . . that was done meticulously, for every meal . . .[47]

All kitchen utensils were also meticulously sterilised and, where possible, Newton sited latrines—and supervised their maintenance—according to Hinder's advice. Lieutenant Frank Ramsbotham (affectionately known as 'sheep's arse') referred to 'the old bottle outside the latrine' and 'told the men to wash your hands where you could.' He remembered a Dutchman caught defecating in the open who had his nose rubbed 'in it'. When a Dutch officer complained to Ramsbotham, he was told that '. . . don't worry I'll issue instructions for my men to do it every time they see you fellows shitting where they shouldn't be . . .'[48] However, all the precautions, no matter how stringently enforced, could only minimise the killer called dysentery. In treating it, Hinder variously used charcoal by the tablespoon, Epsom salts (to 'flush' the system already being cruelly 'flushed') and Condys crystals wrapped in rice paper and taken with water. For the very lucky and very

few, emetine hydrochloride or Sergeant Frank Baker's dwindling supply of
sulphanilamide might be administered.

———◆———

On 4 April 1943, 'U' Battalion was taken from Kanchanaburi by truck to
Tarsau, which was the Japanese HQ for Number 4 Group, and also that
group's base hospital. Here Newton met the British CO, Lieutenant-Colonel
Knights, and arranged that half of his officers' pay for each month was to be
spent on any of his men sent back to hospital. The Battalion's work at and
around Tarsau consisted mainly of building embankments and the digging
of cuttings. At this time Major Quick's 'T' Battalion was employed further
back at Wampo on the construction of a viaduct and an embankment, and
Major Schneider's 'S' Battalion was forward at Kinsayok and later Hintok.
Newton did not, at this time, know of the whereabouts of Lieutenant-Colonel
McEachern and Cough's 'V' Battalion. Judging by the ration scale mentioned
by Newton for his men at Tarsau, and the availability of extras from the
British canteen there, 'U' Battalion's time at that camp was tolerable.

It was at Tarsau that Newton first had to deal with theft amongst his
men. It was a not uncommon problem on the Railway. A watch was stolen,
and when the culprit was caught he received the penalty of having to
run the gauntlet of about a dozen men. Private Jim Stewart was among
them: '... I didn't have the heart to belt him, but some of them did ... but
I remember that bloke came out the end of the gauntlet ... it frightened the
living daylights out of him, he could see what could happen.'[49] But the long-
term penalty far outweighed the short-term physical pain. Sergeant Frank
Baker: 'The humiliation is dreadful, and also the feeling of loneliness ... you
are dependent on those other fellas, no matter what happens you're a part
of that team, and if you are ostracized from that team, you're completely
lost ... a dreadful situation!'[50]

On 1 June 1943, Newton was informed by the Japanese Group 4
commander that 'U' Battalion was to move about five kilometres along
the line to Tonchan South. Before the move, Newton made a number of
astute administrative decisions. The first was the appointment of Captain
Bill Gaden (2/20th Battalion) to stay behind at Tarsau 'to look after
"U" Battalion chaps and Australians generally'.[51] This statement seems

broad and almost bland, but its importance was monumental. In blunt terms, Newton was aware that 'charity would begin at home', and that an Australian administration was best placed to serve Australian interests. Gaden was therefore entrusted with ensuring that officers' and ORs' pay—given at Tarsau—would be spent on the Australians under his care, and that their food would be prepared by cooks left behind. But the critical task given Gaden was to maintain contact with Boon Pong, and arrange for supplies to be redirected to 'U' Battalion further along the line, until Newton could re-establish direct contact.

After a five-kilometre trek carrying their tents, kitchen equipment and gear, Newton's men scaled a narrow, muddy and slippery track and arrived 'onto a flat where there were a large number of British camped under Lieutenant-Colonel "Peanut McKellar"'.[52] Here, on 2 June 1943, Captain 'Roaring Reggie' Newton and the men of 'U' Battalion first met Gunso (Sergeant) Aitaro Hiramatsu, 'the Tiger', and from that very moment a battle of wits and cunning between captor and captives was to rage.

Private Gus Halloran remembered the Tiger as being:

> ... big for a Japanese ... He had a huge chin, he was a big dark skinned fellow ... about five feet nine ... with this big, long, ugly, angular face.
>
> He was obviously a very strong man and he came with a reputation that had preceded him ... a horror man ... he'd had a bad reputation for killing Poms, and we all treated him with a great deal of scepticism. We thought—this is going to be very doubtful.[53]

Private Walter 'Banjo' Patterson: 'He was the ugliest lookin' one I ever seen I think! He looked like some terrible crook!'[54] And he acted like one. Hiramatsu caused no less fear in his own men than in the Australian and British POWs. We have discussed the Japanese propensity to employ corporal punishment on their own. Very soon the Australians witnessed a frequent pattern of brutal bashings by the Tiger—to either POWs or Japanese guards. Sergeant Jack de Loas: 'He was very erratic. Some days he'd be quite alright and other days he'd be completely mad ... he'd call you up and give you a bashing for nothing. He'd stand you up there and he'd give you some punches on the face—three or four.'[55]

As we have seen with our 'A' Force study, each and every Railway force would record its own unique experience of their guards and engineers. The names and locations were different but the behaviour was constant. To the men of 'U' Battalion, such names as 'The Boy Shoko' (a baby-faced young officer), 'Stackem' (given to bashing POWs with a pick handle), 'Silver Bullet', 'The Mad Mongrel' and 'The Kenyu Kid' would become notorious and never forgotten. Gus Halloran: 'You had blokes like the Black Prince who would attempt deliberately to knock a bloke off the bridge. This sort of thing. You had some very unpleasant people who got their kicks out of pure sadism . . .'[56]

But 'U' Battalion did meet what would appear to be a very rare guard. Given to warning the Australians of an impending search, or at times bailing them out of other misdemeanours, the men christened him 'AIF Joe'. Gus Halloran:

He was a pleasant fellow . . . he was big even for a Korean . . . supposedly a Christian; supposedly Catholic . . . but he was certainly kindly disposed and he . . . was very refreshing in a desert of people who were not particularly pleasant. Everyone liked Joe and Joe liked being liked.[57]

Newton called Tonchan South 'not the best of areas, although we were alongside a delightful stream . . .'[58] When you stand beside this 'delightful stream' and Rod Beattie points out that Newton's 'U' Battalion was within some few hundred metres of it, that the 'large' British camp was on the other side, and that a substantial coolie camp was located upstream, it takes some considerable time to fathom how the fortunes of three geographically close camps could have had such diverse—and in two cases utterly tragic—outcomes. And then Private Charles Letts' dictum at the start of chapter 23, that 'it all depends on your *shoko* [officer]' returns to haunt you.

We have quoted the English POW Ian Denys Peek, who said that 'the Gods don't give a damn' in his book, *One Fourteenth of an Elephant*. It is certainly an appropriate theme for our Railway study. Peek chose to mention few names of persons in his book. His chapter 5 deals with his time at Tonchan and his dates and content make it clear that after his arrival there, he came

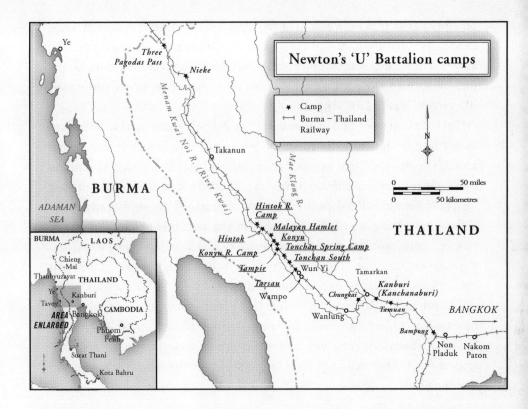

under the command of Lieutenant-Colonel McKellar, and that from 2 June 1943 the men of Newton's 'U' Battalion were his Australian 'neighbours'. If the Gods didn't give a damn, Peek makes it very clear that the British officers at Tonchan South didn't either. The day after his arrival from Wampo as a part of a large contingent of around 1600 men, McKellar addressed the new arrivals. Peek was staggered: '... he is in full uniform, badges of rank, Sam Browne leather all polished, cap exactly right on his barbered head, clean shaven this morning, boots polished and everything laundered and pressed.'[59] With the CO's batman holding his sun umbrella over him, Peek observed that McKellar made it crystal clear that the ragged and emaciated men in front of him 'should have pride in ourselves', and there was an 'unmistakable sneering disdain and a cold hatred in his face as he surveys us'.[60]

Peek also refers to the Tiger, and the fact that the British had heard of his 'exploits' long before their arrival at Tonchan. But the interesting point is that to Peek, the Tiger's name was 'Staff-Sergeant Furobashi'—quite possibly a grim play on words. The fact that there was more than likely only one 'Tiger'; that the dates for Peek's time at Tonchan and Newton's match; and that the Tiger's description by Peek and those recorded during our interviews with the Australians also match would seem ample proof that 'Furobashi' was in fact 'Hiramatsu'.

Peek's accounts of McKellar and the Tiger clearly show that the latter had totally intimidated, humiliated and subsequently dominated the former. In McKellar's eyes the Tiger was junior in rank and had humiliated him to the point where he avoided him at all costs and would not argue, plead or protest on his soldiers' behalf. When the Tiger later threatened the officers and cooks with work if the pace of the Railway construction was not increased, the officers finally protested to him *en masse*, which Peek observed, caused the issue to 'fizzle out', so that 'the cooks go back to their normal duties and the officers to their bridge-playing and books'.[61] And all this while literally hundreds of British ORs at Tonchan South—who had been there for months—were lying around the camp, desperately sick, unable to work, unable to therefore earn pay, and were therefore on absolutely minimal rations—with impending death their persistent companion. Peek observed that they had:

> ... sunken eyes, tight skin over shrunken bodies and stringy muscles, they are little more than skeletons ... Some have the muck of dysentery and raddled bowels trickling down their legs, washed away by the pouring rain. They don't pay any heed to it. It has been their condition for so long, they are past caring and can't stop it anyway. And they simply have nothing to wipe the mess away—not a bit of rag or anything else.[62]

The British camp at Tonchan therefore suffered from a complete breakdown of command. McKellar and his junior officers did not enforce discipline and demonstrated neither courage nor compassion. Peek records the determined efforts of the RMO to sterilise cooking utensils and the men's pannikins, and his efforts to treat his sick with virtually no drugs or instruments, much less with any assistance from the officers in matters of camp hygiene and discipline. In all this, the RMO was virtually a lone hand

operating in an tragic environment of indifference. It is little wonder, therefore, that when the killer called cholera hit Tonchan South the British camp
was decimated. Such hopelessness and despair caused a number of men of
all nationalities on the Railway to quite simply give up on life.

The men of 'U' Battalion were witnesses to the plight of the British. Frank
Baker actually treated a number of them during the cholera outbreak:

> ... this particular Pommy came in, I put him in the tent, and I thought
> he had cholera too, and he was filthy dirty! His clothes were stiff! ...
> I got two of our blokes to wash him. They took him around the back of
> the tent and they scrubbed hell out of him. He was crying! He hadn't
> had a wash ... and there were lots of them like that! So the clothes,
> I wasn't going to do anything with them, I sent them back to his unit.
> And the bloody Pommy [officer] was over to see Reggie Newton! Who
> was I, a miserable sergeant, to send these clothes back to him! ... And
> Reggie looked at the clothes and said, 'Would you wash 'em?' He said,
> 'That's not the point!' And he [Newton] said, 'That is the point! You
> take 'em and wash 'em!' Because Reggie Newton was that sort of bloke.
> And he came to me afterwards and he said, 'What did you do to this
> Pommy?' And I explained, and the matter was closed.[63]

In separate interviews with the author, Privates Gus Halloran and Jim
Stewart both recounted the story of the infamous 'Rin Tin Tin'. Halloran:

> We had two blokes ... we had a tent there at Tonchan, and we had
> tents generally, and we had the Pommies across the creek from us.
> Now we, Newton and Hinder ran a very tight ship; everything was
> boiled, if you were using spoons, forks or ladles they were all sterilized.
> You had boiling water the whole time. And we lost, I think, six or seven
> people. But the Poms really ... we had the classic case of a Sergeant-
> Major_____it was really raining, it was the wet season ... he and
> other sergeants were living in a tent and they had those round mess
> tins and Sergeant-Major_____ had an urgent call of nature and
> shat in his mate's mess tin and used his towel to wipe this [sic] at
> night. And the Poms knew about it and everyone in camp knew

about it . . . the Poms' hygiene was very, very low. He was a very tough
Sar-Major, but he wasn't very disciplined!

It all comes back to your *shoko*. Halloran: '. . . he [McKellar] was a very
polished sort of British officer who didn't do anything for his troops—that's
why, even the Poms referred to him as 'Peanut' McKellar.'[64]

Peek's book raises a further issue of importance to us. Prior to his arrival
at Tonchan, he had been at Wampo (Lieutenant-Colonel McKellar had not
been in command of this camp). Whilst there, Peek had seen British officers
involved in purchasing and carrying parties to the River to meet barges.[65]
Given that the great majority of British officers avoided camp work and
administration, Peek concluded that they were busy buying barge supplies
of food—and one suspects very limited supplies of drugs—and were then
running a canteen. Some items were not available to the ORs. He also
recorded the occasional trip by officers to Tarsau for the purpose of 'camp
business' and 'to meet officers and parties from other camps'.[66] Given that
many of these officers lived and ate separately from their men; that the
purchase and transport of supplies were undertaken by them and them
alone; and that 'occasional trips to Tarsau' were made, it is obvious that
these officers were organising their supplies through Boon Pong—and
possibly others—at Tarsau, and then strictly supervising the control of such
goods. We have stated that the barge supplies were much less likely to be
pilfered in transit than those moved by road and therefore susceptible to
'middlemen'. It is rather heinous therefore, that on occasions the 'pilfering'
took place at the end of the journey and at times, not by the enemy, but by
one's own countrymen.

If the British camp at Tonchan suffered horribly from a lack of leadership, then the coolie camp further upstream was a nightmare. We have
discussed the severe handicaps encountered by the coolies all along the
Railway. There was a lack of camp infrastructure and no leadership
in matters of basic hygiene. Often a coolie's family accompanied him in
the camps. And once the ravages of a multitude of diseases hit them, the
mortality rate was catastrophic.

At Tonchan the British and Australians were detailed to dig mass graves for the coolies, heave or swing the corpses into those pits, and then cover them over. Denys Peek recorded the same shameful behaviour of the Japanese as did our 'U' Battalion veterans. When the numerous corpses were thrown in, the odd 'corpse' would attempt to slowly crawl out—a Japanese rifle butt or a blow with a spade was the solution. Peek noted the Japanese medical orderly sent from Tarsau 'dressed all in white, with a face mask and gumboots', and that his medical aid consisted of having the coolies 'carried to our side of the road and left there for us to bury'.[67] Newton noted that 'we still had room in our hearts to pity them' with their camps 'rotten with the poisoned excrement of all the foul diseases that had struck them . . .'.[68]

———————————

The story of 'U' Battalion's low mortality rate on the Railway is, to a large extent, embodied in the uncompromising hygiene standards planned by Captain Hinder and executed by Newton. But surely one of Newton's greatest triumphs was his relationship with the Tiger. This took two forms. The first was his day-by-day persistent attempts to gain any meagre concession from Hiramatsu. Whilst McKellar considered it beneath his dignity to communicate with, or stand up to the Tiger, Newton impressed him with his soldierly qualities, his discipline and, most likely, his sheer presence. Gus Halloran:

> He [the Tiger] had a good loud voice but nothing like Newton's . . . he couldn't match Newton's! . . . Newton had a battalion voice the whole time, and that would've impressed the Tiger . . . he obviously was a well-trained soldier, and he would have had a regard for another well trained soldier.[69]

But appearances were not everything. There was often a price to pay. Private Len Gooley, 'U' Battalion: 'Reg would go in and be arguing with the Tiger, and he'd be getting belted out the door, and he'd go back again, and go back again . . . the Tiger used to get sick of it before him. Newton could be such a stubborn bugger, he wouldn't give in.'[70] However, if Newton played this daily role with the Tiger with great success, then his business acumen—which amounted to sheer bribery—was even more effective. When cholera descended on Tonchan, the Japanese guards 'kept out of the way' and spent their time gambling with the engineers. Newton and his officers soon discovered that the Tiger had lost very heavily and devised a master stroke. After being given permission to send a party to Tonchan Central to purchase extra canteen supplies, Newton ordered that the party attempt to discover when Boon Pong's next visit was to occur. When his bargeload of supplies arrived four days later, Newton persuaded him [Boon Pong] to offer the Tiger a ten per cent 'levy' on the invoice for the supplies. It was simple bribery.[71] While the Tiger had not a clue that 'U' Battalion was actually helping to pay off his gambling debts, the presence of the Tiger at the barge drop-offs assured Newton of his supplies—unhindered. Not many of the men of 'U' Battalion knew about the Tiger's 'commission', but many knew that he had run up gambling debts with the engineers, and they wondered why the Tiger accompanied Newton to the barges and seemed so 'interested' and compliant with the transactions. Sergeant Frank Baker:

Oh Yes! See this was an arrangement Reggie had. He and Hiramatsu used to go down to the barges. Now Boon Pong was involved... well and truly. They used to go down and they used to do the deals down there... then they'd call for a working party to come and pick up... and there were large quantities! We did pretty well, very well... all due to Reggie's negotiation with him [The Tiger]. Our administration was top!... I don't know of anyone who did better.[72]

When Rod Beattie took us not far along the present day highway from Newton's Tonchan South camp and into the 'bush', we spent an afternoon examining a stretch of about a kilometre of 'U' Battalion's work (as the crow flies). It is composed of four cuttings, one large and three small bridge sites, and the accompanying embankments and ledges. And once again, Beattie was at pains to point out that most of the labour had been provided by the British battalions over months of tedious work, and that 'U' Battalion's job was to add to, or complete, a number of the projects. Yet again there was a recurring message: the quality of the Railway construction engineering is, on the whole, most impressive.

It was eerie walking through the cuttings. The walls are only about five metres high but the methods employed are fascinating: when rock was encountered, the men had to hammer and tap a passage in the rock for dynamite, explode it (often a traumatic experience) and gather the rocks from inside the cutting. Then they had to lift them, or hand them up, or throw them up to the top of the cutting, and then repeat the seemingly never-ending process. 'Hammer and tap' was a slave labour device employed as a substitute for compressors and jackhammers. The work was done in pairs, one man on the crowbar and the other with a sledgehammer. Private Gus Halloran:

> . . . and hammer and tap is no joy . . . you see you turn it [the crowbar] as you go . . . each time he hits it you turn it . . . you're working chips out of the granite . . . usually it was a metre a day . . . it just depends on how good your hammer and tap man was . . . you'd sometimes have to ask the hammer bloke to kindly go away . . . [skinned knuckles or smashed fingers] . . . for embankments, you'd dig holes and shovel that into baskets and the baskets would be carried, or in some cases slings, bags strung between two bamboos, and you'd cart the dirt to the embankment . . .[73]

Rod showed us a cross-section of an embankment where it joined a former bridge, and you can see the quality of the workmanship—over sixty years later, each rock remains in place and fits perfectly into the embankment. Painstaking and accurate work. There is ample evidence along this stretch that the ledges were far easier going, as much of the dirt and rock was simply thrown over the side of the ledge.

From June 1943 until its arrival at Tamuang near the beginning of the Railway in April 1944, Newton's 'U' Battalion would work variously at Konyu No. 3 Camp, Hintok, back to Tonchan, Rin Tin and Tampie camps. In all this, Newton's men were essentially used as 'pinch hitters' to bolster the numbers of workers needed along a given part of the line. And during most of these moves, contact with Boon Pong was maintained, camp sites were strictly administered and supervised, and, at each move, a trusted officer was left behind with funds and equipment to attend to the needs of the sick, until they could be recovered to the next occupied 'U' Battalion camp.

———◆———

In discussing the plight of POWs in the infamous Hellfire Pass area on the Railway, the Australian Official History has recorded that:

> ... the mortality among troops in the Konyu-Hintok area varied from between 12 per cent in the battalions of Dunlop Force to as high as 50 per cent in others. In the period of unrelenting pressure men of various races and differing physiques suffered approximately the same mortality, because, no matter what reserve of physical strength and fortitude an individual possessed, in the long run he was driven to the same level of complete exhaustion and breakdown.[74]

The second sentence contradicts the first. While there were a number of common elements of suffering which influenced the mortality rate for any given area on the Railway, there were other key survival factors.

One of the most important was the duration of time spent on the Railway. Hellfire Pass is a case in point. Rod Beattie: 'The Brits were already working there from November '42, and they were dying from November '42. Dunlop came up in January '43 and then [moved] on, and then the D Force men, Quick, they turned up there in April.'[75] Clearly, the British mortality rate was strongly influenced by the duration of time spent there: two months before Dunlop Force arrived. Further, Dunlop Force was exposed to work on the Railway three months before elements of 'D' Force arrived. Another factor was the utterly obscene one of fate: an individual POW had little or no control over cholera, dysentery, a ravaging tropical ulcer, beriberi, oedema, or a whole host of other medical afflictions; he was subject to accidents and working under harsh physical conditions; he was at the total mercy of unpredictable Japanese or Korean guards.

But the two overriding survival factors on the Railway came down to food and drug supplements, and command competence. The first factor is a complicated one. We have discussed the 'haves' and 'have nots' in Changi, on Singapore work parties and on the Railway. The ability of some POWs to enter Changi with funds or goods, to engage in the black market, to go 'under the wire'—and for that matter to engage in lending schemes—has been discussed. Many of these activities were both fair and understandable. Driver Joe Nimbs is a Changi example. We have also noted Private 'Shorty' Cooper's exploits in scrounging on a large scale with Newton's 'U' Battalion. Again, such exploits were obviously for the individual's good, but they also benefited his mates and sometimes the battalion as a whole.

But what of the plight of the many who could not engage in such ventures for the want of funds, or items for sale, or who lacked the 'street savvy' qualities of others? The answer is that they were totally dependent on the competence of their commanders. We have noted the horrendous plight of the British at Tonchan, caused to a very large degree by a complete and utter breakdown of any sort of command structure. 'D' Force is reckoned to have had a low mortality rate amongst Australian forces on the Railway. It certainly had some advantages over others. When raised, Thompson recorded that it was to be manned by 'only fit men capable of doing heavy manual work';[76] Newton's Battalion was transported forward from Kanchanaburi by rail, and was not therefore subjected to exhausting marches as were some other forces; and there can be little doubt that the River Kwai provided a lifeline of supply that was denied 'A' Force. But underpinning all of this was Newton's dynamic leadership—and that of other resourceful officers such as 'Weary' Dunlop elsewhere.

A tragic illustration of the influence of command is a 'D' Force comparison between Newton's 'U' Battalion and Quick's 'T' Battalion. In his book, *POW Prisoners of War, Australians Under Nippon*, Hank Nelson quotes the experiences of VX 37051 Sergeant Don Moore of the 4th Anti-tank Regiment. Moore does not cite his 'D' Force Battalion, nor his commanding officer by name, but is quoted in the book as saying:

There was one officer known as the White Jap. He was entirely dedicated to his own self-preservation. He was affluent by POW standards. He had money that he could lend where he'd be paid double or three times the price in English currency when he came back. This money had come from the proceeds of a canteen which he ran at a camp of which he was the commander. In this case it was a private enterprise purely and simply for himself. This fellow I speak of has never been back to any reunion that I know of.[77]

Moore was a member of Major Quick's 'T' Battalion.[78] When Newton's Battalion passed through Quick's unit who were with 'Australians from H Force' at a camp called 'Malayan Hamlet', they were confronted by what Newton would later describe as 'some of the first Australian no-hopers we had encountered . . .'[79] They were 'no-hopers' because they had little hope and poor morale—they lacked leadership.

There can be little doubt that conditions around the Konyu–Hintok (Hellfire Pass) area were tough, and that all battalions from all nationalities who camped there had a horrendous time, but the fact remains that Quick's abysmal leadership compounded the problem. Newton's men also served for a time at Hellfire Pass. Further, POWs who did not work there are somewhat—understandably—annoyed that the general public perceive that Hellfire Pass was in some way unique. Their point would seem entirely fair. When you stand in any number of Burmese or Thai railway cuttings, or climb any number of embankments, it is difficult to imagine that a day's work in any of them would have been easier than in Hellfire Pass. Further, the horrendous *speedo* period was not confined to that venue.

The mortality rates of 'U' Battalion and 'T' Battalion bear ample testimony to the issue of leadership. Rod Beattie has extensive records of the Australian Thai–Burma Railway mortality rates: each man's army number; full name; original unit; Railway force; work areas; date of death; place of death; cause(s) of death; his age; next of kin; and his cemetery and plot identification.

Beattie's records show that Newton's 'U' Battalion had 37 deaths on the Railway. The breakdown is intriguing. One man died by accident—a fractured skull caused by a falling tree. Of the 36 who died of sickness, nine died of amoebic dysentery, and three are listed as 'dysentery'. Of the remaining deaths, four cited dysentery as a partial cause. Therefore, dysentery directly claimed 25 per cent of Newton's fatalities and was a partial cause of death in another 11 per cent—dysentery therefore had an influence in 36 per cent of Newton's sickness casualties.[80]

Beattie's records for Quick's 'T' Battalion show 137 deaths on the Railway. Two did not die from sickness: one was bashed over the head with a drill rod at Hellfire Pass, and the other was 'accidentally shot by IJA'. Twenty-four sickness deaths are cited as 'dysentery', and a further thirteen as 'amoebic dysentery'. Dysentery therefore directly claimed 37 or 27 per cent of the deaths. A further 24 deaths (17 per cent) are attributed to dysentery being a contributing cause of death. The incidence of dysentery in 'T' Battalion's deaths is therefore around 45 per cent.[81] While the proportions of deaths due to dysentery are broadly similar, the numbers are not.

We have discussed the multi-layered activities on the Railway with regards to individual and small groups of men being able to scrounge or purchase food and even limited drug supplies. However, for the great majority of POWs who quite simply got up each day and were overworked, abused and beaten, and effectively starved—and were therefore constant victims of the so-called 'killer cycle' identified in the last chapter—the influence of a dynamic unit commander who placed himself in a position almost completely subservient to his RMO, and who could procure even small amounts of food supplements and drugs—for all and sundry and without favour—was a critical survival factor. Upon repatriation to Sydney, Captains Newton and Westbrook were confronted with a Bank of New South Wales cheque account bill for some £770 and £120 respectively![82]

It should be realised that the men of 'U' Battalion suffered under one of the most brutal camp commanders on the line; were exposed to the same working conditions and cruelty from guards as other units; suffered the same weight loss and poor appearance as POWs in other units; but, in the end, the occasional food supplements and limited drugs procured by Newton tipped the balance in favour of survival in the constant fight against that 'killer cycle'.

During pre-war and in combat Captain Newton was an officer who was strongly disliked by his men. He was seen as bombastic, overbearing, and as an officer who quite simply revelled in 'parade ground' pomposity. But from the moment Captain 'Roaring Reggie' Newton entered Pudu Prison, it was as if that incarceration was a preparation, an apprenticeship, that would see him triumph during the most demanding stage of his life. Newton chose his officers with great judgement; he knew the importance of his RMO and his need to 'fire the bullets that Hinder loaded'; he used Boon Pong and the 'V' Organisation adroitly; and above all, he brilliantly tamed and bribed the Tiger.

Private Len Gooley: 'Just about everybody in U Battalion has said the same thing: if we didn't have Reggie Newton, a lot of us wouldn't have come home . . .'[83]

29

'F' FORCE

We have noted that 'D' Force left Changi to work on the Railway in mid-March 1943. Later that month the 1000-strong 'E' Force—of which half were Australians—was sent to Borneo. Like 'B' Force before it, this formation was destined to experience the horror of Sandakan. On 8 April 1943, Major Alan Thompson's Changi diary recorded: 'UP COUNTRY PARTY. Warning order 7,000 party to proceed overland. A.I.F. allocation 125 officers, 3300 O.R.'s 3,425 [total] ... A.I.F. Party to be known as 'F' Force. Personnel to be inoculated & vaccinated.'[1] The men of 'F' Force were indeed 'inoculated & vaccinated,' but because the Japanese raised the force with such speed, only the first of a normal course of two injections against cholera could be given.[2] And from an AIF perspective, that speedy raising and departure of the force was made worse by the fact that the first six of the thirteen trains allotted to its movement to Thailand were occupied by the Australians. The failure of 'F' Force to be adequately inoculated against cholera would have horrific consequences.

'F' Force was the sixth party to be composed of Changi POWs. Command of it was given to the 18th British Division's Lieutenant-Colonel Harris, while the AIF contingent was to be commanded by Lieutenant-Colonel Gus Kappe (8th Division Signals). It will be remembered that whilst in Changi,

Kappe had been in charge of researching and writing the 'official' record of the 8th Australian Division's campaigning in Malaya and Singapore.

The Japanese deceived Malaya Command and AIF HQ from the outset. 'F' Force was to be raised so that 'a large body of prisoners' could be sent 'to an area where food was more plentiful and the climate healthier than on Singapore Island'.[3] Thompson recorded the seemingly generous Japanese concessions: 'Heavy baggage allowed to be taken including cooking equipment, electric light motor, typewriters, batteries, medical equipment and stores.'[4] Some of the 'stores' are of interest: three bands and their instruments—one band per 1000 men; two pianos were to accompany a concert party; and, upon arrival, 'F' Force was to have canteens and access to Thai traders in each of their seven 1000-strong camps. Further, the Japanese stated that transport would be supplied for heavy gear and that there would be no long marches.[5] Sergeant Stan Arneil, 2/30th Battalion: 'The news that we would be taken to Thailand and placed in rest camps was believed by all at Changi and those of us selected to go considered ourselves to be very lucky.'[6] Wigmore has recorded that the AIF portion of 'F' Force consisted mainly of the 27th Brigade which had been 'kept intact since [the] capitulation'.[7] The raising and structure of 'F' Force deserves close scrutiny.

We have discussed (in chapter 25) that very soon after assuming command of the AIF in Changi, Lieutenant-Colonel 'Black Jack' Galleghan had ordered that it was to be completely reorganised to enable it to perform 'any role it might be called upon to do'; that in August 1942 unarmed combat classes were initiated; that area commanders were ordered to supply the names of majors and captains who were fit for field officer duty; and that an officer training syllabus was to begin. In an interview with the author, Signalman Jim Ling (8th Division Signals) confirmed that his unit had been trying to maintain their skills in the event of a breakout, or for any other form of operations.[8] Captain Hardacre, in *The Story of F Force*: 'it was his [Kappe's] original idea of using this Force as a Brigade Group to link up with the British troops fighting in Burma should the opportunity present itself.'[9]

The structure of 'F' Force reflected this combat interpretation of its role rather than the reality of survival in a harsh and unforgiving Thailand POW environment. This view merely demonstrates the difference between a protracted life in Changi and on Singapore work parties, and the experience of soldiers such as Lieutenant-Colonel 'Weary' Dunlop and Captain Reg Newton in camps in Java and at Pudu Prison respectively. When, on 2 May 1943, Kappe and part of his 'F' Force trudged past Dunlop in Thailand, the latter recorded that:

> Lt-Col. Kappe wearing still his blue brigade armband; Col. Kappe was cheerful but very tired. 'The Nipponese have a complete brigade to contend with now, ordnance, AASC [Australian Army Service Corps], and everything complete.' I said, 'Well sir, I hope that you will remain together, because things are pretty rough up here.'[10]

In his history of the 2/19th Battalion, Newton would christen the AIF Changi command organisation of 'F' Force as 'one of the biggest "come in sucker" incidents of the A.I.F. P.O.W. period during the 1939–1945 war'.[11] Blunt but accurate.

Unlike other formations on the Railway, and in keeping with its 'combat' status, 'F' Force Battalions were not named by letters—such as 'D' Force's 'S', 'T', 'U', and 'V' Battalions—or by the names of their commanders. It consisted of four units: the 2/26th Battalion (Major C. P. Tracey); the 2/29th Battalion (Lieutenant-Colonel S. A. F. Pond); the 2/30th Battalion (Major N. Johnston); and a 4th 'support' battalion made up of non-infantry units (Major J. H. Parry of the AASC). It is of interest to note that Galleghan did not retain Lieutenant-Colonel Oakes as CO of the 2/26th, but opted to assign that command to an 'original' officer in Major Tracey. This may well have been a reaction by Galleghan to the controversial withdrawal from the Causeway Sector during the defence of Singapore Island, which, while ordered by Brigadier Maxwell, was led by Oakes. The Senior Medical Officer of 'F' Force was Major Stevens, who was in command of nine medical officers and around 220 other ranks. As per the 'combat' structure of the force, 125 officers were assigned to the command of 3300 ORs. As our story unfolds, we will witness the consequences of Captain Newton's edict that when selecting his 'U' Battalion officers: 'I was determined I would not have a superabundance of officers and then be at the beck and call of all the Nips for having too many drones around the place.'[12] Therefore, whilst Newton left Changi with a ratio of around one officer to 100 ORs, 'F' Force left with a ratio of around one to 27. Subsequent events were to prove that there was to be no shortage of 'drones around the place' in 'F' Force.

On 17 April 1943, Major Thompson recorded the clothing allowance granted to 'F' Force. Given the 'assistance' provided to Dunlop Force before departure, 'Weary' (had he known) would not have been impressed.

> Clothing 25% of all clothing held by Command issued to 'F' Force, A.I.F. issued with 762 boots, 1,344 vests, 138 cardigans, 167 shirts, 245 shorts.
>
>   A.I.F. Kit Store issue 1,000 pullovers, 20 hats, 200 socks, 400 stockings, 1,000 hosetops, 10 bags comforts, 10 bags braces, 100 sports shirts, 200 white bags, 150 underpants, 250 singlets, 100 pyjama coats, 50 gaiters, 100 trousers, 100 jackets, 2 bags clothing material, 6 machine needles, 10 reels cotton, 200 scarves, 150 singlets in lieu of towels, 30 rubber chaplis [footwear].
>
>   I.J.A. state that extra blankets, clothing, boots, mosquito nets being sent to destination in bulk.[13]

The initial standard of health of 'F' Force also deserves mention. Wigmore has stated that the Japanese demanded that the full quota of 7000 men was to be supplied, and as the force was supposed to occupy healthy camps and enjoy better amenities than Changi, up to 30 per cent of its establishment could be composed of unfit men. He quotes the British as sending about a thousand unfit men away and the AIF 'perhaps not more than 125'.[14] Given that a substantial number of the 27th Brigade's POWs had participated in Singapore Island work parties, their health on departure must have been reasonable—comparable to the men of 'D' Force. However, the fate of the thousand British POWs also classified as unfit was to be a dire one.

According to Thompson, 'F' Force was granted around $14 000, at a rate of approximately $4 per man— as per 'D' Force—with the CO of each battalion being given $500.[15] The remaining money was to be administered by Lieutenant-Colonel Kappe.

While 'F' Force was destined to suffer because of deficiencies in structure and planning, and an excess of cumbersome equipment, its most crippling disadvantage would lie in the nature of its Japanese administration. Unlike preceding forces, which were commanded by the Japanese Railway administration in Thailand, 'F' Force was to be administered from Singapore. This would have horrendous consequences, as the supply and management processes were all conducted from afar—and the rigid, compartmentalised nature of the Japanese Army would only exacerbate that disadvantage. On top of all that, 'F' Force was to suffer arguably the worst Australian senior leadership on the Railway.

Our 'F' Force case study, with some digressions, will concentrate on Lieutenant-Colonel Pond's 2/29th Battalion.

Sergeant Stan Arneil, 2/30th Battalion Diary: 'On our last night at Changi we ate lots of little rice cakes and as much stew as we could eat. It was a great feasting just in case the food is not so hot on the trip.'[16] The trip, and certainly the food, would indeed prove to be 'not so hot'. 'F' Force was moved from Changi to Singapore Railway Station by truck convoy, and then boarded thirteen trains each carrying 600 POWs.

As had occurred with previous forces on departure from Changi, the men of 'F' Force encountered their first rude awakening in Singapore. Signalman Jim Ling was a member of train number 1, which left at 6.50 pm on 18 April 1942:

The optimism went out of me and me mates . . . Suddenly there's a new type of Jap!—belting everybody round about, and pushing and screaming . . . from the moment we got on that station and got pushed into the rice trucks . . . God! . . . they were entirely different from the Japs we'd been used to, both on working parties and at Changi.[17]

Lance-Corporal John Roxburgh, 2/29th Battalion:

I don't recall any ventilation . . . we had 28 men in our truck going up. We used to have to work in stages of some standing up while others had a bloody sleep. An absolute nightmare going up. Unbelievable, just shoved in and, 'Kurrah! Kurrah!' [Hurry! Hurry!] And the doors were just slammed and there you were![18]

And as had occurred with 'D' Force, sanitary arrangements during their train journey were non-existent. At railway stations along the route the local population witnessed 'crowds of men bogging all over the station yard'.[19] It was both humiliating and sickening.

After a miserable five-day journey, each trainload of around 600 men arrived at Bampong. The first consisted of Major Parry's Battalion of mixed support units. Upon arrival, each battalion was ordered to stockpile its heavy gear and trunks. Left without adequate supervision, the dump was rapidly rifled by the enthusiastic local population, most likely with the Japanese taking their cut. After being forced to carry their remaining possessions to a camp around a kilometre away—and making two trips for their cooking equipment—two profound shocks awaited them. Their staging camp was the first. Here was no 'holiday' rest camp, but a miserable collection of four dilapidated, filthy huts standing on a sea of fouled ground, with a grimy well which could barely provide enough water for cooking and for filling water bottles.[20] It took the new arrivals a day and a half to 'clean up' the camp. But the biggest shock came with the news that all POWs were to be provided with a number and were to prepare for a ten-day march. Captain Ben Barnett, 8th Division Signals, was a member of Parry's first train, and on 22 April 1943 he recorded that:

> ... the only gear that could be taken was that which could be carried. This was quite contrary to information given at Changi. Men immediately began to repack and sell anything that was not absolutely essential. Officers [sic] trunks and cooking gear could not be taken. These were left stacked and W/O Allen (Englishman) was left behind to look after the gear and endeavour to get it transported to our destination. The time of departure was originally given as midnight, but this was subsequently changed to 24 hours later.[21]

How long Warrant Officer Allen remained at his task is unknown, but the fate of nearly all of that heavy gear and officers' trunks is known: most of it was systematically looted, including some medical supplies.

As had occurred with Newton's 'U' Battalion arrival, a cheap and thriving market almost immediately materialised at Bampong, and after the first

day's march, at Kanchanaburi. A number of experienced scroungers got
up to old tricks. Private Paddy O'Toole, 2/29th Battalion: 'I don't think the
Japs gave a stuff much at Bampong . . . we knocked off a bit of stuff there
too, knocked off a box of tea, a tea chest from the Jap stores . . . and we split
it up, blokes had billy cans . . .'[22] This short 'F' Force interlude at both the
Bampong and Kanchanaburi camps is of interest. While Newton's men
had had a precious week at Kanchanaburi to buy foodstuffs, the 'F' Force
units were able to not only procure food, but also to sell off many more
personal items due to their abundance of gear—despite the fact that their
stay was of a far shorter duration. Sweaters went for $2, shirts $3, sheets $2,
blankets $10 to $15, and despite this frenzy of selling, many men still began
the march with 'assets' which were lugged and sold as soon as possible.[23] We
shall discover that significant numbers of men began the trek with a private
stash of money, or were a part of small groups which pooled their cash and
had the money held by a 'banker'. Another striking feature of the impending
march north would be the unavoidable splintering of trainload formations,
as numbers of men succumbed to the rigours of the trek, or were required
to form carrying parties. As a consequence, they were left behind to the
care of succeeding groups. We have noted Newton's policy of holding
back a trusted officer with limited funds to provide some sort of organisation to those left behind. This would not always be the case with 'F' Force
groups. The issue is a significant one. Private Jack Coffee had travelled in the
second train with his 2/29th Battalion, but had suffered the misfortune of
being left behind at Kanchanaburi because of illness. Later joined by small
numbers of his unit who had dropped out along a succession of camps, he
was subsequently assigned to a unit and to a camp of 'strangers'. He well
remembered the consequences:

> There was no unity, with all these different organizations, there was
> [after the march north] only twenty-three of the 29th and we only had
> two officers [2/29th], maybe three, I might have missed one, but I only
> remember two officers being there, one was the weakest bloke we'd
> ever had there, a fellow by the name of Lieutenant _____ . . . when
> we got up there he lined all us 29th blokes up and said, 'Now look
> fellas, we'll all stick together up here, we don't know what it's going to

be like, but I'll keep you posted.' And that was the last we saw of him till we came out six months later! He was there hidden somewhere, as for reporting to us, no way in the world . . . you're working alongside a couple of 30th blokes or Divvy Sigs, but blokes who you've never seen or heard of before, there's just no unity.[24]

No unity, no organisation, and therefore the battle for survival became that much tougher. Officers too often had been selected for their combat promotion status, and not handpicked for their ability to deal with the very different challenges posed by captivity.

———◆———

The forced march by 'F' Force from Bampong to the Three Pagodas Pass area near the Thailand–Burma border was a nightmare. Private Paddy O'Toole, Pond's 2/29th Battalion:

The first couple of days were alright, the first couple of nights not bad, but the further we went the worse it got. It became very, very difficult because of the situation where you was carrying blokes and carrying gear . . . I very rarely arrived at the next day's camp with my own gear, I usually had someone else's as well . . . 'Give us your pack!' . . . you'd just throw it over the other shoulder . . . hope for the best, expect the worst, and take what you bloody well get! . . . I used to say to them, 'This is your lot, make the most of it!'[25]

It was hard 'to make the most of it'. The men were destined to travel about 275 kilometres in about seventeen days (they had been told ten), marching by night and supposedly resting by day. The first few days were indeed tolerable, as there was a modest gravel road to march on and the men were still feeling the benefit of their purchases of food just days earlier. However, as the road gave way to a narrow, muddy, part corduroy track, potholes and a lack of lighting caused progress to be slow and dangerous. Boots wore out; beatings 'encouraged' the sick and the slow to keep up; water was scarce; and the planned day's rest often didn't eventuate. Men were forced to provide carrying parties for the Japanese and got very little sleep. No matter how tired any man became, to fall behind not only meant a possible beating from a guard, but the prospect of falling into the hands of the trailing Thais. Warrant Officer Bert Mettam, 2/29th Battalion:

> Oh yes! On the march? My bloody oath! Those Thais, they were murderous mongrels! . . . they were following us . . . they [the Australians] called, 'Keep up! Keep up! Bandits back there!' . . . if someone dropped out, or dragged the chain and got behind—it was all at night—there was no torches or anything like that . . . there were two or three cases of blokes getting robbed.[26]

At some camps the medical officers were permitted to leave some of the sick behind, but at others no mercy was shown. The strong carried the weak, carried their equipment, and, despite the fact that a number of carts were rented by individuals and some officers, much of the essential stores were manhandled from camp to camp.

'F' Force's march north was long and gruelling. The men had to contend with the arrival of the monsoon rains and a multitude of fouled and dilapidated staging camps. But then there was the ultimate horror: a new, silent and fatal travelling companion in the form of cholera, one that would only materialise in large numbers at their distant destinations, and which would induce a sense of utter terror and hopelessness amongst the force's exhausted ranks. There would be no deaths in twos, threes or even sixes and sevens here, but a gruesome shredding of a large portion of the force, particularly amongst the far more vulnerable 'unfit' British. According to a report written by a senior medical officer, Lieutenant-Colonel Dillon, this 'silent travelling companion' joined 'F' Force at Konkoita: '. . . the marching parties were quartered in the same camp as a Thai Labour Corps who were suffering from Cholera. The infection was picked up by each of the thirteen parties of marching prisoners.'[27] It was also acquired by drinking from streams on the way through, and the inability to always maintain decent camp hygiene standards when in occupation of a camp for only one or sometimes two nights was another contributor to the rate of infection.

By the end of May 1943, 'F' Force was concentrated in five main camps along a 75-kilometre stretch of the Railway between Konkoita and Three

Pagodas Pass at the Burmese border. Number 1 Camp was at Lower Song-kurai and contained 1800 Australians; Number 2 Camp was at Songkurai (around 1600 British); Number 3 Camp was at Upper Songkurai (393 Australians); Number 4 Camp was at Konkoita (700 Australians); and 700 British POWs were camped at Number 5 Camp at Changaraya. The Force HQ and hospital were initially located at Lower Nieke but soon relocated to Nieke, and as those camps were being occupied, some 550 Australians and 800 British members of the force were still making their weary way forward.

The historian is blessed with five major sources for our 'F' Force study of Lieutenant-Colonel Pond's 2/29th Battalion. First, there is a detailed account written by Pond, a copy of which was given to the author by the 2/29th Battalion Association;[28] second, there is a comprehensive diary written by the battalion's adjutant, Captain Ben Barnett (8th Division Signals), which, at the time of writing, has not been used;[29] third, there is the detailed diary of Captain Adrian Curlewis (HQ, 8th Division, and eventual second-in-command of Pond's battalion). Although much of its content has been published in his daughter's excellent book, additional material is used here not found in that work;[30] fourth, there is the self-published diary of the Battalion's RMO, Captain Roy Mills;[31] and last, we have the oral history interviews with the ORs from the Battalion. It is fascinating, therefore, to observe how four officers and a number of men in the same unit viewed the same experience so differently.

We have noted that the first 'F' Force train to leave Changi was occupied by Major Parry and a mixed contingent of AASC, engineers and signals, and that the second train carried Lieutenant-Colonel Pond's 2/29th Battalion. With Pond's men travelled Lieutenant-Colonel Kappe and his HQ personnel. At 5.30 am on 8 May 1943, Major Parry's advance party reached what Captain Ben Barnett called 'halt number 12', which was Tamarompat, after having dropped off cooks, some sick members and advance party soldiers along the way. At around 8.00 am the next day, Pond and his 2/29th number 2 party arrived. At 7.30 pm that night 253 men still with Parry's party and 447 of Pond's trainload were combined to form a unit under Pond's command (700 strong).[32] Pond's party was destined to work from

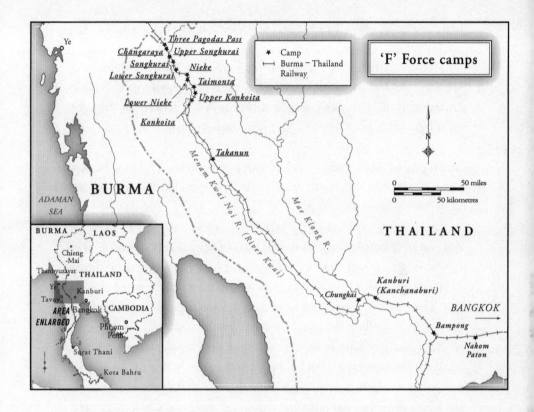

camps between Nieke and Takanun. It was at Tamarompat that the party first met their new master: Lieutenant Murayama. Private Paddy O'Toole, 2/29th Battalion:

A big man, a big man, a very fit bastard too. But he was the biggest Jap I've seen . . . He was a domineering, aggressive type of bastard . . . he'd bash you across the bloody ear no trouble at all! He'd line you up. He gave me a couple the bastard! . . . he'd give you a smack in the jaw and say, 'One more!' He'd say, 'One more!' He flogged blokes, even flogged a bloke with a pick handle one day the bastard! It was in a bloody cutting. He reckoned we weren't going quick enough . . . always pushing, pushing, pushing! The hours got longer, the work got harder, especially when we put in a bloody great cutting at Takanun . . . he pushed us and pushed us, sometimes twelve or fourteen hours a day.[33]

Lance-Corporal John Roxburgh, 2/29th Battalion:

> ... a huge man ... who for the whole period in Thailand remained
> with us. He was the most brutal and inhumane devil I ever struck.
> He hated us just as bitterly as we hated him, and whenever he thought
> fit to beat some poor devil he beat him unmercifully.[34]

The men of Pond's party—and 'F' Force generally—were thus to experience the same arbitrary cruelty from their Japanese guards as others on the
Railway. John Roxburgh:

> And we were detailed to go into this bloody Jap cookhouse and collect
> the food. [There were four of them to carry a watery rice meal in two
> 2.5 foot by 1.5 foot containers]. Two of you would carry one between
> you. These other bloody Japs were coming into the camp, no idea who
> they were. And they reckoned we were pinching the rice, so it didn't
> matter what you bloody said ... we were then tied up by the hands,
> hands behind the back, kneel down, and they just belted us, one Jap in
> particular just belted us with a big bamboo ... across the back, across
> the head, the lower part of your spine ... possibly six or eight times,
> full blast ... undo your ropes and just walk out.[35]

No rhyme nor reason.

———◆———

Pond's party reached the river camp of Konkoita on 10 May 1943, after
covering '176 miles from Bampong to Konkoita in 16 days carrying everything including medical gear, food containers and sick men on stretchers'.[36]
The scenes witnessed on arrival shocked them. The camp was occupied by
a mixture of Malay, Burmese, Tamil and Chinese coolies. It was ravaged
by cholera, the dead and dying and their blood and mucus fouled the ground.
After working for five days cutting a track, the Japanese moved the Australians about six kilometres to Taimonta in an attempt to escape the native
cholera outbreak. At Taimonta the party was engaged in cutting timber and
pile driving on the construction of a twenty-metre bridge. On 20 May 1943,

Ben Barnett recorded that: 'Still on bridge ... Mess still rice onion stew, [7.5 ounces of rice] but men gathering greens & doing a little private cooking.'[37] On 26 May Barnett wrote: '0745 hrs. All party placed in quarantine owing to a suspected cholera case. 0845 hrs. man died. No working parties.'[38] This quarantine period lasted for a further seven days and was marked by a Japanese reduction in the ration because the men were not working.[39] It was also notable for a further deterioration in their health. Captain Adrian Curlewis, 6 June:

> Diarrhoea for third time—nothing can describe the discomfort of 100 yards in rain and mud to slimy fly-blown latrines in the dark, and then squatting on lifeless legs. Acted as Orderly Officer for complete cholera tests in isolation huts ... a hideous night. Roy Mills Medical Officer ill.[40]

On 8 June 1943, the fittest of Pond's party were marched on to Nieke, to be followed two days later by the sick and carrying parties. The work at Nieke consisted of bridge building—cutting pieces of timber for the bridge and standing waist deep in the water and pile driving. Despite the scant ration of only a quarter to a half of a pannikin of rice, the month spent at Nieke was highlighted by the slaughter of five yaks, which added a few days' priceless, if sparse, meat ration to the men's diet. But when Pond's party was ordered to march south, POWs had to pull a number of carts which had been previously hauled by the slaughtered yaks. Pond's party reached Takanun in early July 1943. The party's two-month occupation of that area provides us with an excellent case study of its fortunes on the Railway.

We had been driving for some time along the highway, seemingly in the middle of nowhere, when Rod Beattie turned off the bitumen and drove along a rough, dirt track past two or three small huts, through an open gate and finally over a small bridge. We then crossed another flat-planked bridge across a small creek and then passed through a gate. After a short while Rod stopped the vehicle and informed us that we were standing on the Railway. A brief scraping of a small section of this raised 'track' revealed ballast consisting of washed river stones. And then Beattie pointed to an area of around 70 by 30 metres, and we realised that we were fairly and squarely in the middle of Lieutenant-Colonel Pond's Takanun camp.

When you stand in this pomelo grove, with its neat, orderly rows of trees and its neatly trimmed grass, it is as though it stands as a tranquil memorial to those who suffered here. The backdrop to this peaceful space is a tall wall of not-too-distant trees beyond which flows the River Kwai. During my interviews with 2/29th Battalion veterans, this is the place that evokes the most emotion and the greatest sense of despair for lost comrades.

Beattie then took Frank Taylor and the author along the 'Railway' track over a bridge crossing a substantial stream, to what is now a plantation complex. The manager came out to meet us and generously gave us permission to walk over the area, which is much more extensive than Pond's Takanun camp. It was here in mid-1943 that the British camp existed. This area is also a part of the plantation and has the same neat rows of trees and trimmed grass. When we walked down to a ledge close to the River Kwai, where Thai women were using their rice *kwalis* to cook the evening meal for the plantation workers, we noticed that while the far side of the river was fast-flowing with rocks and white water, the near side was calm and possessed no shortage of barge landing points, with an easy climb to this former English camp. And gazing back over the stream towards Pond's camp, yet again Frank Taylor pointed out a quite wide area where the barges could have turned around or sheltered without running into any white water or rocks. The manager then told us that just to our left there sometimes can be seen the pylons of the bridge that used to go over the stream, linking the two camps.

As at Tonchan, when comparing the location of Newton's camp with the nearby British camp, we immediately wondered why one on one side of a stream could have done so well, and the other, so miserably.

Lieutenant-Colonel Pond:

The march back from Taimonta to Takanun caused dreadful exhaustion. We had ox carts, but they, the luggage, the sick, the tents—were all carried or pulled. The Takanun camp was very bad. 600 men were crowded . . . in an area 35 yards by 75 yards. There was no proper hygiene, 30 men to a leaking tent, so there were lean-to's constructed. The kitchen was unroofed and there were no cookers for rice. The hospital was inadequate, dysentery, malaria, beri beri and then cholera were inevitable. The ground became fouled. (The trench latrines became overfull, and were flooded with water, and seething with maggots were an incredible sight. One's boots were always fouled).[41]

The standard of leadership and camp organisation in Pond's party at Takanun during July–September 1943 deserves examination. As in other battalions or parties on the Railway, we shall identify examples of inspiring officers and ORs, examples of those who were clearly unable to cope, and examples of others who quite consciously avoided their responsibilities. We start with Lieutenant-Colonel Pond. Corporal Jim Kennedy, 2/29th Battalion:

. . . it's human nature, everyone's different. Pondy, being a brigade major, an administrator . . . compassionate, but no where near having a go at a Nip on behalf of his troops. After the war you'd meet him . . . Pondy was a courteous, kind type of person, not one for front lines . . . and as a prisoner of war, I can't recall seeing him . . . and on the railway I can't recall seeing him . . .[42]

Warrant Officer Bert Mettam, 2/29th Battalion: 'He was a solicitor and I think that he'd led a very sheltered life . . . He was a very dour sort of a bloke, he wasn't a humorous type, he didn't have a command [presence] in front of a mob . . . he always seemed to me to be very earnest . . .'[43]

All interviewees agreed with the above assessments. It will be seen that while Lieutenant-Colonel Pond was indeed honest, had a great feeling for his men and always had their best interests at heart, here was a commander bewildered, lost and virtually helpless on the Railway.

His adjutant, Captain Ben Barnett, was a tower of strength. An officer with 8th Division Signals, the 35-year-old Barnett had been Bert Oldfield's wicketkeeping understudy on the 1934 Ashes tour of England and the tour of South Africa in 1935–36. After Oldfield's retirement in Australia during the 1936–37 series, Barnett became the Australian wicketkeeper on the Ashes tour to England in 1938. A number of veterans would recall Captain Ben Barnett's morale-raising Ashes talks given around a fire after a day's despair on the Railway—legendary stories of Bradman, Barnes, Hassett, Hutton, Edrich, Hammond and Compton. Signalman Jim Ling, Pond's party:

> The one man who seemed to be able to handle him [Murayama] pretty well was Ben Barnett. He stood up to him . . . no matter what Murayama turned on to him, or to us, Barnett would agree, or partly agree, or disagree, and he'd take a belting across the head and face and a kick . . .[44]

Barnett's diary contains repeated references to the varying locations and mounting fatalities of his scattered 8th Division Signals comrades, who were caught in the situation of being unable to congregate as a unit, and therefore lacked unity of command, mutual support and amenities which were much more accessible to the infantry battalions in 'F' Force.

In continually attempting to protect the sick and dying, Barnett was ably assisted by the RSM, Warrant Officer Bert Mettam. Corporal Bob Christie:

> He was responsible to the Japs, he'd take the party out, and he'd have to try and interpret what they wanted done, and we'd be told what we had to do, and if we didn't do it properly, or he gave us the wrong instructions, he'd get belted. He was a tough bloke Bert Mettam.[45]

The RMO of Pond's party was Captain Roy Mills. First impressions can be misleading. Signalman Jim Ling well remembered Mills being introduced to the men when Parry's group and Pond's men were formed into a single party at Tamarompat. 'He was over six feet, looked like a great big boy, exactly what he looked like. Rosy cheeked. And I can remember one of our fellows in the back row saying, "Jesus, we're getting a school boy for a bloody doctor!"'[46]

Corporal Bob Christie, 2/29th Battalion:

> He was a gentle man; a very quiet man; a very kind looking man . . . when we went to Thailand, he had virtually no equipment . . . and

almost immediately cholera came on ... the various diseases ... he looked after those men ... he walked up and down that line from Konkoita to Taimonta to Takanun, time and time again, to the different camps, because he was the only doctor ... and Mills got belted up on more than one occasion.[47]

Lance-Corporal John Roxburgh, 2/29th Battalion: 'I can remember Roy Mills when the Japs came and grabbed these blokes out of the hospital, really bloody sick blokes, and he'd cry, he'd just bloody openly cry, about what these bastards were doing to our really sick blokes.'[48]

As we have recorded with RMOs such as Captain Rowley Richards with 'A' Force and Captain Dave Hinder with Newton's 'U' Battalion of 'D' Force, all of them had to work in total isolation from colleagues; they had next to no basic drugs and equipment with which to work; and they had to try and combat the appalling squalor and filth of the camps. And underpinning all of this, one is struck yet again by the extreme youth of many of these doctors who, virtually at the beginning of their careers (Mills was 26 on the Railway) were placed in an unimaginable environment of filth, pain and suffering—and compounded by Japanese cruelty and abuse. And yet, totally trusted by their hundreds of patients, they triumphed.

While every POW on the Railway should have been classified as unfit for work, Captain Mills, in much the same fashion as Captains Richards and Hinder, employed an elaborate written classification system in an attempt to create a priceless day or days off. Mills used seven categories: 'H' for an in-patient in hospital; 'No' for no work at all; 'L3' for very light work; 'L2' for moderately light work; 'L1' for light work; 'MD' for medicine and duty; and where there was no entry, the POW was fit for duty.[49] By the use of such a detailed system, Mills hoped that by moving a POW's name between categories, he might gain some small recovery time. His records also contained a history of each man's illnesses. However, no amount of detailed categories for the sick, or a manipulation of that register, could allow for the arrival of an angry and violent Murayama or one or more of his soldiers demanding additional numbers for the day's slavery. Abuse, kicks, rifle butts and punches repeatedly forced men lying on a bamboo floor or in the mud to stagger to their feet and fill work quotas.

Captain Roy Mills was faced with two horrific cholera outbreaks—one at Taimonta and the other at Takanun:

> Stools burnt on blazing fires. Bed pans too small to cope with profuse stools—some almost 2 quarts [about 2.5 litres] in quantity . . .
>   Dehydration of cholera patient has to be seen to be believed. Nose looks really sharp, cheek bones terribly prominent—eyes roll upward giving dreadful appearance—skin of hands feet very wrinkled. Cramps in abdomen and legs almost unbearable—agonising but given immediate (almost) relief following commencement of saline.[50]

The origin of the 'almost immediate relief' was a masterstroke of improvisation. When his first cholera cases occurred at Taimonta, Mills filtered his saline into Japanese beer bottles and then 'boiled 300 cc Ampoule'. He then joined his stethoscope rubber to a cut thermometer case, and then to either a needle or bamboo cannula. Two saline infusions each of about 2.27 litres (about 4 pints) often saved a life.[51] At Takanun Captain Roy Mills treated 63 cholera cases of whom 25 died. During the two outbreaks of cholera he treated 102 patients for 44 deaths. Walker, in the Australian Official Medical History, would record that 'in the circumstances the results were remarkable'.[52]

Such was the despair of being taken to the cholera tent that some men, despite the best of treatment and care that could be given under the circumstances, considered it a death sentence. Corporal Bob Christie took to self-diagnosis and treatment:

> Suddenly I started to vomit and I started to pass motions—worms, everything came out. They took me straight back to camp, tested me and they said, 'You're a cholera carrier.' So they put me straight into the cholera tent, and in the cholera tent there were eight blokes . . . the eight blokes were laying in mud, it was teeming with rain, the tent was leaking, no floor boards . . . and I was put in there with a fellow named Henderson . . . and I said to Henderson, 'If we stay here we die, let's get out of here!' So we crawled out to the bamboo . . . and we laid in the bamboo with a ground sheet over us, I think it was for a day or

two days, and the disease went right through us and we came good. Nobody came near us, we never ate anything, we never did anything. When we were right, we were able to walk down to the gate—they had a fence around the cholera area—with rice for the blokes who were in the other tents, and we fed the other blokes. And there were orderlies there too. And then we built the funeral pyres to burn the fellows who died. I remember the first one we did the bloke sat up! We knew the blokes we were cremating—dreadful![53]

Captain Roy Mills won universal respect and admiration amongst all members of Pond's party. At a postwar reunion, Private Paddy O'Toole—a forthright man—would recall that: '. . . he said, "How are you?" And I said, "I'm good." And I shook him by the hand, and all I could say to him was, "Thanks very much, Sir!" I was dumbfounded!'[54]

The quantity, quality and availability of goods through both established canteens and the black market in the Takanun area are central to our understanding—and assessment—of the fortunes of Lieutenant-Colonel Pond's party at that camp, and by extension, his leadership. Lieutenant-Colonel Pond:

At Takanun troops had virtually no meat at all for the first month and the same policy of starving the sick was insisted upon again. Practically no vegetables at all were available either, though at nearby English camps each man was having ½ lb meat and plenty of green vegetables daily. The latter period at Takanun was better but still poor except for the party detached to the 2 Kilo camp who, under the guard OKAMURA, lived remarkably well with 1 lb meat per man per day and vegetables in proportion—an indication that food was available, as indeed was well known, for the troops [in transit and during carrying parties] had seen large quantities of tinned foods in local stores. With working hours up to 16 to 18 per day a rapid deterioration of health occurred here.[55]

We deal first with the sources and availability of money and goods.

It will be recalled that an examination was made in the last chapter of Boon Pong's contract with the Japanese to supply them along the Railway; of his relationship with the underground 'V' Organisation in the movement of money, extra food and limited drug supplies along the River Kwai; and his thriving business with POWs in the sale of watches, jewellery and other personal items. Further, it will be recalled that Boon Pong was not the sole barge trader along the River Kwai, but that his unique involvement with the 'V' Organisation and his contract with the Japanese certainly made him the most influential.

We have identified in the last chapter, Lieutenant-Colonel McEachern's citing of two fascinating 'V' Organisation sums of money: 'Up River Camps' 17 400.00 ticals and 'Various' 65 236.34 ticals.[56] The 'up-river' and 'various' were camps such as Tampie, Rin Tin, Takanun and as far north as Nieke. The extent of these donations which arrived in the British Takanun camp is therefore unclear, but it is highly likely that they were substantial. But we do have some concept of Boon Pong's activities. J. Coast in his *Railway of Death* has recorded that Boon Pong 'used to bring supplies by barge and "Pom Pom" right up to our area [Takanun] and beyond', and that he brought the British 'food, news and sometimes even free drugs'. As with Newton's 'U' Battalion, Coast also stated that Boon Pong 'advanced us generous sums against watches, rings and cigarette cases'.[57] Whilst Nieke was a far tougher proposition for Boon Pong's barges during the wet season, Takanun was always within his reach.

Mention should also be made of the significance of Nieke to the supply of goods. When passing through that village after the completion of the Railway, 'A' Force's Captain Rowley Richards observed its commercial wealth: '. . . it seemed beyond belief that we were now strolling through a relatively sophisticated village. We had re-entered civilisation, where people operated shops and markets, drove elephants and were policed by men in gold-braided uniforms.'[58]

Nieke, at the end of the River Kwai, was thus the northernmost point of commercial 'affluence' along that river lifeline. It should be understood that the British at Takanun were not well fed or watered, but what is asserted is that like Newton's 'U' Battalion further south, a critical trickle of money, food and drugs often tipped the balance between life and death. And the fact that the British chose to make generous donations to Pond's party when the general attitude on the Railway was quite understandably 'charity begins at home' is ample testimony to their ability to procure money and black market goods. Lieutenant-Colonel Pond:

> Mention must be made of the help given by English camps to the 700 party at Takanun. The officers at one English camp contributed $248—to buy food for the sick and medical treatment supplies and assistance were given by another hospital camp. In this regard it is desired to single out Lt. Col. WILLIAMSON, Lt. Col. LARKIN (I.A.), Maj. PYCOCK (R.A.O.C), Maj. PEMBERTON (R.A.M.C.) and Capt. LORD (R.A.S.C.) for the pains they went to, to actually get and bring food to our sick men.[59]

The truth is that Lieutenant-Colonel Pond failed to employ the very same sources of help for his men as had the British. In his papers, Pond would record that:

> In the first three months (in Thailand) I had no sickness personally, probably my system was better used to [words unclear, appears to be 'famine like'] foods than most, on account of my porridge eating at home. I was well fed as a child. Religious faith and thoughts of Jessie were a great standby in trouble.[60]

In the same document he recorded that:

> The English officers brought canteen supplies for us which were isolated (by the presence of cholera). (I noted) prices, eggs 15 cents each, condensed milk $2.50 a tin, herrings (in sauce) large $2.50 per tin, small 80 cents. We also got sugar, gula malacca [native sugar], peanuts, soya beans, sardines, whitebait, coffee, tea, biscuits ($3.50 per tin). These items (from the canteen) were a great help to the sick as the Japanese rations were very, very poor . . .

I was able to buy eggs, milk, sugar, biscuits, fish. (We did a little) private cooking (and produced) tapioca custard, omelettes, milky [unclear] tea etc (it should not be thought that these supplies were ever constant or even plentiful, but every now and again something became available).[61]

There would have been no shortage of POWs in his party who had a loving mother who fed them porridge as a child, had the love of a parent, wife or sweetheart at home, and who possessed ample 'religious faith'. But unlike their commander, many men in Pond's party regularly undertook between twelve and fourteen hours of hard labour daily; did not have any money nor goods to sell, and therefore did not have access to the barge supplies, nor the kindness of the British. The RSM, Warrant Officer Bert Mettam, is a case in point. Busily engaged in organising work party numbers with the adjutant each morning, and then accompanying the men out to a cutting, or ledge, or bridge—and often receiving a beating in the process—he quite simply had nothing to sell (his watch was stolen in Changi), and, whilst he knew of the British camp, never, at any time, could he remember receiving any 'extra' rations, goods or supplies. Lance-Corporal Roxburgh and Corporal Jim Kennedy are other examples of men who quite simply ate the 'normal' ration and suffered accordingly. Further, the officers' quarters were near the kitchen and as Corporal Bob Christie recorded: 'We wouldn't know what they were fed because we didn't see them eating, you see they never ate with the men.'[62] This in no way implies that all officers were necessarily given a privileged share of the rations, but, in terms of morale, the notion that they should have been seen to share their men's fate—and rations—would have been desirable. When some officers are perceived to live a privileged life and contribute virtually nothing around a camp, there are those who will react in the interests of self-preservation. It should be mentioned, in fairness, that Captain Barnett's diary records that Pond's party was paid twice on the Railway, which is confirmed by Corporal Christie's diary. Both Pond and Barnett also record that some items were purchased on a few occasions from the adjoining British camp for the hospital.

However, the resourcefulness of 'street savvy' POWs was no less prevalent in Pond's party than in others. Paddy O'Toole identified the purchase of such local goods as eggs, gula malacca and fruit from passing coolies. But scrounging items such as tinned fish and condensed milk from the barges was another matter, because Pond's party lacked the infrastructure and organisation of units such as Newton's 'U' Battalion. Paddy O'Toole:

> Well, it depends on the blokes working on the barge. Gangs might have gone down, ten men, or something like that, to unload the barge under Jap supervision. Now, it depends how cunning the blokes were. Like [Private] Dougy Cameron, he used to put stuff down his shirt, put stuff over the side of the barge [to someone in the water or to be picked up later]. Dougy Cameron, he was one of the best scroungers . . . C Company 2/29th Battalion.
>
> I came across the river one night with a box of the bastards! A box of condensed milk . . . I knocked it off from the stack [from the Jap supplies] We buried it in the camp under the fire place . . . At night time when things are quiet, you make up a billy full of milk . . . take it into your mates that are crook. Occasionally tinned fish, most stuff bobbed up, occasionally bobbed up.[63]

Corporal Jim Kennedy remembered Private J. C. (Jackie) Smerdon: 'he got it [food] for the sick blokes. He didn't get it to sell or anything like that.'[64] And such commodities as rice occasionally 'bobbed up' on carrying parties where POWs were ordered to carry stores from one venue to another. Paddy O'Toole: 'Fill your fucking pocket! You see a hand full [sic] of rice makes a good bowl full of rice once it's cooked.'[65]

When discussing his men's morale, Lieutenant-Colonel Pond concluded that:

> This was at times low, and petty thefts and evidence of selfishness occurred but morale greatly improved in latter months. Discipline among R.A.E. [Royal Australian Engineers] personnel was poor . . .
>
> A good deal of selling of personal effects and clothing occurred. Although every endeavour was made to stop this it was hard to blame troops for trying to obtain food by this means at a time when they were on starvation diet and had received no money.[66]

Blame them indeed. Some of the other ranks did engage in theft and were selfish. Stealing did take place, and morality aside, desperate men do desperate things. In an interview with the author, Corporal Jim Kennedy simply stated that: '... [stealing] drugs, yes, on the Railway, yes, there was one fella did it and he didn't survive. It wasn't the Japs that did him.'[67] The notion that Pond could condemn 'the selling of personal effects', and that 'every endeavour was made to stop this', smacks of an appalling set of double standards. Captain Adrian Curlewis, diary, 30 June 1943:

A morning drying out my pack and clothes and then the hardest decision I have ever made. For five weeks a sentry has tried to buy my watch. I have starved, literally, rather than part with it. Gula malacca and bananas became available in a kampong so from $25 I pushed him to $70. Starvation and sentiment do not go together, so I sold, paid my debts, made loans and felt stronger than ever ... To bed, not hungry for the first time for weeks.[68]

Captain Roy Mills, diary, 29 July 1943:

An I.J.A. soldier took a great fancy to my watch and after days of haggling on his part—myself having told him I wanted $110 for it more to scare him off than anything, since I must have a watch, he produced another waterproof watch and I accepted 47 dollars and his watch for mine—so I am wearing a watch originally owned by VX 53067 Pte L.P. Wallace with that name on the back and a Nippon soldier wears what I once owned. I think he is trading in watches. So I can pay $22 I owe and now really own a pair of boots costing $15. I was stony broke on the trip up and other officers were very generous in helping me out. Now I can repay the compliment.[69]

Curlewis's and Mills's diaries reveal the ability to procure tinned fish, gula malacca, condensed milk and fruit, and further, each were able to visit the British across the stream for the odd meal. Neither Curlewis or Mills were involved in anything other than a perfectly legitimate attempt to survive by trading their personal possessions. It is hard to escape the conclusion that when officers eat separately from their men and when a number of them dodge work and any form of responsibility for the care of those soldiers, the men would feel contempt for them and ill discipline would ensue.

A number of officers in Pond's party chose to flee Takanun and their responsibilities. Captain Ben Barnett, diary, 11 August 1943:

1700 hrs. I.J.A. Doctor asked Capt Mills to supply names of 150 men who should be evacuated to WYNYEA [Tarsau Base Hospital] ... Number to be evacuated to WYNYEA tomorrow increased to 80. Four more signals included—sigmn Ford, Newberry, Collins and Turnbull. Total 8 offrs (no signals) & 72 O/Rs.[70]

On the 14th, Barnett recorded that this number had been reduced to 70, and the probable date of departure was the 16th.[71] When 80 men were duly evacuated by barge, Captain Roy Mills despaired for the remaining 70 or so very sick men who the Japanese had promised would also go. His diary, 16 August 1943:

... we got away another 80 unfit men by barge down the river ... The information for the preparation of the rolls came one evening to be ready next morning. 150 names required—we got the worst 30 and then added the 8 worst from each company up to about 108. Unfortunately they only sent 80 or so apart from their very worst cases 2 companies missed out. I won't forgive myself for this if another boatload does not go.[72]

Captain Adrian Curlewis was more forthright. His diary, 17 August 1943:

Trench feet and diarrhoea got me. Back at 0400 hours from work. A wash and cup of coffee, half an hour in the latrines got me to bed at 0500. Sick parade at 0900 hours got me the day off. Yesterday another 80 men went down the river as too sick to work, including 10 officers. Selfishness and a sad story of illness got a few away and I am left as the old man of the camp. My reward (as the sick officers were all young men) was to overhear several conversations among the men, and some

to my face, of support and comradeship for me while they despised
their own officers of 2/29th.[73]

Paddy O'Toole, 2/29th Battalion: 'I thought he was alright. I thought
Curlewis, among the senior officers, was as good as there was.'[74] When given
a list of officers in Pond's party and asked to comment on their performance on the Railway, Corporal Bob Christie, the long-serving secretary of
the 2/29th Battalion Association and the keeper of exhaustive records of the
unit, used the diplomatic terms 'first class', 'active', 'occasionally active' and
'evacuated by barge Wanyea [sic]' to the author's list of officers. Whilst Mills,
Barnett, Curlewis and an additional few featured in the 'first class' category,
it is of interest to note that a number—not all—who were cited as 'evacuated
by barge Wanyea [sic]' simply had a blank by their names.[75] The ORs have
long memories. When, after the war, 2/29th Battalion reunions occurred,
there would be bitter recollections of officers in the swamp near Bakri who
absconded with all of the maps and compasses, and of a number of those
same officers who had been 'drones' around Takanun, and had left them for
Wanyea on 16 August 1943.

After completion of their work at Takanun in early September 1943,
Pond's party was moved through Tamarompat, Krian Krai, and through to
Taimonta, where they were engaged again in a prolonged stay. The period
was notable for repeated and exhausting work parties engaged in carrying
railway equipment from 'Nieke to Taimonta or from Taimonta to Konkoita'
with each party covering a return trek of around 24 kilometres.[76] Pond's
party's final agony came with the march to Nieke in early November 1943,
which was a prelude to their movement back to Kanchanaburi. Once again
there were instances of never-ending devotion to duty and service from some,
and despair and physical collapse in the case of others. On 6 November 1943,
Lance-Corporal John Roxburgh and Corporal Jim Kennedy witnessed both
in their 2/29th Battalion. John Roxburgh:

At one stage Bertie passed, I heard Bert Mettam going past...his
comment was, 'Pitches, [Private John Pitches] you don't deserve this,'
[he was carrying him] he was a signaller with us...and the background of Pitches was that when we'd first become POWs Pitches

isolated himself from everyone. He went out on working parties but he very much concentrated on Pitches by himself. Never had a mate . . . and he was older compared to James [Kennedy] and myself [Pitches was 37] . . . But in this march on this particular night, Mettam went past carrying Pitches [fireman hold]. When it was starting to get light, Bert went past again and he's got Pitches and he said, 'You don't deserve this Pitches, there's so many blokes a lot sicker than you are.' And Pitches' only comment in a drawl sort of voice was, 'You don't have to worry Mettam, I'll be dead by tomorrow.' And he died the next day.[77]

Private John Pitches succumbed to cardiac beriberi.[78] He sleeps in Than-byuzayat Cemetery in Burma—one trek too many. According to Rod Beattie's records, Pond's party suffered 142 deaths on the Railway.

※

In the end, Pond's party is a striking example of a commander on the Railway who, despite the best of intentions, was incapable of availing himself of the very same supply opportunities that prevailed just across the stream at the British camp. In short, the very plight experienced by the British when compared to the Australians at Tonchan, applied in reverse at Takanun. Lieutenant-Colonel Pond:

> Full advantage could not, however, be taken for the benefit of the men until the last month or so at TAIMONTA for a Japanese soldier was always in charge of the kitchen and dictated policy therein completely, even to the extent of giving orders which resulted in good food often being ruined and made unpalatable. It was always a struggle to get food from the Japanese and the provision of food by the party would have resulted in less being provided by the Japanese. Separate cooking however was always done for the sick 'under the lap' and latterly we were able to cook additional food in the kitchen.[79]

In an interview with the author, Private Paddy O'Toole, a most impressive scrounger, was asked whether Pond might have been able to recruit the services of some of his scroungers within the unit for the greater good. The answer was both rapid and blunt: 'Yes!'

Lance-Corporal John Roxburgh: 'Put it this way, I think we were what you'd call a disorganised bloody rabble, we had no bloody blokes [senior officers] in charge of us.'[80] Captains Ben Barnett, Adrian Curlewis and Roy Mills and his orderlies were, in addition to WO Bert Mettam, acknowledged by Roxburgh and others during interviews with the author as being notable exceptions. Unlike Captain Newton, Pond made few demands of his officers, was lax in establishing camp infrastructure and was unable or unwilling to rort the system to save his men. Lieutenant-Colonel Pond was certainly no Captain Reg Newton.

Konkoita, Taimonta and Nieke are but three Railway camps now lying under the vast Vajiralongkorn Dam. Rod Beattie has, during periods of low rainfall and corresponding low dam water levels, located the sites of a number of these camps, and found artefacts there. Along the approach to the dam, Rod pointed out the occasional embankment and the course of the Railway. We drove north, to where Nieke used to be. Soon we arrived at one of the most notorious camps along the infamous Thai–Burma Railway: Shimo (Lower) Songkurai. In mid-May 1943, the 2/30th and 2/26th Battalions occupied this camp for some two months.

We stood on a large rise and surveyed the surrounding landscape. Beattie: 'You're standing on Cholera Hill.' It was terribly hard not to develop an almost immediate state of depression there. The 2/30th's George Aspinall took a series of forbidden photos during his service as a POW. His photo of Cholera Hill is easy to relate to when you stand on the hill. To have been carried there and deposited in this two-tent 'hospital' with its bamboo floor, to have had a bamboo disc fitted to your wrist for identification purposes, while your life was literally draining away with gushes of vomiting and white diarrhoea, was to know that the end was probably near. Incredibly, as we stood there, Rod scratched in the discoloured earth of the cremation site and noticed a small metal disc just showing above the soil. He picked it up, cleaned it and handed it over to be deciphered. We found it read 'The Great World No 2577'. It seemed to be some sort of token. One can only ponder about its owner. Possibly it belonged to a despairing patient or an orderly who was jeopardising his chances of survival in the selfless care of others. That token must have evoked memories of taxi dancers, drinks and side shows, and of better times—that's what most Railway POWs longed for. They longed for Changi, Changi was home.[81] The disc is now in the hands of Rod Beattie and his Kanchanaburi museum.

On the morning of 15 May 1943, the men of trains 3 and some of 4 (chiefly the 2/26th Battalion), under the command of Major Tracey, arrived at Lower Songkurai. Later, 581 members of the 2/30th Battalion who had left Changi on train number 5, with a further 70 on train 6, arrived there on 17 May, under the command of Major Noel Johnston. After the torment of their forced march to the 'promised land' of better camps, food and facilities, the scenes that greeted them were devastating: '. . . a collection of roofless and dilapidated native huts . . . four 100-yard huts . . . a smaller hut for the guards and a little hut for the kitchen. The whole area of the camp was less than three hundred by one hundred yards.'[82]

A small stream lay at each end of the Lower Songkurai camp, which was to constitute the sole water supply for some 1800 Australians. Cholera hit Lower Songkurai immediately. Captain Lloyd Cahill (Australian Army Medical Corps) diagnosed the first case on 17 May and when he became sick, two medical officers were sent forward. We now come to the arrival in our story of another Railway hero, one who, like 'A' Force's Lieutenant-Colonel Bertie Coates, deserves the same status and fame as 'Weary' Dunlop.

Major Bruce Atlee Hunt was born at Glebe in Sydney on 23 February 1899. He had served in the Great War with the 8th Field Artillery Brigade in 1917, and after the Armistice, had journeyed to London where he completed a year's study in medicine at King's College London. After subsequently graduating in medicine at Melbourne University, and serving in a number of Melbourne hospitals, Hunt qualified as a Fellow of the Royal College of Physicians in 1928. He then moved to Perth, where he joined the Second AIF in August 1941. The following month, Hunt sailed to Malaya with the 2/13th Australian General Hospital. He was '. . . broad shouldered, balding early, with aquiline features and walked with a curious short-stepped shamble'.[83]

Hunt's work in Changi at the combined hospital was notable for combating a dysentery outbreak and for undertaking a dietary analysis of the Changi ration. But it was on the Railway, against all the odds, that Bruce Hunt triumphed.

In a POW environment, news of acts of selflessness, great determination and sheer guts travel like wildfire. Hunt had established such a reputation from the time 'F' Force left Bampong. Private John Boehm had been left behind by his 2/29th Battalion early on the trek through illness. He would subsequently join the 2/30th at Lower Songkurai:

> I was with him [Hunt] on the way up, I remember marching beside him, he was talking about the First World War. He was a man of over six feet . . . a raw boned man, wiry, he'd march like no one's business . . . very straight to the point, no mucking around—a very likable bloke.[84]

Hunt repeatedly marched back and forth along his column, instructing his orderlies how to best look after the sick and struggling, carried men's packs and arranged where possible for those in need of a brief respite to stay behind under the care of others. But it was at Tarsau that the legend of Bruce Hunt really began.

Prior to the departure of his party from that camp, Hunt had gained a Japanese doctor's permission to leave 37 men behind—27 with infected feet and ten dysentery cases. However, the Japanese guard gave permission for only ten of the 37 to stay. When Hunt defiantly paraded the 37 and stood out in front of them, the Japanese corporal immediately attacked the interpreter, Major Wild, and set upon him with a fist to the face and an even more painful bamboo stick to the crutch. Hunt was next, and wrote that he: '. . . was immediately set upon by three guards. One tripped me, while others pushed me to the ground. The three men set about me with bamboos, causing extensive bruising of the skull, hands and arms, and a fractured left 5 metacarpal bone.'[85] Inspiring, but hardly a new occurrence on the Railway. According to a bystander, it was what happened next that was truly stirring. When the watching POWs became restive, a nasty but futile incident might have occurred, but the defiant Hunt exclaimed: 'Keep out of this you blokes, this is my fight!'[86] When approached to travel north by truck, Hunt 'deeply resented' the idea and further exclaimed, 'My duty is to protect the men!'[87]

Hunt, Captain John Taylor and fifteen orderlies arrived at Lower Song-kurai to assist Captain Lloyd Cahill on 18 May 1943. The night before, one man died of cholera. On the 18th, twelve suspects were immediately placed in the new cholera ward: 'Cholera Hill.' Despite the fact that the whole camp was inoculated on 19 May, cholera deaths mounted. We are blessed with a comprehensive diary written by the 2/30th Battalion's intelligence officer, Lieutenant Ron Eaton, in which a consistent record of Hunt's activities at Lower Songkurai becomes clear. Eaton, 27 May 1943:

> There have been 22 cholera deaths to date ... Total cases at present 55—situation now all but out of hand medically. Major Hunt, S.M.O., places responsibility on us to help ourselves. He and John Taylor and Lloyd Cahill have been lion men—marvellous show—goodness knows how they keep up. Bob Howells after chat with us in which we agreed if any action were to be started it would have to come from Bruce Hunt and selves. Went to B.H. this morning and put position frankly. Whole show just plainly up to us alone. Recce of area—jobs to be done at which camp C.O. plus Bn. COs attended then straight to Japs. B.H. put fear of death into them.
>
> Immediate result—300 men in camp remain in camp and put to work in camp for balance of day plus assurance of staying for 3 days to put camp in livable order—whole camp ...
>
> B. Hunt now has hospital as follows: Cholera on hill—Dysentery ward, Fever ward, total patients 586, which compares with an A.G.H. [Advanced General Hospital].[88]

Hunt immediately ordered that fires were to be kept in each hut for the purpose of sterilising eating utensils; all water was to be boiled before consumption; the surface filth from the camp was to be scraped from the area and burnt; old and nearly full latrines were to be fired and new ones dug; and, finally, he gave the POWs of Lower Songkurai a chilling message: 'If a fly alights on the rice you are about to eat, the grains it lands on must be spooned out and burnt, for I assure you, if one contracts cholera, one dies in great distress.'[89] And in a stirring response to his plea for volunteers for the cholera and dysentery patients, Hunt received more offers than he required—75 men responded.

On 29 May Eaton recorded that the Japanese had 'broken their promise and we sent out 750 men to work', which impinged upon the desperately needed work around the camp. This did not deter Hunt. Arriving back at Lower Songkurai that day, he immediately wrote a scathing document which was signed by Johnston, Anderson and Tracey. We have recorded the futility of worded protests. However, in Hunt's case the document was accompanied by the force of his personality and by the 'scare tactics' of a forceful implication that death and suffering were in store not only for the POWs, but for the Japanese, if inoculation and hygiene measures were not observed. Eaton also recorded that while the above-named officers signed the document, they were 'HIS [Hunt's] demands', and that it produced 'immediate results'.[90] Once again, numbers of men were allowed to work in camp rather than on the Railway. Two days later, Eaton reported that Lower Songkurai was under the command of a 'medical dictatorship' and 'advisably so'.[91] At this time, there were about 90 patients on Cholera Hill and there had been over 40 deaths. Before the second cholera needle could be given, and before Hunt's dynamic leadership initiatives could be thoroughly implemented, 101 men out of 209 diagnosed succumbed to this wretched killer.

Our focus upon the dreaded cholera outbreak amongst the men of 'F' Force should not cloud the multitude of other—and common—Railway medical conditions which also took their toll amongst the force. Corporal Arthur Isaac, 2/30th Battalion:

> I had a bloke in my section Tommy Lee . . . a bloke from up the north coast [of NSW] . . . a round faced bloke, not very big, and I went to the hospital hut one day, and Tommy was there. It took me all my time to recognise him, he had beri beri, and it had all gone to the top half of his body. He was almost twice his size . . . and beside him was another bloke, who wasn't in my section but I knew him very well. He had beri beri and it affected his mid-section, and you'd think he was pregnant, his stomach was out like that. I went and saw them this afternoon, late, I was talking to them there, next morning they'd gone.[92]

And there were the 'usual' numbers of tropical ulcers. Private Neville Riley, 2/30th Battalion:

When I was in the hospital . . . an ulcer on the foot, I couldn't get out, I couldn't walk. The fluid would start running out of the ulcer . . . pus . . . you'd have a bandage if you were lucky, and they'd take you out, and scrape it out with a spoon . . . scrape the bad flesh out until it started to bleed. The bandage you had, you didn't get one every day, that was your bandage. What they used to do was take the bandage off . . . and these camps were full of a lot of blow flies . . . and they'd come in droves. And you'd put your bandages there full of pus and muck from your ulcer, and let the flies clean the bloody bandage . . . and if you had a bit of warm water at all, you'd try and rinse the bandage in that, and then you'd put it back over your foot that had been scraped out by the spoon. And that was it! . . . it started off with a bamboo spike that stabbed me just above the toe nail, and it gradually got worse and worse, and it spread between my toes and up my foot . . .

When I was in the hospital ward up there . . . they didn't waste anything from the yak, they used to cook the blood and make a little cube about two inches square and about three quarters of an inch thick, and the bloke used to come around the hospital ward. And they'd have a few of these to hand out to some of the blokes. And they'd look around to see who would benefit most. And you'd think, 'Gee, I hope he picks me!' . . . a little bit of cooked blood![93]

On 3 June, Eaton recorded that: 'Bruce Hunt, John Taylor and Lloyd Cahill should all receive highest Award [sic] for their wonderful unceasing efforts. They alone have saved this camp from almost complete destruction.'[94] Throughout 'F' Force's tragic Railway saga, Major Bruce Hunt worked tirelessly for the men. Lieutenant Kelsey, 2/26th Battalion:

Of the scores of memories one has of this remarkable man, one stands out. It is a picture of him visiting the sick, himself exhausted and recently beaten, and pausing to place a hand gently on a feverish forehead, and murmuring in his beautiful accent, 'Poor old boy. God rest his soul.'[95]

But surely, in any military formation, the ORs are the hardest to impress and often offer the most simple, but sincere tributes. Corporal Arthur Isaac, 2/30th Battalion: 'He [Hunt] was in our camp a fair bit but he used to travel to all the other [F Force] camps as well . . . the blokes thought he was God!'[96]

<hr/>

If Major Bruce Hunt was an 'F' Force 'giant' then a number of 'little men' in that force had indeed become very much 'smaller'. Lieutenant Ron Eaton, 27 June 1943:

Will never forget sight of hungry faces, the use of fly blown latrines. The sight of hundreds of our men in tattered clothing . . . returning from a terrible day of work in mud & slush in the dark to a meagre food issue to slump and rest on hard floors only to rise the morrow in the dark and eat and go again. And still they smile. There have been some wonderful examples of manhood here and there have been cases showing a deplorable lack of it. The little men become smaller and the big men become giants. Many have been the disappointments.[97]

As per Pond's party at Takanun, there were a number of officers and NCOs who acted out of a determined sense of duty to their men at Lower Songkurai. Lieutenant Eaton was an example. Corporal Arthur Isaac, 2/30th Battalion: 'He would go close to being the standout leader, yeah.'[98] Corporal Neville Riley held the same view.[99] But dynamic leadership is always required at the top. It would seem that Major Noel Johnston's health suffered from the enormity of events. On 23 May 1943, Eaton recorded that: 'C.O. quit duties'; on 31 May: 'Maj. Johnston to hospital—extreme nervous stomach upset—vomited for 10 hrs—thought at first cholera—needs rest—now much better.'; on 6 June 1943: 'Major Johnston still ill back from hospital but quite ineffective.'; on 7 June 1943: 'Major Johnston back to hospital—nervous dyspepsia—not well and obviously needs rest.'[100]

A number of officers at Lower Songkurai seemed to suffer a similar ailment to some of their 'colleagues' at Takanun. Sergeant Stan Arneil, 2/30th Battalion Diary, 21 September 1943: 'Only *one* officer has died in this camp, they are *all* well, have neither ulcers nor itch and are all well shod. But Burns said! The lice have no class distinctions.'[101] The lice may not have, but there seems to have been definite 'class distinctions' with regards to rations, clothing and privileges at Lower Songkurai.

Arneil's diary cites no small number of indiscretions from his officers. He mentions a $10 Thai money loan made by him and a mate to two officers, which was paid back in 'worthless ruppees'; at number 1 camp Songkurai, he talked of shirts from the dead being taken by needy ORs and a result-ant diatribe from an officer about 'lowness and lack of principle', when, in fact, that very same officer had acquired items in exactly the same way; of supplies brought into the camp and the ORs receiving token amounts while officers were treated most generously; and 'the utter spinelessness of two of our officers in not having the courage to ask the IJA for permission to leave a dying man in the cholera ward instead of carting him across to the main camp' for a check parade. The man died during his short journey.[102] Arneil also cited the hope and anticipation by the ORs of a soon-to-arrive consign-ment of goods for the opening of a canteen. It had taken two carrying parties each of 100 men to bring the supplies into camp. Arneil's diary recorded the generous officer allowance of 3 October 1943: 'Officers drew more than a quart of gula each and the same of sugar, four tins of fish, tins of milk and as much soap, tobacco and oil as they wanted.' The men, Arneil recorded, were limited to '7½ *pints* of sugar for the Company of 250 men'. Further, Arneil recorded, the ORs were given 'no milk or peanuts and only three tins of fish for the Company'.[103] It should again be stressed that such behaviour was *not* universal on the Railway. What is strongly advanced is that the incidence of what Captain Reg Newton described as 'drones around the place' was signifi-cant, and further, that in a number of formations it was common. There was a definite pattern to the consequences of weak leadership in Railway camps. Private Jack Coffee was at Upper Songkurai:

> I was messing in with two other blokes and I was the only one that
> possessed a wallet. As they got any money they'd give it to me and
> I was the banker ... some bugger had got into my haversack during

the night, and he'd taken me wallet and what money we had, and mum had given me a gold watch, stolen me watch, although it was worth big money, I was determined to get this watch home . . .[104]

Private John Boehm had his boots stolen, Stan Arneil and his mate had $15 (a significant sum) taken, and a never-ending market for boots, clothing and all manner of saleable items existed.

By the end of July 1943, the appalling conditions and meagre diet at Lower Songkurai; the difficulties in the transportation of supplies from Nieke along barely serviceable, boggy tracks to it; the terrible toll taken by the cholera outbreak; and the usual Railway deaths from dysentery, diarrhoea and beriberi—had all combined to reduce the number of men fit for work to 375 out of a total of 1854. A staggering 1265 were in hospital and 214 were engaged in camp duties. At Upper Songkurai just over half of its 430 Australian POWs were in 'hospital'. The final Australian 'F' Force deaths up until the end of May 1943 were 1060 out of 3662.[105] (Major Alan Thompson recorded that 3425 had left Changi.)

The British deaths numbered 2036 out of around 3500. Wigmore has recorded that the average British monthly death rate between May and December 1943 was over 360, and that 'dysentery and diarrhoea had combined to kill 832 men, while 637 had died of cholera alone'.[106] We have noted at the beginning of this chapter that the British, out of their quota of around 3500 Changi inmates for 'F' Force, sent about 1000 unfit men, whilst the Australians sent 'not more than 125'. This surely explains in part why their death rate was so high. Wigmore adds another intriguing point:

The Japanese seemed determined to break the British troops and to discriminate between them and the Australians. No Englishmen was permitted to be employed in the cookhouse or on any other camp duty, so that all were available for working parties despite their age or physical condition.[107]

In general terms, therefore, the very high English death rate in 'F' Force is in part explained by the above two critical factors that did not apply to the Australians.

Lieutenant-Colonel Kappe's ineffectual command of 'F' Force began on the train from Changi. It will be recalled that he accompanied Lieutenant-Colonel Pond's 2/29th Battalion on train number 2 from Singapore. Pond:

> (I noted that) the position of Brigadier [referring to his later promotion] C.H. Kappe (who was the senior AIF officer in the F Force party on the Burma Railway) was invidious on the train, on the march and in the Konkoita and Taimonta camps. He was not popular with the troops.[108]

Newton would record that as Pond's battalion passed through his 'U' Battalion camp at Tarsau, Kappe interfered with Pond's command of his battalion, and having been given eggs for the men from Newton's funds, 'was not happy' when Newton asked him for a contribution to that cost, and only paid the next morning just before his party's departure.[109] After Kappe left Pond's party and journeyed to Lower Songkurai, Eaton's diary—and other recollections—provide us with an inexcusable trail of incompetence, sheer neglect and the total abuse of the privileges of command.

Eaton's diary 1 July 1943: 'Lt.Col. Kappe arrived to take over command of camp.' Four days later: 'Kappe still Hors de Combat [outside the fight] . . .' On 11 July: 'Address by Lt.Col. Kappe and Maj Johnston to all Offrs. General blah excuses for Senior Officers.'[110] Private John Boehm well remembered Kappe at Lower Songkurai:

> What I know of him personally, is that he lined us up one evening after work when it was nearly dark, 'I know what you think of me,' he said, 'But I have to look after myself to get home to report all this.' And the boys had a bit of a giggle, And he said, 'I'll find the man that did that.' And so we all had a bit of a giggle, and nothing more was said. And it was just after that he left our camp . . . that is the only time I saw him . . . he didn't have any patched clothes on that's for sure . . . he looked physically well. And I know for a fact that the

doctors and kitchen staffs hated his guts because he . . . demanded what he wanted . . .

His nick name was 'Kappe-yama'.[111]

Kappe most certainly 'demanded what he wanted'. In his autobiography, Captain Fred Stahl (from Kappe's own 8th Division Signals) would write that:

> . . . an Australian Lieutenant Colonel [*sic*] arrived from Nike [*sic* Nieke] to take over command of our troops. One of his first acts was to issue an instruction that he was to receive double rations. The reason was, he said, 'Someone must go back to tell the story of this bastardry and I am the one best qualified to do it.' Despite protests he insisted on his order being carried out.[112]

Eaton's diary, 19 July 1943: 'Some men are low, very low. Kappe has choice so have I . . .' On 28 July: 'Party 300 from Con. Depot left to No. 3 Camp [Upper Songkurai] under Lt.Col. Kappe. Bruce Hunt returns . . . all this Camp to No. 3. How long O Lord How long—'[113] On 6 August 1943, Eaton arrived at Upper Songkurai with a 2/30th Battalion contingent:

> On arrival at No.3 Upper Songkurai it was a sea of mud. Small camp not prepared for recent trebling in numbers. Lt.Col. Kappe completely despondent. Toyama and Fukuda [Japanese commanders] doing just as they please . . .
>
> Arrive new camp to find Kappe completely 'Jap Happy' and the place one large amount of chaos and confusion. Reg Swartz [Major 2/26th Battalion] doing whole task himself. Kappe completely non-active and not accepting any responsibility for camp. No plan latrines huts hell of a mess. Kitchen hell of a mess. Camp on sea of mud.[114]

It will be remembered that this camp was a small one and was made up originally of a mixed contingent of around 393 Australians. Amongst them was the 2/29th's Private Jack Coffee:

Jack Haig [Warrant Officer 2/29th Battalion] had to report to this Colonel Kappe every night, and Colonel Kappe used to say to him, 'Now don't come any closer ... it's imperative that I get home and I don't want to pick up any germs.' And he'd speak to Jack Haig twelve feet away. Haig told me that—that was common knowledge. But I don't think I saw Kappe all the time I was there.[115]

The author has not been able to find any evidence of what amount or proportion of the 'F' Force funds were spent by Lieutenant-Colonel Kappe during its tragic stay on the Railway. Further, no evidence has been found of any sums given to the four battalion commanders by him. But we shall record a final incident in the next chapter concerning the fate of at least a part of that money.

———

In late October 1943, track-laying parties operating from the south and north met near Konkoita. Within two months the Railway was fully operational. We now turn to the fate of the members of our 'A', 'D' and 'F' Force case studies.

30

'WHERE ARE THE REST, MAJOR?'

———⟫•⟪———

Although our Railway case studies have concentrated on units in 'A', 'D' and 'F' Forces, brief mention should be made of subsequent formations containing Australians sent from Changi. On Anzac Day 1943, 1500 men comprising 'G' Force left Singapore by sea for Japan with 200 Australians amongst them; between 5 and 13 May the 2950-strong 'H' Force left Changi for the Railway, which included 600 Australians under the command of Lieutenant-Colonel Oakes; on 15 May, 900 men of 'J' Force sailed for Japan, of whom 300 were Australians (there was no 'I' Force); an officers' party of around 320 including 70 Australians known as 'H6' left Changi for the Railway on the 17th; and, finally, two medical units—'K' and 'L' Forces totalling 30 medical officers and 200 orderlies—were sent for Railway work during June 1943. Those small forces were essentially raised with the same Japanese lies and broken promises that had been made to preceding units. 'H' and the 'H6 Force' were formed to supplement the rapidly diminishing numbers of POWs who were needed to complete the Railway on schedule, whilst 'K' and 'L' Forces consisted of medical personnel belatedly deployed to support coolie units ravaged by poor hygiene standards, malnutrition and disease, with a resultant appalling death rate.

Apart from the retention of small parties from all forces for the purpose of Railway maintenance, the completion of the Railway in late October 1943 saw the Japanese begin to concentrate the bulk of their prisoners in six main camps at Thailand's southern end of the line: Nakom Paton, Nong Pladuk, Tamuang, Kanchanaburi, Tamarkan and Chungkai. This process was completed between late November 1943 and March 1944. We now turn to the fate of the men of our three case studies.

—◦◦◦—

'A' Force in Burma was transported by train to Tamarkan. The process was long and tedious with large numbers of men having to be moved from a number of camps, rolls prepared and the sick accommodated. Brigadier Varley's diary, 20 December 1943:

> Movements would be as follows: 20–25 Dec, 55 K. [kilometre] Hospital camp. 27–29 Dec: 100 K (5 branch); 30 Dec—4 Jan: 105 K. 5–10 Jan: 108–112–114 K. [kilo camps] 11–12 Jan: 131–133 K. The journey will take 2 nights and 2 days. Food and water will be available at 133 K, 207 K. 296 K.[1]

On Christmas Eve 1943, Varley described the 'A' Force move from the 55 Kilo hospital camp:

> Nos. moved nightly as follows: 20 Dec, 221; 21 Dec, 254; 22 Dec, 238; 23 Dec, 254; 24 Dec, 253; 25 Dec, 208. making a total of 1428, comprising 956 Australians, British and Americans, 472 Dutch. Sitting patients 28 per van; stretcher cases 8 plus 2 sitting and 2 orderlies. This leaves 260 all ranks in 55 kilo camp . . .[2]

On 3 January 1944, Brigadier Varley, two other officers and 282 ORs entrained to Kanchanaburi and arrived at Tamarkan on the 4th. Accompanying the 55 Kilo hospital camp personnel was Lieutenant-Colonel Albert Coates, who was posted as the senior medical officer of the Number 3 and 5 Branches at Tamarkan, while Lieutenant-Colonel Ramsay became the camp's CO.

Brief mention should be made of the further outstanding service of Lieutenant-Colonel Albert 'Bertie' Coates. On 5 March 1944, the Japanese appointed him as Chief Medical Officer and consulting surgeon of what was to become the largest of all of the Railway hospital camps: Nakom Paton. From April 1944, batches of about a thousand patients began arriving at the recently completed hospital and by August Coates commanded a staff of over twenty specialists, numerous orderlies and 7353 patients. Nakom Paton contained 50 huts each able to accommodate 200 patients; cubicled latrines were constructed; cookhouses were built at one per thousand POWs; a separate concrete floor surgical block was made with three operating tables; and some measure of the success of the hospital was the fact that around 896 operations were performed by Coates and his team with a mortality count of eighteen.[3] Coates would spend the remainder of the war at Nakom Paton.

In early 1944, in response to a shortage of technical expertise and labour for heavy industry, the Japanese decided to send some 10 000 POWs to Japan. These men were to be drawn chiefly from the Thailand POW groups—which did not include 'F' and 'H' Forces—and were selected by Japanese doctors on the basis of age and health. The fortunes of those 'Japan Parties' were mixed. The Japanese planned that such groups would be first moved to Saigon and then by sea to Japan. While shipping shortages and the mounting menace of American submarines caused some of those parties to stay in Saigon, others, originally sent there, were later sent to Singapore pending shipment to Japan. Two Japan parties are of interest to our story.

On 6 September 1944, 2300 POWs under the command of Brigadier Varley—sent first from the Railway to Saigon and then to Singapore—left by ship for Japan. About one thousand of these were British and sailed on the *Kachidoki Maru*, while a further 716 Australians and 600 British troops boarded the *Rakuyo Maru*.[4] The latter vessel also carried Brigadier Varley, Colonel Melton of the US Air Force and Group Captain Moore of the RAF. Those three officers were to be dropped off at the senior officers' camp in transit to Japan. Upon embarkation neither ship displayed a Red Cross sign. After leaving Singapore the convoy was reinforced off the Philippines, and consisted then of seven transports, two oil tankers and six escorts.

During the early hours of 12 September 1944, the convoy was attacked by American submarines off Hainan. A destroyer escort was torpedoed first and then at around 5.30 am the two tankers were hit. The *Rakuyo Maru*, sailing at the rear of the convoy, almost immediately became silhou-etted against the tankers. It was not long before screaming Japanese on the bridge identified a 'tin fish' approaching. The initial explosion, soon followed by a second, forced water over the ship and down the hold where the POWs were housed. The Japanese crew almost immediately abandoned ship in ten lifeboats; they left two further boats on board which were rusted to the davits and unable to be released. Most of the Australians then took to the water.

Despite its two torpedo hits, the *Rakuyo Maru* remained afloat for about twelve hours. Captain Richards and one of his 2/15th Field Regiment gunners then began to attempt to launch the remaining starboard lifeboat. After a number of men returned to the stricken ship, the lifeboat was released and around 60 men, some in the water and others in the lifeboat, now drifted in the vicinity of the *Rakuyo Maru*. During the mid-afternoon another party returned to the ship, and managed to release the port lifeboat, which was occupied by one officer and about 30 ORs who decided to sail eastwards. They were not seen or heard of again.

During that afternoon, Japanese corvettes returned to the scene and rescued their comrades from the ten lifeboats, which allowed the Austra-lians to occupy them. By the end of the day, and just before the *Rakuyo Maru* sank, there were then four distinct groups of POW survivors: one group of four lifeboats under the command of Captain Richards sailing west; another under Varley's command consisting of seven boats also sailing west; one further boat sailing eastwards; and the last consisted of a number of luckless survivors who remained in the area clinging to rafts and wreckage. Near midnight that night the *Kachidoki Maru* was torpedoed and sank in twenty minutes. Of her 1000-strong POW contingent, about 520 were later rescued.

Fate can be a cruel master. Two days later, on 14 September 1944, Richards's group of four lifeboats, numbering around 80 Australians and 56 British POWs, were rescued by a Japanese frigate. Those 136 men joined the survivors of the *Kachidoki Maru*. The British survivors from that vessel had suffered cruelly—'coated in oil which burned their skins',[5] or badly sunburnt. This large group sailed to Hainan-To Harbour and eventually made their way by sea to Moji, Japan.

The fate of the other seven lifeboats is tragic indeed. In an interview with the author, Private Wal Williams distinctly remembered hearing gunfire in the distance just before being picked up.[6] In his book, *A Doctor's War*, Captain Rowley Richards would record that he had, on a number of occasions, asked the Japanese commander what had happened to Brigadier Varley's group of seven lifeboats. The Japanese answer gave him little satisfaction. He merely pointed to the other corvettes. Captain Richards would later record that:

> Varley's group of boats was never seen again nor, to my knowledge, has any evidence ever surfaced to suggest the absolute truth of their fate. Those of us who heard the gunfire shortly before we were rescued have only ever believed that their end was swift.[7]

Here we have yet another example of the almost total unpredictability of Japanese behaviour: one group rescued, the other murdered. So much for a labour shortage in Japan. Varley's end was a tragic one for a soldier who had given his all as a battalion commander on the Malay Peninsula, as a newly promoted brigadier during the fighting on Singapore Island and as the CO of 'A' Force in Burma.

Perhaps the luckless, oil-covered survivors of the *Rakuyo Maru* who, unable to gain a lifeboat passage, had clung to rafts and wreckage and had been forced to remain in the area would have stood the least chance of survival. But providence decreed otherwise. During the period 13–17 September 1944 some 141 of them—including 80 Australians—were rescued by American submarines and taken to Saipan and then several of them to Australia. These men provided some of the first news of captivity under Nippon, and gave chilling accounts of conditions on the Thai–Burma Railway.

Of the 2300 POWs under Varley's command who had left Singapore on the two ships, a total of about 656 were rescued by the Japanese. Ahead lay more hard labour and deprivation in Japan before war's end.

Captain Reg Newton's 'U' Battalion of 'D' Force found themselves at Rin Tin camp around the time of the completion of the Railway. Having heard that there was a camp in the area containing a number of Australians and that they were 'in a bad way', Newton trekked some ten kilometres to investigate. What he found yet again illustrates the peculiar mix of factors which could mean the difference between life and death for POWs in any given battalion on the Railway. The camp was called Kewie and here Newton found approximately 1500 Dutch POWs amongst whom was Major Alf Cough's 'V' Battalion of 'D' Force (mainly men from the 2/4th Machine Gun Battalion). Newton would later write:

> Things had gone hard with them with the Japanese 'treatment' and being under the Dutch command as they had no control of their work figures and always received the thin end from the Dutchies; they had had little medical attention as it was centered mainly on the Indonesians and above all they had no representation on the rations and in the kitchens and consequently had to take what they were given. Alf Cough had never received any of the Changi funds nor stores and had little canteen contact, and depended wholly on what he was given by the Dutch.[8]

And that wasn't much.

One of Newton's great qualities as a Railway commander was his ability to not only rort the system for the benefit of his 'U' Battalion men, but where possible, for others. 'Roaring Reggie' 'arranged', as he called it, for Cough to make contact with the Japanese commander—a privilege denied Cough by the Dutch CO—and promptly organised a 'V' Battalion carrying party to journey down to Rin Tin where Newton would give them 'what we could' and further arranged for Boon Pong to land supplies at Kewie.[9] Newton lost contact with Cough after this visit, but the meeting raises a number of interesting Railway issues. First, it seems clear that the funds taken from Changi by force commanders, whilst difficult to administer after battalions became dispersed, were at times used for questionable, and on some occasions, immoral purposes. Second, Cough's plight displays the frequent tendency of national groups—and often battalions—to adopt a self-centered approach to the limited money, food supplies and drugs that made their way along the River Kwai and, in the case of foodstuffs, through local sources.

Third, the incident is a vivid illustration of the fact that mortality rates on the Railway are misleading when given per force rather than by battalion. Whilst a POW's chances of survival on the Railway were influenced by such factors as his geographical location, whether or not he succumbed to any number of diseases, and his treatment by the Japanese, the predominant survival factor was his *shoko*, his unit commander. When this officer worked efficiently for, and together with the RMO, his chances significantly increased.

On 5 April 1944, 'U' Battalion was entrained to Tamuang (about eleven kilometres south of Kanchanaburi) and arrived there on the 6th. Eight days later Captain Gaden and the unit's hospital sick arrived from Chungkai. On 10 June Newton was informed that 'all fit men would go to Japan from the Thailand area and there would be three forces of 2500 each'.[10] The Japanese had originally planned that Varley would command the first, Newton the second and Lieutenant-Colonel McEachern the third. It later transpired that McEachern's group did not make the trip—partly due to the US Navy's submarine presence—and spent their remaining time in captivity in Thailand.

Newton left Captain Keith Westbrook (2/19th Battalion and 'U' Battalion) in charge of those members of his unit who were to be left behind in Thailand and took Captains Hinder and Parker as his RMOs. Ever even-handed with his funds, he gave Westbrook his proportion and then determined how best to use the remaining $942. As the currency would be of no value in Japan, Newton made cash purchases of cigarettes with the idea of selling them in Singapore to facilitate food supplements both there and during the voyage to Japan. The cigarettes were duly bought—560 cartons—and spread amongst the men for secure passage to Singapore. Ever the astute businessman, Newton was 'sure we could make some contact with Chinese traders in Singapore particularly as The Tiger was going with us and he would be looking for his rake-off'.[11]

Newton Force arrived in Singapore by train on 26 June 1944 and were sent to River Valley Road camp. Although three-quarters of the cigarettes were sold for an impressive threefold profit, the acute shortage of goods for sale and highly inflated prices made the purchasing of goods difficult. No matter. Newton managed to buy coconuts and peanuts for his men, and when still faced with the problem of excess money and few goods, he approached the Tiger and 56 pounds of sun-dried fish and 24 pounds of fish paste were procured (with, undoubtedly, a cut going to the Tiger).[12] This transaction would mark the end of 'business' for Newton. Japan would offer no such chances. Newton Force (2250 men) departed in two ships from Singapore on 1 July 1944 and after stops in Borneo, the Philippines and Formosa arrived at Moji, Japan on 8 September. There would be no cohesion of units in Japan. Newton's 'U' Battalion was dispersed, and his Japan Party would henceforth consist of men from the 2/19th, the 2/3rd Machine Gun Battalion and a number of sailors from the *Perth*.

We have recorded that the POWs of 'F' and 'H' Forces were not under the command of the Thailand Japanese Railway administration, and as such were to be returned to Changi after the completion of the line. Nieke was used as a concentration point for 'F' Force pending a Railway trip to Kanchanaburi, which was to be followed by either a train or ship journey back to Singapore. As was the case with other forces, the completion of the Railway came too late for some—particularly a number of patients from Tanbaya Hospital.

Tanbaya had been a belated response from the Japanese in late July 1943 for an 'F' Force hospital, which was to be situated in Burma at the then deserted 50 Kilo camp—50 kilometres from the northern end of the Railway at Thanbyuzayat. Major Bruce Hunt had been a passionate advocate for such a hospital, which the Japanese ruled could house up to 2000 patients, but was to be occupied only by POWs who had permanent disabilities, or were unlikely to recover within two months for heavy work.

Captain Fred Stahl, 8th Division Signals, was the Tanbaya Hospital adjutant. He would later recall that upon arrival in early August as a member of the advanced party, the camp 'inspired no pleasure'.[13] As the rain continued to fall, and in the 'complete absence of drains', the area was a sea of mud upon which stood huts in very poor condition; there were no initial cooking facilities; few tools; the operating 'theatre' was a small bamboo hut with a bamboo operating table; and the hospital was destined to have no chaplain at any time during its existence.

Between 8 August and 7 September 1943, eighteen parties of British
and Australian patients arrived at Tanbaya.[14] The fact that its patients were
exceedingly ill before their departure caused them to arrive at the hospital
in a deplorable condition. Stahl recorded that many of them were in 'their
final days of life, with absolutely no hope of survival', while a number were
found dead on arrival.[15] The total Tanbaya intake of patients was 1924 and
of those 661 died by 24 November 1943.[16]

Religious or spiritual matters aside, the absence of a chaplain would
seem innocuous. But on 13 August, only days after their arrival, two English
soldiers died. Unable to have graves dug because of an absence of fit men,
Captain Fred Stahl had to resort to cremating the dead. He would later recall:

> . . . before leaving Shimo Sonkrai [sic] I had obtained from the
> Anglican Chaplain a copy of a brief funeral service. I co-opted
> Warrant Officer John Kerr to assist me and together we built a
> funeral pyre . . . the two bodies were laid on the top of the pile of
> wood and bamboos and the fire was lit . . .
>
> I was walking past the fire a little later with our surgeon Frank
> Cahill, when Frank suddenly exclaimed, 'My God, he's waving to us.'
> It was almost literally true. Quite inexperienced in the art of crema-
> tion we had put the bodies on the pyre face-up, and, no doubt caused
> by the contraction of the sinews and tendons, one of the dead bodies
> had taken a sitting position and as we passed one arm slowly rose.
> We learned from experience and in all subsequent cremations the
> bodies were laid face-down.[17]

Upon arrival at Tanbaya, Stahl could not have contemplated that he
would preside over as many as nineteen cremations a day, and a total of 661
in just over three months.

> . . . as can be imagined it was a heartbreaking task. I imagine that
> an Undertaker's work becomes quite impersonal, for he deals in the
> main, with unknown bodies. For me, however, the situation was
> quite different. Each man had been a comrade in arms, many were
> lads from my own Unit, quite a few were personal friends.[18]

In an appendix to the War Diary, Hunt would record that it was hoped that in a hospital camp, with Japanese assurances of no work, a better diet and the provision of necessary drugs and dressings, Tanbaya might be the 'means of saving hundreds of lives'.[19] He cited the failure of the hospital to achieve this objective as being caused by the advanced state of disease among many patients (particularly from the British Number 2 Camp at Songkurai); the poor nutrition of a number of patients who had arrived from camps where some of the medical officers had not insisted upon the patients receiving 'the full ration'; the effects of the journey from the working camps to Tanbaya; an acute shortage of drugs; and the fact that malaria 'of a particularly severe type was endemic'.[20]

But there was another critical issue in Tanbaya's failure as a force base hospital—and whether Hunt was aware of it would seem doubtful. Given Tanbaya's geographical isolation, and further, its distance from the River Kwai and its barge supply and the 'V' Organisation, supplies of extra foodstuffs and limited drugs were non-existent. Other hospitals and camps were more fortunate: Chungkai would receive over 72 000 ticals of assistance; Tarakan some 42 000 ticals; Kanburi 17 000; Tonchan 14 000; Tarsau 35 000; and, even allowing for our already cited 'Up-River Camps' (17 000 ticals), Tanbaya therefore stood as an outpost of seclusion, despair and a horrendous mortality rate.[21] And to compound this cruel disadvantage, Captain Fred Stahl noted a further impediment to Tanbaya's supply:

> We knew from past experience that a portion of our rations always disappeared en route from source of supply and ultimate delivery to us . . . with food in short supply for the civilian population it was easy for the Japs to line their pockets at the expense of the P.O.W.
>
> Naturally the Japanese wished to keep this blackmarket trading with the Burmese natives as their own private lurk, and they took a very dim view of any effort by the P.O.W. to trade with the civilian population.[22]

Despite those severe conditions at Tanbaya—preceded by the same conditions at 'F' Force work camps—Major Bruce Hunt not only established a magnificent reputation for his medical expertise, but also for his innovative administration. Throughout those camps, he instigated a highly efficient system of 'wardmastering'. By appointing an officer or a NCO as a ward-master, 'firewood, fires, hot water and cold boiled water'[23] were provided, hygiene standards were rigidly enforced and the limited number of trained orderlies were supplemented by volunteers to maintain suitable standards of nursing and care. In all this, it should be stated that the order-lies, across all forces, were among the unsung heroes of the Thai–Burma Railway. They worked long hours; were given limited training on the job; exposed themselves continually to the disease and plight of those whom they nursed (particularly during outbreaks of cholera); and, inevitably, some of them paid the ultimate price for their selflessness and devotion.

The reader will recall the service of Captain Alf Menz, 8th Division Provost Company, during the final stages of the fight for Singapore and in Changi. After the completion of the Railway, when the majority of POWs from 'F' Force arrived by rail at Kanchanaburi, Menz soon joined them. His Railway experience is illuminating. Menz had been a member of 'F' Force and had marched north with it. His diary:

12 May 43:
Here I am in a Dutch Hospital . . . We have been marching 12 to 15 miles almost every night since leaving Bampong and it has been mighty tough too, very dark & wet roads. Both my heels have blis-tered and are very bad and my left knee had to be opened. I hope I'm not here too long, too much dysentery. All the others have gone on, I wonder if I will catch them up again.

4 June 43:
At last we get away from Kinsayok and travel down river by barge & reach Tarso [sic 'Tarsau'] where we stay over night, its [sic] a grim show, some of the 40 of the party are in a terrible state. I have to carry one chap on my back and at the end of a mile he gets heavy. A recent attack of fever has weakened me.

5 June 43:
Left Tarso with 53 sick, some very bad, kept in rain for 3 hours and again for 1½ hours arrived CHUNKAI [sic 'Chungkai'] at 0200 hours,

bedded down in scabies hut. I am feeling done, have carried one man pick-a-back for miles through mud, he is also feeling very sore.

29 June 43:
Today I have taken over control of the Camp Police and am rated Provost Marshal under Lt. Col. Outram have 30 police (English) and another officer Colin Burn also a Dutch Officer and Sgt.[24]

We now turn to a brief examination of the base camps. In his book *The Thailand–Burma Railway, 1942–1946: Documents and Selected Writings*, Paul H. Kratoska has stated that although there were numerous acts of selfless behaviour in these camps, there was also 'a great deal of self-serving behaviour, and incidents of theft by individuals and organised gangs'.[25] He also states that, driven by hunger, some individuals stole from their comrades and officers, while 'several gangs . . . stole on an organised basis, and they had Thai agents who would buy anything that they had managed to collect'.[26] Further, he stated that there was a market for drugs and clothing which was stolen in Chungkai and sold to the Thais. All this is essentially true, except for one critical point. As we have chronicled a number of times, to lay the blame purely on the ORs is quite simply unfair. Captain Alf Menz, as Chungkai's Provost Marshal, had a different story to tell:

31 July 43:
A big typewriter has been stolen from the Q.M. store and we are very busy trying to locate it. I have had two sleepless nights questioning possible suspects. A reward of 50 ticals is offered for its recovery.

21 August 43:
Last night we caught some of the 'dead-legs' who we have been after for some time, we got them with the goods on them, five of 'em. Drugs & clothing & Hyperdemic Syringes was their line. Maybe I can get a couple of officers Court-Marshalled [*sic*] over it, they are guilty.

15 September 43:
Last night I got the No 1 criminal of the camp, a Dutch soldier named _____, have been after him for a long time. Got him for selling

blankets clothing etc to the value of $197.50 to the Thais, it was only
four days ago that he swore to me that he was not dealing in blankets
or clothes any more.

   Also got a lot more Dutch & British for selling to him. Am after
3 Aussies for the same thing.[27]

Not only were officers involved in such crimes, it seems that a number
became actively involved in obstructing Menz's investigations. His diary,
17 September 1943:

There always seems to be someone trying to get the better of the
police, people who should know better. Officers of Field Rank
making allegations about 3rd degree over _____ [the Dutchman's] case, even if I had he would have deserved it. The more I see
of some of these British officers the more remarkable I think it will
be if we win this war, surely to goodness they can't all be like some of
the collection we have in this camp.[28]

In fairness, it should be stated that Menz had not been present at
Lower Songkurai or Takanun during 'F' Force's time at those locations,
and therefore had not witnessed the behaviour of a number of Australian
officers. He was later moved to Kanchanaburi pending the final concentration of 'F' Force to that camp.

After their slavery on the Railway, Kanchanaburi was heaven for the
men of 'F' Force. Stan Arneil, 2/30th Battalion, recorded that after arriving
there on 23 November 1943, and then being sent to the hospital the following day with beriberi, he found that 'a wonderful vegetable stew, thick with
delicious celery and pumpkin' was like a 'home away from home'.[29] The
following day he and a mate spent the equivalent of $1.50 on brown sugar,
peanuts and four eggs to supplement their 'special diet'. Arneil was in a new
world. 'Fancy special diets for beri beri! Though my feet are swollen like
footballs, they would not be noticed up north.'[30] Captain Adrian Curlewis
of Pond's 'F' Force party arrived at Kanchanaburi on 21 November 1943 and
was served an omelette made by a mate. The following day he noted 'parties
still pouring in by every train'.[31] On 25 November, Curlewis recorded that

there were still 'eggs of all kinds—nine for the day. Party of 1000 to move at any time.'[32] A number of men would not be in the 1000-strong party to 'move at any time'. The sick, under the care of Major Bruce Hunt (himself ill with acute cardiac beriberi), were destined to remain there until April 1944, while Captains Ben Barnett and Fred Stahl also remained as quartermaster and registrar respectively.

On 2 December 1943, the first 500 of the 1000 fittest men were sent to Bangkok to be returned to Singapore by ship. Lieutenant-Colonel Kappe led them.[33] We now come to more controversy.

Signalman Keith 'Curly' Meakin, (8th Division Signals) has been quoted as claiming that after arriving at Bangkok, the Japanese permitted the party to purchase goods. On 10 December 1943, as the men began boarding a barge for transportation to a ship, Kappe was ordered to report to the Japanese. In his absence, his cases were taken on board the barge and immediately rifled by the men. Cartons of Virginia cigarettes, tinned fish and other tinned foodstuffs were found. Signalman Meakin:

... when it [the vessel] was underway Lt.Col. Kappe ordered officers to conduct a thorough search for his boxes—nothing was found. He ordered a parade and criticised the men for stealing the food. There are many versions of what he was reported to have said, the most common account was that he stood up on the bridge, took off his shirt (displaying his good healthy condition) and offered to fight the culprits, he was jeered and 'booed' by the men who, by this time, were all smoking the Virginia cigarettes and the aroma was wafting past Kappe as he said, 'You fools! It was your money I used to purchase that food for you to have on the voyage back to Singapore!' and he was given more boos.[34]

The initial party of about a thousand men of 'F' Force arrived back in Changi over five nights: Kappe's first party of around five hundred arrived by ship and anchored on 15 December. The following day they arrived by truck near Birdwood Camp and were welcomed by Lieutenant-Colonel 'Black Jack' Galleghan, a number of other officers and Changi inmates. They were 'almost unrecognisable shadows of the men who had gone away;

many were hatless, bootless and obviously ill on their feet . . .'[35] When they alighted from the trucks Galleghan was informed that all were 'present and correct'. 'Black Jack' was dumbfounded.

'Where are the rest, Major [Major Noel Johnston, 2/30th Battalion]?'

'They're all here, Sir.'[36]

According to his biographer, Galleghan was silent as he walked along a line of his 2/30th Battalion survivors 'patting the shoulders of a man here and there, the tears streaming down his face'.[37]

The POW Thai–Burma Railway experience is a paradox. After the war, Major Bruce Hunt would give a veiled clue to this paradox by stating that: 'Some of the things I saw with F Force made me very proud to be an Australian.'[38] Some. When human beings are thrust into a prolonged environment of starvation, cruelty, slavery and despair, their strengths and weaknesses are exposed. Lieutenant Norm Couch, personal orderly officer to Major Bruce Hunt, has arguably left us with the most succinct and honest summing up of the Railway experience:

> No man has the command of words needed for conveying, in comprehensible terms, the courage and cowardness; the loyalty and treachery; the dedication and dereliction; the strengths and frailties; the kindness and brutality; the integrity and depravity; the magnificence and enormities of men, as revealed by and to those who fated to pass through the entrails of hell, in Thailand Burma [sic], during and after the Railway was built in 1943.[39]

In the end, the ability to survive the Railway experience came down to mateship. When it was abused, and corruption at times became treachery, everyone suffered. But where a dynamic leader or doctor—or both— grasped the reins of responsibility and employed a communal approach for the common good, then the odds of survival dramatically improved.

In some camps it was a near-run thing. If the gods and a number of leaders and individuals didn't give a damn, there were enough inspirational officers and other ranks who did.

PART V
SINGAPORE

. . . the orphan

—⟫◦⟪—

Victory has a thousand fathers, but defeat is an orphan

variously attributed

31

RECKONING

———◦———

This work has offered an analysis of the campaign and drawn its conclusions as to the fall of Singapore. But various postwar perspectives and the fate of a number of the participants are of interest.

Winston Churchill, in *The Second World War*, Volume IV:

> I judged it impossible to hold an inquiry by Royal Commission into the circumstances of the fall of Singapore while the war was raging. We could not spare the men, the time, or the energy. Parliament accepted this view; but I certainly thought that in justice to the officers and men concerned there should be an inquiry into all the circumstances as soon as the fighting stopped. This however has not been instituted by the Government of the day [Attlee's Labour Government]. Years have passed and many of the witnesses are dead. It may well be that we shall never have a formal pronouncement by a competent court upon the worst disaster and largest capitulation in British history.[1]

Churchill had, on 14 June 1941, directed that ample men, energy and time be found to conduct an official inquiry into the loss of Crete. His real reason for not instigating a wartime Singapore inquiry came down to the contents

of his secret speech to Parliament on 23 April 1942, in which he stated—
not without substance—that a wartime inquiry would merely open wounds
between allies. The Australians had been critical of the Indian performance
during the campaign, whilst 'other credible witnesses reflected badly on the
Australians'.[2] This last statement will be examined shortly.

At the end of the war, Prime Minister Attlee sought guidance from his
senior military advisors. Hack and Blackburn in their *Did Singapore Have
To Fall?* have stated that the Vice Chiefs of Staff and the Joint Planning Staff
told Attlee that an inquiry would only serve to further increase tension
between Australia and India over the 'collapse of morale in Singapore and
their troops' part in this'. Moreover, they pointed out that the colonial
administration, the local commanders and Britain's interwar defence
policies would also be placed under intense scrutiny. Further, such an
inquiry 'would necessitate calling people of the highest rank, including Churchill himself'.[3] In short, any inquiry would prove an unsavoury
business. But the final recommendation given Attlee deserves the strongest condemnation. His military advisors suggested that no action should be
taken until the commanders had had their despatches published, and that
if a full inquiry was instigated, its terms of reference should be confined to
only 'the period in February 1942 when Singapore was besieged'.[4] By any
standard, this was an appalling attempt to whitewash the causes of Singapore's demise to a mere month in time, and would have most assuredly
caused an outcry, particularly from the Australians and Indians, who would
have featured predominantly in such a limited investigation. The Labour
Government decided against a Royal Commission.

Churchill's assertion that 'years have passed and many of the witnesses
are dead' is a feeble statement. He returned to power in 1951, only six years
after war's end, and there was still no shortage of senior political and military
leaders—including himself—available to give evidence. Further, such was
his influence, even after he left office, that had he really desired an inquiry,
it would most likely have occurred. The truth is that a properly constituted inquiry into the fall of Singapore would have reflected poorly upon
British prewar policy, the politicians, the Colonial Office and the conduct of
the campaign. The fact is that Churchill declined the opportunity for a Royal
Commission for the very same reasons as had Attlee.

The reality is that Singapore had to fall. In fact, one is tempted to ask, with equal authenticity, as to why France fell, or why the Low Countries fell, or indeed Greece or Crete, or why reverses were suffered in the Middle East. The answer is that the western democracies were unprepared for war, and when a world conflict emerged their limited resources had to be spread globally. Two years would pass before the full measure of the Allies' potential industrialisation would materialise, their massive reserves of manpower employed and trained, and their services' doctrines developed. Few historians have questioned the wisdom of allotting most of the men and equipment to the defeat of Nazi Germany—the Allies adopted a 'beat Hitler first' policy and it was right. The question asked of Churchill, therefore, is not as to whether he should have prioritised his limited resources to the Middle East and Russia, but whether or not he might have decisively influenced events in Malaya and Singapore with resources *that he could spare*. This work has recorded that even a small number of the available fighters, limited air crews, tanks and trained reinforcements would have dramatically helped the cause, and would hardly have been responsible for a reverse of Russian fortunes. The fact that Percival was denied those few priceless resources would certainly have resulted in acute condemnation during any fair inquiry. But in the end such assistance would have merely delayed the inevitable: Singapore had to fall.

From an Australian perspective, there are three issues regarding our account of the fall of Singapore that demand examination: General Gordon Bennett's escape and his subsequent fate; the behaviour of Australian troops in Singapore Town during the last days before the capitulation; and the 8th Australian Division's performance during the campaign.

The reasons behind Major-General Gordon Bennett's escape from Singapore are the subject of great debate and controversy. In *Why Singapore Fell*, Bennett would write that:

> I, personally, had made this decision [to escape] some time previously, having decided that I would not fall into Japanese hands. My decision was fortified by the resolve that I must at all costs return to Australia

to tell our people the story of our conflict with the Japanese, to warn them of the danger to Australia, and to advise them of the best means of defeating the Japanese tactics.[5]

There can be no doubt that Bennett did indeed act out of a sense of patriotism and the desire to pass on his knowledge of fighting against the Japanese. However, there is also strong evidence that he still believed his destiny was to command the Australian Military Forces, or at worst, lead a corps or division in the avenging battles in the Pacific War. Rowell would record that: 'I'm sure that Bennett's motives were a mixture of ambition and patriotism. Setting aside his antipathy for Blamey, which was very much reciprocated, he felt that he, and he alone, could save Australia.'[6] Gavin Long, the Official Historian, was more blunt: 'I believe he thought he was such a great man that we couldn't possibly win the war without him.'[7]

Bennett arrived by plane at Broome, Western Australia, at 5.00 pm on 27 February 1942. His escape to Australia had taken twelve days. After flying from Broome to Alice Springs, then Charleville in Queensland to Sydney, Bennett finally flew to Melbourne and arrived there on 2 March. His first meeting was at the Victoria Barracks with the Chief of the General Staff, Lieutenant-General Vernon Sturdee. General Bennett:

To my dismay, my reception was cold and hostile. No other member of the Military Board called in to see me. After a few minutes' formal conversation, Sturdee told me that my escape was ill-advised, or words to that effect. I was too shocked to say much. He then went on with his work, leaving me to stand aside in his room.[8]

It was a different story at a meeting with the War Cabinet that same day. Sturdee was also present. Bennett would later record that:

. . . I gave the story of the fall of Singapore. The Prime Minister was friendly and made a short but kind speech thanking me for my work in Malaya and assuring me of the confidence of the Government in me. I then broached the subject of the escape and the criticism from a certain quarter. I told the Cabinet that I left my headquarters in

Singapore well after the surrender was signed, sealed and delivered, and after I had organized units in rest areas and collected arms and equipment. The Prime Minister and other ministers assured me that they were quite satisfied that I had taken the right step.[9]

Clearly the Government and the Chief of the General Staff were 'out of step'. After the Cabinet meeting, Prime Minister Curtin approved the following press release:

War Cabinet and the Chiefs of Staff today met Major-General Gordon Bennett. He reported fully on the Malayan Campaign, including the battle for and the surrender of Singapore.

I desire to inform the nation that *we* [author's italics] are proud to pay tribute to the efficiency, gallantry and devotion of our forces throughout the struggle.

We have expressed to Major-General Gordon Bennett our confidence in him. His leadership and conduct were in complete conformity with his duty to the men under his command and to his country. He remained with his men until the end, completed all formalities in connection with the surrender and then took the opportunity and risk of escaping.[10]

Sturdee was shocked when he read the release: 'They never at any time asked me for my opinion as to the ethics etc. of his actions, and never gave me an opportunity of giving them.'[11]

While Bennett would have taken great heart from his political and public reception upon his return to Australia, the reaction of the Military Board and the majority of his peers shocked him. But worse was to follow. Any hopes Major-General Gordon Bennett had of a fighting command, let alone a senior one, were dashed a mere 21 days after his meeting with the War Cabinet when General Blamey arrived in Perth by ship to be informed that he (Blamey) had been appointed C-in-C Australian Military Forces. From the moment that appointment was made, Bennett's fate was sealed. We have discussed the longstanding and bitter rivalry between Bennett and Blamey.

When Blamey saw Major-General Rowell (Deputy Chief of the General Staff) in Melbourne upon his arrival, he was 'very angry', and told Rowell that 'Bennett should be tried by his peers'. Rowell:

> I urged him to move with caution as he had yet to consolidate his position ... I reminded him that Bennett had a good deal of political sympathy in Sydney, that the Cabinet had seen him and made a statement about his future, and that he (Blamey) would be unwise to challenge the Government so soon unless he was quite sure of success. So he bided his time.[12]

Blamey was no fool. He promoted Bennett to Lieutenant-General and posted him as GOC III Australian Corps in Western Australia. For all intents and purposes, while Bennett's supporters had at least been partly appeased by his promotion and posting, Bennett was now out of the way. Despite his repeated requests for a fighting command, this was denied him. Near the end of 1943, after some twenty months spent languishing in Western Australia, during which the receding tide of the Pacific War had reduced both the size of his command and the relevance of his posting, Bennett made a final desperate effort to secure a South-West Pacific command: he requested a meeting with Blamey in Melbourne. The 'meeting' was nothing more than a stormy and futile confrontation.

Bennett asked 'why he should be held back'. Blamey replied that he had been 'associated with a failure', that he had 'wrongly escaped from Singapore', and, most cutting of all, that he 'had no confidence in me as a commander'.[13] And then, according to Bennett, he (Bennett) inquired as to whether Blamey had been right in escaping from Greece but it had been wrong for him to have escaped from Singapore, and whether Greece had been a success or a failure. 'Blamey hit the roof and shouted loudly his resentment at my insolence. In such circumstances, I kept my head and said no more.'[14]

There was nothing more to say. The truth is that Blamey was ordered out of Greece—Bennett was not ordered out of Singapore. In the end, the sheer hatred between Blamey and Bennett meant that once Blamey was appointed C-in-C Australian Military Forces, Bennett's career was ruined. And it is highly probable that had Bennett ever assumed such power, Blamey would have been similarly sidelined.

The controversy did not end with Bennett's retirement on 15 April 1944. Blamey was not finished with Bennett and had indeed 'bided his time'.

On 31 August 1945, General Blamey flew to Yokohama in preparation for his part in the Japanese surrender, which was to be conducted on 2 September in Tokyo Bay aboard the American battleship *Missouri*. While in Yokohama, Blamey met General Percival and requested that he write a letter confirming the contents of one he had written on 8 March 1943 whilst in captivity, explaining his promotion of Brigadier Callaghan to command the AIF in Singapore in Bennett's absence. Part of Percival's March 1943 letter stated that:

> I have to report that Major-General H. Gordon Bennett, G.O.C., A.I.F., Malaya, voluntarily and without permission relinquished command of the A.I.F on 15 Feb. 1942—the date on which the capitulation of the British Forces in Malaya took place. The command passed to Brigadier C. A. Callaghan.[15]

Having now created a means of destroying Bennett, Blamey then sent a letter to the Minister for the Army in support of Callaghan's promotion, but accusing Bennett of desertion.[16] Blamey now convened a military court of inquiry into Bennett's escape, which met at Victoria Barracks in Sydney on 26 October 1945. The composition of the court deserves examination. It consisted of three members: the president was Lieutenant-General Sir Leslie Morshead, and the other two were Major-General George Wootten and Major-General Victor Stantke. While there is no evidence that Morshead or Wootten were biased in any way towards Bennett, Stantke's participation was entirely unfair, and an example of Blamey's unqualified hatred and determination to ruin Bennett—by any means.

It is extraordinary to note that Lodge, in *The Fall of General Gordon Bennett*, points out that when Bennett had wanted his HQ to be deployed in Malaya in early 1941 'it was rumoured that a senior officer of the Staff Corps had threatened that the 8th Division would never function as a complete formation under Bennett's command', and that Bennett believed the officer to be Stantke;[17] Lodge has further recorded that during early 1941, when Bennett wanted to report directly to the Minister for the Army and chafed under the control of the Military Board, he was confronted by 'the apparent obstruction of the Adjutant-General, Stantke';[18] and, further, that Bennett's suspicions were 'not unreasonable for there is evidence that Stantke was trying to place Bennett in a poor light in Australia', and that 'Bennett's assessment of Stantke was probably correct'.[19] In the interests of common justice therefore, Major-General Victor Stantke should not have been a member of the court of inquiry.

Shortly after the court assembled, Bennett's counsel, Mr B. Clancy, KC submitted that the inquiry should be made public; that a military court was not appropriate on the grounds that its three-man tribunal was not under oath; and, when these submissions were rejected by the tribunal, that finally, and with great substance, Stantke was a biased member and should not be involved in the inquiry. Clancy then tabled a statutory declaration. Lodge simply cites the author of the declaration as 'Mr C R McKerihan', while Bennett's biographer described him as 'one of Australia's best known and most highly respected bankers'.[20] In essence, the declaration cited a luncheon held on 2 March 1945—the very day of Bennett's arrival in Melbourne—in which McKerihan was told by Stantke that he (Stantke), after being asked to do so, had not invited Bennett to the luncheon because 'he had not met him on arrival' and 'was not interested in him'. McKerihan concluded by stating that it was apparent to him 'from his [Stantke's] manner of speech that he was hostile to Major-General Bennett'.[21] There was a short adjournment which was followed by Stantke's denial of bias and the court's rejection of Clancy's submission, whereupon Bennett and Clancy left the proceedings in protest.

On 31 October 1945, the court found that Bennett had not had Percival's permission to leave Singapore; that he did not have POW status when he left; that he had given an order that all AIF personnel were to remain in the final AIF perimeter; and that he was therefore not justified in escaping from Singapore.

The military court of inquiry into Major-General Gordon Bennett's escape from Singapore was nothing more than a 'kangaroo court' contrived by Blamey. And yet Lodge cheaply dismisses Bennett's right to a fair and unbiased trial by stating that:

Although there is little doubt that Stantke was to some degree prejudiced against Bennett, there is equally little doubt that, upon the evidence, any other three general officers of the Australian army would have reached the same conclusions as did Morshead, Wootten and Stantke.[22]

On the basis of the evidence Lodge cites, Stantke's prejudice against Bennett 'to some degree' is a gross understatement, and the notion that any defendant in any court should be subjected to a prejudiced tribunal constitutes nothing less than a miscarriage of justice. Further, Lodge's claim that 'any other three general officers of the Australian army would have reached the same conclusions' is little more than biased conjecture.

Blamey passed on the court's findings to Frank Forde, the Minister for the Army, with the observation that under normal circumstances, Bennett would now be charged with desertion and face a General Court Martial. He added that should the government determine not to allow a Court Martial, that Bennett should be either retired from the army, or face a Royal Commission. Predictably, Blamey suggested the former option.

However, there were other Australians who deplored Bennett's treatment: ten members of parliament including Menzies (a staunch Blamey supporter); the Victorian, New South Wales and Western Australian branches of the RSL; the 8th Division Association; and Bennett's old First AIF 6th Battalion Association. All supported a Royal Commission.

On 17 November 1945, the government appointed Justice George Ligertwood, a judge of the South Australian Supreme Court, to preside over a Royal Commission into Bennett's escape. Adelaide barrister Mark Clisby, in his book *Guilty or Innocent? The Gordon Bennett Case*:

Five issues had to be addressed: whether Bennett had relinquished his command; whether he had permission to do so; whether he was at any material time a POW; whether he had a duty to remain with the forces under his command; and whether he was justified in relinquishing his command and leaving Singapore. Mr W. R. Dovey KC, and Mr R. Chambers were appointed as counsel assisting the commissioner, and Mr B. Clancy KC, and Mr F. C. Stephen appeared on behalf of General Gordon Bennett. Twenty-three witnesses were examined and 25 exhibits of evidence were tendered. The transcripts of evidence covered 580 foolscap pages. All nine witnesses who gave evidence at the Military Court gave evidence again. Of the 14 new witnesses, Bennett himself was the most important. He was examined and cross-examined under oath in the witness box for two full days.[23]

While the Royal Commission found Bennett guilty on all five counts, it also stated that he had believed that the cease-fire had been the point at which he had become a POW; that he believed he had done all he could for his men and would, in any case, be segregated from them after internment; that his escape had been 'a hazardous enterprise and involved no reflection upon General Bennett's personal courage'; that Bennett did 'bring back valuable information to Australia which was used in the training of the A.I.F. in jungle warfare'; and, finally, that his escape was inspired by patriotism and 'the belief that he was acting in the best interests of his country'.[24]

Two further points are of interest. In 1948, Mr T. P. Fry wrote an article which took issue with Ligertwood's findings. Amongst a number of points raised, Fry maintained that as a consequence of his charter, Bennett had 'been made directly responsible to the Australian Government and not to General Percival' as to the AIF soldiers under his command, and with respect to 'his own actions as commander of it [the AIF]'. According to Fry, therefore, Percival 'had no lawful authority to sanction or prohibit General Bennett proceeding to Australia to report to the Minister'.[25] Fry also claimed that Ligertwood had not denied that all of the officers and ORs of the AIF were 'ordinarily under a national duty, both legal and moral in its nature, to escape at the earliest possible moment should they be taken prisoners of war'.[26]

Amidst the mountain of evidence and the terms of reference of both the military court of inquiry and the Ligertwood Royal Commission, surely Mark Clisby has identified the salient point:

... the crucial issue in the Gordon Bennett case is the issue of *the time of the surrender*. Related to that are the issues of *the time when*

Gordon Bennett became a prisoner of war, as well as the issue of the duty of a soldier *when he no longer has the capacity to resist* [the italics are Clisby's].[27]

After observing that the military court of inquiry stated that the surrender of Singapore occurred in four phases—the cease-fire at 8.30 pm on 15 February; the initial 'official' contact with the Japanese at the AIF perimeter at 10.00 am the following day; the beginning of the AIF move to Changi on the 17th; and the completion of that movement on the 20th—Clisby quite rightly asserts with some frustration that: '. . . incredibly, it could not determine when the actual surrender took place!'[28] On the other hand, Ligertwood ruled that the surrender had occurred only when the last of the AIF were in Changi, and therefore Bennett had left before the surrender.[29] Clisby has maintained that, legally, the surrender took place at 8.30 pm on 15 February 1942. His evidence is impressive. He points out that while Lodge identified the time of the surrender as dawn on the 16th, the AIF had 'already handed in their ammunition and had begun stockpiling their weapons'; that the Japanese had already moved into the AIF perimeter and had begun issuing orders and 'removing various items of equipment'; and that the 'Australians had no capacity, either physically or legally, to resist after 8.30 pm'.[30] This last point is crucial. Percival and Yamashita had agreed that a cease-fire would commence at that time and Percival had signed the instrument of surrender at 6.10 pm. Thus, while Clisby cites the time of surrender at 8.30 pm, it is the contention of this work that the surrender of Singapore occurred at 6.10 pm on 15 February 1942. In other words, from the moment of the formal surrender, or at the very least, when the resulting cease-fire occurred at 8.30 pm, surely the surrender had occurred.

In conclusion, the war correspondent Ian Morrison made a succinct point:

Intellectually, I think it was the right decision. He fought until the capitulation, and, when the capitulation had gone into effect, he made good his escape, like many other men . . .

And yet I confess I have that sentimental, emotional feeling that a commanding officer should stay with his men through thick and thin, through the victories and through the defeats. I remain open-minded on the question. The view one takes of his escape depends largely on the extent to which one is emotionally or intellectually inclined.[31]

In the end neither the Chifley Government or the army took any action against Bennett. The government initially declined to pay his £1500 costs, but after the 8th Division Association announced that it would raise that sum, the government paid up. In a letter to Kent Hughes on 14 March 1946, Bennett stated that: 'Morally I won the fight, I think. Legally the decision was all hooey.'[32]

The British and Australian Official Histories are of considerable interest, as few historians have been placed under such close scrutiny both during their research and after publication. Major-General Woodburn Kirby was selected to write the British Official History. The resulting book, *The War Against Japan, Volume 1, The Loss of Singapore* (1957), was a scholarly effort which painstakingly traced the roots of the fall of Singapore back to the failed fiscal and strategic decisions of the interwar period, and then presented a detailed campaign analysis. It is uncertain what constraints Kirby wrote under, either self-imposed or external, but his *The Chain of Disaster* (1971) was certainly a far more forthright work, and, significantly, included an examination of both Percival and Simmons's failure to use the expertise of Brigadier Simson, the Chief Engineer.

Lionel Wigmore was chosen to write the fourth volume of the Australian Official History Army Series (*The Japanese Thrust*). The general editor was Gavin Long. He corresponded with and interviewed a comprehensive number of the participants and gained access to numerous diaries and documents during his research and the writing of his volume. Three other sources—one made available and two denied him—are of great interest. It is at this juncture that a familiar character re-enters our story.

In May 1951, Prime Minister Robert Menzies promoted the member for the federal seat of Chisholm, the Honourable Wilfred Kent Hughes, to the portfolio of Minister for the Interior and Works and Housing.

It will be remembered that Colonel Kent Hughes had been the AA&QMG, 8th Division AIF, at the time of the fall of Singapore. The Australian War Memorial and therefore the Official Histories were the political responsibility of the Minister for the Interior.

The first of the three historical sources of interest is the *Report on Operations of 8th Australian Division Australian Imperial Force in Malaya*, compiled by Colonel Thyer 'from the narrative prepared by Colonel C H Kappe', which Wigmore had a copy of. The fate of the second is fascinating. Just before the fall of Singapore, Kent Hughes had passed a personal diary—which dealt with the period between the arrival of the 8th Division in Singapore and the beginning of hostilities—to Captain John Blanche, who had been ordered to return to Australia. Kent Hughes ordered Blanche to deposit the diary and other papers at Army HQ Melbourne. The third source of interest are the cables sent by General Gordon Bennett before and during the campaign to General Sturdee, Chief of the General Staff.

It is the contention of this work that Kappe's narrative of the campaign in Thyer's document is invaluable to the historian; however, where Thyer analyses command decisions—particularly concerning Bennett—it is heavily biased. One merely needs to look at Thyer's muddled last six paragraphs of his introduction to see a man who was no fair judge of the decisions and actions of not only Bennett, but of a number of Australian senior commanders during the campaign as well.

General BENNETT left Singapore after the surrender and I was very displeased with the manner of his departure. Then for three and a half years, I was forced into the company of men who shared my views. It is very probable that these circumstances may have given me a bias against General BENNETT which is reflected in the criticisms and opinions.

In the case of Brigadier TAYLOR, this officer at all times displayed an antipathy towards Major-General CALLAGHAN. This resulted in a prolonged antagonism during the period of captivity when they were thrown closely together. I throughout this period, was the buffer between the two; but my responsibilities as G.S.O.1 of the Division made my sympathies lean towards General CALLAGHAN. I was therefore constantly critical of Brigadier TAYLOR during the period when any animosity would be aggravated.

Regarding Brigadier MAXWELL, this officer had a constant sympathy towards Brigadier TAYLOR. He consequently developed an animosity towards General CALLAGHAN which was felt by me. In the end, there was therefore much the same reaction between Brigadier MAXWELL and me, as existed between Brigadier TAYLOR and me, although the personal relationships between the three were quite friendly.

In preparing the report, I have been conscious of these reactions and have endeavoured to counter them and to approach the subject dispassionately. I have also tried to minimize any feelings by allowing time to mellow them.

In short, the report has been prepared by a subordinate and somewhat biased officer who is conscious of his defects.

These remarks do not apply to the pure narrative which is the work of Colonel KAPPE.[33]

Thyer made a number of extraordinary statements in his last chapter that surely prejudice the integrity of his report. We have examined the relationship between Bennett and Malaya Command, and the difficulties he faced in implementing the terms of his charter. We have also noted that similar difficulties were experienced by Blamey in the Middle East. Thyer stated that: '... Major-General Bennett was incapable of subordinating himself to Malaya Command or of cooperating wholeheartedly with other commanders'.[34] He noted that 'from discussions in captivity' with the likes of Percival, Heath, Key and Simmons, that the relations 'were more strained than the above statement would indicate'.[35] And yet, in his very next paragraph, he acknowledged that 'his [Bennett's] attitude may have been entirely impersonal and that he was at all times battling for the rights and entity of the A.I.F. That may be perfectly true, but the result was the same ...'.[36] The 'result' may well have been the same, but Thyer's second paragraph immediately answered his very general charge in the preceding statement.

But Thyer saved some of his more ill-informed and vague comments for the troops. The Australians, he claimed, fought reasonably well in Malaya, but:

... the A.I.F. did not measure up to the task required of it in a heart-breaking withdrawal. Ultimately, the morale deteriorated, and in the last stages only 2/3 *at most* of those fit to fight were manning the final perimeter.

It is known that the units in Libya and Greece behaved in a similar manner in parallel circumstances. There can be only one explanation for this and it is submitted that the Australian, in the early stages of a war, lacks military virtue.[37]

The reader is left to contemplate Thyer's long-distance comments concerning the 'military virtue' of the AIF in Libya and Greece; the lack of 'military virtue' of 2/19th and 2/29th Battalions—and the 4th Anti-Tank Regiment and 2/15th Field Regiment—at Bakri; and the performance of the 2/30th at Gemas. With regards to the British, Thyer simply stated that 'the above remarks apply equally to the British troops in Malaya'.[38] Once again, the comment is a sweeping generalisation, one to which commanders such as Stewart and his Argylls might legitimately have taken exception.

The circulation of Thyer's report is of interest. While the number of copies printed is unclear, fifteen were stored at Army HQ. Wigmore and the War Memorial were given copies, Thyer and Kappe obviously had copies, Kent Hughes possessed one, but Bennett did not. On 5 January 1951, the Deputy Chief of the General Staff, General Hopkins, gave permission for the Australian War Memorial to send a copy of the report to the British Official Historian.[39]

As draft chapters of Wigmore's *Japanese Thrust* became available, Kent Hughes became concerned about Wigmore's seeming predominant use of Brigadier Taylor's diary and Thyer's report. In short, he considered Wigmore's early drafts biased. But much of his angst was directed at what he saw as the calculated destruction by Staff Corps officers of two critical historical sources that provided another perspective. The plain and simple truth is that Army HQ destroyed Kent Hughes's diary and the cables sent by Bennett to Sturdee. The Minister for the Interior now began a determined effort to achieve what he considered to be a balanced history.

In February 1952, General Rowell (now Chief of the General Staff) wrote to the Minister for the Army and made three points. First, he distanced himself—and the Army—from Thyer's report, stating that it was 'in no sense an Army Headquarters document' and that it did not 'purport to represent the opinion of Army Headquarters'.[40] But Rowell did defend the report's writers, after a blunt plea by Kent Hughes that another search for his diary should be undertaken:

> I can not close this minute without recording a feeling of disgust at the immoderate language in which Mr. Kent Hughes' letter is written. It is well known that there were many schisms in the AIF in Malaya and many clashes of personality. But both Colonel Thyer and Brigadier Kappe, in addition to being R.M.C. [Duntroon] graduates, are men of honour and of the highest personal integrity. What they have written is purely a personal account, but we can be certain that they both have the sincere conviction that it is a true story.[41]

In the same letter, Rowell claimed that 'no trace' of Kent Hughes's diary could be found, 'nor is there any record of it having been received'. If Army HQ had no record of Kent Hughes's diary being received, Kent Hughes did. In a letter to Rowell on 10 August 1953 he stated that:

> I have in my possession a copy of letter No. 7665 written by the Military Board (Adjutant-General) 19th May 1942, which reads as follows:—
>   'Forwarded herein is the private diary of the above mentioned named Officer who has been reported as missing in Malaya . . .
>   The diary is to be held in safe custody as portion of the effects of this officer.'
>   The letter was addressed to the O.C. 3 MD Records Office, and signed by an indecipherable Captain for Officer i/c 2nd Echelon.[42]

In the same letter, Kent Hughes pointed out that Blanche had recently returned from London and had told him that he (Blanche) had handed the diary to none other than Major-General Stantke and Rowell at Victoria Barracks. When asked by Rowell to comment on Kent Hughes's letter, Stantke replied on 1 September 1953 that he 'could give no information as to where the diary of Kent Hughes is or where it was last seen'.

He denied taking Blanche to Rowell and 'had no knowledge of the material' in the diary.[43]

The Minister for the Interior proved to be a tenacious adversary. A sample of his considerable correspondence is illuminating. In a letter to Gavin Long on 12 June 1953, he stated that:

One of the main troubles with the 8th Division was that the G.O.C. never had the loyalty of many of the professional soldiers on his staff. This is perhaps a bit too controversial and a bit too hot even for a war historian to hold. The reason why I am somewhat emphatic on this point is that the true story was told in a day-to-day diary kept by the D.A.Q.M.G. in Malaya [Kent Hughes], sent off before the capitulation and handed in by Captain Blanche at Victoria Barracks for safe keeping. Nobody has ever seen it from that day to this and I do not have to guess far for the reason. It was in a book desk diary form, fully bound, and could not possibly have been lost by accident. The only thing I can conclude is that it was destroyed by design.[44]

On 18 June he wrote again to Gavin Long in response to a number of Wigmore's draft chapters:

I CAN NOW UNDERSTAND MORE THAN EVERY [sic 'ever'] WHY ARMY HEADQUARTERS LOST MY DIARY, as it had the complete record of Brigadier Taylor's refusal to obey orders, and the difficulties which the G.O.C. encountered with his own staff officers; the difficulties the A.I.F. encountered with Malaya Command and with the lack of knowledge of their own Army Command in Australia; the refusal of the Australian authorities to let us purchase webbing equipment which could have been obtained months ahead of what we ultimately received; the fight we had with Malaya Command to maintain our 16 ounce meat ration, and on and on and on far into the night.

If there are no records of these matters, surely the historian would go to General Bennett or the man who was head of the administrative side for all but two or three months of the time we were in Malaya before the battle began, namely myself. Nobody has ever at any time asked me for any information whatsoever. Colonel Broadbent went back to Australia, I think on duty, once, and another time in order to have a medical test, as a result of which he actually did very little administrative work in Malaya until about October, when I was promoted to A.A. & Q.M.G. Admin. Headquarters. Up to this time I had written every administration order, bar one, in Malaya. Major Kappe, who was G.2 until Thyer took over, would know the G. side in the early days, but Colonel Rourke arrived very late and did little G. work before he arranged his own transfer to the Middle East because he was determined not to work with the G.O.C. He said so himself in the Mess the night before the General arrived at Rosebery Racecourse camp. I do not for one minute suggest all these personal grudges and childlike idiosyncrasies should be included in a war history, but the fact remains that they had a very big influence on the difficulties which the G.O.C. had to face in Malaya before the war.[45]

On 3 September 1953, Kent Hughes wrote to the Minister for Defence, Sir Philip McBride:

Dear Mr. Minister,

This morning I had a discussion with the Official Historian concerning the War History of the Malayan Campaign. In the course of the discussion he informed me that he has been authorized to allow Lt. Gen. Gordon Bennett to have a copy of the document written by Col. Thyer on the narrative originally written by Brigadier (then Lt. Col.) Kappe. This document was roneoed and issued by the Army on 'Restricted' circulation. It is not marked 'Confidential' or 'secret'.

About eighteen months ago I wrote asking who had authorised the circulation of this document and asked to be informed as to who had been the recipients. It is included in a cartridge cover entitled 'Operations of the 8th Division in Malaya' and has all the appearance of being an official document when actually it is only one individual's opinion. The author states this very clearly in the introduction.

I now find that a copy has been given to the official British Historian and another copy is to be included in the official archives. I have had one copy in my safe for over a year as I considered it so inflamatory that if left lying about it would start a conflagration which would burn an untold number of reputations. If a copy is sent to General Bennett I do not have to be a thought reader to know what his reactions will be as in some respects his mind and mine work on parallel lines. The first thing that will happen will be an explosion, compared to which the H-bomb would be a Chinese cracker, and this will be followed by a chain reaction of several libel suits which I think he would have a very good chance of winning.

My own suggestion is that there should be a conference between yourself, the Minister for the Army and myself as to what is the best course to take. If the document is to be preserved in the official archives, every person concerning whom defammatory [sic] statements are made in the document, must have an opportunity of putting his point of view and having this also included in the archives. I feel that it is absolutely outrageous that the British Official Historian should have been given an unabridged and uncensored copy of this document as it must, even if only subconsciously, affect what he will write with regard to certain persons. It is written by an officer who is a very great personal friend of mine and I have no desire whatsoever to upset that friendship, but if you ask me for a general comment it is this: 'It is written by a permanent officer with the unfortunate usual bias against a C.M.F. officer and against C.M.F. troops. It is written by an officer who never saw any service prior to Malaya and therefore had no opportunity to compare the reactions of troops in the atmosphere of a retreat and a defeat as compared to the reactions of the same troops in a successful engagement. He admits that he is biased but it is so biased that it is definitely libellous and, furthermore, so lacking in perspective that it is literally untrue in its general comments.

I have therefore retained the document which I obtained from the Official Historian, and have not allowed it to be forwarded to the G.O.C. Unless the Army is prepared to recall every copy it has issued and rectify the damage already done to the individuals concerned,

I shall feel I have no course of action open to me but to forward the copy that I hold direct to General Bennett.[46]

It would seem that Army HQ not only experienced difficulties in storing diaries, but also in keeping records of cables between Bennett and the Chief of the General Staff (Sturdee). Kent Hughes tried assiduously to find the cables, and the War Memorial tried equally hard—but also in vain. After his return to Australia in January 1946, General Rowell had ordered the destruction of papers concerning General Gordon Bennett and the campaign in Malaya, because they were 'politically embarrassing'.[47] The truth is that Army HQ would have figured very prominently in such 'political embarrassment'.

The pressure upon Lionel Wigmore and Gavin Long can be imagined. However, the voluminous correspondence between them and the participants shows a scholarly and open-minded persistence in balanced research and an equally fair and balanced Official History. Few, if any, of the senior officers of the 8th Division would have agreed with every stance taken by Wigmore, but there would seem to be no major criticisms of the final work. Lodge in *The Fall of General Gordon Bennett* has claimed that by the time the Official History was published Wigmore had developed a dislike for Bennett 'and had little respect for him', but that there was no foundation for an accusation that this dislike had affected his writing. He has also pointed out that 'Black Jack' Galleghan—amongst others—had accused Wigmore of being 'anti-Bennett'.[48]

The impression that Bennett regarded the final Official History as biased is simply not accurate. Some testimony to the final quality of Wigmore's work—and Long's support of him—is surely the final reaction of their most bitter initial protagonist. On 19 November 1957, Bennett wrote to Kent Hughes:

Dear Bill,
At last our war history is published and I have had the opportunity to glance through it. It is not recognizable with the original interpretations of the happenings in Malaya. Our protests evidently had some effect—especially the last ones. There are one or two minor

inaccuracies but the story seems to be fairly accurate. We seem to have removed the ugly inferences and prejudices.[49]

The controversy surrounding the fall of Singapore has never really stopped. From an Indian Army perspective, there is the issue of its large scale defection to join the 'Indian National Army'. According to Alan Warren, 55 000 Indians were taken prisoner either on the mainland or in Singapore, and of those around 20 000 joined the INA. In the second half of 1942, a further 20 000 enlisted, leaving 15 000 as POWs. Some who joined were sent to fight in Burma, while many of the POWs were deployed as labourers across Japan's Pacific conquests.[50]

From an Australian perspective, the release by the British Public Records Office in 1993 of a secret report signed by General Wavell caused shock waves of indignation. In his book, *Singapore: The Pregnable Fortress*, Peter Elphick took to Wavell's report with some relish. He cites an appendix to Wavell's report which states that 'for the fall of Singapore itself, the Australians are held responsible'.[51] Elphick also claimed that 'the shortness of the siege of Singapore was caused by desertion, desertion on a scale never before known in the annals of British history'.[52]

In their book, *Did Singapore Have to Fall?*, Hack and Blackburn have stated that:

> The report contained the sort of retrospective opinions from survivors that one might have expected a commander to forward to his superiors. Unfortunately, much of the opinion made for uncomfortable reading in Canberra and Melbourne. In comments that appeared to reveal the dark side of the Australian self-image as individualistic diggers, who disdained pointless authority, it evoked a picture of indiscipline, desertion and even rape.[53]

The point that a report might have contained such 'retrospective opinions' is fair, but such a report might have included the behaviour of the Indians, or indeed the British. In a letter to Gavin Long on 14 February 1954, General Gordon Bennett wrote that:

Indian stragglers in the city numbered thousands and they looked ugly at one stage. I personally was bailed up at the point of the bayonet on the outskirts of the city by some stragglers of Gordon Highlanders ...

The AIF Provost appeared to be the only ones working on the straggler problems. The Indian units had none. In fact they would have needed an army of Provosts to handle their stragglers. So many Indian units stormed out of battle in panic that it seemed impossible to check them. Their own officers did not appear to attempt it.[54]

In the end, any account of 'stragglers' or 'deserters' on Singapore Island during the last days before the capitulation comes down to claims and counter claims depending on which nationality of troops are being defended or criticised. The truth is that those last days were ones of confusion, despair and, in some instances, of drunkenness, of intimidation to board ships and, possibly, of rape.

It is fascinating to observe that Elphick makes questionable mathematical calculations in an attempt to trace the whereabouts of the Australians during the last days of Singapore's demise. His calculations make no attempt to trace the numbers or whereabouts of the substantial number of Indians and British stragglers on the island, nor the behaviour of either nationality.

Elphick's claim that 'the shortness of the siege of Singapore was caused by desertion' is a shallow argument. We have discussed the impossible task given Brigadier Taylor's 22nd Brigade on the north-west coast of the Island; the total failure of General Simmons—the 'Fortress Commander'—to prepare the northern coast defences and the Kranji–Jurong Line; the appalling decision not to employ the expertise of the Chief Engineer, because 'defences were bad for morale'; and the critical decision not to create a 'fortress' reserve worthy of the name. To then claim, as Elphick has done, that desertions on the Island were the cause of the failure to defend it verges on the comical.

In the end, Elphick might have chosen to analyse what percentage of the final defenders of Singapore were base personnel, untrained Indian and Australian reinforcements, or unacclimatised British troops who had just arrived. When such soldiers are deployed against experienced troops such as the Japanese; when they are manning threadbare defensive lines; when they are facing an artillery bombardment such as that experienced by the 22nd Brigade on the north-west shore; and when, throughout their time in the campaign, have been subjected to an intense enemy air superiority, the end result will be mass confusion and no small number of stragglers. And, in fairness, amongst all the talk of Singapore's stragglers, it should be stated that no small number of trained—and untrained—soldiers of all nationalities stood and fought, and made the supreme sacrifice during those last days on the Island.

—————◆—————

The postwar fate of a few of our central characters are of interest.

General Percival's biographer has recorded the 'icy silence' given Percival by the British Government and the Chiefs of Staff after his repatriation. When Percival later attended Buckingham Palace to receive the CB awarded him earlier during the war, King George 'was sensitive and understanding enough to have a private conversation with him after the ceremony . . .'.[55] The 'understanding and sensitivity' ended there: there was no knighthood, 'the normal reward for the services of an officer of his rank', and despite the fact Percival had borne the title and responsibilities of a lieutenant-general, this rank was not confirmed after his return home, and he was retired with the rank of major-general and his pension paid accordingly.[56]

Percival ran into more trouble when it came time to write his despatch. The RAF was sensitive as to what he had to say 'about the way pre-war decisions that had been taken over the siting of airfields in Malaya', and their foolhardy claim that 40 per cent casualties would be inflicted by them upon any Japanese invasion force. The Colonial Office was also sensitive to the issues of Shenton Thomas and his colonial government's cooperation with the services and 'its actions in the civil defence field'.[57] In the end, Percival's despatch very much anticipated his later book, *The War In Malaya*: he was diplomatic and essentially loyal to his subordinates and superiors.

Although this work has identified the extent of Percival's command failures, in a very real sense he was, as his biographer has claimed, a scapegoat for a multitude of government and individual sins which made his task of defending Malaya and Singapore nigh on impossible with the resources at his disposal. His postwar years were devoted to the welfare of his fellow

POWs, as President of the Hertfordshire Red Cross, and as Colonel of his old unit, the 22nd Cheshire Regiment. Percival died on 31 January 1966, aged 79.

—➤●●◀—

Lieutenant-General Gordon Bennett remains one of the most controversial soldiers in Australian history. After a Great War career of such distinction, few would have then guessed at the controversial nature of his interwar and Second World War service. His open and forthright prewar criticisms of the Staff Corps and the Military Board, and his insistence that only citizen soldiers were suited to field commands, merely served to make him powerful enemies. As a consequence, when tensions had already existed between regular and citizen soldiers, Bennett could never have been entrusted with the command of the Australian Military Forces. Those rifts, already serious, would have turned into irreparable wartime divisions between the two.

That said, this work has shown that the difficulties Bennett experienced in Malaya both before the outbreak of hostilities, and during the campaign, were not all of his own making. We have examined the intransigence of a number of Staff Corps officers both on his 8th Division Staff and in Australia; the difficulties Bennett experienced with regards to the implementation of his charter; the behaviour of a number of Staff Corps officers in suppressing evidence that properly belonged in the hands of the Official Historian and, in the long term, the nation's archives; and the poisonous and vindictive manner in which Blamey sought Bennett's demise.

In the end, Bennett's controversial escape from Singapore, which was surely driven equally by ambition and self-interest as it was by a sense of patriotism and the desire to serve, constituted—rightly or wrongly—the final and all-consuming end of his career. Lieutenant-General Gordon Bennett died in Dural NSW on 1 August 1962, aged 75.

—➤●●◀—

Colonel Wilfred Kent Hughes served on the Liberal Government's front bench until 1955 when Menzies dropped him from the ministry. He was knighted in 1957 for his work as chairman of the organising committee for the Melbourne Olympic Games of 1956. He died—still as a federal member—on 31 July 1970, aged 75.

We have recorded Captain Reg Newton's exploits in Pudu Prison and on the Thai–Burma Railway as the CO of 'U' Battalion, 'D' Force. It will be recalled that Newton had procured a Bank of New South Wales cheque book from Sergeant John French's (2/20th Battalion) haversack while lightening a number of his troops' haversacks, just prior to leaving Kanchanaburi for work on the Railway. Newton had crossed out the Wahroonga Branch on each cheque and promptly labelled them all 'Head Office Sydney' where he (Newton) had an account. It will be also recalled that Boon Pong had agreed to hold the cheques until after the war when 'Head Office' Sydney would redeem them from Newton's account. Newton would later write that:

> . . . it did not take Boon Pong long to place the cheques into his bank, the Hong Kong and Shanghai Bank, in Kanchanaburi for collection on 9th September 1945 and the cheques were paid and cleared at the Bank of Wales Head Office in Sydney in February 1946.
> Newton then applied to the Australian Army to be reimbursed and was refused on the grounds that he was not authorised to operate an imprest account for local purchase.[58]

After some time, Newton decided to take legal action against the government. It was not until, by chance, a Sydney journalist and former war correspondent named David McNicoll published a series of articles in the *Sydney Daily Telegraph* that the issue was resolved. The Red Cross paid Newton back his £770 and Captain Westbrook £120 (a fellow officer also able to sign the cheques), and the matter was closed.[59]

In summing up the 8th Australian Division's experience in Malaya and Singapore, Alan Warren has left us with a thoughtful beginning: '. . . their battalions dominated the known casualty list. Losses are an indication of fighting spirit; at least up to the point at which a unit disintegrates, when the Australian story at Singapore had its share of dark moments.'[60]

The soldiers of the 8th Division in Malaya and Singapore were soldiers first and POWs second. Their fighting exploits at Bakri, at Gemas, and during numerous other fighting withdrawals along the Malay Peninsula— and the casualties they took—bear ample testament to their prowess as soldiers. The Australians were well placed to succeed in their early battles, as they had been well trained in Australia before their arrival and had embarked on a comprehensive training program in Malaya before the outbreak of hostilities.

After its heavy casualties in Malaya, the division was reinforced by nearly 2000 poorly trained soldiers. During the Japanese landings on Singapore's north-west coast, the Australian effort literally disintegrated during the confused and bloody fighting against an enemy easily able to infiltrate its woefully thin and exposed perimeter, which caused—along with other units on the Island—the destruction of many of its soldiers' morale. While the campaign was over in 70 days, the remainder of the war constituted a very different fight. The rules changed, and the heroes of the campaign were not necessarily the heroes in captivity. A very different form of bravery was required for a very different fight, and, in the end, despite the hardships and the despicable cruelty and the unrelenting labour, that war was won.

Perhaps the Roman poet Virgil, writing almost 2000 years ago, has best summed up the 8th Division's campaigning and their prisoner of war experience:

The descent into hell is easy . . . but to climb back again, to retrace one's steps to the upper air . . . there's the difficult task.

ACKNOWLEDGEMENTS

Throughout the nine years spent on the research and writing of this book, I have been privileged to have had invaluable assistance and inspiration from a number of 8th Division AIF veterans, their unit associations, and numerous colleagues and friends.

Dr Rowley Richards has, throughout the project, been a constant source of knowledge concerning the medical conditions, available procedures and drugs, and the workings and leadership of 'A' Force on the Thai–Burma Railway. His tireless patience, his friendship, his proofreading of the entire manuscript, and his generous foreword are most gratefully acknowledged and appreciated.

Much of my research concerning the 2/29th Battalion's role in both the campaign and its POW experience, was facilitated by Corporal Bob Christie. Apart from a number of interviews with me, Bob was able to provide additional files and further interviews which have greatly contributed to my knowledge. I most sincerely thank Bob and the 2/29th Battalion Association.

Similar guidance and contacts were provided by Bob Pink, Secretary of the 19th Battalion, Royal NSW Regiment Association (incorporating the 2/19th Battalion Association). Amongst those interviews, the late Gus Halloran, the late Jim Stewart, the late Jim Howard, the late Bert Donaldson and the late Jack de Loas, made extraordinary contributions. Gone but never forgotten. I also thank Charles Edwards, 2/19th Battalion, for his detailed Parit Sulong, Pudu Jail and Railway interviews.

I am indebted to Jim Kerr, 4th Anti-tank Regiment; to Len Gooley and the late Walter 'Banjo' Patterson, 8th Ammunition Sub Park; to Philippa Poole, daughter of Captain Adrian Curlewis, who granted me access to her father's diaries and letters; to the 2/30th Battalion Association for contacts for interviews and various sources; to Canberra historian Janet Uhr who presented me with a wealth of original diaries and documents—particularly those of Gunner Richard Haynes, 2/10th Field Regiment; to Joe Nimbs Junior who gave me access to his father's manuscript concerning Changi; to the late Mrs Muriel Yates, the sister of Captain Alf Menz, who allowed me to examine and use his diary; to Anthea Taylor for her proof reading; and, to all who offered interviews, lent me diaries, letters and documents. They are listed in the bibliography.

As has repeatedly been the case throughout a number of my works, I have found Professor David Horner's advice invaluable; the late Hank Nelson's POW advice was astute; Associate Professor Brian Dickey's counsel is appreciated; and, over many years I have found Neil McDonald's proof-reading and advice of great benefit.

As was repeatedly the case with my previous works on the Papuan Campaign, Frank Taylor of Australian Military History Tours facilitated my every wish during a comprehensive tour of the battlegrounds of Singapore and Malaysia, and then the Thai–Burma Railway in 2007. Our meeting with Rod Beattie in Kanchanaburi and a detailed journey along the Railway to Three Pagoda Pass was invaluable to both the research and writing of the book. Rod's extensive records—collected over years of painstaking research—and his extensive knowledge of the Railway, have proved priceless. I also owe both Frank and Rod an enormous debt for their proof reading of the manuscript.

Joyce Bradley's comprehensive knowledge of the AWM Collection in Canberra has proved of enormous worth. Her work as my research assistant unearthed both voluminous and critical research—Captain Ben Barnett's elusive diary is but one example of her expertise. I thank her. I should also wish to thank the Australian War Memorial for permission to use selected

photos from their extensive collection, and, the many families of participants who allowed me to reproduce photos of veterans.

I acknowledge those who have contributed priceless previous works:
chiefly the Australian and British Official Historians (Lionel Wigmore and
Major-General Woodburn Kirby); and, Alan Warren's *Singapore 1942*.

Throughout the writing and publication of the last five of my seven
books, Ian Bowring has been my publisher at Allen & Unwin. His most
astute advice, his judgement, his enthusiasm and friendship, are appreciated and never forgotten. To Rebecca Kaiser, Editorial Director at
Allen & Unwin, I owe a great debt. Her patience, expertise, tolerance and
hard work in the production of a work so large has been most appreciated.
I thank her sincerely.

I owe an enormous debt to my editor, Neil Thomas. *Descent into Hell* is
the fourth of my books which owe much of whatever merit is given them to
him. He is demanding, astute, has a great eye for detail and a great intuition
for structure. I am in his debt.

The reader should appreciate that despite the best efforts of others, the
conclusions reached in *Descent into Hell*—at times controversial—are not
necessarily those of other persons. I stand by what I have written.

Last, I hope this work will amplify our understanding of both the fall of
Singapore, and the POW experience in Pudu, Changi and along the Thai–
Burma Railway—warts and all. The soldiers of the 8th Division AIF deserve
no less.

Peter Brune
Adelaide
May 2014

NOTES

———⊰●⊱———

PROLOGUE

1   Although this passage has been taken from the late Joe Nimbs's unpublished manuscript entitled *Survival Changi*, it is not an exact copy. The author has placed the whole text into the present tense, and has, on the basis of his experience of visiting St Andrew's Cathedral in January 2008, added to the description of Nimbs's account of that makeshift hospital. This was done by interviewing Mrs Monica Lim, a guide and church historian, and by touring the church and grounds. Almost all of the passage—the tense and description of the church aside—is Nimbs's work. The passage was written and produced here with the permission of his family.

PART I   PRELUDE TO WAR

1   THE SUN NEVER SETS

1   Ellis, John and Cox Mike., *The World War 1 Databook: The Essential Facts and Figures for All the Combatants* (2002).

2   The Treaty of Versailles, Part V, Military, Naval and Air Clauses.

3   Quoted in Churchill, *The Second World War, Volume 1, The Gathering Storm*, p. 6.

4   Kirby, *History of the Second World War, United Kingdom Military Series, The War Against Japan*, p. 3. (This text will be cited from here on as 'Kirby' with the appropriate page number.)

5   Kirby, p. 3.

6   ibid. p. 4.

7   Kirby, p. 4.

8   ibid.

2 THE FAR EAST AND NEAR NORTH

1 Kirby, *The Chain of Disaster*, p. 6. (This text should not be confused with Kirby's Official British History. As mentioned earlier, where the Official History is cited, the note will state 'Kirby' and the appropriate page number, while *The Chain of Disaster* will be identified by its title and page number.)

2 Three British examples were: Lieutenant-Colonel Repington, a noted British military theorist; Admiral Sir Percy Scott; and Lieutenant-Commander J.M. Kenworthy.

3 Quoted in Gill, *Australia in the War of 1939–1945, Royal Australian Navy, 1939–1942*, p. 15.

4 ibid. p. 19.

5 Quoted in Gavin Long, *To Benghazi*, p. 5.

6 Kirby, *The Chain of Disaster*, pp. 14–15.

7 Kirby, p. 8.

8 Quoted in Wigmore, *The Japanese Thrust*, pp. 1–2.

9 Quoted in G. Herman Gill, *The Royal Australian Navy, 1939–1942*, p. 11, (footnote).

10 Gavin Long, *To Benghazi*, pp. 4–5.

11 Quoted in Hasluck, *The Government and the People, 1939–1941*, p. 16.

12 ibid. p. 17.

13 ibid.

14 Quoted in G. Herman Gill, *The Royal Australian Navy, 1939–1942*, p. 19.

15 ibid.

16 ibid.

17 Paul Hasluck, *The Government and the People, 1939–1941*, p. 31.

18 Gavin Long, *To Benghazi*, p. 5.

19 ibid. p. 10, (footnote).

20 ibid. p. 10.

21 *The Army Quarterly*, April 1927, p. 18.

22 ibid. p. 20.

23 ibid. p. 22.

24 ibid. p. 28.

25 ibid. p. 34.

26 ibid.

3 SINGING FROM DIFFERENT HYMN SHEETS

1 Wigmore, *The Japanese Thrust*, p. 63.

2 It was just under a quarter of the size of the ACT in the early 1960s. Since then a number of Singapore governments have reclaimed land.

3 Tsuji, Masanobu, *Singapore The Japanese Version*, p. 216.

4 The road quality and width was raised and confirmed with numerous participant interviewees, e.g. Lieutenant Jim Howard, Carrier Platoon, 2/19th Battalion. The author also had the opportunity to both examine and measure the old road system, e.g., at Gemas.

5 Kirby, p. 157.

6 Although these figures are approximate, they would seem to be close to the mark. See Kirby, p. 155; Wigmore pp. 64–5 and the footnote on p. 64; and during an excellent

description of prewar Singapore and its society, Hack and Blackburn in *Did Singapore Have to Fall? Churchill and the Impregnable Fortress* give Singapore's population as 560 000.

7 ibid. Kirby lists the European population as 18 000 in 1939. He then goes on to say that 20 per cent were non-British. This would account for about 14 000 who were.

8 Morrison, *Malayan Postscript*, p. 28.

9 Kirby, p. 13.

10 ibid. p. 11.

11 ibid. p. 12.

12 Karl Hack and Kevin Blackburn, *Did Singapore Have to Fall?* pp. 32–6.

13 Lieutenant-General A. E. Percival, *The War in Malaya*, p. 15.

14 Clifford Kinvig, *Scapegoat, General Percival of Singapore*, p. 6.

15 ibid.

16 Wigmore, *The Japanese Thrust*, p. 78.

17 ibid.

18 Peter Elphick, *Singapore: The Pregnable Fortress*, p. 160.

19 These are his biographer's words; see Clifford Kinvig, *Scapegoat, General Percival of Singapore*, p. 226.

20 Key's words, quoted in Kinvig, p. 226.

21 Clifford Kinvig, *Scapegoat, General Percival of Singapore*, p. 108.

22 Kirby, p. 15.

23 Clifford Kinvig, *Scapegoat, General Percival of Singapore*, p. 104.

24 Kirby, *The Chain Of Disaster*, pp. 32–3.

25 ibid. p. 33.

26 Clifford Kinvig, *Scapegoat, General Percival of Singapore*, p. 105.

27 ibid. p. 104.

28 Kirby, *The Chain of Disaster*, p. 30.

29 Sergeant Jack de Loas, 2/19th Battalion, interview with the author, Bomaderry, New South Wales, 13 January 2005.

30 Peter Elphick, *Far Eastern File*, p. 136.

31 ibid.

32 ibid.

33 Clifford Kinvig, *Scapegoat, General Percival of Singapore*, p. 106.

34 Peter Elphick, *Far Eastern File*, p. 144.

35 ibid.

36 ibid. p. 145.

37 Peter Elphick, *Far Eastern File*, p. 146.

38 ibid. p. 151.

39 Kirby, *The Chain of Disaster*, p. 31.

40 Kirby, p. 21.

41 ibid.

42 Brian Montgomery, *Shenton of Singapore*, p. 203.

43 Wigmore, *The Japanese Thrust*, p. 204.

44 Kirby, *The Chain of Disaster*, pp. 40–1.

45 Brian Montgomery, *Shenton of Singapore*, p. 60.

46 Vlieland, quoted in Brian Montgomery, *Shenton of Singapore*, p. 61.

47 ibid.

48 ibid.

49 Kirby, *The Chain of Disaster*, p. 39.

50 ibid. p. 41.

51 ibid. p. 44.

52 ibid.

53 ibid. p. 46.

54 Winston Churchill, *The Second World War, Volume 2, Their Finest Hour*, p. 102.

55 Clifford Kinvig, *Scapegoat, General Percival of Singapore*, p. 118.

56 Kirby, p. 35.

57 Winston Churchill, *The Second World War, Volume 2, Their Finest Hour*, p. 385.

58 ibid. p. 386.

59 ibid. pp. 591–2.

60 ibid. p. 592.

61 Clifford Kinvig, *Scapegoat, General Percival of Singapore*, p. 119.

4 RAISING NEW DIVISIONS

1 David Horner, *Blamey, The Commander-in-Chief*, p. 128. Confirmed with the possible addition of Mackay by Professor David Horner, telephone conversation 6 October 2008.

2 Frank Legg, *The Gordon Bennett Story*, p. 9.

3 Wigmore, *The Japanese Thrust*, pp. 32–3.

4 Gavin Long, *To Benghazi*, p. 46.

5 'Suggestions for the Improvement in Enlistments in the Citizen Forces AMF', Bennett Papers, Mitchell Library, MSS 807/6.

6 The Sydney *Sunday Sun and Guardian*, 28 November 1937.

7 ibid.

8 ibid.

9 The Sydney *Sunday Sun and Guardian*, 5 December 1937.

10 ibid. 12 December 1937.

11 Quoted in Lodge, *The Fall of General Bennett*, p. 14.

12 ibid. p. 15.

13 Bennett in Frank Legg, *The Gordon Bennett Story*, p. 153.

14 David Horner, *Blamey, The Commander-in-Chief*, p. 129.

15 Australian Archives, A 2653 1940, Volume 4, Promotion and Selection Committee, Appointment of Divisional Commanders, 1st and 2nd Divisions, Eastern Command, 2 May 1940.

16 ibid. White is identified as the president of the committee and Miles as a member.

17 Australian Archives, A 2653 1940, Volume 4, letter Sturdee to Miles, 9 May 1940. Quoted in A. B. Lodge, *The Fall of General Gordon Bennett*, p. 26.

18 Australian Archives, A 2653 1940, Volume 4, letter Sturdee to Miles, 9 May 1940.

19 ibid. Lodge p. 26.

20 Australian Archives, A 2653 1940, Volume 4, letter Sturdee to Miles, 9 May 1940.

21 ibid.

22 Australian Archives, A 2653 1940, Volume 4, letter Sturdee to Miles, 9 May 1940. Quoted in A. B. Lodge, *The Fall of General Gordon Bennett*, p. 26.

23 Australian Archives, A 2653 1940, Volume 4, letter Sturdee to Miles, 9 May 1940.

24 Australian Archives, A 2653 1940, Volume 4, letter Sturdee to Miles, 9 May 1940. Quoted in A. B. Lodge, *The Fall of General Gordon Bennett*, p. 26.

25 Australian Archives, A 2653 1940, Volume 4, letter Sturdee to Miles, 9 May 1940.

26 Australian Archives, A 2653 1940, Volume 4, Promotion and Selection Committee, Appointment of Divisional Commanders, 1st and 2nd Divisions, Eastern Command, 2 May 1940.

27 Bennett to Menzies, 2 September 1940, Bennett Papers, Mitchell Library, Sydney, MSS 807/2.

28 Lodge, *The Fall of General Gordon Bennett*, p. 28.

29 Kent Hughes, letter to McBride, AWM 113 4/1/11 part 3. Kent Hughes also refers to this incident in a letter to the Official Historian (Gavin Long) on 18 June 1953; see Kent Hughes Papers, National Library of Australia, MS 4856, Box 9, Series 2, Folder 64, Correspondence with the Official Historian 1953.

30 In an interview with Lionel Wigmore on 23 February 1952, Kent Hughes again names Rourke and cites Broadbent as the second officer (AWM 93 50/2/23/542).

31 AWM 73/46, Wigmore, interview with Rourke, Melbourne June 1952.

32 Lodge, *The Fall of General Gordon Bennett*, p. 34.

33 ibid. pp. 42–3.

34 In the *Defence Force Journal* No. 26, January–February 1981, David Horner lists the mentioned Staff Corps officers as examples of successful senior commanders. The author has added Lavarack.

35 Wigmore, *The Japanese Thrust*, p. 28.

36 See notes 29 and 30 of this chapter.

37 Wigmore, *The Japanese Thrust*, p. 28.

38 ibid. p. 29.

39 ibid.

40 Wigmore, *The Japanese Thrust*, p. 29.

41 Lieutenant Jim Howard, 2/19th Battalion, interview with the author, Port Macquarie, NSW, 28 September 2004.

42 Wall, *Singapore and Beyond*, p. 1.

43 AWM 1/5/17 8th Division General Staff Branch, January 1941.

44 Rourke believed this to be so. He had served in the Middle East before his posting to 8th Division. See interview with the Official Historian, Melbourne, June 1952, AWM 73/46. See Lodge, *The Fall of General Gordon Bennett*, p. 34. Also, the 8th Division employed the same form of training as had the 6th and 7th, and had a comparable amount of time in training in Australia before leaving.

45 Wigmore, *The Japanese Thrust*, p. 60.

46 Lodge, *The Fall of General Gordon Bennett*, p. 34.

47 Wigmore, *The Japanese Thrust*, p. 60 (footnote).

48 AWM 52, 8/3/18, the 2/18th Battalion Unit Diary, the February Diary 1941.

49 Lieutenant Jim Howard, 2/19th Battalion, interview with the author, Port Macquarie, NSW, 28 September 2004.

50 Wall, *Singapore and Beyond*, p. 13.

51 Newton, *The Grim Glory of the 2/19 Battalion AIF*, p. 61.

52 Wigmore, *The Japanese Thrust*, p. 62.

5 MALAYA COMMAND

1 Wigmore, *The Japanese Thrust*, p. 46.

2 ibid. (footnote).

3 Quoted in Clifford Kinvig, *Scapegoat, General Percival of Singapore*, p. 125.

4 Vlieland, quoted in Brian Montgomery, *Shenton of Singapore*, p. 75.

5 Kirby, *The Chain of Disaster*, p. 54.

6 ibid.

7 ibid.

8 Kirby, *The Chain of Disaster*, p. 55.

9 Wigmore, *The Japanese Thrust*, p. 78.

10 Christopher Shores and Brian Cull, *Bloody Shambles*, p. 65.

11 Douglas Gillison, *Australia in the War of 1939–1945: Royal Australian Air Force 1939–1942*, p. 196 (footnote).

12 ibid.

13 Christopher Shores and Brian Cull, *Bloody Shambles*, p. 68.

14 ibid. p. 69.

15 Kirby, p. 162.

16 Douglas Gillison, *Australia in the War of 1939–1945, Royal Australian Air Force*, p. 152 (footnote).

17 ibid. p. 168.

18 Christopher Shores and Brian Cull, *Bloody Shambles*, p. 42.

19 ibid. p. 40.

20 Quoted in Gillison, *Australia in the War of 1939–1945: Royal Australian Air Force*, p. 151.

21 ibid. p. 170.

22 Quoted in David Day, *The Great Betrayal*, p. 190.

23 Douglas Gillison, *Australia in the War of 1939–1945, Royal Australian Air Force*, p. 170 (footnote).

24 Quoted in David Day, *The Great Betrayal*, p. 191.

25 Christopher Shores and Brian Cull, *Bloody Shambles*, p. 32.

26 Douglas Gillison, *Australia in the War of 1939–1945, Royal Australian Air Force*, pp. 163–4.

27 ibid. p. 164.

28 ibid.

29 Douglas Gillison, *Australia in the War of 1939–1945, Royal Australian Air Force*, p. 164.

30 ibid. pp. 164–5.

31 ibid. p. 165.

32 Douglas Gillison, *Australia in the War of 1939–1945, Royal Australian Air Force*, p. 165.

33 Kirby, p. 163.

34 Clifford Kinvig, *Scapegoat, General Percival of Singapore*, p. 126.

35 Kirby, p. 513.

36 Wigmore, *The Japanese Thrust*, p. 104.

37 Alan Warren, in *Singapore 1942, Britain's Greatest Defeat*, provides an excellent account of the Indian Army during this period (pp. 31–4).

38 Warren, *Singapore 1942, Britain's Greatest Defeat*, pp. 32–3.

39 Kirby, p. 514.

40 Warren, *Singapore 1942, Britain's Greatest Defeat*, p. 30.

41 Kirby, p. 165.

42 Kirby, *The Chain of Disaster*, p. 91.

43 ibid. pp. 91–2.

44 Kirby, *The Chain of Disaster*, p. 92.

45 Ivan Simson, *Singapore Too Little, Too Late* p. 23.

46 ibid.

47 ibid.

48 ibid.

49 ibid. p. 24.

50 ibid.

51 Ivan Simson, *Singapore Too Little, Too Late*, p. 27.

52 ibid.

53 ibid. p. 33.

54 Ivan Simson, *Singapore Too Little, Too Late*, pp. 33–4.

55 ibid. p. 34.

56 ibid. pp. 35–6.

57 Clifford Kinvig, *Scapegoat, General Percival of Singapore*, p. 131.

58 Kirby, *The Chain of Disaster* p. 117.

59 The Australian Army, *The Fundamentals of Land Warfare*, p. 105.

60 The Argylls' Captain David Wilson quoted in Thompson, *The Battle for Singapore*, p. 33.

61 Thompson, *The Battle for Singapore*, p. 33.

62 Simson, *Singapore Too Little, Too Late*, p. 42.

63 I. M. Stewart, *History of the Argyll & Sutherland Highlanders 2nd Battalion*, p. 2.

64 ibid.

65 ibid. p. 4.

66 I. M. Stewart, *History of the Argyll & Sutherland Highlanders 2nd Battalion*, p. 4.

67 Simson, *Singapore Too Little, Too Late*, p. 36. (footnote)

68 I. M. Stewart, *History of the Argyll & Sutherland Highlanders 2nd Battalion*, p. 4.

69 ibid. p. 5.

70 Simson, *Singapore Too Little, Too Late*, p. 43.

71 Galleghan, interview with the Official Historian, Canberra 1 February 1950. AWM 73/51.

6 INTERNAL DISSENSION

1 Wigmore, *The Japanese Thrust*, p. 69.

2 Gordon Bennett Papers: Mitchell Library, ML MSS 773 CY783, (hereafter referred to as 'Bennett Diary' or, where applicable, the 'Bennett Papers'.

3 Bennett Diary.

4 Lieutenant Jim Howard, 2/19th Battalion, interview with the author, Port Macquarie, New South Wales, 28, 29 September 2004.

5 AWM 52 8/3/19 The 2/19th Unit Diary, April–June 1941.

6 Wigmore, *The Japanese Thrust*, p. 67 (footnote).

7 ibid. p. 68 (footnote).

8 ibid. p. 70.

9 Frank Legg, *The Gordon Bennett Story*, p. 170.

10 Bennett Diary.

11 ibid.

12 ibid.

13 Taylor, quoted in Lodge, *The Fall of General Gordon Bennett*, p. 52.

14 Lodge, *The Fall of General Gordon Bennett*, p. 53.

15 ibid.

16 Bennett Diary.

17 Kent Hughes Papers, The National Library of Australia: MS 4856 Letter Kent Hughes to Gavin Long, 18 June 1953. The box at the National Library is listed as 'correspondence with the Official Historian 1953'. It would therefore appear in the AWM collection. Kent Hughes's correspondence from his papers will henceforth be titled 'Kent Hughes Papers'.

18 Wigmore, *The Japanese Thrust*, p. 70.

19 Bennett Diary.

20 ibid.

21 ibid.

22 Bennett Diary.

23 ibid.

24 Taylor, quoted in Lodge, *The Fall of General Gordon Bennett*, p. 55.

25 Bennett Diary.

26 ibid.

27 ibid.

28 Bennett Diary.

29 ibid.

30 ibid.

31 Bennett Diary.

32 ibid.

33 Walker, *Clinical Problems of War*, p. 72.

34 AWM 52, 1/5/17, 8 Australian Division General Staff Branch, August–October 1941.

35 Bennett Diary.

36 Lodge, *The Fall of General Gordon Bennett*, pp. 42–3.

37 Lodge, *The Fall of General Gordon Bennett*, p. 58.

38 ibid. pp. 58–9.

39 ibid. p. 60.

40 Lodge, *The Fall of General Gordon Bennett*, p. 30.

41 Wigmore, *The Japanese Thrust*, pp. 28–9.

42 Horner, *Blamey, The Commander-in-Chief*, p. 135.

43 ibid.

44 ibid. pp. 135–6.

45 Horner, *Blamey, The Commander-in-Chief*, p. 137.

46 Rowell, *Full Circle*, pp. 48–9.
47 Bennett's charter as quoted by Wigmore, *The Japanese Thrust*, p. 65.
48 Bennett Diary.
49 ibid.
50 Wigmore, *The Japanese Thrust*, p. 73.
51 Bennett Diary.
52 Wahlert, *The Other Enemy?* P. 146.
53 ibid. p. 144.
54 ibid. p. 146.
55 Bennett Diary.
56 AWM 52, 1/5/17, 8th Australian Division Administrative HQ, August–October 1941.
57 ibid.
58 Bennett Diary.
59 AWM 52, 1/5/17, 8th Australian Division Administrative HQ, August–October 1941.
60 ibid.
61 Bennett Diary.
62 ibid.
63 Wahlert, *The Other Enemy?* p. 145.
64 Kinvig, *Scapegoat, General Percival of Singapore*, p. 127.
65 Bennett Diary.
66 Wigmore, *The Japanese Thrust*, p. 73.
67 ibid.
68 Lodge, *The Fall of General Gordon Bennett* p. 49.
69 Bennett Diary.
70 Kent Hughes Papers, The National Library of Australia: MS 4856, MS 4856/2/10 Correspondence with Gordon Bennett: 1942–68.
71 Sir Charles Moses, interview with Neil McDonald, Sydney 6 February 1985. Copy most kindly given to the author by McDonald, January 2010.

7 THE ENEMY

1 Quoted in James Clark, *Understanding the Japanese Mind*, p. 104.
2 Janet E. Hunter, *The Emergence of Modern Japan*, pp. 170–1.
3 ibid. pp. 111–12.
4 Quoted in James Clark, *Understanding the Japanese Mind*, p. 67.
5 Kirby, p. 10.
6 ibid.
7 Meirion & Susie Harries, *Soldiers of the Sun*, p. 161.
8 James Clark, *Understanding the Japanese Mind*, p. 19.
9 Ei Yamaguchi in *Hell in the Pacific, Programme 1: Inferno*, written, produced and directed by Jonathon Lewis, for Carlton UK Productions Ltd, 2001.
10 Private A. J. (Gus) Halloran, 2/19th Battalion, interview with the author, Port Macquarie, New South Wales, 19 April 2005.
11 Masao Maeda in *Hell in the Pacific, Programme 1: Inferno*, written, produced and directed by Jonathon Lewis, for Carlton UK Productions Ltd, 2001.

12 Tominaga Shozo in Haruko Taya Cook & Theodore F. Cook, *Japan at War, An Oral History*, p. 40.

13 ibid. p. 41.

14 ibid.

15 ibid.

16 Tominaga Shozo in Haruko Taya Cook & Theodore F. Cook, *Japan at War, An Oral History*, p. 42.

17 ibid.

18 Shiro Azuma in *Hell in the Pacific, Programme 1: Inferno*, written, produced and directed by Jonathon Lewis, for Carlton UK Productions Ltd, 2001.

19 ibid.

20 Wigmore, *The Japanese Thrust*, p. 113.

21 Meirion & Susie Harries, *Soldiers of the Sun*, p. 146.

22 Quoted in, G. Hermon Gill, *Royal Australian Navy 1939–1942*, p. 465.

23 Masanobu Tsuji, *Singapore, The Japanese Version*, pp. 35, 191.

24 Wigmore, *The Japanese Thrust*, p. 91.

25 Three British examples were: Lieutenant-Colonel Repington, a noted British military theorist (July 1923); Admiral Sir Percy Scott; and Lieutenant-Commander J.M. Kenworthy. Also, Kirby has recorded that even staff and students at the Imperial Defence College had repeatedly predicted that the Japanese would attack during the north-east monsoon and without a formal declaration of war. Kirby, *The Chain of Disaster*, p. 33.

PART II THE CAMPAIGN

8 AN UNPLEASANT SURPRISE

1 Douglas Gillison, *Royal Australian Air Force 1939–1942*, p. 195.

2 ibid. p. 196.

3 Winston Churchill, *The Second World War*, Vol III, p. 390.

4 ibid. p. 768.

5 ibid.

6 G. Hermon Gill, *Royal Australian Navy, 1939–1942*, pp. 442–3.

7 ibid. p. 445.

8 Douglas Gillison, *Royal Australian Air Force 1939–1942*, p. 198.

9 ibid. p. 199.

10 Masanobu Tsuji, *Singapore, The Japanese Version*, p. 74.

11 Douglas Gillison, *Royal Australian Air Force 1939–1942*, p. 200 (and footnote).

12 ibid. p. 201.

13 Masanobu Tsuji, *Singapore, The Japanese Version*, p. 76.

14 Douglas Gillison, *Royal Australian Air Force 1939–1942*, p. 202.

15 The figures for the British aircraft strength are from Gillison, p. 205, and the Japanese from Kirby, p. 524.

16 Kirby, p. 173.

17 ibid. p. 175.

18 Peter Thompson, *The Battle for Singapore*, p. 115.

19 Brooke-Popham's Despatch, the *London Gazette*, 26 February 1948.

20 Kirby, *The Chain of Disaster*, p. 124.
21 A. E. Percival, *The War in Malaya*, p. 106.
22 ibid. p. 108.
23 ibid.
24 Masanobu Tsuji, *Singapore, The Japanese Version*, p. 80.
25 ibid. p. 92.
26 Douglas Gillison, *Royal Australian Air Force 1939–1942*, p. 219.
27 ibid.
28 Alan Warren, *Singapore 1942, Britain's Greatest Defeat*, p. 59.
29 Thompson, *The Battle for Singapore*, pp. 123–5, and p. 434 note 19.
30 Masanobu Tsuji, *Singapore, The Japanese Version*, p. 95.
31 Douglas Gillison, *Royal Australian Air Force 1939–1942*, p. 208.
32 ibid.
33 Christopher Shores and Brian Cull, *Bloody Shambles*, p. 80.
34 Douglas Gillison, *Royal Australian Air Force 1939–1942*, p. 211.
35 Alan Warren, *Singapore 1942, Britain's Greatest Defeat*, p. 62.
36 ibid.
37 Christopher Shores and Brian Cull, *Bloody Shambles*, p. 81.
38 Douglas Gillison, *Royal Australian Air Force 1939–1942*, p. 215.
39 A. E. Percival, *The War in Malaya*, p. 113.
40 Douglas Gillison, *Royal Australian Air Force 1939–1942*, p. 220.

9 BAD NEWS FOR THE HOUSE
 1 Kirby, p. 193.
 2 Brian Montgomery, *Shenton of Singapore*, p. 5.
 3 The description of the meeting given is based completely on Montgomery's account. Brian Montgomery, *Shenton of Singapore*, pp. 5–7.
 4 Brian Montgomery, *Shenton of Singapore*, p. 7.
 5 ibid. p. 8.
 6 ibid. p. 9.
 7 G. Hermon Gill, *Royal Australian Navy, 1939–1942*, p. 477.
 8 ibid. p. 477.
 9 ibid. pp. 477–8.
10 ibid. p. 478.
11 G. Hermon Gill, *Royal Australian Navy, 1939–1942*, p. 479.
12 Warren, *Singapore 1942, Britain's Greatest Defeat*, p. 72.
13 Christopher Shores and Brian Cull, *Bloody Shambles*, p. 111.
14 ibid. pp. 113–14.
15 ibid. p. 116.
16 G. Hermon Gill, *Royal Australian Navy, 1939–1942*, p. 480.
17 ibid.
18 Christopher Shores and Brian Cull, *Bloody Shambles*, p. 120.
19 G. Hermon Gill, *Royal Australian Navy, 1939–1942*, p. 481.
20 ibid. p. 482.

21 Quoted in Warren, *Singapore 1942, Britain's Greatest Defeat*, p. 77.

22 ibid. p. 552.

23 Marder, *Old Friends, New Enemies*, p. 497.

24 Quoted in Douglas Gillison, *Royal Australian Air Force 1939–1942*, p. 254.

25 Warren, *Singapore 1942, Britain's Greatest Defeat*, p. 74.

26 Winston Churchill, *The Second World War*, Vol III, p. 551.

27 ibid.

10 THE JITRA LINE

1 From notes taken by the Official Historians and quoted in Elphick, *Singapore: The Pregnable Fortress*, p. 220.

2 Kinvig, *Scapegoat, General Percival of Singapore*, p. 143.

3 ibid.

4 ibid.

5 ibid.

6 Wigmore, *The Japanese Thrust*, p. 140.

7 Masanobu Tsuji, *Singapore, The Japanese Version*, pp. 90–1.

8 Quoted in Thompson, *The Battle for Singapore*, p.157.

9 Kinvig, *Scapegoat, General Percival of Singapore*, p. 144

10 Underhill, *The Royal Leicestershire Regiment*, p. 91.

11 ibid. p. 90.

12 ibid.

13 Simson, *Singapore Too Little, Too Late*, p. 48.

14 Kirby, p. 204.

15 Warren, *Singapore 1942, Britain's Greatest Defeat*, p. 83.

16 ibid.

17 Wigmore, *The Japanese Thrust*, p. 147.

18 Warren, *Singapore 1942, Britain's Greatest Defeat*, p. 85.

19 Wigmore, *The Japanese Thrust*, pp. 148–9.

20 Kirby, *The Chain of Disaster*, p. 143.

21 Lieutenant-General A. E. Percival, 'Operations of Malaya Command from 08.12.1941 to 15.02.1942', *London Gazette*.

22 Kirby, p. 208.

23 Warren, *Singapore 1942, Britain's Greatest Defeat*, p. 93.

24 Kirby, p. 209.

25 Kinvig, *Scapegoat, General Percival of Singapore*, p. 156.

26 Kirby, p. 210.

27 Underhill, *The Royal Leicestershire Regiment*, p. 94.

28 ibid.

29 Masanobu Tsuji, *Singapore, The Japanese Version*, p. 126.

30 ibid.

31 Murray-Lyon to Kirby, quoted in Warren, *Singapore 1942, Britain's Greatest Defeat*, p. 95.

32 Wigmore, *The Japanese Thrust*, p. 151.

11 THE DEFENCE OF GURUN

1 Kirby, p. 213.
2 Murray-Lyon, quoted in Warren, *Singapore 1942, Britain's Greatest Defeat*, p. 100.
3 A. E. Percival, *The War in Malaya*, p. 141.
4 Lieutenant-General A. E. Percival, 'Operations of Malaya Command from 08.12.1941 to 15.02.1942', *London Gazette*.
5 Kinvig, *Scapegoat, General Percival of Singapore*, p. 164.
6 Kirby, p. 215.
7 Quoted in Warren, *Singapore 1942, Britain's Greatest Defeat*, pp. 104–5.
8 ibid. p. 105.
9 Kirby, pp. 215–16.
10 ibid. p. 216.
11 Quoted in Warren, *Singapore 1942, Britain's Greatest Defeat*, p. 108.
12 Lieutenant-General A. E. Percival, 'Operations of Malaya Command from 08.12.1941 to 15.02.1942', *London Gazette*.
13 Peter Thompson, *The Battle for Singapore*, p.169.
14 ibid.
15 Wigmore, *The Japanese Thrust*, p. 160.
16 ibid.
17 Kirby, p. 230.
18 I. M. Stewart, *History of the Argyll & Sutherland Highlanders 2nd Battalion*, p. 19.
19 ibid. p. 22.
20 ibid.
21 ibid. p. 23.
22 I. M. Stewart, *History of the Argyll & Sutherland Highlanders 2nd Battalion*, p. 23.
23 ibid.
24 ibid. p. 24.
25 ibid. p. 25.
26 Lieutenant-General A. E. Percival, 'Operations of Malaya Command from 08.12.1941 to 15.02.1942', *London Gazette*.
27 ibid.
28 ibid.
29 ibid.
30 Lieutenant-General A. E. Percival, 'Operations of Malaya Command from 08.12.1941 to 15.02.1942', *London Gazette*.
31 ibid.
32 Bennett Diary.
33 Douglas Gillison, *Royal Australian Air Force 1939–1942*, p. 281.
34 ibid.
35 ibid. (footnote).
36 Winston Churchill, *The Second World War*, Vol III, p. 565.
37 ibid.
38 Wigmore, *The Japanese Thrust*, p. 164.
39 Winston Churchill, *The Second World War*, Vol III, p. 566.

40 Wigmore, *The Japanese Thrust*, p. 163.
41 General H. Gordon Bennett, *Why Singapore Fell*, p. 69.
42 ibid.
43 ibid. p. 74.
44 Australian Archives: A981.
45 Australian Archives: A3830, 1941, 3539.
46 Australian Archives: A3196, 1941, 0.22268.
47 Australian Archives: A891.
48 Winston Churchill, *The Second World War*, Vol III, pp. 568–71.
49 Quoted in Warren, *Singapore 1942, Britain's Greatest Defeat*, pp. 117–18.
50 Winston Churchill, *The Second World War*, Vol III, p. 597.
51 ibid.
52 Kirby, p. 528
53 ibid.
54 ibid. p. 261.
55 National Library of Australia, Kent Hughes Papers, MS 4856: Box 35: series 7: folder 19: 'Administrative HQ AIF Malaya'.
56 Wigmore, *The Japanese Thrust*, p. 258.
57 ibid. p. 96.
58 ibid. p. 258 (footnote).

12 THE WITHDRAWAL FROM KAMPAR

1 I. M. Stewart, *History of the Argyll & Sutherland Highlanders 2nd Battalion*, p. 29.
2 ibid. p. 32.
3 ibid. p. 35.
4 ibid. p. 38.
5 Wigmore, *The Japanese Thrust*, p. 166.
6 A. E. Percival, *The War in Malaya*, p. 156.
7 I. M. Stewart, *History of the Argyll & Sutherland Highlanders 2nd Battalion*, p. 14.
8 Masanobu Tsuji, *Singapore, The Japanese Version*, p. 142.
9 ibid. p. 143.
10 Lieutenant-General A. E. Percival, 'Operations of Malaya Command from 08.12.1941 to 15.02.1942', *London Gazette*.
11 Kirby, p. 242.
12 ibid.
13 Simson, *Singapore Too Little, Too Late*, p. 61.
14 ibid.
15 ibid. p. 62.
16 Kirby, p.242.
17 ibid.
18 Simson, *Singapore Too Little, Too Late*, p. 63.
19 ibid. p. 69.
20 ibid. p. 71.
21 ibid. p. 73.

22 I. M. Stewart, *History of the Argyll & Sutherland Highlanders 2nd Battalion*, p. 49.

23 ibid. p. 50.

24 Warren, *Singapore 1942, Britain's Greatest Defeat*, p. 120.

25 Kirby, p. 244.

26 I. M. Stewart, *History of the Argyll & Sutherland Highlanders 2nd Battalion*, p. 58.

27 Kirby, p. 246.

28 ibid. p. 247.

29 ibid.

30 Warren, *Singapore 1942, Britain's Greatest Defeat*, p. 124.

31 Heath, quoted in Kirby, p. 270.

32 Barstow quoted in Kirby, p. 270.

33 Kirby, p. 271.

34 Kirby, footnote, p. 270.

35 Kirby, p. 272.

36 Warren, *Singapore 1942, Britain's Greatest Defeat*, p. 129.

37 Masanobu Tsuji, *Singapore, The Japanese Version*, p. 151.

13 SLIM RIVER

1 Simson, *Singapore Too Little, Too Late*, p. 67.

2 Kirby, pp. 275–6.

3 Alan Warren, *Singapore 1942, Britain's Greatest Defeat*, p. 134.

4 ibid.

5 Masanobu Tsuji, *Singapore 1942, The Japanese Version*, p. 171.

6 Kirby, p. 276.

7 Deakin, quoted in Kirby, p. 277.

8 I. M. Stewart, *History of the Argyll & Sutherland Highlanders 2nd Battalion*, p. 80.

9 Simson, *Singapore Too Little, Too Late*, p. 44.

10 Kirby, p. 279.

11 These figures are quoted in Kirby, p. 281 (footnote).

12 Lieutenant-General A. E. Percival, 'Operations of Malaya Command from 08.12.1941 to 15.02.1942', *London Gazette*.

13 Kirby, *The Chain of Disaster*, p. 180.

14 Kinvig, *Scapegoat, General Percival of Singapore*, p. 178.

15 Bennett Diary.

16 Kinvig, *Scapegoat, General Percival of Singapore*, p. 178.

17 Wavell to the Chiefs of Staff, 9 January, quoted in Connell, *Wavell, Supreme Commander*, p. 87.

18 Kirby, p. 285.

14 GEMAS

1 Alan Warren, *Singapore 1942, Britain's Greatest Defeat*, p. 150.

2 Kirby, p. 289.

3 Alan Warren, *Singapore 1942, Britain's Greatest Defeat*, p. 150.

4 Lieutenant-General A. E. Percival, 'Operations of Malaya Command from 08.12.1941 to 15.02.1942', *London Gazette*.

5 Percival, *The War In Malaya*, p. 214.

6 Wigmore, *The Japanese Thrust*, p. 30.

7 ibid. p. 36.

8 Maston quoted in *Recollections*, 2/30th Battalion AIF Association, a five DVD disc set, 1994.

9 Lieutenant Albert Farr, Signals Officer, 2/30th Battalion, interview with the author, Sydney, 17 April 2007.

10 Captain Rowley Richards, RMO 2/15th Field Regiment, interview with the author, Sydney, 16 April 2007.

11 Quoted in a number of works e.g., Garth Pratten, *Australian Battalion Commanders in the Second World War*, p. 140.

12 Wigmore, *The Japanese Thrust*, p. 211.

13 Wigmore, *The Japanese Thrust*, p. 212.

14 AWM 52 8/3/30, the 2/30th Battalion Unit Diary. A detailed map is shown in the January–February 1942 Diary.

15 A. W. Penfold, W. C. Baylis, K. E. Crispin, *Galleghans's Greyhounds*, pp. 81–2.

16 Private Ray Brown quoted in *Recollections 2/30th Battalion AIF Association*, a five DVD disc set, 1994.

17 Corporal Harry Holden quoted in *Recollections 2/30th Battalion AIF Association*, a five DVD disc set, 1994.

18 A. W. Penfold, W. C. Baylis, K. E. Crispin, *Galleghans's Greyhounds*, p. 89.

19 Corporal Harry Holden quoted in *Recollections 2/30th Battalion AIF Association*, a five DVD disc set, 1994.

20 A. W. Penfold, W. C. Baylis, K. E. Crispin, *Galleghan's Greyhounds*, p. 88.

21 Private Ray Brown quoted in *Recollections 2/30th Battalion AIF Association*, a five DVD disc set, 1994.

22 Corporal Harry Holden quoted in *Recollections 2/30th Battalion AIF Association*, a five DVD disc set, 1994.

23 Lieutenant Lyn Booth quoted in *Recollections 2/30th Battalion AIF Association*, a five DVD disc set, 1994.

24 Kenneth Harrison, *The Brave Japanese*, p. 25.

25 ibid. p. 26.

26 Wigmore, *The Japanese Thrust*, p. 217.

27 AWM 52 8/3/30, the 2/30th Battalion Unit Diary. The January Diary 1942.

28 ibid.

29 ibid.

30 A. W. Penfold, W. C. Baylis, K. E. Crispin, *Galleghan's Greyhounds*, p. 111.

31 AWM 52 8/3/30, the 2/30th Battalion Unit Diary. The January Diary 1942.

32 A. W. Penfold, W. C. Baylis, K. E. Crispin, *Galleghan's Greyhounds*, pp. 121–2.

33 Ian Morrison, *Malayan Postscript*, p.114.

15 THE BATTLE OF MUAR

1 Kirby, p. 304.

2 ibid.

3 Alan Warren, *Singapore 1942, Britain's Greatest Defeat*, p. 161.

4 Corporal Bob Christie, 2/29th Battalion, interview with the author, Melbourne, 6 January 2005.

5 Captain Victor Brand, RMO, 2/29th Battalion, interview with the author, Melbourne, 5 January 2005.

6 Captain Bill Bowring in R. W. Christie (editor), *A History of the 2/29 Battalion 8th Division AIF*, p. 45.

7 Wigmore, *The Japanese Thrust*, p. 226.

8 Colin E. Finkemeyer, *It Happened To Us*, p. 34.

9 Corporal Jim Kennedy, 2/29th Battalion, interview with the author, Albury NSW, 10 January 2005.

10 Colin E. Finkemeyer, *It Happened To Us*, p. 32.

11 ibid.

12 Captain Victor Brand, RMO, 2/29th Battalion, interview with the author, Melbourne, 5 January 2005.

13 AWM 52 8/3/29, the 2/29th Battalion Unit Diary. The January Diary 1942.

14 Colin E. Finkemeyer, *It Happened To Us*, p. 34.

15 ibid.

16 Kenneth Harrison, *The Brave Japanese*, p. 48.

17 Lance-Corporal John Roxburgh, 2/29th Battalion, interview with the author, Albury NSW, 10 January 2005.

18 Private John Boehm, B Company, 2/29th Battalion, interview with the author, Geelong Victoria, 28 December 2005.

19 Captain Victor Brand, RMO, 2/29th Battalion, interview with the author, Melbourne, 5 January 2005.

20 ibid.

21 ibid.

22 Captain Bill Bowring in R. W. Christie (editor), *A History of the 2/29 Battalion 8th Division AIF* p. 45.

23 Captain Victor Brand, RMO, 2/29th Battalion, interview with the author, Melbourne, 5 January 2005.

24 Lieutenant Jim Howard, Carrier Platoon, 2/19th Battalion, interview with the author, Port Macquarie, NSW, 28 September 2004.

25 Private Gus Halloran, Signals 2/19th Battalion, interview with the author, Port Macquarie, NSW, 29 September 2004.

26 Private Jim Stewart, Signals, 2/19th Battalion, interview with the author, Sydney, 1 October 2004.

27 Lieutenant Jim Howard, Carrier Platoon, 2/19th Battalion, interview with the author, Port Macquarie, NSW, 28 September 2004.

28 ibid.

29 Captain Bill Bowring in R. W. Christie (editor), *A History of the 2/29 Battalion 8th Division AIF* p. 47.

30 Wigmore, *The Japanese Thrust*, p. 231.

31 Newton, *The Grim Glory of the 2/19 Battalion AIF*, p. 200.

32 ibid.

33 Lieutenant Ben Hackney quoted in Wigmore, *The Japanese Thrust*, p. 233. (footnote).

16 TO PARIT SULONG

1 Sergeant Bert Mettam, Mortar Platoon, 2/29th Battalion, interview with the author, Adelaide, August 2005.

2 Lance-Corporal John Roxburgh, HQ Company, 2/29th Battalion, War Diary, copy kindly given to the author 5 October 2005.

3 AWM 52 8/3/29, the 2/29th Battalion Unit Diary. The January Diary 1942.

4 Newton, *The Grim Glory of the 2/19 Battalion AIF*, p. 205.

5 AWM 52 8/3/29, the 2/29th Battalion Unit Diary. The January Diary 1942.

6 Corporal Bob Christie, 2/29th Battalion, interview with the author, Melbourne, 6 January 2005.

7 Lance-Corporal John Roxburgh, HQ Company, 2/29th Battalion, War Diary, copy kindly given to the author 5 October 2005.

8 Corporal Bob Christie, 2/29th Battalion, interview with the author, Melbourne, 6 January 2005.

9 Captain Victor Brand, RMO, 2/29th Battalion, interview with the author, Melbourne, 5 January 2005.

10 Sergeant Bert Mettam, Mortar Platoon, 2/29th Battalion, interview with the author, Adelaide, August 2005.

11 Brand in John Lack, *No Lost Battalion*, p. 92.

12 ibid.

13 Wigmore (p. 234) states the strength of the 2/29th remnant at Bakri as seven officers and 190 other ranks. It would appear that he arrived at this figure at least partly using the 2/19th Unit Diary, which states ' A Coy 50, B Coy 100, C Coy 50' but does not state the number of officers.

14 Sergeant Bert Mettam, Mortar Platoon, 2/29th Battalion, interview with the author, Adelaide, August 2005.

15 Lance-Corporal John Roxburgh, 2/29th Battalion, interview with the author, Albury NSW, 10 January 2005.

16 Sergeant Bert Mettam, Mortar Platoon, 2/29th Battalion, interview with the author, Adelaide, August 2005.

17 Corporal Bob Christie, 2/29th Battalion, interview with the author, Melbourne, 6 January 2005.

18 Corporal Jim Kennedy, 2/29th Battalion, interview with the author, Albury NSW, 10 January 2005.

19 John Lack, *No Lost Battalion*, p. 94.

20 Private Gus Halloran, Signals, 2/19th Battalion, interview with the author, Port Macquarie, NSW, 29 September 2004.

21 The structure and order of withdrawal of Anderson's column is taken from the 2/19th Unit Diary and Anderson's account published in Newton's *The Grim Glory of the 2/19 Battalion AIF*.

22 AWM 52 8/3/19, the 2/19th Battalion Unit Diary. The January Diary 1942. There is a detailed map provided in the Diary.

23 Karl Hack and Kevin Blackburn, *Did Singapore Have To Fall?* p. 157.

24 Private Gus Halloran, Signals, 2/19th Battalion, interview with the author, Port Macquarie, NSW, 29 September 2004.

25 Newton, *The Grim Glory of the 2/19 Battalion AIF*, p. 211.

26 Private Jim Stewart, Signals, 2/19th Battalion, interview with the author, Sydney, 1 October 2004.

27 Wigmore, *The Japanese Thrust*, p. 239.

28 Private Gus Halloran, Signals, 2/19th Battalion, interview with the author, Port Macquarie, NSW, 29 September 2004.

29 Gunner Jim Kerr, 4th Anti-Tank Regiment, interview with the author, Melbourne, 20 April 2007.

30 Wigmore, *The Japanese Thrust*, p. 249.

31 Gunner Jim Kerr, 4th Anti-Tank Regiment, interview with the author, Melbourne 20 April 2007.

32 AWM 52 8/3/19, the 2/19th Battalion Unit Diary. The January Diary 1942.

33 Lieutenant Jim Howard, Carrier Platoon, 2/19th Battalion, interview with the author, Port Macquarie, NSW, 28 September, 2004.

34 Captain Victor Brand, RMO, 2/29th Battalion, interview with the author, Melbourne, 5 January 2005.

35 Private Jim Stewart, Signals, 2/19th Battalion, interview with the author, Sydney, 1 October 2004.

36 Russell Braddon, *The Naked Island*, p. 78.

37 Lieutenant Jim Howard, Carrier Platoon, 2/19th Battalion, interview with the author, Port Macquarie, NSW, 28 September, 2004.

38 The 2/19th Unit Diary.

39 Private Charles Edwards, 2/19th Battalion, interview with the author, Melbourne, 17 February 2007.

40 Lionel Wigmore, *The Japanese Thrust*, p. 249.

41 Lieutenant Jim Howard, Carrier Platoon, 2/19th Battalion, interview with the author, Port Macquarie, NSW, 28 September, 2004.

42 Lynette Ramsay Silver, *The Bridge at Parit Sulong*, p. 177.

43 ibid. p. 182.

44 ibid. p. 185.

45 Percival, *The War in Malaya*, p. 233.

17 A GREAT SCANDAL

1 Kirby, p.306.

2 ibid. p. 307.

3 Wigmore, *The Japanese Thrust*, pp. 235–6.

4 AWM 553/5/23, *Operations of 8 Aust Division in Malaya 1941–1942*, Colonel J. H. Thyer, Part 1, p. 53.

5 Wigmore, *The Japanese Thrust*, p. 236.

6 ibid.

7 AWM 52, 1/5/17, 8 Australian Division General Staff Branch Diary, January–February 1942.

8 AWM 553/5/23, *Operations of 8 Aust Division in Malaya 1941–1942*, Colonel J. H. Thyer, Part 1, p. 53.

9 Percival, *The War in Malaya*, p. 231.

10 AWM 553/5/23, *Operations of 8 Aust Division in Malaya 1941–1942*, Colonel J. H. Thyer, Part 1, p. 53.

11 AWM 52, 1/5/17, 8th Australian Division General Staff Branch Diary, January–February 1942.

12 AWM 553/5/23, *Operations of 8 Aust Division in Malaya 1941–1942*, Colonel J. H. Thyer, Part 1, p. 53.

13 ibid.

14 ibid.

15 ibid. pp. 53–4.

16 AWM 553/5/23, *Operations of 8 Aust Division in Malaya 1941–1942*, Colonel J. H. Thyer, Part 1, p. 54.

17 ibid.

18 ibid.

19 ibid.

20 Percival, *The War in Malaya*, p. 232.

21 ibid.

22 Quoted in Lodge, *The Fall of General Gordon Bennett*, p. 104.

23 Kirby, p. 314.

24 Wigmore, *The Japanese Thrust*, p. 231.

25 Captain C. G. T. Dean, *The Loyal Regiment (North Lancashire) 1919–1953*, pp. 75–7 and pp. 131–5.

26 Bennett Diary.

27 Quoted in Connell, *Wavell, Supreme Commander*, p. 110.

28 Quoted in Connell, *Wavell, Supreme Commander*, pp. 110–11.

29 ibid. p. 111.

30 Quoted in Connell, *Wavell, Supreme Commander*, p. 112.

31 ibid. pp. 112–13.

32 Winston Churchill, *The Second World War*, Vol. IV, p. 43.

33 ibid. p. 44.

34 Kirby, p. 329.

35 ibid.

36 Kirby, *The Chain of Disaster*, p. 207.

37 Wigmore, *The Japanese Thrust*, p. 262.

38 AWM 52 8/3/18, The 2/18th Battalion Unit Diary. The January–February Diary 1942.

39 ibid.

40 ibid.

41 ibid.

42 AWM 52 8/3/18, The 2/18th Battalion Unit Diary. The January–February Diary 1942.

43 Wigmore, *The Japanese Thrust*, p. 268.

44 Warren, *Singapore 1942, Britain's Greatest Defeat*, p. 191.

45 Wigmore, *The Japanese Thrust*, p. 269.

18 TO THE CAUSEWAY

1 A. W. Penfold, W. C. Baylis, K. E. Crispin, *Galleghan's Greyhounds*, p. 148.

2 AWM 52 8/3/30, The 2/30th Battalion Unit Diary, The January–February Diary 1942. Dispositions taken from a map, 'Appendix B'.

3 A. W. Penfold, W. C Baylis, K. E. Crispin, *Galleghan's Greyhounds*, p. 152.

4 ibid. p. 153.

5 The timing of the attack and enemy strength is taken from the 2/30th Battalion Unit Diary, while its location is derived from the 2/30th unit history.

6 A. W. Penfold, W. C. Baylis, K. E. Crispin, *Galleghan's Greyhounds*, p. 155.

7 ibid. p. 158.

8 AWM 52 8/3/30, The 2/30th Battalion Unit Diary, The January–February Diary 1942.

9 ibid.

10 Wigmore, *The Japanese Thrust*, p. 269.

11 Kirby, p. 335.

12 AWM 54 553/5/23, *Operations of 8 Aust Division in Malaya 1941–1942*, Colonel J. H. Thyer, Part 1, p. 65.

13 Wigmore, *The Japanese Thrust*, p. 269.

14 AWM 54 553/5/23, *Operations of 8 Aust Division in Malaya 1941–1942*, Colonel J. H. Thyer, Part 1, p. 65.

15 Kirby, p. 335.

16 AWM 52 8/3/26, The 2/26th Battalion Unit Diary, The January–February Diary 1942.

17 ibid.

18 ibid.

19 The description of the ground at the Namazie Rubber Estate and the dispositions are taken from: a map in AWM 52 8/3/26; the 2/26th Battalion Unit Diary; the January–February Diary 1942; and a map, descriptions and dispositions in A. W. Penfold, W. C. Baylis, K. E. Crispin, *Galleghan's Greyhounds*, p. 163.

20 A. W. Penfold, W. C. Baylis, K. E. Crispin, *Galleghan's Greyhounds*, p. 165.

21 AWM 52 8/3/26, The 2/26th Battalion Unit Diary, The January–February Diary 1942.

22 Wigmore, *The Japanese Thrust*, p. 276.

23 AWM 52 8/3/30, The 2/30th Battalion Unit Diary, The January–February Diary 1942.

24 ibid.

25 Bennett Diary.

26 Wigmore, *The Japanese Thrust*, p. 277.

27 A. W. Penfold, W. C. Baylis, K. E. Crispin, *Galleghan's Greyhounds*, pp. 173–4.

28 AWM 52 8/3/26, The 2/26th Battalion Unit Diary, The January–February Diary 1942.

29 ibid.

30 ibid.

31 AWM 52 8/3/26, The 2/26th Battalion Unit Diary, The January–February Diary 1942.

32 ibid.

33 ibid.

34 Wigmore, *The Japanese Thrust*, p. 279.

35 ibid. p. 257.

36 ibid. p. 270.

37 Kirby, p. 335.

38 ibid. p. 337.

39 ibid. p. 336.

40 Moses Papers (held by Neil McDonald in Sydney: various parts kindly copied and given to the author October 2004). The quoted Trott account is included.

41 Moses letter 19 July 1982 (Moses Papers).

42 General H. Gordon Bennett, *Why Singapore Fell*, p. 157.

43 Moses, letter 19 July 1982 (Moses Papers).

44 John Wyett, *Staff Wallah*, p. 82.

19 'COMETH THE HOUR...'

1 Percival, *The War in Malaya*, pp. 259–60.

2 Morrison, *Malayan Postscript*, p. 156.

3 ibid.

4 ibid.

5 Kirby, pp. 234–5, p. 295.

6 Percival, *The War in Malaya*, p. 184.

7 Warren, *Singapore 1942, Britain's Greatest Defeat*, p. 211.

8 Kirby, *The Chain of Disaster*, p. 213.

9 Percival, *The War in Malaya*, p. 184.

10 ibid.

11 A detailed account of these events is given in Christopher Shores and Brian Cull, *Bloody Shambles*, p. 150.

12 Simson, *Singapore Too Little, Too Late*, pp. 83–91.

13 Kirby, *The Chain of Disaster*, footnote, p. 213, also Simson, *Singapore Too Little, Too Late*, p. 106.

14 Kirby, p. 361.

15 Wigmore, *The Japanese Thrust*, p. 292.

16 Kirby, p. 370.

17 Kirby, *The Chain of Disaster*, p. 221.

18 Percival, *The War in Malaya*, p. 263.

19 Warren, *Singapore 1942, Britain's Greatest Defeat*, p. 215.

20 Kirby, footnote, p. 364.

21 Percival, *The War in Malaya*, p. 262.

22 Kirby, *The Chain of Disaster*, p. 221.

23 Wigmore, *The Japanese Thrust*, footnote, p. 297.

24 ibid. p. 290.

25 Wigmore, *The Japanese Thrust*, p. 296, AWM 52 8/3/19, The 2/19th Battalion Unit Diary, the January–February Diary 1942; Newton, R. W., *The Grim Glory of the 2/19 Battalion AIF*, pp. 255–6.

26 John Lack, *No Lost Battalion*, p. 108.

27 ibid. p.109.

28 Corporal Jim Kennedy, 2/29th Battalion, interview with the author, Albury, NSW, 10 January 2005.

29 Wigmore, *The Japanese Thrust*, p. 302.

30 Corporal Jim Kennedy and Lance-Corporal John Roxburgh, 2/29th Battalion, interview with the author, Albury, NSW, 10 January 2005.

31 Wigmore, *The Japanese Thrust*, p. 304.

32 AWM 54 553/5/23, *Operations of 8 Aust Division in Malaya 1941–1942*, Colonel J. H. Thyer, Part 1, p. 94.

33 ibid.

34 Warren, *Singapore 1942, Britain's Greatest Defeat*, p. 217.

35 ibid. p. 213.

36 Simson, *Singapore Too Little, Too Late*, p. 36.

37 AWM 54 553/5/23, *Operations of 8 Aust Division in Malaya 1941–1942*, Colonel J. H. Thyer, Part 1, p. 98.

38 Warren, *Singapore 1942, Britain's Greatest Defeat*, p. 214.

39 Newton, R. W., *The Grim Glory of the 2/19 Battalion AIF*, pp. 293–5.

40 Wall, Don, *Singapore and Beyond, The Story of the 2/20 Battalion AIF*, p. 56.

41 ibid.

42 AWM 52, 1/5/17 8th Australian Division General Staff Branch, January–February 1942.

43 Kirby, p. 374.

44 Warren, *Singapore 1942, Britain's Greatest Defeat*, p. 222.

45 ibid.

46 AWM 54 553/5/23, *Operations of 8 Aust Division in Malaya 1941–1942*, Colonel J. H. Thyer, Part 1, p. 102.

20 'I DREW MY MEN BACK . . .'

1 Wigmore, *The Japanese Thrust*, p. 334.

2 Kirby, *The Chain of Disaster*, p. 226.

3 ibid. p. 227.

4 ibid.

5 Wigmore, *The Japanese Thrust*, (footnote), p. 311.

6 ibid.

7 Cliff Whitelocke, *Gunners in the Jungle*, p. 119.

8 Warren, *Singapore 1942, Britain's Greatest Defeat*, p. 225.

9 AWM 3DRL/2691, Papers of Brigadier A. L. Varley, Folder 3.

10 Newton, R W., *The Grim Glory of the 2/19 Battalion AIF*, pp. 298–9.

11 Kirby, p. 371.

12 Newton, R. W., *The Grim Glory of the 2/19 Battalion AIF*, p. 302.

13 ibid.

14 13 Platoon's 2/4th dispositions are taken from a map compiled by Major Cough, 2/4th M G Bn and sent to historian Don Wall, 2/20th Battalion. A copy of the map and accounts of the action that night collected by Cough were kindly given to the author by the 2/4th historian Neville Browning in May 2012. Future references to this material will be cited as 'Neville Browning'.

15 Wall, *Singapore and Beyond, The Story of the Men of the 2/20 Battalion AIF*, p. 64.

16 Neville Browning.

17 ibid.

18 Wall, *Singapore and Beyond, The Story of the Men of the 2/20 Battalion AIF*, pp. 70–1.

19 Shelly, quoted in Wall, *Singapore and Beyond, The Story of the Men of the 2/20 Battalion AIF*, pp. 66–7.

20 AWM 3DRL/2691, Papers of Brigadier A. L. Varley, Folder 3.

21 ibid.

22 Wigmore, *The Japanese Thrust*, p. 315.

23 ibid.

24 Newton, R. W., *The Grim Glory of the 2/19 Battalion AIF*, p. 307.

25 ibid.

26 Private Ron Stanton, C Company, 2/19th Battalion, interview with the author, Bega, New South Wales, 12 January 2005.

27 Sergeant Bert Donaldson, D Company, 2/19th Battalion, interview with the author Temora, New South Wales, 8 October 2005.

28 Wall, *Singapore and Beyond, The Story of the Men of the 2/20 Battalion AIF*, p. 85.

29 AWM 3DRL/2691, Papers of Brigadier A. L. Varley, Folder 3.

30 Cody, *Ghosts in Khaki, The History of the 2/4th Machine Gun Battalion*, p. 123.

31 Newton, R. W., *The Grim Glory of the 2/19 Battalion AIF*, p. 318.

32 ibid.

33 ibid. p. 319.

34 AWM 54 553/5/23, *Operations of 8 Aust Division in Malaya 1941–1942*, Colonel J. H. Thyer, p. 125.

35 AWM 52 8/3/29, the 2/29th Battalion Unit Diary. The February Diary 1942. 'Comments by CO and Additions to Unit War Diary for Period subsequent to 25 Jan 42.'

36 Neville Browning.

37 Cough letter to Wall, Neville Browning.

38 The six men concerned were not last minute reinforcements in Perth, and had fought well with Wankey's shoreline guns. Confirmed by their records held by Neville Browning. Telephone conversation with Browning, 3 June 2012.

39 Christopher Shores and Brian Cull, *Bloody Shambles*, p. 373.

40 ibid.

41 Wigmore, *The Japanese Thrust*, p. 323.

42 AWM 52 8/2/22 The 22nd Brigade War Diary, the February Diary 1942, and Appendix B.

43 Wigmore, *The Japanese Thrust*, p. 298.

44 Magarry, Ron., *The Battalion Story, 2/26th Infantry Battalion, 8th Division—AIF*, p. 125.

45 ibid.

46 AWM 52 8/2/27 The 27th Brigade War Diary, the February Diary 1942.

47 AWM 52 8/3/19, the 2/19th Battalion Unit Diary, the February Diary 1942.

48 Quoted in Warren, *Singapore 1942, Britain's Greatest Defeat*, p. 233.

49 Magarry, Ron, *The Battalion Story, 2/26th Infantry Battalion, 8th Division—AIF*, p. 130. Also, Pratten, Garth, *Australian Battalion Commanders in the Second World War*, p. 137.

50 Wigmore, *The Japanese Thrust*, p. 329.

51 ibid.

52 AWM 73/7 Official War Historian working notes, correspondence and source material (Kirby and Wigmore); and AWM 54 553/5/23, *Operations of 8 Aust Division in Malaya 1941 1942*, Colonel J. H. Thyer, pp. 130 and 198.

53 AWM 52 8/2/27 The 27th Brigade War Diary, the February Diary 1942.

54 AWM 93 50/2/23/285 Galleghan to Wigmore, 26 March 1954, p. 18.

55 AWM 73/7 Official War Historian working notes, correspondence and source material (Kirby and Wigmore).

56 ibid.

57 Pratten, *Australian Battalion Commanders in the Second World War*, pp. 161–2.

58 AWM 73/7 Official War Historian working notes, correspondence and source material (Kirby and Wigmore). Interview with Galleghan, 22 January 1953.

59 AWM 67, 3/36, Wigmore interview with Blackburn, 21 January 1953. Also quoted by Blackburn's biographer, Faukner, Andrew *Arthur Blackburn VC*, p. 390.

60 AWM 52 8/3/26, the 2/26th Battalion Unit Diary, the February Diary 1942.

61 Wigmore, *The Japanese Thrust*, p. 333.

62 ibid. p. 330.

63 AWM 52 8/3/26, the 2/26th Battalion Unit Diary, the February Diary 1942.

64 Masanobu Tsuji, *Singapore, The Japanese Version*, p. 244.

65 ibid. p. 243.

66 ibid. p. 245.

67 ibid.

68 Kirby, p. 380.

69 Wigmore, *The Japanese Thrust*, p. 337.

70 A. W. Penfold, W. C. Baylis, K. E. Crispin, *Galleghan's Greyhounds*, p. 199.

21 FURTHER RETREATS

1 Morrison, *Malayan Postscript*, p. 177.

2 ibid.

3 ibid. p. 178.

4 Kirby, p. 383.

5 AWM 52 8/3/30, the 2/30th Battalion Unit Diary, the February Diary 1942.

6 AWM 52 8/2/27 The 27th Brigade War Diary, the February Diary 1942.

7 AWM 73/7 Official War Historian working notes, correspondence and source material (Kirby and Wigmore). Copy of a letter dated 19 November 1952, Harrison to Kirby.

8 Kirby, Appendix 27, p. 350.

9 Wigmore, *The Japanese Thrust*, p. 337.

10 AWM 54 553/5/23, *Operations of 8 Aust Division in Malaya 1941–1942*, Colonel J. H. Thyer, p. 127.

11 Warren, *Singapore 1942, Britain's Greatest Defeat*, p. 240.

12 Taylor, quoted in Warren, *Singapore 1942, Britain's Greatest Defeat*, p. 240.

13 Winston Churchill, *The Second World War*, Vol. IV, pp. 87–8.

14 Kinvig, *Scapegoat, General Percival of Singapore*, p. 209.

15 AWM 54 553/5/23, *Operations of 8 Aust Division in Malaya 1941–1942*, Colonel J. H. Thyer. Appendix B.

16 ibid. p. 137.

17 Kirby, p. 391.

18 AWM 54 553/5/23, *Operations of 8 Aust Division in Malaya 1941–1942*, Colonel J. H. Thyer, p. 137.

19 AWM 52 8/3/29, The 2/29th Battalion Unit Diary, the February Diary 1942.

20 Newton, R. W., *The Grim Glory of the 2/19 Battalion AIF*, p. 328.

21 Wall, *Singapore and Beyond, The Story of the 2/20th Battalion AIF*, p. 92.

22 AWM 54 553/5/23, *Operations of 8 Aust Division in Malaya 1941–1942*, Colonel J. H. Thyer, p. 138.

23 ibid.

24 Wigmore, *The Japanese Thrust*, p. 347.

25 Wall, *Singapore and Beyond, The Story of the Men of the 2/20 Battalion AIF*, p. 95.

26 ibid.

27 AWM 54 553/5/23, *Operations of 8 Aust Division in Malaya 1941–1942*, Colonel J. H. Thyer, p. 140.

28 Kirby, p. 391.

29 AWM 54 553/5/23, *Operations of 8 Aust Division in Malaya 1941–1942*, Colonel J. H. Thyer, p. 137.

30 Kirby, p. 391.

31 Wigmore, *The Japanese Thrust*, footnote, p. 348.

32 ibid. p. 353.

33 Warren, *Singapore 1942, Britain's Greatest Defeat*, p. 247.

34 Kirby, p. 395.

35 Warren, *Singapore 1942, Britain's Greatest Defeat*, p. 248.

36 Wigmore, *The Japanese Thrust*, footnote, p. 354.

37 ibid. footnote. Wigmore's statement that 'Maxwell has recorded emphatically that it [the order] came from General Percival' comes from an interview with Maxwell by Wigmore and Kirby on 26 January 1953. AWM 73/7.

38 Kirby, p. 399.

39 Percival, *The War in Malaya*, p. 281.

40 Shenton Diary, quoted in Brian Montgomery, *Shenton of Singapore*, p. 132.

41 ibid.

42 Papers of Brigadier Taylor, AWM PR 85/42, 419/49/34.

22 FINAL DAYS

1 AWM 52 18/2/21, The 8th Division Provost Company Unit Diary.

 2 ibid.

 3 ibid.

 4 ibid.

 5 AWM PR 84/252, 419/18/25, Chambers wrote 'Five Days In Singapore' while in Changi during the period Feb–April 1942. (Further reference to this work will be cited as 'Chambers, *Five Days in Singapore*'.)

 6 AWM 52 18/2/21, The 8th Division Provost Company Unit Diary.

 7 Wigmore, *The Japanese Thrust*, footnote, p. 370.

 8 AWM 54 553/5/23, *Operations of 8 Aust Division in Malaya 1941–1942*, Colonel J. H. Thyer, p. 137.

 9 Quoted in, Winston Churchill, *The Second World War*, Vol. IV, p. 91.

10 Kinvig, *Scapegoat, General Percival of Singapore*, p. 213, and Warren, *Singapore 1942, Britain's Greatest Defeat*, p. 258; both cite Percival's record of the conversation in the Imperial War Museum.

11 Kinvig, *Scapegoat, General Percival of Singapore*, p. 213.

12 Percival, *The War in Malaya*, p. 286.

13 Quoted in Winston Churchill, *The Second World War*, Vol. IV, p. 91.

14 ibid.

15 ibid.

16 Chambers, *Five Days in Singapore*.

17 AWM 52 18/2/21, The 8th Division Provost Company Unit Diary.

18 Chambers, *Five Days in Singapore*.

19 Masanobu Tsuji, *Singapore, The Japanese Version*, p. 259.

20 Wigmore, *The Japanese Thrust*, footnote, p. 374.

21 AWM 52 18/2/21, The 8th Division Provost Company Unit Diary.

22 Menz, Captain A. (Alf), 8 Australian Division Provost Company, personal Diary, copy most kindly lent to the author, by his sister, Muriel Yates 10 March 2007. Cited hereafter as 'Menz Diary'.

23 Quoted in Winston Churchill, *The Second World War*, Vol. IV, pp. 92–4.

24 Quoted in Warren, *Singapore 1942, Britain's Greatest Defeat*, p. 265.

25 Private Gus Halloran, 2/19th Battalion, interview with the author, Port Macquarie, NSW, 18 April 2005.

26 Private Paddy O'Toole, 2/29th Battalion, interview with the author, Melbourne, 4 January 2006.

27 Sergeant Frank Baker, 2/20th Battalion, interview with the author, Sydney, 9 January 2006.

28 Stan Arneil, *One Man's War*, p. 9.

29 Gunner Richard Haynes, 2/10th Field Regiment, Diary and Papers. Haynes collection was given to the author in Canberra by historian Janet Uhr on 6 April 2010.

PART III   PUDU AND CHANGI

23 'ROARING REGGIE'

1 Private Charles Letts, Malay Volunteers, interview Singapore, 4 January 2008. The interview was not taped at Letts's insistence, but a record of the interview, undertaken with the author and Frank Taylor, was committed to paper later that day.

2 Newton, R. W., *The Grim Glory of the 2/19 Battalion AIF*, p. 471.

3 Private Charles Edwards, 2/19th Battalion, interview with the author, Melbourne, 17 February 2007. Edwards paced out and recorded the dimensions of Pudu while in captivity. He also drew a comprehensive map of the prison, which is reproduced in the narrative with accompanying notes taken from the interview with the author.

4 Russell Braddon, *The Naked Island*, p. 100.

5 Thornton in Colin E. Finkemeyer, *It Happened To Us*, p. 43.

6 Kenneth Harrison, *The Brave Japanese*, p. 101.

7 ibid.

8 Private Charles Edwards, 2/19th Battalion, interview with the author, Melbourne, 17 February 2007; Sergeant Jack de Loas, 2/19th Battalion, interview with the author, Bomaderry, NSW, 13 January 2005; Gunner Jim Kerr, 4th Anti-Tank Regiment, interview with the author, Melbourne, 20 April 2007. Newton, R. W., *The Grim Glory of the 2/19 Battalion AIF*, pp. 471 and 477.

9 Newton, R. W., *The Grim Glory of the 2/19 Battalion AIF*, p. 472.

10 Private Charles Edwards, 2/19th Battalion, interview with the author, Melbourne, 17 February 2007.

11 Russell Braddon, *The Naked Island*, p. 102.

12 ibid. p. 113.

13 Private Charles Edwards, 2/19th Battalion, interview with the author, Melbourne, 17 February 2007.

14 ibid.

15 Private Gus Halloran, 2/19th Battalion, interview with the author, Port Macquarie, NSW, 29 September 2004.

16 Sergeant Jack de Loas, 2/19th Battalion, interview with the author, Bomaderry, NSW, 13 January 2005.

17 ibid.

18 Private Charles Edwards, 2/19th Battalion, interview with the author, Melbourne, 17 February 2007.

19 Newton, R. W., *The Grim Glory of the 2/19 Battalion AIF*, p. 471.

20 Private Charles Edwards, 2/19th Battalion, interview with the author, Melbourne, 17 February 2007.

21 Russell Braddon, *The Naked Island*, p. 118.

22 Private Charles Edwards, 2/19th Battalion, interview with the author, Melbourne, 17 February 2007.

23 Russell Braddon, *The Naked Island*, p. 109.

24 Newton, R. W., *The Grim Glory of the 2/19 Battalion AIF*, p. 473.

25 ibid. p. 473.

26 Lieutenant Ken Archer quoted in Newton, R. W., *The Grim Glory of the 2/19 Battalion AIF*, p. 473.

27 Private Charles Edwards, 2/19th Battalion, interview with the author, Melbourne, 17 February 2007.

28 Newton, R. W., *The Grim Glory of the 2/19 Battalion AIF*, p. 475.

29 Sergeant Jack de Loas, 2/19th Battalion, interview with the author, Bomaderry, NSW, 13 January 2005; Gunner Jim Kerr, 4th Anti-Tank Regiment, interview with the author, Melbourne, 20 April 2007; Private Charles Edwards, 2/19th Battalion, interview with the author, Melbourne, 17 February 2007.

30 Newton, R. W., *The Grim Glory of the 2/19 Battalion AIF*, p. 476.

31 Private Charles Edwards, 2/19th Battalion, interview with the author, Melbourne, 17 February 2007.

32 ibid.

33 Newton, R. W., *The Grim Glory of the 2/19 Battalion AIF*, p. 477.

34 Private Charles Edwards, 2/19th Battalion, interview with the author, Melbourne, 17 February 2007.

35 ibid.

36 Newton, R. W., *The Grim Glory of the 2/19 Battalion AIF*, p. 478.

37 Kenneth Harrison, *The Brave Japanese*, p. 125.

38 Newton, R. W., *The Grim Glory of the 2/19 Battalion AIF*, p. 479.

39 Lynette Ramsay Silver, *The Bridge at Parit Sulong*, p. 260.

40 Lynette Ramsay Silver provides us with an excellent and detailed account of the escape and fate of both parties in *The Bridge at Parit Sulong*, pp. 255–61.

41 Newton, R. W., *The Grim Glory of the 2/19 Battalion AIF*, p. 480.

42 Kenneth Harrison, *The Brave Japanese*, p. 122.

43 Newton, R. W., *The Grim Glory of the 2/19 Battalion AIF*, pp. 481–2.

44 ibid. p. 482.

24 LIGHT OF THE SOUTH

1 Wigmore, *The Japanese Thrust*, p. 511. The Australian Official History has Lionel Wigmore as its author. However, the prisoner of war section was written by A. J. Sweeting. Thus, when the Australian Official History is cited, it will continue as 'Wigmore, *The Japanese Thrust*', although the reader should be aware that Sweeting wrote the section.

2 Wigmore, *The Japanese Thrust*, p. 511.

3 Newton, R. W., *The Grim Glory of the 2/19 Battalion AIF*, p. 390.

4 Kinvig, *Scapegoat, General Percival of Singapore*, p. 221.

5 ibid.

6 Rowley Richards, *A Doctor's War*, p. 71.

7 ibid.

8 Private Gus Halloran, 2/19th Battalion, interview with the author, Port Macquarie, NSW, 29 September 2004.

9 Gunner Richard Haynes, 2/10th Field Regiment, Diary and Papers. Haynes's collection was given to the author in Canberra by historian Janet Uhr on 6 April 2010. Referred to hereafter as 'Gunner Richard Haynes, 2/10th Field Regiment, diary and papers'.

10 Russell Braddon, *The Naked Island*, pp. 153–4.

11 Private Gus Halloran, 2/19th Battalion, interview with the author, Port Macquarie, NSW, 29 September 2004.

12 R. P. W. Havers, *Reassessing the Japanese prisoner of War Experience, The Changi POW Camp, Singapore, 1942–45*, p. 41.

13 Menz Diary.

14 Driver Joe Nimbs's unpublished manuscript, a copy of which was kindly given to the author by his family. Referred to hereafter as 'Nimbs MS.'

15 Nimbs MS.

16 ibid.

17 ibid.

18 Private Jim Stewart, Signals, 2/19th Battalion, interview with the author, Sydney, 1 October 2004.

19 Private Gus Halloran, 2/19th Battalion, interview with the author, Port Macquarie, NSW, 29 September 2004.

20 Corporal Jim Kennedy and Lance-Corporal John Roxburgh, 2/29th Battalion, interview with the author, Albury, NSW, 10 January 2005.

21 Private W. (Wal), Williams, 2/19th Battalion, interview with the author, Sydney, 30 September 2004, 23 April, 24 April 2005.

22 ibid.

23 Warrant Officer 2 Bert Mettam, 2/29th Battalion, interview with the author, Adelaide, 6 March 2005.

24 Gunner Richard Haynes, 2/10th Field Regiment, Diary and Papers.

25 ibid.

26 Warren, *Singapore 1942, Britain's Greatest Defeat*, p. 279.

25 PURGATORY

1   AWM PR00016, file 92/0049, Papers of Major A. Thompson. The papers are divided into four folders. The material from the papers will henceforth be cited as 'Thompson Papers' and the folder number.

2   Most individuals and units took ample initial supplies in with them, and when Nimbs arrived five days after the capitulation, they were still prevalent. Nimbs MS.

3   Thompson Papers, folder 2 of 4.

4   Allan S. Walker, *Australia in the War of 1939–1945, Medical Series, Middle East and Far East*, p. 541.

5   Thompson Papers, folder 2 of 4.

6   Allan S. Walker, *Australia in the War of 1939–1945, Medical Series, Middle East and Far East*, pp. 545–9.

7   ibid. p. 549.

8   Thompson Papers, folder 2 of 4.

9   ibid.

10 Allan S. Walker, *Australia in the War of 1939–1945, Medical Series, Middle East and Far East*, p. 527.

11 Thompson Papers, folder 2 of 4.

12 Wigmore, *The Japanese Thrust*, p. 512.

13 ibid. p. 515.

14 R. P. W. Havers, *Reassessing the Japanese Prisoner of War Experience, The Changi POW Camp, Singapore, 1942–45*, pp. 36–9.

15 AWM 52: 15/1/6, 8th Division Pay Corps Unit Diary, Jan–Dec 1941 and Feb 1942.

16 AWM: PR00531 Papers of WO 1 K. J. Browne.

17 AWM 52: 15/1/6, 8th Division Pay Corps Unit Diary, Jan–Dec 1941 and Feb 1942.

18 AWM 91/0023 Papers of Sir Wilfred Kent Hughes, File 6 of 6.

19 Private John Boehm, 2/29th Battalion, interview with the author, Barwon Heads, Geelong, 29 December 2005.

20 Thompson Papers, folder 2 of 4.

21 ibid.

22 ibid.

23 Thompson Papers, folder 2 of 4.

24 ibid.

25 Thompson Papers, folder 2 of 4; and A. W. Penfold, W. C. Baylis, K. E. Crispin, *Galleghan's Greyhounds*, pp. 239–49.

26 AWM 52: 1/5/19 8 Australian Division Administrative HQ AIF (Prisoner of War) No. 1 Prisoner of War Camp Changi. April 1943, part 3, Prisoners of War (Appendix 18).

27 ibid.

28 Warrant Officer 2 Bert Mettam, 2/29th Battalion, interview with the author, Adelaide, 6 March 2005.

29 Private Gus Halloran, 2/19th Battalion, interview with the author, Port Macquarie, NSW, 29 September 2004.

30 Thompson Papers, folder 2 of 4.

31 The Kent Hughes Papers, National Library of Australia, MS 4856 Box 11, series 3, folder 2.

32 ibid.

33 Menz Diary.

34 In his Diary, Menz identified both the culprit and his informant by their names and army numbers. The 2/29th Unit History records the culprit's fate in Burma (once again by name and army number), and the 2/19th Unit History does the same for the informant.

35 AWM 52: 1/5/19, 8 Australian Division Administrative HQ AIF (Prisoner of War) No. 1 Prisoner of War Camp Changi. April 1943, part 3, Prisoners of war.

36 Menz Diary.

37 ibid.

38 ibid.

39 AWM 52: 1/5/19, 8 Australian Division Administrative HQ AIF (Prisoner of War) No. 1 Prisoner of War Camp Changi. April 1943, part 3, Prisoners of war.

40 Menz Diary.

41 AWM 52: 1/5/19, 8 Australian Division Administrative HQ AIF (Prisoner of War) No. 1 Prisoner of War Camp Changi. March 1943, Prisoners of war.

42 ibid.

43 Russell Braddon, *The Naked Island*, pp.154–5.

44 AWM 52: 1/5/19, 8 Australian Division Administrative HQ AIF (Prisoner of War) No. 1 Prisoner of War Camp Changi. April 1943, part 3, Prisoners of war.

45 ibid.

46 Warrant Officer 2 Bert Mettam, 2/29th Battalion, interview with the author, Adelaide, 6 March 2005.

47 AWM 52: 1/5/19, 8th Australian Division Administrative HQ AIF (Prisoner of War) No. 1 Prisoner of War Camp Changi. April 1943, part 1, Prisoners of War.

48 ibid.

49 ibid.

50 Thompson Papers, folder 2 of 4.

51 Nimbs MS.

52 Menz Diary.

53 ibid.

54 Nimbs MS.

55 Thompson Papers, folder 2 of 4.

56 Nimbs MS.

57 The National Library of Australia: MS 4856, the Kent Hughes Papers, Box 11, Series 3, folder 2.

58 Gunner Richard Haynes, 2/10th Field Regiment, diary and papers.

59 Nimbs MS.

60 ibid.

61 Newton, R. W., *The Grim Glory of the 2/19 Battalion AIF*, p. 404.

62 Private Paddy O'Toole, 2/29th Battalion, interview with the author, Melbourne, 4 January 2006.

63 Wigmore, *The Japanese Thrust*, pp. 518–19.

64 Captain Adrian Curlewis, 8th Division HQ, Diary.

65 The National Library of Australia: MS 4856, the Kent Hughes Papers, Box 11, Series 3, folder 2.

66 Nimbs MS.

67 Private Paddy O'Toole, 2/29th Battalion, interview with the author, Melbourne, 4 January 2006.

68 ibid. The author took particular care to mention Nimbs's prices, manner of sales, Chinese contacts and opinions towards officer involvement etc. O'Toole agreed with almost all of Nimbs's opinions. When I finally told O'Toole of Nimbs's name, he had a vague recollection of him.

69 Wigmore, *The Japanese Thrust*, p. 519.

70 Private Paddy O'Toole, 2/29th Battalion, interview with the author, Melbourne, 4 January 2006.

71 Warrant Officer 2 Bert Mettam, 2/29th Battalion, interview with the author, Adelaide, 6 March 2005.

72 ibid.

73 The National Library of Australia: MS 4856, the Kent Hughes Papers, Box 11, Series 3, folder 2.

74 Thompson Papers, folder 2 of 4.

75 ibid.

76 ibid.

77 Thompson Papers, folder 2 of 4.

78 Wigmore, *The Japanese Thrust*, p. 523.

79 Thompson Papers, folder 2 of 4, and Wigmore, *The Japanese Thrust*, p. 523.

80 Thompson Papers, folder 2 of 4.

81 Galleghan quoted in Wigmore, *The Japanese Thrust*, p. 523.

82 Newton, R. W., *The Grim Glory of the 2/19 Battalion AIF*, pp. 481–2.

83 ibid. p. 481.

84 Thompson Papers, folder 2 of 4. Newton, in his *The Grim Glory of the 2/19 Battalion AIF*, stated that he brought '179 others' with him from Pudu, p. 412.

85 Newton, R. W., *The Grim Glory of the 2/19 Battalion AIF*, p. 412.

86 E. E. Dunlop, *The War Diaries of Weary Dunlop, Java and the Burma Thailand Railway 1942–1945*, p. 141.

87 ibid. p. 143.

88 ibid. p. 144.

89 ibid.

90 E. E. Dunlop, *The War Diaries of Weary Dunlop, Java and the Burma Thailand Railway 1942–1945*, p. 144.

91 Sue Ebury, *Weary, The Life of Sir Edward Dunlop*, p. 371.

92 ibid.

93 E. E. Dunlop, *The War Diaries of Weary Dunlop, Java and the Burma Thailand Railway 1942–1945*, p. 146.

94 Ray Parkin, *Into the Smother*, p. 390.

95 Corporal Jim Kennedy and Lance-Corporal John Roxburgh, 2/29th Battalion, interview with the author, Albury, NSW, 10 January 2005.

96 Nimbs MS.

97 ibid.

26 THE SINGAPORE WORK CAMPS

1 Thompson Papers, folder 2 of 4.

2 Thompson Papers, folder 2 of 4. Thompson does not actually cite the River Valley Road Camp number. However, he states that 3400 were sent out on 12 March and, further, that the Great World had 2109 on 31 March. Therefore, it is assumed that the other 1291 were at River Valley Road.

3 Gunner Richard Haynes, 2/10th Field Regiment, Diary and Papers.

4 Private Gus Halloran, 2/19th Battalion, interview with the author, Port Macquarie, NSW, 18 April 2005.

5 Stan Arneil, *One Man's War*, p. 27.

6 Exercise book, Curlewis Papers, Mrs Philippa Poole.

7 ibid.

8 Sergeant Frank Baker, 2/20th Battalion, interview with the author, Sydney, 9 January 2006.

9 ibid.

10 Such means of scrounging were recounted to the author in a multitude of interviews. For example, Gunner Richard Haynes, 2/10th Field Regiment, Diary and Papers. Private Gus Halloran, 2/19th Battalion, interview with the author, Port Macquarie, NSW, 18 April 2005, Sergeant Frank Baker, 2/20th Battalion, interview with the author, Sydney, 9 January 2006.

11 Gunner Richard Haynes, 2/10th Field Regiment, Diary and Papers.

12 ibid.

13 Private Gus Halloran, 2/19th Battalion, interview with the author, Port Macquarie, NSW, 18 April 2005.

14 Sergeant Frank Baker, 2/20th Battalion, interview with the author, Sydney, 9 January 2006.

15 Private W. (Wal) Williams, 2/19th Battalion, interviews with the author, Sydney, 30 September 2004, 23 April, 24 April 2005.

16 Corporal Jim Kennedy and Lance-Corporal John Roxburgh, 2/29th Battalion, interview with the author, Albury, NSW, 10 January 2005.

17 Gunner Richard Haynes, 2/10th Field Regiment, Diary and Papers.

18 Hank Nelson, *P.O.W Prisoners of War, Australians Under Nippon*, p. 29.

19 Gunner Richard Haynes, 2/10th Field Regiment, Diary and Papers.

20 Stan Arneil, *One Man's War*, p. 41.

21 Private W. (Wal) Williams, 2/19th Battalion, interviews with the author, Sydney, 30 September 2004, 23 April, 24 April 2005.

22 Col. S. A. F. Pond's 'General Notes taken from diary kept while a POW and expanded here and there.' After the heading it says: 'Written more than 30 years later'. Lieutenant-Colonel Pond's notes were given to Corporal Bob Christie, Secretary of the 2/29th Battalion Association. Christie gave the author copies of the originals on 11 October 2006. These notes, to be used in this chapter and for material in the chapters on the Thai–Burma Railway, will hereafter be cited as 'Pond Papers.'

23 Pond Papers.

24 Stan Arneil, *One Man's War*, p. 29.

25 Private Jim Stewart, Signals, 2/19th Battalion, interview with the author, Sydney, 1 October 2004; telephone conversation, 4 February 2007.

26 Private Paddy O'Toole, 2/29th Battalion, interview with the author, Melbourne, 4 January 2006.

27 Sergeant Frank Baker, 2/20th Battalion, interview with the author, Sydney, 9 January 2006.
28 ibid.
29 ibid.
30 Pond Papers.
31 ibid.
32 ibid.
33 Thompson Papers, folder 2 of 4.
34 Newton, R. W., *The Grim Glory of the 2/19 Battalion AIF*, p. 416.
35 Pond Papers.
36 AWM 52: 1/5/19 8 Australian Division Administrative HQ AIF (Prisoner of War) No. 1 Prisoner of War Camp Changi. April 1943, part 3, Prisoners of War (Appendix 18).
37 Pond Papers.
38 Sergeant Bert Donaldson, 2/19th Battalion, interview with the author, Temora, NSW, 8 October 2005.

PART IV   THE THAI–BURMA RAILWAY

27 THE KILLER CYCLE

1 Sergeant Frank Baker, 2/20th Battalion, interview with the author, Sydney, 10 January 2006.
2 Private Paddy O'Toole, 2/29th Battalion, interview with the author, Melbourne, 5 January 2006.
3 Warrant Officer 2 Bert Mettam, 2/29th Battalion, interview with the author, Adelaide, 6 March 2005.
4 Private Wal Williams, 2/19th Battalion, interview with the author, Sydney, 24 April 2005.
5 Captain Adrian Curlewis, 8th Division HQ, Diary, 29 June 1943. Curlewis's daughter Philippa Poole allowed the author to examine the diary and copy material not published in her book, *Of Love and War, The letters and diaries of Captain Adrian Curlewis and his family 1939–1945*. Referred to henceforth as 'Captain Adrian Curlewis, 8th Division HQ, Diary' and the date.
6 Captain Adrian Curlewis, 8th Division HQ, Diary, 30 August 1943.
7 Sergeant Frank Baker, 2/20th Battalion, interview with the author, Sydney, 10 January 2006.
8 Private Jack Coffee, 2/29th Battalion, interview with the author, Melbourne, 9 October 2006.
9 Warmenhoven Report. Copy kindly given to the author by Rod Beattie.
10 These statistics are taken from: Rod Beattie, *The Death Railway, A Brief History*, p. 20.
11 Wigmore, *The Japanese Thrust*, p. 545.
12 Rod Beattie, interview with the author, Kanchanaburi, Thailand, 13 January 2008.
13 ibid.
14 AWM 54, 554/2/5, Report by Lieutenant-Colonel G. E. Ramsay, on conditions of Prisoners of War Camps under Command during period February 1942–August 1944, with general comments only to subsequent events. Cited hereafter as 'Ramsay Report' and page number.
15 Ramsay Report, p. 4.
16 Thompson Papers, folder 2 of 4.

17 AWM PR 2DRL 2691, Papers of Varley, Brigadier R. L. WW2; transcript of diary. This diary will henceforth be cited as 'Varley Diary' and the date.

18 Captain Rowley Richards, RMO 2/15 Field Regiment, RMO Anderson Battalion, A Force, interview with the author, Sydney, 16 April 2007.

19 Varley Diary, 13 May 1942.

20 R. H. Whitecross, *Slaves of the Son of Heaven*, p. 19; and Leslie Hall, *The Blue Haze*, pp. 4–5.

21 Private Wal Williams, 2/19th Battalion and Ramsay Battalion, interview with the author, Sydney, 22 April 2005.

22 Varley Diary, 14 May 1942.

23 Report, Major J. S. Chambers, Australian Army Medical Corps, quoted in Leslie Hall, *The Blue Haze*, pp. 6–7.

24 ibid.

25 ibid.

26 Varley Diary, 20 May 1942.

27 ibid. 22 May 1942.

28 ibid. 24 May 1942.

29 Private Wal Williams, 2/19th Battalion and Ramsay Battalion, interview with the author, Sydney, 22 April 2005.

30 Ramsay Report, pp. 18–19.

31 ibid. p. 18.

32 ibid.

33 Varley Diary, 28 May 1942.

34 ibid.

35 Varley Diary, 6 June 1942.

36 ibid.

37 ibid. 22 June 1942.

38 ibid. 28 June 1942.

39 Varley Diary, 15 July 1942.

40 ibid. 11 July 1942.

41 Captain Rowley Richards, telephone conversation, 17 February 2013.

42 Varley Diary, 24 August 1942.

43 Private Wal Williams, 2/19th Battalion and Ramsay Force, interview with the author, Sydney, 23 April 2005.

44 ibid.

45 Leslie Hall, *The Blue Haze*, p. 108.

46 Varley Diary, 3 October 1942.

47 Private Wal Williams, 2/19th Battalion and Ramsay Force, interview with the author, Sydney, 23 April 2005.

48 ibid.

49 R. H. Whitecross, *Slaves of the Son of Heaven*, pp. 47–8.

50 Sergeant Jim Forbes, 2/19th Battalion and Ramsay Force, interview with the author, Sydney, 20 April 2005.

51 ibid.

52 Rowley Richards, *A Doctor's War*, p. 108.

53 ibid. p. 113.

54 Varley Diary, 18 November 1942.

55 ibid.

56 ibid. 20 November 1942.

57 Varley Diary, 11 November 1942.

58 Private Wal Williams, 2/19th Battalion and Ramsay Force, interview with the author, Sydney, 23 April 2005.

59 Rowley Richards, *A Doctor's War*, p. 132.

60 Sergeant Frank Baker, 2/20th Battalion, interview with the author, Sydney, 10 January 2006.

61 Rod Beattie, *The Death Railway, A Brief History*, p. 52. Beattie points out that these figures are approximate, because records concerning the Asian numbers on the Railway were destroyed.

62 Private Wal Williams, 2/19th Battalion and Ramsay Force, interview with the author, Sydney, 23 April 2005.

63 Rod Beattie, *The Death Railway, A Brief History*, pp. 46–7.

64 Private Wal Williams, 2/19th Battalion and Ramsay Force, interview with the author, Sydney, 23 April 2005.

65 Whitecross, quoted in Wigmore, *The Japanese Thrust*, p. 556.

66 Lieutenant-Colonel Albert Coates, quoted in Rosalind Hearder, *Keep The Men Alive, Australian POW Doctors in Japanese Captivity*, p. 39.

67 Captain Rowley Richards, RMO 2/15 Field Regiment, RMO Anderson Battalion, A Force, interview with the author, Sydney, 16 April 2007.

68 Dunlop, quoted in *The Australian Dictionary of Biography*, for Lieutenant-Colonel Albert Coates, written by Rowan Webb.

69 Wigmore, *The Japanese Thrust*, footnote, p. 550.

70 Allan S. Walker, *Australia In The War of 1939–1945, Medical Series, Middle East and Far East*, p. 589.

71 ibid. p. 589.

72 ibid. p. 590.

73 *The Australian Dictionary of Biography*, for Lieutenant-Colonel Albert Coates, written by Rowan Webb.

74 Private Wal Williams, 2/19th Battalion and Ramsay Force, interview with the author, Sydney, 23 April 2005.

75 Captain Rowley Richards, RMO 2/15 Field Regiment, RMO Anderson Battalion, A Force, interview with the author, Sydney, 16 April 2007.

76 ibid.

77 ibid.

78 Captain Rowley Richards, RMO 2/15 Field Regiment, RMO Anderson Battalion, A Force, interview with the author, Sydney, 16 April 2007.

79 ibid.

80 Rowley Richards, *A Doctor's War*, p. 118.

81 Anderson quoted in Wigmore, *The Japanese Thrust*, p. 561.

82 ibid. p. 551 (in text and in a footnote).

83 Captain Rowley Richards, letter to the author, 10 March 2013.

84 Rowley Richards, *A Doctor's War*, pp. 123–4.

85 Wigmore, *The Japanese Thrust*, p. 561.

28 'U' BATTALION

1 Thompson Papers, folder 2 of 4.
2 ibid.
3 ibid.
4 Hank Nelson, *POW Prisoners of War, Australians Under Nippon*, p. 62.
5 Pond Papers.
6 Sergeant Frank Baker, 2/20th Battalion, interview with the author, Sydney, 9 January 2006.
7 Private Walter Patterson, 8th Division Ammunition Sub Park, 'U' Battalion, interview with the author, Adelaide, 18 July 2005.
8 Sergeant Bert Donaldson, 2/19th and 'U' Battalions, interview with the author, Temora, NSW, 8 October 2005.
9 Thompson Papers, folder 2 of 4.
10 ibid.
11 Newton, R W., *The Grim Glory of the 2/19 Battalion AIF*, p. 571.
12 ibid. p. 420.
13 ibid. p. 575.
14 Private Gus Halloran, 2/19th Battalion, 'U' Battalion, interview with the author, Port Macquarie, NSW, 18 April 2005.
15 Private Walter Patterson, 8th Division Ammunition Sub Park, 'U' Battalion, interview with the author, Adelaide, 18 July 2005.
16 Newton, R. W., *The Grim Glory of the 2/19 Battalion AIF*, p. 576.
17 Private Charles Edwards, 2/19th Battalion, interview with the author Melbourne, 17 February 2007.
18 Private Gus Halloran, 2/19th Battalion, 'U' Battalion, interview with the author, Port Macquarie, NSW, 18 April 2005.
19 Newton, R. W., *The Grim Glory of the 2/19 Battalion AIF*, p. 578.
20 ibid.
21 ibid. p. 579.
22 Private Gus Halloran, 2/19th Battalion, 'U' Battalion, interview with the author, Port Macquarie, NSW, 18 April 2005.
23 Private Charles Letts, Malay Volunteers, interview with the author, Singapore 4 January 2008. The interview was not taped at Letts's insistence, but a record of the interview, undertaken with the author and Frank Taylor, was committed to paper later that day. Letts knew of Hempson, Gairdner and Heath through prewar business and social dealings.
24 *Aid To Prisoners of War in South Thailand, Internment Camp, Tha Pracharn, November 28th 1943*, written by Heath and Hempson. A copy of this report was given to the author by Private Gus Halloran.
25 Ibid. Gus Halloran. Extracts from further report dated 25 July 1945 at Civilian Internment Camp Vajiravudh, and also written and signed by Heath and Hempson.
26 *Personal Account of 'V' Organisation* by Lt. Col. Knights, Commanding Officer of 4th Bn. Royal Norfolk Regt. Copy from Newton's papers and given to the author by Gus Halloran, 20 July 2006.
27 AWM 54 554/2/1C, Brigadier C.A. McEachern, *Report on Conditions, Life and work of POWs in Burma and Siam 1942–1945*.
28 Extracts from further report dated 25 July 1945 at Civilian Internment Camp Vajiravudh, written and signed by Heath and Hempson. Copy from Newton's papers and given to the author by Gus Halloran, 20 July 2006.

29 ibid.

30 Rod Beattie, interview with the author, Kanchanaburi, Thailand, 13 January 2008.

31 Private Jim Stewart, 2/19th Battalion, 'U' Battalion, interview with the author, Sydney, 1 October 2004.

32 ibid.

33 Sergeant Frank Baker, 2/20th Battalion, interview with the author, Sydney, 9 January 2006.

34 Sergeant Bert Donaldson, 2/19th and 'U' Battalions, interview with the author, Temora, NSW, 8 October 2005.

35 Private Charles Edwards, 2/19th Battalion, interview with the author, Melbourne, 17 February 2007.

36 Private Len Gooley, 8th Division Ammunition Sub Park, 'U' Battalion, interview with the author, Adelaide, 18 July 2005.

37 Private Gus Halloran, 2/19th Battalion, 'U' Battalion, interview with the author, Port Macquarie, NSW, 18 April 2005.

38 Newton, R. W., *The Grim Glory of the 2/19 Battalion AIF*, p. 572.

39 Sergeant Frank Baker, 2/20th Battalion, interview with the author, Sydney, 10 January 2006.

40 ibid.

41 ibid.

42 ibid.

43 Private Jim Stewart, 2/19th Battalion, 'U' Battalion, interview with the author, Sydney, 1 October 2004.

44 Sergeant Jack de Loas, 2/19th Battalion, interview with the author, Bomaderry, NSW, 13 January 2005.

45 Sergeant Bert Donaldson, 2/19th, 'U' Battalion, interview with the author, Temora, NSW, 8 October 2005.

46 In a telephone conversation with the author (15 March 2013), Captain Rowley Richards coined the term 'faeces, food, fingers, flies', and pointed out that the expression was fairly widely used on the Railway. He further stated the incidence of dysentery on the line often came down to the ability of camps to instigate rigorous standards of hygiene.

47 Sergeant Frank Baker, 2/20th Battalion, interview with the author, Sydney, 10 January 2006.

48 Lieutenant Frank Ramsbotham quoted in Don Wall, *Singapore and Beyond*, p. 160.

49 Private Jim Stewart, 2/19th Battalion, 'U' Battalion, interview with the author, Sydney, 1 October 2004.

50 Sergeant Frank Baker, 2/20th Battalion, interview with the author, Sydney, 10 January 2006.

51 Newton, R. W., *The Grim Glory of the 2/19 Battalion AIF*, p. 587.

52 ibid. p. 588.

53 Private Gus Halloran, 2/19th Battalion, 'U' Battalion, interview with the author, Port Macquarie, NSW, 19 April 2005.

54 Private Walter Patterson, 8th Division Ammunition Sub Park, 'U' Battalion, interview with the author, Adelaide, 18 July 2005.

55 Sergeant Jack de Loas, 2/19th Battalion, interview with the author, Bomaderry, NSW, 13 January 2005.

56 Private Gus Halloran, 2/19th Battalion, 'U' Battalion, interview with the author, Port Macquarie, NSW, 19 April 2005.

57 ibid.

58 Newton, R. W., *The Grim Glory of the 2/19 Battalion AIF*, p. 588.

59 Ian Denys Peek, *One Fourteenth of an Elephant*, p. 146.

60 ibid.

61 ibid. p. 155.

62 ibid. p. 147.

63 Sergeant Frank Baker, 2/20th Battalion, interview with the author, Sydney, 9 January 2006.

64 Private Gus Halloran, 2/19th Battalion, 'U' Battalion, interview with the author, Port Macquarie, NSW, 19 April 2005. Private Jim Stewart, 2/19th Battalion, 'U' Battalion, interview with the author, Sydney, 1 October 2004.

65 Ian Denys Peek, *One Fourteenth of an Elephant*, p. 23.

66 ibid. p. 118.

67 ibid. p. 175.

68 Newton, R. W., *The Grim Glory of the 2/19 Battalion AIF*, p. 595.

69 Private Gus Halloran, 2/19th Battalion, 'U' Battalion, interview with the author, Port Macquarie, NSW, 19 April 2005.

70 Private Len Gooley, 8th Division Ammunition Sub Park, 'U' Battalion, interview with the author, Adelaide, 18 July 2005.

71 Newton, R. W., *The Grim Glory of the 2/19 Battalion AIF*, p. 597.

72 Sergeant Frank Baker, 2/20th Battalion, interview with the author, Sydney, 9 January 2006.

73 Private Gus Halloran, 2/19th Battalion, 'U' Battalion, interview with the author, Port Macquarie, NSW, 18 April 2005.

74 Wigmore, *The Japanese Thrust*, p. 571.

75 Rod Beattie, interview with the author, Kanchanaburi, Thailand, 13 January 2008.

76 Thompson Papers, folder 2 of 4.

77 Hank Nelson, *POW Prisoners of War, Australians Under Nippon*, p. 59.

78 Moore could have only been in either 'S' Battalion or 'T' Battalion, which was partly made up of 4th Anti-tank Regiment members; and Rod Beattie was able to furnish the author with Moore's railway record: 'Moore was in T Battalion. So Wang Pho [*sic* Wampo] then Konnyu [*sic* Konyu] then to Japan. Recovered from Fukuoka.' Email Beattie to author, 15/3/2013.

79 Newton, R. W., *The Grim Glory of the 2/19 Battalion AIF*, p. 600.

80 Rod Beattie gave the author a copy of his statistics for 'U' Battalion while the author was in Kanchanaburi with him in January 2008.

81 ibid. 'T' Battalion.

82 Newton, R. W., *The Grim Glory of the 2/19 Battalion AIF*, pp. 643–4.

83 Private Len Gooley, 8th Division Ammunition Sub Park, 'U' Battalion, interview with the author, Adelaide, 18 July 2005.

29 'F' FORCE

1 Thompson Papers. Folder 2.

2 Allan S. Walker, *Australia In The War of 1939–1945, Medical Series, Middle East and Far East*, p. 593.

3 Wigmore, *The Japanese Thrust*, pp. 571–2.

4 Thompson Papers. Folder 2.

5 Newton, R. W., *The Grim Glory of the 2/19 Battalion AIF*, p. 646; and Beattie, *The Death Railway, A Brief History*, p. 21.

6 Stan Arneil, *One Man's War*, p. 71.

7 Wigmore, *The Japanese Thrust*, p. 572.

8 Jim Ling, 8th Division Signals, interview with the author, Sydney, 14 July, 2006.

9 *The Story of F Force*, by J. F. Hardacre. A copy of this document was most kindly given to the author by Rod Beattie, in Kanchanaburi, 13 January 2008.

10 E. E. Dunlop, *The War Diaries of Weary Dunlop, Java and the Burma-Thailand Railway 1942–1945*, p. 221.

11 Newton, R. W., *The Grim Glory of the 2/19 Battalion AIF*, p. 646.

12 Hank Nelson, *POW Prisoners of War, Australians Under Nippon*, p. 62.

13 Thompson Papers. Folder 2.

14 Wigmore, *The Japanese Thrust*, p. 572.

15 Thompson Papers. Folder 2.

16 Stan Arneil, *One Man's War*, p. 71.

17 Jim Ling, 8th Division Signals, interview with the author, Sydney, 14 July, 2006.

18 Lance-Corporal John Roxburgh, 2/29th Battalion, interview with the author, Albury, NSW, 6 October 2005.

19 Stan Arneil, *One Man's War*, p. 72.

20 Allan S. Walker, *Australia In The War of 1939–1945, Medical Series, Middle East and Far East*, p. 589.

21 AWM 54 253/1/1, Diary written by VX 29818 Captain B. A. Barnett.

22 Private Paddy O'Toole, 2/29th Battalion, interview with the author, Melbourne, 5 January 2006.

23 Stan Arneil, *One Man's War*, p. 75.

24 Private Jack Coffee, 2/29th Battalion, interview with the author, Melbourne, 9 October, 2006.

25 Private Paddy O'Toole, 2/29th Battalion, interview with the author, Melbourne, 5 January 2006.

26 Warrant Officer 2 Bert Mettam, 2/29th Battalion, interview with the author, Adelaide, 22 October, 2006.

27 Copy of a report written by Dillon and given to George Beard. Copied and sent to the author, 5 July 2007.

28 Col. S. A. F. Pond's 'General Notes taken from diary kept while a POW and expanded here and there.' After the heading it says: 'Written more than 30 years later.' Lieutenant-Colonel Pond's notes were given to Corporal Bob Christie, Secretary of the 2/29th Battalion Association. Christie gave the author copies of the originals on 11 October 2006. These notes will hereafter be cited as 'Pond Papers.'

29 AWM 54 253/1/1, diary written by VX 29818 Captain B. A. Barnett. This diary was discovered by Joyce Bradley at the AWM. It had been wrongly catalogued many years ago when donated, and is quoted for the first time in this work. Hereafter to be referred to as 'Barnett Diary' and the date.

30 Captain Adrian Curlewis, 8th Division HQ, diary. Curlewis's daughter, Philippa Poole, allowed the author to examine the diary and copy material not published in her book,

Of Love and War, The letters and diaries of Captain Adrian Curlewis and his family 1939–1945. Referred to henceforth as 'Curlewis Diary' and the date.

31 Mills, Roy, *Doctor's Diary and Memoirs, Pond's Party, F Force, Thai–Burma Railway*.

32 Barnett Diary, 8–9 May 1943.

33 Private Paddy O'Toole, 2/29th Battalion, interview with the author, Melbourne, 5 January 2006.

34 Lance-Corporal John Roxburgh, 2/29th Battalion, account of his experiences during the campaign, and as a POW, written up straight after the Japanese surrender. Copy most kindly given to the author in Albury, NSW, October 2005.

35 Lance-Corporal John Roxburgh, 2/29th Battalion, interview with the author, Albury, NSW, 6 October 2005.

36 Pond Papers.

37 Barnett Diary, 20 May 1943.

38 ibid. 26 May 1943.

39 ibid. 27 May–3 June 1943.

40 Curlewis Diary, 6 June 1943.

41 Pond Papers.

42 Corporal Jim Kennedy, 2/29th Battalion, interview with the author, Albury, NSW, 6 October, 2005.

43 Warrant Officer 2 Bert Mettam, 2/29th Battalion, interview with the author, Adelaide, 22 October, 2006.

44 Jim Ling, 8th Division Signals, interview with the author, Sydney, 14 July, 2006.

45 Corporal Bob Christie, 2/29th Battalion, interview with the author, Melbourne, 5 January 2006.

46 Jim Ling, 8th Division Signals, interview with the author, Sydney, 14 July, 2006.

47 Corporal Bob Christie, 2/29th Battalion, interview with the author, Melbourne, 5 January 2006.

48 Lance-Corporal John Roxburgh, 2/29th Battalion, interview with the author, Albury, NSW, 5 October 2005.

49 Mills, Roy, *Doctor's Diary and Memoirs, Pond's Party, F Force, Thai–Burma Railway*, p. 64.

50 ibid. p. 62.

51 ibid. p. 62.

52 Allan S. Walker, *Australia In The War of 1939–1945, Medical Series, Middle East and Far East*, p. 606.

53 Corporal Bob Christie, 2/29th Battalion, interview with the author, Melbourne, 4 January 2006.

54 Private Paddy O'Toole, 2/29th Battalion, interview with the author, Melbourne, 5 January 2006.

55 Pond Papers.

56 AWM 54 554/2/1C, Brigadier C.A. McEachern, *Report on Conditions, Life and work of POWs in Burma and Siam 1942–1945*.

57 Coast, J., quoted in *Railway of Death*, p. 123.

58 Rowley Richards, *A Doctor's War*, p. 190.

59 Pond Papers.

60 ibid.

61 ibid.

62 Corporal Bob Christie, 2/29th Battalion, interview with the author, Melbourne, 5 January 2006.

63 Private Paddy O'Toole, 2/29th Battalion, interview with the author, Melbourne, 11 October 2006.

64 Corporal Jim Kennedy, 2/29th Battalion, interview with the author, Albury, NSW, 5 October, 2005.

65 Private Paddy O'Toole, 2/29th Battalion, interview with the author, Melbourne, 11 October 2006.

66 Pond Papers.

67 Corporal Jim Kennedy, 2/29th Battalion, interview with the author, Albury, NSW, 5 October, 2005.

68 Curlewis Diary, 30 June 1943.

69 Mills, Roy, *Doctor's Diary and Memoirs, Pond's Party, F Force, Thai–Burma Railway*, p. 91.

70 Barnett Diary, 11 August 1943.

71 ibid. 16 August 1943.

72 Mills, Roy, *Doctor's Diary and Memoirs, Pond's Party, F Force, Thai–Burma Railway*, p. 94.

73 Curlewis Diary, 17 August 1943.

74 Private Paddy O'Toole, 2/29th Battalion, interview with the author, Melbourne, 11 October 2006.

75 Corporal Bob Christie, 2/29th Battalion, letter to the author from Melbourne, 2 November 2006.

76 Wigmore, *The Japanese Thrust*, p. 580.

77 Lance-Corporal John Roxburgh, 2/29th Battalion, interview with the author, Albury, NSW, 6 October 2005.

78 Rod Beattie's records, Pond's party.

79 Pond Papers.

80 Lance-Corporal John Roxburgh, 2/29th Battalion, interview with the author, Albury, NSW, 6 October 2005.

81 During interviews with veterans, it was fascinating to hear that nearly all of them on the Railway perceived a return to Changi as their goal. Changi was indeed called 'home'.

82 A. W. Penfold, W. C. Baylis, K. E. Crispin, *Galleghan's Greyhounds*, p. 291.

83 From Hunt's entry in the *Australian Dictionary of Biography*.

84 Private John Boehm, 2/29th Battalion, interview with the author, Barwon Heads, Geelong, 29 December 2005.

85 Hunt quoted in Wigmore, *The Japanese Thrust*, p. 573.

86 Wall, *Heroes of F Force*, p. 9.

87 ibid.

88 A complete copy of Lieutenant Ron Eaton's diary was kindly sent from Sydney to the author by his daughter, Mrs Catherine Goodings. Cited hereafter as 'Eaton Diary' and the date.

89 Lieutenant Kelsey, 2/26th Battalion, in Wall, *Heroes of F Force*, p. 137.

90 Eaton Diary, 29 May 1943.

91 ibid. 31 May 1943.

92 Corporal Arthur Isaac, 2/30th Battalion, interview with the author, Sydney, 17 April, 2007.

93 Private Neville Riley, 2/30th Battalion, interview with the author, Sydney, 17 April, 2007.

94 Eaton Diary, 3 June 1943.

95 Lieutenant Kelsey, 2/26th Battalion, in Wall, *Heroes of F Force*, p. 139.

96 Corporal Arthur Isaac, 2/30th Battalion, interview with the author, Sydney, 17 April, 2007.

97 Eaton Diary, 27 June 1943.

98 Corporal Arthur Isaac, 2/30th Battalion, interview with the author, Sydney, 17 April, 2007.

99 Private Neville Riley, 2/30th Battalion, interview with the author, Sydney, 17 April, 2007.

100 Eaton Diary.

101 Stan Arneil, *One Man's War*, p. 130.

102 ibid. pp. 125–33.

103 ibid. p. 133.

104 Private Jack Coffee, 2/29th Battalion, interview with the author, Melbourne, 9 October, 2006.

105 Wigmore, *The Japanese Thrust*, p. 581.

106 ibid.

107 ibid. p. 580.

108 Pond Papers.

109 Newton, R. W., *The Grim Glory of the 2/19 Battalion AIF*, p. 646; and Beattie, *The Death Railway, A Brief History*, p. 586.

110 Eaton Diary, 1, 5, 11 July 1943.

111 Private John Boehm, 2/29th Battalion, interview with the author, Barwon Heads, Geelong, 29 December 2005.

112 Stahl, F. E., *Autobiography of a P.W,(J)* p. 43.

113 Eaton Diary, 19, 28, July 1943.

114 ibid. 6 August 1943.

115 Private Jack Coffee, 2/29th Battalion, interview with the author, Melbourne, 9 October, 2006.

30 'WHERE ARE THE REST, MAJOR?'

1 Varley Diary, 20 December 1943.

2 ibid. 24 December 1943.

3 Allan S. Walker, *Australia In The War of 1939–1945, Medical Series, Middle East and Far East*, p. 638–9.

4 Wigmore's spelling is 'Rokyu Maru', whilst Captain Rowley Richards—who was aboard the vessel—has 'Rakuyo Maru', both in his book and in writing to the author. The latter is used in this work. The subsequent fate of the two vessels is chiefly taken from Richards's book, *A Doctor's War*, and from correspondence between him and the author during late May 2013.

5 Wigmore, *The Japanese Thrust*, p. 615.

6 Private Wal Williams, 2/19th Battalion, interview with the author, Sydney, 24 April 2005.

7 Rowley Richards, *A Doctor's War*, p. 241.

8 Newton, R. W., *The Grim Glory of the 2/19 Battalion AIF*, p. 617.

9 ibid. p. 619.

10 ibid. p. 634.

11 ibid. p. 670.

12 Newton, R. W., *The Grim Glory of the 2/19 Battalion AIF*, p. 671.

13 Stahl, F. E., *Autobiography of a P.W.(J)* p. 47.

14 *War Diary of Thanbaya Hospital Camp*, by Captain Stahl (Australian Signals). A copy of this report was most kindly given to the author by Rod Beattie. Stahl spelt Tanbaya as 'Thanbaya'. Cited hereafter as 'Stahl, Tanbaya War Diary.'

15 Stahl, F. E., *Autobiography of a P.W,(J)* p. 49.

16 Stahl, Tanbaya War Diary.

17 Stahl, F. E., *Autobiography of a P.W,(J)* pp. 48–9.

18 ibid. p. 49.

19 Hunt, Appendix D, Tanbaya War Diary.

20 ibid.

21 AWM 54 554/2/1C Report on Conditions, Life and Work of POWs in Burma and Siam 1942–1945, submitted by C.A. McEachern, Brig. RAA, Senior Ex PW Siam.

22 Stahl, F. E., *Autobiography of a P.W,(J)* p. 51.

23 Allan S. Walker, *Australia In The War of 1939–1945, Medical Series, Middle East and Far East*, p. 604.

24 Menz Diary.

25 Kratoska, Paul, *The Thailand–Burma Railway, 1942–1946: Documents and Selected Writings*, p. 37.

26 ibid.

27 Menz Diary.

28 ibid.

29 Stan Arneil, *One Man's War*, p. 149.

30 ibid.

31 Curlewis Diary, 22 November 1943.

32 ibid. 25 November 1943.

33 Barnett Diary, 2 December 1943.

34 Meakin, quoted in Don Wall, *Heroes of F Force*, p. 126.

35 A. W. Penfold, W. C. Baylis, K. E. Crispin, *Galleghan's Greyhounds*, p. 317.

36 Stan Arneil, *Black Jack, The Life and Times of Brigadier Sir Frederick Galleghan*, p. 122.

37 ibid. p. 123.

38 Broadcast by Bruce Hunt, from Singapore Radio about 9 September 1945, quoted in Don Wall, *Heroes of F Force*, p. ix.

39 Couch, in Don Wall, *Heroes of F Force*, p. 132.

PART V   SINGAPORE

31 RECKONING

1 Winston Churchill, *The Second World War*, Vol. IV, p. 81.

2 Karl Hack and Kevin Blackburn, *Did Singapore Have To Fall?, Churchill and the impregnable fortress*, p. 183.

3 ibid. pp. 183–4.

4 ibid. p. 184.

5 General H. Gordon Bennett, *Why Singapore Fell*, p. 198.

6 AWM, 3DRL 6224, Hetherington Papers, Rowell to Hetherington 13 July 1971.

7 Long quoted in Hetherington, *Blamey, Controversial Soldier*, p. 343.

8 General H. Gordon Bennett, *Why Singapore Fell*, p. 217.

9 ibid. pp. 217–18.

10 Quoted in Lodge, *The Fall of General Gordon Bennett*, p. 202.

11 ibid.

12 S. F. Rowell, *Full Circle*, pp. 104–5.

13 Legg, Frank, *The Gordon Bennett Story: From Gallipoli to Singapore*, p. 274.

14 ibid. p. 275.

15 Quoted in Lodge, *The Fall of General Gordon Bennett*, p. 247.

16 ibid. p. 248.

17 ibid. p. 34.

18 ibid. p. 42.

19 Lodge, *The Fall of General Gordon Bennett*, pp. 42–3.

20 Lodge, *The Fall of General Gordon Bennett*, p. 252; and Legg, Frank, *The Gordon Bennett Story: From Gallipoli to Singapore*, p. 279.

21 Lodge, *The Fall of General Gordon Bennett*, p. 252.

22 ibid. p. 260.

23 Clisby, Mark, *Guilty or Innocent?, The Gordon Bennett Case*, p. 26.

24 Quoted in Wigmore, *The Japanese Thrust*, p. 651.

25 Clisby, Mark, *Guilty or Innocent?, The Gordon Bennett Case*, p. 47.

26 ibid. p. 53.

27 ibid. p. 108.

28 ibid. p. 109.

29 Clisby, Mark, *Guilty or Innocent?, The Gordon Bennett Case*, p. 109.

30 ibid. pp. 113–14.

31 Morrison, Ian, *Malayan Postscript*, pp. 157–8.

32 Kent Hughes Papers, National Library of Australia, MS 4856/2/10, Box 3, Series 2, Folder 10, Correspondence with Gordon Bennett: 1942 to 1968.

33 AWM 54 553/5/23, *Operations of 8 Aust Division in Malaya 1941–1942*, Colonel J. H. Thyer, Introduction Part 1. p.v.

34 ibid. p. 191.

35 ibid.

36 ibid.

37 AWM 54 553/5/23, *Operations of 8 Aust Division in Malaya 1941–1942*, Colonel J. H. Thyer, p. 193.

38 ibid.

39 AWM 113 4/1/11 Part 2, Hopkins to Treloar 5 January 1951.

40 AWM 113 4/1/11 Part 2.

41 ibid.

42 AWM 93 50/2/23/542, Records of the War of 1939–45, The Hon. W. Kent Hughes, Kent Hughes to Rowell, 10 August 1953.

43 AWM 113 4/1/11 Part 3.

44 ibid.

45 ibid.

46 AWM 113 4/1/11 Part 2.

47 Lodge, *The Fall of General Gordon Bennett*, p. 299.

48 ibid. p. 306.

49 Kent Hughes Papers, National Library of Australia, MS 4856/2/10, Box 3, Series 2, Folder 10, Correspondence with Gordon Bennett: 1942 to 1968.

50 Alan Warren, *Singapore 1942, Britain's Greatest Defeat*, pp. 274–7.

51 Peter Elphick, *Singapore: The Pregnable Fortress*, p. 363.

52 ibid.

53 Karl Hack and Kevin Blackburn, *Did Singapore Have To Fall?, Churchill and the impregnable fortress*, p. 158.

54 Gordon Bennett Papers: Mitchell Library, ML MSS 807/2–5: Correspondence: 1924 to 1961.

55 Kinvig, *Scapegoat, General Percival of Singapore*, p. 238.

56 ibid.

57 ibid. pp. 238–41.

58 Newton, R. W., *The Grim Glory of the 2/19 Battalion AIF*, p. 643.

59 ibid. p. 644.

60 Alan Warren, *Singapore 1942, Britain's Greatest Defeat*, p. 292.

BIBLIOGRAPHY

AUSTRALIAN WAR MEMORIAL, CANBERRA
AWM 52
AIF and Militia Unit War Diaries 1940–42
8/3/18 The 2/18th Battalion War Diary
8/3/19 The 2/19th Battalion War Diary
8/3/20 The 2/20th Battalion War Diary
8/3/26 The 2/26th Battalion War Diary
8/3/29 The 2/29th Battalion War Diary
8/3/30 The 2/30th Battalion War Diary
AWM 54

AWM WRITTEN RECORDS, 1939–46
253/1/1 Diary written by Captain B.A. Barnett, 8th Division Signals, and F Force
553/5/5 Summary of Malayan Campaign by Lieutenant-Colonel Kappe, Commanding Officer, 8th Division Signals
553/5/23 Operations of 8 Aust Division in Malaya 1941–42. Compiled by Colonel J. H.Thyer from narrative prepared by Colonel C.H. Kappe
554/11/38 Notes by Colonel J.H. Thyer and Colonel C.H. Kappe on the departure of General Gordon Bennett, from Malaya, and conditions in Changi POW Camp during prisoner of war period
AWM 71
Correspondence between Gavin Long and Major-General Kirby
AWM 73

Official History, 1939–45 War, Series 1 (Army) Volume IV: Records of Lionel Wigmore

Item 2, Letter, Gavin Long to Lionel Wigmore, 1 August 1950

Item 5, Letter, Gavin Long to Lionel Wigmore, 23 May 1949

Item 46, Notes of interviews Lionel Wigmore with Brigadier Taylor, August 1949; Brigadier Rourke, June 1952; Brigadier Mawwell, December 1946

Item 51, Notes of interview with Major-General F. Galleghan, 1 February 1950

Item 59, Extracts from a letter from Wilfred Kent Hughes to McBride (AWM) 24 January 1952

Item 71, Notes of an interview of General Bennett with Lionel Wigmore

AWM 93

AWM CORRESPONDENCE FILES, 1951–58

419/54/101 Lieutenant-Colonel C.H. Kappe

50/2/23/64 L.N. Roach

50/2/23/136 Colonel J.J. Scanlan

50/2/23/224 Colonel B.J. Callinan

50/2/23/280 Brigadier W.C.D. Veale

50/2/23/294 Brigadier Duncan Maxwell

50/2/23/461 Lieutenant-Colonel H.H. Carr

50/2/23/480 Colonel J.H.Thyer

50/2/23/482 Captain W.B. Bowring

50/2/23/518 Lieutenant-General V.A.H. Sturdee

50/2/23/542 Records of the War 1939–45. Hon. W.S. Kent Hughes

50/2/23/551 Lieutenant-Colonel W.E. Fraser

50/2/23/554 Lieutenant-Colonel R.F. Oakes

50/2/23/563 Lieutenant-Colonel W.J.K. Scott

50/2/28/2A Report on Operations of 8 Div in Malaya (Correspondence)

50/9/3/3/4B Volume IV Wigmore, Source Material

AWM 113

Military History Section files and historical records, 1923–45

4/1/11 (parts 1, 2, 3)

1/5/17 Correspondence dealing with missing files from Malayan Campaign

AWM PERSONAL RECORDS

PR00016 Papers of Major A. Thompson 92/0049 (in 4 parts)

Brigadier Varley Diary, 3DRL/2691 Folders 1–3

National Library of Australia, Canberra

Mitchell Library, Sydney

Bennett Papers, MSS 807

Moses Papers (held by Neil McDonald in Sydney: various parts kindly copied and given to the author October 2004)

NATIONAL LIBRARY OF AUSTRALIA, CANBERRA

Papers of Sir Wilfred Kent Hughes (1895–1970), MS 4856

UNPUBLISHED MANUSCRIPTS AND PAPERS

Blackburn, Brigadier Arthur, a copy of his Diary in captivity, 1942–44, most kindly lent to the author by his biographer, Andrew Faulkner, 14 December 2008

Brand, Captain V., Section of Diary concerning his service at Tamarompat, Thai–Burma Railway, (copy given to the author by Mr Bob Christie, 2/29th Battalion Association, October 2006)

Ellerman, Lieutenant Austin, 2/29th Battalion, a copy of his reminiscences, kindly given to the author by his son, Andrew Ellerman, 26 February 2008

Haynes, Gunner Richard, 2/10th Field Regiment, a three-part account of his experiences of the fall of Singapore; Changi and various work parties, and the Thai–Burma Railway. This document was most kindly given to the author by historian Janet Uhr in Canberra on 6 April 2010

Lancaster, W.E., Straits Settlements Volunteer Forces, an account of his time in action and as a POW. The original exercise books kindly lent to the author by his widow, Mrs Kathie Lancaster, 17 March 2007

McNamara, H.J., *Nor All Thy Tears*

Menz, Captain A. (Alf), 8th Australian Division Provost Company, Diary, copy most kindly lent to the author, by his sister, Muriel Yates 10 March 2007

Nimbs, E.G. (Joe), Survival Changi (copy and original diaries kindly given to the author by his son, Joe Nimbs)

Pond, Lieutenant-Colonel S.A.F., (the following material kindly given to the author by Mr Bob Christie, 2/29th Battalion Association, October 2006):
    Report on F Force Working Party In Thailand
    Written evidence for the War Crimes Trial of Captain Murayama
    General notes taken from Pond's Diary kept while POW, with some additional comments

INTERVIEWS

Baker, Sergeant F.J. (Frank), 2/20th Battalion, Sydney, 9 January, 10 January 2006

Barron, Private W.V., 2/19th Battalion, Sydney, 30 September 2004

Beattie, Rod., Historian and Manager of Commonwealth War Graves, Kanchanaburi, Thailand, interview Kanchanaburi, 13 January 2008

Boehm, Private J.W., 2/29th Battalion, Barwon Heads, Geelong, 28 December, 29 December 2005

Brand, Captain V., 2/29th Battalion, Melbourne, 5 January 2005

Christie, Corporal R.W., 2/29th Battalion, Melbourne, 4 January, 5 January, 6 January 2005, 6 January 2006, 10 October, 11 October 2006

Clarke, Private L.G. (Leo), 2/29th Battalion, Barwon Heads, Geelong, Victoria, 28 December 2005

Coffee, Private J., 2/29th Battalion, Melbourne, 9 October 2006

de Loas, Sergeant R., 2/19th Battalion, Bomaderry, New South Wales, 13 January 2005

Donaldson, Sergeant Bert, 2/19th Battalion, Temora, New South Wales, 8 October 2005

Edwards, Private C.A. (Charles), 2/19th Battalion, Melbourne, 17 February 2007

Farlow, Lance-Corporal C., 2/19th Battalion, Hay, New South Wales, 17 January 2005

Farr, Lieutenant A. I., 2/30th Battalion, Sydney, 17 April 2007

Forbes, Sergeant J., 2/19th Battalion, Sydney, 20 April 2005

Glossop, Private V.E., 2/29th Battalion, Melbourne, 10 October, 2006

Gooley, Private L.W., 8th Division Ammunition Sub Park, Adelaide, 18 July 2005

Grant, Private R.L., 2/19th Battalion, Sydney, 2 October 2004

Halloran, Private A.J., (Gus), 2/19th Battalion, Port Macquarie, New South Wales, 29 September 2004, 18 April, 19 April 2005

Harvey, Sergeant C., 2/19th Battalion, Sydney, 4 October 2004

Howard, Lieutenant J.A., 2/19th Battalion, Port Macquarie, New South Wales, 28 September, 29 September 2004

Isaac, Corporal Arthur, 2/30th Battalion, Sydney, 17 April 2007

Kennedy, Corporal J., 2/29th Battalion, Albury, New South Wales, 10 January, 5 October, 6 October, 7 October, 2005

Kerr, Gunner Jim, 4th Anti-Tank Regiment, Melbourne, 20 April 2007

Ling, Private J.M., 8th Division Signals, Sydney, 14 July, 15 July 2006

Mettam, Warrant Officer 2 Bert, 2/29th Battalion, Adelaide, 6 March, August 2005, 22 October 2006, 22 July 2007

Moses, Sir Charles, 8th Division Headquarters, interviews by Neil McDonald, Sydney, 6 February 1985, 22 August 1986, copies kindly given to the author by Neil McDonald, October 2004 and January 2010

O'Toole, Private L.J. (Paddy), 2/29th Battalion, Melbourne, 4 January, 5 January, 6 January 2006

Parkes, John, 8th Division Signals, Sydney, 14 July 2006

Patterson, Private W.G., 8th Division Ammunition Sub Park, Adelaide, 18 July 2005

Pearson, Private A.T., 2/19th Battalion, Sydney, 1 October 2004

Perceval, Private R.L., 2/19th Battalion, Temora, New South Wales, 14 January 2005

Piggott, Private R.P., 2/19th Battalion, Sydney, 3 October 2004

Richards, Captain Rowley, RMO 2/15th Field Regiment, Sydney, 16 April 2007

Riley, Private Neville, 2/30th Battalion, Sydney, 17 April 2007

Roxburgh, Lance-Corporal J., 2/29th Battalion, Albury, New South Wales, 10 January 2005, 5 October, 6 October, 7 October 2005

Sanderson, Private J., 2/19th Battalion, Sydney, 4 October 2004, 22 April 2005

Sizeland, Private F.J.R. (Fred), 2/29th Battalion, Geelong, Victoria, 28 December 2005

Stanton, Private R., 2/19th Battalion, Bega, New South Wales, 12 January 2005

Stewart, Private J.T., 2/19th Battalion, Sydney, 1 October 2004, 12 July, 13 July 2006

Thompson, Warrant Officer 2 S.W., 2/19th Battalion, Sydney, 1987, interview by Ivan Chapman, copy most kindly given to the author by Neil McDonald, October 2004

Webb, Dr Mark, interview Adelaide, 17 November 2006

Williams, Private W., (Wal), 2/19th Battalion, Sydney, 30 September 2004, 22 April, 23 April, 24 April 2005

CORRESPONDENCE: DIARIES, QUESTIONNAIRES, LETTERS, TAPES

Browning, Neville, Historian, 2/4th Machine Gun Battalion, copies of letters June 1984 from A.J. Gough, 2/4th Machine Gun Battalion to Historian Don Wall

Christie, Corporal R.W., 2/29th Battalion, letter from Melbourne, 2 November 2006; letter, July 2007

Edwards, Private Charles, letter from Melbourne, 11 March 2008

Halloran, Private A.J., copy of F Force Report, from Sydney, 5 July 2007

Ling, Private J.M., 8th Division Signals, letter from Sydney, July 2007

Richards, Dr R., questionnaire reply, received from Sydney, 17 August 2007

Roxburgh, Lance-Corporal J., 2/29th Battalion, Diary written shortly after the end of the war. Copy most kindly given to the author, January 2005

Williams, Private W., (Wal), 2/19th Battalion, letter from Sydney, 22 December 2004

BOOKS

Allbury, A.G., *Bamboo and Bushido*, Robert Hale Ltd, London, 1955

Arneil, Stan, *Black Jack, The Life and Times of Brigadier Sir Frederick Galleghan*, MacMillan, Melbourne, 1983

—— *One Man's War*, Sun Books, South Melbourne, 1982

Attiwell, Kenneth, *The Singapore Story*, Frederick Muller Ltd, London, 1959

Australian Army (Headquarters Training Command), *The Fundamentals of Land Warfare*, Sydney, 1993

Beasley, W.G., *The Rise of Modern Japan*, St Martin's Press, New York, 1995

Beattie, Rod, *The Death Railway, A Brief History*, Image Makers Co, Ltd, Bangkok, 2006

Bell A.C., *History of the Manchester Regiment, The First and Second Battalions, 1922–1948*, John Sherratt and Son, Altrincham, 1954

Bennett, H. Gordon, *Why Singapore Fell*, Angus and Robertson, Sydney, 1944

Bergamini, David, *Japan's Imperial Conspiracy*, William Morrow and Company, New York, 1971

Boi, Lee Geok, *The Syonan Years, Singapore Under Japanese Rule, 1942–1945*, National Archives of Singapore and Epigram Pty Ltd, Singapore, 2005

Bose, Romen, *Secrets of the Battlebox, The History and Role of Britain's Command HQ in the Malayan Campaign*, Marshall Cavendish, Singapore, 2005

Bowden, Tim, *Changi Photographer: George Aspinall's Record of Captivity*, ABC Books, Sydney, 1984

Braddon, Russell, *The Naked Island*, Werner Laurie, London, 1952

Chapman, Ivan, *Tokyo Calling: The Charles Cousens Case*, Hale & Iremonger, Sydney, 1990

Christie, R.W., (editor), *A History of the 2/29th Battalion—8th Division AIF*, High Country Publishing, Melbourne, 1985

Christie, R.W., (edited John Lack), *Surviving Captivity, The Campaign and POW Diary of Bob Christie 2/29th Battalion AIF 1942–1945*, Australian Scholarly Publishing, Melbourne, 2010

Churchill, Winston S., *The Second World War*, Cassell, London, six volumes, 1948–54

Clisby, Mark, *Guilty or Innocent?: The Gordon Bennett Case*, Allen & Unwin, Sydney, 1992

Cody, Les, *Ghosts in Khaki, The History of the 2/4 Machine Gun Battalion, 8th Division A.I.F.*, Hesperian Press, Perth, 1997

Connell, John, *Wavell: Supreme Commander*, Collins, London, 1969

Cook, Haruko Taya and Theodore F., *Japan at War, An Oral History*, Phoenix Press, London, 2000

Daniel, David Scott, *History of the East Surrey Regiment*, Ernest Benn Ltd, London, 1957

Davies, Peter N., *The Man Behind The Bridge, Colonel Toosey and the River Kwai*, The Athlone Press, London, 1991

Day, David, *The Great Betrayal: Britain, Australia and the Onset of the Pacific War 1939–42*, Oxford University Press, Melbourne, 1988

Dean, Captain C.G.T., *The Loyal Regiment (North Lancashire), 1919–1953*, Regimental Headquarters, The Loyal Regiment (north Lancashire) Preston, 1955

Dunlop, E.E., *The War Diaries of Weary Dunlop: Java, the Burma–Thailand Railway, 1942–1945*, Viking Books, Melbourne, 1989

Durnford, John, *Branch Line to Burma, Slave labourers built a line to hell*, Four Square Books, London, 1966

Ebury, Sue, *Weary: The Life and Times of Sir Edward Dunlop*, Viking, Melbourne, 1994

Edwards, Norman and Keys, Peter, *Singapore, A Guide to Buildings, Streets, Places*, Times Books International, Singapore, 1988

Elphick, Peter, *Far Eastern File, The Intelligence War in the Far East*, Hodder & Stoughton, London, 1997

—— *Singapore: The Pregnable Fortress*, Hodder & Stoughton, London, 1995

Elphick, Peter and Smith, Michael, *Odd Man Out, The Story of the Singapore Traitor*, Hodder & Stoughton, London, 1993

Faulkner, Andrew, *Arthur Blackburn VC, An Australian hero, his men, and their two world wars*, Wakefield Press, Adelaide, 2008

Finkemeyer, Colin E., *It Happened To Us*, C.E. and D.J. Kinkemeyer, Melbourne, 1992

Forbes, Cameron, *Hellfire: The Story of Australia, Japan and the Prisoners of War*, Macmillan, Sydney, 2005

Gill, Hermon G., *Australia in the War of 1939–1945, Royal Australian Navy 1939–1942*, Australian War Memorial, Canberra, 1957

Gillison, Douglas, *Australia in the War of 1939–1945, Royal Australian Air Force 1939–1942*, Australian War Memorial, Canberra, 1962

Goodwin, Bob, *Mates and Memories, Recollections of the 2/10th Field Regiment*, Boolarong Press, Brisbane, 1995

Grey, Jeffrey, *A Military History of Australia*, Cambridge University Press, Cambridge, 1990

Hack, Karl and Blackburn, Kevin, *Did Singapore Have to Fall? Churchill and the Impregnable Fortress*, Routledge, London, 2005

Hall, Leslie, *The Blue Haze*, self-published, Sydney, 1985

Harries, Meirion and Susie, *Soldiers of the Sun: The Rise and Fall of the Imperial Japanese Army 1868–1945*, Heinemann, London, 1991

Harrison, Kenneth, *The Brave Japanese*, Rigby, Adelaide, 1966

Hasluck, Paul, *Australia in the War of 1939–1945, The Government and the People 1939–1941*, Australian War Memorial, Canberra, 1952

Havers, R.P.W., *Reassessing the Japanese Prisoner of War Experience, The Changi POW Camp, Singapore, 1942–45*, Routledge Curzon, London, 2003

Hearder, Rosalind, *Keep the Men Alive: Australian POW Doctors in Japanese Captivity*, Allen & Unwin, Sydney, 2009

Hetherington, John, *Blamey, Controversial Soldier*, The Australian War Memorial and the Australian Government Publishing Service, Canberra, 1973

Horner, David, *Blamey: The Commander-in-Chief*, Allen & Unwin, Sydney, 1998

—— (ed.), *The Commanders: Australian Military Leadership in the Twentieth Century*, George Allen & Unwin, Sydney, 1984

—— *General Vasey's War*, Melbourne University Press, 1992

Howard, Frederick, *Kent Hughes, A Biography*, MacMillan, Melbourne, 1972 .

Hunter, Janet, E., *The Emergence of Modern Japan, An Introductory History Since 1853*, Longman, London, 1989

Jacobs, J.W. and Bridgland R.J., (ed.), *Through: The Story of the Signals 8 Australian Division and Signals A.I.F. Malaya*, 8 Division Signals Association, Sydney, 1949

Kent Hughes, W.S., *Slaves of the Samurai*, Oxford University Press, Melbourne, 1946

Kinvig, Clifford, *Scapegoat, General Percival of Singapore*, Brassey's, London, 1996

Kirby, Major-General S. Woodburn, *The Chain of Disaster, A controversial account of Britain's humiliation in the Far East*, MacMillan, New York, 1971

—— *The War Against Japan, Volume 1: The Loss of Singapore*, His Majesty's Stationery Office, London, 1957

Kratoska, Paul H., *The Thailand–Burma Railway, 1942–1946: Documents and Selected Writings*, Routledge, 2005

Lack, John (ed.), *No Lost Battalion: An Oral History of the 2/29th Battalion AIF*, Slouch Hat Publications, McCrae, Australia, 2005

Lamont-Brown, Raymond, *Kempeitai, Japan's Dreaded Military Police*, Budding Books, England, 1998

Legg, Frank, *The Gordon Bennett Story: From Gallipoli to Singapore*, Angus and Robertson, Sydney, 1965

Lodge, Brett, *Lavarack, Rival General*, Allen & Unwin, Sydney, 1998

—— *The Fall of General Gordon Bennett*, Allen & Unwin, Sydney, 1986

Long, G., *Australia in the War of 1939–1945, To Benghazi*, Australian War Memorial, Canberra, 1952

Low, N.I., *When Singapore was Syonan-To*, Times Editions, Marshall Cavendish, Singapore, 1973

MacArthur, Brian, *Surviving the Sword, Prisoners of the Japanese, 1942–45*, Time Warner Books, London, 2005

Magarry, Ron, *The Battalion Story, 2/26th Infantry Battalion, 8th Division—AIF*, self-published, Brisbane, 1994

Mant, Gilbert, *The Singapore Surrender: The Greatest Disaster In British Military History*, Kangaroo Press, Sydney, 1992

Marder, Arthur J., *Old Friends, New Enemies*, Clarendon Press, Oxford, 1981

Mason, Philip, *A Matter of Honour, An Account of the Indian Army, its Officers and Men*, Papermac, London, 1986

Merriman, Thaddeus (editor-in-chief) and Wiggin, Thos. H. (associate editor), *American Civil Engineers' Handbook*, John Wiley & Sons Inc., New York, 1925

Mills, Roy, *Doctor's Diary and Memoirs: Pond's Party, F Force, Thai–Burma Railway*, Self-Published, New Lambton, NSW, 1994

Moloney, James Clark, *Understanding the Japanese Mind*, Philosophical Library, New York, 1954

Montgomery, Brian, *Shenton of Singapore: Governor and Prisoner of War*, Times Books International, Singapore, 1984

Morrison, Ian, *Malayan Postscript*, Angus and Robertson, Sydney, 1943

Nelson, Gordon, *Men Of The Line, Building The Burma–Thai Railway 1942–1945*, Australian Military History Publications, Sydney, 2005

Nelson, Hank, *Prisoners of War: Australians Under Nippon*, Australian Broadcasting Commission, Sydney, 1985

Newton, R.W., (and various unit members), *The Grim Glory of the 2/19 Battalion A.I.F.*, 2/19th Battalion AIF Association, Sydney, 1975

Parkin, R., *Wartime Trilogy*, Melbourne University Press, Melbourne, 1999

Peek, Ian Denys, *One Fourteenth of an Elephant*, Macmillan, Sydney, 2003

Penfold, A. W., Baylis, W. C., Crispin, K. E., *Galleghan's Greyhounds, The Story of the 2/30th Australian Infantry Battalion*, 2/30th Bn A.I.F. Association, Sydney, 1949

Percival, Lieutenant-General A.E., *The War in Malaya*, Eyre & Spottiswoode, London, 1949

Perkins, M., *Tropic Tide: An Adventurer's Life*, Bantam, Sydney, 1998

Poole, Philippa, *Of Love and War: The Letters and Diaries of Captain Adrian Curlewis and his family 1939–1945*, Collins, Sydney, no date

Pratten, Garth, *Australian Battalion Commanders in the Second World War*, Cambridge University Press, Port Melbourne, 2009

Ramsay Silver, Lynette, *Sandakan: A Conspiracy of Silence*, Sally Milner Publishing, Burra Creek, New South Wales, 1998

—— *The Bridge at Parit Sulong: An Investigation of Mass Murder, Malaya 1942*, The Watermark Press, Sydney, 2004

Richards, Rowley, *A Doctor's War*, HarperCollins, Sydney, 2005

Rowell, S.F., *Full Circle*, Melbourne University Press, Melbourne, 1974

Rowland, Robin, *A River Kwai Story, The Sonkrai Tribunal*, Allen & Unwin, Sydney, 2007

Saggers, Ian, *To Hell-Fire, Purgatory and Back*, Optima Press, Perth, 2000

Shores, Christopher, Cull, Brian, with Yasudo Izawa, *Bloody Shambles, The First Comprehensive Account of Air Operations Over South-East Asia December 1941–April 1942*, Volume I, Grub Street, London, 1992

Simson, Ivan, *Singapore: Too Little, Too Late*, Leo Cooper, London, 1970

Smith, Neil C., *Tid-Apa, The History of the 4th Anti-Tank Regiment*, Mostly Unsung Military History Research and Publications, Melbourne, 1992

Stahl, F.E., *Autobiography of a PW*, Victoria Branch Printing Department of the AMP Society, Melbourne, 1974

Stewart, I.M., *History of the Argyll and Sutherland Highlanders 2nd Battalion (The Thin Red Line) Malayan Campaign, 1941–42*, Thomas Nelson & Sons Ltd, London, 1947

Strabolgi, Lord, *Singapore and After*, Hutchinson & Co., London, 1942

Summers, Julie, *The Colonel of Tamarkan: Philip Toosey and the Bridge on the River Kwai*, Simon & Schuster, London, 2005

Thompson, Peter, *The Battle for Singapore: The True Story of the Greatest Castastrophe of World War II*, Portrait, London, 2005

Tsuji, Colonel Masanobu, *Singapore: The Japanese Version*, Ure Smith, Sydney, 1960

Tsunoda, Ryusaku *et al.*, *Sources of Japanese Tradition*, Columbia University Press, New York, 1958

Uhr, Janet, *Against the Sun, The AIF in Malaya, 1941–42*, Allen & Unwin, Sydney, 1998

Underhill, Brigadier W. E., *The Royal Leicestershire Regiment 17th Foot, A History of The Years 1928–1956*, N&M Press, UK, 2010

Wahlert, Glenn, *The Other Enemy? Australian Soldiers and the Military Police*, Oxford University Press, Melbourne, 1999

Walker, Allan S., *Australia In the War Of 1939–1945, Medical Series, Middle East And Far East*, Australian War Memorial, Canberra, 1953

—— *Australia In the War Of 1939–1945, Medical Series, Clinical Problems of War,* Australian War Memorial, Canberra, 1952

Wall, Don, *Heroes of F Force,* Self-Published, Mona Vale, Sydney, 1993

—— *Singapore and Beyond: The Story of The Men Of The 2/20 Battalion,* The 2/20th Battalion Association, Sydney, 1985

Ward, Ian, *The Killer They Called God,* Media Masters, Singapore, 1992

Warren, Alan, *Singapore 1942: Britain's Greatest Defeat,* Talisman, Hardie Grant Books, Melbourne, 2002

Whitecross, R.H., *Slaves of the Son of Heaven,* Corgi Books, London, 1980

Whitelocke, Cliff, *Gunners in the Jungle: A Story of the 2/15 Field Regiment, Royal Australian Artillery, 8 Division, Australian Imperial Force,* 2/15 Field Regiment Association, Sydney, 1983

Wigmore, Lionel, *The Japanese Thrust,* Australian War Memorial, Canberra, 1957

Wyett, John, *Staff Wallah, At the fall of Singapore,* Allen & Unwin, Sydney, 1996

NEWSPAPERS

The Sydney *Sun,* November, December 1937

JOURNALS

The Army Quarterly, April 1928

The Australian Army Journal, Volume II, Number 1

The Defence Force Journal, Number 26 January–February 1981

The *London Gazette,* Lieutenant-General A. E. Percival, 'Operations of Malaya Command from 08.12.1941 to 15.02.1942'

DVDS, VIDEOS

Hell in the Pacific, written and produced and directed by Jonathon Lewis, for Carlton UK Productions Ltd, 2001

Recollections 2/30th Battalion AIF Association, a five DVD disc set, 1994

INDEX